Lecture Notes in Computer Science 2127

Edited by G. Goos, J. Hartmanis and J. van Leeuwen

Springer

Berlin
Heidelberg
New York
Barcelona
Hong Kong
London
Milan
Paris
Tokyo

Victor Malyshkin (Ed.)

Parallel Computing Technologies

6th International Conference, PaCT 2001
Novosibirsk, Russia, September 3-7, 2001
Proceedings

 Springer

Series Editors

Gerhard Goos, Karlsruhe University, Germany
Juris Hartmanis, Cornell University, NY, USA
Jan van Leeuwen, Utrecht University, The Netherlands

Volume Editor

Victor Malyshkin
Supercomputer Software Department
ICM and MG SB RAS
pr. Lavrentiev 6, 630090 Novosibirsk, Russia
E-mail: malysh@ssd.sscc.ru

Cataloging-in-Publication Data applied for

Die Deutsche Bibliothek - CIP-Einheitsaufnahme

Parallel computing technologies : 6th international conference ; proceedings
/ PaCT 2001, Novosibirsk, Russia, September 3 - 7, 2001. Victor Malyshkin
(ed.). - Berlin ; Heidelberg ; New York ; Barcelona ; Hong Kong ; London ;
Milan ; Paris ; Tokyo : Springer, 2001
    (Lecture notes in computer science ; Vol. 2127)
    ISBN 3-540-42522-5

CR Subject Classification (1998): D, F.1-2, C, I.6

ISSN 0302-9743
ISBN 3-540-42522-5 Springer-Verlag Berlin Heidelberg New York

Springer-Verlag Berlin Heidelberg New York
a member of BertelsmannSpringer Science+Business Media GmbH

http://www.springer.de

© Springer-Verlag Berlin Heidelberg 2001
Printed in Germany

Typesetting: Camera-ready by author, data conversion by Olgun Computergrafik
Printed on acid-free paper   SPIN 10839972   06/3142   5 4 3 2 1 0

Preface

The PaCT-2001 (Parallel Computing Technologies) conference was a four-day conference held in Akademgorodok (Novosibirsk), September 3–7, 2001. This was the sixth international conference in the PaCT series, organized in Russia every odd year.

The first conference, PaCT-91, was held in Novosibirsk (Academgorodok), September 7–11, 1991. The next PaCT conferences were held in Obninsk (near Moscow), August 30 – September 4, 1993; in St.Petersburg, September 12–15, 1995; in Yaroslavl September 9–12, 1997; and in Pushkin (near St.Petersburg) from September 6–10, 1999. The PaCT proceedings are published by Springer-Verlag in the LNCS series.

PaCT-2001 was jointly organized by the Institute of Computational Mathematics and Mathematical Geophysics of the Russian Academy of Sciences (Novosibirsk), the State University, and the State Technical University of Novosibirsk.

The purpose of the conference was to bring together scientists working with theory, architecture, software, hardware, and solution of large-scale problems in order to provide integrated discussions on parallel computing technologies. The conference attracted about 100 participants from around the world. Authors from 17 countries submitted 81 papers. Of those submitted, 36 papers were selected for the conference as regular ones; there were also 4 invited papers. In addition there were a number of posters presented. All the papers were internationally reviewed by at least three referees. As usual a demo session was organized for the participants.

Many thanks to our sponsors: the Russian Academy of Sciences, the Russian Fund for Basic Research, the Russian State Committee of Higher Education, the European Commission (Future and Emerging Technologies, Directorate General–Information Society) for their financial support. Organizers highly appreciated the help of the Association Antenne-Provence (France).

June 2001   Victor Malyshkin
                                                    Novosibirsk, Academgorodok

Organization

PaCT 2001 was organized by the Supercomputer Software Department of the Institute of Computational Mathematics and Mathematical Geophysics SB RAS in cooperation with the State University of Novosibirsk and the State Technical University of Novosibirsk.

Program Committee

V. Malyshkin	Program Chair (Russian Academy of Sciences)
F. Arbab	(Centre for MCS, The Netherlands)
O. Bandman	(Russian Academy of Sciences)
A. Bode	(Technical University of Munich, Germany)
T. Casavant	(University of Iowa, USA)
P. Ciancarini	(University of Bologna, Italy)
P. Degano	(State University of Pisa, Italy)
A. Doroshenko	(Academy of Sciences, Ukraine)
D. Etiemble	(University of Toronto, Canada)
B. Goossens	(University Paris 7 Denis Diderot, France)
S. Gorlatch	(Technical University of Berlin, Germany)
A. Hurson	(Pennsylvania State University, USA)
V. Ivannikov	(Russian Academy of Sciences)
Y. Karpov	(State Technical University, St.Petersburg)
B. Lecussan	(State University of Toulouse, France)
J. Li	(University of Tsukuba, Japan)
T. Ludwig	(Technical University of Munich, Germany)
G. Mauri	(University of Milan, Italy)
N. Mirenkov	(The University of Aizu, Japan)
I. Pottosin	(Russian Academy of Sciences)
M. Raynal	(IRISA, Rennes, France)
B. Roux	(Institut de Mecanique des Fluides de Marseilles, France)
G. Silberman	(IBM TJ Watson Research Center, USA)
P. Sloot	(University of Amsterdam. The Netherlands)
V. Vshivkov	(Russian Academy of Sciences)

Organizing Committee

N. Dikansky
V. Malyshkin
B. Mikhailenko
G. Shvedenkov
A. Vostrikov
S. Achasova   Financial Director
O. Bandman   Publication Chair
A. Selikhov   Secretariat
N. Kuchin
S. Piskunov
S. Pudov
A. Usov
I. Virbitskaite

Referees

S. Achasova	A. Hameurlain	A. Nepomniaschaya
F. Arbab	J.-M. Helary	V. Nepomniaschy
P. Baldan	T. Herault	M. Ostapkevich
O. Bandman	R. Hoffmann	S. Pallotino
D. Beletkov	A. Hurson	S. Pelagatti
A. Bernasconi	V. Il'in	B. Philippe
O. Bessonov	H.A. Jacobsen	S. Piskunov
A. Bode	N. Kalinina	T. Plaks
H. Cai	M. Kandemir	I. Pottosin
T. Casavant	Yu. Karpov	P. Raghavan
J. Cazin	V. Korneev	M. Raynal
P. Ciancarini	N. Kuchin	S. Rogazinsky
M. Danelutto	M. Kutrib	B. Roux
P. Degano	Sh. Kutten	S. Sharyi
A. Doroshenko	R. Lechtchinsky	G. Silberman
D. Etiemble	B. Lecussan	P. Sloot
K. Everaars	J. Li	A. Vasilache
E. Fleury	T. Ludwig	A. Vazhenin
P. Fraigniaud	T. Lyubimova	I. Virbitskaite
F. Gartner	V. Markova	V. Vshivkov
C. Germain	G. Mauri	A. Zavanella
B. Goossens	N. Mirenkov	E. Zehendner
R. Gori	V. Morozov	V. Zissimopoulos
S. Gorlatch	A. Mostefaoui	
J. Guillen-Scholten	V. Narayanan	

Table of Contents

Theory

Software and Architecture

Applications

A Hybrid Approach
to Reaction-Diffusion Processes Simulation

Olga Bandman

Supercomputer Software Department
ICMMG, Siberian Branch
Russian Academy of Science
Pr. Lavrentieva, 6, Novosibirsk, 630090, Russia
bandman@ssd.sscc.ru

Abstract. A hybrid approach for simulating reaction-diffusion processes is proposed. It combines into a single iterative procedure Boolean operations of Cellular Automata Diffusion with real number computation of nonlinear reaction function. The kernel of the proposed approach is in constructing methods for transforming reals into spatial distribution of Boolean values. Two algorithms are proposed and illustrated by the simulation of some well studied typical reaction-diffusion phenomena. Computational features of the methods are discussed and problems for future research are outlined.

1 Introduction

There is a number of well known Cellular Automata diffusion and Gas-Lattice models [1,2,3], as well as some trials to find cellular automata simulating kinetic and chemical processes. Following [4], all these models should be considered as "alternatives rather than approximations of Partial Differential Equations (PDE) solutions". These discrete models have a number of computational advantages, the most important being the absolute stability of computation and the absence of rounding off errors. These properties attract the mathematicians, while the specialists in chemistry, biology and physics are interested in creating models of phenomena, which have no mathematical description at all. Such Cellular Automata (CA) are constructed on the basis of kinetic or chemical microscopic dynamics. Boolean cell states simulate the existence or the absence of an abstract particle (molecule, velocity component, concentration, etc.) at certain points of time and space. Cell operations are represented as Boolean functions of states in the cell neighborhood. To obtain physical interpretation of Boolean results, a sum of state values over an area around each cell is calculated. Two prominent examples are a deterministic chemical CA, proposed in [5], and a "Stochastic Cellular Automaton" from [6], which are intended for simulation chemical processes in active media. In [7] a reaction-diffusion CA is presented, based on a neurolike model, whose elementary automaton executes a threshold function and has a refractory period after the active state. In [8,9] many very interesting industrial application of Cellular-Automata models are presented.

V. Malyshkin (Ed.): PaCT 2001, LNCS 2127, pp. 1–16, 2001.

An important problem not yet completely solved in the above approaches is to prove the correspondence of the cellular array evolution to the modeled phenomenon, as well as the way of accounting physical parameters (density, viscosity, diffusion coefficient, pressure, etc) in the array function parameters. The most correct approach to solve these problems might be a natural experiment which, however, is impractical. But such experiments are sometimes impractical. Certain particular results have been obtained theoretically for the CA-diffusion with Margolus neighborhood [2] and for Gas-Lattice FHP-model [10]. In both cases the proofs of the CA evolution correspondence to the modeled phenomenon are done by reducing the CA to the PDE of the modeled phenomenon.

There are many problems also in studying reaction-diffusion processes by PDE analysis. They are investigated literally by the piece (equations of Gordon, Fitz-Nagumo, Belousov-Zhabotinsky, etc.), and with much difficulty, because analytical solutions are impossible due to the nonlinearity, and numerical methods are limited by stability and accuracy problems [12,13].

Unfortunately up to now no method is known for determining a CA-model of process when its PDE description is known. The latter is a system of first order PDEs, having in their right sides two additive terms: 1) a Laplacian to represent the diffusion, and 2) a nonlinear function to represent the reaction (in chemistry) or the advective process (in hydrodynamics), phase conversion (in crystallization), population evolution (in ecology). The first is perfectly modeled by CA, and the second is easy to count without the danger to make the computation unstable.

From the above it follows, that it makes sense to find methods which combine CA-diffusion with calculation of reaction function in reals. We propose to state the problem as follows: given a reaction-diffusion PDE, a discrete cellular algorithm is to be constructed whose evolution approximate that of finite-difference PDE. Obviously, it should be an iterative algorithm, at each step performing the operation of transforming spatially distributed Boolean values into the averaged and reals and the inverse operation referred to as allocation procedure. The latter is precisely the most crucial point of the algorithm. Thus, we propose to exploit well studied CA-models of a diffusion [3] combining it with the integer approximation of reaction function.

The motivation for such an approach contains two arguments. The first is based on the wish to use the great experience of nonlinear phenomena study by PDE solving. The second reason is to obtain rather simple discrete models to replace PDEs, the solution of which is sometimes impractical. We do not know attempts to use such an approach, so we shall try to fill the gap.

To give a mathematical background of the proposed methods the formalism of *Parallel Substitution Algorithm* (PSA) [14] is used, which allows to combine real number and Boolean computation in a unique iterative process.

Apart from Introduction and Conclusion the paper contains four sections. In the second section main concepts and formalisms used in the paper are presented. The general scheme and two algorithms of transforming PDE into a discrete cellular automaton are presented in the third section. In the forth section the computer simulation results are given. In the short fifth section the properties of proposed methods are discussed and problems for future investigation are outlined.

2 Continuous and Discrete Forms of Spatial Dynamics Representation

2.1 Reaction-Diffusion Partial-Differential Equations

Let us consider reaction-diffusion process as a function of concentration of a certain substance of time and space. The traditional representation of the most simple one-dimensional reaction-diffusion process has the form of the following PDE;

$$\frac{du}{dt} = d\left(\frac{\partial^2 u}{\partial x^2}\right) + F(u) \tag{1}$$

where u is a variable with the normalized domain from 0 to 1, t, x are continuous time and space, d is a diffusion coefficient, $F(u)$ a differentiable nonlinear function, satisfying certain conditions, which in [11] are given as follows.

$$F(0) = F(1) = 0; \qquad F(u) > 0 \qquad \text{if } 0 < u < 1;$$
$$F'(0) = \alpha; \quad \alpha > 0; \qquad F'(u) < \alpha; \quad \text{if } 0 < u < 1; \tag{2}$$

The conditions (2) are met by a second order polinome (Fig. 1a) of the form

$$F(u) = \alpha u(1 - u); \tag{3}$$

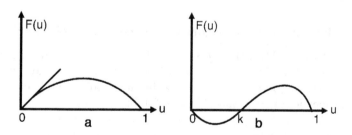

Fig. 1. The nonlinear functions used in typical reaction-diffusion equation

Equation (3) describes also the propagating front of the autocatalitic reaction (Field-Noyes model [15]). The equation (1) with $F(u)$ like (2) is studied in details [11,14]. It is known, that with the initial conditions

$$u(x,0) = \begin{cases} 1 & \text{if } x < 0, \\ 0 & \text{if } x \geq 0. \end{cases} \tag{4}$$

it generates an autowave of the type *propagating front*, which moves (at $t \to \infty$) with the velocity

$$V = 2\sqrt{d\alpha}, \tag{5}$$

In ecological research functions satisfying (2) are classified as *logistic* ones and considered to be basic, although some others are also studied, for example, those represented by third order polinomes (Fig. 1b), such as

$$F(u) = \alpha u(1 - u)(u - k), \quad 0 < k < 1, \tag{6}$$

which meet the following conditions:

$$\begin{aligned}
&F(0) = F(k) = F(1) = 0, \quad 0 < k < 1; \\
&F(u) < 0 \quad \text{if} \ \ 0 < u < k; \\
&F(u) > 0 \quad \text{if} \ \ k < u < 1; \\
&F'(0) < 0, \quad F'(k) > 0, \quad F'(1) < 0,
\end{aligned} \tag{7}$$

With $F(u)$ of the form (6) the propagating front velocity is

$$V = \sqrt{\alpha/2}(1 - 2k) \tag{8}$$

Moreover, when the initial condition have the form

$$u(x, 0) = \begin{cases} u_0 & \text{if} \ \ |x| \le l, \ k < u_0 \le 1, \\ 0 & \text{if} \ \ |x| > l, \end{cases} \tag{9}$$

referred to as a "flash", then the wave may attenuate, if $F(u)_{max}$ is not sufficiently large.

The above analytical characteristics of some simple and well studied reaction-diffusion phenomena are further used for comparing them with the similar ones obtained by simulation of CAs. Obviously, their correspondence would confirm the correctness of the proposed method.

2.2   Parallel Substitution Algorithm for Discrete Cellular Simulation

Parallel Substitution Algorithm (PSA) [14], is a convenient formalism for representing spatially distributed processes. It suits well to be used for our purpose, due to the fact that it allows to deal both with Boolean and real data. The following properties of PSA make it powerful for this purpose.

• PSA processes *cellular arrays*, which are sets of cells given as pairs $C(A, M) = \{(a, m)\}$, where $a \in A$ is a cell *state*, and $m \in M$ is a cell *name*. A - is an alphabet (in our case it is Boolean or real). M is a *naming set* (in general case a countable one). On the set M naming functions $\phi_l : M \to M$ are defined. The naming set is the set of discrete Cartesian coordinates, given as $m = \langle i, j, k \rangle$. In our case only shift naming functions are used. A set of namimg functions form determines the names of any cell *neighborhood*.

• Operations over a cellular array are specified by a set $\Phi = \{\Theta_i\}, i = 1, \dots, n$, of parallel substitutions of the form

$$\Theta_i : C_i(m) * S_i(m) \to S'_i(m). \tag{10}$$

where

$$C_i(m) = \{(y_{ik}, \phi_{ik}(m)) : k = 0, \ldots, q_y\},$$
$$S_i(m) = \{(x_{ij}, \phi_{ij}(m)) : j = 0, \ldots, q_x\}, \qquad (11)$$
$$S_i'(m) = \{(f_{ij}(X, Y), \phi_{ij}(m) : j = 0, \ldots, q_x\},$$

In (10,11) $C_i(m), S_i(m)$ and $S_i'(m)$ are *local configurations*, $*$ meaning their union for any $m \in M$. Further only stationary parallel substitutions are used, in which the neighborhoods of $S_i(m)$ and $S_i'(m)$ are formed by identical sets of naming functions, which contain an identical naming function $\phi(m) = m$ referred to as a *central* cell of the substitution. A parallel substitution should meet the following conditions:

1) no pair of naming functions values in (11) are equal,

2) $x_{ij} \in X, y_{ik} \in Y$ are state variables or constants and $f_{il}(X, Y)$ are cellular functions with the domain from A.

- A substitution *is applicable* to $\mathbf{C}(A, M)$, if there is at least one cell named $m \in M$ such that $C_i(m) \cup S_i(m) \subseteq \mathbf{C}(A, M)$. Application of a substitution at a cell $(a, m) \in \mathbf{C}(A, M)$ yields changing cell states in $S_i(m)$ called *the base* by the corresponding ones from $S_i'(m)$, the set of cells $C_i(m)$ (called *a context*) remaining unchanged.

- There are three modes of parallel substitutions application.

1) *Synchronous mode*, when at each step all substitutions are applied at all cells at once. At this case in order to provide determinism of the computation, one should be careful not to allow the substitutions be contradictory when $|S_i'(m)| > 1$ [14].

2) *Asynchronous mode*, when any substitution is applied at any cell, one application being allowed at a time. There is no danger of contradictoriness in this case, but a generator of random numbers should be used to determine a next cell to which the substitutions are to be applied each time .

3) *2-step synchronous mode*, when cellular array under processing is to be partitioned into two parts, and at each time-step the substitutions act at one of them only.

- A Parallel Substitution Algorithm (PSA) is a set of substitutions together with indication of the mode of application. Implementation of a PSA over a cellular array $\mathbf{C}$ is an iterative procedure, where at each step the substitution set is executed at a set of cells, according to the given mode. The algorithm stops when no substitution is applicable to the array.

- A PSA may process not only one but a number of interacting arrays $\mathbf{C} = \{\mathbf{C}_1, \ldots, \mathbf{C}_n\}$ as well. In the latter case each substitution Θ_i is allowed to be applied to only one array. It means that its base $S_i(m)$ is located in only one $C_l \in \mathbf{C}$, i.e. $m \in M_l$. As for the context $C_i(m)$, it may be located at any array, moreover, it may be composed of a number of local configurations, located in different arrays, i.e.

$$C_i(m) = C_1(m_1) * \ldots * C_k(m_k), \quad k \leq n; m_j \in M_j. \qquad (12)$$

PSA is further used to represent reaction-diffusion processes by discrete fine-grained parallel algorithms.

3   Combining CA-Diffusion with Finite-Difference Reaction

3.1   General Scheme of the Computational Process

Without loss of generality let's consider the two-dimensional case. After time and space are transformed to the discrete form resulting in $x = hi, y = hj, t = n\tau$, where i, j, n are integers, $h = 1$, the equation (1) looks as follows.

$$u'_{ij}(t + 1) = u'_{ij} + \tau dL(u'_{ij}) + \tau F(u'_{ij}, \tag{13}$$

where $L(u'_{ij})$ is a Laplacian, $u_{ij}\prime = u_{ij}\prime(t)$ are variable values in real numbers.

Let us now focus on the most discrete form of process representation, when concentration values are given in Boolean form, i.e. $u \in \{0, 1\}$. Using the PSA notation we consider coordinates i,j as cell names $\langle i, j \rangle \in M$, and concentration values as cell states $a \in A$, the process to be simulated being given by a set of parallel substitutions acting on the cellular array $C \in A \times M$. The correspondence between continuous and discrete forms of representation is that $u'_{ij}(t + 1)$ and $u'_{ij}(t)$ are averaged values over a certain area $Av(ij)$ around a cell named $\langle i, j \rangle$, referred to further as *averaging area*,

$$u'_{ij} = \sum_{Av(ij)} u_{ij}. \tag{14}$$

When $F(u) = 0$, then (1) and (13) describe a "pure diffusion" which has some simple and well studied CA-models. The most known of them called *Block-Rotation CA-model* is theoretically proved [2] to be equivalent to Laplace equation with $d = 3/2$ (in 2D case). Moreover, in [3] it is shown how to use the model with any diffusion coefficient.

The above approves the possibility to decompose each step of the iterative simulation procedure into three operations: application of a CA-diffusion rule, computation of the reaction function and combining the result.

Accordingly, the array C under simulation is partitioned into three parts: *diffusion array* C_D with Boolean cell states, *reaction array* C_R and *resulting array* C' both with real cell states, the naming sets of the parts being in one-to-one correspondence.

CA-diffusion rules are applied to the diffusion array resulting in $C_D(t + 1)$. As for the reaction function computation, it may be accomplished only in reals, resulting in $C_R(t + 1)$. At last, to obtain the next state both results should be combined in such a way that the result of the t-th iteration satisfies the following conditions:

$$C\prime(t + 1) = (C'_D(t + 1)) \oplus C_R(t + 1), \quad C'(t + 1) = Av(C(t + 1)), \tag{15}$$

where "$\oplus$" means cell-wise states summing, $Av(C_D(t+1))$ has states obtained by (14) applied to corresponding states of $C_D(t+1)$. Both cellular arrays $C(t+1)$ and $C'(t+1)$, representing t-th iteration result in Boolean and real form respectively, are the initial arrays for the next iteration (Fig. 2).

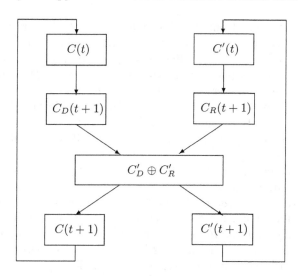

Fig. 2. General scheme of one iteration of the iterative hybrid method of simulation the reaction-diffusion process given by an equation of the form (13)

The main problem to be solved for constructing the computational algorithms according to the general scheme given in Fig. 2 is to find the procedure which is inverse to averaging. It comprises the distribution of "ones" over the cellular array in a way, that guaranties given averaged values and is referred to further as *allocation procedure*. Allocation is just the problem that constitutes the kernel of the proposed approach. Two allocation procedures determine two algorithms for combining Boolean and real computations into a single iterative procedure. The first is called a *multilayer method*. It requires one dimension to be added to the diffusion cellular space. So, the array is treated as a multilayer one. An iteration of CA-diffusion algorithm is executed in all diffusion layers independently, and the averaging and the allocation is performed over the subarray, containing corresponding cells names, i.e. differing only by the layer number. The second method is referred to as a *three-layer method*. In it the CA-diffusion is performed in only one layer of the array where the averaging and allocation is performed over the averaging area which contains cells whose spatial coordinates differ in no more than a constant ρ, referred to as a radius of averaging. The allocation is done by inverting the cell state with a probability, depending of the number of bits to be allocated and the neighborhood size.

In the following subsections the above methods are given formally in terms of PSA. CA-diffusion algorithms used in the methods are not discribed there, they are given in brief in the examples of section 5.

3.2 A Multilayer Reaction-Diffusion Method

To simulate a reaction-diffusion process in an n-dimensional space an (n+1)-dimensional cellular array should be taken, which is further considered as a multilayer n-dimensional one. So, the naming set of the array in 2D case is $M = \{\langle i, j, k \rangle\}$, where $i, j = \ldots, 0, 1, 2, \ldots,$ – are coordinates of 2D infinite space, further referred to as *spatial coordinates*, and $k \in \{0, \ldots, L\}$ is a *layer number*. The naming set is partitioned into two subsets: $M = M_D \cup M_R$, $M_R = \{\langle i, j, 0 \rangle\}$ contains the names of the zero layer cells, M_D – the cell names of all other layers. M_D in its turn is partitioned into subsets of names, differing only by the layer numbers: $M_D = \cup_{i,j} M_{ij}$, where $M_{ij} = \{\langle i, j, k \rangle : k = 1, \ldots, L\}$ is the average area forming the averaging subarray C_{ij} of the cell, with spatial coordinates (i, j).

Cells with names from M_D and M_R have the state alphabets $A_D = \{0, 1\}$ and $A_R = \mathbf{R}$, respectively.

The subarray $C_R = \{(v, \langle i, j, 0 \rangle) : v \in A_R, \langle i, j, 0 \rangle \in M_R\}$ plays a twofold role: it is destined for computing the nonlinear function and storing the averaged result. In each k-th layer from the diffusion part $C_D = \{(u, \langle i, j, k \rangle) : u \in A_D, \langle i, j, k \rangle \in M_D\}$ one of the chosen 2D CA-diffusion algorithm is realized.

The scheme of the multilayer algorithm is as follows.

Given an initial cellular array $C(0) = C_D(0) \cup C_R(0)$ of finite size $G \times H \times L$ where $M = \{\langle i, j, k \rangle : i = 0, 1, \ldots, G - 1, /j = 0, 1, \ldots, H - 1, /k = 0, \ldots L\}$, and cells of diffusion layers $(k = 1, \ldots, L)$ have Boolean states, zeros and ones being distributed over the layer in such a way that the number of ones in the averaging subarray of the cell is equal to the initial concentration of the substance in the space under simulation. These concentration values $v_{ij} = u'_{ij0}$ given in real numbers are cell states of the reaction layer $(k = 0)$.

The computation is an iterative procedure, each t-th iteration being composed of the following steps.

• *Step 1.* In all diffusion layers an iteration of CA-diffusion transition rule is performed. It results in changing the cell states of $C_D(t)$, i.e.

$$C_D(t + 1) = Dif(C_D(t)). \qquad (16)$$

It should be noted, that at this step there is no interactions between the layers.

• *Step 2.* In each cell $(v, \langle i, j, 0 \rangle) \in C_R$ the nonlinear function $F(v)$ is computed and the nearest integer to the result becomes the cell state.

$$\Theta_1 : \{(v, \langle i, j, 0 \rangle)\} \rightarrow \{(y, \langle i, j, 0 \rangle)\}, \text{ where } y = \text{Int}(F(v)). \qquad (17)$$

• *Step 3.* Allocation operation is performed as follow. In each subset $C_{ij} \in C_D$ the amount of cells equal to the state of the cell $(y, \langle i, j, 0 \rangle)$ is inverted according to its sign. If $y > 0$, then cell states $u = 1$ are inverted, else, if $y < 0$, the same is done with cell states $u = 0$.

$$\begin{aligned} \Theta_2 &: \{(|y| > 1, \langle i, j, 0 \rangle)\} * \{(u, \langle i, j, k \rangle)\} \rightarrow \{(\bar{u}, \langle i, j, k \rangle)\} \\ \Theta_3 &: \{(|y| > 1, \langle i, j, 0 \rangle)\} \rightarrow \{(|y| - 1, \langle i, j, 0 \rangle)\}, \end{aligned} \qquad (18)$$

k ranging from 1 to L.

Allocation operation results in the subarray $C_D(t + 1)$.

• *Step 4.* Averaging operation over all M_{ij} is performed according to (14).

$$\Theta_4 : \{(u_1, \langle i, j, 1 \rangle), \ldots, (u_L, \langle i, j, L \rangle)\} * \{(v, \langle i, j, 0 \rangle)\} \rightarrow \{(u', \langle i, j, 0 \rangle)\} \qquad (19)$$

where

$$u\prime = \sum_{k=1}^{L} u_{ijk}, \tag{20}$$

Averaging operation results in the subarray $C_R(t+1)$.

• *Step 5.* If the whole computation is not completed, i.e. $t+1 < T$, then the subarrays obtained in step 3 and 4 are taken as the initial ones for the next iteration, else the computation is considered to be completed and $C(t+1) = C_D(t+1) \cup C_R(t+1)$ is its result.

In section 4.1 this algorithm is illustrated by simulation results of two types of autowaves: 1D and 2D propagating fronts.

3.3   Three-Layer Reaction-Diffusion Method

Three-layer hybrid method provides for a three-layer array, whose spatial coordonates together with the layer number ($k = 0, 1, 2$) form the naming set. For definiteness 2D-case is further considered. Let the layer with $k = 0$ be the reaction subarray $C_R = \{(y, \langle i, j, 0 \rangle)\}$, the layer with $k = 1$ – the diffusion layer $C_D = \{(u, \langle i, j, 1 \rangle)\}$ and the last one with $k = 2$ – the layer storing the averaged result it contains and counts the averaged diffusion results $C' = \{(v, \langle i, j, 2 \rangle)\}$. Respectively, $u \in A_D, y, v \in A_R$. Averaging is performed over the neighborhood $Q = \{\langle i + h, j + l, 1 \rangle : h, l = -r, \ldots, r\}$. Initially $C_(0)$ and $C'(0)$ contain the Boolean distribution and averaged values of concentration at $t = 0$, $C_R(0)$ has zero-states in all cells.

The simulation procedure is an iterative one with the t-th iteration consisting of the following steps.

• *Step 1.* In the diffusion layer an iteration of a CA-diffusion algorithm is executed resulting in

$$C_D(t+1) = \{(u, \langle i, j, 1 \rangle) : i = 0, \ldots, M - 1; j = 0, \ldots, N - 1\}.$$

Step 2. In the cells of reaction subarray C_R the nearest integer to the function $F(v)$ value is computed according to the substitution

$$\Theta_5 : \{(v, \langle i, j, 2 \rangle)\} * \{(0, \langle i, j, 0 \rangle)\} \rightarrow \{(y, \langle i, j, 0 \rangle)\}, \text{ where}/y = Int(F(v)). \tag{21}$$

• *Step 3.* Allocation operation is performed by inverting cell states in the diffusion layer according to the following probabilities.

$$\begin{array}{ll} p = \frac{y}{|Q|-v} & \text{if } x = 0 \ \& \ y_{>}0 \\ p' = y/v & \text{if } y < 0. \end{array} \tag{22}$$

Two parallel substitutions executing this operation are as follows.

$$\begin{aligned} &\Theta_6 : \{(v, \langle i, j, 2 \rangle), (y, \langle i, j, 0 \rangle)\} * \{(u, \langle i, j, 1 \rangle)\} \rightarrow \{(\phi(u, v, y), \langle i, j, 1 \rangle)\}. \\ &\Theta_7 : \{(v, \langle i, j, 2 \rangle), (y, \langle i, j, 0 \rangle)\} \rightarrow \{(0, \langle i, j, 2 \rangle), (0, \langle i, j, 0 \rangle)\}, \end{aligned} \tag{23}$$

where

$$\phi(u, v, y) = \begin{cases} 1, & \text{if}(u = 0)\&(y > 0)\&(rand(1) < p); \\ 0, & \text{if}(u = 1)\&(y < 0)\&(rand(1) < p'); \end{cases} \tag{24}$$

- *Step 4.* Averaging operation is performed in all cells of the averaging subarray C'_D according to the substitution

$$\Theta_8 : \{(u_{i_r, j-r}\langle i - r, j - r, 1\rangle), \dots, (u_{i+r, j+r}\langle i + r, j + r, 1\rangle)\} * \{(0, \langle i, j, 2\rangle)\} \\ \rightarrow \{v, \langle i, j, 2\rangle)\}, \tag{25}$$

where

$$v = \sum_{h=-r}^{h=r} \sum_{l=-r}^{l=r} u_{i+h, j+l} \tag{26}$$

- *Step 5.* If the whole computation is not completed, i.e. $t + 1 < T$, then the subarrays obtained in steps 3 and 4 are taken as the initial ones for the next iteration, else the computation is considered to be completed and $C(t + 1) = C_D(t + 1) \cup C'$ is its result.

The above method of allocation is approximate. It is absolutely accurate only in case of uniform probability distribution over the cell neighborhood. In case of p_{ij} variation, the expectation $\mathcal{M}$ of the event Y meaning that the number of inversed cell-states in the neighborhood is y_{ij} is equal to

$$\mathcal{M}(Y) = \sum_Q p_{ij} \simeq y_{ij}.$$

Moreover the approximation error approaches to zero when the deviations are of different signs. At any case some corrective coefficients may be provided to reduce the error to any small value.

4   Computer Simulation Results

4.1   Simulating 1D Propagating Front by Multilayer Method

As it was mentiomed above, the use of hybrid simulation methods suggests to choose appropriate CA diffusion model to be included in the algorithms.

Comparative analysis of CA diffusion models presented in [3] allows to make the following conclusion: the model, called a *naive CA-diffusion* should be used for 1D-case, and the *Block-Rotation method* (BR-method) is the best for the 2D one. The diffusion coefficient of naive CA-diffusion is not known. So, it has been obtained by simulation by comparing the results with those obtained solving PDE, the result being $d = 1.1$. So, the hybrid method of one-dimensional propagating front combines *1D naive CA-diffusion* [3] with the nonlinear function of the form (3).

Naive CA-diffusion is the most simple model of equalizing the concentration by local stirring along one direction. Let it be the direction along the axis j of the 1D $(L + 1)$-layer cellular array $C = \{(u_{jk}, \langle j, k\rangle) : j = 0, 1, \dots, G; k =$

$0, \ldots, L\}$, $C = C_D \cup C_R$. The diffusion subarray C_D, which contains the layers $(k = 1, \ldots, L)$ uses the alphabet $A = \{0, 1\}$, the variables being specified by u_{jk}. Naive CA-diffusion dictates to each cell to exchange states with one of its randomly chosen neighbor. To avoid contradictoriness the asynchronous mode of execution is used. It means, that at each time only one (randomly chosen) pair of cells exchanges states. So, one iteration which corresponds to Step 1 of the general scheme comprises $G \times L$ times, each time the following operations should be executed.

1) Two random numbers $j, k,\ 0 \leq j < G, 1 \leq k < L$, are obtained. They indicate the cell, to which the algorithm is applied.

2) A context cell (α, m_0) is introduced to indicate the neighbor with whom the cell should interact. The neighbor is determined according to the probability $p = 1/2$. So, if a random number $r \leq 1/2, (0 < r < 1)$, then $\alpha = 1$, which means, that the neighbor to interact with is at the right side of the cell $\langle i, j \rangle$. If $r > 1/2$ then $\alpha = 0$ and the left neighbor is chosen.

3) The following parallel substitutions are applied to a chosen cell of C_D.

$$\Theta_9 : \ (1, m_0) * \{(u, \langle j, k \rangle), (u', \langle j+1, k \rangle)\} \rightarrow \{(u', \langle j, k \rangle), (u, \langle j+1, k \rangle)\};$$
$$(27)$$
$$\Theta_{10} : (0, m) * \{(u, \langle j, k \rangle), (u', \langle j-1, k \rangle)\} \rightarrow \{(u', \langle j, k \rangle), (u, \langle j-1, k \rangle)\};$$

The other steps are executed in complete accordance with the general scheme (section 3.2). The difference is only in the absence of coordinate i in the names.

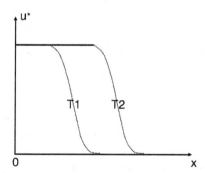

Fig. 3. A pair of snapshots of the profiles of 1D propagating front, obtained by the multilayer method with naive asynchronous CA-diffusion and and nonlinear function of the form (3)

In Fig. 3a two profiles of 1D propagating front are given. They have been obtained by simulation using the multilayer algorithm with $N = 128, L = 32, F(u)$ of the form (3) with $\alpha = 1.2$ Propagation velocity has been determined by analyzing the fronts profiles, obtained from the series of similar experiments. The coincidence with that, obtained by formula (5) is in the limits of the accuracy of the experiment. For example, in accordance with the well known character of propagating front behavior [11,14] its propagating velocity decreases with time, approaching (according to (5)) at $t = \infty$ to $V_0 = 2.3$ (with $\alpha = 1.2, d = 1.1$).

4.2   Simulating 2D Propagating Front by Multilayer Method

The algorithm to be presented here combines the 2D BR-diffusion with a non-linear functions (3) and (6). BR-diffusion, which is referred to in [2] as a *CA with Margolus neighborhood*, works in a two-step mode of execution over a cellular array $C = \{(u, \langle i, j, k \rangle) : i = 0, \ldots G - 1, j = 0, \ldots, H - 1, k = 0, \ldots, L\}$. In the diffusion layers $(k = 1, \ldots, L)$, two types of cells are distinguished: *even cells* and *odd cells*. Even cells have both i and j even, odd cells have both i and j odd. A cell from the even (odd) subset is considered to be a central one for each k-th layer block $B(i, j, k) = \{(u_1, \langle i, j, k \rangle), (u_2, \langle i, j + 1, k \rangle), (u_3, \langle i + 1, j + 1, k \rangle), (u_4, \langle i + 1, j, k \rangle\}$. Similar blocks are formed by cells belonging to the even subset. Clearly, the intersections between blocks from one the same subset are empty, from which follows the noncontradictoriness. To indicate the type of blocks an additional context cell (β, m_0) is introduced, $\beta = 0, \beta = 1$ corresponding to even and odd cells, respectively.

Each diffusion iteration (Step 1) consists of two times: at the even time even blocks turn with probability $p = 1/2$ to $\pi/2$ either clockwise or counterclockwise. To indicate the rotation direction an additional context cell (γ, m_1) is introduced. If $\gamma = 1$ then the rotation is clockwise, else – counterclockwise. In PSA notation it looks like this.

$$
\begin{aligned}
\Theta_{11} : \ & \{(1, m_0)(1, m_1)\} * \{(u_1, \langle i, j, k \rangle), (u_2, \langle i, j + 1, k \rangle), (u_3, \langle i + 1, j + 1, k \rangle), \\
& (u_4, \langle i + 1, j, k \rangle)\} \rightarrow \{(u_4, \langle i, j, k \rangle), (u_1, \langle i, j + 1, k \rangle), (u_2, \langle i + 1, j + 1, k \rangle), \\
& (u_3, \langle i + 1, j, k \rangle)\}; \\
\Theta_{12} : \ & \{(1, m_0)(0, m_1)\} * \{(u_1, \langle i, j, k \rangle), (u_2, \langle i, j + 1, k \rangle), (u_3, \langle i + 1, j + 1, k \rangle), \\
& (u_4, \langle i + 1, j, k \rangle)\} \rightarrow \{(u_2, \langle i, j, k \rangle), (u_3, \langle i, j + 1, k \rangle), (u_4, \langle i + 1, j + 1, k \rangle), \\
& (u_1, \langle i + 1, j, k \rangle)\}
\end{aligned}
$$
$$(28)$$

For the odd times the substitutions differ from (30) only by the context cell (β, m_0), which is in this case $(0, m_0)$. Other steps are in accordance with the general scheme of the algorithm.

2D propagation front simulation has been done for the cellular array with $G = H = 64, L = 32$ with two different nonlinear functions, given by (3) and by (6). The initial array had the cells states $u = 1$ in the cells from $\{(u, \langle i, j, k \rangle) : (G/2 - g) < i < (G/2 + g); (H/2 - g) < j < (H/2 + g); k = 1, \ldots, L\}, g = 6$, the rest of cells had $u = 0$. Such initial states are referred to as a *flash* in the ecological research. In Fig. 4a two snapshots of front profile propagating from the flash are shown, the reaction function being of the form (3) with $\alpha = 1.2$. In Fig. 4b two snapshots are shown, which are obtained simulating diffusion-reaction with the function $F(u)$ of the form given by (6) having $F_{max}(u)$ not sufficiently large to support tyhe front to propagate. In this case the flash diminishes and disappears.

In Fig. 5 a diffusion two propagating towards each other fronts array shown after $T = 16$ iterations (Fig. 5b), being initiated by two dense spots (Fig. 5a).

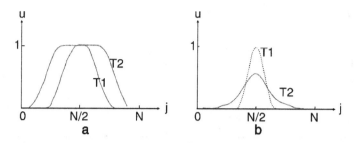

Fig. 4. Snapshots, obtained by simulating 2D reaction-diffusion with $F(u)$ of the form (6). a) propagating front profiles, b) profiles of a damping flash

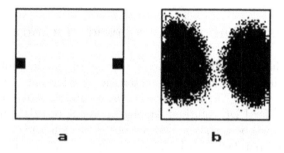

Fig. 5. The initial state and the snapshot at $T = 16$ of two propagating fronts

4.3 Simulating 1D Propagating Front by Three-Layer Method

Let us combine naive 2-step CA-diffusion with reaction function of the form (3). The array has three 1D layers: $C_R, (k = 0)$, $C_D (k = 1)$ and $C', (k = 2)$. One-dimensional 2-step naive diffusion is similar to the Block-Rotation diffusion. The array is partitioned into two subsets: a subset of even cells, which form even blocks: $\{(u_1, \langle j, 0 \rangle), (u_2, \langle j+1, 0 \rangle) : j = 0, 2, \ldots, N-2\}$, and a subset of odd ones: $\{(u_1, \langle j, 0 \rangle), (u_2, \langle j+1, 0 \rangle) : j = 1, 3, \ldots, N-1\}$. Each diffusion iteration consists of two times: at even time cells of even blocks exchange states . The same do the odd blocks at odd times. Substitution of state exchange is as follows.

$$\Theta_{13} : \{(u_1, \langle j, 0 \rangle), (u_2, \langle j + 1, 0 \rangle)\} \rightarrow \{(u_2, \langle j, 0 \rangle), (u_1, \langle j + 1, 0 \rangle)\}. \qquad (29)$$

The averaging (step 2) is performed using Θ_8, neighborhood size being chosen according to the required accuracy. Reaction function (step 2 of the algorithms in section 4.3) is computed in cells of C_R according to Θ_2.

The allocation procedure is performed in the cells of C_D with the account of corresponding probabilities counted by (22) and (23). In Fig. 6 two snapshots of a propagating front obtained by this method are shown, propagation speed being in good accordance with the theoretic value.

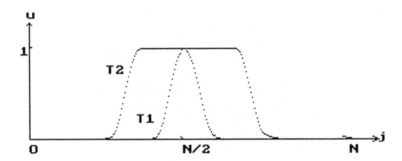

Fig. 6. Two snapshots of propagating front profiles, obtained by stochastic method

5 Characterisation of the Proposed Method

To make a conclusion about the proposed method of reaction-diffusion phenomena simulation, its computational characteristics (performance, accuracy, stability) should be assessed. The most correct way to do this is to compare them to the similar ones, for PDE solution. Among the scope of PDE solution methods the finite-difference one is chosen, because of the two following reasons. The first is its fine-grained parallelism, which is considered as a very important feature, due to its simplicity and capability of decomposition. The second is its simulation similarity to a CA evolution, which allows to consider the comparison to be correct.

On this stage of proposed method development only qualitative comparison is possible. The qualitative assessment may be done after a long and hard work both theoretical and experimental. Here only some considerations can be applied to the problems of the above characteristics determining. They are as follows.

Accuracy. The accuracy is determined by two types of errors. The round off errors and approximation errors. Round off errors are very small in the proposed method, because the CA-diffusion is absolutely free of them, as for averaging and reaction function calculation they might be done in integers. Approximation errors emerge in the procedures of counting the reaction function, as well as in the stochastic updating cell neighborhood. Since these errors depend on the size of the averaging space, the price for the accuracy is the size of the array.

Stability of the computation. According to the finite-difference PDE theory the stability of the iterative algorithm to compute Laplace operator is conditioned by a relationship among a diffusion coefficient, and spatial (h) and time discretization (τ) steps. To meet these conditions the steps are to be chosen sufficiently small, which yields in large time of computation. When the proposed CA-method is used, no restriction on computation stability is imposed. The choice of discretization steps is done according to required accuracy and smoothness of the resulting dependencies (absence of "CA noise").

Performance, which is the inverse of the time, needed to solve a given problem may be assessed by three time parameters: 1) number of iterations for reaching the result, 2) number of elementary operations in each iteration, and 3) number of cells (grid nodes in PDE) needed to provide the required properties. Each of the above time parameters needs to be of assessed with the account of many factors: kind of nonlinearity, spatial dimension, number of variables, etc. At this stage of study the following remarks may be done. The amount of iteration is expected to be less than when the corresponding PDE is solved. The number of elementary operations, the amount of bit-operations should be computed and compared to that needed for PDE solution. It is obvious, that the amount of bit operations is less for CA-diffusion in each iteration, but the averaging and updating procedures may override the difference. As for the size of the array, on one hand it can be smaller than for the PDE solution because the value of h is not restricted by stability conditions, on the other hand, it should be larger to diminish the CA-noise.

The above considerations show that a correct comparison of CA-model with finite-difference solution is a separate hard task, which may be solved basing on the considerable body of experience. This task is most likely to be formulated as follows: for certain class of reaction-diffusion PDEs the domain of parameters should be found such that the proposed approach is preferable.

6   Conclusion

Two methods for constructing CA representation of reaction-diffusion PDE are presented, both using the approach of combining known CA diffusion models with conventional computation of nonlinear function. The methods are illustrated by simulation on array of limited size. Simulation results coincide with those known from the corresponding PDE analysis. Some considerations are applied to the assessment of the approach and future investigations, among which the most important is to promote applications and accumulate experience.

References

1. Toffoli T., Margolus M.: Cellular Automata Machines. MIT Press (1987) 280 p.
2. Malinetski G.G., Stepantsov M.E.: Modelling diffusive processes by cellular automata with Margolus neighborhood. Zhurnal Vychislitelnoy Matematiki i Matematicheskoy Physiki, vol.36, N 6, (1998) 1017-1021 (in Russian).
3. Bandman O.L.: Comparative Study of Cellular-Automata Diffusion Models. In: Malyshkin V.(ed.): Lecture Notes in Computer Science. Vol. 1662. Srringer-Verlag, berlin (1999) 395-409.
4. Toffoli T.: Cellular Automata as an alternative to (rather than an approximation of) differential equations in modeling physics. Physica. 10D (1984) 117-127.
5. Adamatsky A.: Reaction-Diffusion and Excitable processors: a sense of the unconventional. Parallel and Distributed Computing Practices. N1 (1999).
6. Latkin E.: SCAM: a chemical computer. Vychislitelnye systemy. Vol.152. Institute of Mathematics, Novosibirsk (1995) 140-152 (in Russian).
7. Allouche J.P., Reder C.: Oscillations Spatio-Temporelles Engendrees par un Automate Cellullaire. Disc.Appl.Math.(1984) 215-254.

8. Bandini S., Illy E., Simone C., F.S.Liverani F.S.: A Computational Model Based on the Reaction-Diffusion Machine to Simulate Transportation Phenomena: the case of Coffee Percolation. In: Bandini S., Serra R., Liverani F.S. (eds): Cellular Automata: Research Towards Industry. Springer-Verlag (1998) 157-164.

9. Bandini S., Mauri G., Pavesi G., Simone C.: A Parallel Model Based on Cellular Automata for the Simulation of Pesticide Percolation in the Soil. In: Malyshkin V.(ed.): Lecture Notes in Computer Science. Vol. 1662. Springer-Verlag (1999) 382-394.

10. Rothman D.H., Zaleski S.: Lattice-Gas Cellular Automata. Simple Models of Complex Hydrodynamics. Cambridge University Press (1997) 293 pp.

11. Kolmogorov A.N., Petrovski I.N., Piskunov N.S.: A study of diffusion equation combined with the increase of substance, and its implementation to a biological problem. Bulletin of Moscow State University. Vol.1, series A, issue B.(1937) (in Russian)

12. Madore B.F., Freedman W.L..: Computer Simulation of the Belousov-Zhabotinsky Reaction. In.: S.Wolfram (ed.). Theory and Application of Cellular Automata. Singapore, World Scientific (1986), 311-312.

13. Young D.A.. A Local Activator-Inhibitor model of Vertebrate Skin Patterns. In: S.Wolfram (ed.). Theory and Application of Cellular Automata. Singapore, World Scientific (1986), 320-327.

14. Achasova S., Bandman O., Markova V., Piskunov S.: Parallel Substitution Algorithm. Theory and Application. World Scientific, Singapore (1994) 240 pp.

Formal Verification of Coherence for a Shared Memory Multiprocessor Model

Manuel Barrio-Solórzano[1], M. Encarnación Beato[2], Carlos E. Cuesta[1], and Pablo de la Fuente[1]

[1] Departamento de Informática. Universidad de Valladolid, Spain
[2] Escuela de Informática. Universidad Pontificia de Salamanca, Spain

Abstract. The specification and verification of shared-memory multi-processor cache coherence protocols is a paradigmatic example of parallel technologies where formal methods can be applied. In this paper we present the specification and verification of a cache protocol and a set of formalisms which are based on *'process theory'*. System correctness is not established by simple techniques such as testing and simulation, but 'ensured' in terms of the underlying formalism. In order to manipulate the specification and verify the properties we have used an automated tool —namely the 'Edinburgh Concurrency Workbench' (CWB).

1 Introduction

Formal methods are mathematically based techniques for specifying and verifying complex hardware and software systems [3]. This paper emphasizes their application to parallel processing and distributed computing systems, where the main source of complexity is due to the co-existence of multiple, simultaneously active, and interacting agents. The specification and verification of shared-memory multiprocessor cache coherence protocols is a paradigmatic example of parallel technologies where formal methods can be applied. This kind of systems are composed of a set of elements which need to be coordinated by means of a reliable communication protocol.

In this paper we have chosen a cache coherence protocol as working example which will be developed through several stages of specification and verification. Cache coherence protocols range from simple *"snooping"* ones to complex *"directory-based"* frameworks [12]. In order to make a first approximation to the subject we will stick to one that belongs to the second group: the CC-NUMA protocol. Although its description is relatively simple it allows the definition of non-trivial properties. The verification of these properties illustrates the expressiveness and potentiality of the formalisms and how they could be applied to more complex examples.

In order to deal with a formal specification and verification of the cache coherence protocol, it is essential to use a mathematically-based technique or formal method. There are several formalisms that could be used to tackle this problem. Any protocol can be successfully described in terms of *processes* (con-

V. Malyshkin (Ed.): PaCT 2001, LNCS 2127, pp. 17–26, 2001.
© Springer-Verlag Berlin Heidelberg 2001

current agents which interact in accordance with a predefined pattern of communication [4]) and consequently modelled by using a process-based formalism. Specifically, we have used a process algebra —CCS [9]— for the specification, and an associated temporal logic —μ-calculus [7,13]— for the coherence verification. Furthermore, for these formal methods an automated tool —'Edinburgh Concurrency Workbench[1]', CWB [1]— is available. Basically, it allows the definition, manipulation and verification of processes and temporal properties.

This paper has been structured in four sections following this first introduction. Section 2 deals with process-oriented specification and verification of protocols; a justification of the chosen formalisms can be found here. Section 3 describes the CC-NUMA cache coherence protocol. First of all, its specification in terms of communicating processes is presented; secondly, coherence restrictions are defined in terms of temporal properties which are then automatically verified with regard to the previous specification. A brief summary and conclusions, as well as future lines of research, are discussed in Section 4.

2   Specification and Verification of Protocols in CCS

Cache coherence protocols (in general, any communication protocol) can be described in terms of *'objects'* [10] which operate concurrently and interact in accordance with a predefined pattern of communication. This idea of communicating objects fits with the concept of *process* which allows the definition of an observable behaviour by means of all possible communications.

There are different process theories, most of them with a notion of behaviour pattern of objects [5] or machine for performing actions [4]. Moreover, some of them are based on a well-founded underlying formalism and so are suitable to be used to formally specify, manipulate and verify cache coherence protocols. From all existing formal process theories we have chosen the process algebra CCS ('Calculus of Communicating Systems' [9] and the μ-calculus [14,13] as a complementary temporal logic which allows the definition of properties to be verified in relation to the specified processes (other formal methods can lead to valid results as well). The main features are:

1. The CCS is a process theory which allows a formal manipulation of concurrent communicating processes.
2. There are higher-order extensions where dynamic structures communicating not only interaction channels but whole processes can be modelled.
3. The CCS is complemented by a temporal logic —the μ-calculus— which allows the definition of temporal properties. The process of verifying whether a certain process satisfies a property can be automated.
4. An automated tool —the CWB [1]— is available.

---

[1] See http://www.dcs.ed.ac.uk/home/cwb/index.html (29/10/1999)

3   The CC-NUMA Model

A cache-coherent shared-memory multiprocessor system allows the users to have a logical perspective where all the processors have access to a shared global memory. This operation must be performed in such a way that it is transparent to the user the fact that memory is physically distributed and there must exist multiple copies of the same data element throughout the private caches of each processor. Whereas private caches improve system performance, they introduce the *cache coherence problem*. This means that an update of a memory element in any of the caches must be visible to all other processors in order to keep consistent cached copies of the same data element. This is achieved through a coherence protocol which is defined as a set of rules coordinating cache and memory controllers [11,12].

Among different existing cache coherence protocols we have chosen the CC-NUMA protocol [11] as the running example of this paper. It considers three states for cached blocks: *invalid, shared, dirty*. Invalid is the initial state of all the caches and the one where the block is considered to have been invalidated. The state of shared means that the local copy is valid and can be read. Finally, the state will be dirty if the local copy is valid and it can be written (ownership of the copy).

On the other hand, the shared memory can show one of the following three states: *Uncached,* (initial state) where a block copy is found at the memory and not at the caches; *Shared,* at least one cache holds a copy which can be read; *Dirty,* memory information is obsolete due to a previous cache modification.

3.1   Algorithm

Taking into account that caches can perform read, write and replacement operations, the protocol algorithm (from the perspective of cache C_i) can be described as follows:

1. Read Hit. No cache coherence actions need to be done.
2. Read Miss. When the block is not cached, a memory request is to be issued. In case the copy ownership is held by another cache, the memory should be updated (shared) and a copy transmitted to the demanding cache.
3. Write Hit. A write operation is issued and the cache memory has a copy. If the block is *dirty*, then no action is performed. If it is *shared*, an ownership request is issued.
4. Write Miss. Similar to write hit but the block cannot be found in the cache and a memory request is issued. If there is a copy owner, the information should be updated. Subsequently, the block copy will be transmitted to the waiting cache, along with its ownership. If the block copy is shared by several caches, then the memory will invalidate all the copies, giving a valid copy to the one trying a write operation. Finally, if there is no valid copy, then the memory will provide it (and ownership).
5. Replacement. Update action of the main memory with a cache copy.

3.2 Specification

The CC-NUMA protocol has been modelled —using CCS— for the particular
case of 3 caches. This is due to the fact that we use a model checking technique
where the size of the system's state space grows exponentially with the number
of subsystems. We have avoided the simplest examples (1–2 caches) but we have
also tried to limit our problem difficulty to the extent of being able to keep track
of all possible evolutions. Moreover, we present a well-structured specification
and so it should not be difficult to increase the number of caches of our example.

Other techniques not attempted here permit verification of parameterised
systems, i.e. to perform formal reasoning in terms of the number of caches [2,8].

Processors send to their caches which operation is to be performed next. The
protocol specification uses two different kinds of actions, *visible* and *internal*.
Visible actions are used for cache-processor communications (read, write, repl).
Every operation invocation is matched with an acknowledgement action (*g
ending), also visible. Internal actions are used for the rest of the communications.
This set of actions includes all the communications from caches to the memory
and vice versa.

From cache to memory: rmiss − req, request to the memory when 'read
miss', wmiss − req, for a write operation, own − req, the cache holds a valid
copy and a write operation has been issued, inv − ack, acknowledgement reply
due to a memory invalidation, wback, the cache has updated the memory copy.

From memory to cache: nack, operation denied, miss − reply, reply to a read
request, miss − reply − own, reply to a write request, own − reply, reply to a
own − req request, inv − req, invalidation request, wback − req, update request
to the copy owner, wback − req − own, update request to the copy owner which
is required to go to the invalid state.

The following is the specification of the CC-NUMA protocol in CCS (CWB
notation). For the sake of brevity, we specify just one cache (Cache1) since all
of them share the same behaviour (instances of the same agent with different
communication channels).

```
*Inv1, block invalid
 agent Inv1=read1.PE-RO1 + write1.PE-RW-INV1 + repl1.Inv1 +
   inv-req1.'inv-ack1.Inv1 + wback-req1.Inv1 + wback-req-own1.Inv1;
*PE-RO1: cache is to comm. read operation to memory.
 agent PE-RO1='rmiss-req1.P-RO1 + inv-req1.'inv-ack1.PE-RO1 +
   wback-req1.PE-RO1 + wback-req-own1.PE-RO1;
*PE-RW-INV1: cache is to comm. write operation to memory (invalid copy)
 agent PE-RW-INV1='wmiss-req1.P-RW-INV1 + inv-req1.'inv-ack1.PE-RW-INV1 +
   wback-req1.PE-RW-INV1 + wback-req-own1.PE-RW-INV1;
*RO1: valid copy that can be read
 agent RO1=read1.'readg1.RO1 + write1.PE-RW-VAL1 + repl1.Inv1 +
   inv-req1.'inv-ack1.Inv1;
*PE-RW-VAL1: cache is to comm. write operation to memory (valid copy)
 agent PE-RW-VAL1='own-req1.P-RW-VAL1 + inv-req1.'inv-ack1.PE-RW-INV1;
*RW1: valid copy that can be written
 agent RW1=read1.'readg1.RW1 + write1.'writeg1.RW1 + repl1.PE-Remp-RW1 +
```

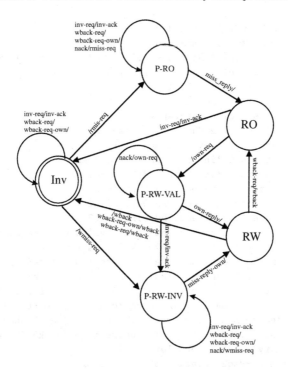

Fig. 1. CC-NUMA protocol (cache point of view)

```
   wback-req1.'update1.'wback1.RO1+wback-req-own1.'update1.'wback.Inv1;
  agent PE-Remp-RW1='update1.'wback1.Inv1 +
   wback-req1.'update1.'wback1.RO1+wback-req-own1.'update1.'wback.Inv1;
*P-RO1: cache waiting to complete read operation (read reply)
  agent P-RO1=miss-reply1.'readg1.RO1 + inv-req1.'inv-ack1.P-RO1 +
   wback-req1.P-RO1 + wback-req-own1.P-RO1 + nack1.PE-RO1;
*P-RW-INV1: cache waiting to complete write operation (invalid copy)
  agent P-RW-INV1=miss-reply-own1.'writeg1.RW1 +
   wback-req1.P-RW-INV1 + wback-req-own1.P-RW-INV1 +
   inv-req1.'inv-ack1.P-RW-INV1 + nack1.PE-RW-INV1;
*P-RW-VAL1: cache waiting to complete write operation (valid copy)
  agent P-RW-VAL1=own-reply1.'writeg1.RW1 + inv-req1.'inv-ack1.P-RW-INV1 +
   nack1.PE-RW-VAL1;
```

Figure 1 shows the state transition diagram of the CC-NUMA model. Only internal actions have been represented, and so transitions are due to communications between the caches and the memory. Whenever a transition is triggered by an input action and requires an output action, it has been denoted by *input action / output action*.

The shared memory agent (see Fig.2 for the state transition diagram) is defined as follows:

```
*Uncached: no cache holds a valid copy
 agent Uncached=rmiss-req1.'miss-reply1.Shared +
   rmiss-req2.'miss-reply2.Shared + rmiss-req3.'miss-reply3.Shared +
   wmiss-req1.'miss-reply-own1.Dirty1+wmiss-req2.'miss-reply-own2.Dirty2+
   wmiss-req3.'miss-reply-own3.Dirty3;
*Shared: at least one cache has a copy
 agent Shared=rmiss-req1.'miss-reply1.Shared +
   rmiss-req2.'miss-reply2.Shared + rmiss-req3.'miss-reply3.Shared +
   wmiss-req1.'inv-req2.'inv-req3.Shd-Dirty-Miss1 +
   wmiss-req2.'inv-req1.'inv-req3.Shd-Dirty-Miss2 +
   wmiss-req3.'inv-req1.'inv-req2.Shd-Dirty-Miss3 +
   own-req1.'inv-req2.'inv-req3.Shd-Dirty-Own1 +
   own-req2.'inv-req1.'inv-req3.Shd-Dirty-Own2 +
   own-req3.'inv-req1.'inv-req2.Shd-Dirty-Own3;
*Shd-Dirty-Miss: from Shared, cache with invalid copy requests write
 agent Shd-Dirty-Miss1=inv-ack2.inv-ack3.'miss-reply-own1.Dirty1 +
   rmiss-req2.'nack2.Shd-Dirty-Miss1 + rmiss-req3.'nack3.Shd-Dirty-Miss1+
   wmiss-req2.'nack2.Shd-Dirty-Miss1 + wmiss-req3.'nack3.Shd-Dirty-Miss1;
*Shd-Dirty-Own: from Shared with two copies, one tries write
 agent Shd-Dirty-Own1=inv-ack2.inv-ack3.'own-reply1.Dirty1 +
   rmiss-req2.'nack2.Shd-Dirty-Own1 + rmiss-req3.'nack3.Shd-Dirty-Own1 +
   wmiss-req2.'nack2.Shd-Dirty-Own1 + wmiss-req3.'nack3.Shd-Dirty-Own1;
*Dirty: the memory value is obsolete
 agent Dirty1=rmiss-req2.'wback-req1.Dirty-Shd2 +
   rmiss-req3.'wback-req1.Dirty-Shd3 +
   wmiss-req2.'wback-req-own1.Dirty-Dirty2 +
   wmiss-req3.'wback-req-own1.Dirty-Dirty3 + wback1.Uncached;
*Dirty-Shd: from Dirty, cache without valid copy issues read
 agent Dirty-Shd1=wback2.'miss-reply1.Shared +
   wback3.'miss-reply1.Shared +
   rmiss-req2.'nack2.Dirty-Shd1 + wmiss-req2.'nack2.Dirty-Shd1 +
   rmiss-req3.'nack3.Dirty-Shd1 + wmiss-req3.'nack3.Dirty-Shd1;
*Dirty-Dirty: from Dirty, cache without valid copy issues write
 agent Dirty-Dirty1=wback2.'miss-reply-own1.Dirty1 +
   wback3.'miss-reply-own1.Dirty1 + rmiss-req2.'nack2.Dirty-Dirty1 +
   wmiss-req2.'nack2.Dirty-Dirty1 + rmiss-req3.'nack3.Dirty-Dirty1 +
   wmiss-req3.'nack3.Dirty-Dirty1;
```

This is not the complete specification but a reduced version where all the requests are issued by the cache 1. The complete model includes the other possibilities —Dirty2, Dirty3, Shd-Dirty-Miss2, Shd-Dirty-Miss3, Shd-Dirty-Own2, Shd-Dirty-Own3, Dirty-Shd2, Dirty-Shd3, Dirty-Dirty2, Dirty-Dirty3— which are constructed in a similar way.

Now it is possible to model the whole protocol as the concurrent composition of all the agents —caches and memory— where all the internal actions have been restricted so that no other 'external' agent can interfere with them. Initially, the protocol is considered to have an uncached copy.

```
agent Protocol=(Inv1|Inv2|Inv3|Uncached)\Inter;
```

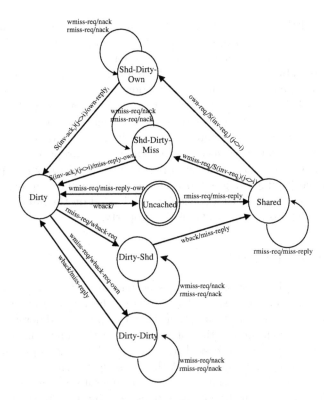

Fig. 2. CC-NUMA protocol (memory point of view)

3.3   Verification of Coherence Properties

Cache coherence is accepted as far as it can be verified in terms of data consistency (otherwise inconsistent data copies may be observed when a processor modifies that data copy in its private cache [12]).

Traditionally, simple protocol correctness has been established by using techniques such as testing and simulations. However, the need for high performance and scalable machines has made coherence protocols much more complex so that new techniques are needed. Some of the most promising verifying techniques are based on formal methods and mechanical checking procedures (see [11] for a comparison): (1) *state enumeration* of all possible agent interactions, (2) *symbolic state model* [11], where equivalence relations among global states are defined in order to represent a canonical state model, and (3) *model checking* [6], where it is verified whether a given state system is a model for a property specification or not.

In this paper we have used a *temporal model checking* [3] technique. Model checking verification is based on the possibility of assuring that a particular state (agent with a certain state) satisfies a specification. This specification is, precisely, the property to be verified. In our case, the property will represent data consistency and the state will be the agent (or set of agents) implementing the protocol. Data coherence properties are represented as *modal-temporal* properties. This is due to the implicit temporal character of the coherence constraint: "it is *never* possible to reach a state where an invalid read takes place". The temporal logic we use in this paper is the modal μ-calculus [7,13] which includes temporal modalities that allow the description and reasoning of time-varying behaviour —how the truth values of assertions change over time. Indeed, the modal mu-calculus is a very expressive propositional temporal logic which can be used to describe safety, liveness, fairness and cyclic properties.

The problem of verifying whether a particular process satisfies a property or not is decidable (taking for granted that the total amount of possible states is finite). Nevertheless, the actual efficiency will depend on the number of possible states and the intrinsic complexity of the property.

3.4   Coherence Property

Coherence means data consistency. This notion, excessively general to be represented as such, can be described in terms of the agents taking part in the protocol and the communication actions they can perform. Therefore, it is possible to make a second description of coherence in the following terms: data is consistent if whenever it is accessed by an agent, the value is precisely the last that was assigned (by any processor). A third description characterizes coherence as a *"future-tense"* specification: after a write operation of a data block (new value), no later access will be possible unless a value update takes place. This new property description can be considered to be equivalent to the previous ones and more appropriate for proving that it is satisfied by the described protocol.

In order to keep the verification as simple as possible, it has been considered that one single data position is managed. For notation purposes, let the index i refer to the writing cache, and j, k to the other ones.

The μ-calculus is a recursive propositional temporal logic including[2]: propositional variables, Z, boolean connectives, modal operators, [], <> —immediate *necessity* and *capability*— respectively, and fixed-point operators —*least* and *greatest*— max, min. An intuitive explanation of fixed-points is usually given in the following terms: min does not allow an infinite behaviour without something (good?) *eventually* to happen (*liveness*), whereas max enforces something (not bad?) *invariantly* to happen (*safety*).

The coherence property —as stated above— is specified by the following μ-calculus formula:

```
prop Coherence_i = max(X. [-'writeg_i]X &
                      ['writeg_i](max(Z. ['readg_{j,k}, 'writeg_{j,k}]F &
                                      [-'update_i]Z)))
```

---

[2] For a full description of modal and temporal logics for processes, and the μ-calculus see [13].

1. The first greatest fixed-point (X) establishes that after any action other than a write operation, the same (coherence) property has to be satisfied. This is a safety component of coherence.

2. After the write operation, a second greatest fixed-point (Z) establishes that, (a) no other cache can complete any access [$'readg_{j,k}$,$'writeg_{j,k}$]F —either read or write— and (b) recursively continues to hold (Z) upon doing any derivation other than update. The only way to "get out" of this construction and allow other read/write operations is by means of a previous update.

3. Yet another safety construction could have been added to state that this write-update schema holds onwards.

Verifying that the CC-NUMA protocol satisfies this coherence property has been accomplished using the CWB, an automated tool which caters for the manipulation and analysis of concurrent systems. In particular, the CWB allows for various equivalence, preorder and model checking using a variety of different process semantics.

The number of states of a finite-state agent is a good indication of the model *size*. For the particular case of three caches, the CWB has found 1273 states. Other interesting commands give users the possibility of listing all the *states*, the *transitions* of an agent, running a *simulation* of an agent interactively, finding the *derivatives* of an agent via a given action, and many others.

As far as model checking is concerned, it is possible to verify predefined properties —dead- or lived-locked states and traces leading to them— and user-defined formulas —e.g., the coherence property stated above. Proving coherence is defined in the CWB as a command that checks the proposition **Coherence** over the agent **Protocol** (does the agent satisfy the formula?). This is answered using a *game-based* model checking algorithm which generates a winning strategy for the corresponding model checking game (see [13] for a complete description of this technique).

The CWB execution of **checkprop(Protocol, Coherence)** gives a 'true' result, and the corresponding winning strategy constitutes a proof of the coherence property with respect to the specified CC-NUMA protocol. Indeed, there were intermediate specifications which could not be proved to be correct due to different modelling errors. The usefulness of the CWB lies in the possibility of playing model checking games against the tool. Game traces help to understand why a process does or does not satisfy a formula. This feature allowed us to detect the modelling errors until having a correct specification.

4   Conclusions and Future Work

In this paper we have described an application of formal methods to the specification and verification of a cache coherence protocol. Specifically, the protocol has been specified as a set of interacting processes in CCS and the coherence constraints have been described as temporal propositions in the μ-calculus. The results we have presented allow us to conclude that these formalisms are of a great interest and potentiality since: (1) the advantages of a formal specification are evident —e.g., the lack of ambiguity and the possibility of automatic manipulation, (2) automatic verification (tool assisted) allows the user to propose different properties and to check whether the protocol satisfies them or not.

We think that there are very promising research lines related to this subject. It is clear that the specification and verification techniques used in this paper could be used for the case of more complex protocols. Theoretically, this is possible no matter how sophisticated the protocol is. The only limitation is that the number of possible states is finite. In practical terms, we can make use of powerful tools which allow us to manipulate specification and to automatise the verification of properties.

It would be interesting to make a systematic study of how different consistency and coherence properties could be characterised in terms of temporal propositions. The application of specification and verification techniques could be applied not only to coherence protocols but to any other communication protocol. Moreover, they could be applied to any *"process-oriented"* system —i.e., a system that can be accurately modelled as a set of communicating processes that interact and exchange information.

References

1. Rance Cleaveland, Joachim Parrow, and Bernhard Steffen. The Concurrency Workbench. Technical Report ECS-LFCS-89-83, LFCS, Department of Computer Science, University of Edinburgh, 1989.
2. G. Delzanno. Automatic verification of parameterized cache coherence protocols. In *Proceedings of CAV'2000*, vol.1885 of *LNCS*, pages 53–68. Springer-Verlag, 2000.
3. E. M. Clarke and J. M. Wing. Formal methods: State of the art and future directions. Technical Report CMU-CS-96-178, September 1996.
4. Matthew Hennessy. *Algebraic Theory of Processes*. MIT Press, Cambridge, 1988.
5. C.A.R. Hoare. *Communicating Sequential Processes*. Prentice Hall, 1985.
6. K.L. McMillan. *Symbolic Model Checking: An Approach to the State Explosion Problem*. PhD thesis, School of Computer Science, CMU, May 1992.
7. Dexter Kozen. Results on the Propositional μ-Calculus. *Theoretical Computer Science*, 27(3):333–354, December 1983.
8. Ladkin, Lamport, Olivier, and Roegel. Lazy caching in TLA. *Distributed Computing*, 12, 1999.
9. Robin Milner. *Communication and Concurrency*. Prentice Hall, 1989.
10. A.K. Nanda and L.N. Bhuyan. A formal specification and verification technique for cache coherence protocols. In *Proceedings of the 1992 International Conference on Parallel Processing*, pages 122–126, 1992.
11. Fong Pong and Michel Dubois. Verification techniques for cache coherence protocols. *ACM Computing Surveys*, 29(1):82–126, March 1997.
12. Per Stenström. A Survey of Cache Coherence Schemes for Multiprocessors. *IEEE Computer*, 23(6):12–24, June 1990.
13. C. Stirling. Modal and temporal logics for processes. Technical Report ECS-LFCS-92-221, LFCS, Dep. of Computer Science, University of Edinburgh, June 1992.
14. Colin Stirling. An introduction to modal and temporal logic for ccs. In *Proc. 1989 UK/Japan Workshop on Concurrency, LNCS* 491, pages 2–20. Springer 1991.

Static Analysis for Secrecy and Non-interference in Networks of Processes*

C. Bodei[1], P. Degano[1], F. Nielson[2], and H. Riis Nielson[2]

[1] Dipartimento di Informatica, Università di Pisa
Corso Italia 40, I-56125 Pisa, Italy
{chiara,degano}@di.unipi.it

[2] Informatics & Mathematical Modelling, The Technical University of Denmark
Richard Petersens Plads bld 321,
DK-2800 Kongens Lyngby, Denmark
{nielson,riis}@imm.dtu.dk

Abstract. We introduce the νSPI-calculus that strengthens the notion of "perfect symmetric cryptography" of the spi-calculus by taking time into account. This involves defining an operational semantics, defining a control flow analysis (CFA) in the form of a flow logic, and proving semantic correctness. Our first result is that secrecy in the sense of Dolev-Yao can be expressed in terms of the CFA. Our second result is that also non-interference in the sense of Abadi can be expressed in terms of the CFA; unlike Abadi we find the non-interference property to be an extension of the Dolev-Yao property.

1 Introduction

The widespread usage of distributed systems and networks has furnished a great number of interesting scenarios in which security plays a significant role. Well established and well founded process algebraic theories offer a fertile ground to express distributed and concurrent systems in pure form, and to study their properties. In particular, protocols and security protocols can be conveniently written in the spi-calculus [1,5], an extension of the π-calculus with primitives for encryption and decryption. These are based on symmetric cryptography that is assumed to be perfect; as usual this is formulated in an algebraic manner: that encryption and decryption are inverses of one another. This facilitates expressing cryptographic protocols and one can reason on them exploiting the rich variety of techniques and tools, developed for calculi of computation and programming languages.

As observed in [1] the notion of perfect encryption embodied in the spi-calculus is too weak to guard against certain attacks based on comparing ciphertexts. As an example, consider a process that first communicates *true* encrypted under some key, then *false* encrypted under the same key, and finally a secret

---

* The first two authors have been partially supported by the Progetti MURST TOSCA and AI, TS & CFA.

V. Malyshkin (Ed.): PaCT 2001, LNCS 2127, pp. 27–41, 2001.
© Springer-Verlag Berlin Heidelberg 2001

boolean b encrypted under the same key; then confidentiality of b is not guaranteed because its value can be obtained by comparison of ciphertexts. To guard against this form of attack a type system is developed that enforces placement of so-called confounders in all encryptions [1].

By contrast our approach is based on the observation that many symmetric cryptosystems, e.g. DES operating in a suitable chaining mode, are *always* initialised with a random initialisation vector, thereby dealing with a notion of confounders dynamically. To be closer to real implementations, we therefore use a slight modification of the spi-calculus, called νSPI. We semantically model the randomization of the encryption function, by adding to each plaintext M a new and fresh value r, making any two encryptions of M different from each other. In other words, we obtain a notion of history dependent cryptography. Recent and independent developments along a similar line of thought may be found in [20,3]. Indeed, it seems unlikely that any approach only based on algebraic identities (and consideration of the free theory generated) will be able to mimic our semantics-based development.

In preparation for the applications to security we then develop in Section 3 a Control Flow Analysis (CFA) in the form of a Flow Logic [21]. Its specification is in line with previous developments for the π-calculus [8,7] and the same goes for its semantic correctness by means of a subject-reduction result and the existence of least solutions. However, the techniques needed for obtaining the least solution in polynomial time (actually $O(n^3)$) are more involved than before because the specification operates over an infinite universe [23,25].

Our first application to security in Section 4 is to show that CFA helps in showing that a protocol has no *direct* flows that violate confidentiality. The static condition, called *confinement*, merely inspects the CFA information to make sure that only public messages flow along public channels. The dynamic condition, called *carefulness*, then guarantees for all executions that no secrets are output on public channels. Correctness of the static analysis then follows from the subject-reduction result. This notion of security essentially says that no attacker, not even an active saboteur, can decipher a secret message sent on the network; actually, we show that if a process is careful then it preserves the secrecy of messages according to the notion originally advocated by Dolev and Yao [16,2]. A similar result has independently been achieved by [4] using a type system on a slightly different calculus.

Our second application to security in Section 5 is to show that CFA also helps in checking that a protocol has no *indirect* flows that violate confidentiality. In the formulation of Abadi [1] the static condition is formulated using a type system and the dynamic condition then compares executions using testing equivalence [13,10]. In our formulation the static condition, called *invariance*, is formulated as yet another check on the CFA information, and we retain the dynamic notion, which we prefer to call *message independence*. (Both our and Abadi's dynamic notions say that the active attacker cannot detect whatsoever information about the message sent, even by inspecting and changing the behaviour of a secure protocol; but this does not quite amount to non-interference in the sense of [17].) While inspired by [24, Section 5.3] this represents the first use of CFA for establishing testing equivalence for processes allowing cryptography. In our approach, confinement is a prerequisite for invariance, thus suggesting a deeper connection between Dolev-Yao and Non-Interference than reported by Abadi [2].

A more widely used alternative approach for calculi of computation and security is based on Type Systems [1,32,31,29,30,19,27,28,12,11]. Here security requirements are seen as static information about the objects of a system [1,32,12,11]. Our approach builds on the more "classical" approaches to static analysis and thus links up with the pioneering approach taken in the very early studies by Denning [14,15]; it also features a very good computational complexity.

Because of lack of space, we dispense with the proofs, which often use techniques similar to those of [7] and that can in part be found in the extended version of the paper.

2   History Dependent Cryptography

Syntax. We define the νSPI-calculus by modifying the spi-calculus [5] (we consider here its monadic form, for simplicity) so that the encryption primitive becomes history dependent. Roughly, this amounts to saying that every time we encrypt a message we get a different ciphertext, even if the message is the same and the key is the same. We do so by changing the semantics: each encryption necessarily generates a fresh confounder that is part of the message (corresponding to the random initialisation vector used when running DES in an appropriate chaining mode); therefore our analysis does not need to enforce this property (unlike the type system in [1]). This naturally leads to modifying the semantics to evaluate a message before it is actually sent; in other words we define a call-by-value programming language. — To aid the intuitions of the reader familiar with the spi-calculus we have also changed the syntax by letting each encryption contain a construct for generating the confounder; however this syntactic change is in no way essential (quite unlike the semantic change).

The formulation of the CFA of the νSPI-calculus, in Section 3, is facilitated by making a few assumptions. Mainly, we slightly extend the standard syntax by mechanically assigning "labels" to the occurrences of terms; these are nothing but explicit notations for program points and in an actual implementation can be taken to be pointers into the syntax tree. Furthermore, to deal with the α-renaming of bound names in a simple and "implicit" way, we assume that names are "stable", i.e. that each name a is the canonical representative for its class of α-convertible names. To this aim, we define the set of names $\mathcal{N}'$ as the disjoint union of sets of indexed names, $\mathcal{N}' = \uplus_{a \in \mathcal{N}} \{a, a_0, a_1, \cdots\}$, and we write $\lfloor a_i \rfloor = a$ for the canonical name a associated to each actual name a_i. Then we restrict α-conversion so that we only allow a name a_i to be substituted for the name b_j, if $\lfloor a_i \rfloor = \lfloor b_j \rfloor$. In this way, we statically maintain the identity of names that may be lost by freely applying α-conversions. (For a more "explicit" approach using marker environments see [8,6].)

Definition 1. *Let* $l, l', l_i \in \mathcal{L}$ *be labels,* $n, m, \cdots \in \mathcal{N}'$ *be names and* $x, y, \cdots \in \mathcal{V}$ *be variables. Then (labelled) expressions,* $E, V \in \mathcal{E}$, *(unlabelled) terms,* $M, N \in \mathcal{M}$, *values* $w, v \in Val'$, *and processes,* $P, P_i, Q, R, \cdots \in \mathcal{P}$, *are all built according to the following syntax:*

$$E, V ::= M^l$$
$$M, N ::= n \mid x \mid (E, E') \mid 0 \mid suc(E) \mid \{E_1, \cdots, E_k, (\nu r) \; r\}_{E_0} \mid w$$
$$w, v ::= n \mid pair(w, w') \mid 0 \mid suc(w) \mid enc\{w_1, \cdots, w_k, r\}_{w_0}$$
$$P, Q ::= 0 \mid \overline{E}\langle V\rangle.P \mid E(x).P \mid P|P \mid (\nu n)P \mid$$
$$[E \; is \; V]P \mid \; !P \mid let \; (x, y) = E \; in \; P \mid$$
$$case \; E \; of \; 0 : P \; suc(x) : Q \mid case \; E \; of \; \{x_1, \cdots, x_k\}_V \; in \; P$$

Here $E(x).P$ *binds the variable* x *in* P, *while* $(\nu n)P$ *binds the name* n *in* P. *We dispense with defining the standard notions of free and bound names (fn and resp. bn) and of free and bound variables fv (resp. bv). We often omit the trailing* 0 *and write* ⁓ *to denote tuples of objects.*

The νSPI-calculus slightly extends the spi-calculus, that in turn extends the π-calculus (with which we assume the reader to be familiar) with more structured terms (numbers, pairs and encryptions) and process constructs dealing with them. Moreover, our term $\{E_1, \cdots, E_k, (\nu r) \; r\}_{E_0}$ represents the unevaluated encryption of $E_1, \cdots, E_k$ under the symmetric key E_0. Its evaluation results in the actual value $enc\{w_1, \cdots, w_k, r\}_{w_0}$, where w_i is the value of E_i and the restriction (νr) will make sure that the confounder (or initialisation vector) r is fresh (see below). The process $case \; E \; of \; \{x_1, \cdots, x_k\}_V \; in \; P$ attempts to decrypt E with the key V: if E is on the form $\{E_1, \cdots, E_k\}_V$ then the process behaves as $P[\tilde{E}_i/\tilde{x}_i]$, otherwise the process is stuck. Similarly, $let \; (x, y) = E \; in \; P$ attempts to split the pair E and $case \; E \; of \; 0 : P \; suc(x) : Q$ tries to establish if E is either 0 or a successor of some term.

Note that, unlike the π-calculus, names and variables are considered distinct. Finally we extend $\lfloor \cdots \rfloor$ to operate on values by the straightforward structural definition. We write Val for the set of canonical values, i.e. those values v such that $\lfloor v \rfloor = v$.

Entities are considered equal whenever they are α-convertible; so $P = Q$ means that P is α-convertible to Q. Substitution of terms, $\cdots [M/x]$, is standard; substitution of expressions, $\cdots [E/x]$, really denotes substitution of terms, so it preserves labels, hence $x^{l_x}[M^l/x]$ is M^{l_x}; finally, substitution of restricted values, $\cdots [(\nu r)w/x]$, acts as substitution of values, $\cdots [w/x]$, with the restriction moved out of any expressions, e.g. $\overline{n}\langle x\rangle[(\nu r)r/x] = (\nu r)\overline{n}\langle r\rangle$. We shall write $P \equiv Q$ to mean that P and Q are equal except that restriction operators may be placed differently as long as their effect is the same, e.g. $(\nu r)\overline{n}\langle s\rangle.\overline{m}\langle r\rangle \equiv \overline{n}\langle s\rangle.(\nu r)\overline{m}\langle r\rangle$.

Semantics. The semantics is built out of three relations: the evaluation, the reduction and the commitment relations. In all of them we will apply our disciplined α-conversion when needed. They all operate on *closed* entities, i.e. entities without free variables.

Table 1. The semantics of νSPI: the evaluation relation, $\gg$; the reduction relation, $>$; and the commitment relation, $\xrightarrow{\alpha}$ (without symmetric rules).

---

1. $n^l \gg n$　　2. $0^l \gg 0$　　3. $\dfrac{E_i \gg (\nu\tilde{r}_i)\, w_i,\ i = 1,2,\ \tilde{r}_1\tilde{r}_2 \text{ w.o. duplicates}}{(E_1, E_2) \gg (\nu\tilde{r}_1\tilde{r}_2)\, pair(w_1, w_2)}$

4. $\dfrac{E \gg (\nu\tilde{r})\, w}{suc(E) \gg (\nu\tilde{r})\, suc(w)}$

5. $\dfrac{E_i \gg (\nu\tilde{r}_i)\, w_i,\ i = 0 \cdots k,\ \tilde{r}_1 \cdots \tilde{r}_k\tilde{r}_0 r \text{ w.o. duplicates}}{\{E_1, \cdots, E_k, (\nu r)\, r\}_{E_0} \gg (\nu\tilde{r}_1 \cdots \tilde{r}_k\tilde{r}_0 r)\, enc\{w_1, \cdots, w_k, r\}_{w_0}}$

$Match:$ $\dfrac{E_i \gg (\nu\tilde{r}_i)\, w_i,\ i = 1,2}{[E_1 \text{ is } E_2]P > (\nu\tilde{r}_1\tilde{r}_2)\, P}$ 　$(\nu\tilde{r}_1\tilde{r}_2)\, w_1 = (\nu\tilde{r}_1\tilde{r}_2)\, w_2;\ \tilde{r}_1\tilde{r}_2 fn(P) \text{ w.o. duplicates}$

$Let:$ $\dfrac{E \gg (\nu\tilde{r})\, pair(w_1, w_2)}{let\ (x,y) = E \text{ in } P > (\nu\tilde{r})\, P[w_1/x, w_2/y]}$ 　$\tilde{r} fn(P) \text{ w.o. duplicates}$

$Zero:$ $\dfrac{E \gg 0}{case\ E \text{ of } 0 : P\ suc(x) : Q > P}$ 　　$Rep:$ $\dfrac{}{!P > P\,|!P}$

$Suc:$ $\dfrac{E \gg (\nu\tilde{r})\, suc(w)}{case\ E \text{ of } 0 : P\ suc(x) : Q > (\nu\tilde{r})\, Q[w/x]}$ 　$\tilde{r} fn(Q) \text{ w.o. duplicates}$

$Enc:$ $\dfrac{E \gg (\nu\tilde{r}_0)\, enc\{w_1, \cdots, w_k, s\}_{w_0},\ V \gg (\nu\tilde{r}_1)\, v}{case\ E \text{ of } \{x_1, \cdots, x_k\}_V \text{ in } P > (\nu\tilde{r}_0)\, P[w_1/x_1, \cdots, w_k/x_k]}$
$\tilde{r}_0\tilde{r}_1 fn(P) \text{ w.o. duplicates}; (\nu\tilde{r}_0\tilde{r}_1)\, w_0 = (\nu\tilde{r}_0\tilde{r}_1)\, v$

$In:$ $m(x).P \xrightarrow{m} (x)P$ 　　　$Out:$ $\dfrac{M^l \gg (\nu\tilde{r})\, w}{\overline{m}\langle M^l \rangle.P \xrightarrow{\overline{m}} (\nu\tilde{r})\langle w^l \rangle P}$ 　$\tilde{r} fn(P) \text{ w.o. duplicates}$

$Inter:$ $\dfrac{P \xrightarrow{m} F \quad Q \xrightarrow{\overline{m}} C}{P|Q \xrightarrow{\tau} F@C}$ 　　$Par:$ $\dfrac{P \xrightarrow{\alpha} A}{P|Q \xrightarrow{\alpha} A|Q}$

$Red:$ $\dfrac{P > Q \quad Q \xrightarrow{\alpha} A}{P \xrightarrow{\alpha} A}$ 　　　$Res:$ $\dfrac{P \xrightarrow{\alpha} A}{(\nu m)P \xrightarrow{\alpha} (\nu m)A}$ 　$\alpha \notin \{m, \overline{m}\}$

$Congr:$ $\dfrac{P \equiv Q \quad Q \xrightarrow{\alpha} A \quad A \equiv B}{P \xrightarrow{\alpha} B}$

The evaluation relation $\gg$ in the upper part of Table 1 reduces an expression E to a value w. Although it is not part of the standard semantics of the spi-calculus, it is quite natural from a programming language point of view, and it is crucial in specifying history dependent encryption. As it will be clear soon, a term has to be fully evaluated before it is used either in a reduction (e.g. when matching or a decryption takes place) or as a message. So to speak, our variant of the calculus is a call-by-value one. The central rule is that for encryption: the restriction (νr) acting on the confounder r is pushed in the outermost position, so that every other name in the process is and will be different from r.

Two different occurrences, M^l and $M^{l'}$ (with $l \neq l'$), of a term containing an unevaluated encryption operator, never evaluate to the same values, $(\nu\tilde{r})w$ and

$(\nu \tilde{r}')w'$, where $w = w'$ and the concatenation of vectors of names $\tilde{r}$ and $\tilde{r}'$ has no name occurring more than once (abbreviated $\tilde{r}\tilde{r}'$ w.o. duplicates).

This is crucial for matching; indeed, $[\{0,(\nu r)r\}_w^l$ is $\{0,(\nu r)r\}_w^{l'}]P$ never reduces to P, because every time we encrypt 0, even if under exactly the same evaluated key, we get a different value. The *reduction* rules in the central part of Table 1 govern the evaluation of guards. They only differ from the standard spi-calculus ones because, as mentioned above, the terms occurring in P that drive the reduction $P > Q$ have to be evaluated. This step may introduce some new restricted names, in particular when the terms include an encryption to be evaluated. This restriction is placed around Q, so as to make sure that the new names are indeed fresh and that there will be no captures. The side condition "$\tilde{r}_1\tilde{r}_2 fn(P)$ w.o. duplicates" in the rule *Match* ensures that the scopes are preserved even though the restrictions are placed differently; similarly for the other side conditions. Finally, note that after a decryption, the process P has no access to the confounder s.

To define the *commitment relation*, we need the usual notions of abstraction $F = (x)P$ and of concretion $C = (\nu\tilde{n})\langle w^l \rangle Q$ (assuming that $(x)P \mid Q = (x)(P \mid Q)$, if $x \notin fv(Q)$, that $(\nu\tilde{n})\langle w^l \rangle Q \mid R = (\nu\tilde{n})\langle w^l \rangle (Q \mid R)$, if $\tilde{n} \cap fn(R) = \emptyset$, and the symmetric rules). Note that the message sent must be an actual value. The interaction $F@C$ (and symmetrically for $C@F$) is then the following, provided that $\{\tilde{n}\} \cap fn(P) = \emptyset$:

$$F@C = (\nu\tilde{n})(P[w^l/x] \mid Q)$$

The structural operational semantic rules for the commitment relation are in the lower part of Table 1; they are standard apart from rule *Out* that requires the evaluation of the message sent, and introduces the new restricted names $\tilde{r}$ (possibly causing also some α-conversions).

3   Control Flow Analysis (CFA)

Writing $\widehat{Val} = \wp(Val)$ the result of our analysis for a process P is a triple (ρ, κ, ζ), where:

- $\rho : \mathcal{V} \to \widehat{Val}$ is the *abstract environment* that associates variables with the values that they can be bound to; more precisely, $\rho(x)$ must include the set of values that x could assume at run-time.
- $\kappa : \mathcal{N} \to \widehat{Val}$ is the *abstract channel environment* that associates canonical names with the values that can be communicated over them; more precisely, $\kappa(n)$ must include the set of values that can be communicated over the channel n.
- $\zeta : \mathcal{L} \to \widehat{Val}$ is the *abstract cache* that associates labels with the values that can arise there; more precisely $\zeta(l)$ must include the set of the possible actual values of the term labelled l.

Acceptability. To define the *acceptability* of a proposed estimate (ρ, κ, ζ) we state a set of clauses operating upon flow logic judgments on the forms $(\rho, \kappa, \zeta) \models M$ and $(\rho, \kappa, \zeta) \models P$.

The analysis of expressions and of processes are in Table 2. Our rules make use of canonical names and values and of the following abbreviations, where $W \in \widehat{Val}$:

- SUC(W) for $\{suc(w)|w \in W\}$;
- PAIR(W, W') for $\{pair(w, w')|w \in W, w' \in W'\}$;
- ENC$\{W_1, \cdots, W_k, r\}_{W_0}$ for $\{enc\{w_1, \cdots, w_k, r\}_{w_0}|\forall i : w_i \in W_i\}$.

All the rules for validating a compound term or a process require that the components are validated. The rules for an expression M^l demand that $\zeta(l)$ contains all the values associated with its components. Moreover, the rule for output requires that the set of values associated with the message N can be passed on each channel associated with M. Symmetrically, the rule for input requires that each value passing along M is contained in the set of possible values of x, i.e. $\rho(x)$. The last three rules check the ith sub-components of each value associated with the expression to split, compare or decrypt. Each sub-component must be contained in the corresponding $\rho(x_i)$.

Finally, the analysis is extended to concretions and abstractions in the last part of Table 2.

Correctness. To establish the semantic correctness of our analysis we establish subject-reduction results for the evaluation, the reduction and the commitment relations of the previous section.

Theorem 1 (Subject Reduction for $\gg$, $>$ and $\xrightarrow{\alpha}$).
Let $M^l \in \mathcal{E}$; if $(\rho, \kappa, \zeta) \models M^l$ and $M^l \gg (\nu\tilde{r})\, w$ then $\lfloor w \rfloor \in \zeta(l)$.

Let P be a closed process such that $(\rho, \kappa, \zeta) \models P$;

(1) if $P > Q$ then $(\rho, \kappa, \zeta) \models Q$.

(2) if $P \xrightarrow{\tau} Q$ then $(\rho, \kappa, \zeta) \models Q$;

(3) if $P \xrightarrow{\overline{m}} (\nu\tilde{n})\langle w^l \rangle Q$ then $(\rho, \kappa, \zeta) \models (\nu\tilde{n})\langle w^l \rangle Q$ and $\zeta(l) \subseteq \kappa(\lfloor m \rfloor)$;

(4) if $P \xrightarrow{m} (\nu\tilde{n})(x)Q$ then $(\rho, \kappa, \zeta) \models (\nu\tilde{n})(x)Q$ and $\kappa(\lfloor m \rfloor) \subseteq \rho(x)$.

Existence. So far we have only considered a procedure for validating whether or not a proposed estimate (ρ, κ, ζ) is in fact acceptable. Now, we show that there always exists a least choice of (ρ, κ, ζ) acceptable in the manner of Table 2.

It is quite standard to partially order the set of proposed estimates by setting $(\rho, \kappa, \zeta) \sqsubseteq (\rho', \kappa', \zeta')$ if and only if $\forall x \in \mathcal{V} : \rho(x) \subseteq \rho'(x)$, $\forall n \in \mathcal{N} : \kappa(n) \subseteq \kappa'(n)$ and $\forall l \in \mathcal{L} : \zeta(l) \subseteq \zeta'(l)$. Furthermore, a *Moore family* $\mathcal{I}$ is a set that contains $\sqcap \mathcal{J}$ for all $\mathcal{J} \subseteq \mathcal{I}$, where $\sqcap$ is the greatest lower bound operator (defined pointwise). One important property of a Moore family is that it always contains a least element. The following theorem then guarantees that there is always a least estimate to the specification in Table 2. Its statement concerns processes and the proof relies on analogous statements for expressions; this also holds for some of the following results.

Theorem 2. *The set $\{(\rho, \kappa, \zeta)|(\rho, \kappa, \zeta) \models P\}$ is a Moore family for all P.*

Table 2. CFA for expressions, processes, concretions and abstractions.

$(\rho, \kappa, \varsigma) \models n^l$	iff	$\{\lfloor n \rfloor\} \subseteq \varsigma(l)$
$(\rho, \kappa, \varsigma) \models x^l$	iff	$\rho(x) \subseteq \varsigma(l)$
$(\rho, \kappa, \varsigma) \models (M^{l_1}, N^{l_2})^l$	iff	$(\rho, \kappa, \varsigma) \models M^{l_1} \wedge (\rho, \kappa, \varsigma) \models N^{l_2} \wedge$ $\mathrm{PAIR}(\varsigma(l_1), \varsigma(l_2)) \subseteq \varsigma(l)$
$(\rho, \kappa, \varsigma) \models 0^l$	iff	$\{0\} \subseteq \varsigma(l)$
$(\rho, \kappa, \varsigma) \models suc(M^{l_M})^l$	iff	$(\rho, \kappa, \varsigma) \models M^{l_M} \wedge \mathrm{SUC}(\varsigma(l_M)) \subseteq \varsigma(l)$
$(\rho, \kappa, \varsigma) \models \{M_1^{l_1}, \cdots, M_k^{l_k}, (\nu r)\, r\}_{M_0^{l_0}}^l$	iff	$\forall i = 0, .., k : (\rho, \kappa, \varsigma) \models M_i^{l_i} \wedge$ $\mathrm{ENC}\{\varsigma(l_1), \cdots, \varsigma(l_k), \{\lfloor r \rfloor\}\}_{\varsigma(l_0)} \subseteq \varsigma(l)$
$(\rho, \kappa, \varsigma) \models w^l$	iff	$\{\lfloor w \rfloor\} \subseteq \varsigma(l)$
$(\rho, \kappa, \varsigma) \models \mathbf{0}$	iff	*true*
$(\rho, \kappa, \varsigma) \models \overline{M^l}\langle N^{l'} \rangle.P$	iff	$(\rho, \kappa, \varsigma) \models M^l \wedge (\rho, \kappa, \varsigma) \models N^{l'} \wedge$ $(\rho, \kappa, \varsigma) \models P \wedge \forall n \in \varsigma(l) : \varsigma(l') \subseteq \kappa(n)$
$(\rho, \kappa, \varsigma) \models M^l(x).P$	iff	$(\rho, \kappa, \varsigma) \models M^l \wedge (\rho, \kappa, \varsigma) \models P \wedge \forall n \in \varsigma(l) : \kappa(n) \subseteq \rho(x)$
$(\rho, \kappa, \varsigma) \models P_1 | P_2$	iff	$(\rho, \kappa, \varsigma) \models P_1 \wedge (\rho, \kappa, \varsigma) \models P_2$
$(\rho, \kappa, \varsigma) \models (\nu n)P$	iff	$(\rho, \kappa, \varsigma) \models P$
$(\rho, \kappa, \varsigma) \models\, !P$	iff	$(\rho, \kappa, \varsigma) \models P$
$(\rho, \kappa, \varsigma) \models [M^l\ is\ N^{l'}]P$	iff	$(\rho, \kappa, \varsigma) \models M^l \wedge (\rho, \kappa, \varsigma) \models N^{l'} \wedge (\rho, \kappa, \varsigma) \models P$
$(\rho, \kappa, \varsigma) \models let\ (x_1, x_2) = M^l in\ P$	iff	$(\rho, \kappa, \varsigma) \models M^l \wedge (\rho, \kappa, \varsigma) \models P \wedge$ $\forall pair(v, w) \in \varsigma(l) : \{v\} \subseteq \rho(x_1) \wedge \{w\} \subseteq \rho(x_2)$
$(\rho, \kappa, \varsigma) \models \begin{array}{l} case\ M^l\ of \\ 0 : P\ suc(x) : Q \end{array}$	iff	$(\rho, \kappa, \varsigma) \models M^l \wedge (\rho, \kappa, \varsigma) \models P \wedge$ $(\rho, \kappa, \varsigma) \models Q \wedge \forall\, suc(w) \in \varsigma(l) : \{w\} \subseteq \rho(x)$
$(\rho, \kappa, \varsigma) \models \begin{array}{l} case\ M^l\ of \\ \{x_1, \cdots, x_k\}_{N^{l'}} \\ in\ P \end{array}$	iff	$(\rho, \kappa, \varsigma) \models M^l \wedge (\rho, \kappa, \varsigma) \models N^{l'} \wedge (\rho, \kappa, \varsigma) \models P \wedge$ $\forall\, enc\{w_1, \cdots, w_m, r\}_w \in \varsigma(l) : \mathrm{if}\ m = k \wedge w \in \varsigma(l')$ $\mathrm{then}\ \forall i = 1, \cdots, k : \{w_i\} \subseteq \rho(x_i)$
$(\rho, \kappa, \varsigma) \models (\nu \tilde{m})\langle w^l \rangle P$	iff $(\rho, \kappa, \varsigma) \models P \wedge (\rho, \kappa, \varsigma) \models w^l$	
$(\rho, \kappa, \varsigma) \models (x)P$	iff $(\rho, \kappa, \varsigma) \models P$	

Polynomial Time Construction. In [7] we developed a polynomial time procedure for calculating least solutions. This development does *not* immediately carry over because we now operate over an *infinite* universe of values due to the expressions present in the calculus. Therefore the specification in Table 2 needs to be interpreted as defining a regular tree grammar whose least solution can be computed in polynomial time. A recent result [25] in fact shows that the time complexity can be reduced to cubic time.

4   CFA and Dolev-Yao Secrecy

In this section, we extend to the νSPI-calculus the static property of confinement, studied in [8] for the π-calculus. We then show that our notion corresponds to that of Dolev and Yao [16,9,26,2].

The Dynamic Notion. The names, $\mathcal{N}'$, are partitioned into the public ones, $\mathcal{P}$, and the secret ones, $\mathcal{S}$, in such a way that $n \in \mathcal{S}$ iff $\mathcal{N}_n \subseteq \mathcal{S}$. We demand that the free names of processes under analysis are all public; it follows that the secret names either do not occur at all or are restricted within a process. This partition is used as a basis for partitioning (also non canonical) values according to the two kinds s (for secret) and P (for public). The intention is that a single "drop" of secret makes the entire value secret except for what is encrypted with a secret key, which is anyway public. We do not consider confounders as they are discarded by decryptions.

Definition 2. *The operator* $kind : Val' \to \{s, P\}$ *is defined as*

- $kind(n) = \begin{cases} s & \text{if } n \in \mathcal{S} \\ P & \text{if } n \in \mathcal{P} \end{cases}$

- $kind(0) = P;$ $- \; kind(suc(w)) = kind(w);$

- $kind(pair(w, w')) = \begin{cases} s & \text{if } (kind(w) = s \ \vee \ kind(w') = s) \\ P & \text{otherwise;} \end{cases}$

- $kind(enc\{w_1, \cdots, w_k, r\}_{w_0}) = \begin{cases} P & \text{if } kind(w_0) = s \ \vee \ k = 0 \\ kind(\{w_1, \cdots, w_k\}) & \text{otherwise,} \end{cases}$

where, by abuse of notation, $kind(W) = \begin{cases} s \text{ if } \exists w \in W : kind(w) = s \\ P \text{ if } \forall w \in W : kind(w) = P. \end{cases}$ *We shall write* ValP *for the set of canonical values of kind* P.

To define the dynamic notion of secrecy we write $P \to^* Q$ to mean that $P \xrightarrow{\tau} \cdots \xrightarrow{\tau} Q$. Then carefulness means that no secrets are sent in clear on public channels:

Definition 3. *A process P is careful w.r.t. $\mathcal{S}$ iff whenever $P \to^* P' \xrightarrow{\alpha} P''$, with the last step deduced with the premise $R \xrightarrow{\overline{m}} (\nu\tilde{r})\langle w^l \rangle R'$, then $m \in \mathcal{P}$ implies $kind(w) = P$.*

The Static Notion. We now define the confinement property for the νSPI-calculus. It predicts at compile time that a process is careful. A check suffices on the κ component of a solution: the set of values that can flow on each public name n must be all the ones that have kind P.

Definition 4. *A process P is confined w.r.t. $\mathcal{S}$ and (ρ, κ, ζ) if and only if $(\rho, \kappa, \zeta) \models P$ and $\forall n \in \mathcal{P} : \kappa(n) = $ ValP.*

The subject reduction theorem extends trivially to confined processes thereby paving the way for showing that the static notion implies the dynamic one.

Theorem 3. *If P is confined w.r.t. $\mathcal{S}$ then P is careful w.r.t. $\mathcal{S}$.*

Example 1. We consider here an adaptation of the Wide Mouthed Frog key exchange protocol as presented in [5]. The two processes A and B share keys

K_{AS} and K_{BS} with a trusted server S. In order to establish a secure channel with B, A sends a fresh key K_{AB} encrypted with K_{AS} to S. Then, S decrypts the key and forwards it to B, this time encrypted with K_{BS}. Now A can send a message M encrypted with K_{AB} to B (for simplicity, M is a name). The analysis guarantees that M is kept secret. The protocol and its specification are as follows:

$$\text{Message 1}\ \ A \to S\ :\ \{K_{AB}\}_{K_{AS}}$$
$$\text{Message 2}\ \ S \to B\ :\ \{K_{AB}\}_{K_{BS}}$$
$$\text{Message 3}\ \ A \to B\ :\ \{M\}_{K_{AB}}$$

$$P = (\nu K_{AS})(\nu K_{BS})(\ (A|B)\ |\ S)$$
$$A = (\nu K_{AB})(\overline{c_{AS}^{l_{c1}}}\langle\{K_{AB}^{l_{k3}}, (\nu r_1)r_1\}_{K_{AS}^{l_{k1}}}\rangle . \overline{c_{AB}^{l_{c3}}}\langle\{M^{l_M}, (\nu r_2)r_2\}_{K_{AB}^{l_{k3}}}\rangle)$$
$$S = c_{AS}^{l_{c1}}(x).case\ x^{l_x}\ of\ \{s\}_{K_{AS}^{l_{k1}}}\ in\ \overline{c_{BS}}\langle\{s^{l_s}, (\nu r_3)r_3\}_{K_{BS}^{l_{k2}}}\rangle$$
$$B = c_{BS}^{l_{c2}}(t).case\ t^{l_t}\ of\ \{y\}_{K_{BS}^{l_{k2}}}\ in\ c_{AB}^{l_{c3}}(z).case\ z^{l_z}\ of\ \{q\}_{y^{l_y}}\ in\ B'(q)$$

Let $\mathcal{S} = \{K_{AS}, K_{BS}, K_{AB}, M\}$ and $\mathcal{P} = \{c_{AS}, c_{BS}, c_{AB}\}$; the relevant part of an estimate for P (disregarding $B'(q)$) is:

$$\rho(bv) = \begin{cases} \mathsf{ValP} & \text{if } bv \in \{x, s, t, y, z, q\} \\ \emptyset & \text{otherwise} \end{cases} \qquad \kappa(c) = \begin{cases} \mathsf{ValP} & \text{if } c \in \{c_{AS}, c_{BS}, c_{AB}\} \\ \emptyset & \text{otherwise} \end{cases}$$

Moreover, $\zeta(l_{bv}) = \rho(bv)$ for $bv \in \{x, s, t, y, z, q\}$ and $\zeta(l) = \{n\}$. for all the names n^l occurring in P. It is now easy to check that P is confined, hence the secrecy of M is guaranteed. ∎

The Formulation of Dolev and Yao. We now show that our notion of confinement enforces secrecy in the sense of Dolev and Yao [16,9,26,2]. Its inductive definition simulates the placement of a process P in a hostile environment that initially has some public knowledge, and thus knows all the values computable from it. Then, the environment may increase its knowledge by communicating with P. The secrecy requirement is that a message M is never revealed by P if the environment cannot reconstruct M from the initial knowledge and the knowledge it has acquired by interacting with the process P.

In our case the initial knowledge is given by the numbers and by all the names that are not considered secret, among which those free in the process under consideration. In other words, we are interested in keeping secrets of honest parties, only. The values whose secrecy should be preserved are composed of at least a secret name, except for secret terms, when encrypted (and therefore protected) under a secret key.

We first make precise which messages are computable from a given set of canonical messages $W \subseteq Val$. The function $C : \widehat{Val} \to \widehat{Val}$ is specified as the closure operator (meaning that C is idempotent and extensive: $C(C(W)) = C(W) \supseteq W$) associated with the following inductive definition (where "iff" is short for a rule with "if" and one with "only if"):

- $0 \in C(W)$; $-W \subseteq C(W)$; $-w \in C(W)$ iff $suc(w) \in C(W)$;
- $pair(w, w') \in C(W)$ iff $w \in C(W)$ and $w' \in C(W)$;
- if $\forall i : w_i \in C(W)$ then $\forall r \in W : enc\{w_1, \cdots, w_k, r\}_{w_0} \in C(W)$;
- if $enc\{w_1, \cdots, w_k, r\}_{w_0} \in C(W)$, $w_0 \in C(W)$ then $w_1, \cdots, w_k \in C(W)$.

The following relation $\mathcal{R}$ (or $\mathcal{R}_{K_0, P_0}$ to be pedantic) specifies how the environment, which knows a set of names K_0, can acquire some additional knowledge by interacting with a process P_0:

- $\mathcal{R}(P_0, C(K_0))$;
- if $\mathcal{R}(P, W)$ and $P \xrightarrow{\tau} Q$ then $\mathcal{R}(Q, W)$;
- if $\mathcal{R}(P, W)$, $P \xrightarrow{m} (x)Q$, $\lfloor m \rfloor \in W$ and $\lfloor w \rfloor \in W$ then $\mathcal{R}(Q[w/x], W)$;
- if $\mathcal{R}(P, W)$, $P \xrightarrow{\overline{m}} (\nu\tilde{n})\langle w^l \rangle Q$ and $\lfloor m \rfloor \in W$ then $\mathcal{R}((\nu\tilde{n})Q,$
  $C(W \cup \{\lfloor w \rfloor\}))$.

The notion of secrecy put forward by Dolev and Yao can now be phrased as follows. (Recall that $fn(P_0) \subseteq \mathcal{P}$; P_0 is closed; and that the names $\mathcal{N}'$ are partitioned in $\mathcal{S}$ and $\mathcal{P}$.)

Definition 5. *The process P_0 may reveal M from $K_0 \subseteq \mathcal{P}$, with $M \gg (\nu\tilde{r})w$ and $kind(w) = s$, if $\exists P', W'$ s.t. $\mathcal{R}(P', W')$ and $\lfloor w \rfloor \in W'$.*

The Comparison. Next, we consider the *most powerful* attacker or saboteur S, and define the format of its estimate, which therefore will be an estimate for any other attacker. From this estimate and one confining P, we can construct an estimate showing that $P \mid S$ is also confined. In other words, P can be placed in any context without disclosing its secrets. Typically, the estimate for S will involve expressions of kind p, only. This and the following lemma deeply depend on the Moore family property (Theorem 2). To state this succinctly define the restrictions $\rho_{|B}$, $\kappa_{|C}$, $\zeta_{|L}$ ($B \subseteq \mathcal{V}, C \subseteq \mathcal{N}, L \subseteq \mathcal{L}$) as follows:

$$(\rho_{|B})(x) = \begin{cases} \rho(x) & \text{if } x \in B \\ \emptyset & \text{o.w.} \end{cases} \quad (\kappa_{|C})(n) = \begin{cases} \kappa(n) & \text{if } n \in C \\ \emptyset & \text{o.w.} \end{cases} \quad (\zeta_{|L})(l) = \begin{cases} \zeta(l) & \text{if } l \in L \\ \emptyset & \text{o.w.} \end{cases}$$

We now characterize the shape of estimates for an attacker Q.

Lemma 1. *Let Q be a closed process with all names in $\mathcal{P}$; then $(\rho', \kappa'_{|\mathcal{P}}, \zeta') \models Q$ where $\forall x, \forall n \in \mathcal{P}, \forall l : \rho'(x) = \kappa'_{|\mathcal{P}}(n) = \zeta'(l) = \mathsf{ValP}$.*

Given an estimate for P, we can reduce it to act on the variables and labels of P only.

Lemma 2. *Let B and L be the sets of variables and labels in P, then $(\rho, \kappa, \zeta) \models P$ if and only if $(\rho_{|B}, \kappa, \zeta_{|L}) \models P$.*

From the estimate confining P, we can construct an estimate confining $P \mid Q$, using the above estimate for Q and the above lemma.

Proposition 1. *Let P be confined w.r.t. S; and let Q be a closed process with names all in P, and such that all variables and labels occurring inside Q do not occur inside P. Then P | Q is confined w.r.t. S.*

Due to this proposition, there is *no need* to actually compute the estimate for the most powerful attacker S or for any attacker Q and more importantly that for P | S: the estimate for P as defined in Defn. 4 suffices for checking secrecy. Indeed, since P is confined, so is P | Q which also is careful, by Theorem 3. This suffices for proving that P never reveals secret messages to an attacker knowing only public data.

It follows that our static notion of confinement suffices to guarantee Dolev and Yao's property of secrecy. Indeed, a confined (and thus careful) process never sends secrets in clear on public channels.

Theorem 4. *A process P confined w.r.t. S, does not reveal any message M, with $M \gg (\nu \tilde{r})w$ and $kind(w) = s$, from any $K_0 \subseteq \mathcal{P}$.*

5   CFA and Message-Independence

The notion of secrecy seen above does not guarantee absence of implicit information flow, cf. [2] for more explanation. A typical case of implicit flow is when a protocol P behaves differently, according to the result of comparing a secret value against a public one. In this case, an attacker can detect some information about a message sent by noticing, e.g., that the message is *not* the number 0. In this section, we follow Abadi's approach [1], and consider the case in which a message received does not influence the overall behaviour of the protocol, even in presence of an active attacker Q. Note however that Q running in parallel with P *may* change the behaviour of P, e.g. by sending a message that permits to pass a matching. We shall show that our CFA can guarantee this form of non-interference, that we call *message independence*.

More precisely, we shall make sure that no attacker can detect whether a process $P(x)$ (where for simplicity, x is the only free variable) uses a message M or a different one M' in place of x. To interface with the developments of Section 4 we shall focus on a specific canonical channel $n_* \in S$ not otherwise used; it will be used to track the places where the value of x may reach. Technically, we can either assume that all solutions (ρ, κ, ζ) considered have $\rho(x) = \{n_*\}$ or else substitute n_* for x in all instances where we invoke the analysis and the notion of confinement.

To cater for this development, we assign two sorts to values, according to whether they contain n_* or not (again, encryption is an exception). Intuitively, a value w has sort I if either n_* does not occur in w, or it appears encrypted; otherwise n_* is "visible" in w that then gets sort E. Also, note that if $kind(w) = P$ then $sort(w) = I$.

Definition 6. *The operator $sort : Val' \rightarrow \{I, E\}$ is defined as*

$$- \ sort(n) = \begin{cases} I & \text{if } n \neq \lfloor n_* \rfloor \\ E & \text{if } n = \lfloor n_* \rfloor \end{cases}$$

$$- \quad sort(0) = I; \quad - \ sort(suc(w)) = sort(w);$$

$$- \ sort(pair(w, w')) = \begin{cases} I & \text{if } sort(w) = sort(w') = I \\ E & \text{otherwise}; \end{cases}$$

$$- \ sort(enc\{w_1, \cdots, w_k, r\}_{w_0}) = I$$

Again, by abuse of notation, $sort(W) = \begin{cases} E \text{ if } \exists w \in W : sort(w) = E \\ I \text{ if } \forall w \in W : sort(w) = I. \end{cases}$

With our next definition, we statically check if a process uses (the value that will bind) x in points where an attacker can grasp it. More in detail, we consider as sensitive data those terms that are used as channels or as keys or in comparisons, and check that they will never depend on the message M. Otherwise, in the first case, the attacker may establish different communications with $P[M/x]$ and $P[M'/x]$; in the second case, the attacker may decrypt a message if M turns out to be public; in the last case, the attacker may detect some information about M (e.g. if it is not 0, see above). The static check controls that the special name n_* never belongs to the sets of values that are associated by the ζ component of estimates to each occurrence of these sensitive data. Note that we allow decomposing a term containing x; we only forbid, in a lazy way, that x is used to alter the flow of control.

Definition 7. *The process $P(x)$ is invariant w.r.t. x and (ρ, κ, ζ) if and only if for all occurrences of*
- *terms $\{V_1, \cdots, V_k, (\nu r) r\}_{N^l}$, are s.t. $sort(\zeta(l)) = I$;*
- *prefixes $\overline{M^l} \langle V \rangle.P$ and $M^l(y).P$ and constructs let $(y, z) = M^l$ in P; case M^l of $0 : P$ suc$(y) : Q$; case M^l of $\{y_1, \cdots, y_k\}_{N^{l'}}$ in P, are s.t. $n_* \notin \zeta(l)$ and $sort(\zeta(l')) = I$;*
- *constructs $[M^l$ is $N^{l'}]P$, are s.t. $sort(\zeta(l)) = sort(\zeta(l')) = I$.*

Before defining our notion of message independence we need to adapt testing equivalence. Basically two processes are testing equivalent [13,10] if they pass exactly the same set of tests, i.e. if one process is ready to communicate with any partner then so is the other, and viceversa.

Definition 8. *Let P, P' and Q be closed processes and let β be m or $\overline{m}$. The process P passes a public test (Q, β) if and only if $fn(Q) \subseteq \mathcal{P}$ and $(P|Q) \xrightarrow{\tau} Q_1 \cdots \xrightarrow{\tau} Q_n \xrightarrow{\beta} A$, for some $n \geq 0$, some processes $Q_1, \cdots, Q_n$ and some agent A. The two processes P and P' are public testing equivalent, in symbols $P \sim P'$, if $\forall (Q, \beta)$, if P passes (Q, β) then P' passes (Q, β) and viceversa.*

Message independence of a process $P(x)$ then merely says that no external observer can determine the term instantiating the variable x.

Definition 9. *A process $P(x)$ is message independent iff $P[M/x] \sim P[M'/x]$ for all closed messages M and M'.*

Finally, we establish that a confined and invariant process is message independent; our formulation offers an alternative to Abadi's approach, based on type systems. Moreover, our formulation sheds light on the role played by confidentiality in non interference. It is crucial to keep confidential secrets for not exposing, either directly or indirectly, the values that can be bound to the free variable x.

Theorem 5. *If $P(x)$ is confined (w.r.t. S containing n_*) and invariant (w.r.t. x and the same solution), then it is message independent.*

6   Conclusion

Control Flow Analysis has already been successfully used for studies of security in the π-calculus [8] (focusing on direct flows violating confidentiality) and for studies of mobility in the Mobile Ambients [22,18] (focusing on firewalls).

Here, we have proved that our overall approach to direct flows does scale up to a calculus with perfect cryptography, despite the need to use more advanced techniques for efficiently implementing the analysis. Prior to that, we have also overcome a weakness in previous formulations of perfect symmetric cryptography, usually formulated using algebraic identities, by defining its properties as part of the semantics of the νSPI-calculus.

Our second technical result was to show that our approach is also amenable to the treatment of indirect flows, in the form of non-interference results, thereby obtaining results similar to those obtained using type systems. Indeed, we have factored confidentiality out of non interference. This separation of concerns may clarify the relationship between the two properties and may help checking them separately.

References

1. M. Abadi. Secrecy by Typing In Security protocols. *Journal of the ACM*, 5(46):18–36, September 1999.
2. M. Abadi. Security protocols and specifications. In *FoSSaCS'99, LNCS 1578*, pages 1–13. Springer, 1999.
3. M. Abadi, C. Fournet. Mobile Values, New names, and Secure Communication. In *POPL'01*, ACM, 2001.
4. M. Abadi, B. Blanchet. Secrecy Types for Asymmetric Communication. In *FoSSaCS'01, LNCS 2030*, pages 25–41. Springer, 2001.
5. M. Abadi and A. D. Gordon. A calculus for cryptographic protocols - The Spi calculus. *Information and Computation 148*, 1:1–70, January 1999.
6. C. Bodei. *Security Issues in Process Calculi*. PhD thesis, Dipartimento di Informatica, Università di Pisa. TD-2/00, March, 2000.
7. C. Bodei, P. Degano, F. Nielson, and H. Riis Nielson. Static analysis for the π-calculus with their application to security. To appear in *I&C*. Available at http://www.di.unipi.it/~chiara/publ-40/BDNNi00.ps.
8. C. Bodei, P. Degano, F. Nielson, and H. Riis Nielson. Control flow analysis for the π-calculus. In *CONCUR'98, LNCS 1466*, pages 84–98. Springer, 1998.

9. D. Bolignano. An approach to the formal verification of cryptographic protocols. In *3rd ACM Conf. on Computer and Communications Security*, pages 106–118. ACM Press, 1996.

10. M. Boreale and R. De Nicola. Testing equivalence for mobile processes. *Information and Computation*, 120(2):279–303, August 1995.

11. L. Cardelli and A.D. Gordon. Types for mobile ambients. In *POPL'99*, pages 79–92. ACM Press, 1999.

12. R. De Nicola, G. Ferrari, and R. Pugliese, B. Venneri. Types for access control. *Theoretical Computer Science* 240(1): 215-254, June 2000.

13. R. De Nicola and M.C.B. Hennessy. Testing equivalence for processes. *Theoretical Computer Science*, 34:83–133, 1984.

14. D. E. Denning. A Lattice Model of Secure Information Flow. *Communications of the ACM*, pages 236–243, May 1976.

15. D. E. Denning and P. J. Denning. Certification of Programs for Secure Information Flow. *Communications of the ACM*, pages 504–513, July 1977.

16. D. Dolev and A.C. Yao. On the security of public key protocols. *IEEE Transactions on Information Theory*, IT-29(12):198–208, March 1983.

17. J.A. Goguen and J. Meseguer. Security policy and security models. In *1982 IEEE Symposium on Research on Security and Privacy*, pages 11–20. IEEE Press, 1982.

18. R. R. Hansen, J. G. Jensen, F. Nielson, and H. R. Nielson. Abstract interpretation of mobile ambients. In *SAS'99, LNCS 1694*, pages 135–148, 1999.

19. N. Heintze and J.G Riecke. The SLam calculus: Programming with secrecy and integrity. In *POPL'98*, pages 365–377. ACM Press, 1998.

20. J. Jürjens. Bridging the Gap: Formal vs. Complexity-theoretical Reasoning about Cryptography. Security through Analysis and Verification, Dagstuhl Dec. 2000.

21. F. Nielson and H. R. Nielson. Flow logics and operational semantics. *Electronic Notes of Theoretical Computer Science*, 10, 1998.

22. F. Nielson, H. R. Nielson, R. R. Hansen, and J. G. Jensen. Validating firewalls in mobile ambients. In *CONCUR'99, LNCS 1664*, pages 463–477, 1999.

23. F. Nielson, H. Seidl. Control-Flow Analysis in Cubic Time. In *ESOP'01, LNCS 2028*, pages 252–268, 2001.

24. H. Riis Nielson and F. Nielson. *Semantics with Applications: A Formal Introduction*. Wiley Professional Computing. Wiley, 1992.

25. H. Riis Nielson, F. Nielson, H. Seidl. Cryptographic Analysis in Cubic Time. Manuscript, 2001.

26. L.C. Paulson. Proving properties of security protocols by induction. In *CSFW'97*, pages 70–83. IEEE, 1997.

27. J. Riely and M. Hennessy. A typed language for distributed mobile processes. In *POPL'98*, pages 378–390. ACM Press, 1998.

28. J. Riely and M. Hennessy. Trust and partial typing in open systems of mobile agents. In *POPL'99*, pages 93–104. ACM Press, 1999.

29. D. Volpano and G. Smith. Language Issues in Mobile Program Security. In *Mobile Agent Security*, LNCS 1419, pages 25–43. Springer, 1998.

30. D. Volpano and G. Smith. Probabilistic noninterference in a concurrent language. In *CSFW'98*, pages 34–43. IEEE, 1998.

31. D. Volpano and G. Smith. Secure information flow in a multi-threaded imperative language. In *POPL'98*, pages 355–364. ACM Press, 1998.

32. D. Volpano, G. Smith, and C. Irvine. A sound type system for secure flow analysis. *Journal of Computer Security*, 4:4–21, 1996.

Consensus in One Communication Step

Francisco Brasileiro, Fabíola Greve*, Achour Mostefaoui, and Michel Raynal

IRISA, Université de Rennes 1
Campus de Beaulieu, 35042 Rennes Cedex, France
{fbrasile,fgreve,achour,raynal}@irisa.fr

Abstract. This paper presents a very simple consensus protocol that converges in a single communication step in favorable circumstances. Those situations occur when "enough" processes propose the same value. ("Enough" means "at least $(n - f)$" where f is the maximum number of processes that can crash in a set of n processes.) The protocol requires $f < n/3$. It is shown that this requirement is necessary. Moreover, if all the processes that propose a value do propose the same value, the protocol always terminates in one communication step. It is also shown that additional assumptions can help weaken the $f < n/3$ requirement to $f < n/2$.

Keywords: Asynchronous Distributed System, Consensus, Crash Failure, Message Passing.

1 Introduction

The *Consensus* problem is now recognized as being one of the most important problems to solve when one has to design or to implement reliable applications on top of an unreliable asynchronous distributed system. Informally, the Consensus problem is defined in the following way. Each process proposes a value, and all non-crashed processes have to agree on a common value which has to be one of the proposed values. The most important practical agreement problems (such as Atomic Broadcast, View Synchrony, Weak Atomic Commitment, Atomic Multicast, etc.) can be reduced to Consensus, which can be seen as their *"greatest common sub-problem"*. Consequently, a distributed module implementing Consensus constitutes a basic building block on top of which solutions to practical agreement problems can be built. This explains why the Consensus is a fundamental, and justifies the large interest the literature has brought to it.

Solving the Consensus problem in asynchronous distributed systems is far from being a trivial task. In fact, it has been shown by Fischer, Lynch and Paterson [4] that there is no (deterministic) solution to this problem as soon as processes (even only one) may crash. Two major approaches have been proposed to circumvent this impossibility result. One lies in the use of randomized protocols [2]. The other lies in the *unreliable failure detector* concept, proposed and investigated by Chandra and Toueg [3]. Several failure detector-based consensus protocols have been designed ([11] presents a general approach to solve

---

* This author is supported by a grant of the CNPq/Brazil #200323-97.

V. Malyshkin (Ed.): PaCT 2001, LNCS 2127, pp. 42–50, 2001.

the consensus problem in asynchronous systems equipped with Chandra-Toueg's failure detectors). Interestingly, a *Hybrid* approach combining failure detectors and random number generators has also been investigated [1,12].

To converge towards a single decided value, a consensus protocol makes the processes exchange proposed values. Each exchange constitutes a communication step. So, an interesting measure of the efficiency of a protocol is the number of communication steps it requires. In the best scenario, the consensus protocols proposed so far require that processes execute at least two communication steps.

This paper presents a novel and surprisingly simple consensus protocol that allows processes to decide in a single communication step when "enough" processes propose the same value. "Enough" means at least $(n - f)$, where n is the number of processes and f is the maximum number of them that can be faulty. This protocol requires $f < n/3$. Although failures do occur, they are rare in practice. This observation shows that the $f < n/3$ requirement is not really constraining. Moreover, it is shown that it is actually necessary when the initial knowledge of processes is limited to n and f. The paper also shows that, when the processes are initially supplied with more information, the $f < n/3$ requirement can be weakened to $f < n/2$.

2   System Model and Consensus

Asynchronous System. The system model is patterned after the one described in [3,4]. It consists of a finite set Π of $n > 1$ processes, namely, $\Pi = \{p_1, \ldots, p_n\}$. A process can fail by *crashing*, i.e., by prematurely halting; a crashed process does not recover. A process behaves correctly (i.e., according to its specification) until it (possibly) crashes. By definition, a *correct* process is a process that does not crash. A *faulty* process is a process that is not correct. As indicated in the Introduction, f denotes the maximum number of processes that may crash.

Processes communicate and synchronize by broadcasting and receiving messages through channels. Communication is reliable: there is no message creation, alteration, duplication or loss. If a process crashes while broadcasting a message m, only a subset of processes can receive m. There are assumptions neither on the relative speed of processes nor on message transfer delays.

The Consensus Problem. In the Consensus problem, every process p_i *proposes* a value v_i and all correct processes have to *decide* on some value v, in relation to the set of proposed values. More precisely, the *Consensus problem* is defined by the following three properties [3,4]:

- Termination: Every correct process eventually decides some value.
- Validity: If a process decides v, then v was proposed by some process.
- Agreement: No two processes (correct or not) decide differently.

Additional assumption. Our aim is to provide a consensus protocol that terminates in one communication step in good scenarios (i.e., when enough processes

Function Consensus(v_i)

Task $T1$:
      (1) *broadcast* PROPOSED(v_i);
      (2) **wait until** (($n - f$) PROPOSED messages have been received);
      (3) **if** (these messages carry the same estimate value v)
      (4)   **then** *broadcast* DECISION(v); *return*(v)
      (5)   **else if** (($n - 2f$) PROPOSED messages carry the same value v)
      (6)   **then** $v_i \leftarrow v$ **endif**;
      (7)   *return*(Underlying_Consensus(v_i))
      (8) **endif**

Task $T2$:
      (9) **upon** *reception* **of** DECISION(v): *broadcast* DECISION(v); *return*(v)

Fig. 1. The Consensus protocol

do propose the same value), but also terminates in bad scenarios. So, we consider that the underlying asynchronous distributed system allows to solve the consensus problem. More precisely, we assume it is equipped with a black box solving the consensus problem, and we provide a protocol that decides in one communication step in good scenarios and uses the underlying consensus protocol in the other cases. A process p_i locally invokes it by calling Underlying_Consensus(v_i) where v_i is the value it proposes.

3   The Protocol

Underlying Principle. The idea that underlies the design of the protocol is very simple. It comes from the following observation: if all the processes initially propose the same value, then this value is necessarily the decided value, whatever the protocol and the system behavior. Hence, the proposed protocol executes a first communication step during which the processes exchange the values they propose. Then, each process checks whether all the processes have the same initial value (actually, ($n - f$) identical values are sufficient). If it is the case, this value is decided. If it is not, the underlying protocol is used.

The Protocol. The protocol is described in Figure 1. A process p_i starts a Consensus execution by invoking Consensus(v_i). It terminates it when it executes the statement *return* which provides it with the decided value (at line 4, 7 or 9). To prevent a process from blocking forever (i.e., waiting for a value from a process that has already decided), a process that decides, uses a reliable broadcast [3] to disseminate its decision value. To this end the Consensus function is made of two tasks, namely, $T1$ and $T2$. $T1$ implements the core of the protocol. Line 4 and $T2$ implement the reliable broadcast.

One Communication Step Decision. Let us consider the case where all the processes that propose a value (those are the processes that have not initially crashed) propose the same value. The protocol makes the processes that do not crash decide in exactly one communication step[1].

If less than $(n - f)$ processes propose the same value v, then the consensus is solved by the Underlying_Consensus protocol. When there is a set of $(n - f)$ processes that propose the same value v, there are two cases according to the set of PROPOSED messages received by a process p_i at line 2:

• Case 1: The $(n - f)$ PROPOSED messages received by p_i carry v. It follows from lines 2-4 that p_i decides after one communication step.

• Case 2: One of the $(n - f)$ PROPOSED messages received by p_i carries a value different from v. Let us notice that, as there are $(n - f)$ PROPOSED messages carrying v and $3f < n$, it follows that necessarily p_i receives at least $(n - 2f)$ PROPOSED messages carrying v, and consequently adopts v at line 6. It follows that when $(n - f)$ processes propose the same value v, all the processes that do not decide at line 4, invoke Underlying_Consensus withe same value v. Interestingly, some consensus protocols expedite the decision when processes propose the same value[2].

4   Proof

The proof of the Validity property (a decided value is a proposed value) is left to the reader.

Theorem 1. (Termination) *If a process p_i is correct, then it eventually decides.*

Proof   As there are at least $(n - f)$ correct processes, let us first note that no correct process can block forever at line 2. Hence, they all execute line 3. According to the results of the test there are two cases:

– A process decides at line 4.
  In that case, this process has previously sent a DECISION message to all other processes. Due to the reliable channel assumption, it follows that if a correct process has not yet decided when it receives this message, it executes line 9 and consequently decides.

– No process decides at line 4.
  In that case, all the processes that have not crashed during the first communication step invoke the underlying consensus protocol. Due to its Termination property, all the correct processes eventually decide.

$$\square_{Theorem\ 1}$$

---

[1] It is important to notice that, in the same situation, the randomized protocols, the failure detector-based protocols and the hybrid protocols presented in [1,2,3,11,12] do not allow a one step decision.

[2] In that case, [2] allows the processes to decide in two communication steps, while [12] requires three steps. Due to the possibilty of false suspicions, failure detector-based protocols [3,11] do not enjoy this interesting property.

Theorem 2. (Agreement) *Let $f < n/3$. No two processes decide differently.*

Proof Let us first notice that a process that decides at line 9, decides a value v that has been sent by a process at line 4. So, we only consider the decision at line 4 and line 7. The proof considers three cases.

- Let us first consider the case where two processes p_i and p_j decide at line 4. This means p_i received $(n - f)$ PROPOSED messages carrying the same value v. Similarly, p_j received $(n - f)$ PROPOSED messages carrying the same value w. Moreover, each process sends a single PROPOSED message to the other processes. As $f < n/3$, we have $(n - f) > n/2$. It follows that at least one PROPOSED(v) message and one PROPOSED(w) message have been sent by the same process. Consequently $v = w$.
- If no process executes line 4, then the processes that decide execute line 7. In that case, due to the Agreement property of the underlying consensus protocol, they decide the same value.
- Let us now consider the case where some processes decide a value (say v) at line 4, while other processes decide at line 7. We claim[3] that the variable v_j of any process p_j that executes line 7 has been previously set to v at line 6. Then, all the processes that execute the underlying protocol propose the same value v to this consensus. Due to the Validity property of the underlying consensus, they can only decide v.

  Proof of the claim. Let p_i be a process that executes line 4 and p_j be a process that executes line 5. We have the following:

  1. p_i received $(n - f)$ PROPOSED(v) messages. Hence, no more than f PROPOSED messages carry a value different from v.
  2. p_j received $(n - f)$ PROPOSED messages. Due to (1), at most f of them carry a value different from v. (In the worst case, those f values are equal.)
  3. From (1) and (2) we conclude that at least $(n - 2f)$ PROPOSED messages received by p_j carry the value v.
  4. As $n > 3f$, we have $(n - 2f) > f$. This means that the value v is a majority value among the values received by p_j.
  5. From the test done at line 5, we conclude that p_j updates v_i to v, which concludes the proof of the claim.

$\square_{Theorem\ 2}$

5   A Necessary Condition

This section considers an asynchronous distributed system in which the consensus problem can be solved. Let $\mathcal{P}$ be the family of consensus protocols where the global knowledge of a process p_i is the pair (n, f).

---

[3] Using traditional terminology [3], this claim states how a value decided during the first communication step is *"locked"*.

Theorem 3. *Let $P \in \mathcal{P}$. If P allows processes to decide during the first communication step, then $f < n/3$.*

Proof Let us first introduce the following parameters related to $P \in \mathcal{P}$:
- ℓ: number of processes from which a process has to receive a value before deciding after one communication step (note that $\ell \leq (n - f)$, otherwise the protocol could block forever).
- x: number of messages containing the same value v, that allows a process p_i to decide that value after the first communication step (note that $x \leq \ell$).
  Let us observe that, as two processes that decide at the end of the first communication step have to decide the same value, it is necessary that $x > n/2$. (If this was not the case, p_i could decide v_1 because it received x copies of it, while p_j could independently decide $v_2 \neq v_1$ because it received x copies of it).

The proof is by contradiction. Let us assume that P works in a system made up of $n = 3k$ processes with $k \leq f$. The processes are partitioned into three subsets G_1, G_2 and G_3 of size k. Combining $3f \geq 3k = n$ with $x \leq \ell \leq (n - f)$ and $x > n/2$, we get $k = n/3 < n/2 < x \leq \ell \leq (n - f) \leq (n - k) = 2k \leq 2f$. From $\ell \leq 2k$, we deduce $\ell - k \leq k < x$. Hence, $\max(k, \ell - k) < x$. Let us consider the following scenario.

- No process has initially crashed. The processes of G_1 propose v; the processes of G_2 propose v; and the processes of G_3 propose w $(\neq v)$.
- Each process $p_i \in G_1$ receives values from $\ell \leq 2k \leq 2f$ processes of G_1 and G_2. As $x \leq \ell$, each process $p_i \in G_1$ receives enough copies of v to decide (definition of x). So each process of G_1 decides v. Then, after having decided, the processes of G_1 crash.
- Each process $p_i \in G_2 \cup G_3$ receives values from $\ell \leq 2k \leq 2f$ processes of G_2 and G_3. More precisely, let us consider the scenario where:
  - Each process of G_2 receives k copies of v and $(\ell - k)$ copies of w.
  - Each process of G_3 receives $(\ell - k)$ copies of v and k copies of w.

From $\max(k, \ell - k) < x$, we conclude that no process $p_i \in G_2 \cup G_3$ can decide. It follows that any $p_i \in G_2 \cup G_3$ neither decides nor is blocked during the first communication step. Consequently, the processes of $G_2 \cup G_3$ continue executing P. Moreover, there is no way for them to know whether processes of G_1 have decided. The subsets of processes G_2 and G_3 are symmetric with respect to the number of copies of v and w they have. Hence, whatever P, the processes of $G_2 \cup G_3$ can indistinctly decide v or w. The Uniform Agreement property is violated in all the runs of P that decide w.

This shows that there is no protocol P when $n = 3k$ with $k \leq f$. A contradiction.
$$\square_{Theorem\ 3}$$

Corollary 1. *The protocol presented in Section 3 is optimal with respect to the number of process crashes that can be tolerated by the protocols of $\mathcal{P}$.*

Function Consensus(v_i)

Task $T1$: *broadcast* PROPOSED(v_i);
          wait until (PROPOSED messages received from a majority of processes);
          if (all the received values are equal to α)
                 then *broadcast* DECISION(α); *return*(α)
                 else if (α received from a process) **then** $v_i \leftarrow \alpha$ **endif**;
                        return(Underlying_Consensus(v_i))
          endif

Task $T2$: **upon** *reception* **of** DECISION(v): *broadcast* DECISION(v); *return*(v)

Fig. 2. Use of a privileged value ($f < n/2$)

Proof The protocol presented in Section 3 trivially belongs to the family $\mathcal{P}$. The corollary follows directly from Theorem 3. $\square_{Corollary\ 1}$

6   Considering Additional Assumptions

This section shows that the previous necessary requirement can be weakened when the system satisfies additional assumptions. Those assumptions basically enrich the initial knowledge of processes, more precisely they define an "a priori agreement" among the processes. We give here two protocols that, with the help of such additional assumptions, allow one step decision when $f < n/2$.

- In the first protocol the a priori agreement is "value oriented": there is a statically predetermined value that is decided when it is proposed by a majority of processes. Hence, here, from an intuitive point of view, the values that can be proposed have not the same "power".
- In the second protocol the a priori agreement is "control oriented": there is a statically predetemined majority set of processes explicitly used by the protocol. Hence, here, from an intuitive point of view, all the processes have not the same "power".

Existence of a Privileged Value. Let Let α be a predetermined value of the set of values that can be proposed. Moreover, let us assume that α is initially known by each process. The a priori knowledge of such a predetermined value can help expedite the decision when $f < n/2$ as shown in Figure 2. The idea of the protocol is very simple: a process is allowed to decide α in one communication step as soon as it knows that α has been proposed by a majority of processes[4].

Predefined Set of Processes. Let us assume that there is a predefined set of processes S that is initially known by each process. The protocol described in

---

[4] When consensus is used as a sub-protocol to solve the atomic commit problem (see [6]), COMMIT can be considered as privileged with respect to ABORT.

Function Consensus(v_i)

Task $T1$:   *broadcast* PROPOSED(v_i);
       wait until (PROPOSED messages received from $(n - f)$ processes);
       if (the same value v has been received from each process $\in S$)
           then *broadcast* DECISION(v); *return*(v)
           else $v_i \leftarrow$ a value from a process $\in S$;
                   return(Underlying_Consensus(v_i))
       endif

Task $T2$:   **upon** *reception* **of** DECISION(v): *broadcast* DECISION(v); *return*(v)

Fig. 3. Predefined set of processes ($f < n/2$)

Figure 3 uses this a priori knowledge to decide in one communication step when all the processes of S propose the same value. It requires $f < n/2 < |S|$. In this solution, the processes are no longer anonymous: their identities are used by the protocol.

7   Concluding Remark

This paper has presented a consensus protocol that makes the processes decide in one communication step when the processes that propose a value propose the same value. It has been shown that this protocol requires $f < n/3$ and that this requirement is necessary. It has also been shown how additional assumptions allow to weaken the $f < n/3$ requirement.

As noted in the Introduction, in practice failures occur but are rare. Moreover, in some practical agreement problems, processes usually propose the same value. This is the case of the atomic commitment problem where, nearly always, the processes do propose COMMIT [5]. A reduction of atomic broadcast to consensus is described in [6] (this reduction involves a preliminary message exchange to allow each process to transform the votes it receives into a COMMIT/ABORT proposal). The proposed consensus protocol is particularly attractive to solve these agreement problems.

Very recently, a new and promising *Condition-based* approach has been proposed to solve the consensus problem [7]. It consists in identifying sets of input vectors for which it is possible to design a consensus protocol that works despite up to f faults. Such conditions actually define a strict hierarchy [8]. The efficiency of the associated condition-based protocols is investigated in [10]. Moreover, this approach reveals to be very general, as it allows to solve more general agreement problems [9].

References

1. Aguilera M.K. and Toueg S., Failure Detection and Randomization: a Hybrid Approach to Solve Consensus. SIAM Journal of Computing, 28(3):890-903, 1998.

1. Aguilera M.K. and Toueg S., Failure Detection and Randomization: a Hybrid Approach to Solve Consensus. SIAM Journal of Computing, 28(3):890-903, 1998.
2. Ben-Or M., Another Advantage of Free Choice: Completely Asynchronous Agreement Protocols. 2nd ACM Symposium on Principles of Distributed Computing, (PODC'83), Montréal (CA), pp. 27-30, 1983.
3. Chandra T. and Toueg S., Unreliable Failure Detectors for Reliable Distributed Systems. Journal of the ACM, 43(2):225-267, 1996.
4. Fischer M.J., Lynch N. and Paterson M.S., Impossibility of Distributed Consensus with One Faulty Process. Journal of the ACM, 32(2):374-382, 1985.
5. Gray J. and Reuter A., Transaction Processing: Concepts and Techniques. Morgan Kaufmann, 1993.
6. Guerraoui R., Hurfin M., Mostefaoui A., Oliveira R., Raynal M. and Schiper A., Consensus in Asynchronous Distributed Systems: a Concise Guided Tour. In Advances in Distributed Systems, Springer-Verlag LNCS #1752 (Krakowiak S. and Shrivastava S. Eds), pp. 33-47, 2000.
7. Mostefaoui A., Rajsbaum S. and Raynal M., Conditions on Input Vectors for Consensus Solvability in Asynchronous Distributed Systems. Proc. 33rd ACM Symposium on Theory of Computing (STOC'01), ACM Press, Crete (Greece), July 2001.
8. Mostefaoui A., Rajsbaum S., Raynal M. and Roy M., A Hierarchy of Conditions for Consensus Solvability. Proc. 20th ACM Symposium on Principles of Distributed Computing (PODC'01), ACM Press, Newport (RI), August 2001.
9. Mostefaoui A., Rajsbaum S., Raynal M. and Roy M., Condition-Based Protocols for Set Agreement Problems. Research Report #1393, IRISA, University of Rennes, France, April 2001, 21 pages.
   http://www.irisa.fr/bibli/publi/pi/2001/1393/1393.html.
10. Mostefaoui A., Rajsbaum S., Raynal M. and Roy M., Efficient Condition-Based Consensus. 8th Int. Colloquium on Structural Information and Communication Complexity (SIROCCO'00), Carleton Univ. Press, Val de Nuria, Catalonia (Spain), June 2001.
11. Mostéfaoui A. and Raynal M., Solving Consensus Using Chandra-Toueg's Unreliable Failure Detectors: a General Quorum-Based Approach. 13th Int. Symposium on DIStributed Computing (DISC'99), Springer-Verlag LNCS #1693 (P. Jayanti Ed.), pp. 49-63, 1999.
12. Mostéfaoui A., Raynal M. and Tronel F., The Best of Both Worlds: a Hybrid Approach to Solve Consensus. Int. Conference on Dependable Systems and Networks (DSN'00, Formerly FTCS), IEEE Computer Society Press, New-York City, pp. 513-522, June 2000.

Design Space Exploration
for Massively Parallel Processor Arrays*

Frank Hannig and Jürgen Teich

University of Paderborn, D-33098 Paderborn, Germany,
{hannig,teich}@date.upb.de
http://www-date.upb.de

Abstract. In this paper, we describe an approach for the optimization of dedicated co-processors that are implemented either in hardware (ASIC) or configware (FPGA). Such massively parallel co-processors are typically part of a heterogeneous hardware/software-system. Each co-processor is a massive parallel system consisting of an array of processing elements (PEs). In order to decide whether to map a computational intensive task into hardware, existing approaches either try to optimize for performance or for cost with the other objective being a secondary goal. Our approach presented here, instead, a) considers multiple objectives simultaneously. For a given specification, we explore *space-time-mappings* leading to different degrees of parallelism and cost, and different optimal hardware solutions. b) We show that the hardware cost may be efficiently determined in terms of the chosen space-time mapping by using state-of-the-art techniques in polyhedral theory. c) Finally, we introduce ideas to drastically reduce dimension and size of the search space of mapping candidates. d) The feasibility of our approach is shown for two realistic examples.

1   Introduction

Technical analysts foresee the dilemma of not being able to focus next generation hardware complexity because of a lack of mapping tools. On the other hand, the next generation of ULSI chips will allow to implement arrays of 10×10 32-bit micro-processors on a single die and more. Hence, parallelization techniques and compilers will be of utmost importance in order to map computational-intensive algorithms efficiently to these processor arrays.

Through this advance in technology, also reconfigurable hardware, sometimes also called *configware* such as FPGAs (field-programmable gate-arrays) [8], becomes more and more attractive as co-processors for the following three reasons: 1) Chips with up to 10 million gate counts allow to implement arithmetic co-processors with hundreds of processing elements, e.g., for image processing and linear algebra algorithms, see, e.g., in Fig. 1. Shown is an FPGA placement visualized by the tool BoardScope by Xilinx [16] with a square array of processing

---

* Supported in part by the German Science Foundation (DFG) Project SFB 376 "Massively Parallel Computation".

V. Malyshkin (Ed.): PaCT 2001, LNCS 2127, pp. 51–65, 2001.

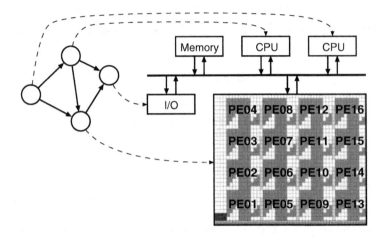

Fig. 1. Heterogeneous application, architecture, and hardware/software partition including a massively parallel co-processor implemented in hardware (ASIC) or configware (FPGA).

elements (PEs), each consisting of an array-multiplier, an adder, registers, and some control logic. 2) Configware has the major advantage of being able to reuse silicon for time-variant co-processor functions by means of reconfiguration. 3) Support for regular designs: standards such as the Java API JBits [16] allow to specify the regular design within Java-loops such that lower-level mapping may be accomplished efficiently and independent of the problem-size.

In the eighties and early nineties, higher-level mapping techniques for so-called *systolic arrays* have been in its fancy. They pretty much dealt with the problem of mapping a certain algorithm specified by a loop program onto a parallel processor array such as a systolic array, and architectural extensions thereof with time-dependent and control-dependent processor functions [12]. By the use of linear space-time mappings, the relationship between a regular array of communicating PEs and the temporal execution of operations of loop algorithms has been described. Unfortunately, dedicated hardware chips proposed for certain algorithms were too rigid, implementing just a single problem, or too slow and expensive due to long time-to-market.

With the above mentioned advances of silicon technology, and the advent of configware, the necessity of mapping tools for parallel hardware processors has been rethought and its application scope and processor capabilities broadened. Some important recent approaches include the PICO-N system by Hewlett-Packard [11] that specifies a methodology for synthesizing an array of customized VLIW processors starting with a loop program with uniform data dependencies and VHDL code at the RTL-level. From a given irregular program, parts are automatically extracted, mapped to hardware, and finally, the specification is modified to make use of this accelerator. Another approach that embeds regular array design into heterogeneous hardware/software targets is the Compaan system [4]. There, Matlab applications are transformed into a network of sequential, communicating processes where each process is responsible for computing some variables of a nested loop program.

In this realm, our paper deals with the specific problem of exploring cost/performance tradeoffs when mapping a certain class of loop-specified computations called *piecewise regular algorithms* [12] onto a dedicated co-processor. The main new ideas of our approach are summarized as follows:

- Simultaneous consideration of multiple objectives: For a given *piecewise regular algorithm*, we explore *space-time-mappings*[1] leading to different degrees of parallelism and cost, and different optimal hardware solutions. Existing approaches such as [3] consider solutions that find a schedule first (time-mapping) such to minimize latency and minimize cost as a secondary goal, or the other way round. Such design points are not necessarily so-called *Pareto-optimal* [9] points.
- Efficient computation of objectives: We show that hardware cost may be efficiently determined in terms of the chosen space-time mapping by using state-of-the-art techniques in polyhedral theory.
- Search space reduction: We introduce several ideas to drastically reduce dimension and size of the search space of mapping candidates.

The rest of the paper is structured as follows. Section 2 introduces the class of algorithms we are dealing with. In Section 3, the exploration algorithm for finding Pareto-optimal space-time mappings is given. There, the objective functions for cost and performance (latency) are explained including the reduction of the search space. Finally, results are presented in Section 4.

2   Notation and Background

2.1   Algorithms

In this paper the class of algorithms we are dealing with is a class of recurrence equations defined as follows:

Definition 1. *(Piecewise Regular Algorithm). A piecewise regular algorithm contains N quantified equations*

$$S_1[I], \ldots, S_i[I], \ldots, S_N[I]$$

Each equation $S_i[I]$ is of the form

$$x_i[I] = f_i(\ldots, x_j[I - d_{ji}], \ldots)$$

where $I \in \mathcal{I}_i \subseteq \mathbb{Z}^n$, $x_i[I]$ are indexed variables, f_i are arbitrary functions, $d_{ji} \in \mathbb{Z}^n$ are constant data dependence vectors, and ... denote similar arguments.

---

[1] Although we are able to handle also more general classes of algorithms and mappings, introducing them here would unnecessarily complicate the notation and hinder to present the main ideas of the exploration approach.

The domains $\mathcal{I}_i$ are called index spaces, and in our case defined as follows:

Definition 2. *(Linearly Bounded Lattice). A linearly bounded lattice denotes an index space of the form*

$$\mathcal{I} \ = \ \{I \in \mathbb{Z}^n \mid I = M\kappa + c \ \wedge \ A\kappa \geq b\}$$

where $\kappa \in \mathbb{Z}^l$, $M \in \mathbb{Z}^{n \times l}$, $c \in \mathbb{Z}^n$, $A \in \mathbb{Z}^{m \times l}$ *and* $b \in \mathbb{Z}^m$. $\{\kappa \in \mathbb{Z}^l \mid A\kappa \geq b\}$ *defines an integral convex polyhedron or in case of boundedness a polytope in* $\mathbb{Z}^l$. *This set is affinely mapped onto iteration vectors* I *using an affine transformation* $(I = M\kappa + c)$.

Throughout the paper, we assume that the matrix M is square and of full rank. Then, each vector κ is uniquely mapped to an index point I. Furthermore, we require that the index space is bounded.

    For illustration purposes throughout the paper, the following simple example is used.

Example 1. Consider a piecewise regular algorithm which consists of three quantified indexed equations

$$
\begin{aligned}
a[i,j] &= \ f(a[i-1,j]), & \forall(i\ j)^{\mathrm{T}} = I \in \mathcal{I} \\
b[i,j] &= \ g(b[i,j-1]), & \forall(i\ j)^{\mathrm{T}} = I \in \mathcal{I} \\
c[i,j] &= \ a[i,j] \text{ op } b[i,j], & \forall(i\ j)^{\mathrm{T}} = I \in \mathcal{I}.
\end{aligned}
$$

The data dependence vectors are $d_{aa} = (1\ 0)^{\mathrm{T}}$, $d_{bb} = (0\ 1)^{\mathrm{T}}$, $d_{ac} = (0\ 0)^{\mathrm{T}}$, and $d_{bc} = (0\ 0)^{\mathrm{T}}$. The index space is given by

$$
\mathcal{I} \ = \ \left\{ I \in \mathbb{Z}^2 \ \middle| \ \begin{pmatrix} 1 & -1 \\ -3 & -5 \\ 3 & 4 \\ -4 & 5 \end{pmatrix} \begin{pmatrix} i \\ j \end{pmatrix} \geq \begin{pmatrix} -3 \\ -63 \\ 26 \\ -14 \end{pmatrix} \right\}.
$$

Computations of piecewise regular algorithms may be represented by a *dependence graph* (DG). The DG of the algorithm of Example 1 is shown in Fig. 3(a). The DG expresses the partial order between the operations. Each variable of the algorithm is represented at every index point $I \in \mathcal{I}$ by one node. The edges correspond to the data dependencies of the algorithm. They are *regular* throughout the algorithm, i.e. $a[i,j]$ is directly dependent on $a[i-1,j]$. The DG specifies implicitly all legal execution orderings of operations: if there is a directed path in the DG from one node $a[J]$ to a node $c[K]$ where $J, K \in \mathcal{I}$, then the computation of $a[J]$ must precede the computation of $c[K]$.

    Henceforth, and without loss of generality[2], we assume that all indexed variables are embedded in a common index space $\mathcal{I}$. Then, the corresponding dependence graphs can be represented in a reduced form.

Definition 3. *(Reduced Dependence Graph). A reduced dependence graph (RDG)* $G = (V, E, D, \mathcal{I})$ *of dimension* n *is a network where* V *is a set of nodes and* $E \subseteq V \times V$ *is a set of edges. To each edge* $e = (v_i, v_j)$ *there is associated a dependence vector* $d_{ij} \in \mathbb{Z}^n$.

---

[2] All described methods can also applied for each quantification individually.

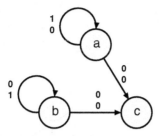

Fig. 2. Reduced dependence graph.

Example 2. In Fig. 2, the RDG of the algorithm introduced in Example 1 is shown.

2.2   Space-Time Mapping

Linear transformations as in Equation (1) are used as *space-time mappings* [7,6] in order to assign a *processor index* $p \in \mathbb{Z}^{n-1}$ (space) and a *sequencing index* $t \in \mathbb{Z}$ (time) to index vectors $I \in \mathcal{I}$.

$$\begin{pmatrix} p \\ t \end{pmatrix} = \begin{pmatrix} Q \\ \lambda \end{pmatrix} I \tag{1}$$

In Eq. (1), $Q \in \mathbb{Z}^{(n-1)\times n}$ and $\lambda \in \mathbb{Z}^{1 \times n}$. The main reasons for using linear allocation and scheduling functions is that the data flow between PEs is local and regular which is essential for VLSI implementations. The interpretation of such a linear transformation is as follows: The set of operations defined at index points $\lambda \cdot I = $ const. are scheduled at the same time step. The index space of allocated processing elements (*processor space*) is denoted by $\mathcal{Q}$ and is given by the set $\mathcal{Q} = \{p \mid p = Q \cdot I \wedge I \in \mathcal{I}\}$. This set can also be obtained by choosing a projection of the dependence graph along a vector $u \in \mathbb{Z}^n$, i.e. any coprime[3] vector u satisfying $Q \cdot u = 0$ [5] describes the allocation equivalently.

Allocation and scheduling must satisfy that no data dependencies in the DG are violated. This is ensured by the well-known *causality constraint*

$$\lambda \cdot d_{ij} \geq 0 \quad \forall (v_i, v_j) \in E. \tag{2}$$

A sufficient condition for guaranteeing that no two or more index points are assigned to a processing element at the same time step is given by

$$\text{rank}\begin{pmatrix} Q \\ \lambda \end{pmatrix} = n. \tag{3}$$

Using the projection vector u satisfying $Q \cdot u = 0$, this condition is equivalent to $\lambda \cdot u \neq 0$ [10].

---

[3] A vector x is said to be *coprime* if the absolute value of the greatest value of the greatest common divisor of its elements is one.

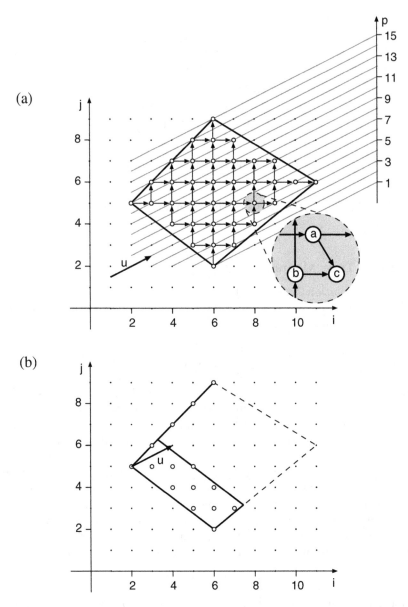

Fig. 3. In (a), the dependence graph of the algorithm introduced in Example 1 is shown. Also an allocation given by a projection vector u is illustrated. Counting the number of processors is equal to counting the number of integral points in a transformed polytope shown in (b) which may be accomplished using Ehrhart polynomials [2].

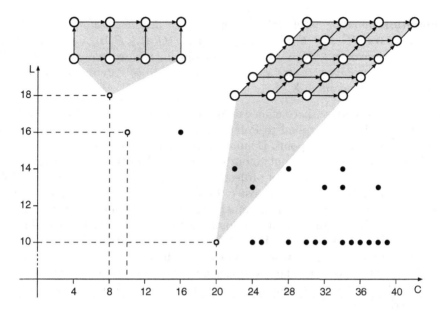

Fig. 4. Pareto-points for the matrix multiplication example in the objective space of latency (L) and cost (C).

3   Methodology

Based on the class of piecewise regular algorithms, we want to explore space-time mappings systematically in order to find optimal implementations. Thereby, we want to simultaneously minimize several objectives, a multiobjective optimization problem (MOP). In this paper, we consider the two objectives *latency* $L(Q, \lambda)$ as a measure for the performance, and *cost* $C(Q, \lambda)$ of a processor array.

As C and L are dependent on Q and λ, the search space contains $n \times n$ parameters. But as already mentioned, a linear allocation can be described equivalently through a coprime projection vector u. Thus, the dimension of the search space can be reduced to $2 \times n$ (vector u, vector λ).

Fig. 4 shows a typical tradeoff curve between cost and performance for a matrix multiplication algorithm. Different pairs of latency and cost correspond to different space-time mappings. As we are concerned with a MOP, there is not only one optimal solution but typically a set of optimal solutions, so called *Pareto-optimal* solutions. Our MOP consists of two objective functions $C(u, \lambda)$ and $L(u, \lambda)$, where the parameters u and λ are denoted as decision variables. The optimization goal is to simultaneously minimize $C(u, \lambda)$ and $L(u, \lambda)$ within a search space of feasible space-time mappings.

Definition 4. *(Search Space, Decision Vector). Let $x = (u\ \lambda)^{\mathrm{T}} \in \mathbb{Z}^{2n}$ denote a decision vector and $\mathbf{X}$ denote decision space of all vectors x satisfying Eq. (1), (2) and (3).*

Definition 5. *(Pareto-optimality). For any two decision vectors* $\mathbf{a}, \mathbf{b} \in \mathbf{X}$, *a dominates* $\mathbf{b}$ *iff* $(C(\mathbf{a}) < C(\mathbf{b}) \wedge L(\mathbf{a}) \leq L(\mathbf{b})) \vee (C(\mathbf{a}) \leq C(\mathbf{b}) \wedge L(\mathbf{a}) < L(\mathbf{b}))$. *A decision vector* $\mathbf{x} \in \mathbf{X}$ *is said to be* non-dominated *regarding a set* $\mathbf{A} \subseteq \mathbf{X}$ *iff* $\nexists\ \mathbf{a} \in \mathbf{A} : \mathbf{a}$ *dominates* $\mathbf{x}$. *Moreover,* $\mathbf{x}$ *is said to be* Pareto-optimal *iff* $\mathbf{x}$ *is non-dominated regarding* $\mathbf{X}$.

In Fig. 4, the objective space of an example discussed later in Section 4 is shown. The white points correspond to Pareto-optimal solutions because they are not dominated by any other point. Dominated points are shown in black.

Now, we are able to formulate our exploration algorithm. For a given RDG $G = (V, E, D, \mathcal{I})$ and a set U of projection vectors u, our exploration methodology works as follows: First, the cost C for a given projection vector u is determined. For this allocation, the minimal latency L is computed. Afterwards, we determine if the design point is non-dominated with respect to the actual set of Pareto-optimal solutions. If it is non-dominated, the decision vector $(u\ \lambda)^{\mathrm{T}}$ is added to the Pareto-optimal set, denoted $\mathcal{O}$ in the following. Subsequently, the set $\mathcal{O}$ has to be updated if the new decision vector dominates some other vectors in $\mathcal{O}$. In the following algorithm, the main ideas of our exploration methodology are described.

EXPLORE
      IN: RDG, set U of projection vector candidates
      OUT: Pareto-optimal set $\mathcal{O}$
      BEGIN
         FOR each candidate $u \in U$ DO
            $C \leftarrow$ determineNoOfPEs(u)
            $L \leftarrow$ minimize$_\lambda \{L(u, \lambda)\}$
            IF $(u\ \lambda)^{\mathrm{T}}$ is non-dominated with respect to $\mathcal{O}$ THEN
               $\mathcal{O} \leftarrow \mathcal{O} \cup \{(u\ \lambda)^{\mathrm{T}}\}$
               update$(\mathcal{O})$
            ENDIF
         ENDFOR
      END

Next, we briefly describe how the cost C and the latency L may be computed. Afterwards, we describe how to reduce the set U of candidate vectors u that must be investigated.

3.1   Cost

For a regular processor array, we are able to approximate the cost, as being proportional to the processor count.

$$C(u, \lambda) = \#PE(u) \cdot (c_{\mathrm{FU}} + c_{\mathrm{Rg}}(\lambda) + c_{\mathrm{Wire}}(u)) \tag{4}$$

In Eq. (4), $\#PE(u)$ denotes the number of projected index points when projecting the index space $\mathcal{I}$ along u (see, e.g., Fig. 3(a)). The cost for functional units, registers and wiring is denoted by c_{FU}, c_{Rg} and c_{Wire}. In the following, we assume that processor arrays are resource-dominant: This means that $c_{FU} \gg c_{Rg}(\lambda) + c_{Wire}(u)$. Under these assumptions, we obtain the approximation:

$$C(u, \lambda) \approx C(u) = \#PE(u) \cdot c_{FU} \qquad (5)$$

As a consequence, the cost of an array is independent of the schedule and proportional to the number of points in the projected polytope $\mathcal{I}$. This is also the reason why we are able to investigate only the projection vector candidates $u \in U$ and minimize the latency L.

It remains to determine the number of processor elements for a given linear allocation. Here, a geometrical approach recently proposed in [1] is applied, for illustration, see Fig. 3. In (a), the index space of the algorithm described in Example 1 and a projection vector $u = (2\ 1)^T$ is shown. This linear allocation leads to an array of 15 processors. This number of processor elements can be determined by a transformation of the given polytope $\mathcal{I}$. The number of integral points inside this transformed polytope is equal to the number of processor elements obtained by the projection along u. In [1], it has been shown that this problem is equal to a counting problem of the number of integral points in a transformed polytope, see e.g. the polytope shown in Fig. 3(b) for the algorithm of Example 1. The number of processors using the projection vector $u = (2\ 1)^T$ results in 15 different projected PEs. This is exactly the number of integral points inside the polytope shown in Fig. 3(b), see [1] for details. A state-of-the-art solution to the final counting problem is to use so-called *Ehrhart polynomials*[4] [2].

3.2 Latency

In this section, a short description is given how the latency for a given piecewise regular algorithm and a given schedule vector λ is determined. For approximation of the latency, the following term is used

$$L = \max_{I \in \mathcal{I}} \{\lambda \cdot I\} - \min_{I \in \mathcal{I}} \{\lambda \cdot I\} = \max_{I_1, I_2 \in \mathcal{I}} \{\lambda \cdot (I_2 - I_1)\}.$$

The latency minimization problem in algorithm **EXPLORE** may be formulated as a mixed integer linear program (MILP) [14,13]. This well-known method is used here during exploration as a subroutine. In this MILP, the number of resources inside each processing element can be limited (determining c_{FU}). Also given is the possibility that an operation can be mapped onto different resource types (module selection), and pipelining is also possible. As a result of the MILP, we obtain:

- the minimal latency L,
- the according optimal schedule vector λ,
- the iteration interval[5] P,

---

[4] Due to space limits, we omit the details of this procedure.

[5] The iteration interval P of an allocated and scheduled piecewise regular algorithm is the number of time instances between the evaluation of two successive instances of a variable within one processing element [14].

- the start times of each $v_i \in V$, within the iteration interval
- the selected resource type for each $v_i \in V$.

Here, only the latency is used for rating the performance. The other values, however, are necessary for simulation and synthesis. We will present a detailed example of this procedure in Section 4.

In the following, we introduce two new additional methods how to reduce the search space for Pareto-optimal space-time mappings.

3.3   Projection Vector Candidates

Let $\mathcal{I} \subset \mathbb{Z}^n$ be a linearly bounded lattice according to Definition 2. In the following, we investigate projection vectors for the polytope $\mathcal{P} = \{\kappa \in \mathbb{Z}^n \mid A\kappa \geq b\}$. By our assumption that the lattice matrix M has full rank, projection vectors $u' \in \mathbb{Z}^n$ for $\mathcal{P}$ may be transformed to a corresponding projection vector $u \in \mathbb{Z}^n$ in $\mathcal{I}$ by $u = Mu'$.

For the exploration, it is necessary to determine a set U of projection vector candidates. This search space may be bounded as follows: Note that a projection vector may not be optimal if not at least two points $\kappa_1, \kappa_2 \in \mathcal{P}$ are projected onto each other:

$$\kappa_1 - \kappa_2 = \alpha u', \qquad \alpha \in \mathbb{Z}. \tag{6}$$

Hence, the search space may be bounded by the set of possible differences of two points in $\mathcal{P}$, the so-called *difference body* $\mathcal{D}$ of $\mathcal{P}$ [15], which again is a polytope.

$$\mathcal{D} = \{\kappa \in \mathbb{Z}^n \mid \kappa = \kappa_1 - \kappa_2 \ \wedge \ \kappa_1, \kappa_2 \in \mathcal{P}\}.$$

The *dual* $\mathcal{P}^-$ of $\mathcal{D}$ is convex and symmetric about the origin (see, e.g., in Fig. 5 for the polytope $\mathcal{P}$ in Fig. 3(a)). From duality, $\mathcal{P}^- = \{\kappa \in \mathbb{Z}^n \mid A^-\kappa \geq b^-\}$ is the intersection of closed half-spaces. Furthermore, let $\mathcal{B} \subset \mathbb{Z}^n$ be the smallest n-dimensional box (*bounding box*) containing $\mathcal{P}^-$.

In the following, a procedure for the reduction of suitable projection vector candidates is described:

- Compute all vertices $\mathcal{V}$ of the polytope $\mathcal{P}$.
- For each pair $v_i, v_j \in \mathcal{V}$ compute the vertex difference $v_i - v_j$. The set of vertex differences is denoted by $\mathcal{V}^-$.
- Determine the dual representation of $\mathcal{V}^-$. This is the convex polytope $\mathcal{P}^-$. Also determine the bounding box $\mathcal{B}$ of $\mathcal{V}^-$.
- Iterate over all points $u' \in \mathcal{B}$. For the reason $\mathcal{P}^-$ is symmetric about the origin, also $\mathcal{B}$ is symmetric about the origin. Due to symmetry, it is only necessary to consider, e.g., for the first component of u' all positive values. Furthermore, the selected projection vectors u' have to be coprime. Finally, test if u' is in $\mathcal{P}^-$. If $u' \in \mathcal{P}^-$, the condition in Eq. (6) that at least two point mapped onto each other is satisfied.

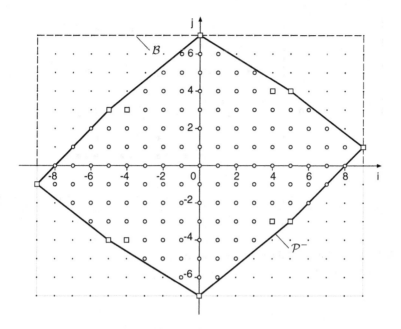

Fig. 5. Difference body of the convex polytope from Fig. 3(a).

Example 3. Reconsider the polytope shown in Fig. 3(a) with the vertices

$$v_1 = \begin{pmatrix} 2 \\ 5 \end{pmatrix}, \quad v_2 = \begin{pmatrix} 6 \\ 9 \end{pmatrix}, \quad v_3 = \begin{pmatrix} 11 \\ 6 \end{pmatrix}, \quad v_4 = \begin{pmatrix} 6 \\ 2 \end{pmatrix}.$$

All differences $v_i - v_j$, $i,j \in [1,4]$, $i \neq j$ are marked in Fig. 5 as white small boxes. $\mathcal{P}^-$ is bounded by the black, $\mathcal{B}$ by the dashed line. Due to symmetry, only the upper half-space has to be explored. All coprime integral points $(i\ j)^\mathrm{T}$, $i \in [-9,9]$, $j \in [0,7]$ which lie inside $\mathcal{P}^-$ are projection vector candidates.

3.4   Further Reduction of the Search Space

The order in our exploration algorithm to determine the cost first has the advantage that possibly the search space can be reduced further by adding a more restrictive constraint to the MILP for latency minimization: Let $\mathcal{O}$ be the set of so far determined Pareto-points (see Fig. 6). The dashed line denotes the computed cost of a design point $(u_j\ \lambda_j)^\mathrm{T}$. If this design point shall be Pareto-optimal, obviously $L(\lambda_j)$ must be smaller or equal to the latency $L(\lambda_i)$ of all such points $o_i \in \mathcal{O}$ for which the cost $C(u_i)$ is smaller or equal to $C(u_j)$:

IF $(\exists\ o_i = (u_i\ \lambda_i)^\mathrm{T} \in \mathcal{O} \mid C(u_i) \leq C(u_j))$ THEN
    let $o_i \in \mathcal{O}$ be the Pareto-point for which
    $\max_{o_i \in \mathcal{O}}\{C(u_i) \mid C(u_i) \leq C(u_j)\}$ holds

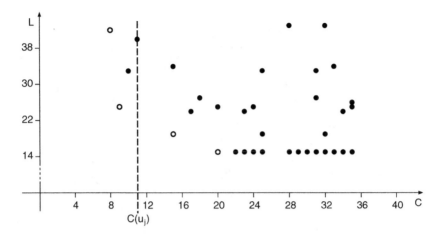

Fig. 6. Pareto-points obtained through design space exploration for the algorithm introduced in Example 1.

```
IF (C(uᵢ) < C(uⱼ)) THEN
    add constraint L(λⱼ)  <  L(λᵢ) to MILP
ELSE
    IF (C(uᵢ) = C(uⱼ)) THEN
        add constraint L(λⱼ)  ≤  L(λᵢ) to MILP
    ENDIF
ENDIF
ENDIF
```

4   Results

First, space-time mappings for the algorithm introduced in Example 1 are explored. The bounding box (Fig. 5) contains 295 integral points as candidates for projection vectors. When symmetry is explored and only coprime vectors are considered, U is reduced to 45 candidates. For each of these projection vectors, the cost C is determined. Subsequently, the latency is minimized. The results are visualized in Fig. 6, the Pareto-optimal solutions are the white points and presented in Table 1. The MILP was solved for execution times of 1 unit for $f(a)$ and $g(b)$. For op, we considered 4 time units. From the solution of the MILP, we obtain the schedule vector λ, the iteration interval P and as well all starting times for each operation within the iteration interval. In the following, we take a closer look at the solution for $u = (2\ 1)^T$. The corresponding iteration interval is 4 and the starting points are $\tau(a) = 0$, $\tau(b) = 0$, and $\tau(c) = 1$. In Fig. 7, the scheduling for the processors $p = 3$, 4, and 5 is shown. The data dependencies between adjacent index points are visualized by arcs.

The second example is a matrix multiplication algorithm. The product $C = A \cdot B$ of two matrices $A \in \mathbb{R}^{N_1 \times N_3}$ and $B \in \mathbb{R}^{N_3 \times N_2}$ is defined as follows

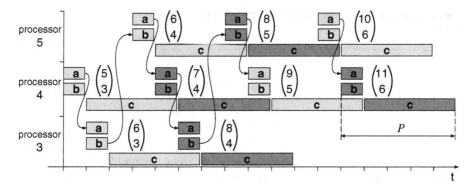

Fig. 7. Bar chart of scheduled algorithm.

Table 1. Pareto-points of the design space exploration for the algorithm in Example 1.

u	λ	C	L
$(1\ 0)^{\mathrm{T}}$	$(4\ 1)$	8	42
$(1\ 1)^{\mathrm{T}}$	$(2\ 2)$	9	25
$(2\ 1)^{\mathrm{T}}$	$(1\ 2)$	15	19
$(3\ 1)^{\mathrm{T}}$	$(1\ 1)$	20	15

$$c_{ij} = \sum_{k=1}^{N_3} a_{ik}b_{kj} \quad \forall\ 1 \le i \le N_1 \ \wedge\ 1 \le j \le N_2.$$

A corresponding piecewise regular algorithm is given by

input operations

$a[i,0,k] \leftarrow a_{ik}$ $1 \le i \le N_1\ \wedge\ 1 \le k \le N_3$

$b[0,j,k] \leftarrow b_{kj}$ $1 \le j \le N_2\ \wedge\ 1 \le k \le N_3$

$c[i,j,0] \leftarrow 0$ $1 \le i \le N_1\ \wedge\ 1 \le j \le N_2$

computations

$a[i,j,k] \leftarrow a[i,j-1,k]$ $1 \le i \le N_1\ \wedge\ 1 \le j \le N_2\ \wedge\ 1 \le k \le N_3$

$b[i,j,k] \leftarrow b[i-1,j,k]$ $1 \le i \le N_1\ \wedge\ 1 \le j \le N_2\ \wedge\ 1 \le k \le N_3$

$z[i,j,k] \leftarrow a[i,j,k] \cdot b[i,j,k]$ $1 \le i \le N_1\ \wedge\ 1 \le j \le N_2\ \wedge\ 1 \le k \le N_3$

$c[i,j,k] \leftarrow c[i,j,k-1] + z[i,j,k]$ $1 \le i \le N_1\ \wedge\ 1 \le j \le N_2\ \wedge\ 1 \le k \le N_3$

output operations

$c_{ij} \quad\quad \leftarrow c[i,j,N_3]$ $1 \le i \le N_1\ \wedge\ 1 \le j \le N_2$

where the index space is

$$\mathcal{I} = \{I = (i\ j\ k)^{\mathrm{T}} \in \mathbb{Z}^3 \mid 1 \le i \le N_1\ \wedge\ 1 \le j \le N_2\ \wedge\ 1 \le k \le N_3\}.$$

The input operations a and b are mapped each to one resource of type *input*. The execution times of these operations are zero. This is equivalent to a multi-cast without delay to a set of index points. For the multiplication (variable z), an

Table 2. Pareto-points of the design space exploration for the matrix multiplication algorithm.

u	λ	C	L
$(1\ 0\ 0)^{\mathrm{T}}$	$(2\ 0\ 3)$	10	16
$(0\ 1\ 0)^{\mathrm{T}}$	$(0\ 2\ 3)$	8	18
$(0\ 0\ 1)^{\mathrm{T}}$	$(0\ 0\ 3)$	20	10

execution time of 4 time units is considered, whereby the multiplier is pipelined, being able to start a new execution every two time units. The addition (variable c) takes three time units and by use of pipelining is able to start each time unit a new operation.

An exploration for $N_1 = 4$, $N_2 = 5$ and $N_3 = 2$ has been performed. The search space of $\|[-4, 4]\| \cdot \|[-5, 5]\| \cdot \|[-2, 2]\| = 9 \cdot 11 \cdot 5 = 495$ projection vector candidates can be reduced to 83 using our reduction techniques. The results are visualized in Fig. 4. We obtain three Pareto-optimal solutions shown in Table 2.

5   Conclusion and Future Work

We have presented a first approach for systematically exploring Pareto-optimal space-time mappings for a class of algorithms with uniform data dependencies. The considered objective functions are cost and performance (latency). In our exploration algorithm we introduced also several new techniques for reduction of search space for Pareto-optimal space-time mappings.

Our exploration framework is part of the PARO[6] design system that supports also the automated synthesis of regular circuits.

In the future, we would like to extend the presented results to include energy consumption as an additional objective and to perform symbolic design space exploration for parameterized index spaces.

References

1. Philippe Clauss. Counting Solutions to Linear and Nonlinear Constraints through Ehrhart polynomials: Applications to Analyse and Transform Scientific Programs. In Tenth ACM International Conference on Supercomputing, Philadelphia, Pennsylvania, May 1996.
2. Philippe Clauss and Vincent Loechner. Parametric Analysis of Polyhedral Iteration Spaces. Journal of VLSI Signal Processing, 19(2):179–194, July 1998.
3. Dirk Fimmel and Renate Merker. Determination of Processor Allocation in the Design of Processor Arrays. Microprocessors and Microsystems, 22(3–4):149–155, 1998.

---

[6] PARO is a design system project for modeling, transforming, optimization, and processor synthesis for the class of piecewise linear algorithms. For further information, check the website: `http://www-date.upb.de/research/paro/`.

4. Bart Kienhuis, Edwin Rijpkema, Ed F. Deprettere, and Paul Lieverse. High Level Modeling for Parallel Executions of Nested Loop Algorithms. In IEEE International Conference on Application-specific Systems, Architectures and Processors, pages 79–91, Boston, Massachusetts, 2000.

5. Robert H. Kuhn. Transforming Algorithms for Single-Stage and VLSI Architectures. In Workshop on Interconnection Networks for Parallel and Distributed Processing, pages 11–19, West Layfaette, IN, April 1980.

6. Christian Lengauer. Loop Parallelization in the Polytope Model. In Eike Best, editor, CONCUR'93, Lecture Notes in Computer Science 715, pages 398–416. Springer-Verlag, 1993.

7. Dan I. Moldovan. On the Design of Algorithms for VLSI Systolic Arrays. In Proceedings of the IEEE, volume 71, pages 113–120, January 1983.

8. John V. Oldfield and Richard C. Dorf. Field Programmable Gate Arrays: Reconfigurable Logic for Rapid Prototyping and Implementation of Digital Systems. John Wiley & Sons, Chichester, New York, 1995.

9. Vilfredo Pareto. Cours d'Économie Politique, volume 1. F. Rouge & Cie., Lausanne, Switzerland, 1896.

10. S. K. Rao. Regular Iterative Algorithms and their Implementations on Processor Arrays. PhD thesis, Stanford University, 1985.

11. Robert Schreiber, Shail Aditya, B. Ramakrishna Rau, Vinod Kathail, Scott Mahlke, Santosh Abraham, and Greg Snider. High-Level Synthesis of Nonprogrammable Hardware Accelerators. In IEEE International Conference on Application-specific Systems, Architectures and Processors, pages 113–124, Boston, Massachusetts, 2000.

12. Jürgen Teich. A Compiler for Application-Specific Processor Arrays. PhD thesis, Institut für Mikroelektronik, Universität des Saarlandes, Saarbrücken, Germany, 1993.

13. Jürgen Teich, Lothar Thiele, and Li Zhang. Scheduling of Partitioned Regular Algorithms on Processor Arrays with Constrained Resources. Journal of VLSI Signal Processing, 17(1):5–20, September 1997.

14. Lothar Thiele. Resource Constrained Scheduling of Uniform Algorithms. Journal of VLSI Signal Processing, 10:295–310, 1995.

15. Yiwan Wong and Jean-Marc Delosme. Optimization of Processor Count for Systolic Arrays. Technical Report YALEEU/DCS/RR-697, Yale University, Department of Computer Science, New Haven, Conneticut, 1989.

16. Xilinx, Inc. http://www.xilinx.com/products/software/jbits/

GCA: Global Cellular Automata.
A Flexible Parallel Model

Rolf Hoffmann, Klaus-Peter Völkmann,
Stefan Waldschmidt, and Wolfgang Heenes

Darmstadt University of Technology,
Alexanderstr. 10, D-64283 Darmstadt, Germany
{hoffmann,voelk,waldsch,heenes}@informatik.tu-darmstadt.de

Abstract. A model called global cellular automata (GCA) will be introduced. The new model preserves the good features of the cellular automata but overcomes its restrictions. In the GCA the cell state consists of a data field and additional pointers. Via these pointers, each cell has read access to any other cell in the cell field, and the pointers may be changed from generation to generation. Compared to the cellular automata the neighbourhood is dynamic and differs from cell to cell. For many applications parallel algorithms can be found straight forward and can directly be mapped on this model. As the model is also massive parallel in a simple way, it can efficiently be supported by hardware.

1 Motivation

The classical cellular automata model (CA) can be characterised by the following features

- The CA consists of a n–dimensional field of cells. Each cell can be identified by its coordinates.
- The neighbours are fixed and are defined by relative coordinates.
- Each cell has local read access to the states of its neighbours. Each cell contains a local rule. The local rule defines the next state depending on the cell state and the states of the neighbours.
- The cells are updated synchronously, the new generation of cells (new cell states) depend on the old generation (old cell states).
- The model is massive parallel, because all next states can be computed and updated in parallel.
- Space or time dependent rules can be implemented by the use of special space or time information coded in the state.

The CA is very well suited to problems and algorithms, which need only access to their fixed local neighbours [7]. Algorithms with global (long distance) communication can only indirectly be implemented by CA. In this case the information must be transported step by step along the line from the source cell to the destination cell, which needs a lot of time. Therefore the CA is not an efficient model for global algorithms.

V. Malyshkin (Ed.): PaCT 2001, LNCS 2127, pp. 66–73, 2001.

We have searched for a new model, which preserves the good features of the CA but overcomes the local communication restriction. The new model shall be still massive parallel, but at the same time suited to any kind of global algorithm. Thus we will be able to describe more complex algorithms in a more efficient and direct way. We have also investigated how this model can efficiently be implemented in hardware.

2   The GCA Model

The model is called *global automata model* (GCA). The GCA can be characterised by the following features

- A GCA consists of a n–dimensional field of cells. Each cell can be identified by its coordinates.
- Each cell has n individual neighbours which are variable and may change from generation to generation. The neighbours are defined by relative coordinates (addresses, pointers).
- The state of a cell contains a data field and n address fields.
  State = (Data, Address1, Address2, ...)
- Each cell has global read access to the states of its neighbours by the use of the address fields.
- Each cell contains a *local rule*. The local rule defines the next state depending on the cell state and the states of the neighbours. By changing the state, the addresses may also be changed, meaning that in the next generation different neighbours will be accessed.
- The cells are updated synchronously, the new generation of cells depends on the old generation.
- The model is massive parallel, because all next states can be computed and updated in parallel.
- Space or time dependent rules can be implemented by the use of special space or time information coded in the state.

A one–dimensional GCA with two address fields will be defined in a formal way, using a PASCAL like notation:

1. The cell field

```
Cell = array [0..n-1] of State
```

2. The State of each cell

```
State = record
  Data: Datatype
  Address1: 0..n-1
  Address2: 0..n-1
endrecord
```

3. The definition of the local rule

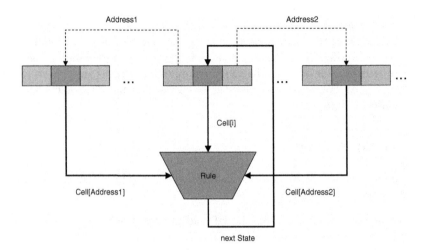

Fig. 1. The GCA model.

```
function Rule(Self:State,
    Neighbour1:State,Neighbour2:State):State
```

4. The computation of the next generation

```
for i:=0..n-1 do in parallel
    Cell[i]:= Rule(Cell[i], Cell[Address1], Cell[Address2])
endfor
```

Fig. 1 shows the principle of the GCA model. Cell[i] reads two other cell states and computes its next state, using its own state and the states of the two other cells in access. In the next state, Cell[i] may point to two different cells.

The above model can be defined in a more general way with respect to the following features

- The number k of addresses can be 1, 2, 3... If $k=1$ we call it a *one-handed* GCA, if $k=2$ we call it a *two-handed* GCA and so forth.
- The number k may vary in time and from cell to cell, in this case it will be a *variable-handed* GCA.
- Names could be used for the identification of the cells, instead of ordered addresses. In this case the cells can be considered as an unordered set of cells.
- A special *passive* state may be used to indicate that the cell state shall not be changed any more. It can be used to indicate the end of the computation or the deletion of a cell. A cell which is not in the *passive* state is called *active*. An active cell may turn a passive cell to active.

Similar models (pointer machines) have been proposed before[4,5]. In these models nodes are accessed step by step via fixed pointers stored in a tree–like structure. In our model any node can immediately be accessed because the whole pointer–structure can be changed from generation to generation through address calculations. The PSA–model [1] is a model which allows parallel state substitutions on arbitrary cells in the field. In the PSA–model each cell (or all complex) tries to perform the same set of substitution rules, on the same set of neighbours. In our model each cell has access to individual neighbours and each cell may compute a new neighbourhood from generation to generation.

3   Mapping Problems on the GCA Model

The GCA has a very simple and direct programming model. The programming model is the way how the programmer has to think in order to map an algorithm to a certain model, which is interpreted by a machine. In our case, the programmer has to keep in mind, that a machine exists which interpretes and executes the GCA model.

Many problems can easily and efficiently be mapped to the GCA model, e.g.

- sorting of numbers
- reducing a vector, like sum of vector elements
- matrix multiplication
- permutation of vector elements
- graph algorithms

The following examples are written in the cellular programming language CDL[2]. CDL was designed to facilitate the description of cellular rules based on a rectangular n-dimensional grid with a local neighbourhood. The locality of the neighbourhood radius was asserted and controlled by the declaration of distance=$radius$. For the GCA the new keyword infinity was introduced for the declaration of the $radius$.

In CDL the unary operator * is used (like in C) to dereference the relative address of a cell in order to obtain the state of the referenced cell. The following examples are *one–handed* GCAs, showing how useful unlimited read-access to any other cell is.

3.1   Example 1: Fast Fourier Transformation

The Fast Fourier transformation (FFT) is our first example. The FFT is used to transform a time–discret signal into there frequency components. We do not explain the algorithm in detail, because you can find it in many books, e.g.[6]. The example is used to demonstrate that a complex algorithm can

- easily be mapped onto the GCA model
- concisely be described
- efficiently be executed in parallel

Each cell contains a complex number (r,i) which is calculated in every time step from its own number and the number contained in another cell. The address

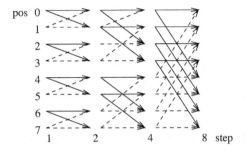

pos 0

1

2

3

4

5

6

7

1   2   4   8 step

Fig. 2. The FFT access pattern.

of the other cell depends on its own absolute address (`position`) and the time
step in the way shown in fig. 2.

For example, the cell at position 2 reads the cell at position 3 in the first
step, the cell at position 0 in the next step, and the cell at position 6 in the last
time step. Obviously this access pattern can not be implemented efficiently on
a classical cellular automaton using strict locality.

```
(1) cellular automaton fft;
(2)
(3) const dimension = 1;
(4)        distance  = infinity;
(5)
(6) const pi = 3.141592654;
(7)
(8) type celltype=record
(9)        r,i     : float;   /* the complex value  */
(10)       step    : integer; /* initialised with 1 */
(11)       position: integer; /* init with 0..(2^k)-1, n = 2^k */
(12)       end;
(13)
(14) var other    :celladdress;
(15)     a,wr,wi :float;
(16)
(17) #define cell *[0] /*    *[0] means "state of center cell" */
(18)
(19) rule begin
(20)    /* calculate relative address of other cell */
(21)    other := [(cell.position xor cell.step)-cell.position];
(22)
(23)    /* calculate new values for local r and i */
(24)    a:=(-pi * (cell.position + (cell.step-1)))/ cell.step;
(25)
(26)    wr:=cos(a);
(27)    wi:=sin(a);
```

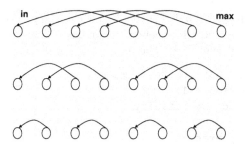

Fig. 3. Bitonic sequenz access pattern.

```
(28)
(29)   if (other.x > 0) then
(30)   begin
(31)   /* other cell has higher number */
(32)
(33)     cell.r := cell.r + wr * (*other.r) - wi * (*other.i);
(34)     cell.i := cell.i + wr * (*other.i) + wi * (*other.r);
(35)   end
(36)   else
(37)   begin
(38)   /* other cell has lower number */
(39)
(40)     cell.r := *other.r - (wr * cell.r - wi * cell.i);
(41)     cell.i := *other.i - (wr * cell.i + wi * cell.r);
(42)   end;
(43)
(44)   /* step = 1,2,4,8,... */
(45)   cell.step := 2 * cell.step;
(46)
(47) end;
```

The algorithm is concise and efficient because the address of the neighbour is calculated (line (21)) and thereby an individual neighbour is accessed (lines (33) and (34)). The listing of the FFT without using this feature would be at least twice as long and the calculation would take significantly more time. The time complexity is $O(n) = ld(n)$, with n = number of cells/positions ($n = 2^k$).

3.2   Example 2: Bitonic Merge

The bitonic merge algorithm sorts a bitonic sequence. A sequence of numbers is called bitonic, if the first part of the sequence is ascending and the second part is descending, or if the sequence is cyclically shifted. Consider a sequence of length $n = 2^k$. In the first step cells with distance 2^{k-1} are compared, fig. 3.

Their data values are exchanged if necessary to get the minimum to the left and the maximum to the right. In each of the following steps the distance for the cells to be compared is halve of the distance of the preceding step. Also with each step the number of subsequences is doubled. There is no communication between different subsequences. The number of parallel steps is $K = ld(n)$.

```
(1)  cellular automaton bitonic_merge;
(2)  const dimension = 1;
(3)        distance  = infinity;
(4)
(5)  type celltype=record
(6)  /* data is initialized by a bitonic sequence */
(7)        data       : integer;
(8)  /* own_pos is initialized by 0..(2^k)-1 */
(9)        own_pos    : integer;
(10) /* other_pos initialized by (2^k)/2 */
(11)       other_pos  : integer;
(12)       end;
(13)
(14) var other : celladdress;
(15)     w,a   : integer;
(16)
(17) #define cell *[0]
(18)
(19) rule begin
(20)   if ((cell.own_pos and cell.other_pos) = 0 ) then
(21)     begin
(22)       /* relative address of cells with higher numbers */
(23)       other := [cell.other_pos];
(24)       w := *other.data;
(25)       a := cell.data;
(26)       /* comparator */
(27)       if (w < a) then cell.data := w;
(28)     end
(29)   else
(30)     begin
(31)       /* relative address of cells with lower numbers */
(32)       other := [-cell.other_pos];
(33)       w := *other.data;
(34)       a := cell.data;
(35)       /* comparator */
(36)       if (a < w) then cell.data := w;
(37)     end;
(38)
(39)   /* access-pattern is (2^k)/2,...,4,2,1 */
(40) cell.other_pos := cell.other_pos / 2;
(41) end;
```

4   Conclusion

We have introduced a powerful model, called *global cellular automata* (GCA). The cell state is composed of a data field and n pointers which point to n arbitrary other cells. The new cell state is computed by a local rule, which takes into account its own state and the states of the other cells which are in access via the pointers. In the next generation the pointers may point to different cells. Each cell changes its state independently from the other cells, there are no write conflicts. Therefore the GCA model is massive parallel meaning that it has a great potential to be efficiently supported by hardware. We plan do implement the GCA model on the CEPRA-S processor[3].

Parallel algorithms can easily be described and mapped onto the GCA. Compared to the CA model it is much more flexible although it is only a little more complex.

References

1. S. Achasova, O. Bandman, V. Markova, and S. Piskunov. *Parallel Substitution Algorithm*. World Scientific, P O BOX 128, Farrer Road, Singapore 9128, 1994.
2. Christian Hochberger, Rolf Hoffmann, and Stefan Waldschmidt. Compilation of CDL for different target architecures. In Viktor Malyshkin, editor, *Parallel Computing Technologies*, pages 169–179, Berlin, Heidelberg, 1995. Springer.
3. Rolf Hoffmann, Bernd Ulmann, Klaus-Peter Völkmann, and Stefan Waldschmidt. A stream processor architecture based on the configurabel CEPRA-S. In Reiner W. Hartenstein and Herbert Grünbacher, editors, *Field–Programmable Logic and Applications*, pages 822–825, Berlin, Heidelberg, 2000. Springer.
4. A.N. Kolmogorov and V.A. Uspenskii. On the definition of an algorithm. In *American Mathematical Society Translations*, volume 9 of *Series 2*, pages 217–245. American Mathematical Society, 1963.
5. Arnold Schönhage. Real-time simulation of multidimensional turing machines by storage modification machines. *SIAM Journal on Computing*, 9(3):490–508, August 1980.
6. Samuel D. Stearns. *Digital Signal Analysis*. Hayden Book Company, Rochelle Park, New Jersey, 1975.
7. T. Toffoli and N. Margolus. *Cellular Automata Machines*. MIT Press, Cambridge Mass., 1987.

Cellular-Pipelined Algorithm Architecture for Polynomial Computing

Valentina Markova

Supercomputer Software Department
ICMMG, Siberian Branch
Russian Academy of Science
Pr. Lavrentieva, 6, Novosibirsk, 630090, Russia
markova@ssd.sscc.ru
Tel.: (3832) 343994, Fax.: (3832) 324259

Abstract. This paper is oriented to algorithm architecture for computation of polynomials. The algorithm is based on "divide and conquer" method and performed in terms of a model of fine-grained parallelism – Parallel Substitution Algorithm.

1   Introduction

It is known that the efficiency of computation of most numerical functions is in strong dependence on the efficiency of polynomial computation. In such a way, the problem of polynomial approximation is standard and often-used operation. As a result, more attention is paid to designing high-speed algorithms for polynomial computation, which are also suitable for VLSI implementation.

In this paper we describe a cellular-pipelined architecture of the algorithm for polynomial computation. The interest in cellular algorithms is associated with their properties: homogeneity, maximal parallelism and high-tech mapping into VLSI.

Parallel Substitution Algorithm (PSA) [1,2] is used for the above algorithm design and modeling. Unlike other cellular models, PSA properties and expressive capabilities allow to represent any complex algorithm. Moreover, there is one-to-one correspondence between PSA and automata net, that forms the basis for the architectural design. Traditionally, the Horner scheme is used for polynomial computation. It requires $O(n)$ steps, where n is a degree of a polynomial. Systolic algorithms for polynomial computation are widely covered in the literature. To reduce the time complexity of algorithm to $O(\log n)$ steps, we employ "divide and conquer" method [3]. (FFT is the best illustration of use of this method and properties of complex roots of one [3].) Degree of exploitation of the method parallelism is determined by the size of a cellular array.

The presented algorithm computes polynomials in an array of restricted size in time $(l + 13)\lceil \log n \rceil + \lceil \log l \rceil - 2$, where l is the length of the polynomial coefficients and the variable, $\lceil x \rceil$ identifies the ceilling of x.

The article is organized as follows. In the second section "divide and conquer" method for computing polynomials is given. The cellular-pipelined algorithm

V. Malyshkin (Ed.): PaCT 2001, LNCS 2127, pp. 74–79, 2001.

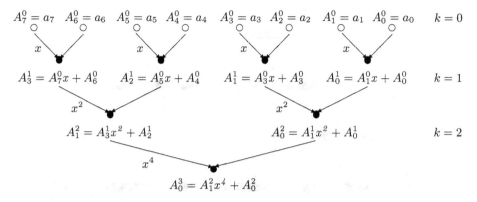

Fig. 1. The computational tree

architecture for computing polynomials and its time complexity are discussed in the third section.

2   Method for Computing Polynomials

Let $P(x) = a_n x^n + a_{n-1} x^{n-1} + \cdots + a_0$, $a_n \neq 0$, be a polynomial of degree n and let $n = 2^i - 1$. Then

$$P(x) = a_{2^i - 1} x^{2^i - 1} + a_{2^i - 2} x^{2^i - 2} + \cdots + a_0. \tag{1}$$

Using "divide and conquer" method, the polynomial (1) is represented as

$$P(x) = \sum_{m=0}^{2^{(i-k)} - 1} A_m^k(x) x^{2^k m},$$

where $A_m^0(x) = a_m$, $A_m^k(x)$ is m-th *partial* polynomial of degree less or equal to 2^{k-1}. Since

$$P(x) = \sum_{m=0}^{2^{(i-k)} - 1} A_m^k(x) x^{2^k m} = \sum_{m=0}^{2^{(i-(k+1)+1)} - 1} A_m^{k+1}(x) x^{2^{k+1} m},$$

we have the following recurrence

$$A_m^{k+1}(x) = A_{2m+1}^k(x) x^{2^k} + A_{2m}^k(x), \quad 0 \le k \le i - 1, \quad 0 \le m \le 2^{i-k} - 1, \tag{2}$$

where k is the index of recursion. Let us call $A_{2m+1}^k(x)$ and $A_{2m}^k(x)$ in (2) *the first and the second coefficient* of m-th partial polynomial, respectively.

So, computation of $P(x)$ of degree n is reduced to recursive computation of the partial polynomials (2) and their composition. The result is formed in time $O(\log n)$. In Fig. 1 an example of computation of a polynomial of degree 7 is given.

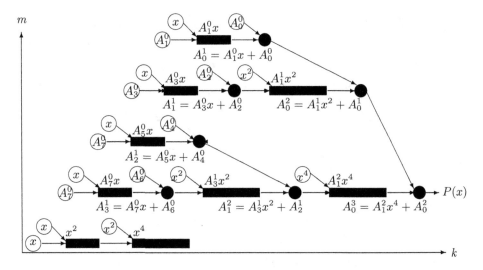

Fig. 2. The scheme of the cellular-pipelined algorithm

3   Cellular-Pipelined Algorithm Architecture

In this section, at first we discuss computational scheme of the presented algorithm then we take a quick look at the cellular algorithm architecture and estimate the time complexity of the presented algorithm.

3.1   Calculation Scheme of Algorithm

Let $P(x)$ be a polynomial of degree n. For simplicity, we shall make the following assumptions: $0 \le a < 1$, $p = 0, 1, \ldots n$, $0 \le x < 1$, $\sum_{i=0}^{n} a_i < 1$, the initial and immediate data are l-bit binary numbers, and $l > n$. It is required to calculate $P(x)$ in an array of size $(l \times l)$ for multiplying.

The cellular-pipelined algorithm for computing sum of products [2] is used for forming the partial polynomials and the squares. The algorithm carries out the products in a redundant form in an array of size $(l \times l)$ with the period equal to 4 steps. High pipelining is achieved due to the following. The multipliers are loaded digit serially, the least significant bit first. The multiplicands are loaded digit parallelly at 4 step intervals. The fast carry-save technique is used for summing. The first product is obtained at the $(l+1)$-th step, the second product – in 4 steps, and so on.

The computational scheme of the algorithm is shown in Fig. 2. It is obtained from the scheme (Fig. 1) by the computation pipelining by two parameters : by k, $k = 0, 1, \ldots, i-1$, and by m, $m = 2^{i-k} - 1, \ldots, 0$. For given k the square of number x^{2^k} $(x^{2^k} x^{2^k} = x^{2^{k+1}})$ is carried out at first and then the products $A_{2m+1}^k(x) x^{2^k}$ are computed beginning from maximum value of m. Let us call the partial polynomial $A_m^{k+1}(x)$ for maximum value of m a *leading* polynomial of degree less or equal to 2^k. Using algorithm [2], the leading polynomial of degree

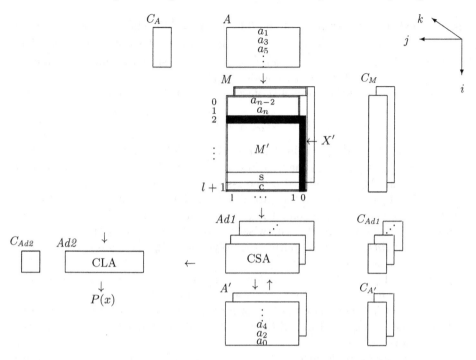

Fig. 3. Architecture for computing a polynomial

1 (A_3^1) is ready at the ($l + 8$)-th step (the summation requires 3 steps). Hence, beginning from the 9-th step the algorithm can compute the leading polynomial of degree 2.

All intermediate results are in the redundant form. Only the square is transformed into a nonredundant form. This transformation does not require an additional time. In this case computing the products $A_{2m+1}^k(x)x^{2^k}$ and the square $x^{2^{k+1}}$, $k \geq 1$, are reduced to two multiplications and one summation.

3.2 Cellular-Pipelined Algorithm Architecture

Algorithm architecture corresponds to its calculational scheme and is given in Fig. 3. Data to be processed are allocated in 10 arrays.

The initial data are placed as follows. X' stores the multiplier (x). A', A and two first rows of the 0-th layer of the array M' of size (($l + 2$) $\times l \times 2$) store the multiplications (the coefficients of $P(x)$), moreover, the even coefficients are stored in the 0-th of A'. In Fig. 3 the first pair (x, x) to be multiplied is marked. In the array X' the least significant bit of x is placed in the top cell, in the array M' the least significant bit of x – in the rightmost cell of the 2-nd row of M'.

The 0-th layer of the array M of size ($l + 2$) $\times$ ($l + 1$) $\times 2$ is intended for computing the products and the squares. Each result (a two-row code) (c, s)

is obtained in two last rows of the 0-th layer of M'. The code of the square $x^{2^{k+1}} = (c,s)^{2^{k+1}}$ is transferred into two first rows of the 1-st layer of M'. The two-row code of product $A_{2m+1}^k(x)x^{2^k} = (c,s)_m^{k+1}$ is supplied number serially in the 0-th layer of $Ad1$ (Carry save adder (CSA)).

The 0-th layer of the array $Ad1$ of size $3 \times l \times (n/4+1)$ is used for computing

$$A_m^{k+1}(x) = A_{2m+1}^k(x)x^{2^k} + A_{2m}^k(x). \tag{3}$$

The coefficient $A_{2m}^k(x)$ is loaded from A' into $Ad1$ in advance. If $k = 0$, then $A_{2m}^k(x) = a_{2m}^0$ is placed in the 2-nd row of $Ad1$. If $k \geq 1$, then two-row code of coefficient the $A_{2m}^k(x)$ is placed in the 1-st and the 2-nd rows of $Ad1$.

So, the algorithm formed the partial polynomial. If the obtained result is the first coefficient of the polynomial $A_m^{k+2}(x)$, then its code is placed in two first rows of the 0-th layer of M'. Otherwise the obtained code is dropped into one of the layers of $Ad1$. Before computing the polynomial $A_m^{k+2}(x)$, this code is turned back into the 0-th layer of $Ad1$.

The 1-st layer of the array M forms the one row code of the square. The obtained result is loaded into X' digit serially, starting from the 1-st digit.

The result is accumulated in the form of the two-row code in the array $Ad1$, which is then transferred into $Ad2$ (carry-look-ahead adder (CLA)) to sum the last numbers.

Data loading is performed under the control of the arrays C_A, C_M, $C_{A'}$. Data processing is performed under the control of C_M, C_{Ad1}, $C_{A'}$, and C_{Ad2}.

The cellular algorithm consists of two procedures carried out successively

- *computing the partial polynomials and the square,*
- *transformation of two-row code of the square.*

The procedure of computing the partial polynomials and the squares is based on the cellular-pipelined algorithm for computing a sum of products.

The transformation procedure is reduced to peformence the transformation $(c,s)^{2^k} \to x^{2^k}$. It takes $(l+1)$ steps. Each step consists of adding two boolean integers c^{2^k} and s^{2^k} and shifting of the result (sum and carry) one digit to the write. Four rules $(\Theta_1, \Theta_2, \Theta_3$ and $\Theta_4)$ and the example are given in Fig. 4.

3.3   Time Complexity

The time complexity of the cellular algorithm is the following sum

$$T = t_{2^1} + \sum_{j=2}^{\lceil \log n \rceil - 1} t_{2^j} + t_p + t_l + t_{CLA}.$$

Here t_{2^1} and t_{2^j} – the time needed to compute the squaters x^{2^1} and x^{2^j}, $j = 2, 3, \ldots, \lceil \log n \rceil - 1$, respectively. $t_{2^1} = (l+3)$ steps (2 steps is required to load two-row code of x^{2^1} into $Ad1$). $t_{2^j} = (l+13)$ steps (5 steps is required to transfer two-row code of x^{2^j} into the 1-st layer of M and to obtain the first digit

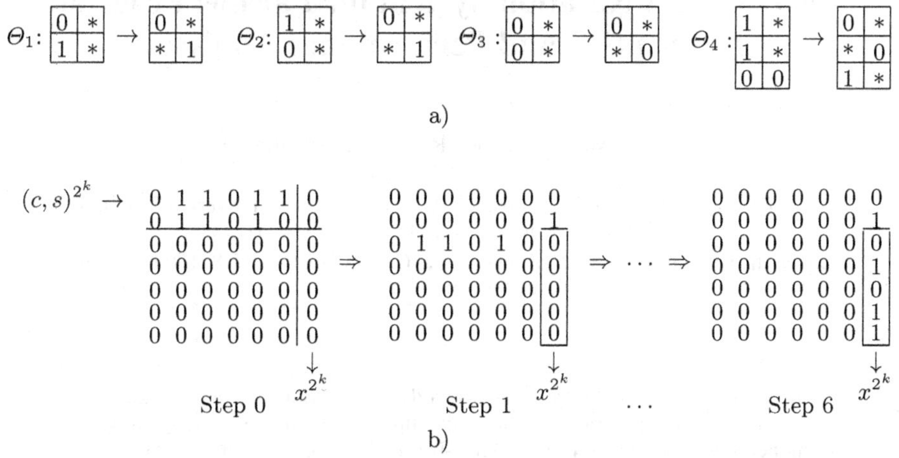

a)

b)

Fig. 4. Transformation procedure: a) the summation rules, b) the example of the transformation $2 \rightarrow 1$ in the 1-st layer of M

of its one-row code, $(l+8)$ steps needed to compute two-row code of $x^{2^{j+1}}$). As the algorithm computes the leading polynomial of degree 2^j 8 steps after the computation of the squarer $x^{2^{j+1}}$, $j > 1$, $t_p = 8$. t_l – the time needed to generate the last leading partial polynomial $(P(x))$, $t_l = (l+11)$ steps. t_{CLA} – the time is required to transfer the result from CSA into CLA (2 steps) and to sum up two last numbers ($\lceil \log l \rceil$ steps). So, the algorithm computes a polynomial in time $T = (l+13)\lceil \log n \rceil - 2 + \lceil \log l \rceil$.

4 Conclusion

In this paper, we present the new cellular algorithm architecture for computing polynomials of degree n. The algorithm computes a polynomial in time $(l+13)\lceil \log n \rceil + \lceil \log l \rceil - 2$.

References

1. S. Achasova, O. Bandman, V. Markova, S. Piskunov. Parallel Substitution Algorithm. Theory and Application. World Scientific. Singapore. 1994. 220 p.
2. V. Markova, S. Piskunov, Yu. Pogudin. Formal Methods and Tools for Design of Cellular Algorithms and Architectures. Programmirovanie, 4, 1996, pp. 24-36. (in Russian)
3. T. Cormen, C. Leiserson, R.Rivest. Introduction to Algorithms. The MIT Press. Cambridge. 1990. 960 p.

MetaPL: A Notation System for Parallel Program Description and Performance Analysis

N. Mazzocca[1], M. Rak[1], and U. Villano[2]

[1] DII, Seconda Universita' di Napoli, via Roma 29, 81031 Aversa (CE), Italy
`n.mazzocca@unina.it, maxrak@iol.it`
[2] Universita' del Sannio, Facolta' di Ingegneria, C.so Garibaldi 107, 82100 Benevento, Italy
`villano@unisannio.it`

Abstract. This paper introduces MetaPL, a notation system designed to describe parallel programs both in the direct and in the reverse software engineering cycle. MetaPL is an XML-based Tag language, and exploits XML extension capabilities to describe programs written in different programming paradigms, interaction models and programming languages. The possibility to include timing information in the program description promotes the use of performance analysis during software development. After a description of the main features of the notation system, its use to obtain two particular program descriptions (*views*) is shown as an example.

1 Introduction

Currently the use of parallel hardware and parallel programs for solving computation-intensive problems is customary. Unfortunately, the development of parallel software is still carried out ignoring systematically software engineering principles and methods. Most of the times, the obtained programs are badly structured, difficult to understand, not easy to maintain or re-use. Sometimes, they even fail to meet the desired performance, which is the primary reason for resorting to parallelism. The first cause of this state of affairs is the absence of a unifying programming approach. Traditional sequential software developers have a clear idea of how program statements will be executed, and can pay attention to software quality. Parallel programmers are instead mobilized for the holy war between the supporters of shared memory and message-passing paradigms.

A second complementary issue is the relatively scarce interest taken by software engineering researchers in performance issues. The traditional targets of software engineering are functional requirements and how to build software that has few bugs and can be easily maintained. In fact, performance-oriented techniques have rarely been adopted throughout the software life cycle. It should be also noted that the scenario is quite changed, due to the more intensive use of structured software design approaches, such as component-based development. Currently there is a widespread interest in techniques that allow the design of software for performance. It is worth pointing out that, oddly enough, performance problems have not been eliminated, not even mitigated, by the availability of cheap and fast hardware. The newness of

V. Malyshkin (Ed.): PaCT 2001, LNCS 2127, pp. 80–93, 2001.

software environments and hardware, along with the consequent inexperience of developers, increases the risk of performance failures. This is particularly true for parallel systems, where hidden, non-intuitive and inter-related performance factors, computer environment heterogeneity and complexity, and the wide range of possible design choices make it very difficult to obtain satisfactory performance levels.

Software performance engineering (SPE) methods, successfully used for years in the context of sequential software, are the obvious solution for the development of responsive parallel software systems. The SPE process begins early in the software life cycle, and uses quantitative methods to identify among the possible development choices the designs that are more likely to be satisfactory in terms of performance. Stated another way, SPE makes it possible to discriminate between successful and unsuccessful (as far as performance is concerned) designs, before significant time and effort is invested in detailed design, coding, testing and benchmarking [1], [2], [3], [4], [5]. Starting from the performance problems and the need to study them at the early stages of development, new software life-cycles, graphical software views and CASE tools were developed, oriented to the development of parallel software [4], [5], [6], [7]. Unfortunately, the research efforts in this field have been carried out in many different directions in a completely uncoordinated way, thus producing incompatible tools based on alternative approaches.

It is interesting to point out that for sequential software, and in particular for Object-Oriented Programming, there are instead many widely accepted standards, such as UML, as graphical notation systems. New standards are under development, such as XMI [8] for data interchanging between CASE tools. Tools based on these standards, initially developed for traditional sequential programming, are beginning to be used in distributed systems, and in particular for distributed object systems like Corba. However, they are not easily re-utilizable for general parallel programming, as the existence of many non-standard UML extensions for parallel programming clearly shows.

Our research group has been active for several years in the field of heterogeneous distributed system simulation for performance analysis [1], [9], [10], [11]. The development of parallel applications on top of a high-performance simulator, running on a workstation or on a scaled-down distributed environment rather than directly on the target computing system, has proven to be a simple and profitable solution, able to improve software quality and to reduce development costs, even in the absence of integration with customary software engineering methodologies.

Probably the most interesting possibility offered by software development in simulation environments is the iterative refinement and performance evaluation of program *prototypes*. Prototypes are incomplete program designs, skeletons of code where (some of) the computations interleaved between concurrent process interactions are not fully specified. In a prototype, these local[1] computations are represented for simulation purposes by delays equal to the (expected) time that will be spent in the actual code. The use of prototypes has shown that this synthetic way of describing the behavior of a parallel program is very powerful: it is language- and platform-independent, shows only the essential features of software, and can be used for performance analysis at the early development stages.

---

[1] By "local" computation, we mean a sequence of executed statements that entail no interaction (whether by shared memory or by message-exchange) with other concurrent processes or threads.

In this paper we describe MetaPL, a notation system designed to be the evolution of the concept of prototypes. MetaPL is an XML-based Tag language, and provides predefined elements for the description of parallel programs at different levels of detail. Using XML peculiar extension characteristics, the capabilities of the notation system can be freely expanded whenever necessary. In fact, MetaPL is composed of a minimal "core" language; through the introduction of suitable extensions, it is possible for the software developer to describe virtually any parallel/distributed software system. The extension mechanism is also used to obtain particular *views* of the developed software, such us graphical representations, program documentation or program activity traces to be used as input for trace-based simulators. The main features of MetaPL are the following:

- *flexibility,* since it may be used in conjunction with any type of programming language or parallel programming paradigm;
- *completeness,* as every single line of code contained in the source code program can be represented, if necessary. Conversely, the source code can be easily recovered from the description;
- *simplicity,* as it supports code examination and understanding though graphical views which define simple transformations that can be used as input for graphical tools, or to generate human-readable code documentation;
- *suitability for performance evaluation*: the program description allow the insertion of information on response times of portions of code, thus promoting the integration with performance evaluation tools.

The use of a single, flexible notation system may help the development of CASE tools and data interchanging between them. Furthermore, its suitability for simulation promotes the use of performance analysis techniques in the early stages of the software development cycle.

This paper is structured as follows. In the next section the key concepts of the language are introduced, along with a description of its structure and of the main solutions adopted. The core of the notation is presented, introducing the extension system and a simple message-passing extension. Then the concept of views and two examples of their use are dealt with. Finally, the conclusions are drawn.

2   Meta-language Overview

Owing to the great research efforts of the last decades in the field of parallel and distributed programming, there is currently a very high number of imperative parallel/concurrent programming languages, based on alternative memory models (shared-memory, message-passing, hybrid solutions). They allow (with some restrictions, of course) different kinds of interaction models to be exploited (client-server, peer-to-peer, master-slave, processor farm, ...). All the above can be targeted to radically different target hardware/software systems, exploiting run-time libraries in stand-alone computers, run-time libraries or O.S. calls on the top of communication protocol software in networked systems, or even resorting to specialized communication hardware.

In this paper we describe a single unifying notation whose objective is to (try to) tame this complexity, assisting the software developer in:

- the development of high-performance parallel software from scratch by intensive use of prototypes and by performance prediction techniques integrated with software development tools (*direct parallel software engineering*, DPSE);
- the examination, comprehension, refinement and performance improvement of fully-developed programs by simplified program *views* such as diagrams, animations, simulations (*reverse parallel software engineering*, RPSE).

In DPSE, our development procedure requires the description of the basic structure of the algorithm through prototypes. These are static flow graphs made up of nodes corresponding to blocks of sequential code (i.e., sequences of executable statements involving no interaction with other tasks), and nodes corresponding to a basic set of parallel programming primitives (parallel activation and termination, wait for child task termination, communication, synchronization, ...). Once the blocks of sequential code have been annotated with execution time estimates, found by direct measurement on available code or by speculative benchmarking, it is possible to evaluate the time required for task interaction by simulation tools [11] or analytic models. Predicting the final performance, even at the very early stages of software development, makes it possible to adopt a cyclic software evolution technique. The (predicted) performance is validated against problem specifications. If the results are not satisfactory, it is necessary to revise (some of) the choices made in the previous development steps. Otherwise, the prototypes are refined, replacing nodes with sub-graphs or even with real code. Performance is validated once again, the design is further detailed, and so on. When the process stops, the original prototypes have been replaced with a fully-developed code compatible with the initial performance objectives. The whole process, represented graphically for a simple two-task program in Fig. 1 (left to right), requires a language- and paradigm-independent notation, made up of a simple set of primitives for expressing explicit parallelism, plus the ability to encapsulate opaque code or blocks of sequential statements.

In RPSE, instead, a fully-developed program is to be represented as a prototype. This requires the construction of a static flow graph made up of nodes corresponding to concurrent programming constructs and nodes corresponding to sections of sequential code involving no interaction with other tasks. It should be noted that this requires some knowledge about the sequential programming language adopted, as well as the full range concurrent constructs exploited. An issue of paramount importance for the developer is to have the possibility to recover actual code from the prototype-like notation and vice versa. The RPSE process is also shown in Fig. 1, following the arrows from right to left.

The main issue dealt with in this paper is the design of a notation able to support both direct and reverse development cycles. In light of the above, these have different representation requirements. In DPSE, it is important to manage hierarchical structures of code blocks, which are to be progressively detailed. In RPSE, instead, complete program codes have to be suitably handled. It should be explicitly pointed out that our proposal, MetaPL, is not decidedly a parallel programming language (as mentioned earlier, there is plenty of parallel languages), but just a simple and concise notation to support forward and reverse development cycles. It should also be clear that it is not possible to devise a notation able to support the totality of parallel programming languages and notations. The basic assumption made here is that the program is written in a conventional imperative sequential language (maybe an object-oriented one), extended with commands/functions for performing the basic tasks linked to parallel programming (e.g., activation and termination of tasks, message/passing and/or shared-memory synchronization, ...). Each task runs until completion, executing its statements in a sequential fashion, communicating and synchronizing with other tasks on a single processor, or on multiple processors communicating by a network, a shared memory or a combination of the two. This is not a particularly restrictive assumption, as the majority of existing parallel/ distributed programs satisfies these requirements.

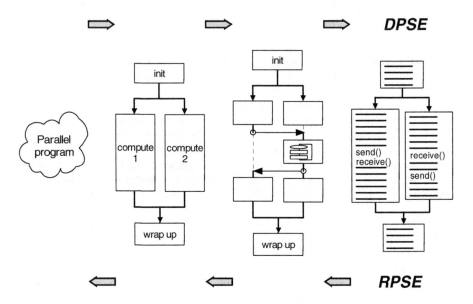

Fig. 1. The direct and reverse parallel software development cycles

As briefly mentioned in the introduction, the main characteristic of the notation system, namely its flexibility, has been obtained by defining not a single notation, but an extensible language. MetaPL is composed of a *core*, a minimal set of language- and paradigm-independent commands for expressing high level prototypes of concurrent computations, plus language-, model- and paradigm-based extensions that can be added to the core notation, thus making it possible to represent real code at any level of detail in prototype-like form. As a matter of fact, extendibility is one of the key characteristics of XML [12]. In XML, a Document Type Definition (DTD) defines the Tags of the language and their composition rules. Hence it has been a natural choice to develop MetaPL as a collection of DTDs for XML. A further advantage linked to the use of XML is the possibility to use existing tools (e.g., Xerces, libxml, IE, Quilt, Swig) for parsing, querying (extracting information) or editing the XML documents describing a parallel program.

In the subsequent language description we will define *XML elements*,[2] their attributes and composition rules, explaining how they can represent parallel programs

---

[2] An XML document is composed of *elements*, the boundaries of which are either delimited by start-tags and end-tags, or, for empty elements, by an empty-element tag.

concepts. It is also worth pointing out that, unless otherwise noted, we will consider for expositive convenience only the direct cycle, showing the use of MetaPL in the DPSE context. However, the proposed notation can support RPSE as well.

3 The Language Core

The MetaPL core has a very limited description capability. This choice was made purposely, in order to avoid a unifying programming approach, which would lead to the impossibility to describe alternative programming paradigms and models. The objective of the core notation is to describe in a simplified way only the high-level structure of the parallel code (task activation and termination, plus minimal synchronization statements) and generic sequential code. In fact, parallel programs are made up of sequential code augmented with concurrency, communications and synchronization constructs typical of the programming paradigm adopted. Hence, facilities for describing sequential code are at the base of every parallel program description.

A MetaPL description is essentially a hierarchical structure whose building blocks are different types of blocks of code. All blocks encapsulate sections of code, and may have attributes associates with them, such as the actual code contained, the expected execution time or the name of a cost function, which gives the (expected) execution time as a function of program inputs. It should be noted that the description by blocks encapsulating hierarchically the code at different levels of detail is indeed useful for prototype code in the direct cycle. It is less advantageous in RPSE, when complete programs have to be modeled. In the latter case, a *complete* description (in that every line of code contained in the source code program can be represented) can be obtained by exploiting the concept of "vagueness": all the source code statements that are not directly supported by the notation system can be marked as GenericCommand, keeping the original code into the notation system. Whenever a new extension is applied to the description, the unknown commands are analyzed and, if recognized, replaced with a more detailed description.

The basic type of block is the CodeBlock. By definition a CodeBlock is an opaque object, made up internally of a sequence of executable statements written in a conventional (sequential) programming language. A parallel program can be described as a set of CodeBlocks, along with commands that describe the high-level structure of the code. These commands[3] can either be *concurrent* or *sequential*, depending on whether they involve some form of interaction among concurrent tasks, or not. Sequences of CodeBlocks and sequential commands can be combined into SequentialBlocks. In their turn, SequentialBlocks and concurrent commands compose the Block, which is the basic program unit assigned to a processor, and is executed as a separate task.

---

[3] As the word "commands" may be misleading, it is worth pointing out that in this context a command is not an executable statement, as MetaPL is just a notation for describing a computation, and not a programming language. However, a command corresponds to executable statements (or sequences of executable statements) in the described code.

3.1 Variables

Even if MetaPL is not a programming language, and so there is no need for data management, the introduction of variables is of great help to describe an algorithm. Furthermore, it is useful to evaluate its performance in the presence of variable input data (e.g., the problem dimension). For this reasons, a MetaPL description may include Variable elements. They are identified by the name attribute, may contain an initial value attribute, and a further attribute describing the type. Instead of a constant initial value, it is possible to use the ASK predefined value. In this case, it is up to the user to supply interactively the value, whenever the value is actually required (typically, when a view is built from the program description). It is worth pointing out that MetaPL variables are meta-variables, i.e., they have only descriptive validity, and should never be confused with any variables possibly present in the encapsulated code.

3.2 Sequential Commands: Loop and Switch

The possibility to describe programs that have alternative paths (even at high level), or that perform an activity a number of times that depends on user input, is the primary reason for the inclusion in the MetaPL core of conventional sequential commands such as *loop* and *switch*.

The Loop available in MetaPL is a *for* cycle executed a known number of times. The attributes of a Loop include the name of the loop control variable and the number of iterations; optional attributes (start, end, step) can be used to vary in a more complex way the values of the control variable. It should be noted that the coherence of the attribute values is not verified in the description system. For example, a loop to be repeated 8 times, controlled by a variable with start value 1, end value 5, step 1, is well-formed, even not semantically correct.

The following is a simple example that shows the use of Loop:

```
<Code><Loop variable="i" iterations="1">
<CodeBlock type="opaque"> <description> Get the i-th element
of the first vector, get the i-th element of the second
vector and sum them </description></CodeBlock>
</Loop></Code>
```

The next example shows the use of cost functions and how the loop can be hidden in an opaque CodeBlock.

```
<Code>
<CodeBlock type="opaque" costfunction="VectorMul">
<description> Multiply two vectors and store the result in a
single variable. The dimension is n </description>
</CodeBlock>
</Code>
```

```
<CostFunction name="VectorMul"> The time spent is 0.15ms
</CostFunction>
```

The `Switch` command enables the description of statements such as *if-then-else*. It contains a sequence of `Case` elements, and each of them contains the action to be performed.

The `Case` element has two attributes:

- `prob`, the probability that the option of the switch is selected;
- `condition`, that describes the condition leading to the selection of a switch option.

The two attributes may be used together, as shown in the following example.

```
<Switch>
<Case prob="5%" condition="condition description">
<CodeBlock> Do something </CodeBlock> </Case>
<Case prob="95%" condition="condition description">
<CodeBlock> Do something else </CodeBlock> </Case>
</Switch>
```

3.3 Concurrent Commands: Spawn, Exit and Wait

Concurrent commands are required to introduce into MetaPL the concept of a program composed of many concurrent tasks.[4] A parallel program and its task structure is described as in the following example:

```
<ParallelProgram>
<TaskDecl name="father" id="1"> This is the father
task</TaskDecl>
<TaskDecl name="son" id="2"> This is the son task</TaskDecl>
</ParallelProgram>
```

The task code description is given in the `Task` element, characterized by the `name` attribute; the code is composed of the MetaPL core statements introduced above, plus the concurrent commands shown below.

The `Spawn` command is characterized by two attributes, the name of the spawned task, defined elsewhere along with the enclosed code, and its identifier.

The `Wait` statement is used for the description of synchronization on task exit: the task that contains this element waits for the termination of the task whose `id` is reported in the `waitforid` attribute, or for the termination of the number of spawned tasks reported in the attribute `number`. The two attributes can never be present at the same time.

The `Exit` statement indicates the end of a task and is used to terminate the corresponding `Wait`.

The following example shows two tasks, synchronized by means of a `Wait` command.

---

[4] A "concurrent task" is the basic schedulable unit that can be assigned to a processor. In practice, it can be implemented by a process or by a thread, depending on the execution environment.

```
<Task name="master"><Code>
<Spawn spawnedname="son" spawnedid="2" ></Spawn>
<CodeBlock time="0.1" > Do something and close </CodeBlock>
<Wait waitforid="2" />
<Exit />
</Code></Task>

<Task name="son"><Code>
<CodeBlock time="0.3" > Do something and close </CodeBlock>
<Exit />
</Code></Task>
```

4 The Language Extensions

The notation system introduced until now is equivalent to other existing program description languages. However, MetaPL can gain major flexibility and expressive power by the use of extensions. Extensions are used to enable the notation system to describe programs that contain notations that cannot be converted into the ones defined in the MetaPL language core.

The extensions to the language can be divided into two major classes:

- *language extensions,* which expand the description capability of the core language, adding new commands typical of new programming paradigms or specific to a library or a programming language;
- *filters,* which define the rules that can be used to obtain less complete and structured, though simpler, representations of the software (*views*). Typical program views are diagrams, traces or prototypes for simulation.

There is a wide range of language extensions (some already developed, other only planned) that allow the description using MetaPL of the most widely used parallel and concurrent languages and notations. In this Section, we will propose as an example the Message Passing Extension (MPE).

Figure 2 shows the relationship between a document describing a parallel program, the language extension used, which define further programming concepts typical of the adopted programming paradigm, and the filters used to obtain traces for simulation and an HTML program view.

4.1 The Message-Passing Extension (MPE)

The MPE extends the core set of MetaPL commands with the introduction of non-blocking send (Send) and blocking receive (Receive). These basic commands are sufficient to describe the majority of message-passing task interactions. It should be explicitly noted that, as far as program description is concerned, information on the contents of exchanged message is useless, unless it influences the number of times a loop is performed, or the choice of one switch branch or another. However, this is not possible in MetaPL, owing to the (rather restrictive) way in which loops and switches are defined.

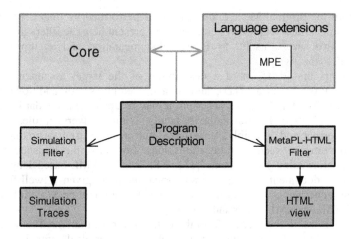

Fig. 2. A parallel program description and MetaPL extensions

The Send element is characterized by three attributes:

- receiver, the id of the task that has to receive the message. This attribute is mandatory;
- dim, the dimension in bytes of the message. This attribute is not mandatory, but it is useful for performance evaluation purposes;
- msgtag, which can be used to identify a specific message.

An example of Send element is the following:

```
<Send receiver="2" msgtag="1" dim="10"></Send>
```

The Receive element, instead, has only the attributes sender and msgtag, both of which are not mandatory. If a sender is not specified, the receiver can get the message from any sender, as in the following example:

```
<Receive></Receive>
```

Similarly, the absence of a msgtag attribute is representative of a situation in which the receiver is willing to accept any type of message.

5 The Views

By exploiting suitably-defined extensions, MetaPL can describe most parallel and distributed programs. However, even if the number of defined elements is not high, the resulting description can be neither concise, nor particularly easy to manage, because of XML language redundancy. As mentioned in the language overview, the *views* are descriptions less complete and structured than the MetaPL one, but able to highlight specific aspects of the program. For example, they could be UML sequence diagrams, portions of code, automatically-generated documentation of the program, prototypes or program traces useful for simulation purposes [11]. The derivation of views from the original MetaPL description is performed by *filters*, which formally are extensions to the notation system.[5] We will present here the filters that can be used to derive two views, useful as HTML documentation and as input for HeSSE simulation, respectively.

The filters are made up of a description of the target document format (this description typically is a DTD), and of a non-empty set of additional documents (*translators*). The target format description may be absent if a standard output format (e.g., HTML) is used. The translators basically contain conversion rules from MetaPL to a new format and (possibly) vice versa, but are also used to produce additional support documents, such as translations logs. Formally, the translators are XSLT (XSL Transformations) documents [13]. XSLT is an XML-based language; XSLT well-formed documents define a transformation that, given a well-formed XML document, generates a new text document. The target could be a "traditional" format, such as HTML or XMI, or a brand new one.

In some cases, in order to perform the defined transformations it may be necessary to supply additional information. This problem can be dealt with in two different ways. A first possibility is simply to report the absence of the data needed for translation in the output document. Later on, the user can supply them, and repeat the transformation process. Alternatively, the additional information can be asked to the user at translation time.

The same technique used to extend the core language of MetaPL is also used for the filters. The core filter is able to handle only the notation defined in the MetaPL core. It may be suitably extended by *filter extensions*, which allow the conversion of elements not belonging to the core set.

5.1 The MetaPL-HTML Filter

The *MetaPL-HTML* filter produces a simple hypertextual view of the program, which highlights the computational steps carried out, and enables the developer to navigate through his/her code. Since the filter output format is HTML (a well-know format), the filter is made up only of an XSLT document (the translator) that defines the transformation from the MetaPL description to the HTML document.

The generated HTML page is very simple. It starts with the declaration contained in the MetaPL element `ParallelProgram`, that is, with a marked list of the declared task names, each of which is a link to the task code description. In particular, the first XSLT definition in the translator associates the MetaPL XML document heading with the heading of the HTML document. The `ParallelProgram` MetaPL tag is associated with a first level heading (H1) whose content is the element attribute `name`. The `Task` element is substituted with an HTML second level heading, whose content is "`Task name id`". The `id` attributes of the `Task` and `ProcessDecl` elements are used as names for an HTML bookmark to the heading. Each element defined in the language core is reported with the name in bold; its contents are provided in the form of an HTML paragraph.

---

[5] They are called here simply "filters" and not "filter extensions" because they are in their turn extensible. Hence by "filter extension" we will mean an extension to a filter.

Message-passing extensions to the filter make it also possible to handle `Send` and `Receive` commands, reporting them in bold font with hyperlinks to the bookmarks whose names are given by the `sender` and `receiver` attributes.

5.2 The Simulation Filter

As mentioned in the introduction, one of the primary design objectives of the MetaPL notation system is to promote the use of performance prediction tools at the early stages of software development. The simulation filter briefly described here can automatically perform the generation of traces that can be used to drive the HeSSE simulator [11] in order to obtain predictions of program performance on a given (real or fictitious) distributed heterogeneous computing platform.

The output format of the *Simulation* filter is the trace format accepted as input by the HeSSE Simulator. Obviously, this format is textual, not an XML document. HeSSE traces are sequences of events corresponding to the basic actions that the system can simulate, such as CPU bursts (*Workload* event) or message-passing calls (*Send* or *Receive*). Formally, each event is a *HeSSE System Call*, and may have parameters (e.g., the *receiver* for a *Send* event). Each trace starts with a control symbol sequence ("`PST`").

The filter contains two translators. The first XSLT, the *MetaPL-HeSSE* translator, is used to generate the trace input for simulation. The second one, *Simulation-checker*, is instead used to check if all information needed to simulate a program description is available. In fact, sometimes some values required for program simulation cannot be obtained by the code description and have to be supplied by the user. The translator generates an output log file wherein all the encountered problems are reported. The suggested filtering procedure is to test the description through the Simulation-checker first, to analyze the output log and, finally, to generate the output traces.

5.2.1 The MetaPL-HeSSE Translator

The *MetaPL-HeSSE* translator produces HeSSE trace files. It assumes that the MetaPL description can be translated; otherwise, the result may be inconsistent. The goal is to produce usable HeSSE trace files; the translator does not handle their subdivision according to the system configuration (HeSSE needs a separate file for each simulated task). Hence the XSLT simply generates a single text document, which can be successively subdivided since each task trace is marked by the control symbol sequence PST.

Just to give the reader the flavor of the translation carried out, we will informally mention the transformations made under the assumption that `Variable`, `Switch` and `CostFunction` elements are not used, and that loops are not nested:

- each `CodeBlock` is replaced with a `Workload` event and the content of its `time` attribute;
- each `Loop` is unrolled: its content is analyzed a number of times equal to the value of the `iteration` attribute;
- each `Spawn` and `Wait` is replaced with the corresponding HeSSE System Call, giving as parameter their attributes;
- the `Exit` is replaced with the equivalent HeSSE System Call.

In addition, if the MetaPL-HeSSE filter extension handling message-passing is used:

· for each `Send` (`Receive`) in the MetaPL description, a HeSSE *Send* (*Receive*) event is written to the output file. The `sender`, `dim`, `msgtag` attributes are reported as parameters of the HeSSE System Call.

5.2.2 The Simulation-Checker Translator

The output of this XSLT is a text file showing all the additional information that has to be supplied in order to be able to simulate the description. Even if simulation is possible and no further input is necessary, the output file may be non-empty, and contain additional information useful for simulation purposes.

In practice, the *Simulation-Checker* translator checks that all the attribute values needed in the translation to HeSSE simulation traces can be obtained from values of MetaPL variables in scope. A typical example of missing value is the number of iterations of a loop where the final value of the control variable is supplied only at run-time. In this case, the MetaPL description is (necessarily) incomplete as far as simulation is concerned, and the value has to be supplied during the trace generation process.

6   Conclusions

This paper has introduced MetaPL, a notation system designed to describe parallel programs both in the direct and in the reverse software engineering cycle. The main features of MetaPL are:

- *flexibility,* since it may be used in conjunction with any type of programming language or parallel programming paradigm;
- *completeness,* as every single line of code contained in the source code program can be represented, if necessary. Conversely, the source code can be easily recovered from the description;
- *simplicity,* as it supports code examination and understanding though views, which can be used as input for graphical tools, to generate human-readable code documentation, or as input for trace-driven simulations;
- *suitability for performance evaluation*: the program description allows the insertion of information on the response times of portions of code, thus promoting the integration with performance evaluation tools.

These characteristics have been obtained by exploiting heavily XML extension capabilities. In fact, MetaPL can describe programs code based on different memory models, interaction structures and programming languages. The possibility to include timing information in the program description makes it possible to analyze performance during software development.

After a description of the main features of the notation system, we have shown its use to obtain two completely different kinds of views as an example. The first one is an automatically generated documentation on the Parallel Program in HTML, which enables the navigation of the code description by a simple web browser. The second view enables the performance evaluation of a parallel program from the MetaPL description, producing a set of traces that can be used as input for the HeSSE simulator environment.

References

1. Aversa, R., Mazzeo, A., Mazzocca, N., Villano, U.: Developing Applications for Heterogeneous Computing Environments using Simulation: a Case Study. Parallel Computing 24 (1998) 741-761
2. Smith, C. U., Williams, L. G.: Performance Evaluation of a Distributed Software Architecture. In: Proc. CMG, CMG, Anaheim, USA (1998)
3. Smith, C. U., Williams, L. G.: Software Performance Engineering for Object-Oriented Systems. In: Proc. CMG, CMG, Orlando, USA (1997)
4. Smith, C. U., Williams, L. G.: Performance Engineering Evaluation of Object-Oriented Systems with SPE·ED. In: R. Marie et. al. (eds.): Computer Performance Evaluation Modeling Techniques and tools, Lecture Notes in Computer Science, Vol.   1245, Springer-Verlag, Berlin (1997)
5. Woodside, C. M.: A Three-View Model for Performance Engineering of Concurrent Software. IEEE Trans. on Software Engineering 21 (1995) 754-767
6. Gorton, I., Jelly, I., Gray, J.: Parallel Software Engineering with PARSE. In: Proc. IEEE COMPSAC 17th Int Computer Science and Applications Conference, IEEE Press, Phoenix, USA (1993) 124–130
7. Winter, S. C.: Software Engineering for Parallel Processing. In: IEEE Colloquium on High Performance Computing for Advanced Control, IEEE Press (1994) 8/1-8/7
8. XML Metadata Interchange (XMI). ftp://ftp.omg.org/pub/docs/ad/99-10-02.pdf
9. Aversa, R., Mazzocca, N., Villano, U.: Design of a Simulator of Heterogeneous Computing Enviroments. Simulation – Practice and Theory 4 (1996) 97-117
10. Aversa, R., Mazzeo, A., Mazzocca, N., Villano, U.: Heterogeneous System Performance Prediction and Analysis using PS. IEEE Concurrency 6 (1998) 20-29
11. Mazzocca, N., Rak, M., Villano, U.: The Transition from a PVM Program Simulator to a Heterogeneous System Simulator: the HeSSE Project. In: J. Dongarra et al. (eds.): Recent Advances in Parallel Virtual Machine and Message Passing Interface, Lecture Notes in Computer Science, Vol. 1908, Springer-Verlag, Berlin (2000) 266-273
12. Extensible Markup Language (XML) 1.0 (Second edition). http://www.w3.org/TR/2000/REC-xml-20001006
13. XSL Transformation (XSLT) Version 1.0. http://www.w3.org/TR/1999/REC-xslt-19991116

First-Order 2D Cellular Neural Networks Investigation and Learning*

Sergey Pudov

Supercomputer Software Department, ICMMG of SB RAS
Pr. Lavrentieva, 6, Novosibirsk, 630090, Russia
pudov@ssd.sscc.ru

Abstract. In this paper first order 2D cellular neural networks (CNN's) with homogeneous weight structure are investigated. It is proved that all CNN's are divided into equivalence classes by respect to formed patterns properties. The method of learning first order CNN is proposed, which allows to find the parameters of CNN weight template if an example of stable state is given.

1 Introduction

There are a lot of natural phenomena including some reaction-diffusion processes of dissipative structures formation which have no adequate mathematical models up to day. For example this can be said about some chemical reactions, crystallization processes, as well as natural area of biological species, ecological phenomena and so on. So, the new models of spatial dynamics are currently under active investigation. They should not only explain qualitatively the existing phenomena but also are to be applicable for technological implementation on the modern parallel computing systems. In other words, they should have the properties of fine-grained parallelism with local interconnections. So the investigations of cellular automata (e.g., [1]) and CNN [2,3] simulative properties are of great interest.

CNN consists of local interconnected elements (named *cells*). The connections are weighted, and each cell computes its output(s) as a nonlinear function of it internal state(s). In a discrete-time CNN all cells calculate their next states in parallel, i.e. iteratively and synchronously. The computation starts when all cells are set in an initial state, and stops at a stable state, when no cell changes its output state any more. The order of CNN is determined by the amount of variables representing the internal (or output) cell states. First order CNN stable state considered as a *pattern* in the form of the set of output cell states. In this work the simulative properties of first order homogeneous CNN's for pattern formation are investigated. A method of their learning if the example of stable state is given is suggested.

---

* Supported by RFBR, grants 00-01-00026, 01-01-06261

V. Malyshkin (Ed.): PaCT 2001, LNCS 2127, pp. 94–97, 2001.

2   Formal Model Presentation

Notions in this paper are based on those used in [4]. We suppose that a 2D
CNN consists of N cells which are enumerated in some way, i.e. each cell has an
unique *name*. Connection structure in a CNN is characterized by a *connection
template* T, which for each cell i consists of a set of its neighbor names, i.e.
$T(i) = \{j_0, \ldots, j_q\}$, $(j_0 = i)$, where q is the cardinality of the cell neighborhood.
A real number a_k denotes the weight value of the connection between a cell
named i and its neighbor $j_k \in T(i)$, the set of all neighbors weights is referred to
a *weight template* $A = \{p, a_1, \ldots, a_q\}$, where $p = a_0$ is a *self-connection weight*.

For each cell the set of its neighbors states forms a *neighborhood state* $X_i =
\{x_0, \ldots, x_q\}$, where x_k is the state of the neighbor j_k of the cell i. The output
state y_i of the cell i is a non-linear function of x_i, i.e. $y_i = f(x_i)$. Here we use
the following piece-wise function

$$f(x) = \frac{1}{2}(|x + 1| - |x - 1|). \tag{1}$$

A cell i with $-1 \le x_i \le 1$ is called a *linear cell*, otherwise it is called a *saturated
cell*. Further $Y_i = f(X_i)$ denotes the *neighborhood output state* of the cell i. With
the above notations a weighted sum of neighbors output states can be written as
follows: $A \times Y_i = \sum_{j \in T} a_j y_j$. Depending of this sum the cell changes its state x_i
in time in a discrete time CNN according to the following synchronous updating
rule

$$x_i(t + 1) = x_i(t) + \tau(-x_i(t) + A \times Y_i(t)) \tag{2}$$

where τ is a time discretization parameter. Computation either lasts endlessly,
or it stops at a stable state (in this case we say that CNN *forms a pattern* which
is the set of output state of all cells $\{y_i, i = 1, \ldots, N\}$) when no cell output state
is changed in time any more.

In this paper we consider only space invariant templates, i.e. symmetric ones,
because CNN's with such templates are known to be stable [5]. A given state
is stable if and only if for all cells the following set of linear equalities and
inequalities holds [3]:

$$\begin{aligned}
y_i \left(\sum_{j \in T} a_j y_j \right) &> 0 \quad \text{if } |x_i| > 1 \\
\sum_{j \in T} a_j y_j &= x_i \quad \text{if } |x_i| \le 1
\end{aligned} \tag{3}$$

3   Properties of Patterns Formed by 2D CNN

The main goal of CNN investigation in this paper is to describe the possible
stable states in relation to connection template properties. Some results for 2D
CNN were obtained in [3] but they mostly concern *mosaic* patterns with the
output state of each cell is from the set $\{-1, 0, +1\}$.

Here we are not restricted by mosaic states allowing cell outputs to be in $[-1, 1]$. Before new results presentation let's tell some words about the formed patterns. Here we have in mind that a pattern is characterized by the areas made up of pictures repeated more or less systematically called in [3] *motives* (dense black, chessboards, stripes etc.). There exists a boundary (probably with zero width) between neighbour areas with different motives. So, each pattern is characterized by a set of inherent properties such as a set of motives and boundary parameters: width and maximal curvature. Consequently, each CNN with the weight template A can be characterized by the properties of all possible patterns formed.

At first let's look at the following problem: does it exists the one-to-one correspondence between the weight template and properties of possible stable states? Let a CNN have the weight template A, and C is its stable state. From (3) it follows that there is an infinite set of weight templates which provide the stability of a given pattern C. It can be shown in the following way. Let A be the template which satisfies the conditions (3) for the pattern C. If we multiply all elements of A by a constant $b > 0$, then these conditions may not hold for all cells. Particularly, for a linear cell i with the state c_i and the neighbourhood state C_i:

$$b(A \times C_i) = bc_i \neq c_i, \quad \text{when } b \neq 1. \tag{4}$$

In order to correct (4) it is enough to add the value $(1 - b)$ to the selfconnection weight in bA (the obtained template is further denoted as $A(b)$):

$$(A(b) \times C_i) = bc_i + (1 - b)c_i = c_i. \tag{5}$$

It is easy to show that the template $A(b)$, $b > 0$ satisfies (3) for all saturated cells. Consequently we have an infinite set of weight templates *(equivalence class)*, each of them can form the given pattern C. Moreover, the equivalence class $A(b)$ of weight templates is described by the following system of parametric equations:

$$s(b) = sb, \quad p(b) = 1 + (p - 1)b, \\ b > 0, \tag{6}$$

where p and s – the parameters of weight template A. From (6) it follows that the selfconnection weight value in $A(b)$ is calculated by the following formula: $p(b) = 1 + (p - 1)b$. Since $b > 0$, then if the value p in A is greater than 1 then $p(b)$ can have any value above the 1 and vice versa, if $p < 1$ then $p(b) < 1$. Consequently, the set of all equivalence classes of weight templates consists of three disjoint subsets: 1) with $p < 1$; 2) with $p > 1$; and 3) with $p = 1$.

This result is useful for investigation of stable states in homogeneous CNN because it reduces the amount of independent weight parameters. Moreover we can fix the selfconnection weight during the learning process in order to obtain the concrete weight template from the equivalence class. So it is possible to use for CNN learning the methods based on the Perceptron Learning Rule [7].

For weight template with not more than three independed weight parameters we should investigate the equivalence classes described by not more than two independed parameters. This can be done by building the 2D diagrams [6], any restricted area of them is visually presents the properties of patterns which might be formed by CNN with the weight template parameters equal to the coordinates of the diagram.

4   Method of CNN Learning

Let the pattern C be given, the size and weight parameters of template A should be found such that the stability conditions (3) are satisfied. Based on this problem statement a learning method is elaborated [6] meeting the following conditions: 1) it should be local; 2) it should guarantee the individual stability of *prototypes* (patterns which are to be stored); 3) the number of prototypes should be as large as possible. This method based on Perceptron Learning Rule [7], and extensive simulation showd that the proposed method allows to find the parameters of weight template (one of the equivalence class) if the example of stable state is given.

5   Conclusion

In this paper the pattern formation properties of homogeneous 2D CNN are investigated. It is shown that all weight templates are devided into equivalence classess by respect to properties of possible stable states. Method of CNN learning is suggested, which allows to find the parameters of weight template if example of stable state is given.

References

1. Simons N.R., Briges G.E., Cuhaci M.A: lattice gas automaton capable of modeling tree-dimensional Electromagnetic Fields. – Journ. of Computational Physics **151**, 1999, pp.816-835.
2. Leon O. Chua: CNN: a Paradigm for Complexity. World Scientific, Series on Nonlinear Science, Vol. 31, 1998.
3. Thiran P., Crounse K., Chua L.O., HaslerM.: Pattern Formation Properties of Autonomous Cellular Neural Networks. IEEE trans. on circ. and syst.-1: fund. theory and appl., vol.42, NO. 10, October 1995.
4. Bandman O.L.: Cellular-Neural Computations, Formal Model and Possible Applications. Lecture Notes in Computer Science, 964, 1995, p.21–35.
5. Chua L.O., Yang L.: Cellular Neural Networks: Theory and Application. IEEE Trans. Circuits and Systems, **CAS-35**, 1257 - 1290 (1988).
6. Pudov S.: Learning of Cellular Neural Networks. Future Gen. Comp. Syst. 17 (2001), pp. 689-697.
7. Rosenblatt F.: Principles of Neurodynamics. Washington, Spartan, 1959.

Quiescent Uniform Reliable Broadcast as an Introduction to Failure Detector Oracles

Michel Raynal

IRISA – Campus de Beaulieu, 35042 Rennes Cedex, France
raynal@irisa.fr

Abstract. This paper is a short and informal introduction to failure detector oracles for asynchronous distributed systems prone to process crashes and fair lossy channels. A distributed coordination problem (the implementation of Uniform Reliable Broadcast with a quiescent protocol) is used as a paradigm to visit two types of such oracles. One of them is a "guessing" oracle in the sense that it provides a process with information that the processes could only approximate if they had to compute it. The other is a "hiding" oracle in the sense that it allows to isolate and encapsulate the part of a protocol that has not the required behavioral properties. A quiescent uniform reliable broadcast protocol is described. The guessing oracle is used to ensure the "uniformity" requirement stated in the problem specification. The hiding oracle is used to ensure the additional "quiescence" property that the protocol behavior has to satisfy.

Keywords: Asynchronous Distributed Systems, Failure Detectors, Fair Lossy Channels, Fault-Tolerance, Oracles, Process Crashes, Quiescent Protocol, Uniform Reliable Broadcast.

1 Introduction

One of the most striking and disturbing fact of the fault-tolerant asynchronous distributed computing field is the number of impossibility results that have been stated and proved in the past years [20,21]. One of the most outstanding of those results is related to the *Consensus* problem. This problem is defined as follows: each process proposes a value and the processes that do not crash have to agree (termination) on the same value which has to be one of the proposed values (safety). It has been shown by Fischer, Lynch and Paterson that this apparently simple problem actually has no deterministic solution as soon as even only one process can crash [14]. This is the famous FLP impossibility result. On the other side, it is also important to note that a characterization of the problems that can be solved in presence of at most one process crash has also been proposed [8].

When a problem cannot be solved in a given model (representing a particular context) several attitudes are possible. One consists in modifying the problem statement in order to get solutions to a close (but "modified") problem. For the consensus problem, this has consisted in weakening some of its properties. For

V. Malyshkin (Ed.): PaCT 2001, LNCS 2127, pp. 98–111, 2001.

example, the weakening the termination property has given rise to probabilistic protocols [7]. Other studies have considered the weakening of the agreement property (e.g., ε-agreement [12], and k-set agreement [11]). Another attitude consists in enriching the underlying fault-prone asynchronous distributed system with appropriate oracles in order that the problem becomes solvable in the augmented system.

The *oracle* notion has first been introduced as a *language* whose words can be recognized in one step from a particular state of a Turing machine [15,19]. The main characteristic of such oracles is to *hide* a sequence of computation steps in a single step, or to *guess* the result of a non-computable function. They have been used to define equivalence classes of problems and hierarchies of problems when they are considered with respect to the assumptions they require to be solved. In our case, the *oracle* notion is related to the detection of failures. These oracles do not change the pattern of failures that affect the execution in which they are used. Their main characteristic is not related to the number of computation steps they hide, but to the guess they provide about failures. Such oracles have been proposed and investigated in the past years. Following their designers (mainly S. Toueg) they are usually called *failure detectors* [4,2,9]. A given failure detector oracle is related to a problem (or a class of related problems). Of course, it has to be strong enough to allow to solve the concerned problem, but, maybe more important, it has to be as weak as possible in order to fix the "failure detector" borderline beyond which the problem cannot be solved.

When we consider the consensus problem, several failure detector classes have been defined to solve it [9]. It has also been shown that one of these classes is the weakest that can be used to solve consensus [10]. A failure detector belongs to this class if it satisfies the following two properties. *Completeness*: Eventually, every process that crashes is suspected by every correct process. *Eventual Weak Accuracy*: Eventually, there is a correct process that is not suspected by the correct processes. As we can see, the completeness is on the actual detection of crashes, while the accuracy limits the mistakes a failure detector can make. Several consensus protocols based on this weakest failure detector oracle have been designed [9,25]. It is important to note that a failure detector satisfying the previous properties cannot be implemented in an asynchronous distributed system prone to process crashes (if it was, it would contradict the FLP impossibility result!). However, a failure detector that does its best to approximate these properties can be built. When the behavior of the underlying system allows it to satisfy the completeness and the eventual accuracy properties during long enough time, the current execution of the consensus protocol can terminate, and consequently the current instance of the consensus problem can be solved.

This paper is an introductory visit to failure detector oracles for asynchronous distributed systems where processes can fail by crashing and links can fail by dropping messages. To do this visit, we consider a distributed computing problem related to distributed coordination, namely the *Uniform Reliable Broadcast* (URB) problem [16]. This is an important problem as it constitutes a basic distributed computing building block. Informally, URB is defined by two primitives

(Broadcast and Deliver), such that (1) if a process delivers a message m then all processes that do not crash eventually deliver m, and (2) each process that does not crash eventually delivers at least the messages it broadcasts. By interpreting the pair Broadcast/Deliver as This_is_an_order/Execute_it, it is easy to see that URB abstracts a family of distributed coordination problems [4,17].

Furthermore, in order to fully benefit from the visit, we are interested in solving the URB problem with a *quiescent* protocol. This means that, for each application message m that is broadcast by a process, the protocol eventually stops sending protocol messages. This is a very important property: it guarantees that the network load generated by the calls to the Broadcast primitive remains finite despite process and links failures.

The paper is made up of seven sections. Section 2 introduces the underlying system layer and Section 3 reminds a few results related to the net effect of process and links failures. Then, Section 4 defines the URB problem. Section 5 presents a "guessing" and a "hiding" failure detector oracles (that have been introduced for the first time in [4] and [2], respectively). These oracles are then used in Section 6 as underlying building blocks to define a quiescent URB protocol. Section 7 concludes the paper.

2   Asynchronous Distributed System Model

The system model consists of a finite set of processes, namely, $\Pi = \{p_1, \dots, p_n\}$. They communicate and synchronize by sending and receiving messages through channels. Every pair of processes p_i and p_j is connected by a channel which is denoted (p_i, p_j).

2.1   Processes with Crash Failures

A process can fail by *crashing*, i.e., by prematurely halting. A crashed process does not recover. A process behaves correctly (i.e., according to its specification) until it (possibly) crashes. By definition, a *correct* process is a process that never crash. A *faulty* process is a process that is not correct. In the following, f denotes the maximum number of processes that may be faulty ($f \leq n - 1$). There is no assumption on the relative speed of processes.

2.2   Fair Lossy Channels

In addition to process crashes, we consider that channels can fail by dropping messages. Nevertheless, they are assumed to be fair lossy. This means that for each channel (p_i, p_j) we have the following properties:

- FLC-Fairness (Termination): If p_i sends a message m to p_j an infinite number of times and p_j is correct, then eventually p_j receives m.
- FLC-Validity: If p_j receives a message m from p_i, then p_i previously sent m to p_j.

– FLC-Integrity: If p_j receives a message m infinitely often from p_i, then p_i sends m infinitely often to p_j.

It is important to note that (1) there is no a priori assumption on the message transfer delays, and (2) a message can be duplicated a finite number of times. The basic communication primitives used by a process p_i are: send () to p_j, and receive () from p_j.

3   A Few Results

3.1   The Case of a Single Channel

When we consider a system as simple as one made up of two processes connected by a channel, there are some impossibility results related to the effect of process crashes, channel unreliability, or the constraint to use only bounded sequence numbers (see [21] -chapter 22- for an in-depth presentation of these results). Let a reliable channel c_{rel} be a channel such that there is no loss, no duplication, no creation, and no reordering. Let us consider two processors connected by a channel c. The aim is to design on top of c a protocol offering a reliable channel c_{rel}.

– Let us assume that c is reliable, each processor can crash and recover but has not access to a non-volatile memory. There is no protocol that builds a reliable channel c_{rel} and that tolerates the crash/recovery of the processors [13]. To tolerate it, a non-volatile memory is necessary in order that the processor state can survive crashes.
– Let us assume that the processors cannot crash, and the underlying channel c can duplicate or reorder messages (but it does not create or lose messages). Moreover, only bounded sequence numbers are allowed. It is impossible to design a protocol that implements a reliable channel c_{rel} on top of c [30].
– Let us assume that the underlying channel c can lose and reorder messages but cannot duplicate them. Moreover, the processors do not crash, and only bounded sequence numbers are allowed. There is a protocol that builds c_{rel} on top of c, but this protocol is highly inefficient [1].

3.2   Simulation of Reliable Channels in Presence of Process Crashes

The effect of lossy channels on the solvability of problems in general is discussed in [6]. Two main results are stated.

– The first concerns a specific class of problems, namely those whose specification does not refer to faulty processes. This is the class of *correct-restricted* problems. An algorithm is provided that transforms any protocol solving a correct-restricted problem and working with process crashes and reliable channels into a protocol working with process crashes and fair lossy links.

– The second result is more general in the sense that it does not consider a particular class of problems. It presents a protocol that, given a system with fair lossy channels and a majority of correct processes, simulates a system with reliable channels. Informally, this shows that a majority of correct processes is powerful enough to cope with message losses when channels are fair.

The two proposed transformations do not provide quiescent protocols.

4   Uniform Reliable Broadcast

4.1   Definition

The *Uniform Reliable Broadcast* problem (URB) is defined in terms of two communication primitives: Broadcast() and Deliver(). When a process issues Broadcast(m), we say that it *"broadcasts"* m. Similarly, when a process issues Deliver(m), we say that it *"delivers"* m. Every broadcast message is unique[1]. This means that if an application process invokes *Broadcast*(m_1) and *Broadcast*(m_2) with m_1 and m_2 having the same content, m_1 and m_2 are considered as two different messages by the underlying layer.

Uniform Reliable Broadcast is formally defined by the following set of properties [16]:

– URB-Termination: If a correct process *broadcasts* m, then any correct process *delivers* m (no messages from correct processes are lost).
– URB-Validity: If a process *delivers* m, then m has been *broadcast* by some process (no spurious message).
– URB-Integrity: A process *delivers* a message m at most once (no duplication).
– URB-Agreement: If a (correct or not) process *delivers* m, then any correct process *delivers* m (no message UR-delivered by a process is missed by a correct process).

The last property is sometimes called "Uniform Agreement". Its non-uniform counterpart would be: "If a correct process *delivers* m, then any correct process *delivers* m". The Uniformity requirement obliges to also consider the messages delivered by faulty processes. The *Reliable Broadcast* problem is similar to URB except for the Agreement property that is non-uniform.

Let us remark that, differently from the other properties, the URB-Termination property does not apply to faulty processes. This means that the correct processes deliver the same set of messages S, and that the set of messages delivered by a faulty process is always a subset of S.

---

[1] This can easily be realized, at the underlying level, by associating with each application message m a pair made up of its sender identity, plus a sequence number.

4.2   URB with Reliable Channels

Figure 1 describes a simple quiescent protocol (defined in [16]) that solves the URB problem in asynchronous distributed systems made up of processes that (1) can crash, and (2) are fully connected by reliable channels (no loss, no duplication, and no creation of messages). To broadcast a message m, a process p_i sends it to itself. Then, when a process receives a message m for the first time, it forwards it before delivering it. Consequently, due to channel reliability, it follows that the four URB properties are satisfied.

---

(1) **Procedure** Broadcast(m):
(2)   send msg(m) to p_i

(3) **when** msg(m) *received from* p_k:
(4)   **if** (first reception of m) **then**
(5) $\forall j \neq i, k$ **do** *send* msg(m) *to* p_j **enddo**;
(6)   Deliver(m)
(7)   **endif**

Fig. 1. A quiescent URB protocol for reliable channels

5   Enriching the System with Appropriate Oracles

A main difficulty in solving the URB problem in presence of fair lossy links lies in ensuring the URB-Agreement property which states: "If a process delivers a message m, then any correct process delivers m". This means that a process can deliver a message only when it is sure that this message will eventually be received by each correct process. It has been shown that failure detector oracles are required to overcome this problem [4,17]. The failure detector (called Θ) described below is an answer to this problem. It has been introduced in [4].

Although Θ is the weakest failure detector that can be used to ensure the URB-Agreement property [4], its only use is not sufficient to get a quiescent protocol: the broadcast of an application message can still generate an infinite number of network messages. Actually, ensuring the quiescence property requires that a process p_i be able to know if another process p_j is still alive: if p_j is not, p_i can stop sending messages to p_j even if the last message it sent to it has not yet been acknowledged. Several failure detectors can be designed to allow a process p_i to get this information. Some (as Θ) provide outputs with bounded size. Others provide outputs whose size is not bounded. It has been shown that the failure detector oracles of the first category cannot be implemented [9], while some of the second category can be. Hence, in the following we present an oracle of the second category called *Heartbeat* that can be implemented. This oracle has been introduced in [2].

5.1 A Guessing Failure Detector Oracle: Θ

This failure detector [4] is defined by the following properties. Each process p_i is endowed with a local variable TRUSTED$_i$ whose aim is to contain identities of processes that are currently perceived as non-crashed by p_i (this variable is updated by Θ and read by p_i). The failure detector Θ ensures that these variables satisfy the following properties:

- Θ-Completeness: There is a time after which, for any process p_i, TRUSTED$_i$ does not include faulty processes.
- Θ-Accuracy: At every time, for any process p_i, TRUSTED$_i$ includes at least one correct process. (Note that the correct process trusted by p_i is allowed to change over time.)

In the general case ($f < n$), the Θ oracle cannot be implemented in an asynchronous distributed system. That is why we place it in the family of "guessing" failure detector oracles. Differently, when the system satisfies the additional assumption $f < n/2$, it can be implemented (such an implementation is described in [4]).

5.2 A Hiding Failure Detector Oracle: *Heartbeat*

The *Heartbeat* failure detector oracle [2] provides each process p_i with an array of counters HB$_i[1..n]$ (initialized to $[0, \ldots, 0]$) such that:

- HB-Completeness: For each process p_i, HB$_i[j]$ stops increasing if p_j is faulty.
- HB-Accuracy: HB$_i[j]$ never decreases, and HB$_i[j]$ never stops increasing if p_i and p_j are correct.

A Hearbeat failure detector can be easily implemented, e.g., by requiring each process to periodically send "I am alive" messages. This implementation entails the sending of an infinite number of messages by each correct process: it is not quiescent. That is the reason why we place it in the family of "hiding" failure detector oracles. A set of modules (one per process) realizing a Hearbeat oracle can be used to encapsulate and isolate the non-quiescent part of a protocol and thereby hides its undesirable behaviors.

6 A Protocol

6.1 Description of the Protocol

A quiescent URB protocol is described in Figure 2 for a process p_i. It is based on the previously described failure detectors and the classical acknowledgement mechanism. An important local data managed by a process p_i is $rec\_by_i[m]$

which records the processes that, to p_i's knowledge, have received a copy of the application message m. The protocol uses two types of messages, tagged "msg" and "ack", respectively. They are called *protocol messages*, to distinguish them from the messages broadcast by the application. Each protocol message tagged "msg" carries an application message, while one tagged "ack" carries only the identity of an application message.

To broadcast an application message m, a process p_i sends a protocol message tagged "msg" and including m to itself (line 2). When, it receives a protocol message carrying an application message m for the first time (line 12), a process p_i activates the task *Diffuse(m)* which repeatedly (lines 5-10) sends m to the processes that, from p_i's point of view, have no copy of m and are alive. The Heartbeat failure detector is used by p_i to know which processes are locally perceived as being alive. It is important to note that, as soon as the test at line 7 remains permanently false for all j, then p_i stops sending messages (but does not necessarily terminate as it can keep on executing the loop if the condition of line 10 remains false[2]). Each time p_i receives a protocol message tagged "msg", it sends back an "ack" message to inform the sender that it has got a copy of m (line 16). When a process receives an "ack" message, it updates accordingly the local data $rec\_by_i[m]$ (line 18).

Finally, if p_i has not yet delivered an application message m, it does it as soon as it knows that at least one correct process got it (condition TRUSTED$_i \subseteq rec\_by_i[m]$ at line 19).

6.2   Proof

The proof that the protocol described in Figure 2 satisfies URB-Integrity (no duplication of an application message) and URB-Validity (no creation of application messages) are left to the reader. The proof has the same structure as the proof given in [4].

Lemma 1. *If a correct process starts Diffuse(m), eventually all correct processes start Diffuse(m).*

Proof Let us first observe that if the identity k belongs to $rec\_by_i[m]$, this is because p_i received msg(m) or ack(m) from p_k and updated consequently $rec\_by_i[m]$ at line 13, 15 or 18, from which we conclude that p_k has a copy of m.

Let us consider a correct process p_i that starts Diffuse(m). It launches this task at line 14 when it receives m for the first time. Let p_j be a correct process. As p_j is correct, HB$_i[j]$ keeps on increasing and the subcondition $(prev\_hb_i[m][j] < cur\_hb_i[j])$ is infinitely often true. We consider two cases:

- Case ($j \in rec\_by_i[m]$). In that case, due to the previous observation, p_j has a copy of m. We conclude from the protocol text, that p_j started Diffuse(m) when it received m for the first time.

---

[2] It is important not to confuse a *quiescent* protocol and a *terminating* protocol. Ensuring termination requires stronger failure detector oracles, namely, oracles that allow to know exactly which processes have crashed and which have not [18].

```
(1)  Procedure Broadcast(m):
(2)          send msg(m) to p_i

(3)  Task Diffuse(m):
(4)          prev_hb_i[m] ← [-1,...,-1];
(5)          repeat periodically
(6)              cur_hb_i ← HB_i;
(7)              ∀j ≠ i: if ((prev_hb_i[m][j] < cur_hb_i[j]) ∧ (j ∉ rec_by_i[m]))
(8)                          then send msg(m) to p_j endif;
(9)              prev_hb_i[m] ← cur_hb_i;
(10)         until   (∀j ∈ [1..n] : (j ∈ rec_by_i[m]) ) endrepeat

(11) when msg(m) is received from p_k:
(12)         if (first reception of m)
(13)             then rec_by_i[m] ← {i,k};
(14)                  activate task Diffuse(m)
(15)             else  rec_by_i[m] ← rec_by_i[m] ∪ {k} endif;
(16)         send ack(m) to p_k

(17) when ack(m) is received from p_k:
(18)         rec_by_i[m] ← rec_by_i[m] ∪ {k}

(19) when ((p_i has not yet delivered m) ∧ (TRUSTED_i ⊆ rec_by_i[m]))
(20)         do Deliver(m) enddo
```

Fig. 2. A quiescent uniform reliable broadcast protocol

– Case $(j \notin rec\_by_i[m])$. In that case p_i keeps on sending copies of m to p_j (at line 8). Due to the FLC-Fairness property of the channel (p_i, p_j), p_j eventually receives m from p_i and, if not yet done, starts $Diffuse(m)$.

$$\square_{Lemma\ 1}$$

Lemma 2. *If all correct processes start* Diffuse(m), *they eventually execute* Deliver(m).

Proof Let us assume that all the correct processes execute $Diffuse(m)$ and let p_i and p_j be two correct processes. So, p_i sends m to p_j until it knows that m has been received by p_j (i.e., until $j \in rec\_by_i[m]$). Due to the acknowledgment mechanism and the FLC-Fairness property of the underlying channels, this eventually occurs. It follows that, for each correct process p_i, $rec\_by_i[m]$ eventually includes all correct processes.

Let us now consider the set TRUSTED$_i$. Due to the Θ-Completeness property of the Θ failure detector, TRUSTED$_i$ eventually does not include faulty processes. It follows that the condition (TRUSTED$_i \subseteq rec\_by_i[m]$) eventually becomes true, and then p_i executes Deliver(m). $\square_{Lemma\ 2}$

Theorem 1. URB-Termination. *If a correct process executes* Broadcast(m), *then all correct processes execute* Deliver(m).

Proof If a correct process p_i executes Broadcast(m), it sends msg(m) to itself (line 2) and consequently starts the task *Diffuse*(m) (lines 12-14). Then, due to Lemma 1, all correct processes start *Diffuse*(m), and due to Lemma 2, they all execute Deliver(m). $\Box_{Theorem\ 1}$

Theorem 2. URB-Agreement. *If a process executes* Deliver(m), *then all correct processes execute* Deliver(m).

Proof If a (correct or not) process p_i executes Deliver(m), then the condition (TRUSTED$_i$ $\subseteq$ $rec\_by_i[m]$) was satisfied just before it executes it. Due to the Θ-Accuracy property of the Θ failure detector, TRUSTED$_i$ includes at least one correct process p_j. Hence, $p_j \in rec\_by_i[m]$, from which we conclude that there is at least one correct process that received m (at line 11). As p_j is correct, it started the task *Diffuse*(m) when it received m for the first time. It then follows from Lemmas 1 and 2 that each correct process executes Deliver(m). $\Box_{Theorem\ 2}$

Theorem 3. Quiescence. *Each invocation of* Broadcast(m) *gives rise to a finite number of protocol messages.*

Proof Let us observe that the reception of an "ack" protocol message never entails the sending of a protocol message. It follows that we only have to show that, for any application message m, eventually no process sends protocol messages of the form msg(m).

A msg(m) protocol message is sent at line 8 by the task *Diffuse*(m). So, we have to show that any process p_i eventually stops executing line 8. This is trivial if p_i crashes. So, let us consider that p_i is correct. There are two cases according to the destination process p_j:

– Case 1: p_j is faulty. Then due to the HB-Completeness, HB$_i[j]$ eventually stops increasing, and from then on $prev\_hb_i[m][j] = cur\_hb_i[j] =HB_i[j]$ is permanently true, from which we conclude that p_i stops sending messages to p_j.

– Case 2: p_j is correct. In that case the subcondition ($prev\_hb_i[m][j] < cur\_hb_i[j]$) is infinitely often true. So, let us consider the second subcondition, namely, ($j \notin rec\_by_i[m]$). Let us assume that the subcondition ($j \in rec\_by_i[m]$) is never satisfied. We show a contradiction.

If ($j \in rec\_by_i[m]$) is never satisfied, it follows that p_i sends an infinite number of protocol messages msg(m) to p_j. Due to the FLC-Fairness property of the channel (p_i, p_j), p_j eventually receives an infinite number of copies of m. Each time it receives msg(m), p_j sent back ack(m) to p_i (line 16). It then follows that, due to FLC-Fairness property of the channel (p_j, p_i), p_i receives an ack(m) protocol message from p_j. At the first reception of such a protocol message, p_i includes j in $rec\_by_i[m]$ (line 18). Finally, let us note that a process identity is never removed from $rec\_by_i[m]$. So from now on, the condition ($j \in rec\_by_i[m]$) remains permanently true. A contradiction. $\Box_{Theorem\ 3}$

6.3 Favoring Early Quiescence

This guideline in the design of the protocol described in Figure 2 was simplicity. It is possible to improve the protocol by allowing early quiescence (in some cases, this can also reduce the number of protocol messages that are exchanged). To favor early quiescence, the variable $rec\_by_i[m]$ of each process has to be updated as soon as possible. This can be done in the following way:

- (1) add the current content of $rec\_by_i[m]$ to each protocol message sent by a process p_i;
- (2) add to each "ack" message the corresponding application message (instead of only its identity);
- (3) send "ack" messages to all the processes (instead of only the sender of the corresponding "msg" message).

The resulting protocol is described in Figure 3. Its improved behavior is obtained at the price of bigger protocol messages. Its proof is similar to the proof of Section 6.2. The main difference lies in the way it is proved that $j \in rec\_by_i[m]$ means that p_j has got a copy of m.

```
(1) Procedure Broadcast(m):
(2)            send msg(m, ∅) to p_i

(3) Task Diffuse(m):
(4)            prev_hb_i[m] ← [−1, ... , −1];
(5)            repeat periodically
(6)                 cur_hb_i ← HB_i;
(7)                 ∀j ≠ i: if ((prev_hb_i[m][j] < cur_hb_i[j]) ∧ (j ∉ rec_by_i[m]))
(8)                         then send msg(m, rec_by_i[m]) to p_j endif;
(9)                 prev_hb_i[m] ← cur_hb_i;
(10)           until   (∀j ∈ [1..n] : (j ∈ rec_by_i[m]) ) endrepeat

(11) when type(m, rec_by) is received from p_k:
(12)           if (first reception of m)
(13)                then rec_by_i[m] ← {i} ∪ rec_by;
(14)                     activate task Diffuse(m)
(15)                else  rec_by_i[m] ← rec_by_i[m] ∪ rec_by endif;
(16)           if ((type ≠ ack) ∨ (first reception of m)) ∧(k ≠ i))
(17)                then ∀j ≠ i do send ack(m, rec_by_i[m]) to p_j enddo endif

(18) when ((p_i has not yet delivered m) ∧ (TRUSTED_i ⊆ rec_by_i[m]))
(19)           do Deliver(m) enddo
```

Fig. 3. An improved quiescent URB protocol

6.4   Strong Uniform Reliable Broadcast

The URB-Termination property of the URB problem is only on the correct processes. Said another way, a message broadcast by a process that crashes (either during the broadcast or even later) is not required to be delivered. Its actual delivery depends on the system behavior. This can be a drawback for some applications. So, let us define *Strong Uniform Reliable Broadcast* (S_URB). We define this communication service as being similar to URB except for the termination property which is:

- S_URB-Termination: If a process completes the execution of Broadcast(m), then a correct process delivers m. (This means that, whatever the future behavior of its sender, no message that has been broadcast is lost).

We conclude from the combination of URB-Agreement and S_URB-Termination that each correct process delivers all the messages whose broadcasts have been completed.

The S_URB-Termination property can easily be implemented. When we consider Figure 2, only a very simple modification of the procedure Broadcast(m) is required. Namely, the only statement **wait** (TRUSTED$_i$ ⊆ $rec\_by_i[m]$) has to be added at the end of this procedure. It ensures that when a broadcast completes, the corresponding application message is known by at least one correct process (that will disseminate it in its *Diffuse* task).

7   Conclusion

Failure detector oracles are becoming a fundamental issue in the design of fault-tolerant distributed applications designed to run on fault-prone distributed systems. The aim of this paper was to provide a simple introduction to their philosophy and to illustrate it with some of them, namely, a "guessing" oracle and a "hiding" oracle.

The design of a quiescent protocol solving the Uniform Reliable Broadcast problem has been used as a paradigm to show why failure detector oracles are required and how they can be used. The guideline for the design of this protocol was simplicity (as we have seen, more efficient protocols can be designed).

The reader interested in more details on the concept of failure detector oracles, the problems they can help to solve, and their uses, can consult [2,4,9,10,17,18,25,29].

As far as the consensus problem is concerned, the randomization approach has been investigated in [7]. The combined use of random oracles and failure detectors oracles for consensus has ben investigated in [3,26]. Failure detectors appropriate to solve the k-set agreement problem have been investigated in [26,31]. Recently, a randomzation approach to solve this problem has been proposed in [27].

Very recently, a new *Condition-based* approach has been proposed to solve the consensus problem [22]. It consists in identifying sets of input vectors for which it is possible to design a consensus protocol that works despite up to f faults. Such conditions actually define a strict hierarchy [23]. Moreover, this approach can be extended to solve more gernal agreement problems [24].

Acknowledgments

I would like to thank referee for comments that helped improve parts of the presentation.

References

1. Afek Y., Attiya H., Fekete A.D., Fischer M., Lynch N., Mansour Y., Wang D. and Zuck L., Reliable Communication over Unreliable Channels. *Journal of the ACM*, 41(6):1267-1297, 1994.
2. Aguilera M.K., Chen W. and Toueg S., On Quiescent Reliable Communication. *SIAM Journal of Computing*, 29(6):2040-2073, 2000.
3. Aguilera M.K. and Toueg S., Failure Detection and Randomization: a Hybrid Approach to Solve Consensus. *SIAM Journal of Computing*, 28(3):890-903, 1998.
4. Aguilera M.K., Toueg S. and Deianov B., Revisiting the Weakest Failure Detector for Uniform Reliable Broadcast. *Proc. 13th Int. Symposium on DIStributed Computing (DISC'99)*, Springer -Verlag LNCS #1693, pp. 21-34, 1999.
5. Attiya H. and Welch J., *Distributed Computing: Fundamentals, Simulations and Advanced Topics,* McGraw–Hill, 451 pages, 1998.
6. Basu A., Charron-Bost B. and Toueg S., Simulating Reliable Links with Unreliable Links in the Presence of Process Crashes. *Proc. 10th Int. Workshop on Distributed Algorithms (now, DISC)*, Springer -Verlag LNCS #1051, pp. 105-121, 1996.
7. Ben-Or M., Another Advantage of Free Choice: Completely Asynchronous Agreement Protocols. *Proc. 2nd ACM Symposium on Principles of Distributed Computing (PODC'83)*, ACM Press, pp. 27-30, Montréal (Canada), 1983.
8. Biran O., Moran S. and Zaks S., A Combinatorial Characterization of the Distributed 1-Solvable Tasks. *Journal of Algorithms*, 11:420-440, 1990.
9. Chandra T. and Toueg S., Unreliable Failure Detectors for Reliable Distributed Systems. *Journal of the ACM*, 43(2):225-267, 1996.
10. Chandra T., Hadzilacos V. and Toueg S., The Weakest Failure Detector for Solving Consensus. *Journal of the ACM*, 43(4):685–722, July 1996.
11. Chaudhuri S., More *Choices* Allow More *Faults:* Set Consensus Problems in Totally Asynchronous Systems. *Information and Computation,* 105:132-158, 1993.
12. Dolev D., Lynch N., Pinter S., Stark E.W., and Weihl W.E., Reaching Approximate Agreement in the Presence of Faults. *Journal of the ACM*, 33(3):499-516, 1986.
13. Fekete A.D., Lynch N., Mansour Y. and Spinelli J., The Impossibility of Implementing Reliable Communication in Face of Crashes. *Journal of the ACM*, 40(5):1087-1107, 1993.
14. Fischer M.J., Lynch N. and Paterson M.S., Impossibility of Distributed Consensus with One Faulty Process. *Journal of the ACM*, 32(2):374–382, 1985.
15. Garey M.R. and Johnson D.S., *Computers and Intractability: A Guide to the Theory of NP-Completeness.* Freeman W.H. & Co, New York, 340 pages, 1979.
16. Hadzilacos V. and Toueg S., Reliable Broadcast and Related Problems. In *Distributed Systems,* ACM Press (S. Mullender Ed.), New-York, pp. 97-145, 1993.

17. Halpern J.Y. and Ricciardi A., A Knowledge-Theoretic Analysis of Uniform Distributed Coordination and Failure Detectors. *Proc. 18th ACM Symposium on Principles of Distributed Computing (PODC'99)*, pp. 73-82, Atlanta (GA), 1999.

18. Hélary J.-M., Hurfin M., Mostefaoui A., Raynal M. and Tronel F., Computing Global Functions in Asynchronous Distributed Systems with Perfect Failure Detectors. *IEEE Transactions on Parallel and Distributed Systems*, 11(9):897-909, 2000.

19. Hopcroft J.E. and Ullman J.D. *Introduction to Automata Theory, Languages and Computation.* Addison Wesley, Reading (MA), 418 pages, 1979.

20. Lynch N., A Hundred Impossibility Proofs for Distributed Computing. *Invited Talk, Proc. 8th ACM Symposium on Principles of Distributed Computing (PODC'89)*, ACM Press, pp. 1-27, Edmonton (Canada), 1989.

21. Lynch N., *Distributed Algorithms.* Morgan Kaufmann Pub., San Francisco (CA), 872 pages, 1996.

22. Mostefaoui A., Rajsbaum S. and Raynal M., Conditions on Input Vectors for Consensus Solvability in Asynchronous Distributed Systems. *Proc. 33rd ACM Symposium on Theory of Computing (STOC'01)*, ACM Press, Crete (Greece), July 2001.

23. Mostefaoui A., Rajsbaum S., Raynal M. and Roy M., A Hierarchy of Conditions for Consensus Solvability. *Proc. 20th ACM Symposium on Principles of Distributed Computing (PODC'01)*, ACM Press, Newport (RI), August 2001.

24. Mostefaoui A., Rajsbaum S., Raynal M. and Roy M., Condition-Based Protocols for Set Agreement Problems. *Research Report #1393*, IRISA, University of Rennes, France, April 2001, 21 pages.
    http://www.irisa.fr/bibli/publi/pi/2001/1393/1393.html.

25. Mostefaoui A. and Raynal M., Solving Consensus Using Chandra-Toueg's Unreliable Failure Detectors: a General Quorum-Based Approach. *Proc. 13th Symp. on DIStributed Computing (DISC'99)*, Springer Verlag LNCS #1693, pp. 49-63, 1999.

26. Mostefaoui A. and Raynal M., *k*-Set Agreement with Limited Accuracy Failure Detectors. *Proc. 19th ACM Symposium on Principles of Distributed Computing (PODC'00)*, Portland (OR), pp. 143-152, 2000.

27. Mostefaoui A. and Raynal M., Randomized *k*-Set Agreement. *Proc. 13th th ACM Symposium on Parallel Algorithms and Architectures (SPAA'01)*, ACM Press, Crete (Greece), July 2001. *Research Report #1340*, IRISA, University of Rennes, France, July 2000, 14 pages.
    http://www.irisa.fr/bibli/publi/pi/2000/1340/1340.html.

28. Mostefaoui A., Raynal M. and Tronel F., The Best of Both Worlds: a Hybrid Approach to Solve Consensus. *Proc. Int. Conference on Dependable Systems and Networks (DSN'00, previously FTCS)*, IEEE Computer Society Press, pp. 513-522, New-York City, June 2000.

29. Raynal M. and Tronel F., Restricted Failure Detectors: Definition and Reduction Protocols. *Information Processing Letters*, 72:9197, 1999.

30. Wang D.-W. and Zuck L.D., Tight Bounds for the Sequence Transmission Problem. *Proc. 8th ACM Symposium on Principles of Distributed Computing (PODC'89)*, ACM Press, pp. 73-83, Edmonton (Canada), 1989.

31. Yang J., Neiger G. and Gafni E., Structured Derivations of Consensus Algorithms for Failure Detectors. *Proc. 17th ACM Symposium on Principles of Distributed Computing (PODC'98)*, Puerto Vallarta (Mexico), pp.297-308, 1998.

A Transaction Processing Model
for the Mobile Data Access System

K. Segun[1], A.R. Hurson[1], and A. Spink[2]

[1] Computer Science and Engineering Department,
The Pennsylvania State University, University Park, PA 16802, USA
[2] School of Information Sciences and Technologies,
The Pennsylvania State University, University Park, PA 16802, USA

Abstract. Advances in wireless networking technology and portable computing devices have led to the emergence of a new computing paradigm known as mobile computing and a number of applications. As a result, software applications have to be redesigned to take advantage of this environment while accommodating the new challenges posed by mobility.
As mobile users wander about, they are bound to encounter a variety of different information sources (databases) that are often autonomous and heterogeneous in nature. Such a collection of autonomous and heterogeneous database is often known as a multidatabase. The existing multidatabase systems do not readily support mobile computing. A new class of multidatabase that provides access to a large collection of data via a wireless networking connection is proposed — a Mobile Data Access System (MDAS). Within the scope of MDAS, a new transaction-processing model is proposed that allows timely and reliable access to heterogeneous and autonomous data sources while coping with the mobility issue. The proposed model extends the existing multidatabase system without any adverse effect to the preexisting local and global users. This is accomplished through the implementation of multi tiered mobile transaction proxies that manage the execution of mobile transactions on behalf of the mobile user. The proposed transaction-processing model is simulated and the results are analyzed.

1   Introduction

The mobile computing paradigm has emerged due to advances in wireless networking technology and portable computing devices. Mobile computing enables users equipped with portable computing devices to access information services through a shared infrastructure, regardless of physical location or movement. The mobile computing environment is a distributed computing platform with the following differences: the mobility of users and their access devices, frequent disconnection, limited bandwidth and the mobile resource constrains — limited computational and power sources.

Mobile users now have the ability to send and retrieve emails, receive updates on stock prices and weather, and obtain driving directions while in motion using cellular phones, pagers, and PDAs. Wireless transmission media across wide-area tele-

V. Malyshkin (Ed.): PaCT 2001, LNCS 2127, pp. 112–127, 2001.

communication networks are also an important element in the technological infrastructure of E-commerce [21]. The effective development of guided and wireless-media networks will support the delivery of World Wide Web functionality over the Internet. Using mobile technologies will enable users to purchase E-commerce goods and services anywhere and anytime. Naturally, mobile users also desire the same functionality available to them at a stationary computer on a wired network — edit and save changes to documents stored on a file server or to query and update shared data in private or corporate databases. The focus of this paper is on the latter.

As mobile users wander about, they are bound to encounter a variety of different information sources (databases) that are often autonomous and heterogeneous in nature. It would be advantageous if a uniform interface can be presented to the mobile users freeing them from the need to have knowledge of the data representation or data access method employed at different data sources. Organizing a collection of autonomous databases into a multidatabase is therefore desirable. A multidatabase integrates pre-existing autonomous and heterogeneous databases to form a global distributed information-sharing paradigm. To support mobile users, it is necessary to augment the existing multidatabases with wireless networking capabilities. This augmented multidatabase is known as a Mobile Data Access System (MDAS) [13].

The MDAS must have the capability of supporting a large number of mobile users. It is necessary that the MDAS provide timely and reliable access to shared data. Multidatabases have been designed to meet these requirements, albeit within the scope of the fixed networking environment. However, these systems have not been designed to cope with the effects of mobility.

Transactions are the means of access to shared data in databases; this is also the case in a multidatabase and a MDAS. Transaction management in an MDAS environment has some inherent problems due to the full autonomy of local nodes over the execution of transactions and the limitations imposed by the mobile computing environment. In this environment, the global transaction manager (GTM) must be able to deal with: i) different local transaction management systems; ii) different local concurrency control mechanisms; iii) lack of communication with local nodes, and iv) limitations of the mobile computing environment.

Concurrency control is needed in order to increase throughput and to allow timely and reliable access to shared data and must therefore support simultaneous execution and interleaving of multiple transactions. In an MDAS environment, the concurrency control algorithm has to overcome the effects of the local autonomy, in addition to constraints imposed by the mobile units.

As an example, consider a transaction in execution on a stationary computer on a wired network. The occurrence of a disconnection is often treated as a failure in the network thus, when this occurs the executing transaction is aborted. In a mobile computing environment, which is characterized by frequent disconnection (users may choose to disconnect voluntarily, for instance to conserve battery life), disconnection cannot be treated as a failure in the network.

Transactions issued from mobile clients tend to be long-lived. Thus, transactions issued by mobile users are exposed to a larger number of disconnections. Another effect of long-lived transactions is that it could result in low system throughput. Long-lived transactions are more likely to result in conflicts. Pessimistic locking schemes in the implementation of concurrency control could result in blocking of concurrently executing transactions, resulting in deadlocks and aborted transactions. On the other hand, employment of optimistic concurrency control could result in a high rate of transaction restarts. Thus, a new transaction model is needed for the MDAS environment that manages concurrency control and recovery, handles frequent disconnection, and address the issue of long-lived transactions while at the same time does not violate the autonomy of the local data sources.

The goal of this paper is to present such a transaction processing model. The model is built on the concept of global transactions in multidatabase based on the Summary Schemas Model [6]. This work expands our effort reported in [13] by implementing an additional layer on top of the MDBS that handles mobile transactions, disconnection, and long-lived transaction.

Section 2 addresses the background material on multidatabase systems and mobile computing and the issues that affect the MDAS. Section 3 is a description of the MDAS transaction processing model and the necessary protocols. Section 4 presents the results and analysis of the simulation model of the proposed model. Finally, Section 5 concludes the paper and addresses several future research issues.

2   Background

The basis of the MDAS is the mobile computing environment and the multidatabase. Thus, this section gives a brief overview of the mobile computing environment, multidatabase systems, and the concepts and issues that characterize these environments.

2.1   Mobile Computing Environment

The mobile computing environment is a collection of mobile hosts (MH) and a fixed networking system [8],[10],[13]. The fixed networking system consists of a collection of fixed hosts connected through a wired network. Certain fixed hosts, called base stations or Mobile Support Stations (MSS) are equipped with wireless communication capability. Each MSS can communicate with MHs that are within its coverage area (a cell). MHs can move within a cell or between cells, effectively disconnection from one MSS and connecting to another. At any point in time, a MH can be connected to only one MSS. MHs are portable computers that vary in size, processing power, and memory. Wireless Communication, mobility, and portability are three essential properties of mobile computing that pose difficulties in the design of applications [10].

2.2   Multidatabase Systems

A multidatabase system integrates pre-existing local databases to form a single integrated global distributed database system. It is a collection of autonomous local database systems (LDBS), possibly of different types. The integration of the DBMSs is performed by multiple software sub-systems at the local databases [3],[19]. The local databases are unaware of the existence of the global database [20]. Local autonomy is the key requirement in the design of a multidatabase. In a multidatabase there are two types of users: local users and global users. Local autonomy guarantees that the local users access their own local database independent of, and unaffected by, the existence of the multidatabase and its global users. Autonomy in multidatabases comes in the form of; design autonomy, participation autonomy, communication autonomy, and execution autonomy [3].

2.3   MDAS Issues

The MDAS is a multidatabase system that has been augmented to provide support for wireless access to shared data. Issues that affect multidatabases are therefore applicable to the MDAS. Mobile computing raises additional issues over and above those outlined in the design of a multidatabase. In the following we examine the effects of mobility on query processing and optimization, and transaction processing.

- **Query Processing and Optimization**: The higher communication cost of wireless medium and limited power of a mobile unit may lead to the design of query processing and optimization algorithms that focus on reducing the financial cost of transactions and consideration for query processing strategies for long-lived transactions that do not rely on frequent short communications but longer communications. Query optimization algorithms may also be designed to select plans based on their energy consumption. Approximate answers will be more acceptable in mobile databases than in traditional databases due to the frequent disconnection and the long latency time of transaction execution [1].
- **Transaction Processing**: Since disconnection is a common mode of operation, transaction processing must provide support for disconnected operation. Temporary disconnection should be tolerated with a minimum disruption of transaction processing, and suspension of transactions on either stationary or mobile hosts. In order for users to work effectively during periods of disconnection, mobile computers will require a substantial degree of autonomy [1],[13],[18]. Effects of mobile transactions committed during disconnection should be incorporated into the database while guaranteeing data and transaction correctness upon reconnection [18]. Atomic transactions are the normal mode of access to shared data in traditional databases. Mobile transactions that access shared data cannot be structured using atomic transactions. However, mobile computations need to be organized as a set of transactions some of which execute on mobile hosts and others that execute on the mobile support hosts. The transaction model will need to include aspects of long transaction models and Sagas. Mobile transactions are expected to be lengthy due to the mobility of the data consumers and/or data producers and their interactive nature. Atomic transactions cannot satisfy the ability to handle partial failures and provide different recovery strategies, minimizing the effects of failure [1],[7],[20].
- **Transaction Failure and Recovery**: Disconnection, bandwidth limitations, and higher probability of damage to the mobile devices are some of the possible sources of failure in mobile environments. Special action can be taken on behalf of active transactions at the time a disconnection is predicted — a transaction processes may be migrated to a stationary computer particularly if no further user interaction is required. Remote data may be downloaded in advance of the

predicted disconnection in support of interactive transactions that should continue to execute locally on the mobile machine after disconnection. Log records needed for recovery may be transferred from the mobile host to a stationary host [1].

2.4   Summary Schemas Model

The Summary Schemas Model (SSM) has been proposed in [6] as an efficient means to access data in a heterogeneous multidatabase environment. The SSM uses a hierarchical meta structure that provides an incrementally concise view of the data in the form of summary schemas. The hierarchical data structure of the SSM consists of leaf nodes and summary schema nodes. The leaf nodes represent the portion of local databases that are globally shared. Each higher-level node (summary schema nodes) provides a more concise view of the data by summarizing the semantic contents of its children. The terms in the schema are related through synonym, hypernym and hyponym links. The SSM allows a user to submit a request in his/her own terms. It intelligently resolves a query into a set of subqueries using the semantic contents of the SSM meta data. The overall memory requirements for the SSM, compared to the requirements of a global schema, are drastically reduced by up to 94%. Subsequently, the SSM meta data could be kept in main memory, thus reducing the access time and query processing time. Furthermore, for resource scares MDAS access devices, caching the upper levels of the SSM meta data structure allow a great amount of autonomy to each mobile unit. Finally, the SSM could be used to browse data by "stepping" through the hierarchy, or view semantically similar data through queries.

3   Proposed Transaction Processing Model

The proposed MDAS transaction model is based on a multi tiered approach capable of supporting pre-existing global users on the wired network in addition to mobile users. The proposed transaction model is implemented as a software module on top of the pre-existing multidatabase management system. Integration of the mobile computing with the pre-existing multidatabase system in then the key challenge in MDAS.

3.1   MDAS Transactions

We may distinguish three types of transactions:
- Local transactions that access only local data at each LDBS,
- Global Transactions that access data at more than one LDBS, and
- Mobile transactions that could access data from more than one LDBS.

In reality, a mobile transaction is no different from a global transaction as far as the MDBS layer is concerned. However, a number of factors make it sufficiently different enough to consider it as a separate transaction type in the MDAS:
- Mobile transactions require the support of stationary hosts for their computations and communications.

- Mobile transactions might have to split their computations, with one part executing on a mobile client and the other part executing on a stationary host.
- Mobile transactions might have to share state and data. This is a violation of the revered ACID transactions processing assumptions.
- Mobile transactions might have to be migrated to stationary hosts in order to accommodate the disconnection of the mobile client.
- Mobile transactions tend to be long lived. This is a consequence of the frequent disconnection experienced by the mobile client and the mobility of the mobile client.

3.2   MDAS Transaction Model

The MDAS as we envision it, consists of a software module, called a Mobile Transaction Manager (MTM), implemented above the MDBS layer. The two layers combined form the MDAS. The MTM is responsible for managing the submission of mobile transactions to the MDBS layer and their execution. Thus, the MTM acts as a proxy for the mobile unit, thereby establishing a static presence for the mobile unit on the fixed network. The other half, the GTM is responsible for managing the execution of global transactions submitted by non-mobile users and mobile transactions submitted on behalf of the mobile unit by the MTM.

Our approach is based on the principle that the computation and communication demands of an algorithm should be satisfied within the static segment of the system to the extent possible [2]. In another words, we attempt: i) to localize communication between a fixed host and a mobile host within the same cell, ii) to reduce the number of wireless messages by downloading most of the communication and computation requirements to the fixed segment of the network, and iii) to develop distributed algorithm based on the maintained logical structure among the fixed network.

Mobile transactions are submitted to the MDBS layer in a FIFO order by the MTM. There are two operating modes that reflect the level of delegation of authority to the proxy by the mobile client.

- **Full Delegation Mode**: In this mode the mobile client delegates complete authority of the mobile transaction to the MTM. The MTM has the authority to commit the transaction upon completion. If there is a conflict the MTM may decide to abort the transaction and resubmit it, later on. In any case, the mobile client is notified of the status of the transaction and will receive the results (if any).
- **Partial Delegation Mode**: In this mode more participation is required of the mobile client. The mobile client has the final say on whether or not the transaction should be committed. The MTM submits the transaction to the MDBS and manages its execution on behalf of the mobile client. Upon completion of the operations of the transaction, the mobile client is notified and the MTM waits for the commit or abort message from the mobile client.

In applying the proposed transaction-processing model to the MDAS we may derive the following benefits:

- Our protocol decouples the effects of mobility from the MDBS. Hence, any developed concurrency control and recovery mechanism can be readily adopted into our protocol.

- The MDBS layer does not need to be aware of the mobile nature of some nodes. The mobile transactions are submitted to the MDBS interface by the transaction proxies. The MDBS interacts with the transaction proxy as though it were the mobile unit. In the case of a mobile transaction, most of the communication is within the fixed network and as far as the MDBS is concerned, a static host has initiated the transaction.
- The operations of non-mobile users are unaffected by the transactions of mobile users. The effects of long-lived transactions can be effectively and efficiently handled. Delegating the authority to commit and/or abort a transaction on behalf of the mobile host to the transaction proxy can minimize the effects of long-lived transactions. Thus, transactions initiated by non-mobile users will experience less conflict and as a consequence system throughput and response times are not severely affected.
- The mobile host may disconnect and freely change location since the transaction proxy acts on its behalf without requiring any participation from the mobile host unless it is interested in the outcome.

3.3   Operating Modes

Mobile Host – MSS Relationship. In the proposed MDAS transaction-processing model, communication occurs through the exchange of messages between static and/or mobile hosts. In order to send a message from a mobile host to another host, either fixed or mobile, the message is first sent to the local MSS over the wireless network. The MSS forwards the message to the local MSS of the other mobile host, which forwards it over the wireless network to the other mobile host if it is meant for a mobile host. Otherwise, the message is directly forwarded to the fixed host. The location of a mobile host within the network is neither fixed nor universally known in the network. Thus, when sending a message to a mobile host the MSS that serves the mobile host must first be determined. This is a problem that has been addressed through a variety of routing protocols (e.g. Mobile IP, CDPD) at the network layer [4,11]. We are not concerned with any particular routing protocol for message delivery but instead assume that the network layer addresses this issue.

Each MSS maintains a list of *id*s of mobile hosts that are local to its cell. When a mobile host enters a new cell, it sends a *join message* to the new MSS. The *join message* includes the *id* (usually the IP address) of the mobile host. When the MSS receives the *join message* adds the mobile host to its list of local mobile hosts. To change location, the mobile host must also send a *leave message* to the local MSS. The mobile host neither sends nor receives any further messages within the present cell once the *leave message* has been sent. When the MSS receives the *leave message* from the mobile host, it removes the mobile host *id* from its list of local mobile hosts.

Disconnection is often predictable by a mobile host before it occurs. Therefore, in order to disconnect, the mobile host sends a *disconnect message* to the local MSS. The *disconnect message* is similar to the *leave message*, the only difference being that when a mobile host issues a *leave message* it is bound to reconnect at some other MSS at a later time. A mobile host that has issued a *disconnect message* may or may not reconnect at any MSS later. When the MSS receives the *disconnect message* a *disconnect flag* is set for the particular mobile host id. If an attempt is made to locate a disconnected mobile host the initiator of the search will be informed of the disconnected status of the mobile host.

A mobile host that issues a *leave message* or a *disconnect message* must issue a *reconnect message* to reconnect to a MSS. The *reconnect message* must include the *id*s of the mobile host and the previous MSS at which it was last connected. The *id* of the previous MSS is necessary so that the new MSS and the previous MSS can execute any handoff procedures necessary, for instance, unsetting the *disconnect flag*. When the MSS receives the *reconnect message* it adds the mobile host to its list of local mobile hosts and executes any handoff procedures with the prior MSS.

Mobile Host – MTM Relationship. To initiate a transaction, the mobile host sends a *Begin-Transaction* message to the MTM. The MTM acknowledges the request by returning a transaction sequence number. Each MSS has a MTM associated with it and transaction sequence numbers are assigned in a distributed manner among the MTMs in the system using any distributed ordering algorithm, for example, Lamport's algorithm [12]. The mobile host tags each transaction request message with a transaction *id*, which is composed of the mobile host *id*, and the transaction sequence number. The transaction request message is composed of the mobile host *id*, the transaction sequence number, and the transaction operations. To signify the completion of a transaction request, an *End-Transaction message* is sent to the MTM. Transaction execution is delayed until the receipt of the *End-Transaction message*. This is in order to guarantee that the entire transaction as a whole is submitted to the MDBS.

3.4   Transaction Processing Model Work Flow

The transaction processing model workflow can be described as shown in Fig. 1.

- The mobile host initiates a transaction request message. The message is received by the MSS, and is forwarded to the associated MTM.
- The MTM receives the transaction request from the MSS. The transaction request is logged and the transaction *id* (transaction sequence number + mobile host *id*) is placed in the ready list. A transaction proxy is created to execute the transaction.
- The transaction proxy removes a transaction *id* from the ready list and inserts it into the active list. The transaction proxy translates the transaction request and then submits the transaction to the MDBS for execution.
- The transaction request is executed at the MDBS layer and the results and/or data are returned to the transaction proxy.
- The transaction proxy places the transaction *id* in the output list along with the results and data to be returned to the mobile host.
- The MTM initiates a search for the location of the mobile host and the results are transferred to the mobile host if it is still connected and then the transaction *id* is removed from the ready list.

Mobile transaction   Completed transaction
requests   requests

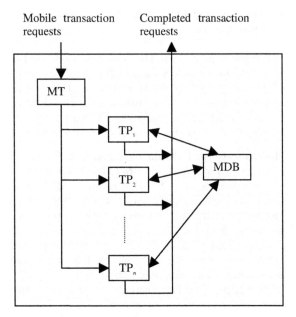

MTM: Mobile Transaction Manager   TP: Transaction Proxy
MDBS: Multidatabase System

Fig. 1. Transaction processing workflow

3.5   Disconnected Operation

We turn our attention to the case where the mobile host is no longer connected to the local MSS while the transaction is still in execution. By handing over transaction execution to transaction proxies, the disconnection of a mobile host or its relocation does not affect the transaction execution. The key issue to be addressed is how to notify the mobile host of the results of the transaction execution. In this case the following actions are taken:

On reconnection at the new MSS the mobile host should supply the *id* of the previous MSS to which it was connected. A handoff procedure is then initiated between the two MSSs.

- As part of the handoff procedure, the MTM at the previous MSS searches its ready list, if the transaction request issued by the mobile host has not yet been processed it is forwarded to the MTM at the new MSS and inserted into its ready list. Thus, control of transaction execution is transferred to the new MSS.
- If the transaction has completed its execution then the results are forwarded to the new MSS, which subsequently returns them to the mobile host.
- If the transaction is still active then control is not transferred but the new MSS places the transaction request in its active list but marks it as being executed at another site. The previous MSS will initiate a search for the new MSS of the mobile host when the transaction is complete in order to transfer the results to it.

4   Simulation Result and Analysis

4.1   Simulator

A simulator was developed to measure the feasibility of the proposed protocol within an MDAS environment. The MDASsim simulator and some results from a comparison between the two modes of operation of the Mobile Transaction Manager (Full Delegation Mode and Partial Delegation Mode) are presented. The simulator is based on the DBsim simulator presented in [15]. However, DBsim has been extended to support the concepts of a multidatabase and the MDAS.

The DBsim is an event driven simulator written in C++. The DBsim was designed as a framework to simulate different scheduling policies. Its architecture is based on an object-oriented paradigm, with all the major components implemented as classes in C++. The simulator is a collection of cooperating objects, comprising of: the event controller, transaction manager (TM), scheduler, data manager (DM), and the bookkeeper. A multidatabase is much more complex to model, compared to a distributed database mainly due to the local autonomy and heterogeneity issues. As a result, the DBsim was enhanced with additional flexibility to simulate the important aspects of the MDAS environment. In order to achieve this we introduced three new concepts to the simulation model:

- The DBsim architecture implemented a single transaction manager. We have departed from the single transaction manager module implemented in the original DBSim simulator by allowing a transaction manager at each of the local nodes.
- An additional layer above the local transaction managers was implemented to manage global and mobile transactions. This is the global transaction manager (GTM). For the purpose of our simulation, the GTM serves as the Mobile Transaction Manager (MTM) as well.
- We have introduced the concepts of global and mobile transactions into the simulation model.
  For each simulated local node we have one data manager (DM) object, one scheduler object and one transaction manager (TM) object. The GTM object is responsible for creating mobile and global subtransactions that generate operations to the transaction managers at each local node. The architecture of our simulator is shown in Fig. 2.

4.2   Global Transaction Manager

A Global Transaction is resolved by the summary schema's meta data. As a result, the global transaction is decomposed into several subtransactions, each resolved at a local node. This process also recognizes a global transaction manager for the global transaction — a global transaction manager is the lowest summary schema node that semantically contains the information space manipulated by the transaction. In our simulated environment, the number of local nodes at which the transaction is resolved is chosen randomly from the number of nodes in the system. The global or mobile transaction makes calls to the local transaction managers to begin execution of the subtransactions.

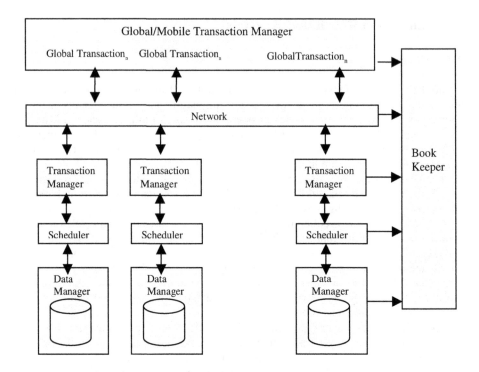

Fig. 2. MDASSim architecture

To allow multiprogramming (MP) level at each local node, the simulator maintains a fixed number of local transactions executing simultaneously at each node — this number is varied for different simulation run. A fixed number of global/mobile transactions are also maintained in the system. The ratio of global to mobile transaction is varied for different simulation runs, as well. Together, the fixed number of simultaneous local transactions and the fixed number of global/mobile transactions serve as an approximation of a system with a constant load. Every time a transaction (local, global or mobile) is terminated, a new one is created after some random delay.

Upon creation (submission) of a transaction (subtransaction) to a local node, its operations (read, write, commit or abort) are begun to schedule for execution. Every time an operation finishes successfully, the transaction, after a short delay, generates a new operation or it decides end the transaction by sending a commit or abort operation.

4.3   Commit Protocol

Each local node implements the two-phase commit (2PC) protocol. In case of a global or mobile subtransaction, the GTM coordinates the commit protocol so as to ensure that either all or none of the subtransactions succeed to preserve the atomicity of the global transaction. A timeout is used to simulate the obtaining of permission to commit the mobile transaction from the mobile unit when there is a need to do so. A commit or abort is returned based on the probability of communication between the MTM and the mobile unit during the timeout period.

4.4   Simulation Parameters

The behavior of our multi-tiered control level protocol is determined based on several parameters. Some of these parameters are hardware, software, and administrative dependent, and others are application dependent. It is very important that reasonable values be selected for each parameter. The system parameters were derived from the underlying platform. Additional parameters for the mobile component of the system were obtained from the work reported in [13]. These parameters are presented in Tables 1-3.

Table 1. Min and max values of interval parameters

Parameter	Min.	Max.
Number of operations in local transactions selected	2	8
Number of operations generated in a burst	3	5
Time between transactions	10ms	100ms
Time between operation requests	1ms	10ms
Time between operations in a burst	1ms	3ms
Time to perform a disk operation	8ms	16ms
Restart delay	500ms	1500ms

Table 2. Application parameters

Parameter	Value
Number of transactions	20000
Size of address space, # of resource units	20000
Hot spot size, # resource units	2000
Hot spot probability	50%
Abort probability	0.1%
Read probability	80%
Burst probability	20%
Block size	4KB

Table 3. Global and Mobile Unit Parameters

Parameter	Default Value
Number of global/mobile transactions in the systems	10
Service time for each communicated message to the mobile unit selected randomly	0.3 – 3 sec
Probability of mobile unit not being found after the timeout	0.20

4.5   Simulations and Results

Our simulations were based on a constant load. The MPL (the number of simultaneous local transactions) at the local sites during each simulation run was constant (varied from 1 to 25) with a mix of global and mobile transactions. At all times, the total number of global transactions (global/mobile) is also constant while the ratio of global to mobile transactions varies for each simulation run (chosen as 20%, 40%, 50%, 60% and 80%). The throughput was used as the performance measure and it was measured against parameters such as: number of simultaneous local transactions (MP-Level), the varying ratio of global to mobile transactions, and the two different operating modes of the MTM (full-delegation and partial delegation modes). In general, as one could expect, at a lower MP-level, the global/mobile throughput was higher due to the fewer local transactions in the system and less likelihood of conflicts among transactions. As the MP-level increased, the global/mobile throughput dropped as a result of more local transactions in the system with increased likelihood of indirect conflicts among global/mobile transactions.

Figs 3 – 5 show the throughput of both global and mobile transactions as the number of simultaneous local transactions and the ratio of global to mobile transactions are varied. The charts compare the results under the Full Delegation mode of operation and the Partial Delegation mode of operation. As can be noted, the performance under the Full Delegation mode (FDM) surpasses that of the Partial Delegation mode (PDM) since the proxy needs to communicate with the mobile unit under the latter scheme. However, such performance degradation is quite tolerable specially, when one considers the flexibility and adaptability of our approach.

5   Conclusion and Future Directions

5.1   Conclusion

This paper proposed a new transaction-processing model for the mobile data access system (MDAS). The proposed multi-tiered transaction model uses the concepts of transaction proxies to manage the execution of mobile transactions. To provide support for mobile transactions, a layer, the Mobile Transaction Manager (MTM), is implemented above the pre-existing multidatabase system. Using proxies the proposed model decouples the effects of mobility – frequent disconnection, limited bandwidth, limited computational resources, etc. – from the multidatabase systems.

Two modes of operation, namely, Full delegation mode and partial delegation mode, were proposed to address the level of participation of a mobile unit in the completion of a mobile transaction. In the Full Delegation mode of operation, the mobile unit relinquishes control of the final commit/abort of a transaction to the MTM. In the Partial Delegation mode of operation, the mobile unit has the final say on whether to commit or abort the transaction. The MTM must communicate with the mobile unit when the transaction is ready to be committed. However, should the mobile unit be unavailable, the MTM is free to abort the transaction after a sufficient time out period.

A simulator written in C++ was developed to evaluate the feasibility and performance of the proposed transaction-processing model. The simulation results showed that the performance of the Full Delegation mode of operation is better than the Partial Delegation mode. This comes about as a result of fewer communications between the mobile unit and the multidatabase system. The performance of the system was evaluated by varying the number of simultaneous local transactions executing at each node and by varying the ratio of global to mobile transactions present in the system.

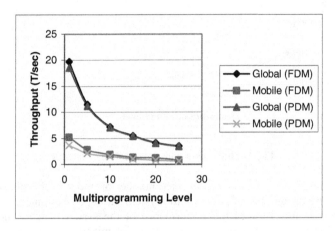

Fig. 3. Throughput with 20% Mobile Transactions

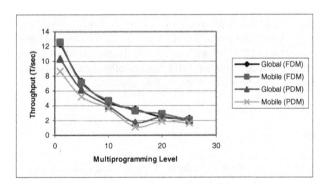

Fig. 4. Throughput with 50% Mobile Transactions

5.2   Future Directions

The proposed transaction processing system can be extended in a number of ways:
- Our simulation results showed the validity of the proposed transaction-processing model. However, it would be interesting to study the model in a real mobile computing environment A potential approach would be to implement the MDAS as part of the Mobile Computing Environment and simulation test bed (MCE) proposed in [16].

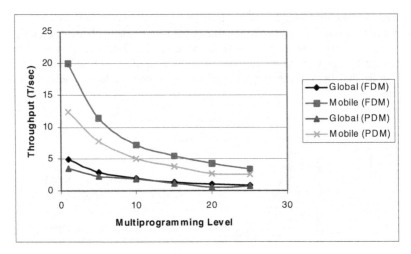

Fig. 5. Throughput with 80% Mobile Transactions

- The simulations were run with a fixed number of nodes in the system. The effect of varying the number of nodes on the system should be examined.
- The test results showed the performance of the system when either of the two operation modes was employed. The effect of mixed operation modes should be examined. It would be interesting to study the effect of mobility at the data sources level, as well.

As the final notes, the development of effective E-commerce technologies is in its formative stage. As E-commerce moves from a largely business-to-business model to include a proliferation of retail seeking channels, the demand for mobile data access will proliferate. The problems of effective mobile data access must be resolved to allow the effective development of electronic markets.

References

1. R. Alonso and H. F. Korth. Database System Issues in Nomadic Computing. ACM SIGMOD Conference on Management of Data, pp. 388-392, 1993.
2. B. R. Badrinath, et al. Structuring Distributed Algorithms for Mobile Hosts. Conference on Distributed Computing Systems, pp. 21-38, 1994.
3. D. Bell and J. Grimson. Distributed Database Systems. Addison-Wesley Publishing Company, 1992.
4. P. Bhagwat and C. E. Perkins. A Mobile Networking System Based on Internet Protocol. symposium on Mobile and Location Independent Computing, 1993.
5. Y. Breitbart, H. Garcia-Molina and A. Silberschatz. Overview of Multidatabase Transaction Management. VLDB 1(2): 181-239, 1992.
6. M. W. Bright, A. R. Hurson and S. Pakzad. Automated Resolution of Semantic Heterogeneity in Multidatabases. ACM TODS, 19(2): 212-253, 1994.
7. P. Chrysanthis. Transaction Processing in Mobile Computing Environment. Workshop on Advances in Parallel and Distributed Systems, pp. 77-82, 1993.
8. R. A. Dirckze and L. Gruenwald. Nomadic Transaction Management. IEEE Potentials, 17(2): 31-33, 1998.

9. M. H. Durham, A. Helal and S. Balakrishnan. A Mobile Transaction Model that Captures both the Data and Movement Behavior. Mobile Network Applications 2 (2): 149-162, 1997.

10. G. H. Forman and J. Zahorjan. The Challenges of Mobile Computing. IEEE Computer Volume: 27(4): 38-47, 1994.

11. J. Ioannidis, D. Duchamp, and G. O. Maguire. IP-based Protocols for Mobile Internetworking. ACM SIGCOMM Symposium, pp. 235-245, 1991.

12. L. Lamport. Time, clocks and the Ordering of Events in Distributed Systems. Communications of the ACM, 21: 558-565, 1978.

13. J. B. Lim, A. R. Hurson and K. M. Kavi. Concurrent Data Access in Mobile Heterogeneous Systems. Hawaii Conference on System Sciences, 1999.

14. S. K. Madria and B. Bhargava. A Transaction Model for Mobile Computing. Database and Engineering Applications Symposium, pp. 92-102, 1998.

15. K. Norvag, O. Sandsta and K. Bratbergsengen. Concurrency Control in Distributed Object-Oriented Database Systems. Proceedings of ADBIS, 1997.

16. R. Rajagopalan, S. Alagar and S. Venkatesan. MCE: An Integrated Mobile Computing Environment and Simulation Test bed. USENIX symposium on Mobile and Location Independent Computing, 1995.

17. A. P. Sheth and J. Larson. Federated Database Systems for Managing Dist. Heterogeneous & Autonomous Databases. Computer, 22(3): 183-236, 1990.

18. M. Wu and C. Lee. On Concurrency Control in Multidatabase Systems. Computer Software and Applications Conference, pp. 386-391, 1994.

19. X. Ye and J. A. Keane. A Distributed Transaction Management Scheme for Multidatabase Systems. International Trends in Electronics, 1: 397-401, 1994.

20. L. H. Yeo and A. Zaslavsky. Submission of Transaction from Mobile Workstations in Cooperative Multidatabase Processing Environment. Conference on Distributed Computing Systems, pp. 372-379, 1994.

21. V. Zwass. Structure and Macro-Level Impacts of Electronic Commerce: From Technological Infrastructure to Electronic Marketplaces. Foundations of Information Systems: [http://www.mhhe.com/business/mis/zwass/ecpaper.html]

Characterizing Timed Net Processes Categorically*

I.B. Virbitskaite

Institute of Informatics Systems
Siberian Division of the Russian Academy of Sciences
6, Acad. Lavrentiev avenue, 630090, Novosibirsk, Russia
virb@iis.nsk.su

Abstract. The paper aims at extending the categorical approach to Petri net based models with time constraints. We define a category of net processes with dense time, and use the general framework of open maps to obtain a notion of bisimulation. We show this to be equivalent to the standard notion of timed bisimulation. Next, decidability of timed bisimulation is shown in the setting of finite net processes. Further, the result on decidability is applied to time safe Petri nets, using a timed version of the McMillan-unfolding.

1 Introduction

Category theory has been used to structure the seemingly confusing world of models for concurrency – see [29] for a survey. The general idea is to formalize that one model is more expressive than another in terms of an 'embedding', most often taking the form of a coreflection, i.e. an adjunction in which the unit is an isomorphism. The models are equipped with behaviour preserving morphisms, to be thought of as kinds of simulations.

An important ingredient of every theory of concurrency is a notion of equivalence between processes. Bisimulation [10] is the best known behavioural equivalence. In an attempt to understand the relationships and differences between the extensive amount of research within the field of bisimulation equivalences, Joyal, Nielsen, and Winskel [12] proposed an abstract category-theoretic definition of bisimulation. They identify spans of morphisms satisfying certain 'path lifting' properties, so-called open maps, as an abstract definition of bisimilarity. Further, in [22] open maps have been used to define different notions of bisimulation for a range of models, but none of these have modelled real-time.

Recently, the demand for correctness analysis of real time systems, i.e. systems whose descriptions involve a quantitative notion of time, increases rapidly. Timed extensions of interleaving models have been investigated thoroughly in the last ten years. Various recipes on how to incorporate time in transition systems – the most prominent interleaving model – are, for example, described in [2,21].

---

* This work is partially supported by the Russian Fund of Basic Research (Grant N 00-01-00898).

V. Malyshkin (Ed.): PaCT 2001, LNCS 2127, pp. 128–141, 2001.

Timed bisimulation was shown decidable for finite timed transition systems by Čerāns in [7], and since then more efficient algorithms have been discovered in [14,27].

On the other hand, the incorporation of quantitative information into non-interleaving models has received scant attention: a few extensions are known of pomsets [6], asynchronous transition systems [1], net processes [3,4,15,26], and event structures [13,20]. In this respect, Petri net models are the only nice exception: various timed generalizations of the models are known in the literature (see [16,24] among others).

In this paper, we present a model of timed net processes which are a timed extension of occurrence nets (e.g., [8]) by associating their events with two timing constraints that indicate earliest and latest occurrence times both with regard to a global clock. Events once ready – i.e., all their causal predecessors have occurred and their timing constraints are respected – are forced to occur, provided they are not disabled by others events. A timed net process progresses through a sequence of states by occurring events at a certain time moment. An event occurrence takes no time. The model appeared to us as a most simple and natural approach to our purpose.

The main contribution of the paper is to show the applicability of the general categorical framework of open maps to true concurrent models with dense time. We first define a category of timed net processes, where the morphisms are to be thought of as simulations, and an accompanying path (sub)category of timed words, which, following [12], provides us with notions of open maps and a bisimulation. Next, we show within the framework of open maps that timed bisimulation is decidable for finite timed net processes. Further, the result on decidability is applied to safe Petri nets with discrete time [16,4], using a timed version of the McMillan-unfolding [19].

There have been several motivations for this work. One has been given by the paper [8] where a theory of branching processes of Petri nets has been proposed. Further, the approach has been successfully extended to timed net models (see [3,15,26]). A next origin has been the papers [17,18,23,25,28], which have extensively studied categorical characterizations of Petri net based models. Furthermore, the paper [5] first establishes a precise connection between morphisms of Petri nets which consider only their static structures and morphisms on their dynamic behaviours, and then applies the results to a discrete timing of Petri nets. Finally, another motivation has been given by the paper [11], which provides an alternative proof of decidability of bisimulation for an interleaving model with dense time (finite timed transition systems) in terms of open maps, and illustrates the use of open maps in presenting timed bisimilarity.

The rest of the paper is organized as follows. The basic notions concerning timed net processes are introduced in the next section. A category of timed net processes and an accompanying path (sub)category of timed words, are defined in Sect. 3. Section 4 introduces the concept of open morphism and shows its decidability in the framework of finite timed net processes. In Sect. 5, basing on spans of open maps, the resulting notion of bisimulation is studied, and established to coincide with the standard notion of timed bisimulation. Further, decidability of timed bisimulation in the setting of finite processes is shown. In Sect. 6 the result on decidability of timed bisimulation is applied to time safe Petri nets.

2   Timed Net Processes

In this section, we shortly define some terminology concerning timed net processes. 'Timed net process' is a timed extension of an occurrence net (e.g. [8]) by associating its events with two timing constraints that indicate earliest and latest occurrence times both with regard to a global clock. Events once ready – i.e., all their causal predecessors have occurred and their timing constraints are respected – are forced to occur, provided they are not disabled by others events. A timed net process progresses through a sequence of states by occurring events at a certain time moment. An event occurrence takes no time.

We start with the well-known concept of a net. A *net* is a triple (B, E, G), where B is a set of conditions; E is a set of events ($B \cap E = \emptyset$); $G \subseteq (B \times E) \cup (E \times B)$ is the flow relation ($E \subseteq dom(G) \cap cod(G)$).

For $x \in B \cup E$, ${}^\bullet x = \{y \in B \cup E \mid (y, x) \in G\}$ and $x^\bullet = \{y \in B \cup E \mid (x, y) \in G\}$ denote the *preset* and *postset* of x, respectively. Note, the definition above exclude events with ${}^\bullet e = \emptyset$ or $e^\bullet = \emptyset$. A net (B, E, G) is *acyclic*, if G^+ (G^+ is the transitive closure of G) is acyclic; (B, E, G) is *finitary*, if for all $x \in B \cup E$ the set $\{y \in B \cup E \mid y \ G^+ \ x\}$ is finite. A net (B', E', G') is a *subnet* of (B, E, G), if $B' \subseteq B$, $E' \subseteq E$, $G' \subseteq G \cap (B' \times E' \cup E' \times B')$. $x, y \in B \cup E$ are *in conflict* iff there exist distinct events $e_1, e_2 \in E$ such that ${}^\bullet e_1 \cap {}^\bullet e_2 \neq \emptyset$ and $(e_1, x), (e_2, y) \in G^*$ (G^* is the reflexive and transitive closure of G).

A *net process* is an acyclic finitary net $N = (B, E, G)$ such that $\mid {}^\bullet b \mid \leq 1$ for all $b \in B$ and $\neg(e \ \# \ e)$ for all $e \in E$.

Let ${}^\bullet N = \{b \in B \mid {}^\bullet b = \emptyset\}$ (the set of *input* conditions of N) and $N^\bullet = \{b \in B \mid b^\bullet = \emptyset\}$ (the set of *output* conditions of N).

A *computation* of a net process $N = (B, E, G)$ is a subnet $\pi = (B_\pi, E_\pi, G_\pi)$ of N such that ${}^\bullet \pi =^\bullet N$ and $\mid b^\bullet \mid \leq 1$ for all $b \in B_\pi$. The *initial computation* π_N is one with $E_{\pi_N} = \emptyset$. Let $Comp(N)$ denote the set of computations of N. For $e \in E$ and $\pi \in Comp(N)$, e is *enabled* after π if ${}^\bullet e \subseteq \pi^\bullet$, otherwise it is *disabled*. Let $En(\pi)$ be the set of events, enabled after π. If some $e \in E$ is enabled after π, we can extend π to a process π' by adding the event e and its postset $e^\bullet$. We write $\pi \xrightarrow{\ e\ } \pi'$ in this case.

Let $Act = \{a, a_1, a_2 \ldots\}$ be a set of actions. A *net process (labelled over Act)* is a tuple $N = (B, E, G, L)$, where N is a net process and $L : E \to Act$ is a labelling function. We define $Act_N = \{a \in Act \mid \exists \ e \in E \diamond l(e) = a\}$.

Before introducing the basic concepts of timed net processes we need to consider some auxiliary notations. Let $\mathbf{N}$ be the set of natural numbers and $\mathbf{R}_0^+$ the set of nonnegative real numbers. We use d, possibly subscripted and/or primed, to range over $\mathbf{R}_0^+$. We now come to the definition of timed net processes labelled over Act.

Definition 1 *A* timed net process *(labelled over Act) is a tuple* $TN = (N = (B,$ $E, G, L), Eot, Lot)$, *where N is a net process (labelled over Act)*; $Eot, Lot : E \rightarrow$ **N** *are functions of the* earliest *and* latest *occurrence times of events, satisfying* $Eot(e) \leq Lot(e)$ *for all* $e \in E$.

Figure 1 shows a simple example of a timed net process, where a pair of numbers near by an event corresponds to its earliest and latest occurrence times.

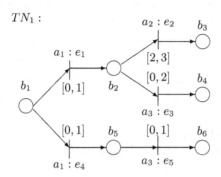

Fig. 1.

Let $\Gamma(TN) = [E \rightarrow \mathbf{R}_0^+]$ be the set of *time assignments* for events from E. Given $\tau \in \Gamma(TN)$, we let $\Delta(\tau) = \sup\{\tau(e) \mid e \in E\}$.

A *state* of TN is a pair (π, τ), where π is a computation and $\tau \in \Gamma(TN)$. The *initial state* of TN is a pair (π_N, τ_{TN}), where $\tau_{TN}(e) = 0$ for all $e \in E$.

The states of TN change, if an event occurs at some global time moment.

In a state (π, τ), an event e *may occur at a time moment* $d \in \mathbf{R}_0^+$, if $e \in \pi^\bullet$, $\Delta(\tau) \leq d$, $Eot(e) \leq d$ and $d \leq Lot(e')$ for all $e' \in En(\pi)$. In this case, the state (π', τ') is obtained by occurring an event e at a time moment $d \in \mathbf{R}_0^+$ (denoted $(\pi, \tau) \xrightarrow{(e,d)} (\pi', \tau')$), if $\pi \xrightarrow{e} \pi'$, $\tau' \mid_{E \setminus \{e\}} = \tau$, and $\tau'(e) = d$. A state (π, τ) is *reachable* if either $(\pi, \tau) = (\pi_N, \tau_{TN})$ or there exists a reachable state (π', τ') such that $(\pi', \tau') \xrightarrow{(e,d)} (\pi, \tau)$ for some $e \in E$ and $d \in \mathbf{R}_0^+$. We use $RS(TN)$ to denote the set of all reachable states of TN.

A *timed word* of an alphabet Act over $\mathbf{R}_0^+$ is a finite sequence of pairs: $w = (a_1, d_1) (a_2, d_2) \ldots (a_n, d_n)$, where for all $1 \leq i \leq n$, $a_i \in Act$, $d_i \in \mathbf{R}_0^+$, and furthermore $d_i \leq d_{i+1}$. We shall write $(\pi, \tau) \xrightarrow{(a,d)} (\pi', \tau')$, if $(\pi, \tau) \xrightarrow{(e,d)} (\pi', \tau')$ and $L(e) = a$. A *run* r of a timed word $w = (a_1, d_1) \ldots (a_n, d_n)$ is a finite sequence of the form: $r = (\pi_N, \tau_{TN}) \xrightarrow{(a_1,d_1)} (\pi_1, \tau_1) \ldots (\pi_{n-1}, \tau_{n-1}) \xrightarrow{(a_n,d_n)} (\pi_n, \tau_n)$. In this case, we say that (π_n, τ_n) is *reachable by a timed word w*.

As an illustration, we construct the set of the timed words corresponding to the runs of the timed net process TN_1 (see Fig. 1): $\{(a_1, d_1), (a_1, d_1)(a_2, d_2), (a_1, d_1)(a_3, d_3) \mid 0 \leq d_1 \leq 1, d_2 = 2, 0 \leq d_3 \leq 2, d_1 \leq d_3\}$.

3   A Category of Timed Net Processes

In this section, we define a category of timed net processes and an accompanying path (sub)category of timed words.

The morphisms of our model category will be simulation morphisms following the approach of [12]. This leads to the following definition of a morphism, consisting of a relation between conditions of the simulated system and simulating conditions of the other, and a function, mapping events of the simulated system to simulating events of the other, satisfying some further requirements.

Definition 2 *A morphism between timed net processes* $TN = (N = (B, E, G, L), Eot, Lot)$ *and* $TN' = (N' = (B', E', G', L'), Eot', Lot'), (\lambda, \mu) : TN \to TN'$, *consists of a relation* $\lambda \subseteq B \times B'$ *and a partial function* $\mu : E \to E'$ *such that:*

- $^{\bullet}\pi_{N'} = \lambda \,^{\bullet}\pi_N;$
- $\lambda \,^{\bullet}e = \,^{\bullet}(\mu(e))$ *and* $\lambda \, e^{\bullet} = (\mu(e))^{\bullet}$ *for all* $e \in E;$
- $\mu(e) = \mu(e') \Rightarrow e = e'$ *for all* $e, e' \in E_\pi$ *and* $\pi \in Comp(N);$
- $L' \circ \mu = L;$
- $Eot'(\mu(e)) \le Eot(e)$ *and* $Lot'(e) \le Lot(\mu(e))$ *for all* $e \in E.$

As an illustration, consider a morphism from the timed net process TN_2 in Fig. 2 to the timed net process TN_1 in Fig.1 mapping conditions b'_i to b_i $(1 \le i \le 4)$ and events e'_j to e_j $(1 \le j \le 3)$. It is easy to check that the constraints in Definition 2 are satisfied.

From now on, we use $(\lambda, \mu) \cdot \pi$ to denote the application of a morphism (λ, μ) to a computation π of some timed net process.

$TN_2 :$

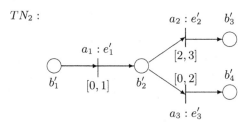

Fig. 2.

Let us consider a simulation property of a morphism defined prior to that.

Theorem 1 *Given a morphism* $(\lambda, \mu) : TN \to TN'$ *and a timed word* (a_1, d_1) $\ldots (a_n, d_n)$. *If* $(\pi_N = \pi_0, \tau_{TN} = \tau_0) \xrightarrow{(a_1, d_1)} (\pi_1, \tau_1) \ldots (\pi_{n-1}, \tau_{n-1}) \xrightarrow{(a_n, d_n)}$ (π_n, τ_n) *is a run in* TN, *then* $(\pi_{N'} = (\lambda, \mu) \cdot \pi_0, \tau_{TN_1} = \tau'_0) \xrightarrow{(a_1, d_1)} ((\lambda, \mu) \cdot \pi_1, \tau'_1) \ldots ((\lambda, \mu) \cdot \pi_{n-1}, \tau'_{n-1}) \xrightarrow{(a_n, d_n)} ((\lambda, \mu) \cdot \pi_n, \tau'_n)$ *is a run in* TN'.

Proof Sketch. It is straightforward by induction on n, using the definitions of a computation, a morphism and the relation $(\pi, \tau) \xrightarrow{(a, d)} (\pi', \tau')$. $\qquad \square$

Thus, in the formal sense of Theorem 1 we have shown that the morphisms from Definition 2 do represent a notion of simulation. Now, define a category of timed net processes as follows.

Definition 3 *Timed net processes (labelled over Act) with morphisms between them form a category of timed net processes CTN_{Act}, in which the composition of two morphisms $(\lambda_1, \mu_1) : TN_0 \longrightarrow TN_1$ and $(\lambda_2, \mu_2) : TN_1 \longrightarrow TN_2$ is $(\lambda_2 \circ \lambda_1, \mu_2 \circ \mu_1) : TN_0 \longrightarrow TN_2$, and the identity morphism has the form $(1_B, 1_E)$ where 1_B and 1_E are the identities on the condition-sets and event-sets, respectively.*

Proposition 1 CTN_{Act} *is a category.*

Following the standards of timed net processes and the paper [12], we would like to choose timed words with word extension so as to form a subcategory of CTN_{Act}. For each timed word w, we shall construct a timed net process as follows.

Definition 4 *Given a timed word $w = (a_1, d_1)(a_2, d_2) \cdots (a_n, d_n)$, we define a timed net process $TN_w = (N_w = (B_w, E_w, G_w, L_w), Eot_w, Lot_w)$ as follows: $B_w = \{1', 2', \cdots, n', n'+1\}$; $E_w = \{1, 2, \cdots, n\}$; $G_w = \{(i', i), (i, i'+1) \mid 1 \le i, i' \le n\}$; $L_w(i) = a_i$, $(i = 1, 2 \cdots n)$; $Eot_w(i) = Lot_w(i) = d_i$ $(i = 1, 2 \cdots n)$.*

The purpose of the construction is to represent the category of timed words with extension inside CTN_{Act}, and to identify runs of w in TN with morphisms from TN_w to TN, as expressed formally in the following two results.

Proposition 2 *The construction of the timed net process TN_w from a timed word w extends to a full and faithful functor from the category of timed words (as objects) and word extensions (as morphisms) into CTN_{Act}.*

Theorem 2 *Consider a timed net process TN and a timed word $w = (a_1, d_1)$ $\cdots (a_n, d_n)$. For all the runs of w in TN, $(\pi_N = \pi_0, \tau_{TN} = \tau_0) \overset{(a_1,d_1)}{\longrightarrow} (\pi_1, \tau_1)$ $\cdots (\pi_{n-1}, \tau_{n-1}) \overset{(a_n,d_n)}{\longrightarrow} (\pi_n, \tau_n)$ such that $\pi_{i-1} \overset{e_i}{\longrightarrow} \pi_i$ $(0 < i \le n)$, we can associate a morphism $(\lambda, \mu) : TN_w \to TN$ such that $\mu(i) = e_i$. Furthermore, this association is a bijection between the runs of w in TN and morphisms $(\lambda, \mu) : TN_w \to TN$.*

Proof Sketch. It directly follows from the definitions of a run of w and a morphism. □

4   *TW*-Open Morphisms

Given our categories of timed net processes and timed words, we can apply the general framework from [12], defining a notion of *TW*-open map.

Definition 5 *A morphism* $(\lambda, \mu) : TN \to TN'$ *in* $\mathcal{CTN}_{Act}$ *is TW-open iff for all timed words w and w', and morphisms such that the following diagram commutes:*

$$
\begin{array}{ccc}
TN_w & \xrightarrow{(\lambda', \mu')} & TN \\
{\scriptstyle (\lambda''', \mu''')}\big\downarrow & & \big\downarrow{\scriptstyle (\lambda, \mu)} \\
TN_{w'} & \xrightarrow[(\lambda'', \mu'')]{} & TN'
\end{array}
$$

there exists a morphism $(\widetilde{\lambda}, \widetilde{\mu}) : TN_{w'} \to TN$ such that in the diagram

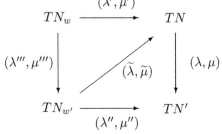

the two triangles commute.

Our next aim is to characterize *TW*-openness of morphisms.

Theorem 3 *Let (π_1, τ_1) and $((\lambda, \mu) \cdot \pi_1, \tau_1')$ be reachable by w in TN and TN' respectively. A morphism $(\lambda, \mu) : TN \to TN'$ is TW-open iff whenever $((\lambda, \mu) \cdot \pi_1, \tau_1') \xrightarrow{(a,d)} (\pi_2', \tau_2')$ in TN' then $(\pi_1, \tau_1) \xrightarrow{(a,d)} (\pi_2, \tau_2)$ in TN and $(\lambda, \mu) \cdot \pi_2 = \pi_2'$.*

Proof Sketch. It follows similar lines as other standard proofs of the characterization the openness of a morphism (see e.g., [11]), using the definition of a morphism and Theorem 2. □

We do not require for the category $\mathcal{CTN}_{Act}$ to have pullbacks. The following weaker result suffices.

Theorem 4 *Given two TW-open morphisms $(\lambda_1, \mu_1) : TN_1 \to TN$ and $(\lambda_2, \mu_2) : TN_2 \to TN$. There exists a timed net process TN_X and TW-open morphisms $(\lambda_1', \mu_1') : TN_X \to TN_1$, $(\lambda_2', \mu_2') : TN_X \to TN_2$ such that the diagram commutes:*

$$
\begin{array}{ccc}
TN_X & \xrightarrow{(\lambda_2', \mu_2')} & TN_2 \\
{\scriptstyle (\lambda_1', \mu_1')}\big\downarrow & & \big\downarrow{\scriptstyle (\lambda_2, \mu_2)} \\
TN_1 & \xrightarrow[(\lambda_1, \mu_1)]{} & TN
\end{array}
$$

Proof Sketch. See Appendix.   □

We next consider the decidability question for openness of a morphism in the setting of finite timed processes, i.e. processes with finite sets of B and E. The subclass of timed net processes is denoted by $\mathbf{TN}_f$. As for many existing results for timed models, including results concerning verification of real-time systems, our decision procedure relies heavily on the idea behind regions [2], which essentially provides a finite description of the state-space of timed net processes.

Given a timed net process TN and $\tau, \tau' \in \Gamma(TN)$, we let $\tau \simeq \tau'$ iff (i) for each $e \in E$ it holds: $\lfloor \tau(e) \rfloor = \lfloor \tau'(e) \rfloor$, and (ii) for each $e, e' \in E$ it holds: $\wr \tau(e) \wr \leq \wr \tau(e') \wr \Leftrightarrow \wr \tau'(e) \wr \leq \wr \tau'(e') \wr$, and $\wr \tau(e) \wr = 0 \Leftrightarrow \wr \tau'(e') \wr = 0$. Here, for $d \in \mathbf{R}_0^+$, $\wr d \wr$ and $\lfloor d \rfloor$ denote its fractional and smallest integer parts, respectively. For $\tau \in \Gamma(TN)$, let $[\tau]$ denote the *region* to which it belongs.

An *extended state* of a timed net process TN is defined as a pair $(\pi, [\tau])$, where $(\pi, \tau) \in RS(TN)$. We consider $(\pi_{TN}, [\tau_{TN}])$ as the *initial extended state* of TN. For extended states $(\pi, [\tau]), (\pi', [\tau'])$, we shall write $(\pi, [\tau]) \xrightarrow{(a,d)} (\pi', [\tau'])$, if $(\pi, \tau) \xrightarrow{(a,d)} (\pi', \tau')$. An extended state $(\pi, [\tau])$ is called *reachable by a timed word w*, if (π, τ) is reachable by a timed word w.

We can now give a characterization of TW-open maps in terms of extended states.

Theorem 5 *Let $TN_1, TN_2 \in \mathbf{TN}_f$, and $(\pi_1, [\tau_1])$, $((\lambda, \mu) \cdot \pi_1, [\tau_1'])$ be extended states reachable by w in TN_1 and TN_2, respectively. A morphism $(\lambda, \mu) : TN_1 \rightarrow TN_2$ is TW-open iff whenever $((\lambda, \mu) \cdot \pi_1, [\tau_1']) \xrightarrow{(a,d)} (\pi_2', [\tau_2'])$ in TN_2, then $(\pi_1, [\tau_1]) \xrightarrow{(a,d)} (\pi_2, [\tau_2])$ in TN_1 and $(\lambda, \mu) \cdot \pi_2 = \pi_2'$.*

Proof Sketch. It follows from Theorem 3 and the definition of a region.   □

Corollary 1 *Openness of a morphism is decidable between $TN, TN' \in \mathbf{TN}_f$.*

5 Timed Bisimulation

In this section, we first introduce a notion of TW-bisimulation, using the concept of TW-open map. Then the standard notion of timed bisimulation is defined in terms of states of timed net processes. Further, the coincidence of the bisimilarity notions is shown. Finally, decidability of timed bisimulation is demonstrated for finite timed net processes.

As was reported in [12], the TW-open map approach provides a general concept of bisimilarity for any categorical model of computation. The definition is given in terms of spans of TW-open maps.

Definition 6 *Timed net processes TN_1 and TN_2 are TW-bisimilar iff there exists a span $TN_1 \xleftarrow{(\lambda, \mu)} TN \xrightarrow{(\lambda', \mu')} TN_2$ with vertex TN of TW-open morphisms.*

Following the approach of [12], it is easy to show that TW-bisimulation is exactly the equivalence generated by TW-open maps, using Theorem 4.

Further, the notion of timed bisimulation [7] is defined in terms of states of timed net processes as follows.

Definition 7 *Two timed net processes TN_1 and TN_2 are timed bisimilar iff there exists a relation $\mathcal{B} \subseteq RS(TN_1) \times RS(TN_2)$, satisfying the following conditions: $((\pi_{N_1}, \tau_{TN_1}), (\pi_{N_2}, \tau_{TN_2})) \in \mathcal{B}$ and for all $((\pi_1, \tau_1), (\pi_2, \tau_2)) \in \mathcal{B}$ it holds:*

(a) if $(\pi_1, \tau_1) \xrightarrow{(a,d)} (\pi_1', \tau_1')$ in TN_1, then $(\pi_2, \tau_2) \xrightarrow{(a,d)} (\pi_2', \tau_2')$ in TN_2 and $((\pi_1', \tau_2'), (\pi_2', \tau_2')) \in \mathcal{B}$ for some $(\pi_2', \tau_2') \in RS(TN_2)$;

(b) if $(\pi_2, \tau_2) \xrightarrow{(a,d)} (\pi_2', \tau_2')$ in TN_2, then $(\pi_1, \tau_1) \xrightarrow{(a,d)} (\pi_1', \tau_1')$ in TN_1 and $((\pi_1', \tau_1'), (\pi_2', \tau_2')) \in \mathcal{B}$ for some $(\pi_1', \tau_1') \in RS(TN_1)$.

Finally, the coincidence of the bisimilarity notions is established.

Theorem 6 *Timed net processes TN_1 and TN_2 are TW-bisimilar iff they are timed bisimilar.*

Proof Sketch. See Appendix. □

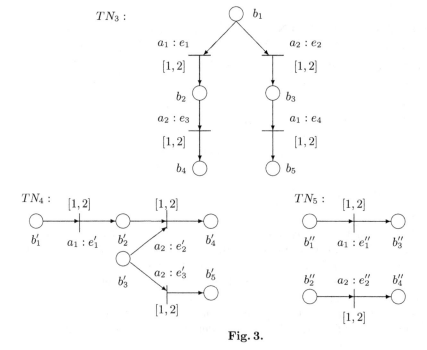

Fig. 3.

The timed net processes TN_1 and TN_2, shown in Fig. 1 and 2 respectively, are not bisimilar. Next, consider the timed net processes in Fig. 3. It is easy to see that there are morphisms from TN_3 to TN_4 and to TN_5, and these morphisms are TW-open. Hence we have a span of TW-open maps between TN_4 and TN_5. Bisimilarity between TN_4 and TN_5 follows from Theorem 6.

Theorem 7 *Let* $TN_1, TN_2 \in \mathbf{TN}_f$. *If there exists a span of* TW*-open maps* $TN_1 \xleftarrow{(\lambda_1, \mu_1)} TN \xrightarrow{(\lambda_2, \mu_2)} TN_2$ *then there exists* $TN' \in \mathbf{TN}_f$ *of size bounded by the size of* TN_1 *and* TN_2 *and with* TW*-open morphisms* $TN_1 \xleftarrow{(\lambda'_1, \mu'_1)} TN' \xrightarrow{(\lambda'_2, \mu'_2)} TN_2$.

Proof Sketch. Since $TN_1 \xleftarrow{(\lambda_1, \mu_1)} TN \xrightarrow{(\lambda_2, \mu_2)} TN_2$ is a span of TW-open maps, then TN_1 and TN_2 are TW-bisimilar, by Theorem 6. This means that there exists a timed bisimulation $\mathcal{B}$ between states of TN_1 and TN_2. Using $\mathcal{B}$ we construct TN' as in the converse part of the proof of Theorem 6. From the construction it follows that $TN' \in \mathbf{TN}_f$. The number of extended states of TN' is bounded by $\mid E \mid! \cdot 2^{2|E|+|B|} \cdot (c+1)^{|E|}$, where $\mid E \mid = \mid E_1 \mid * \mid E_2 \mid$ ($\mid E_i \mid$ is the number of events in TN_i $(i = 1, 2)$), $\mid B \mid = \mid B_1 \mid * \mid B_2 \mid$ ($\mid B_i \mid$ is the number of conditions in TN_i $(i = 1, 2)$), and c is the greatest constant appearing in the time constraints in TN_1 and TN_2. $\qquad \square$

Corollary 2 *Timed bisimulation is decidable for* $TN, TN' \in \mathbf{TN}_f$.

6   Time Petri Nets

Time Petri nets were introduced in [16]. Following the reasoning of [4], we consider time Petri nets with discrete time.

We start with the well-known concept of a Petri net. A *Petri net* (labelled over *Act*) is a tuple $\mathcal{N} = (P, T, F, m_0, l)$, where (P, T, F) is a net (with a finite set P of conditions called *places*, a finite set T of events called *transitions* $(P \cap T = \emptyset)$, and the flow relation $F \subseteq (P \times T) \cup (T \times P)$); $m_0 \subseteq P$ is the initial marking; $l : T \to Act$ is a labelling function. For $t \in T$, we let ${}^\bullet t = \{p \in P \mid (p, t) \in F\}$ and $t^\bullet = \{p \in P \mid (t, p) \in F\}$. To simplify the presentation, we assume that ${}^\bullet t \cap t^\bullet = \emptyset$ for every transition t. A *marking* m of $\mathcal{TN}$ is any subset of P. A transition t is *enabled* in a marking m if ${}^\bullet t \subseteq m$ (all its input places have tokens in m), otherwise it is *disabled*. Let $En(m)$ be the set of transitions, enabled in m. If $t \in En(m)$ then it may *fire*, and its firing leads to a new marking m' (denoted $m \xrightarrow{t} m'$) defined by $m' = (m \setminus {}^\bullet t) \cup t^\bullet$. A marking m is *reachable* if $m = m_0$ or there exists a reachable marking m' such that $m' \xrightarrow{t} m$. A Petri net is called *safe* if for every reachable marking m and for every $t \in En(m)$ it holds: $t^\bullet \cap m = \emptyset$.

Let $\mathcal{N} = (P, T, F, m_0, l)$ be a (labelled) Petri net and $N = (B, E, G, L)$ be a (labelled) net process. Then a mapping $\phi : (B \cup E) \longrightarrow (P \cup T)$ is called *homomorphism* iff $\phi(B) \subseteq P$, $\phi(E) \subseteq T$ and for all $e \in E$ the following hold: (i) the restriction of ϕ to ${}^\bullet e$ is a bijection between ${}^\bullet e$ and ${}^\bullet \phi(e)$; (ii) the restriction of ϕ to $e^\bullet$ is a bijection between $e^\bullet$ and $\phi(e)^\bullet$; (iii) the restriction of ϕ to ${}^\bullet N$ is a bijection between ${}^\bullet N$ and m_0; (vi) $L(e) = l(\phi(e))$. A pair (N, ϕ) is called a *process* of $\mathcal{N}$ iff ϕ is a homomorphism from N to $\mathcal{N}$. For each Petri net $\mathcal{N}$, there exists a unique (up to renaming of conditions and events) *maximal process*, where 'maximal' is related to the prefix ordering (cf. [8]). The McMillan-unfolding of $\mathcal{N}$ (denoted $McM(\mathcal{N})$) was defined in [19] as a finite prefix of the maximal process of $\mathcal{N}$ such that each reachable marking of $\mathcal{N}$ occurs as an image of output conditions of some computation of this prefix. It can be shown to be unique and finite.

The time Petri net is the Petri net whose transitions are labelled by their earliest and latest firing times that denote the minimal and maximal, respectively, number of time units which may pass between the enabling of and the occurrence of the transitions.

Definition 8 *A* time Petri net *(labelled over Act) is a tuple* $\mathcal{TN} = (\mathcal{N} = (P,$ $T,\ F,\ m_0,\ l),\ eft,\ lft)$, *where* $\mathcal{N} = (P,\ T,\ F,\ m_0,\ l)$ *is a safe Petri net (labelled over Act) and* $eft, lft : T \to \mathbf{N}$ *are functions of the* earliest *and* latest *firing times of transitions, satisfying* $eft(t) \leq lft(t)$ *for all* $t \in T$.

Let $\mathcal{V}(\mathcal{TN}) = [T \to \mathbf{N}]$ be the set of *time assignments* for transitions from T. A *state* of $\mathcal{TN}$ is a pair (m, ν), where m is a marking and $\nu \in \mathcal{V}(\mathcal{TN})$. The *initial state* of $\mathcal{TN}$ is a pair (m_0, ν_0), where $\nu_0(t) = 0$ for all $t \in T$. In a state (m, ν), a transition $t \in T$ may *fire after a delay* $\delta \in \mathbf{N}$ if $t \in En(m)$, $eft(t) \leq \delta$, and $\delta \leq lft(t')$ for all $t' \in En(m)$. In this case, the state (m', ν') is obtained by firing t after a delay δ (written $(m, \nu) \overset{(t,\delta)}{\to} (m', \nu')$), if $m \overset{t}{\to} m'$ and for all $t' \in T$ it holds: $\nu'(t') = 0$ if $t' \in En(m') \setminus En(m)$, $\nu'(t') = \delta$ if $t' = t$, otherwise $\nu'(t') = \nu(t')$. A state (m, ν) is *reachable* if $(m, \nu) = (m_0, \nu_0)$ or there exists a reachable state (m', ν') such that $(m', \nu') \overset{(t,\delta)}{\to} (m, \nu)$ for some $t \in T$ and $\delta \in \mathbf{N}$. Let $RS(\mathcal{TN})$ denote the set of all reachable states of $\mathcal{TN}$. A *run* r in $\mathcal{TN}$ is a sequence of the form: $(m_0, \nu_0) \overset{(t_1,\delta_1)}{\to} (m_1, \nu_1) \ldots (m_{n-1}, \nu_{n-1}) \overset{(t_n,\delta_n)}{\to} (m_n, \nu_n) \ldots$. To guarantee that in any run, time is increasing beyond any bound, we need the following *progress condition*: for every set of transitions $\{t_1, t_2, \ldots, t_n\}$ such that $\forall 1 \leq i < n \circ t_i^\bullet \cap {}^\bullet t_{i+1} \neq \emptyset$ and $t_n^\bullet \cap {}^\bullet t_1 \neq \emptyset$ it holds $\sum_{1 \leq i \leq n} eft(t_i) > 0$. In the sequel, $\mathcal{TN}$ will always denote a time Petri net satisfying the progress condition.

Let $\mathcal{TN} = (\mathcal{N} = (P, T, F, m_0, l), eft, lft)$ be a time Petri net, and (N, ϕ) be a process of $\mathcal{N}$. Then

- a mapping $\sigma : E_N \longrightarrow \mathbf{N}$ is called a *timing* of N;
- if $\overline{B} \subseteq B_N$ and $t \in En(\phi(\overline{B}))$, then the *time of enabling* for t in $\overline{B}$ under σ is given by: $TOE_\sigma(\overline{B}, t) = \max(\{\sigma(e) \mid \{e\} = {}^\bullet b, b \in (\overline{B} \setminus {}^\bullet N), \phi(b) \in {}^\bullet t\} \cup \{0\})$;
- a timing σ is *valid* iff for all $e \in E_N$ the following holds: $eft(\phi(e)) \leq \sigma(e) - TOE_\sigma({}^\bullet e, \phi(e)) \leq lft(\phi(e))$. Let $VT(N, \phi)$ denote the set of valid timings of (N, ϕ);
- $(T(N), \phi)$ is called a *timed process* of $\mathcal{TN}$ iff $T(N) = \bigcup((N_\sigma, Eot_\sigma, Lot_\sigma) \mid \sigma \in VT(N, \phi))$, where
  - $N_\sigma = (B, E, G, L)$ with
    - $B_{N_\sigma} = \{b_\sigma \mid b \in B_N\} \cup \{\tilde{b} \mid \tilde{b} \notin B_N\}$;
    - $E_{N_\sigma} = \{e_\sigma \mid e \in E_N\} \cup \{\tilde{e}_\sigma \mid \tilde{e}_\sigma \notin E_N\}$;

$$* \ F_{N_\sigma} = \{(e_\sigma, b_\sigma), (b_\sigma, e_\sigma) \mid (e, b), (b, e) \in F_N\} \cup \{(\widetilde{b}, \widetilde{e}_\sigma)\} \cup$$
$$\{(\widetilde{e}_\sigma, b) \mid b \in {}^\bullet N\};$$
$$* \ L_{N_\sigma}(e_\sigma) = L_N(e) \text{ for all } e_\sigma \in (E_{N_\sigma} \setminus \{\widetilde{e}_\sigma\}), \ L_{N_\sigma}(\widetilde{e}_\sigma) = \widetilde{a} \ (\widetilde{a} \notin Act_N);$$

- $Eot_{N_\sigma}(e_\sigma) = \sigma(e)$ for all $e_\sigma \in (E_{N_\sigma} \setminus \{\widetilde{e}_\sigma\})$, $Eot_{N_\sigma}(\widetilde{e}_\sigma) = 0$;
- $Lot_{N_\sigma}(e_\sigma) = \sigma(e)$ for all $e_\sigma \in (E_{N_\sigma} \setminus \{\widetilde{e}_\sigma\})$, $Lot_{N_\sigma}(\widetilde{e}_\sigma) = 0$.

We call $T(N)$ the *time-expansion* of a process (N, ϕ).

Proposition 3 *Let* $\mathcal{TN} = (\mathcal{N}, eft, lft)$ *be a time Petri net,* (N, ϕ) *be a process of* $\mathcal{N}$, *and* $McM(\mathcal{N}) = (N_u, \phi_u)$ *be the McMillan-unfolding of* $\mathcal{N}$. *Then*

(i) $T(N)$ *is a timed net process;*
(ii) *if* N *is finite, then* $T(N)$ *is finite;*
(iii) *if* $(m, \nu) \in RS(\mathcal{TN})$ *and* t *may fire after* δ *in* (m, ν), *then there exists* $(\pi, \tau) \in RS(T(N_u))$ *and* $e_\sigma \in E_{T(N_u)}$ *such that* $\phi_u \{b \mid b_\sigma \in \pi^\bullet\} = m$, $\phi_u(e) = t$, *and* e_σ *may occur at* $(\delta + TOE_\sigma({}^\bullet e, t))$ *in* (π, τ), *for some* $\sigma \in VT(N_u, \phi_u)$.

We say that two time Petri nets are *timed bisimilar* iff the time expansions of their maximal processes are timed bisimilar.

Given time Petri nets $\mathcal{TN} = (\mathcal{N}, eft, lft)$ and $\mathcal{TN}' = (\mathcal{N}', eft', lft')$, a procedure for checking timed bisimulation between $\mathcal{TN}$ and $\mathcal{TN}'$ consists of the following steps: (1) constructing the McMillan-unfolding of $\mathcal{N}$ and $\mathcal{N}'$, $McM(\mathcal{N}) = (N_u, \phi_u)$ and $McM(\mathcal{N}') = (N'_u, \phi'_u)$, respectively; (2) computing the sets of valid timings of (N_u, ϕ_u) and (N'_u, ϕ'_u), $VT(N_u, \phi_u)$ and $VT(N'_u, \phi'_u)$, respectively; (3) constructing the time net processes $T(N_u)$ and $T(N'_u)$, respectively; (4) checking timed bisimulation between $T(N_u)$ and $T(N'_u)$.

Make some remarks on the complexity of the above procedure: the complexity of the construction of the McMillan-unfolding of a safe Petri net is polynomial in the net's size [9], the complexity of the computation of the set of valid timings is exponential in the size of a time Petri net, and hence, the size of the constructed timed net process is also exponential; the complexity of checking for timed bisimulation between timed net processes is exponential in their sizes (see the sketch proof of Theorem 7), however, for Petri nets with discrete time it can be simplified significantly.

Appendix

Proof Sketch of Theorem 4. We first construct $TN_X = (N, Eot, Lot)$ as follows:

- $N_{TN_X} = \cup(N_{\pi_1 \times \pi_2} \mid \pi_i \in Proc(N_i), \ \exists \pi \in Proc(N) \circ \pi = (\lambda_i, \mu_i) \cdot \pi_i \ (i = 1, 2))$, where $N_{\pi_1 \times \pi_2} = (B, E, G, L)$ with
  - $E_{\pi_1 \times \pi_2} = \{(e_1, e_2) \mid e_i \in E_{\pi_i}, \ \exists e \in E_\pi \circ e = \mu_i(e_i) \ (i = 1, 2)\}$;
  - $B_{\pi_1 \times \pi_2} = \{(b_1, b_2) \mid b_i \in B_{\pi_i}, \ \exists b \in B_\pi \circ b = \lambda_i(b_i) \ (i = 1, 2)\}$;
  - $G_{\pi_1 \times \pi_2} = \{((b_1, b_2), (e_1, e_2)) \mid (b_i, e_i) \in G_{\pi_i} \text{ for some } i = 1, 2\} \cup$
    $\{((e_1, e_2), (b_1, b_2)) \mid (e_i, b_i) \in G_{\pi_i} \text{ for some } i = 1, 2\}$;
  - $L_{\pi_1 \times \pi_2}((e_1, e_2)) = L_{N_1}(e_1) = L_{N_2}(e_2)$;

- $Eot_{TN_X}((e_1, e_2)) = \max\{Eot_{TN_1}(e_1), Eot_{TN_2}(e_2)\};$
- $Lot_{TN_X}((e_1, e_2)) = \min\{Lot_{TN_1}(e_1), Lot_{TN_2}(e_2)\}.$

Basing on the construction, it can be shown that TN_X is a timed net process. Define mappings $(\lambda_i', \mu_i') : TN_X \to TN_i$ as follows: $\lambda_i'((b_1, b_2)) = b_i$ and $\mu_i'((e_1, e_2)) = e_i$ $(i = 1, 2)$. According to the construction of TN_X, these mappings are morphisms. Moreover, it holds that $(\lambda_1', \mu_1') \circ (\lambda_1, \mu_1) = (\lambda_2', \mu_2') \circ (\lambda_2, \mu_2)$. This implies that the diagram (see Theorem 4) commutes. Further using the construction of TN_X and Theorem 3, it is straightforward to show that $(\lambda_i', \mu_i') : TN_X \to TN_i$ is a TW-open morphism for $i = 1, 2$. $\square$

Proof Sketch of Theorem 6.

$(\Rightarrow)$ Let $TN_1 \overset{(\lambda_1, \mu_1)}{\longleftarrow} TN \overset{(\lambda_2, \mu_2)}{\longrightarrow} TN_2$ be a span of TW-open maps. Define a relation $\mathcal{B}$ as follows: $\mathcal{B} = \{((\pi_1, \tau_1), (\pi_2, \tau_2)) \mid (\pi_i, \tau_i) \in RS(TN_i), \exists (\pi, \tau) \in RS(TN) \circ (\lambda_i, \mu_i) \cdot \pi = \pi_i, \tau \mid_{E_\pi} = \tau_i \mid_{\mu_i(E_\pi)} \;\; (i = 1, 2)\}$. We then have $((\pi_{N_1}, \overline{0}), ((\pi_{N_2}, \overline{0})) \in \mathcal{B}$. Since (λ_1, μ_1) and (λ_2, μ_2) are TW-open morphisms, it is straightforward to show that $\mathcal{B}$ is a timed bisimulation, using Theorem 3.

$(\Leftarrow)$ Assume $\mathcal{B}$ be a timed bisimulation between TN_1 and TN_2. We first construct $TN = (N, Eot, Lot)$ as follows:

- $N_{TN} = (B, E, G, L)$ with
  - $E_{N_{TN}} = \{(e_1, e_2) \mid (\pi_i, \tau_i) \overset{(e_i, d)}{\longrightarrow} (\pi_i', \tau_i') \text{ in } TN_i \; (i = 1, 2),$
    $((\pi_1', \tau_1'), (\pi_2', \tau_2')) \in \mathcal{B}, L_{TN_1}(e_1) = L_{TN_2}(e_2)\};$
  - $B_{N_{TN}} = \{(b_1, b_2) \mid \exists (e_1, e_2) \in E_{N_{TN}} \circ b_i \in {}^\bullet e_i \vee b_i \in e_i^\bullet, \; (i = 1, 2)\};$
  - $G_{N_{TN}} = \{((b_1, b_2), (e_1, e_2)) \mid b_i \in \pi_i^\bullet, \; (b_i, e_i) \in G_{N_i} \text{ for some } i = 1, 2\} \cup$
    $\{((e_1, e_2), (b_1, b_2)) \mid b_i \in \pi_i'^\bullet, \; (e_i, b_i) \in G_{N_i} \text{ for some } i = 1, 2\};$
  - $L_{N_{TN}}((e_1, e_2)) = L_{N_1}(e_1) = L_{N_2}(e_2);$
- $Eot_{TN}((e_1, e_2)) = \max\{Eot_{TN_1}(e_1), Eot_{TN_2}(e_2)\};$
- $Lot_{TN}((e_1, e_2)) = \min\{Lot_{TN_1}(e_1), Lot_{TN_2}(e_2)\}.$

Basing on the construction it can be shown that TN is a timed net process. Define mappings $(\lambda_i, \mu_i) : TN \to TN_i$ as $\lambda_i((b_1, b_2)) = b_i$ and $\mu_i((e_1, e_2)) = e_i$ $(i = 1, 2)$. From the construction of TN, it follows that these mappings are morphisms. Further using the definition of timed bisimulation, the construction of TN, and Theorem 3, it is straightforward to show that $(\lambda_i, \mu_i) : TN \to TN_i$ is a TW-open morphism for $i = 1, 2$. $\square$

References

1. L. Aceto, D. Murphi. Timing and causality in process algebra. *Acta Informatica* **33**(4) (1996) 317–350.
2. R. Alur, D. Dill. The theory of timed automata. *Theoretical Computer Science* **126** (1994) 183–235.
3. T. Aura, J. Lilius. Time processes for time Petri nets. *Lecture Notes in Computer Science* **1248** (1997) 136–155.
4. B. Bieber, H. Fleischhack. Model checking of time Petri nets based on partial order semantics. *Lecture Notes in Computer Science* **1662** (1999) 211–225.
5. C. Brown, D. Gurr. Timing Petri nets categorically. *Lecture Notes in Computer Science* **623** (1992) 571–582.

6. R.T. Casley, R.F. Crew, J. Meseguer, V.R. Pratt. Temporal structures. *Mathematical Structures in Computer Science* **1**(2) (1991) 179–213.

7. K. Čerāns. Decidability of bisimulation equivalences for parallel timer processes. *Lecture Notes in Computer Science* **663** (1993) 302–315.

8. J. Engelfriet. Branching processes of Petri nets. *Acta Informatica* **28** (1991) 576–591.

9. J. Esparza, S. Roemer, W.Vogler An improvement of McMillan's unfolding algorithm. *Lecture Notes in Computer Science* **1055** (1996) (87–106).

10. M. Hennessy, R. Milner. Algebraic laws for nondeterminism and concurrency. *Journal of ACM* **32** (1985) 137–162.

11. T. Hune, M. Nielsen. Bisimulation and open maps for timed transition systems. *Fundamenta Informaticae* **38**(1-2) (1999) 61–77.

12. A. Joyal, M. Nielsen, G. Winskel. Bisimulation from open maps. *Information and Computation* **127(2)** (1996) 164–185.

13. J.-P. Katoen, R. Langerak, D. Latella, E. Brinksma. On specifying real-time systems in a causality-based setting. *Lecture Notes in Computer Science* **1135** (1996) 385–404.

14. F. Laroussinie, K.G. Larsen, C. Weise. From timed automata to logic and back. *Lecture Notes in Computer Science* **969** (1995) 529–539.

15. J. Lilius. Efficient state space search for time Petri nets. Proc. MFCS'98 Workshop on Concurrency, August 1998, Brno (Czech Republic), FIMU Report Series, FIMU RS-98-06 (1998) 123–130.

16. P. Merlin, D.J. Faber. Recoverability of communication protocols. *IEEE Trans. of Communication* COM-**24**(9) (1976).

17. J. Meseguer, U. Montanari. Petri nets are monoids. *Information and Computation* **88** (1990) 105–154.

18. J. Meseguer, U. Montanari, V. Sassone. Process versus unfolding semantics for Place/Transition Petri nets. *Theoretical Computer Science* **153** (1996) 171–210.

19. K. McMillan. Symbolic model checking – an aproach to the state explosion problem. PhD Thesis, SCS, Carnegie Mellon University (1992).

20. D. Murphy. Time and duration in noninterleaving concurrency. *Fundamenta Informaticae* **19** (1993) 403–416.

21. X. Nicolin, J. Sifakis. An overview and synthesis on timed process algebras. *Lecture Notes in Computer Science* **600** (1992) 526–548.

22. M. Nielsen, A. Cheng. Observing behaviour categorically. *Lecture Notes in Computer Science* **1026** (1996) 263–278.

23. M. Nielsen, G. Winskel. Petri nets and bisimulation. *Theoretical Computer Science* **153** (1996).

24. C. Ramchandani. Analysis of asynchronous concurrent systems by timed Petri nets. Cambridge, Mass.: MIT, Dept. Electronical Engineering, PhD Thesis, 1974.

25. V. Sassone. On the category of Petri Net Computations. *Lecture Notes in Computer Science* **915** (1995) 334–348.

26. V. Valero, D. de Frutos, F. Cuartero. Timed Processes of Timed Petri Nets. *Lecture Notes in Computer Science* **935** (1995) 490–509.

27. C. Weise, D. Lenzkes. Efficient scaling-invariant checking of timed bisimulation. *Lecture Notes in Computer Science* **1200** (1997) 176–188.

28. G. Winskel. Petri nets, algebras, morphisms, compositionality. *Information and Computation* **72** (1987) 197–238.

29. G. Winskel, M. Nielsen. Models for concurrency. In *Handbook of Logic in Computer Science* **4** (1995).

Mapping Heterogeneous Task Graphs onto Networks: Execution Time Optimization

Natalya Vodovoz (candidate)

Perm State University
Snaiperov st. 11-46, 614022 Russia
vodovoz@permonline.ru

Abstract. The paper presents a formulation for the problem of mapping parallel programs on heterogeneous networks and proposes a distributed recursive (heuristic) algorithm for its solution. This algorithm doesn't require global knowledge of computational state, it uses only information obtained from a neighbours nodes. Parallel programs and networks are presented as weighted graphs. In each stage graph bisection strategy is used to divide all processes of the program on two groups, which farther may be sent to neighbour nodes, where algorithm will be continued in the same way, or be leaved on initial node.

1. Introduction

The task is to distribute processes of a parallel program in a heterogeneous network as to minimize execution time of this program. It would allow adapting the same programs to different network topologies increasing program effectiveness and decreasing communication costs.

2. Models

It is necessary to examine structures of different parallel programs to solve mapping problem. Therefore we should choose a model by which a lot of parallel programs can be presented, i.e. it must be abstract enough. The abstraction of particular network details enhances a model's architecture independence. This enables algorithms and software to be portable across several types of parallel systems. Graph model provides complete abstraction from the explicit expression of parallelism and details of communication and synchronization.

2.1. Graph Model of the Program

A program graph is a directed graph $G=(V, E)$ with

V. Malyshkin (Ed.): PaCT 2001, LNCS 2127, pp. 142–149, 2001.

- $V=\{(v_i, cv_i)\}$ - a set of vertices v_i with complexity of cv_i,
- $E=\{(e_k, ie_k)\}$ - a set of arcs $e_k=(v_i, v_j)$ with communication cost of ie_k.

Let a process complexity be the number of instructions a process will do from its initiation to completion. Let a communication cost from process v_i to v_j be a number of bytes that process v_i sent to v_j during one execution of a program. Then communication cost ie between processes v_i and v_j be the sum of communication costs $v_i \rightarrow v_j$ and $v_j \rightarrow v_i$.

2.2. Graph Model of the Network

The network is modelled by a graph $S=(W, Q)$, where $W=\{(w_i, f_i)\}$ is a set of vertices (nodes, computers) with weight of f_i, and $Q=\{(q_i, g_i)\}$ is a set of arcs (channels) with weight of g_i. As well as for program graph, it is necessary to estimate computer capacities and speed of channels to nominate weights of vertices and arcs.

2.2.1. Computer Capacity Estimate

Computer capacity unit of measurements is the time: the computer, which is carrying out same volume of work for smaller time is faster. The time of performance of any program is measured in seconds. Frequently productivity is measured as speed of occurrence of some number of events per one second, so the smaller time means large productivity.

The time of the central processor for some program can be expressed by two ways: by amount of synchronization steps for the given program multiplied on synchronization step duration, or amount of synchronization steps for the given program, divided on frequency of synchronization. The important characteristic of the processor is the average amount of clock cycles per instruction (CPI). With known amount of carried out instructions in the program this parameter allows to estimate time of the central processor for the given program.

Thus, the productivity of the central processor depends on three parameters: frequencies of synchronization ω, average amount of steps per instruction λ and amount of carried out instructions. When two computers compared it is necessary to consider all three components to get relative capacity.

Thus, executions time if process v_i on processor q_j is

$$\tau_{ij} = \frac{\lambda_j * cv_i}{\omega_j}. \tag{1}$$

But the task executing on the computer occupies processor and resources. Therefore computer capacity for other tasks becomes lower. Then execution time of process v_i on processor q_j is

$$\overline{\tau_{ij}} = \frac{\lambda_j * cv_i}{\omega_j} + \mu, \text{ where } \mu = \sum_k \tau_{kj} \text{ - execution time of previous tasks.} \tag{2}$$

2.2.2 Channel Speed Estimates

The information transfer speed in a network depends on latency and throughput of channels.

Latency is a transfer time of the empty message. Using this size one can measure software delays (time of accessing to a network on the side of the sender and receiver).

Throughput limits from above volume of the traffic which sender can transfer to the receiver for a time unit. With measurement of this characteristic the opportunity of a competition of several flows for throughput should be taken into account.

According to the entered above definitions, the transfer time of the message containing *length* bit on direct connection from one computer to other is defined (determined) as

$$t = latency + length / throughput$$

(3)

The productivity of a network is worsened in conditions of an overload (when there are many messages simultaneously in a network). How the overload will affect on the entered characteristics depends on technology of a particular network.

3. Execution Time Optimization

Execution time of a parallel program is the time that elapses from when the first processor starts executing on the problem to when the last processor completes execution.

During execution, each processor is computing, communicating, or idling Hence, total execution time T can be defined as the sum of computation, communication, and idle times of all p processors:

$$T = \sum_{i=1}^{p} \left(T_{comp}^i + T_{comm}^i + T_{idle}^i \right),$$

(4)

Where T_{comp}^i, T_{comm}^i, T_{idle}^i are the time spent computing, communicating, and idling, respectively, on the ith processor.

Taking into account graph model of a program and a network:

$$T_6^i = \sum_j cv_{tj} * f_i, \quad T_\kappa^i = \sum_k \left(latency + \frac{ie_{tk}}{g_l} \right),$$

(5)

Where process v_{tj} was placed on the vertex w_i for each j (processes with numbers $j_1 \neq j_2$ can be placed to the same vertex of a network).

Both computation and communication times specified explicitly in a parallel algorithm; hence, it is generally straightforward to determine their contribution to execution time. Idle time can be more difficult to determine, however, since it often depends on the order in which operations are performed.

So we can define two strategies in placing processes to the processors.

1. We place different tasks on different processors to decrease computation time.
2. We place tasks that communicate frequently on the same processor to decrease communication time.

Clearly, these two strategies will sometimes conflict, in which case our design will involve tradeoffs. In addition, resource limitations may restrict the number of tasks that can be placed on a single processor.

The mapping problem is known to be NP-complete. Therefore it should be solved approximately or using heuristic knowledge about program and network.

3.1. Recursive Graph Partitioning

In recursive bisection, we partition a domain (e.g., a finite element grid) into sub-domains of approximately equal computational cost while attempting to minimize communication costs, that is, the number of channels crossing task boundaries.

$$\sum_i cv_{i,1} \approx \sum_j cv_{j,2} \text{, where } \left(v_{i,k}, cv_{i,k} \right) \in G_k, k = \overline{1,2} \tag{6}$$

$$\sum_n ie_n \rightarrow \min \text{, where } \left(\left(v_{i,1}, v_{j,2} \right), ie_n \right) \in G \tag{7}$$

The domain is first cut in one dimension to yield two sub-domains. Cuts are then made recursively in the new sub-domains until we have as many sub-domains as we require tasks. Notice that this recursive strategy allows the partitioning algorithm itself to be executed in parallel.

Partitioning into two approximately equal parts is oriented to the parallel computers in which all processes are the same productivity and channels are quick. In the networks it is expediently to accentuate on minimizing sub-domains communication because of low communication speed. We should find a minimum cut of the graph G to solve this problem. But this task has very high complexity and we can't use an exact solution here.

We will use connectivity information to reduce the number of edges crossing sub-domain boundaries, and hence to reduce communication requirements. First we should identify two extremities of the graph v_1 and v_2, that is, the two vertices that are the most separated in terms of graph distance. (The graph distance between two vertices is the smallest number of edges that must be traversed to go between them.) Include extremities in G_1 and G_2. Then for each of remaining vertices calculate its distances to the extremities (r_1 and r_2). If $r_2 > r_1$ then vertex is included into G_1, if $r_2 > r_1$ then in G_2. And if $r_1 = r_2$ then the decision about vertex place is taken on the basis of heuristic knowledge (vertex is included in the smallest graph or in the graph with more incident vertices).

The complexity of this algorithm is $O(N^3)$ in the worst case. The exactness of the solution depends on initial graph class.

3.2. Optimizing Algorithm

Mapping algorithm will be developed within the model "the hierarchical manager/worker". On a first step there are given two graphs G_0 - program graph and S - network graph. It is necessary to map $G_0 \rightarrow S$ with minimum execution time.

1. Let all processes work on one computer. Program performance time estimation is
   $$t_0 = \sum_i cv_i * f .$$ This is a lower bound of T, since the processes interaction does

   not take into account (one process can suspend execution before reception of the data from other process, and it increases general execution time).

2. Let divide G_0 into two graphs G_0^1 and G_0^2 using recursive graph partitioning and calculate program execution time on two nodes w_1 and w_2 connected by arc (e, g):

$$t_1 = \max\left(\sum_i cv_i * f_1, \sum_j cv_j * f_2\right) + \sum_{k=1}^{M}\left(latency + \frac{ie_k}{g} * M\right), \tag{8}$$

where M is a number of arcs between G_0^1 and G_0^2.

   Since the graph of a network can be rather large, it would be not effective to examine all pairs of computers, on which the received groups of processes could be executed. Therefore we shall limit ourselves by neighbours of the current computer, i.e. having direct connection with it. It will strongly reduce complexity of algorithm, though reducing accuracy. Let t_1 be the minimum among all the nodes connected to the initiator.

3. If $t_1 \leq t_0$ then all processes will be placed on two computers.

   If $t_0 \gg \sum_{k=1}^{M}\left(latency + \frac{ie_k}{g} * M\right)$, then dividing program in two groups, we

   will reduce the whole program execution time T, so all processes will be placed on two computers. Go to *step* 5.
4. The program will be executed on initiator. End.
5. Continue algorithm for node w_1 and w_2.

   On the second step we divide initial graph G_0 getting two new graphs G_0^1 and G_0^2. After it a number of arcs connecting G_0^1 and G_0^2 become lost to this graphs. After the first division, they are available through the graph G_0 but further new groups of processes will not have an access to initiator. Sending G_0 with new graphs is not effective because $G_0^i \subset G_0$. It is more convenient to get G_0' from G_0 by indicating in each node, which graph G_0^1 or G_0^2 it is included by (before sending

G_0' on processor w_i we will write on G_0' vertices processor identifier). Therefore, in each step we will know where all groups of processes are situated. Such program graph in vertices of which is written where this vertex is situated will be referred as *mapping graph*.

Lets demonstrate on the simple example how this algorithm works. The initial graph is G_0 (homogenous grid). Network consists of six nodes, where node 5, which is more powerful than others, is the initiator (Fig. 1).

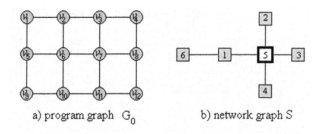

a) program graph G_0 b) network graph S

Fig. 1. Program and network graphs

On the first step we divide vertices of G_0 on two groups, mark them and send one copy of the marked graph to node 1 (Fig. 2). This means that executing processes on two nodes (1 and 5) will take less time than executing on one node.

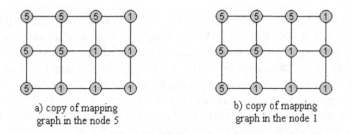

a) copy of mapping   b) copy of mapping
graph in the node 5   graph in the node 1

Fig. 2. First step of the mapping algorithm

On the second step node 1 divides its graph, remarks it and sends copy of new marked graph to the node 6. As node 5 is more powerful, it leaves all processes with mark "5" to be executed on it. On this step we can see two different versions of mapping graph in a network (Fig. 3).

The problem of different copies reduces accuracy of algorithm. However, the error will be small because the processes with direct interconnection placed on the same or close nodes.

Resulting distribution, received by given algorithm, and exact solution, received by exhaustive search, are shown on Fig. 4.

As one can see the difference between exact and heuristic solution is one arc.

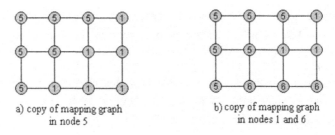

a) copy of mapping graph
in node 5

b) copy of mapping graph
in nodes 1 and 6

Fig. 3. Graph copies on the last step

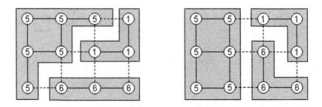

Fig. 4. Resulting distribution (left) and exact solution (right).

Conclusions and Future Work

The distributed heuristic algorithm presented in this paper uses classical presentation of parallel programs and networks as weighted graphs and well-known graph bisection strategy (which though can be replaced by another one). But in implementation of this algorithm one should use more complex presentation of networks (for example, to take into account features of bus networks or stars with hubs). To prevent deadlocks the result program can be organized as hierarchical manager/worker, where each level of hierarchy has its own number mark. Node with larger marks can't be the manager to the node with smaller mark.

Future work will be the implementation of presented algorithm and detailed investigation of its behaviour for different applications and networks.

References

1. Carol A. Ziegler. Programming System Methodologies. Prentice Hall, Inc. Englewood Cliffs, N. J. 1983.
2. Victor Shnitman. Modern supercomputer architectures, 1996. From www.citforum.ru.
3. Steve Steinke. Throughput optimization // LAN/Network magazine, 2/1999, pp.102-107.
4. Ian Foster. Designing and Building Parallel Program: Concepts and Tools for Parallel Software Engineering - Addison-Wesley Publishing Co, 1995.

5. B. Schnor and M.Gehrke. Dynamic-SED for Load Balancing of Parallel Applications in Heterogeneous Systems. Proceedings of the International Conference on Parallel and distributed Processing Techniques and Applications, PDPTA'97, pages 442-449, Las Vegas, NV, July 1997.
6. M.M. Eshaghian and Y.C. Wu. Mapping Heterogeneous Task Graphs onto Heterogeneous System Graphs. Proceedings of the Sixth Heterogeneous Computing Workshop, pages 147-160, Geneva, 1997.
7. Muhammad Kafil and Ishfaq Ahmad. Optimal Task Assignment in Heterogeneous Computing Systems. Proceedings of the Sixth Heterogeneous Computing Workshop, pages 135-146, Geneva, 1997.

An $O\left[\dfrac{n^3}{z^3}\right]$ Reduction Procedure

for Determining the Maximum Degree of Parallelism in Parallel Applications

Igor V. Zotov and Vitaliy S. Titov

Kursk State Technical University, Department of Computer Science,
94, 50 let Oktyabrya, 305040 Kursk, Russian Federation
zotov@kursknet.ru, titov@cafct.kursk.ru

Abstract. In the present work, fine-grain parallel applications of a wide class to be executed on distributed-memory multiprocessors are investigated. The problem of determining the maximum degree of parallelism in the control flow of such applications is under consideration. An efficient procedure (called R-procedure) for solving the indicated problem is introduced and stated. The procedure operates on a control flow graph of an application, and it provides fast calculation of the parallelism degree through the technique of reduction of the control flow graph. The R-procedure is shown to have the time complexity of at most $O\left[\dfrac{n^3}{z^3}\right]$, with n and z standing for the number of processes in the application and parallelism degree, respectively.

1 Introduction and Characteristic of the Problem

In the present work, we investigate fine-grain parallel applications of a wide class, the applications to be executed on distributed-memory multiprocessors (DMMP) [1], [2]. One of the important problems that arise in treating this type of applications is to determine the maximum degree of parallelism in their control flow. If we were able to calculate this degree, we could, for example, get information on how many processors must be involved within a DMMP to optimally implement the application in such a fashion that no pair of mutually parallel modules (processes) are assigned to the same processor. Calculating the parallelism degree for an application, in general, requires exhaustive search among different combinations of processes within the application resulting in exponential time complexity. Thus, we need to take a different approach to reduce the overhead.

We introduce a procedure for efficiently solving the indicated problem. Our procedure provides fast calculation of the parallelism degree through the technique of reduction of a control flow graph of an application. We show the procedure to have the time complexity of at most $O\left[\dfrac{n^3}{z^3}\right]$, with n and z standing for the number of processes in the application and parallelism degree, respectively.

V. Malyshkin (Ed.): PaCT 2001, LNCS 2127, pp. 150–158, 2001.

2 Description of the Procedure

To represent an application to be analyzed, we introduce a single-entry-single-termination control flow graph G [3]. G is a directed graph with a set of vertices V and a set of arcs $E \subseteq V \times V$. Each vertex $a_j \in V$ corresponds to a particular process in the application, and an arc $e_{jm} \equiv (a_j, a_m) \in E$ shows a_m to be a direct successor to a_j in the application's control flow. Graph G contains a vertex a_0 which has no incoming arcs, and a vertex a_* that has no outgoing ones; a_0 is called the initial vertex (the entry point) of G at which the application comes into execution, a_* is said to be the termination vertex (the termination point) at which the application gets dead.

Remark 1. Hereinafter, we use the terms "vertex" and "process" interchangeably.

Remark 2. To help the following analysis, we ignore data flows between processes.

Remark 3. We consider general case control flow graphs in which any vertex may stand for a complex subgraph in turn. Say, a process denoted as a_j in G may have a number of parallel threads whose precedence can be depicted by a separate control flow graph.

Parallel applications of the considered class are known to have conditional and parallel branching points [4]. To incorporate these points in our application model, we introduce two additional sets of vertices, $V^\oplus$ and V^*. A vertex $a_j \in V^\oplus$ will represent a conditional branching point, and a vertex $a_m \in V^*$ will stand for a parallel branching (barrier) point. In the following, we assume that $V^\oplus \cup V^* \subset V$.

Remark 4. Each vertex $a_j \in V^\oplus$ is a predecessor of at least two other vertices $a_{m_1}, a_{m_2} \in V$ (i.e., $(a_j, a_{m_1}), (a_j, a_{m_2}) \in E$) and can transfer control to either a_{m_1} or a_{m_2}.

Remark 5. Each vertex $a_j \in V^*$ is a direct predecessor of at least two vertices $a_{m_1}, a_{m_2} \in V$ (i.e., $(a_j, a_{m_1}), (a_j, a_{m_2}) \in E$) and/or a direct successor for at least two vertices $a_{n_1}, a_{n_2} \in V$ (i.e., $(a_{n_1}, a_j), (a_{n_2}, a_j) \in E$).

Remark 6. Hereinafter, we suppose that the initial graph G contains no cyclic paths (loops); otherwise we transform G by conventionally eliminating some arcs using the following procedure. We trace any path emanating from the initial vertex a_0 until it reaches either the termination vertex a_* or a vertex a_l that has already been passed by. If we have found the vertex a_l, then we eliminate its incoming arc that has led us into a_l. In the same fashion, we eliminate all similar arcs. We denote the graph obtained through the above-mentioned transformation as G^*. Let E^* be the set of arcs in G^*.

Remark 7. The described procedure makes the initial graph have several hypothetical termination points (first is a_*, and the others are vertices devoid of their outgoing arcs due to the above transformation). To avoid these extra termination points, we may introduce additional arcs in such a way that any parallel vertices in G are still parallel in G^*.

To provide formal representation to our procedure, let us define the (indirect) successor σ, disjunction δ, and parallelism π relations on the set V.

Definition 1. A vertex a_j is said to be a successor of a vertex a_m, i.e., $a_j \sigma a_m$, if there exists a path connecting a_m to a_j in G^*.

Definition 2. Two vertices a_m and a_j are supposed to be in the disjunction relation, i.e., $a_j \delta a_m$, if they are covered by two alternative paths emanating from a vertex $a_s \in V^{\oplus}$ in G^*.

Definition 3. Vertices a_m and a_j are assumed to be in the parallelism relation, i.e., $a_j \pi a_m$, if not $a_j \delta a_m$ and not $a_j \sigma a_m$ and not $a_m \sigma a_j$.

Relation π can be represented by a graph $\Pi = \langle V, \pi \rangle$ whose vertices correspond to those of G, and any two vertices a_m and a_j are coupled by an edge iff $a_j \pi a_m$. Graph Π is convenient to refer to as the parallelism relation graph.

In terms of the above-defined relations, we can reformulate the initial problem as searching for a clique within the parallelism relation graph Π. To solve such a problem, it is possible to employ known methods for finding a clique in a graph. In this case, however, we need to supply the graph Π as an input to these methods (i.e., the initial application is first required to transform into Π). We take another approach that makes no need to directly construct a graph Π, and calculates a clique for Π implicitly through graceful reduction of the graph G^*.

To provide a more formal statement to the reduction process, we specify a transformed graph G^* by a system of constructive expressions $\Xi = \{S_i\}_{i=\overline{1,Q}}$ of the following form

$$S_i = \left(i \colon R_1^i \to R_2^i \right), \quad R_1^i, R_2^i \subset V, \quad i = \overline{1,Q},$$

where R_1^i and R_2^i are sets of vertices such that $R_1^i \cap R_2^i = \varnothing$, $\forall a_j \in R_1^i, a_m \in R_2^i \colon (a_j, a_m) \in E$, and both R_1^i and R_2^i are maximal by inclusion.

It is evident that no two vertices of either R_1^i or R_2^i can be each other's direct or indirect successors. Thus, sets R_1^i, R_2^i can be represented in the following generalized constructive (parenthesis) form:

$$R_1^i = a_{m_1} \bullet \dots \bullet a_{m_f} \bullet \left(\tilde{R}_1^1 | \tilde{R}_2^1 | \dots | \tilde{R}_{\rho_1}^1 \right) \bullet \dots \bullet \left(\tilde{R}_1^h | \tilde{R}_2^h | \dots | \tilde{R}_{\rho_h}^h \right), \tag{1}$$

$$R_2^i = a_{l_1} \bullet \dots \bullet a_{l_v} \bullet \left(x_1^1 \overline{R}_1^1 | x_2^1 \overline{R}_2^1 | \dots | x_{\gamma_1}^1 \overline{R}_{\gamma_1}^1 \right) \bullet \dots \bullet \left(x_1^r \overline{R}_1^r | x_2^r \overline{R}_2^r | \dots | x_{\gamma_r}^r \overline{R}_{\gamma_r}^r \right), \tag{2}$$

where $\tilde{R}_{t'}^g$ $\left(g = \overline{1,h}, t' = \overline{1,\rho_g} \right)$ is a subset of vertices ($\tilde{R}_{t'}^g \subseteq R_1^i$) recursively defined in form (1); $\overline{R}_{t''}^g$ $\left(g = \overline{1,r}, t'' = \overline{1,\gamma_g} \right)$ is a subset of vertices ($\overline{R}_{t''}^g \subseteq R_2^i$) recursively defined in form (2); $x_{t''}^g$ is a logic condition that controls the transition from the vertices of R_1^i to the vertices of $\overline{R}_{t''}^g$; "$\bullet$" and "$|$" are constructive separators reflecting the parallelism and disjunction relations, respectively.

Figure 1 illustrates the construction of a system Ξ for a given control flow graph G (in the figure, symbols & and $\oplus$ denote vertices $a_m \in V^\&$ and $a_i \in V^\oplus$, respectively).

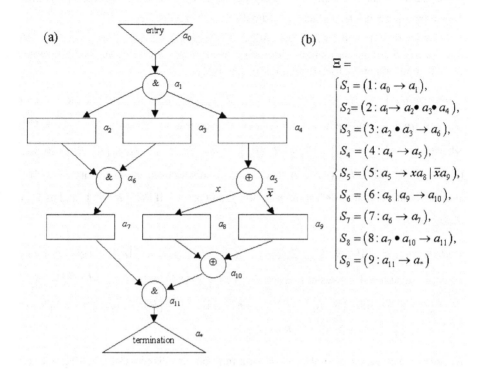

(a)

(b)

$$\Xi = \begin{cases} S_1 = (1 : a_0 \to a_1), \\ S_2 = (2 : a_1 \to a_2 \bullet a_3 \bullet a_4), \\ S_3 = (3 : a_2 \bullet a_3 \to a_6), \\ S_4 = (4 : a_4 \to a_5), \\ S_5 = (5 : a_5 \to x a_8 \mid \bar{x} a_9), \\ S_6 = (6 : a_8 \mid a_9 \to a_{10}), \\ S_7 = (7 : a_6 \to a_7), \\ S_8 = (8 : a_7 \bullet a_{10} \to a_{11}), \\ S_9 = (9 : a_{11} \to a_*) \end{cases}$$

Fig.1. Representation of a control flow graph by a system of constructive expressions (*a - graph G; b - system* Ξ *specifying graph G*

We introduce the relations of strict and non-strict constructive inclusion ([$\subset$] and [$\subseteq$]) possessing the properties of the strict and non-strict inclusion ($\subset$ and $\subseteq$), respectively.

Definition 4. Let R_{i_1} and R_{i_2} be subsets of vertices represented in form (1) (or (2)). We assume that

$$R_{i_2} [\subset] R_{i_1} \Leftrightarrow \left(R_{i_2} \neq R_{i_1} \right) \wedge \left(\exists \varsigma_\lambda^{i_1} \subset R_{i_1} : \varsigma_\lambda^{i_1} = R_{i_2} \right),$$

$$R_{i_2} [\subseteq] R_{i_1} \Leftrightarrow \left(R_{i_2} [\subset] R_{i_1} \right) \vee \left(R_{i_2} = R_{i_1} \right),$$

where $\varsigma_\lambda^{i_1}$ is a subset of vertices enclosed by a parenthesis in R_{i_1}, i.e., what we call "a constructive subset" of R_{i_1}.

Using the constructive inclusion relations gives us a formal and straightforward way to specify the hierarchy of control constructs in a control flow graph.

Let R be a set specified in form (1) (or (2)). R can include a certain number of mutually alternative or/and parallel vertices, taking into account those enclosed by parenthesis. To show the maximum of mutually parallel vertices that constitute R, we introduce a parameter referred to as "π-cardinality" of R and denoted as $|R|^{\pi}$.

Now let us define the operators (rules) of the proposed reduction procedure. We will specify these operators in the following form: if ψ, then fulfill φ, assuming ψ and φ are a condition and a transformation, respectively.

$\uparrow$-*absorption rule.* If $\exists S_i, S_k \in \Xi,\ i \neq k:\ R_1^k \left[\subseteq\right] R_2^i,\ a_* \notin R_2^k,\ \left|R_2^k\right|^{\pi} \geq \left|R_1^k\right|^{\pi}$, then we construct a new reduced subsystem of expressions $\Xi^- = \left[\Xi \backslash \{S_i, S_k\}\right] \cup \{S_i^0\}$, where $S_i^0 = \left(i: R_1^i \rightarrow \tilde{R}_2^i\right)$, $\tilde{R}_2^i = \left(R_2^i \backslash R_1^k\right) \triangleright \mathrm{subst}\left(R_2^k, R_1^k\right)$; $\mathrm{subst}\left(R_2^k, R_1^k\right)$ implies replacing R_2^k with R_1^k (we call this action a substitution, or an absorption); " $\triangleright$ " should be interpreted as "$\bullet$", if $R_1^k \bullet \left(R_2^i \backslash R_1^k\right)$, and as " $|$ ", if $R_1^k \,|\, \left(R_2^i \backslash R_1^k\right)$, and as $\emptyset$, if $R_2^i \backslash R_1^k = \emptyset$.

$\downarrow$-*absorption rule.* If $\exists S_i, S_k \in \Xi,\ i \neq k:\ R_2^i \left[\subseteq\right] R_1^k,\ a_0 \notin R_1^i,\ \left|R_1^i\right|^{\pi} \geq \left|R_2^i\right|^{\pi}$, then we construct a reduced subsystem $\Xi^- = \left[\Xi \backslash \{S_i, S_k\}\right] \cup \{S_k^0\}$, where $S_k^0 = \left(k: \tilde{R}_1^k \rightarrow R_2^k\right)$, $\tilde{R}_1^k = \left(R_1^k \backslash R_2^i\right) \triangleright \mathrm{subst}\left(R_1^i, R_2^i\right)$, " $\triangleright$ " = "$\bullet$", if $R_2^i \bullet \left(R_1^k \backslash R_2^i\right)$, " $\triangleright$ " = " $|$ ", if $R_2^i \,|\, \left(R_1^k \backslash R_2^i\right)$, " $\triangleright$ " = $\emptyset$, if $R_1^k \backslash R_2^i = \emptyset$.

Remark 8. The effect of $\uparrow$-absorption rule may be visualized as eliminating a subset of vertices (R_1^k) from the graph and reconnecting all their incoming arcs to their direct successors (R_2^k). This elimination is subject to the number of parallel vertices in R_2^k exceeds or is equal to that in R_1^k, i.e., $\left|R_2^k\right|^{\pi} \geq \left|R_1^k\right|^{\pi}$. The corresponding illustration is given in Fig.2. The effect of $\downarrow$-absorption rule is about the same, and also can be easily understood through exploring the example in Fig.2.

The above-defined rules allow us to formulate the reduction procedure (referred to as the *R*-procedure in the further) as follows.

1. Choose a pair of expressions $S_i, S_k \in \Xi$ satisfying the conditional part ψ of $\downarrow$-absorption or $\uparrow$-absorption rule. If no such pair is encountered, then terminate.

2. Transform the initial system Ξ to a reduced system Ξ^- according to the chosen rule.

3. Let $\Xi \equiv \Xi^-$ and go to step 1.

The procedure continues until a non-reducible system Ξ' specifying a hypothetical graph is obtained. Our thorough investigation has shown that the following theorem holds.

Theorem. Any system Ξ' resulting in the *R*-procedure always contains a pair of expressions $S_1 = \left(1: a_0 \rightarrow \Omega\right)$, $S_{Q'} = \left(Q': \Omega \rightarrow a_*\right)$, with Ω specifying a clique to be found; the π-cardinality of Ω yields the parallelism degree for the given graph G and the application analyzed ($z = |\Omega|^\pi$).

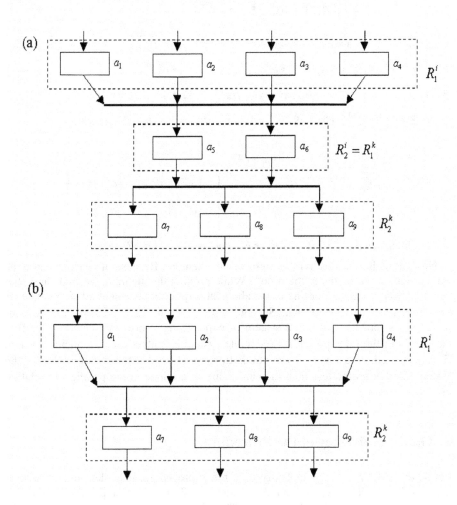

Fig.2. Effect of ↑-absorption rule (*a - a segment of graph, perhaps, partially transformed graph G; b - result in applying ↑-absorption rule to the given segment*)

Before discussing the proof of the theorem, we must mention that these results were found to be valid for those graphs which include no mutually parallel communicating cyclic and/or branching segments. For a graph with such constructs, the reduction process may get dead before it actually yields a system Ξ'. This effect was found to be a consequence of an ambiguity in the representation of the considered constructs by constructive expressions. The illustration to this phenomenon is given in Fig.3. However, the addition of an extra rule (the rule referred to as "regrouping") to our procedure allows us to overcome this problem. The new rule is stated as follows.

If $\exists S_i, S_k \in \Xi$, $i \neq k$: $R_1^k \subseteq R_2^i$, and R_2^i includes a constructive subset $\widehat{R}_2^i$ of the following form

$$\tilde{R} \circ \left(\left[a_1^{\mu_1} | \ldots | a_\beta^{\mu_1} \right] \bullet \ldots \bullet \left[a_1^{\mu_\eta} | \ldots | a_\beta^{\mu_\eta} \right] \right),$$

where $a_\alpha^{\mu_f} \subset V$ is a subset of vertices, $\alpha = \overline{1, \beta}$, $\mu_f = \overline{\mu_1, \mu_\eta}$, $"\circ" \in \{"\bullet", "|"\}$, with

$$R_1^k = \left(a_{\delta_1}^{\mu_1} \bullet \ldots \bullet a_{\delta_1}^{\mu_\eta} \right) | \left(a_{\delta_2}^{\mu_1} \bullet \ldots \bullet a_{\delta_2}^{\mu_\eta} \right) | \ldots | \left(a_{\delta_w}^{\mu_1} \bullet \ldots \bullet a_{\delta_w}^{\mu_\eta} \right),$$

$$\delta_1, \delta_2, \ldots, \delta_w \in \{ 1, 2, \ldots, \beta \}, \ \delta_b \neq \delta_c, \ b \neq c, \ b, c = \overline{1, w}, \text{ then we presume}$$

$$\Xi^- = \left[\Xi \backslash \{ S_i \} \right] \cup \{ \widehat{S}_i \}, \text{ where } \widehat{S}_i = \left(i : R_1^i \to \left(R_2^i \backslash \widehat{R}_2^i \right) \triangleright \tilde{R} \circ \left[R_1^k | R^- \right] \right), \text{ with}$$

$$R^- = \left(a_1^{\mu_1} | \ldots | a_{\delta_1 - 1}^{\mu_1} | a_{\delta_1 + 1}^{\mu_1} | \ldots | a_{\delta_2 - 1}^{\mu_1} | a_{\delta_2 + 1}^{\mu_1} | \ldots | \ldots | a_{\delta_r - 1}^{\mu_1} | a_{\delta_r + 1}^{\mu_1} | \ldots | a_\beta^{\mu_1} \right) \bullet$$
$$\bullet \left(a_1^{\mu_2} | \ldots | a_{\delta_1 - 1}^{\mu_2} | a_{\delta_1 + 1}^{\mu_2} | \ldots | a_{\delta_2 - 1}^{\mu_2} | a_{\delta_2 + 1}^{\mu_2} | \ldots | \ldots | a_{\delta_r - 1}^{\mu_2} | a_{\delta_r + 1}^{\mu_2} | \ldots | a_\beta^{\mu_2} \right) \bullet \ldots \bullet$$
$$\bullet \left(a_1^{\mu_\eta} | \ldots | a_{\delta_1 - 1}^{\mu_\eta} | a_{\delta_1 + 1}^{\mu_\eta} | \ldots | a_{\delta_2 - 1}^{\mu_\eta} | a_{\delta_2 + 1}^{\mu_\eta} | \ldots | \ldots | a_{\delta_r - 1}^{\mu_\eta} | a_{\delta_r + 1}^{\mu_\eta} | \ldots | a_\beta^{\mu_\eta} \right),$$

$" \triangleright "$ interpreted as $"\bullet"$, if $\left(R_2^i \backslash \widehat{R}_2^i \right) \bullet \widehat{R}_2^i$, and as $" | "$, if $\left(R_2^i \backslash \widehat{R}_2^i \right) \| \widehat{R}_2^i$.

Now let us briefly discuss the proof of our theorem. Because of space constraints, we provide only a sketch to the proof.[1] While proving the theorem, we first show that the reduction process according to the above absorption rules can at all start whatever system Ξ is to be transformed. Second, we specify the general form of the non-reducible system for any initial system of expressions. Third, by induction, we find out that both the rules produce a reducible system Ξ^- unless a non-reducible system Ξ' is obtained. And finally, by contradiction, we show that the π-cardinality for the system Ξ' can not be less than the cardinality of a clique in the parallelism relation graph.

3   On the Efficiency of the Procedure

Let us evaluate the time complexity C of the R-procedure. It is clear that its laboriousness T essentially depends on step 1 and step 2, however, step 2 requires a constant time to obtain a reduced system Ξ^-. Therefore, we can state the following

$$T = \sum_{p=1}^{q} \left(\varepsilon + \left| \Xi_p \right| \left(\left| \Xi_p \right| - 1 \right) \right), \tag{3}$$

where $\left| \Xi_p \right|$ is the cardinality of the system Ξ at a pth step (note that $\left| \Xi_1 \right| \equiv \left| \Xi \right| \equiv Q$); q is the total number of steps in the reduction process; ε is the maximal laboriousness of a rule in our procedure.

---

[1] To see a complete and detailed version of the proof, please send a request to
   zotov@kursknet.ru

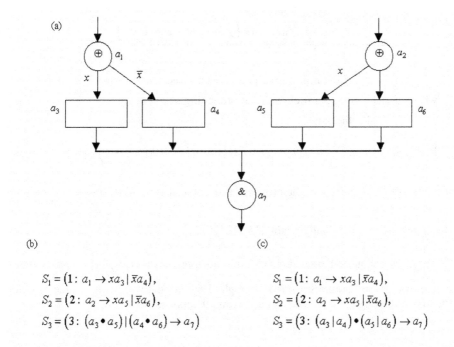

(b)

$$S_1 = \left(1: a_1 \rightarrow xa_3 \,|\, \bar{x}a_4\right),$$
$$S_2 = \left(2: a_2 \rightarrow xa_5 \,|\, \bar{x}a_6\right),$$
$$S_3 = \left(3: \left(a_3 \bullet a_5\right) | \left(a_4 \bullet a_6\right) \rightarrow a_7\right)$$

(c)

$$S_1 = \left(1: a_1 \rightarrow xa_3 \,|\, \bar{x}a_4\right),$$
$$S_2 = \left(2: a_2 \rightarrow xa_5 \,|\, \bar{x}a_6\right),$$
$$S_3 = \left(3: \left(a_3 \,|\, a_4\right) \bullet \left(a_5 \,|\, a_6\right) \rightarrow a_7\right)$$

Fig. 3. Ambiguity in representation of parallel conditional branching in control flow graphs (*a - a segment of graph G; b - first way to specify the segment; c - second way to specify the segment*)

The $\uparrow$-absorption and $\downarrow$-absorption rules decrement the value $|\Xi|$, and the regrouping rule has no effect on $|\Xi|$, therefore $q = |\Xi| + \chi - 2$, where χ is the number of regroupings to be performed on the system being reduced, $\chi = O(1)$. Each vertex of the initial graph G^* can have at most $z = |\Omega|^\pi$ outgoing arcs to other mutually parallel vertices (otherwise we were to state Ω could not specify a clique to be found), hence $|\Xi| \sim \dfrac{d(n-1)}{z}$ and $q \sim \dfrac{d(n-1)}{z} + \chi - 2$, $1 \le d \le z$. Denote χ_p the total number of regroupings followed by a pth reducing step. Then $|\Xi_p| = |\Xi| - (p-1) + \chi_p \sim \dfrac{d(n-1)}{z} - (p-1) + \chi_p$ (in general, $\dfrac{\chi_p}{p} \square\, 1$, with χ_p weakly depending upon the total number of steps; consequently, we may assume that $\chi_{p_1} = \chi_{p_2} \equiv \chi'$, $p_1 \ne p_2$). Having substituted the expressions for $|\Xi_p|$ and q into (3), and having performed some evident algebraic transformations, we shall obtain

$$T \sim \frac{d^3 n^3}{3z^3} + \frac{\tilde{\chi} d^2 n^2}{z^2} + \frac{dn\left(\tilde{\chi}^2 - 2\tilde{\chi} + \varepsilon - 2\frac{1}{3}\right)}{z},$$

where $\tilde{\chi} = \begin{cases} \chi', \text{ if the initial graph contains at least} \\ \quad \text{one parallel cyclic or branching segment, } \chi' > 1; \\ 1 \text{ otherwise.} \end{cases}$

It is evident that $\frac{d^3}{3} = O(1)$, $\tilde{\chi} d^2 = O(1)$, $d\left(\tilde{\chi}^2 - 2\tilde{\chi} + \varepsilon - 2\frac{1}{3}\right) = O(1)$, there-

fore, the time complexity of the proposed procedure will be $C = O\left[\frac{n^3}{z^3}\left(1 + \frac{z}{n} + \frac{z^2}{n^2}\right)\right]$.

Assuming $n \square z$, we finally attain $C = O\left[\frac{n^3}{z^3}\right]$.

Thus, the suggested procedure requires no more than $O\left[\frac{n^3}{z^3}\right]$ steps to find a clique of a given parallelism relation graph. The cardinality z of the clique provides the maximum degree of parallelism in the initial application.

References

1. Paragon XP/S Product Overview, Beaverton, Ore.: Supercomputer Systems Division, Intel Corp. (1991)
2. Duato, J., Yalamanchili, S., Ni, L.M.: Interconnection Networks: An Engineering Approach. Los Alamitos, Calif. IEEE CS Press (1997)
3. Chu, W.W., Lan, L.M-T.: Task Allocation and Precedence Relations for Distributed Real-Time Systems. IEEE Trans. Comput., Vol. C-36. 6 (1987) 667–679
4. Chu, W.W., et al.: Task Allocation in Distributed Data Processing. IEEE Computer. 11 (1980) 57–69

ARTCP: Efficient Algorithm for Transport Protocol for Packet Switched Networks

Igor V. Alekseev and Valery A. Sokolov

Yaroslavl State University, 15000 Yaroslavl, Russian Federation
{Aiv,Sokolov}@uniyar.ac.ru

Abstract. We propose a new algorithm (ARTCP) for transport protocols of packet switching networks.
ARTCP uses scheduling mechanism to smoothly transmit data flow, and does not cause network overload, because it considers temporal characteristics of the flow to self adjust to the available network capacity. ARTCP utilizes inter-segment spacing and round trip time measurements to control the rate of the flow.
In order to study of the characteristics of the ARTCP protocol we have developed and coded imitational programmable model, which is a universal tool for studying processes occurring in communication networks. Built with object-oriented principles, this model allows building simulation network topology of great complexity and setting various environments for simulation experiments. Results of our simulation studies, performed with ARTCP, on our model display substantial advantages, which ARTCP has over standard TCP algorithms. Statistical analysis of ARTCP traffic traces yields the self-similar property of ARTCP traffic, which is in line with other studies of traffic traces in network systems.

1 Introduction

Communication protocols coordinate information transmission processes in distributed systems, such as communication networks. Communication protocols form several levels, separated by their functionality. An ordered set of protocol layers, or a protocol hierarchy, forms network architecture. TCP/IP architecture [1] is one of the most well defined and widely used. All nodes in a TCP/IP network are divided into end systems (network nodes), which are the sources and sinks of information and intermediate systems (routers), which provide the communication path between end systems so that information transmission among the latter can occur.

A two-way information flow in a network between a pair of adjacent systems is provided by a channel, which connects these two systems. A channel can be characterized by the rate of information flow, which can traverse the channel in each direction (bandwidth), transmission delay and bit error probability. At each point of a channel connection to a router there exists a buffer, which holds a queue of data packets awaiting transmission via this particular channel. The buffer space and channel bandwidth are shared resources of the network, that is, all information flows with a common channel have to share resources and compete for the access to them. In the

V. Malyshkin (Ed.): PaCT 2001, LNCS 2127, pp. 159–174, 2001.
© Springer-Verlag Berlin Heidelberg 2001

case when the rate of information arrival to the router exceeds the maximum possible rate of its departure, network congestion will result. This congestion is indicated by buffer overflow and data losses.

The transport layer protocol provides reliable ordered and effective data transmission facility between two end systems, that is, end-to-end. Two systems, communicating using transport protocol can be considered as a self-controlled distributed system. The rules nodes obey, guide how senders access shared resources of the network, therefore transmission protocol's efficiency defines the efficiency of a network in general.

Transmission Control Protocol (TCP) [2-4] is the major transport layer protocol of the TCP/IP network architecture model. TCP provides reliable duplex data transport with congestion control between end systems. The TCP source receives information from its user as a bit sequence. The TCP object than chops this bit sequence to form finite length blocks of user data and control information attached to it (segments). Segments are encapsulated in network packets and put on the network to be delivered to the recipient. The recipient picks packets from the network, takes TCP segments out of them, absorbs control data and resends the reconstructed bit sequence to the user.

A flow of segments between two TCP end systems can pass through an ordered set of routers and channels. The maximum bandwidth of TCP connection is limited by the minimum bandwidth of the channels, through which the flow passes. In general, the channels are shared between several TCP and non-TCP flows. A congestion control algorithm, which is a part of TCP, tries to send segments out at a rate, which does not exceed that of the slowest channel in the path of the connection and does not overflow the receiver (that is, does not exceed the rate at which the receiver absorbs data).

A set of multiple TCP flows sharing a common channel is a complex self-organizing system [5]. TCP algorithms define behavior of every TCP protocol object in such a system, whereas behavior of the system as a whole cannot be described in general by the sum of actions of all system components. Every transmitting protocol object tends to adapt its sending rate to an available network resource with maximum efficiency by cooperating with other entities in the system.

TCP works in the following way: both sender and receiver reserve certain buffer space to hold segments awaiting transmission onto the network (at the sender) or delivery to the user (at the receiver). Each byte of data has a sequence number, which is unique for the connection. A segment consists of the header and payload fields. The header carries control information for this segment, the sequence number of the first byte of its data in particular. The payload field carries user data bytes.

Sending out every segment TCP sets a timer for it. When and if the timer fires the segment, associated with it is considered lost and is retransmitted. By implicitly considering congestion as only source of packet loss in the network, TCP treats each segment loss event as a signal to decrease its sending rate. The TCP receiver sends back to the sender acknowledgement with the sequence numbers of the next expected byte of user data, that is one larger than the last received in-sequence byte of data. Transmission rate of TCP sender is controlled by variable-size sliding window algorithm. The sender is allowed to send all bytes starting from the last acknowledged and falling within the window. While there are no loss indications, TCP grows the sending rate linearly and drops it multiplicatively when the loss event is detected.

TCP is presently known to have a number of substantial inefficiencies:

1. In order to assess available network bandwidth, the TCP congestion control algorithm constantly increases load on the network, pushing it to the saturation point, when packet losses signal the event of network overload to the sender. This artificially created network congestion causes frequent packet losses and subsequent retransmission of lost packets. Excessive retransmissions and high buffer occupancy levels lead to sharp growth of transmission delay and transmission jitter.
2. TCP interprets most packet loss events as signals of network congestion. Thus a TCP sender decreases its transmission rate when data loss occurs, irrespectively to the reason of the loss. Such behavior leads to substantial inefficiency of TCP as data transport protocol for wireless networks, where may loose packets not only as a result of congestion.
3. Local instabilities in TCP sender's algorithms increase probability of packet losses, because the average queue lengths in router buffers are oscillating near the value determined by the total buffering space available. Long queues together with bursts in TCP transmission cause packet losses.

2. Known Improvements of the TCP Congestion Control Algorithm

A great number of research works were aimed at improvement of the TCP performance limited by the shortcomings outlined above.

These works are very interesting and provided a lot for ARTCP development. Among these works we would cite TCP Vegas [6], TRUMP [7], PP [8], NETBLT [9], Tri-S [10], DUAL [11].

In TCP Vegas the segment retransmission is improved by using more precise timing and congestion avoidance mechanism is based on carefully monitored sending rate. DUAL algorithms derive additional hints about network congestion by observing changes in the RTT. In Tri-S scheme the sender's window is slowly changed to see what effect this will have on the throughput. The NETBLT protocol sender uses feedback from the receiver to decide at what rate the next buffer of data is to be transmitted.

Unfortunately, none of these new methods are used in standard network systems. The main drawback of Vegas, Tri-S, DUAL is that they all are based on TCP algorithm, which reacts by rate decrease, when segment loss indication appears and when no loss is detected it drives network linearly to saturation resulting in buffer overflows. TRUMP protocol dictates that all routers should use a form of explicit congestion notification, which is hard to implement everywhere. The authors of PP method propose a very efficient way of measuring network resource availability. Segments are sent in back-to-back pairs whereas separation between segments at the receiver determines the load on the shared network resources. PP scheme can be implemented only in network with separate queuing for each flow, which is hard to achieve in TCP/IP networks.

3. Adaptive Rate TCP (ARTCP)

Our task was to propose a new algorithm for transport protocol, remaining within the scope of TCP/IP architecture, but more efficient than TCP. New protocol should also be universal by being equally usable in wireless and wired network environments without violating the principle of end-to-end connectivity and not requiring modification of internetwork routers or channels.

In the course of this work we have:

- Developed congestion control algorithm for the new transport protocol - ARTCP (Adaptive Rate Transmission Control Protocol). ARTCP utilizes timing characteristics of the data flow as input parameters of the congestion control algorithm and efficiently combines window-based flow control algorithm with individual scheduling of every segment. ARTCP can gradually replace TCP in wired and wireless networks, preserving intermediate compatibility with the former.
- Provided formal description of ARTCP as the code of the C++ class, which models the new protocol.
- Developed universal object-oriented imitational model, which allows construction of networks with complex topologies and simulation of the most important characteristics, which influence the transport protocols.

We have performed a number of experiments using this model and have shown that ARTCP has an advantage over TCP in most use scenarios. We have also discovered self-similarity in ARTCP traffic traces with large number of samples.

New algorithms of ARTCP compared to those in TCP, have several advantages:

- ARTCP does not push a network to the congested state in order to find its maximum bandwidth. Because of this, network with stable state ARTCP flows does not experience packet losses at all. Thus, network infrastructure usage efficiency is increased.
- ARTCP does not interpret segment loss as network congestion indication. Due to this property ARTCP can be used much more efficiently than TCP in networks with high bit error rates.
- ARTCP keeps average queue length of router near the minimum (one packet per flow on the average) because ARTCP not only adapts the sending rate of segments into network to the slowest service rate in this network, but also possesses an overload compensation algorithm. Lower queue lengths lead to shorter transmission delays.
- The ARTCP logic does not preclude the existence of TCP-compatible implementations, so ARTCP can be introduced first to the end systems, where this protocol would be most useful.

4. Considered Characteristics of a Transport Protocol

In our studies of ARTCP behavior we observed the following main characteristics of the protocol:

1. The relative number of lost segments (ratio of the number of lost segments to the number of sent segments).
2. The channel bandwidth utilization efficiency. (ratio of the number of successfully received bytes to the maximum possible number of transferred bytes):

$$U = \frac{bytes\_received}{(channel\_bandwidth) \times run\_time} \tag{1}$$

1. The fairness of resource sharing:

$$F = (\sum_{i=1}^{n} b_i)^2 \bigg/ n \times (\sum_{i=1}^{n} b_i^2), \tag{2}$$

where b_i is i-th connection's bandwidth share.

1. The average queue length Q of bottleneck link router. (Fig. 1)

We have provided comparison of ARTCP and TCP by these characteristics in similar usage scenarios.

5. Formal Model of the System

The network consists of several end systems, two routers, and a number of channels, connecting end systems to the routers and routers with each other. ARTCP protocol object is being executed at each end system, which are grouped into two LANs, each connected to one router (Fig. 1). Routers provide connectivity between two LANs by sending traffic via channel, which models WAN link with relatively small bandwidth and longer delay, than that of the channels within each LAN.

Table 1. Model parameters and variables.

Parameter	Description
S	Segment size (bytes).
$\tau_s(t)$	Inter-segment interval set by the sender.
$\tau_r(t)$	Inter-segment interval measured by the receiver.
$R_s(t)$	Rate of segment departure set by the sender.
$R_r(t)$	Rate of segment arrival measured by the receiver.
$R_e(t)$	Rate of segment arrival to the receiver when the sender learns it from acknowledgements.
$A_c(t_i)$	Compensation area. Represents amount of data, accumulated in network buffers.
$Q(t)$	Router queue length.
Q^{max}	Router buffer size (limits maximum queue).
BER	Bit error ratio.
Speedup	Rate growth probability coefficient.
Slowdown	Rate decrease probability coefficient.
ε	Precision coefficient. Used for comparisons. $\varepsilon \ll 1$.
RTT	Round trip time.

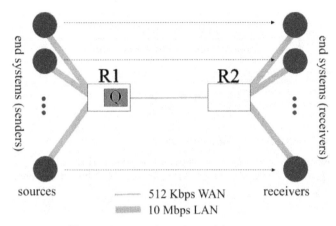

Fig. 1. The general topology of the system.

Each of the end systems in one LAN sends segments to a particular system in another LAN. Segments are sent out by ARTCP spaced in time by interval

$$\tau_s(t) = S/R_S(t), \tag{3}$$

where rate $R_S(t)$ is controlled by the congestion control algorithm of ARTCP. We assume that ARTCP sources always have data to send. Senders and receivers are in different LANs. ARTCP receivers reply with acknowledgements, traveling in the opposite direction as small segments without data. However ARTCP allows for the same piggybacking of control data as TCP does.

The task of the router is in forwarding segment towards its receiver according to the receiver's address in the segments header. FIFO queue of segments is organized in the router R1, where segments wait to be sent to R2 over WAN channel. The queue has finite length

$$Q \leq Q^{\max}. \tag{4}$$

Segment arriving at the output interface of R1 at time t is placed in queue if

$$S \leq Q^{\max} - Q(t), \tag{5}$$

otherwise the segment is lost. The queue at the output interface or R1 router is served at the rate, determined by bandwidth of the channel between R1 and R2.

We consider the following properties of the channels: bandwidth, transmission delay, bit error ratio. Channel bandwidth determines the rate at which bits of segments are accepted to enter the channel. Transmission delay characterizes length of the interval between acceptance of a particular bit into channel and appearance of this bit from the other end of the channel. Bit error probability defines the probability of segment loss depending to bit error probability as

$$1 - (1 - BER)^S. \tag{6}$$

Each ARTCP object performs as follows:

Network congestion for ARTCP is indicated not by lost segments, but by the temporal properties of its flow. ARTCP source concludes that the congestion starts to build up when with growing $R_s(t)$ time RTT starts to grow and rate of the flow arrival rate measured at the receiver stabilizes:

$$R_e(t) < R_S(t - RTT).$$ (7)

ARTCP segments are put onto the network not as a back-to-back burst within window, as TCP does, but spaced by time intervals $\tau_s(t)$ by the scheduler. Measurement of inter-segment intervals $\tau_r(t)$ at the receiver gives the rate of the flow arrival $R_r(t)$. The sender stops increasing sending rate $R_s(t)$ when time RTT starts to increase and the value of segment arrival rate drops below the sending rate of the segments. These two events are indication that the system has reached the state, when average rate of segment arrival reaches the average flow service rate and further sending rate increase will lead to growth of the queue length in router buffers. ARTCP receiver returns observed values of the flow arrival rate $R_r(t)$ along with acknowledgements. Having obtained acknowledgement of a segment RTT seconds after the segment has been sent, ARTCP sender extracts the value of rate at which the flow containing this segment was delivered to its receiver by the network. The sender uses this information $R_e(t)$ as an estimation of available network bandwidth. (Fig. 2)

Congestion control and error correction algorithms of ARTCP are completely independent, because segment loss is not taken as a sign of network overload. Retransmission does not occur immediately, but the segment in error receives higher priority and stays in the transmission queue to be sent first when the scheduler allows.

ARTCP does not unnecessarily stress the network by congesting it. Unlike TCP, ARTCP allows for fast and efficient adaptation to available network resources.

Due to existence of scheduler in ARTCP, it sends segments to the network more smoothly, avoiding bursts and consequent queue overflow. Therefore the need in buffer space in network routers is decreased.

The main difference of ARTCP and TCP is in the congestion control algorithm of ARTCP, which sets the rate of data flow matching available resource by observing values of $R_e(t)$ and RTT.

5.1. Congestion Control Mechanism of ARTCP

ARTCP uses both the standard sliding window of variable size to prevent overflow of the receiver and an innovative rate adaptation function for the sending rate to match the available network bandwidth. All segments within the window announced by the receiver are sent at the rate, determined by the rate adaptation function, whose goal is to send segments out exactly at the rate at which they are served by the network and to compensate for possible overload.

Rate adaptation algorithm has several states of operation (Fig. 3). After the start the algorithm tries to determine available rate as fast as possible and after that enters fine-tuning mode, where the rate of the flow is kept at the value of available rate. Rate control algorithm receiver values of $R_e(t)$ and RTT at its input and depending on these values and its current state makes state transition and calculates the value of $R_s(t)$. $R_s(t)$ is used by the scheduler to set the length of inter-segment delay interval.

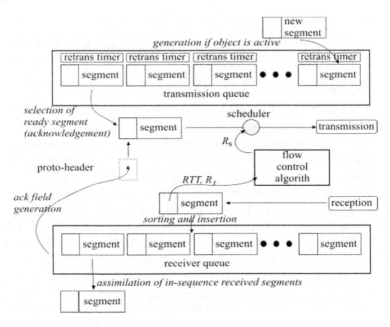

Fig. 2. ARTCP queues and in-object information flows.

5.2. States of the Rate Adaptation Algorithm

At time t the sender estimates available network bandwidth as $R_e(t)$ and can compare the values of flow sending rate as it was at time t-RTT and flow arrival rate to the receiver. At time t the sender obtains acknowledgements for segments sent before time t-RTT.

Fast start state (FS) has the goal to grow the sending rate of the flow from its minimal value to the value permitted by the available bandwidth as fast as possible immediately after connection initialization. In FS mode the flow rate of the sender is grown exponentially. The algorithm exists FS state when

$$R_e(t_i) < (1-\varepsilon) \times R_S(t_i - RTT).$$ (8)

Multiplicative decrease state (MD1) follows the FS state. After the fast start ends the value of $R_s(t)$ will be larger than $R_e(t)$ because it was exponentially growing previously. In MD1 state the flow rate is instantaneously set below $R_e(t)$. After this decrease the algorithm procceds to compensation state.

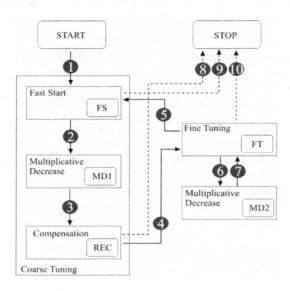

Fig. 3. State diagram of the ARTCP flow control algorithm.

Compensation state (REC) grows the sending rate linearly up to the already known value of available bandwidth $R_e(t)$ compensating the overload, which occurred at FS state. In compensation state the algorithm calculates the compensation area value $A_c(t_i)$ as area of the ABC figure (Fig. 4), formed by the values of $R_s(t$) over $R_e(t_i)$ during the time when

$$R_s(t_i) > R_e(t_i) \tag{9}$$

in FS state. The meaning of $A_c(t_i)$ is that its value represents the amount of excess data accumulated in router buffers while the sending rate of the flow exceeded available network bandwidth. The sending rate in REC state grows linearly in such a way that amount of data sent into network is exactly $A_c(t_i)$ less then the amount which would be sent if sending rate were equal $R_e(t_i)$. This condition geometrically is explained as equality of surface area of CDF triangular and $A_c(t_i)$. State REC is terminated when

$$R_s(t) \geq R_e(t). \tag{10}$$

The fine tuning (FT) state follows the REC state. In FT state the sending rate of the flow slowly adapts to the available bandwidth of the network. Relation of speedup and slowdown coefficients determines rate increase or decrease probability at each clock tick. Speedup coefficient, which represents the rate increase possibility, is in reverse proportionality to current rate of the flow. Slowdown coefficient, which represents the rate decrease possibility, is proportional to the ratio of measured *RTT* to minimal observed value of *RTT*. Speedup is thus smaller for faster flows and is larger for smaller values of $R_s(t)$, which helps slow flows to achieve larger relative share of bandwidth. The value of slowdown is equal for all flows and grows with *RTT*. The FT state gives slower flows possibility to increase their rates and causes all flows to decrease rates equally, when *RTT* grows – that is queues start to build up. The algorithm leaves FT state, when a sharp variation of measured *RTT* occurs.

Multiplicative decrease state 2 (MD2) is needed for fast rate decrease, which is triggered by any sharp growth of the measured RTT. Following the decrease, which may be caused for example by failed network link and routing traffic over slower link, the algorithm reenters FT state. No compensation is needed, because rate was not growing fast in the previous state.

The rate adaptation process of the single ARTCP flow to the network bandwidth of 96 kbps is shown on figure 4.

6. Simulation Model

In order to model ARTCP behavior and compare it to TCP we have developed and implemented imitation programmable model (IPM) of ARTCP itself and of all network components, which determine protocol functionality.

IPM consists of a set of ARTCP protocol objects and all network elements, which influence the behavior of congestion control algorithm. IPM is build as a network of the required amount of interacting objects, arranged in a particular topological scheme. ARTCP protocol object and objects representing all other elements of the network are implemented as C++ classes. The IPM is universal because the set of main objects it contains: node, router, link can be used to build model of any network, while individual settings of each individual object allows to set any possible imitation scenario.

6.1. Object Structure of the Imitation Programmable Model

The network being modeled is constructed of any number of end systems, where protocol objects of ARTCP, TCP or constant bit rate are executed, channels and routers. Segments, generated by the active sources, travel the modeled network passing through its elements towards the receiver. Each node in the model has a unique network address and segments carry source and destination address fields in their headers. All objects of the model create logs of their states and events, which are then analyzed to study the dynamic behavior of the model.

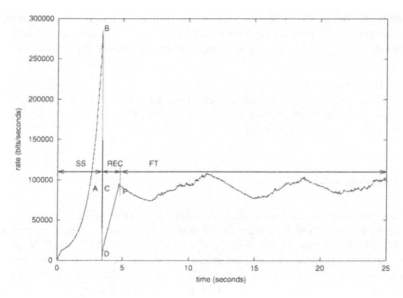

Fig. 4. Adaptation process of the single ARTCP flow to 96 Kbps network bandwidth.

6.1.1. The ARTCP Protocol Object

The object performs initial synchronization of the connection (connection establishment), rate adaptation, generation and scheduling of segments, reception of data from network and generation of acknowledgements, timer based retransmission and fast retransmission [12]. Two ARTCP objects are capable of simultaneous data exchange in both directions. Internal structure of ARTCP class is relatively complex (fig. 2).

6.1.2. Constant Bit Rate (CBR) Protocol Object

This protocol object attempts to send segments into network at configured constant rate without flow control or lost data retransmission. This protocol is used to model multimedia and UDP data flows and study their coexistence with ARTCP.

6.1.3. End System Object

Objects modeling end systems are used as platforms to run ARTCP, TCP or CBR protocol objects. Each end system has unique address within the model. This address has to be set in segment header for the segment to be delivered to a particular node. The end system functions are in passing interrupts to the active protocol object on this system, passing segments between the channels and the active protocol objects.

6.1.4. Router Object

We chose to model a router as an internetwork device with non-blocking switching matrix and output buffering. This is a good model of a contemporary Internet router. The router object of composed of several other objects: interfaces (one per each link the router is connected to) and one switching matrix object, which interconnects interfaces.

The router has to switch segments to an appropriate output interface according to the destination address in the segment header. Each interface maintains a FIFO queue on the output side, where segment awaiting transmission out of this interface are held.

6.1.5. Channel Object
The channel object is used to connect end systems and routers in our model. Each direction of a channel is independently characterized by a certain bit rate, transmission delay and bit error probability.

7. Modeling ARTCP

We have performed a number of simulation studies with the ARTCP protocol.

The goal of our modeling experiments was to determine the important properties of ARTCP (see section 4). We also needed to compare ARTCP and TCP performance. Multiple experiments were run in each of several scenarios, where two LANs were connected via limited bandwidth WAN channel. Each channel within a LAN is characterized by the bandwidth of 10 Mbps, 0.01-second delay and zero bit error ratio. Through varying scenarios we simulate several simultaneous ARTCP flows and a CBR flow, competing for shared network resources.

7.1. Isolated Flow

In order to observe the details of ARTCP rate adaptation process we used a scenario with isolated ARTCP flow through WAN channel with 96 Kbps bandwidth and 0.1-second delay. Maximum queue length in R1 router does not exceed 16 Kbytes. Fig. 4 depicts the plot of flow sending rate versus time. No segment loss occurs in this scenario.

7.2. Two ARTCP and One CBR Flow

For two ARTCP flows coexisting with CBR flow we needed to check the correctness of ARTCP algorithm. In experiments of this scenario we randomly choose the start/stop times of the flows and CBR rates. We used the topology of three source-destination pairs and two routers, connected by 256 Kbps channel with 0.1-second delay. 32 Kbytes limit output buffer of router R1. In every one of every 100 simulation runs of this scenario the first ARTCP flow starts at time $t = 0$, moment of start for the second ARTCP flow and CBR flow are chosen at random from intervals 10-110 and 190-210 seconds respectively. The stop time of the first ARTCP flow is also taken at random from interval of 390-410 seconds. The CBR rate is randomly selected between 50-200 Kbps. We obtained the following results in this scenario: for two ARTCP flows sharing the channel with CBR flow link utilization $U = 0.981 \pm 0.012$; for two ARTCP without CBR flow $U = 0.971 \pm 0.023$; the number of lost segments in all experiments equals zero; for two ARTCP flows with CBR flow the fairness of resource sharing $F = 0.989 \pm 0.011$; without CBR $F = 0.97 \pm 0.028$.

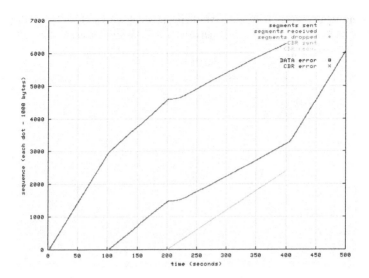

Fig. 5. Segment sequence graph for two ARTCP and one CBR flow.

7.3. Comparison of ARTCP and TCP

In order to study the influence of segment loss not caused by network overload on the protocol performance we set up simulation, where 10 transport protocol traffic flows were sent through 256 Kbps channel with 0.1-second delay and different values of BER. We ran this simulation for both TCP and ARTCP. For each of the values of BER (up to 6×10^{-5}) there were 50 runs, each lasted 500 seconds. All flows started simultaneously at $t = 0$.

As our simulation suggests, the ARTCP has a clear advantage over the TCP, because under the condition of growing BER, the ARTCP flow rate remains nearly constant, whereas the TCP rate goes down sharply. Figure 6. shows the plot of average flow rates (averaged over 50 runs) with mean square deviation vs. BER values.

In the next scenario we compared bandwidth utilization coefficients and fairness of resource sharing for ARTCP and TCP. For each of the protocols 100 simulations were run, each lasted 500 seconds on 10 variants of network topology, containing from 2 to 20 end systems and from 1 to 10 simultaneous flows.

With small number of active flows link utilization is slightly better for TCP. As the number of active flows goes up, link utilization by ARTCP approaches 1, while TCP link utilization starts to deteriorate due to retransmissions (fig. 7). ARTCP flows are fairer in sharing resources between themselves and the fairness coefficient F grows as number of flows increases.

7.4. Self-Similarity of ARTCP Traffic

Experimental studies of TCP/IP traffic [13] have shown that assumption of limited variance of segment interarrival times is invalid and this questions the applicability of the queuing theory to such systems. In their classical works [13-15] V. Willinger and M. Taqqu have shown that TCP/IP network traffic is characterized by self-similarity property.

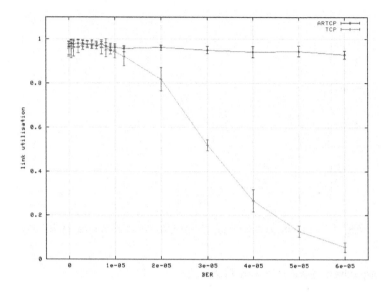

Fig. 6. Throughput of ARTCP and TCP vs. bit error ratio.

At present, the theoretical apparatus of self-similar processes analysis is in its early stage of development and lacks well-studied theoretical models, which could be applied to systems with network traffic. That is why, we believe, that simulation experiment is the main tool for studying such systems with network traffic.

In order to find out, whether traffic trace is characterized by the property of self-similarity, Hurst coefficient is computed over a large volume of samples. To perform such computation of Hurst coefficient for ARTCP traffic we ran simulation to obtain a large number of samples. In our case it was a series with 147036 measurements, each of which is a sum of segment arrival events on R1 router from 10 active ARTCP flows over periods of 0.1 second.

The series was than subject to statistical analysis using rescaled adjusted range (R/S) and aggregated variance methods. Results of application of both methods were used to calculate Hurst coefficient, R/S method yields 0.63, aggregated variance method yields 0.65. Thus we have shown that ARTCP traffic, just as other network traffic [14, 15] is self-similar. Existence of self-similarity in traffic traces, which were obtained by our imitation programmable model, is a good validation of the latter.

8. Conclusions

We have given description of the algorithm for transport protocol, which uses scheduling to smoothly transmit data, which does not cause network overload, by utilizing inter-segment and RTT time measurements to control the rate of the flow. We have described the algorithm of this protocol and created a model implementation as C++ class.

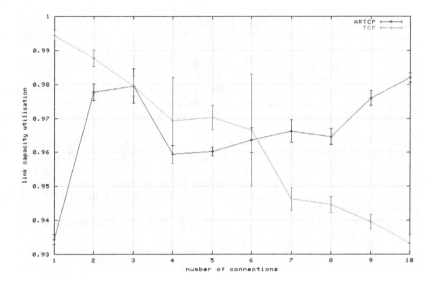

Fig. 7. ARTCP and TCP link utilization coefficient vs. number of connections.

Results of simulation studies performed with ARTCP on our imitational programmable model display substantial advantages, which our new protocol ARTCP has over standard TCP.

Acknowledgements

This research work was supported by the Russian Foundation for Basic Research grant # 01-07-90331.

References

1. Cerf V., Kahn R.: A protocol for packet network intercommunication. IEEE Trans. on communications, Vol. COM-22, N. 5. (1974) 637-648.
2. Postel J.: Transmission Control Protocol. RFC793 (STD7). (1981)
3. Braden R. T.: Requirements for Internet Hosts – Communication Layers. RFC1122. (1989)
4. Jacobson V.: Congestion Avoidance and Control. In proc. ACM SIGCOMM'88. (1988)
5. Haken H.: Synergetics. 2nd edn. Springer-Verlag, Berlin Heidelberg New York (1978)
6. Brakmo L., O'Malley S., Peterson L.: TCP Vegas: New Techniques for Congestion Detection and Avoidance. In proc. ACM SIGCOMM'94. (1994) 24-35.

7.   Tomey C.: Rate-Based Congestion Control Framework for Connectionless Packet-Switched Networks. Doctor of Philosophy Thesis. University of New South Wales Australian Defense Force Academy (1997)
8.   Keshav S.: The Packet Pair Flow Control Protocol. ICSI Tech. Rept. TR-91-028. Computer Science Division, Department of EECS, University of California, Berkeley and International Computer Science Institute. Berkeley (1991)
9.   Clark D., Lambert M., Zhang L.: NETBLT: A Bulk Data Tranfer Protocol. RFC 969 (1987)
10. Wang Z. Routing And Congestion Control In Datagram Networks. Doctor Of Philosophy Thesis. University College London. London (1992)
11. Zhang L., Lefelhocz C., Lyles B., Shenker S.: Congestion Control for Best-Effort Service: Why We Need a New Paradigm. IEEE Network, Vol. 10, N. 1. (1996)
12. Jacobson V., Braden R., Borman D.: TCP Extensions for High Performance. RFC1323 (1992)
13. Leland W., Taqqu M., Willinger W., Wilson D.: On the Self-Similar Nature of Ethernet Traffic (Extended Version). IEEE/ACM Transactions on Networking. Vol. 2(1) (1994) 1-15
14. Willinger W., Taqqu M., Sherman R., Wilson D.: Self-similarity through high variability: Statistical analysis of Ethernet LAN traffic at source level. IEEE/ACM Transactions of Networking. Vol. 5. (1997) 71-86
15. Taqqu M., Teverovsky V., Willinger W.: Is network traffic self-similar or multifractal? Fractals. Vol. 5. (1997) 63-73

Extension of Java Environment by Facilities Supporting Development of SPMD Java-Programs

Arutyun Avetisyan, Serguei Gaissaryan, and Oleg Samovarov

Institute for System Programming Russian Academy of Sciences, 25 B.
Kommunisticheskaya str., Moskow, 109004, Russia
{arut,ssg,samov}@ispras.ru

Abstract. ParJava is extension of Java environment by facilities to support developing of effective scalable portable object-oriented parallel SPMD-programs for homogenous and heterogeneous computing systems with distributed memory. ParJava model is determined by four Java-interfaces, which support the notion of computing space as JavaVM network. ParJava allows to perform parallel programs designed for homogenous system on heterogeneous ones without lost of scalability. These facilities provide base supporting design of high-level object models of parallel programming.

1 Introduction

SPMD-program development and implementation capabilities for multiprocessor distributed computer systems are discussed. The goal consists in design of useful and effective tools supporting development of portable scalable parallel programs running on such systems. Parallel computations in distributed systems are usually executed using processes together with message passing.

Standard high-performance communication equipment (Fast Ethernet, Myrinet etc.) that has recently entered computer markets brought to life computer clusters with distributed memory. Their advantage consists in that they are built on basis of standard prevalent hardware and therefore it is possible to use standard software (e.g., OS Linux, various implementations of MPI and other appropriate software both commercial and free).

There is an opinion that computers having various performance and/or architecture may be united in clusters as well. Such systems are referred as heterogeneous clusters [1]. We will call such systems heterogeneous computer networks (HCN). In particular we have such situation when cluster hardware is partially modified or local computer network (workstations, personal computers etc. connected in network) is used as a cluster.

Distributed memory parallel program design needs special languages facilities. Usually SPMD programs are designed using sequential programming languages (Fortran, C, C++) together with standard message passing interface MPI. When SPMD programs to be executed using HCN are designed, specific problems due to heterogeneity of computer network arise. To solve these problems some new programming language facilities are needed. MPI interface does not provide such

V. Malyshkin (Ed.): PaCT 2001, LNCS 2127, pp. 175–180, 2001.

facilities being developed to support message passing through homogeneous networks.

The collection of such facilities is implemented in ParJava environment [2]. Being an extension of standard Java environment ParJava supports design, implementation, execution, and modification of portable scalable SPMD-programs running on homogeneous and heterogeneous networks of JavaVM. It means that ParJava allows to execute parallel Java programs using supercomputers, homogeneous and heterogeneous clusters, local computer networks, as well as virtual computer networks, utilizing free Internet resources. ParJava supports the following two approaches for implementation, porting, and execution of Java SPMD-programs:

- running one JavaVM on each computer of distributed computer system (homogeneous or heterogeneous), which results in homogeneous or heterogeneous network of Java-executors,
- simulation of homogeneous network of Java-executors on heterogeneous computer system by running several JavaVMs on more productive processors to achieve load balancing.

The last approach supports the design of parallel programs for homogeneous parallel computer system (say, supercomputers or homogeneous clusters) using local network of personal computers and/or workstations.

Main disadvantage of Java environment is comparatively low productivity of virtual processor. However, JIT-compilers integrated with JavaVM allow to obtain highly optimized object code, which is executed on the same speed as Java-programs compiled in native code by corresponding Java native compiler. The speed of optimized native programs obtained from Java source code is close to that of C/C++ programs (loss in speed is about 1.5 times).

It is necessary to point that even Java Native Compilers produce object code, which works slower than that received from C/C++. The point is that Java-program (unlike C/C++) remains object-oriented during execution time. It makes Java-program more flexible and robust but everything has its cost.

ParJava environment consists of

- language facilities: the set of Java interfaces (implemented in several packages), which extend Java environment by means supporting SPMD programming,
- analyzers and other tools that help programmer to develop and implement high quality scalable SPMD Java-programs.

According to requirement avoiding any changes in Java language as well as in JavaVM no new language constructs were added to Java: all extensions supporting parallel programming are introduced by interface and class libraries.

In current paper the basic level of ParJava is presented. No additional assumptions about parallel programs are made. Java packages (methods) implementing basic level environment support low-level data parallel programming for distributed computer systems: all decisions about parallel computations are made by an application programmer and implemented with the help of ParJava facilities. Implementation of higher-level models is beard on basic level and usually uses additional assumptions about computer network's topology, hardware and software properties (e.g., using DVM [3] or HPF model it should be assumed that parallel computer network has one, two or three dimensional grid topology, other high level models will be based on some other assumptions).

2 ParJava Interfaces

Basic level ParJava model is determined by four Java-interfaces, in which the notion of computer space is introduced as JavaVM network executing SPMD program. JavaVM network is represented by a weighted graph: weight of each node is equal to productivity of corresponding JavaVM, the weight of each arc is equal to capacity of corresponding channel.

IJavaNet interface specifies methods of creating JavaVM networks and their sub-networks as well as some network transformations. We call *JavaVM network* any enumerated set of JavaVMs that are able to exchange by messages. No assumptions about homogeneity (or heterogeneity) of network are made on this level. Each JavaVM sub-network also is treated as network, has parent network (sub-network), and may have arbitrary number of child sub-networks. If JavaVM network has no parent network it is called *root* JavaVM network. IJavaNet interface defines methods that allow to create network (sub-network) of Java-executors using nodes of current network, receive the number of nodes (or free nodes) of current network, receive current number of each node of current network, pass to parent network, create new network as union or intersection of current network with some additional network. JavaNet class (implementing IJavaNet interface) may be used to create a computer network (which is assumed to be homogeneous) by starting exactly one Java-executor on each node of parallel computer system.

IFullGraph interface specifies operations on full weighted graph.

Interface INetProperties allows to specify some properties of heterogeneous Java-net, which are used when optimal homogeneous or heterogeneous Java-net is modeled using given heterogeneous computer network. This interface extends interfaces IJavaNet and IFullGraph. It also defines methods allowing to specify SPMD program special requirements to the topology of computer network (e.g., star, grid, line, etc).

When SPMD-program is executed on heterogeneous JavaVM net, optimal use of system resources may be achieved using non-uniform data distribution. Interface IHeterogenNet provides methods that calculate relative productivity of any specified node, create heterogeneous network executing exactly one JavaVM on each node, determine and delete all nodes that do not correspond to scalability conditions, optimize the network according to program requirements, scatter parts of transmission buffer of current node to reception buffers of remaining nodes having various sizes, gather data in reception buffer of given node from transmission buffers of remaining nodes.

When the optimal network of Java-executors is created productivity of each node, measured using appropriate benchmarks (http://www.nas.nasa.gov/Software/NPB/, http://netlib2.cs.utk.edu/benchmark/linpackjava/) should be accounted, as well as program requirements to topology of target network. In cases when execution times of sequential and parallel parts of SPMD-program are comparable, it is necessary to estimate the time needed to execute the sequential parts.

Interface IHomogenNet defines methods supporting creation of homogeneous network of Java-executors on given heterogeneous computer network.

3 ParJava Environment

ParJava environment allows to edit, debug, and execute parallel programs using homogenous or heterogeneous computer networks (supercomputers, clusters, or local networks of workstations and/or personal computers). This environment also enables to model homogeneous computer networks on heterogeneous ones.

A user interface to ParJava environment is started on one of nodes of a parallel computer network (referred further as "root"). When a list of available nodes is displayed, the "root" node is marked by the "root" word.

The "Tools" item of the main menu provides an access to ParJava facilities supporting choice of the network and compilation of Java-program. "Tools" submenu provides the following items: "New Net" allocates new subnet using dialog box, which contains the list of available nodes; a parallel program will be executed on the network consisting of nodes marked in the list. "Hosts Performance" defines relative nodes performances of the allocated network. "Compile" compiles SPMD-program using Java compiler from the JDK 1.2 environment. "Run" executes parallel program on the "root" node in the sequential mode. "Run on Homogeneous Net" executes SPMD-program on a homogeneous network of the JavaVMs, which is modeled on the current network. Number of nodes is defined by the user (in automatic mode it is determined to be optimal). "Run on Heterogeneous Net" executes an SPMD-program using heterogeneous network of the JavaVM (one JavaVM is started on each node). The nodes, which don't satisfy scalability condition, are eliminated.

When a sequential program is being tested and debugged, it is necessary to provide not only its correctness, but also its efficiency, stability and scalability. For this purpose it is useful to know some properties of the program (profiles, traces, slices, etc.). An effective distribution of SPMD-program to nodes of a heterogeneous network demands the knowledge of the program parameters, which define actual speed of the program execution on each node of the network.

The tools allowing to determine these parameters are collected in the "Analyzers" submenu of the main menu, which provides the following items: "Instrumentate" inserts system debugging calls in SPMD-program. "Profile" determines a dynamic profile of a parallel program. These two tools enable to take into account a weight of the sequential part, when a performance of nodes is calculated. "Test_mode" allows to translate a parallel program in the mode using debugging library providing collection of a history of parallel execution of each branch of parallel program in special file. Parallel execution trace is represented as partially ordered set of events. An absolute time of each branch execution and times between parallel events in a branch are presented. The special file contains also additional information about events (a size of the event, a source and a target of the event, etc.) User can visualize the stored history traces by means of the "TraceVizualization" item of the menu. "TraceVizualization" tool displays each parallel branch of SPMD-program as a horizontal line. Calls to the communication library are marked on this line by small squares. A temporal bar is displayed on the top of the image. A time of communication function call can be defined in milliseconds by using this bar. Communication functions on the image are represented by integer numbers, printed within a small square on diagram. For example, number one may represent Init() function, while number two - Finalize() function. When the square with function number is covered by cursor, a hint appears. It contains a name of a communication function and a relative time of it's execution. Some of squares may be connected by green lines, which show that a branch of parallel program invokes a communication function and an expectation for external event is started to complete this function. A length of the green line is proportional to waiting time. If a button on the left side of the image was clicked by the cursor, the idle time of each processor will be calculated (in milliseconds) and shown on a diagram. To get the diagram of all processors it is necessary to click "All" button. The result of program profiling is stored automatically into system files accessible to users by the "TraceVizualization" tool.

4 Example

An example of use of ParJava is Java version of parallel scalable C-program designed for homogeneous parallel computing system (Parsytec GC). The program was converted from C to Java without modification of algorithm. Fig. 1 shows speed-ups of program execution for heterogeneous computer network, which consisted of Intel (Linux) and Sparc (Solaris) platforms for the following three cases: 1) ignoring heterogeneity of the network (gray curve); 2) modeling optimal homogeneous network (dotted curve); 3) launching one JavaVM on each computer (black curve).

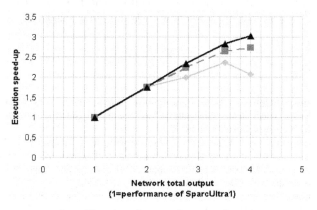

Fig. 1. Results of example executions.

5 Related Works

Possibility of performing effective parallel computations using heterogeneous computer networks is widely discussed in periodic. WINPAR system [4] is one of the successful attempts to solve this problem. It provides an integrated development environment for local area networks of personal computers operated by Windows NT message passing supported by MPI and PVM. It provides a set of tools for parallel program development, simulation, performance prediction, graphical high-level debugging, monitoring, and visualization. Though the system provided very convenient user interface it failed by reason of ineffectiveness of heterogeneous parallel computations. There are several other Java environments for homogeneous and heterogeneous SPMD programming. We can mention Towards [5] system, which adds to Java new language primitives - parallel arrays. It makes Java parallel programs more efficient but removes system out of Java framework. DOGMA [6] is a metacomputing environment, which allows use of heterogeneous clusters. A key feature of DOGMA is its ability to operate as an application server for parallel applications. Project Dome addresses the problems of load balancing in framework of heterogeneous multiuser environment, ease of programming, and fault tolerance [7]. mpC [8] is a high-level parallel language (superset of ANSI C), designed specially to develop portable adaptable applications for heterogeneous networks of computers.

6 Conclusion

Development of sample SPMD programs in ParJava environment approved that it is suitable tool supporting effective scalable parallel programming. ParJava is used for design high-level object models of SPMD programming. Main advantage of ParJava is the possibility to execute parallel program without any modification or transformation on various scalable computing systems (portability).

ParJava environment is in state of evolution. The full-scale debugger of parallel programs is being developed. Some new analyzers are designed.

References

1. B. Paz and M. Gulias. "Cluster Setup and its Administration". In Rajkumar Buyya (ed.) "High Performance Cluster Computing." Programming and Applications. Vol. 1. Prentice Hall PTR, New Jersey, 1999, p. 48-67.
2. A.I. Avetisyan, I.V. Arapov, S.S. Gaissaryan, V.A. Padaryan. "The environment supporting design of parallel Java-programs for homogeneous and heterogeneous networks of JavaVM." In "High Performance Calculations and Applications. Proc.
3. S.S. Gaissaryan, M.V. Domrachev, V.F. Yoch, O.I. Samovarov, A.I. Avetisyan. "Parallel programming of systems with distributed memory in Java environ-ment." Proc. ISP RAS. Vol. 1., Moscow, 2000, p. 39-60.
4. D. Ahr, A. Bäcker, et al. WINPAR - Windows-based Parallel Computing, in E. D'Hollander, G. Joubert, F. Peters and U. Trottenberg (eds), Parallel Computing: Fundamentals, Applications and New Directions, Elsevier, Amsterdam, 1998.
5. B. Carpenter, G. Zhang et al. Towards Java environment for SPMD programming. In D. Pritchard, Je Reeve (eds), 4th Int. Europar Conf., LNCS, 1470, Springer, 1998.
6. DOGMA – Distributed Object Group Metacomputing Architecture. http://www.dogma.byu.edu.
7. J. Arabe, A. Beguelin, et al. Dome Parallel programming in a heterogeneous multi-user environment. Proc. Int. Parallel Processing Sym. 1996.
8. A.Lastovetsky, D.Arapov, A.Kalinov, and I.Ledovskih, "A Parallel Language and Its Programming System for Heterogeneous Networks", *Concurrency: Practice and Experience*, 12(13), 2000, pp.1317-1343.

Mechanisms of Parallel Computing Organization for NeuroCluster

L.K. Babenko, A.G. Chefranov, P.A. Fedorov, A.Yu. Korobko,
and O.B. Makarevich

Taganrog State University of Radio Engineering, , Taganrog, 347928, Russian Federation
chefranov@mopevm.tsure.ru, korobko@mailru.com, mak@tsure.ru

Abstract. Neurocluster based on NM6403 neuroprocessors architecture, system software and programming technology are discussed. Special attention was paid to operating system structure, data and control flow between subsystems, internal data structures, system topology, programming language and general parallel programming ideas.

Introduction

Neurocluster based on NM6403 is a part of a whole in general heterogeneous network cluster. System is developed for SPMD (Single Program Multiple Data) -tasks, but it is possible to execute MIMD (Multiple Instruction Multiple Data) - tasks. Such system has to support data distribution, branch synchronization and fast communications between subtasks [1]. This research is supported by Russian Foundation for Basic Research (project № 00-07-90300).

NM6403 microprocessor was developed by RT Module [2] and current programming technology is uncomfortable for parallel programming. The main reason of this is using low-level language [3]. There is a high level programming language C++, but it does not allow using vector instructions. Programmer has to compose code for parallel processing, communication organization and other supporting code.

Parallel computing systems need high-speed mechanisms for transferring data and system messages between processes. Every processor has two such links with transfer rate of 20Mb/sec. Processors are connected by ring topology using two rings with opposite transferring directions. As an alternative topology we use star topology with communication device in the center. Communication device is based on TMS320C40 signal processors and has memory accessed from neuroprocessors connected to the device. Second communication mechanism is a transferring through PCI or Compact PCI buses, but it is not the fastest way because it depends on number of processors.

There are similar systems [4]. Philips produces Lneuro chip, which consists of 16 processor elements with 16 bit registers. Each processor element can work as 16 1bit, 8 2bit, 4 4bit, 2 8bit or 1 16bit processor element.

Hitachi developed Wafer Scale Integration. Every wafer contains neural network with 576 neurons. Neuron has 64 8bit weight.

V. Malyshkin (Ed.): PaCT 2001, LNCS 2127, pp. 181–185, 2001.

NM6403 has weight matrix 32x64 bit. Weight bit length varies from 1 to 64. But this processor is not only neurochip, but DSP (Digital Signal Processor) too.

1 Operating System

Operating system has module architecture and can be logically separated into
- Global task manager (GTM), which executed on Intel [5] 80x386 compatible microprocessor. There is only one copy of GTM in system. GTM is a central control subsystem, which monitor and communicate with other system modules.
- Local task managers (LTM), which executed on each NM6403 microprocessor. It monitors tasks executed on local processor element and communicates with another LTMs and GTM.
- Remote operating system console. It serves as a communication and control tool between user and GTM.

Global Task Manager

Loading of GTM is the initial procedure for starting of operating system. GTM provides following services: system modules initialization, control and communications with another modules, collision detection, modules unloading and system shutdown.

System modules initialization includes: GTM loading and system tables creation (resource table, processes table, messages queue, etc.), LTM loading and establishing connection with console.

Messages can be of the following types: informational, control and packet messages.

Local Task Manager

LTM provides services for user tasks (communicational, computational, control, etc.). Another function is the communication with GTM and LTM running on connected by links processors. LTM switches between running processes to provide multitasking environment in real time mode.

Dynamic Resource Management

Programmer separates code into branches during writing parallel programs. If program is SPMD task then total number of branches is defined. Programmer doesn't know how many processors and other resources will be available during program execution. Operating system has to provide needed number of processors.

If system contains N processors, SPMD task needs M processors, N<M, and branches don't produce communications to each other, operating system executes N branches and places (M-N) branches to execution queue. But if branches intensively

interact then branches should be executed in parallel. In this case some branches will wait needed resources (e.g. synchronization or communication) and will be "slept" by operating system. "Slept" processes are placed to execution queue.

When process is started it placed in execution queue and its state is starting. If system has unused processor and in execution queue there is only one waiting process then it will be loaded to the free processor (GTM sends branch code and supported data to the LTM). In the case when execution queue contains more waiting processes than number of free processors, execution queue is analyzed. Every process has its priority value (user can set these values to processes). These values are used to choose the next process from queue for execution (see Table 1 for example).

Table 1. Example of Execution Queue

Priority of waiting process	4	1	2	1	3	3	4	1
Execution sequence	2	8	5	7	4	3	1	6
Queue growing				←				

Processes are taken from the execution queue when computing resources are released or some process is slept.

2 Programming Technology

Programming Language

Programmer can divide code on branches, which will be executed on separated processors. Some branches can be executed in parallel. Others should wait for some event. It depends on logic of task. Following construction shows how branch can be declared.

```
branch proc_type branch_name ( parameter_list) { body
},
```

branch is a keyword, which allow to generate special code for load, unload and communication. Proc_type sets type of microprocessor, which allow to execute branch; it can be nm for NM6403. Branch_Name is a unique identifier of branch. Parameter_list is a list of parameters, which passed to branch; body – is the set of operators and commands.

When OS loads branch, process is created, which consists of set of segments: code segment, data segments, stack segment etc. Parameters passed to branch and results of calculation are pushed to stack. When process is terminated, result is returned to main program.

Also parameters and results can be passed with help of MPI [6] (Message Passing Interface) or MPI-RT [7] (Message Passing Interface – Real Time).

Branch can be loaded by branchstart routine. Declaration of this function is following:

```
handle branchstart ( branch, num_param, param_list);
```

branch – identifier of branch , num_param – number of parameters, param_list – list of parameters. Function branchstart returns the process descriptor (ID).

Branchwait routine is used for barrier synchronization. Parameter of this function is a list of process descriptors terminated by 0 (null).

Function branchkill terminates execution of process. Process descriptor is passed as a parameter.

For running SPMD-task, which consists of num_branches branches with the same code and different data, next function is used:

```
handle SPMD_start (num_branches, branch_name,
     num_param, list_param [dist]);
```

branch_name – branch identifier, num_param – number of parameters, list_param – list of parameters, dist – kind of data distribution. Function returns descriptor of SPMD-task.

For barrier synchronization with termination of SPMD-task following routine is used

```
SPMD_wait (handle ID);
```

ID – descriptor of SPMD-task.

Types of Data Distribution

Branches of SPMD-task share data. That is why we need to set method of data distribution between branches. There are following types of data distribution:
1. Cyclic type distributes data between branches one by one (see table 2).
2. Block type distribute data between branches by dividing original data amount into equal blocks. Number of blocks is the same as number of branches.
3. Block-cyclic type is similar to cyclic distribution but data are distributed not by one but by block.

Table 2. Example of cyclic data distribution between 6 branches

Branch 1	Branch 2	Branch 3	Branch 4	Branch 5	Branch 6
1	2	3	4	5	6
7	8	9	10	11	12
...	...	...	...	...	...

Commutation

During the first stage of OS staring detecting of configuration is performed. OS loader sends test message to first processor, which was found. When processor receive message, it "remembers" sender and sends test message with help of own links to another processors. This procedure repeats while there is one (or more) processor, which has not received the message. Then message is returned back and every device adds own identifier and number of link to the end of message. Received sequence is analyzed to build topology of system.

In that case when there is no special commutation device, communication is performed by using host-computer. It means that message is sent to host-computer and then host-computer sends message to target processor. This method of communication is slow and can be used when communication is performed rarely.

If there is special commutation device in the system, then all messages are sent to that device and later to target processor or another commutation device.

When program is compiled compiler checks data requests, which are placed in RAM of another processor. In that case compiler adds code for accessing to that data. Host-computer (or commutation device if it present) has table of data location, which are used during search of data.

Conclusion

Main operating system modules were coded and tested. These modules are Global Task Manager, Local Task Manager and system console. Technology of programming is ready.

Next part of work will include development of communication libraries, system drivers, C and Fortran [8] compilers, system tools and such applications as image processing, image recognition and maps processing (e.g. fingerprint recognition).

References

1. Korobko A.Yu., Chefranov A.G.. Operation System for Computing System Based on NM6403 Neuroprocessors. In proceedings of conference "New Information technologies", 2000, Taganrog, p. 130-132 (in Russian).
2. RC "Module" web-site, NM6403 Documentation, www.module.ru.
3. Neuroprocessor NM6403. Base Software. Assembler Language Description. UFKV.30002-01 35 01, RT Module, 1997, 83 p.
4. Korneev V.V. Parallel Computing Systems. Moscow, Knowledge, 1999, 320 p. (in Russian).
5. Intel Corporation web-site, www.intel.com.
6. "MPI-2: Extensions to the Message-Passing Interface", Message Passing Interface Forum, July 18, 1997.
7. "Document for the Real-Time Message Passing Interface (MPI/RT-1.0)", Real-Time Message Passing Interface (MPI/RT) Forum, March 6, 2000.
8. H. Zima, P. Chapman, H. Moritsch, and P. Mehrotra. Dynamic Data Distributions in Vienna Fortran. In proceedings of Supercomputing `93, Portland, OR, November 1993.

Parallel SPMD-Tasks Graph Description Language for Network Clusters*

L.K. Babenko, A.G. Chefranov, and R.V. Trotsenko

Taganrog State University of Radio-Engineering
Per. Nekrasovskiy, 44, Taganrog, 347928, Russia
roman@mopevm.tsure.ru

Abstract. Language for the description of tasks graph informational-control structure is offered. The tasks graph nodes can represent the SPMD-applications in network cluster. The graph supposes branching, cycles and parametrical adjustment. The questions of organization of dynamic cluster resource management are considered in the process of the tasks graph realization. The example of the description of a tasks graph, demonstrating the basic capabilities of language and system, is given.

Introduction and Problem Statement

A lot of the software for network cluster systems is known: MPI, PVM, mpC [6], Linda [6], T-system [1], Condor [4] and many others. There are many mechanisms of synchronization and parallel processes communications in this software. Such systems, known for the authors, usually do not offer dynamic resource distributions, or impose some restrictions. Dynamics in parallel calculations organization allows to optimize system resources utilization, provides high level of reliability and virtually infinite resources. Also dynamics provides additional security in network.

In our works [2,3,5] cluster network system security problems, questions of remote subtasks launching system realization, their synchronization and data exchange between them were considered. This paper is devoted to task graph description language, which sets sequence of subtasks execution and data exchanges between them. The language also allows easily describing of SPMD-tasks.

MPI, PVM, mpC are based on Unix concept of processes existing simultaneously and having identical codes with several branches. Programming technology coincides with sequential tasks programming that results in hardness of complex parallel tasks programming.

T-system, Linda and Condor cluster system are closest to offered development.

T-system gives an automatic dynamic programs paralleling capability. It is a program system, using dynamic tasks (functions) distribution. In T-system the functional programming principle is applied. The functional programming imposes some restrictions on programs creation methods (for example each function has several inputs and only one output). T-system works on Unix-compatible OS's.

---

* The work is supported by RFBR (project 00-07-90300).

V. Malyshkin (Ed.): PaCT 2001, LNCS 2127, pp. 186–189, 2001.

Linda is similar to T-system, is based on shared memory ideology and has not suitable mechanism of dynamic resource allocation [6].

Condor is a system for dynamic distributed calculations organization. It provides tasks migration mechanism in case of machine failure and dynamic task creation. Condor does not allow or allows with restrictions a task structure setting: sequence of execution, task synchronization, data exchanges.

Task Configuration Language

So, the tasks in the system are described by means of a configuration language, which actually sets a graph of informational links inside a task. The task consists of subtasks or graph nodes. Each subtask is an executable file obtained by means of traditional sequential programming (C for example), which represents a "black box", having the inputs and outputs links.

There two basic inter-subtasks links: after death (actual after task completion) and lifetime (used during task processing). The links are unique system objects. The data transmitted via links, have no type and are represented by a byte raw of information.

Actually task structure is defined by its data links. It is one of the main system novelties. Links inside a task exist all time while the task is processing. They are independent from nodes, which are processed and then finish. Links and subtasks readiness functions define conditions when subtasks have to be started.

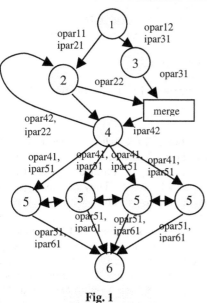

Fig. 1

When it is necessary to start a subtask, system chooses a minimally loaded workstation in the cluster and sends it command to start an executable file of the subtask.

Readiness functions are Boolean functions over combination of subtasks inputs. Subtask input has a true state when it contains data. If readiness function of some subtask is true and subtask is not processing, system starts this subtask. All subtasks have readiness functions. If readiness function is not defined for certain subtask in task configuration script, then it is supposed, that inputs readiness function is AND over all subtask inputs.

A text below describes graph, which is shown in fig.1 and shows main capabilities of the language.

```
//Task name and its input
and output parameters:
Task "sample" in tifile1, tifile2 out tofile;
const{N=4;} //Constant description and definition
//Task input and output data description:
```

```
data{tifile1 "file path"; tifile2 "file path";
     tofile   "file path";}
//Subtasks types description:
node_types{stsk1 "executable file path" in ipar11,
ipar12 out opar11;
stsk2 "executable file path" in ipar21, ipar22 out
opar21, opar22;
stsk3 "executable file path" in ipar31 out opar31;
stsk4 "executable file path" in ipar41, ipar42 out
opar41, opar42;
stsk5 "executable file path" in ipar51 out opar51 live
lpar51;
stsk6 "executable file path" in ipar61 out opar61;}
//Graph description:
graph{stsk1 s1; //Nodes variables definition
stsk2 s2;stsk3 s3;stsk4 s4; stsk5 stsk5m[N]; stsk6 s6;
//Readiness functions definition:
fready s2(ipar21|ipar22);fready s4(ipar41|ipar42);
//Connecting links:
connect tifile1,s1.ipar11;connect tifile2,s1.ipar12;
connect s1.opar11,s2.ipar21;
connect s1.opar11,s3.ipar31;
connect s2.opar21,s4.ipar41;
connect s4.opar42,s2.ipar22; //Making a cycle
//Merge a number of links in one link:
merge s4.ipar42 s2.opar22,s3.opar31;link t[N];
//Distribute data from one link on array of links:
dist s4.opar41(cyclic(100)on t);
rep i=0,N-2//Replicate part of text
{   connect t[i],stsk5m[i].ipar51;
    connect stsk5m[i].lpar51, stsk5m[i+1].lpar51;}
merge s6.ipar61 (stsk5m[i],i=0,N-1);
connect s6.opar61,tofile;}
```

Now we give some comments to the text above. Task, which is described by it, starts in *node 1* and finishes in *node 6*. The task takes data from files, defined in section *data*. This section also defines where will be put output data when the task completes. Then we define node types – our "black boxes". They are just types, not real nodes! Real nodes are defined in *graph* section as variables with types, defined above.

For *node 2* and *node 4* we have to define readiness function. These nodes can organize a cycle. So, usual AND in readiness function cannot be applied for this case, because data can be received from several destinations. If *node 2* starts with data in *ipar22*, it is a cycle, in *ipar21*, it is a direct flow of execution. By analogy, if *node 4* starts with data in *ipar41*, it is a cycle, in *ipar42*, it is a direct flow of execution. Thus, to organize a cycle we need to use readiness functions combined with *merge*. Another way to do this, it is use of additional node, which works like *merge* and unites data from several links into one output link.

The language has several constructions to make easy SPMD tasks creation. They are: merges, which unite data from several links into one link; distributions, which cut data from one link into slices and then put this slices into distribution output links;

arrays of nodes, which multiply one subtask. Thus, to create SPMD task, we need to declare nodes array, to distribute data between these nodes with use of *dist* and to merge output data with use of *merge*, after all subtasks completion.

Conclusion

Thus, in this article the language, allowing describing task structure as a graph with informational links, admitting branching and cycles was described; the example of the graph description was considered. Graph nodes are executable files obtained by mean of traditional sequential programming (C for example).

The task representation in the form of considered above information-control graphs can be useful (effects in virtualizing of resources and system reliability increasing) at the solving such complex tasks, as adaptive mobile objects management in conditions of non-stationary environment, where the complex counting algorithms depend on the movement mode and environment conditions are applied. Also dynamic task distribution provides additional security of cluster system, which works in networks with public access.

At this time the subsystems of security, remote starting and tasks state monitoring with graph handling were partially implemented. In the near future further realization of the system is planned.

References

1. Abramov S.M., Adamovich A.E. T-system – programming environment with automatic dynamic programs paralleling. – In a book: Software systems: Theoretical basis and applications/under ed. A.K. Ailamozyan. –M.: Nauka, 1999, p. 201-213 (in Russian).
2. Babenko L.K., Trotsenko R.V., Chefranov A.G. About methods and means of effective and safe distributed calculations realization development. – Works of All-Russian science conference «High-performance calculations and its applications, Chernogolovka, October 30-November 2, 2000», M.: MSU, 2000, p. 71-72 (in Russian).
3. Babenko L.K., Trotsenko R.V., Chefranov A.G., Yavkin A.A. The network Internet/Intranet clusters: problems and solutions – Works collection of second regional science-practical seminar "Informational security – South of Russia", Taganrog, June 28-30, 2000, Taganrog: TSURE, 2000, p. 114-125 (in Russian).
4. Open systems, 7-8 2000, p. 20-26 (in Russian).
5. Trotsenko R.V. About a problem of multicomputer operating system on Wintel platform creation – Proceedings of V All-Russian science conference of students and post-graduates «Technical cybernetics, radio electronics and control systems», Taganrog, October 12-13, 2000, Taganrog: TSURE, p. 127-128 (in Russian).
6. htttp://www.parallel.ru

Optimizing Metacomputing
with Communication-Computation Overlap

Françoise Baude, Denis Caromel, Nathalie Furmento, and David Sagnol

OASIS – Joint Project CNRS / INRIA / University of Nice Sophia – Antipolis
INRIA - 2004 route des Lucioles - B.P. 93 - 06902 Valbonne Cedex, France
FirstName.LastName@sophia.inria.fr

Abstract. In the framework of distributed object systems, this paper presents the concepts and an implementation of an overlapping mechanism between communication and computation. This mechanism allows to decrease the execution time of a remote method invocation with parameters of large size. Its implementation and related experiments in the C++// language running on top of Globus and Nexus are described.

Keywords: Distributed Objects, C++, Metacomputing, Nexus/Globus, Lightweight Process, Remote Method Invocation, Pipelining, Future, Overlapping communication and computation

1 Introduction

1.1 General Objective

Distributed supercomputing applications require large amounts of computational resources that often only computational grids environments can provide. The price to pay when executing on such environments is the mandatory use of a high latency, low throughput network. As a consequence, any solution that could help to lower communication costs would be worth considering.

A basic idea is to overlap communication with computation, thus yielding to a pipeline effect regarding messages transmission. Any attempt to exploit this opportunity needs to rely on non-blocking elementary communications, such as for instance, asynchronous send and receive primitives as provided by well-known message-passing libraries (e.g. PVM [11] or MPI [15]).

For code readability and portability purposes, one additional requirement is to make the use of the overlapping technique as much transparent as possible for programmers. As such, we reject distributed hand programmed solutions where the programmer would himself split the data to be sent into smaller pieces, asynchronously send each piece in turn thus "feeding" the pipeline, while at the receiver side, explicitly and repetitively receive each new piece and goes on with it in the related computation.

Previous attempts to automatically make use of an overlapping mechanism between communication and computation have been successful in the context of data-parallel compiled languages. But as far as we know, this idea has never been investigated in the area of distributed object-oriented languages.

V. Malyshkin (Ed.): PaCT 2001, LNCS 2127, pp. 190–204, 2001.

1.2   Formulation of the Problem

The general idea featuring the concept of overlapping is that during a remote computation dealing with large data requiring transmission, communication and computation are automatically split in steps with a smaller data volume; then, it is only a question of pipelining these steps in order to achieve overlapping between the current step of the remote computation and the data transmission related to the next step of the remote computation. This requires executing a computation and a transmission step **at the same time**. One way to achieve this is to use non-blocking communications.

Schematically, in the SPMD or SIMD programming models, a similar computation has to be executed on each element of a large but fixed size data structure. So, the compiler or the run-time system is quite easily able to split it into small pieces, send each one in turn, apply the computation on each piece once it is received. If the compiler or the run-time system is not able to automatically decide how to split the data, the programmer can help. Thus, the implementation of this technique has generally been restricted to the field of data-parallel languages for parallel architectures with distributed memory: HPF [3], FortranD [17], but also in LOCCS [8], a library for communication routines and computation.

But, how should the same problem be tackled with, in the area of distributed object-oriented languages ? In this context, the whole computation taking place on the distributed entities can be expressed as remote service invocations through method calls as RMI [16] in Java or RPC in C/C++ [2], even if ultimately very low-level communications, e.g., network communications, are used. In order to exhibit parallelism between distributed computations, a solution is to use asynchronous – or non-blocking – service invocations instead of blocking ones as featured by classical RPCs. Many models and languages have exploited this idea [4]. In particular, we have designed and implemented distributed extensions to object-oriented languages such as Eiffel, C++ and Java, that enforce sequential code reuse in a parallel and distributed setting [6, 7]. In such languages extensions, each service invocation can be executed in parallel with the on-going computation. Once the result of the service is required, a wait-by-necessity mechanism comes to help [5]. More information related to this model will be given in Sect. 3.

In the implementation of such remote method invocation-based settings, all arguments of the method call must generally be received before the method execution starts.

Main idea. The essence of our proposition is thus to **apply a classical pipelining idea to the arguments of a remote call**: once the first part of the arguments has arrived, the method execution will be able to start. Moreover, it is only the type of the arguments that will automatically indicate how to split the data to send. In this way, programmers will be able to express, at a very high level, opportunities to introduce an overlapping of communications with computation operations. Optimisation of the parameter copying process, as in [18] is a different but complementary approach.

As the rest of the paper will show, the way the technique is designed and implemented implies an easy and flexible usage for programmers, and, in some circumstances, remarkable performance gains on a LAN-based environment as well as on a WAN-based one (i.e. on a grid).

1.3 Design Guidelines

To implement this general idea, several problems have to be solved:

1. design and implement elementary mechanisms, such as: data splitting, computation steps that can deal with partial data, ...;
2. make it as much as possible a transparent mechanism for programmers, but give them the possibility to guide the data splitting;
3. try to determine the appropriate size for data packets (i.e. try to estimate the duration of the different steps).

Our contribution is to design, implement, and evaluate it within the context of an object-oriented language extended with mechanisms for parallelism and distribution, C++// [6]. Only points 1 and 2 are resolved in this paper. *Automatically* solving point 3 would require more precise information about the computation and the underlying communication performances (a strategy for data-parallelism languages running on dedicated parallel machines is developed for instance in [8]).

As communication performances in the context of grid computing are quite unpredictable and vary dynamically, solving point 3 would be essentially manual (even if the programmer could be helped by some performance measurement tool) knowing that the benefits of the overlapping would also vary dynamically. As slicing of data into smaller units and also the corresponding slicing of computations seem to have to be manually done by the programmer, our solution can help: it provides an easy way in terms of programming effort, and a cheap way in terms of running cost, to describe and try to take advantage of pipelining in distributed object-oriented applications.

Structure of the paper. In Sect. 2, requirements and steps for point 1 are discussed. Then, strategies for splitting requests (point 2) are presented. Section 3 introduces an implementation for this technique using the C++// language, whose runtime is based on both standard and lightweight processes (through Nexus and Globus). In Sect. 4, we present some benchmarks whose main purpose are to validate the technique and its implementation while exhibiting some cases where the gain is almost optimal. This work is an extension of [1] in the sense that, excepted the design, the implementation, experiments, analysis and learned lessons are new, as they arise in a broader context (multithreading plus metacomputing).

2 Communication/Computation Overlap

This section presents the overlapping technique and the requirements for its implementation.

2.1   Elementary Mechanisms

The following items are the building blocks of the technique:

- send a request in pieces (without taking into account the strategy used for splitting it);
- be able to rebuild a partial request in such a way that service execution can be started;
- be able to integrate missing data when it arrives even if service execution has started;
- be able to block the computation if it tries to use missing data.

Step for Request Creation. In every system that proposes an RPC mechanism, the remote service request has to contain the method ID and the different parameters of the call which are marshalled using a deep (i.e. recursive) copy of the objects graph[1]. After that, the request is sent.

Requirement 1. Have access to the runtime code that sends requests in order to be able to decide *when* to send a request piece.

Step for Request Rebuilding. Once arrived in the remote system, the request is rebuilt: each parameter is reconstructed with the corresponding data and then the service can start. For implementing the overlapping technique, we have to be able to put a mark for the missing data. This mark informs the service that data are, temporarily, unavailable.

Requirement 2. Have access to the runtime code that deals with the unmarshalling of the request in order to manage marks of missing pieces.

When the remote context receives a new part of a request that is already partially rebuilt, the context has to be able to deal with it in an *automatic* and *transparent* way regarding the service that is already executing.

Requirement 3. A mechanism that receives and manages messages transparently.

Step for Service Execution. The service can run without any problem as long as it does not attempt to access missing data. An automatic and transparent blocking mechanism is required when it tries to use a missing data. In the same way, resumption has to be transparent and automatic. This requires a wait-by-necessity mechanism [5]. Such a mechanism is provided by the classical *future* mechanism as originally designed in Multilisp [12].

Requirement 4. Future types available from the programming language.

Assuming the previous requirement is fulfilled, each missing data at the instantiation time of the request object is replaced with a data type presenting a *future* semantic.

---

[1] If a field of an object is a reference to a remote object, i.e. a proxy, we just flatten a copy of this proxy.

2.2   Strategies for Splitting a Request

This section deals with the point 2 mentioned in the introduction. The crucial idea is to break, in the most transparent way for the programmers, the request parameters. It requires a modification of the marshalling/unmarshalling routines of objects. Whether these routines are generic or not, we have to be able to overload them.

Requirement 5. Be able to change the default marshalling/unmarshalling routines.

Strategies can be split in two groups whether they modify or not the class of the objects involved in a request.

With Class Modification A **new** class called *later* is introduced, from which all objects that require to be sent latter have to inherit from (see Code 1 for an example). Objects from these classes must not be sent (eventually also, not be marshalled) during the first inspection of the objects belonging to the request, but later, each one in a new message (as would be done for $m2$ when calling $dom \rightarrow rang(m1, m2)$ in Code 2 for example). According to the previous requirements, *later* objects behave the same as *future* objects: automatic blocking when one tries to access to the value, transparent update of the object with the incoming value.

This technique applies whether objects of *later* type sit at the first level (i.e. they are parameters of the remote call as $m2$ in Code 2), or at lower levels (i.e. they are parts of non-*later* parameters; for example each line of a matrix could be declared *later* whereas the matrix itself not). Notice that if needed, it is possible to cast an object declared as inheriting from *later* to the original type (e.g. from `Matrix_Later` to `Matrix`), and vice-versa. For example, if a *later* object must be used at the very beginning of the next remote call, it would be worth to cast it now to its original type in order to send it immediately.

Code 1 (Definition of a later class).

```
class Matrix_Later :
        public Later, public Matrix {
...
};
```

Without Class Modification. Two kinds of strategies come to mind:

1. either a new routine could replace the one used by default by the language runtime in order to flatten the objects graph corresponding to a request. The new routine would split the graph, each obtained part being subsequently sent in a new message. Splitting strategies could rely on the algorithm used for traversing the graph (either breadth or depth first);

2. or, if the language allows that a class member function be used for the
flatten operation instead of the standard one, a class could define its own
customised flatten-splitting routine, in the same spirit as done when defining
derived datatypes in MPI. For example, assume one parameter of the request
be an instance of a `Matrix` class, the flatten routine overriding the default
one could tell independently for each line how to flatten it and when to send
it.

Considering the first strategy implies that all arguments that need to be marshalled been split, whatever the potential benefit, i.e. without taking into account
the use order of those arguments for instance. Whereas considering the second,
while not transparent, gives the opportunity to give a more adequate splitting
and even sending order. As such, one can consider that these two strategies lie
at the two extremes of the spectrum, while the one using *later* types lies in-
between. Indeed, casting an object to *later* or back to its original type, and be
careful of argument positions in method signatures is a satisfactory compromise:
it is not completely transparent for programmers which thus have some control
on the splitting, but it does not require to define a specific marshalling routine
for each type, which would be quite boring. So, we decided to only experiment
with the strategy which relies on using *later* types.

3   Prototype Environment

We briefly present in this section our implementation of the overlapping mechanism. We use for this a parallel and distributed extension of C++, called C++//,
whose runtime is based on communicating lightweight processes using the NEXUS
library and GLOBUS [9].

3.1   C++//

The C++// language [6] (http://www.inria.fr/oasis/c++ll/) was designed
and implemented with the aim of importing reuse into parallel and concurrent
programming. It does not extend the language syntax, and requires no modification of the C++ compiler, since C++// is implemented as a library and a
preprocessor (relying on a Meta-Object Protocol [13] – MOP).

C++// provides a heterogeneous model with both passive and active objects. Active objects act as sequential processes serving requests (i.e. method
invocations) in a centralized and explicit manner by default (such objects are
instances of subclasses of the specific C++// class `Process`). Communications
towards active objects are systematically asynchronous. There are no shared passive objects (only call-by-value between processes, implying making deep copies
of request/reply parameters, like serialization in Java RMI).

The MOP is centered around points concerning RPC, where some reification
is applied: request send, request receive, reply send, reply receive. These points
manipulate requests or replies as first-class objects. Generic flatten and rebuild

functions are used for these objects. The reply of a service invocation is transparently built as a *future*. Access through method invocation to any object of *future* type is reified and blocks the caller if the result is not back yet.

Part of C++// runtime based on NEXUS. NEXUS [10] is a library used for both communications and lightweight processes (threads) in distributed applications, which provides the notion of remote service execution.

A C++// active object is implemented by using a lightweight process on a possibly remote NEXUS *context*. A requests queue of an active C++// object can be remotely referenced thanks to the definition of a NEXUS global pointer. A request for an active object is remotely queued by invoking a remote service at the NEXUS level (named *Queue_a_request*). This service takes as arguments a C++// service request id, and a list of C++// objects as parameters. Each such object is flattened using the generic flat() method of C++//. Executing a *Queue_a_request* service implies launching a new thread whose code is the effective queuing of the C++// request in the queue of the target C++// object, after its parameters have been unmarshalled (the generic C++// build() method is used for this purpose). Concurrency between request queue filling and request queue extracting is managed with NEXUS local mutual exclusion primitives.

Part of C++// runtime based on GLOBUS. C++//relies on the GRAM mechanism [9] to acquire nodes on a remote host and allocate active objects on a new machine. To help the programmer in this task, C++//provides a simple file to specify the mapping. For example :

```
m0 ll.inria.fr GLOBUS /0/sloop2/dsagnol/ecll/tests/gtk2/sc99Demo_slave
m1 pitcairn.mcs.anl.gov GLOBUS /nfs/dsl-homes02/caromel/sc99Demo_slave
m2 das3fs.tn.tudelft.nl GLOBUS /home/caromel/sc99Demo_slave
m3 bolas.isi.edu GLOBUS /nfs/v6/caromel/sc99Demo_slave
```

The strings $m0 \ldots m3$ are the virtual names of the machines that we use in the program. With this mechanism, we can change the mapping of the application without recompiling it.

3.2   Implementation of the Overlapping Technique in C++//

At the MOP level, the main modification is to write a new generic function to flatten requests (see Requir. 5): this function builds a first fragment which holds the request header and the non-*later* parameters, and then one fragment for each parameter of *later* type. Then at the runtime level (see Requir. 1), the *Queue_a_request* service is remotely called for the first fragment, while a new defined service *Update_Later* is called for the remaining fragments. The *Queue_a_request* service has been slightly modified in order to manage marks for missing objects (see Requir. 2). The newly defined service *Update_Later* transparently updates the corresponding awaited request parameters (see Requir. 3). As seen here, implementing the overlapping technique requires only minor modifications in the C++// language runtime support.

In order to switch from a *later* type to the original type and vice-versa, the MOP of C++// provides two primitives. Being of type *later* implies being accessed through a proxy, casting to the original type means discarding the proxy and returning a pointer to the original object.

4   Validation

4.1   Benchmark

We designed a simple test and benchmarked it. This test must not be considered as a real application, but as a means to validate the effectiveness of the technique.

Program. The test is based on the remote call of the method OpMatrix::rang() (see Code 2) which takes two matrices, squares the first one, and adds the second one. As the second matrix m2 is of type Matrix_Later, it can be used as a parameter of OpMatrix::rang(). The remote service can start as soon as the request id and the non-*later* parameters have been received. Experiments not using the overlapping technique are easily conducted : define m2 as an instance of Matrix instead of Matrix_Later.

Code 2 (Definition and use of a C++// remote service with later parameter).

```
class OpMatrix : public Process {
    virtual int rang(Matrix *m1,
                     Matrix *m2) {
        m1->square();
        m2->plus(m1);
        int res = m2->result();
        return (res);
    }
};
```

```
OpMatrix *dom = CppLL_new(("host"),OpMatrix,());
Matrix *m1 =
        new Matrix(COLUMN, LINE);
Matrix *m2 =
        CppLL_new (Matrix_Later, (COLUMN, LINE));
// set the values for m1 and m2
CLOCK_Call_Time_START;
int res = dom->rang(m1, m2);
CLOCK_Call_Time_STOP;
```

The technique should allow to overlap the remote execution requiring only m1 (i.e. the method m1→square()) with the transmission and reception of the *later* parameter (i.e. the matrix m2) that is only useful for the second part of the service execution (i.e. m2→plus(m1)). Compared with an execution not using the overlapping technique, the duration of m1→square() should increase, since, at the same time, the remote processor has also to manage the reception and update of the matrix m2.

In the framework of this test, we measure various durations (see Fig. 1). The first, *total_duration* is the total duration of the complete call as perceived by the caller. This is the duration that will be reduced using the overlapping technique. Duration $d1$ is the time when using only m1 in the computation (m1→square()), while $d2$ is the time requiring both matrices (i.e. m2→plus(m1)). Both computations depend on the matrix size (for simplicity, both matrices are of the same size). Moreover, in order to experiment with longer computations thus with situations where there is more opportunity for some overlapping to occur, the duration $d1$ can vary: a parameter, say $p \geq 1$, is given to the test, and the computation inside m1→square() is called p times.

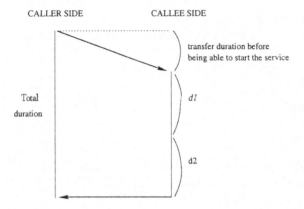

Fig. 1. Temporal decomposition of a – blocking – remote service call

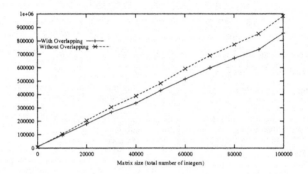

Fig. 2. Execution of the remote service (caller side, total_duration in μs)

4.2 Results using C++//

Apart from proving the correctness of the overlapping technique implementation, we will show that the obtained results are scalable and can yield optimal gains. The formal definition of what we mean by gain will be given at the end of this subsection. We begin by some LAN-based tests (two Sun Solaris 2.6 workstations with 128 MB of RAM, interconnected by a 10 Mbits Ethernet are used), followed by some GLOBUS -based ones.

The two curves plotted in Figs. 2 and 3 show that when the remote computation duration that does not access to *later* parameters increases ($d1$), then the benefit also increases. Indeed, because of the use of lightweight processes, computation using only m1 and reception of m2 have more opportunity to be interleaved when $d1$ increases.

Moreover, the reception related operations do not disturb very much the on-going computation (see Fig. 4), although they arise while m1→square() is being executed. To claim this, we must be sure that the reception related operations indeed arise while m1→square() is being executed (and not latter when

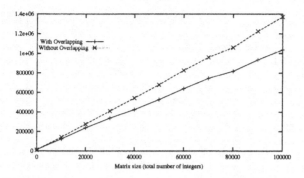

Fig. 3. Execution of the remote service (caller side, total_duration in μs). m1→square() (d1) is 4 times longer than in Fig. 2

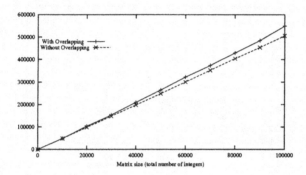

Fig. 4. Duration in μs of the remote computation not using *later* parameters (d1). The tests correspond to those of Fig. 3

m2→plus(m1) is already started). The answer is given by Fig. 5 where one can observe that almost no reception related operations have arisen in m2→plus(m1).

The overlapping technique used in this context where lightweight processes are available, scales very well, as Fig. 6 shows it. As distributed computing on grid environments is mainly justified by huge data sets, this is an interesting property. Moreover, we deduce against our past experiences that only runtime supports using lightweight processes can scale so well. Indeed, benchmarks conducted in the context of C++// on top of PVM [1] proved that the amount of data that could be sent and received while the remote service is in progress, is bounded by the remote receiving buffer size. The fundamental reason is that the transport-level layer can not gain the receiver process attention while this latter is engaged in a remote computation (i.e. m1→square()), due to the lack of a dedicated concurrent receiving thread.

We have also tested the use of a multi-processor workstation for the remote service execution. All experiments we have conducted on this platform occurred while it was unloaded, so that we could assume that at least 2 CPUs were idle. In this case, the computation not using *later* parameters (i.e. m1→square())

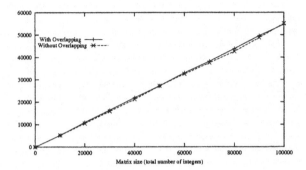

Fig. 5. Duration in μs of the remote computation using *later* parameters (d2). The tests correspond to those of Fig. 3

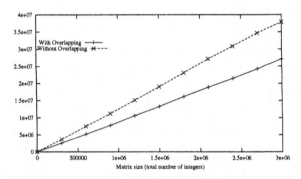

Fig. 6. Execution of the remote service with large matrix sizes (caller side, total_duration in μs). Same configuration as tests of Fig. 3

is absolutely not disturbed compared with experiments where the overlapping technique is not active. This confirms the fact that the reception of *later* parameters is effectively executed in parallel with the computations not using *later* parameters. This gives us confidence that the way the technique is implemented, i.e. based on lightweight processes, provides really concurrent activities that can even be executed in parallel, in this case yielding an unmeasurable overhead.

Gain. Let us define a gain (G) in order to give a concrete estimation of the benefit.

$$G = \frac{duration_{not\_using\_overlap} - duration_{using\_overlap}}{later\_parameters\_transfer\_duration}. \tag{1}$$

$duration_{..\_using\_overlap}$ represents the total duration of the remote service execution in either case (using or not the overlapping technique). The duration for transferring *later* parameters, i.e. m2, is estimated by sending a C++// object of the same size, not counting the – small – additional cost that would be required for managing a *later* parameter (a few milliseconds).

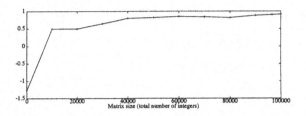

Fig. 7. Benefit (G) obtained from using the overlapping technique on a LAN. Correspond to the tests of Fig. 3

Expected values of G are in $[0, 1[$: it means that the transfer duration of *later* parameters has been overlapped by some useful computation occurring at the callee side (i.e. m1→square()). To avoid negative values for G, the only condition is that *later* parameters and computation duration be sufficiently large, such as to mask the – small – overhead of the technique (see Fig. 7). Obtaining a value of G greater than 1 is not related to the overlapping technique but of the variable network loads (especially noticeable on a WAN, see Fig. 9 and [1]).

4.3   Discussion

Using an environment where computation and reception executions are parallel or pseudo-parallel enables to really take advantage of our technique, thus leading to a gain close to the optimal possible value, as computed by G and shown in Figs. 7 and 8.

But, one should notice that the duration of the remote computation is of course an other crucial point. Indeed, if it is really too short compared with the transmission speed, almost no communication overlapping occurs. This is why the grid-based experiments plotted in Figs. 8 and 9 assigned $d1$ to be 300 times higher than in experiments plotted in Fig. 3. Even if the matrix size was 4 times smaller, this arbitrary choice for such a high value for $d1$ lead to a sufficiently high remote computation duration, in the same order of magnitude as communication delays. It is reasonable to expect that transmitting a large or even huge volume of data to remote computers (especially on a grid) is justified by the need to execute quite costly computations on these data.

An other important factor is related to the transmission delays. If they are very low because either the number of transmitted bytes is small, or the network speed is really good as on a LAN, then the technique can yield to a gain but which can prove in fact to be negligible (for instance, if we spare a few milliseconds only). If we now integrate the overhead oft the technique (a few milliseconds of computation time only), then we can see that the benefit (even if optimal if all the transmission has been overlapped) can sometimes be overridden by the overhead. This can effectively arise on LAN-based environments as Fig. 7 plots it for small matrix sizes (observe the negative values for G). On the contrary, on

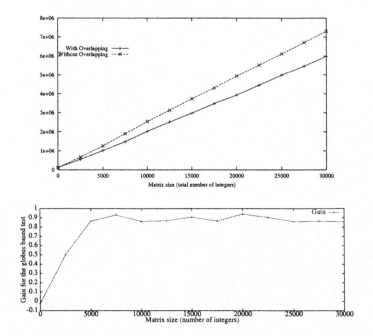

Fig. 8. Execution of the remote service (caller side, total_duration in μs) and corresponding gain. This corresponds to one Globus-based test between Argonne and INRIA during night period, with (d1) 300 times longer than in Fig. 3

WAN-based environments, sparing the transmission time of even a few bytes[2] yields a positive gain that the overhead of the technique can not override (due to so high transmission delays): observe for instance in Fig. 8 the fact that G is greater than 0.

We thus advocate to turn the overlapping technique on for every remote service invocation whose related communications occur on a WAN. Depending on the remote computation algorithm and its parameters usage (which implies how to best split parameters transmission through their cast into *later* type), the benefit can in some cases even rise close to the optimal possible value, i.e. where the whole transmission time of *later* parameters has been spared.

5   Conclusion

In this paper, we have defined and implemented a mechanism to overlap computations with communications in distributed object-oriented languages.

---

[2] More precisely, the total duration for the test in Fig. 8 using matrices $m1$ and $m2$ of 2500 integers decreases from 680816 microseconds not using the overlapping technique to 556446 microseconds when using it.

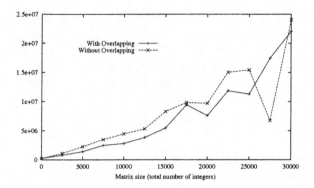

Fig. 9. Execution of the remote service (caller side, total_duration in μs). This corresponds to one Globus-based test between Argonne and INRIA during day period, with (d1) 300 times longer than in Fig. 3

Performances. This mechanism is interesting for environments based on lightweight processes, because they enable to make the transfer of *later* objects parallel with the on-going remote service execution. The technique scales very well, and its use dramatically decreases the total duration of the service execution as soon as operations on non-*later* parameters take enough time to enable the parallel execution of *later* parameters transmission. In this last case, this becomes clearly an advantage for applications running on high latency WANs (see Figs. 8 and 9) where several seconds in transmission time can be spared. Nevertheless, be aware that there is a small overhead when accessing objects of *later* type because the access is reified. An experiments-&-measurements analysis tool could help programmers to decide when to turn the overlapping mechanism on or off. Such a tool could extract the same kind of numerical results than described in Sect. 4 (e.g. extract $d1$, $d2$, ... dn and *total_duration* out of the experiments with or without using the overlapping mechanism, compute the related value for G).

Ease of use. As exemplified in Code 2, the programmer has to manually split data into smaller units, but this only requires to change the type of the parameters (make them inherit from the *later* class). To take advantage of the mechanism, the remote computation does not necessarily need a specific design (or redesign). The only important point is that the order the various parameters are first used should closely follow the order they are sent and received. So, the position of *later* parameters in method signatures becomes important. This ease of use is an argument in favour of a systematic usage of the technique, even if the benefits are not always here as they could depend from unpredictable communication durations especially on the grid.

Implementation. The requirement to implement the overlapping technique in an object-oriented distributed language is mainly to have free access to the transport layer and a MOP for the language. If so, essentially only the flatten and rebuild phases of remote procedure calls need to be modified: the object representing the remote call has to be fragmented into several pieces. Those phases need only to use a mechanism offering a *future* semantic. Transparent reception and management for later fragments is required at the runtime support level. Such a mechanism is of widespread use, and is in particular available in NEXUS, and in PM^2 [14], both of them acting as "low-level" runtime supports for parallel and distributed computations.

References

1. F. Baude, D. Caromel, N. Furmento, and D. Sagnol. Overlapping Communication with Computation in Distributed Object Systems. In HPCN Europe'99 *LNCS 1593*, 744-753, 1999.
2. A.D. Birrell and B.J. Nelson. Implementing Remote Procedure Calls. *ACM Transactions on Computer Systems*, 2(1): 39–59, Feb. 1984.
3. T. Brandes and F. Desprez. Implementing Pipelined Computation and Communication in an HPF Compiler. In *Euro-Par'96*, J:459-462, Aug. 1996.
4. J.-P. Briot, R. Guerraoui and K.-P. Lhr. Concurrency and Distribution in Object-Oriented Programming. *ACM Computing Surveys, 30(3), Sep. 1998.*
5. D. Caromel. Towards a Method of Object-Oriented Concurrent Programming. *Communications of the ACM, 36(9):90-102, Sep. 1993.*
6. D. Caromel, F. Belloncle and Y. Roudier. *Parallel Programming Using C++*, chapter The C++// System, p 257-296. MIT Press, 1996. ISBN 0-262-73118-5.
7. D. Caromel, W. Klauser and J. Vayssiere, *Towards Seamless Computing and Metacomputing in Java*, Concurrency Practice and Experience, 10(11-13), Nov. 1998.
8. F. Desprez, P. Ramet, and J. Roman. Optimal Grain Size Computation for Pipelined Algorithms. In *Euro-Par'96*, T:165-172, Aug. 1996.
9. I. Foster, C. Kesselman. Globus: A Metacomputing Infrastructure Toolkit. *International Journal of Supercomputer Applications*, 11(2):115-128, 1997.
10. I. Foster, C. Kesselman, and S. Tuecke. The Nexus Approach to Integrating Multithreading and Communication. *JPDC*, 37:70-82, 1996.
11. A. Geist *et al.* PVM Parallel Virtual Machine: a user's guide and tutorial for networked parallel computing. *MIT Press, 1994.*
12. R. Halstead. Parallel Symbolic Computing, *Computer*, 19(8):35–43, Aug. 1986
13. G. Kiczales, J. des Rivières, and D.G. Bobrow. *The Art of the Metaobject Protocol.* MIT Press, 1991.
14. R. Namyst and J-F. Méhaut. PM^2: Parallel Multithreaded Machine. A Computing Environment for Distributed Architectures. In *ParCo'95*, Gent, Belgium, Sep. 1995.
15. M. Snir and W. Gropp *et al. MPI: The Complete Reference.* MIT Press, 1998.
16. Sun Microsystems. Java RMI Tutorial, Nov. 1996. http://java.sun.com.
17. C.W. Tseng. *An Optimizing Fortran D Compiler for MIMD Distributed-Memory Machines.* PhD thesis, Rice University, Jan. 1993.
18. C. Videira Lopes. Adaptive Parameter Passing. In *ISOTAS'96*, Mar. 1996.

WebCluster: A Web-Accessible Cluster Computing System Based on Coordination and Mobility

Paolo Ciancarini and Davide Rossi

Dipartimento di Scienze dell'Informazione,
Università di Bologna,
Mura Anteo Zamboni, 7 - 40127, Bologna, Italy
{cianca,rossi}@cs.unibo.it

Abstract. Coordination systems based on multiple tuple spaces, namely those inspired by and extending the Linda coordination language, targeted to design and implement open distributed systems are experiencing some popularity thanks to the flexibility and dinamicity of the Java language: examples are Sun's JavaSpaces and IBM's TSpaces.
By integrating coordination and mobility, a flexible technology supported by the "run-everywhere" feature of Java, we developed WebCluster. WebCluster is a meta-application development system: namely a Web-based system that enables the implementation of Web-accessible, agent oriented, distributed applications. The application target of WebCluster is the class of computationally intensive applications based on the master-worker architecture.

1 Introduction

The integration of existing and new technologies often leads to the development of new applications classes. The most important examples of this concept are the current generation of Web-based, agent-oriented systems. In these systems the Web technology is integrated with existing technologies to improve the remote accessibility of distributed applications which implement some form of agents, namely autonomous programs which cooperate to solve some problem or to offer some service. Examples are applications that are simple front-ends of existing tools (like Web-based e-mail systems, discussion groups and the likes) but also applications that use the Web to enable the integration and the cooperation among multiple components providing a uniform user-interface (a notable example of these systems is the Source Force project [1] that integrates a set of cooperative programming tools like CVS, bug tracking systems, mailing lists and so on).

In most of these systems, however, the relationships among the various components are handled using *ad hoc* programming techniques, usually based on scripting languages. It seems then natural the idea of using some coordination technique to ease the development this kind of software. One of the definition

V. Malyshkin (Ed.): PaCT 2001, LNCS 2127, pp. 205–210, 2001.

of coordination is, in fact, the glue that enables components to cooperate and interact [5]. Starting from the above observation we designed PageSpace [4], a reference architecture to support distributed applications on the WWW based on coordination technologies. The work we introduce in this paper is our first attempt to design a meta-application development system based on the PageSpace concepts. We describe a Web-based environment that enable the users to build their own distributed, Web-accessible applications by using a coordination technology to enable component integration. In this very first system we decided to keep the things as simple as possible and in fact WebCluster, the application we present, is targeted to the development of rather simple application based on a master-worker architecture in a LAN environment. WebCluster itself is a Web-accessible system that integrates the Web with coordination and code mobility [2].

This paper is structured as follows: Sect. 2 introduces Jada, the coordination system on which WebCluster is based; Sect. 3 describes the architecture of WebCluster; in Sect. 4 an example application based on WebCluster is presented; Sect. 5 concludes the paper.

2   Jada

Jada [3] is a coordination language for Java that can be used to coordinate parallel/distributed components inspired by Linda [5]. Jada extends Linda's basic concepts by implementing new primitives, replacing tuple spaces with object spaces (i.e. specialized object containers) and enabling the creation of multiple spaces [6].

Jada's basic coordination entity is the `Space`. Concurrent threads can access a space by using a small yet effective set of primitives that are made available as methods of the `Space` class. `in`, `read` and `out` primitives are used to post an object into a space, to associatively get a copy of on object from a space or to associatively remove a object from a space, respectively. Associative access is performed by passing to the input primitives a *template*, an object that has to match (using a defined matching mechanism) the returned object.

Jada also provides the users with the `readAll` primitive that returns all the objects that match a given template and with the `getAll` and `getAny` primitives that return, respectively, all the objects that match or any object that matches a set of templates. All the input primitives can be associated to a timeout, interpreted as the time within which the primitive has to be performed. Input primitives are never blocking: they return an object that is an instance of the `Result` class. This object provides users with methods to check whether the operation has been successfully performed, whether it has been canceled (either by the user or because the timeout is over), and to gather its result. Gathering the result is a blocking operation: if the result is not yet available, the calling thread blocks until either the operation is successfully performed, or it is canceled. Output primitives can specify an associated time-to-live: when this time is over, the object emitted in the object space can be reclaimed by the garbage collector (the actual time-to-live used is the minimum between the one requested by the agent and the space default one).

The matching policy used by Jada is very simple and easily extensible. Templates (formals) are represented by instances of the `Class` class, the Java meta-class. A template representing an `Integer` class, for instance, matches any `Integer` object. Actual to actual matching is delegated to the standard Java `equals` method in the general case, and to the ad hoc `matches` method when the objects implement the `JadaObject` interface. This mechanism is used in particular to customize the matching in the `Tuple` class, which is an ordered object container used to mimic Linda tuples. This class defines its matching policy by implementing the `matches` method so that two `Tuple` objects a and b match when:

- a and b have the same number of fields;
- each field in a matches the corresponding field in b using the standard Jada matching mechanism.

The same mechanism can be applied to any user-supplied class.

Jada provides users with a client/server based technology that enables distributed components to access an object space uniformly. Moreover, since an object space is a Java object, any application can create several object spaces and even several server objects spaces. The same paradigm can then be used to achieve data driven coordination in both parallel and distributed applications – though the access to a remote object space can obviously fail because of network troubles.

Security in Jada is addressed at two levels: by enforcing access control policies on a per-space basis, and by supporting data encryption when accessing a remote space. While the second mechanism obviously applies to remote spaces only, the first can also be used when concurrent threads access a local, shared object space. One of the advantages of this approach is that adopting a space-based access control enables uniform security policies to be used for both the concurrent and the distributed case, which is particularly useful for mobile agents.

In the last few years Jada has been used for several research projects and to implement quite different systems, from parallel computing to Internet card games, from distributed collaborative applications to mobile agents systems.

3 Architecture of WebCluster

WebCluster is a Web-accessible distributed computation system that allows remote users to upload Java-based workers agents into the run-time environment. Remote applications, or applets, can submit jobs for the workers agents and gather computation results by using Jada object spaces.

Distributed applications on WebCluster are called *projects*. The components of a typical project are:

- an object space used to post jobs and results;

- a set of worker agents (run by the WebCluster run time system on every available host in the remote local area network);
- a master agent, usually an applet that can be downloaded from the Web-Cluster HTTP server.

The components are uploaded by the users to WebCluster by the mean of a Web-based interface that allows the remote administration of the projects. Administration options include:

- the creation of a new project;
- the uploading of updated code for an existing project;
- the activation of an existing project;
- the suspension of an existing project.

When a new project is created the Java code for the workers agents and for the master applet are uploaded into WebCluster (along with an HTML document that is used as the project's homepage and that usually include a reference to the master applet in order to enable access to the project from the Web). When this operation is accomplished the application can be activated.

When a project is activated the WebCluster's `Coordinator` component creates a new Jada object space that can be used by the project agents to post jobs and results. `Coordinator` also uses the WebCluster's main object space to notify available workstations that new workers agents have to be activated. WebCluster is designed so that new workstations can join the system at any time. At this point a user can download the project's homepage to execute the master applet that will post computation jobs into the WebCluster. The architecture of WebCluster is shown in Fig.1. Dashed lines are used to remark the containment of a set of components inside the same physical host. Jada spaces are not shown as contained to remark that they can be created by the `Coordinator` in any available host.

4   The Mandelbrot Set Explorer Application

The Mandelbrot Set Explorer is an application written to be run by WebCluster. The idea is to easily decompose the whole area to calculate in smaller sub-areas, creating a set of *jobs*, and delegate the computation of the jobs to workers agents. In the Frequently Asked Questions of the `comp.parallel` Usenet group, the computation of the Mandelbrot set is defined as "embarrassingly parallel" and this is one of the reasons for choosing it as a test bed for WebCluster. It is not the aim of this paper, in fact, to show how to write an application for WebCluster that exploits some "smart" parallelization technique but, rather, to show how to use WebCluster for a "bare-bone" parallel algorithm.

The components of the Mandelbrot Set Explorer applications are two: the master and the worker(s). The master itself is composed by two sub-components: the engine (the component that splits the whole computation in jobs, posts the jobs into the remote space and gather the results) and the user interface (that reads the user input and displays the calculated set on the screen).

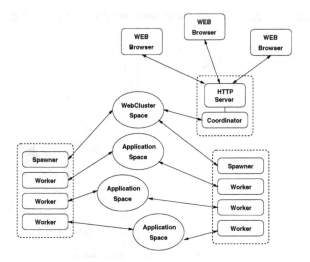

Fig. 1. WebCluster architecture

As with every WebCluster projects, when the Mandelbrot Set Explorer is activated the workers are propagated to the hosts in the cluster. When they start as new computational threads, a reference to the project's space is passed to them by the run-time system. At this point the workers start an endless loop in which they get a new job from the space (a blocking operation), compute the job and put the result back into the space.

Since jobs in the space can come from different concurrent masters (multiple users can, in fact, access the project at the same time) a field in the job descriptor is used to label the generator of the job; a corresponding field is used into the result descriptor so that results can be retried only from the generator of the corresponding jobs.

In order to enable masters to label their jobs with non conflicting labels the `Coordinator` put the (`"index"`, 0) initial tuple into newly created spaces. Masters in the Mandelbrot Set Explorer project use this tuple to generate a sequence of unique labels.

When a remote master is stopped without waiting for all the results to be gathered, unclaimed results objects could pollute the project's spaces. In order to overcome this problem the default time-to-live for the objects in the project spaces is set to a reasonable amount so that when results stay unclaimed for more than one hour they can be claimed by the garbage collector.

Figure 2 shows, on the left, the WebCluster interface for creating a new project and, on the right, the Mandelbrot Set Explorer application running.

5   Conclusions

WebCluster is a a Web-accessible distributed computation system that exploits coordination and mobile code technologies. While it has be implemented mostly

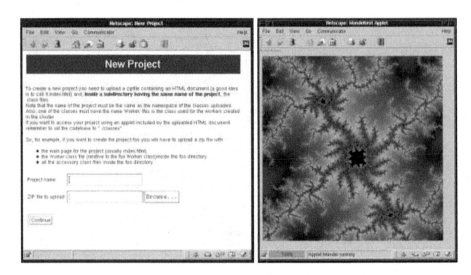

Fig. 2. WebCluster: creating a new project and the Mandelbrot Set Explorer

as a proof of concept for the design of a meta-application development system it is actually a running, usable system. Still, WebCluster lacks some valuable feature like the ability to build three-tier applications moving the master into the WebCluster and leaving just the input/output component into the browser, something that should be possible with a more flexible system. We are currently investigating on how to implement this kind of features while keeping the system as simple as possible. We are also engaged in the design of more generic meta-application development systems for deployment of distributed, collaborative applications accessible from the Web.

References

1. http://sourceforge.net
2. A. Fuggetta and G. Picco and G. Vigna Understanding Code Mobility *IEEE Transactions on Software Engineering* 24(5):342–361, 1998
3. P. Ciancarini and D. Rossi Coordinating Java Agents Over the WWW *World Wide Web Journal* 1(2):87–99, 1998
4. P. Ciancarini and R. Tolksdorf and F. Vitali and D. Rossi and A. Knoche Coordinating Multiagent Applications on the WWW: a Reference Architecture *IEEE Transactions on Software Engineering* 24(5):362–375, 1998
5. N. Carriero and D. Gelernter Coordination Languages and Their Significance *Communications of the ACM* 35(2):97–107,
6. D. Rossi and G. Cabri and E. Denti Tuple-based Technologies for Coordination. in *Coordination of Internet Agents: Models, Technologies, and Applications*, A. Omicini and F. Zambonelli and M. Klusch and R. Tolksdorf editors, Springer-Verlag Berlin/Heidelberg, 83–109, 2001

On Using SPiDER to Examine and Debug Real-World Data-Parallel Applications*

T. Fahringer[1], K. Sowa-Piekło[2], J. Luitz[3], and H. Moritsch[4]

[1] Institute for Software Science, University of Vienna
Liechtensteinstrasse 22, A-1090, Vienna, Austria
tf@par.univie.ac.at
[2] ABB Corporate Research
ul. Starowiślna 13A, 31-038 Kraków, Poland
krzysztof.sowa-pieklo@pl.abb.com
[3] Institute of Physical and Theoretical Chemistry,
Vienna University of Technology
Getreidemarkt 9/156, A-1060 Vienna, Austria
j.luitz@tuwien.ac.at
[4] Department of Business Administration, University of Vienna
Brünner Strasse 72, A-1210 Vienna, Austria
moritsch@finance2.bwl.univie.ac.at

Abstract. Debuggers are used to control the state of many processes, to present distributed information in a concise and clear way, to observe the execution behavior, to detect and to locate programming errors. In this paper we briefly describe the design of SPiDER which is an interactive source-level debugging system for both regular and irregular High Performance Fortran programs. SPiDER allows to inspect a single process of a parallel program or to examine the entire program from a global point of view. A sophisticated visualization system has been developed and included in SPiDER to visualize data distributions, data-to-processor mapping relationships, and array values. SPiDER enables a programmer to dynamically change data distributions as well as array values. For arrays whose distribution can change during program execution, an animated replay displays the distribution sequence together with the associated source code location. Array values can be stored at individual execution points and compared against each other to examine execution behavior (e.g. convergence behavior of a numerical algorithm). SPiDER has been fully implemented and is currently being used for the development of various real-world applications. Several experiments will be presented that demonstrate the usefulness of SPiDER.

1 Introduction

In recent years, parallel processing has evolved to a wider-spread technology for delivering parallel computing capability across a range of parallel architectures.

---

* This research is partially supported by the Austrian Science Fund as part of Aurora Project under contract SFBF1104.

V. Malyshkin (Ed.): PaCT 2001, LNCS 2127, pp. 211–225, 2001.

Unfortunately, availability of parallel systems does not imply ease of use. Hence, there has been an increased emphasis on parallel programming environments, including parallel language systems and tools for performance analysis, debugging, and visualization.

In this paper we briefly describe the design of SPiDER which is an interactive source-level debugging system for High Performance Fortran programs and leverages the HPF language, compiler, and runtime system to address the problem of providing high-level access to distributed data. SPiDER has been developed as part of the long-term AURORA project [1] where several real-world applications have been parallelized based on HPF. For the development of SPiDER in the context of AURORA we had several objectives in mind:

- Support programmers to observe and understand the execution behavior of their programs.
- Detect and locate programming errors at the high-level HPF code instead of low-level message passing program.
- Provide support for debugging an entire program from a global point of view instead of debugging individual processes.
- Enable sophisticated data distribution steering and animation as well as visualization and comparison of array values.
- Provide support to examine the quality of data distribution strategies.
- Develop debugging technology that is capable of handling both regular and irregular parallel programs.

The development of SPiDER is a joint effort among several research groups in Austria, Germany and Poland. SPiDER integrates a base debugging system (Technical University of Munich [17] and AGH Cracow [4]) for message passing programs with a high-level debugger (University of Vienna) that interfaces with VFC (University of Vienna [2]), a Fortran90/HPF compiler. The visualization system of SPiDER which is crucial to achieve the design objectives mentioned above, consists of two subsystems. Firstly, a graphical user interface displays the source code and allows the programmer to control execution, to inspect and to modify the program state. Secondly, GDDT (University of Linz [14]) is a sophisticated system to visualize data distributions and array values, to animate array distribution sequences and to display how well data has been distributed across all processors.

In the next section we give an overview of the VFC compiler and the most important HPF language constructs necessary to describe some of the functionality of SPiDER and are necessary to understand our experiments. In Sects. 3 we describe SPiDER as a multi-layer system comprising of VFC, HPF dependent debugging system, base debugging system, data distribution steering facility, and a graphical user interface. Experiments to demonstrate the usefulness of SPiDER are described in Sects. 4. Related work is discussed in Sect. 5 and concluding remarks are given in Sect. 6.

2   VFC Compiler and High Performance Fortran

The Vienna High Performance Compiler (VFC – [2]) is a command-line source-to-source parallelization system that translates Fortran90/HPF+ programs into Fortran90/MPI message-passing SPMD (single-program-multiple-data) programs. The SPMD model implies that each processor is executing the same program based on a different data domain.

The input language to VFC is Fortran90/HPF+ where HPF+ [2] is an improved variant of HPF (High Performance Fortran) language. HPF consists of a set of language extensions for Fortran to alleviate data parallel programming. The main concept of HPF relies on data distribution. A programmer writes a sequential program and specifies how the data space of a program should be distributed by adding data distribution directives to the declarations of arrays. It is then the responsibility of the compiler to translate a program containing such directives into an efficient parallel SPMD target program using explicit message passing on distributed memory machines.

The core element of HPF is the specification of data distribution, which is expressed by the **DISTRIBUTE** directive. HPF supports a two-level mapping model where arrays must be at first aligned to a template and then the template is distributed onto a processor array. Processor arrays are declared by using the **PROCESSORS** directive. For every array dimension the distribution is specified separately. HPF+ extends the standard HPF set of distribution methods (replicated, block, cyclic, block-cyclic) with the generalized block and indirect distributions which allow for more flexible distribution methods especially useful for irregular problems.

3   SPiDER

SPiDER[4] - an advanced symbolic debugging system for Fortran90/HPF parallel programs enables to control and to monitor program processes at the source code level. Multiple process view of the program enable a programmer to examine a single process of a parallel program or to inspect the entire program from a global point of view. SPiDER allows to examine distributed data structures which are visible as a single global entity, i.e., a programmer can inspect and modify a section or individual elements of distributed arrays without the need to specify on which processor the elements reside. Moreover, SPiDER provides support for regular and irregular applications with several exceptional features for visualization and steering of data distributions. Data distribution can be dynamically changed after stopping program execution at a breakpoint. Sophisticated visualization capabilities provide graphical representation of array values and data distribution with convenient navigation facilities for distributed data and logical processor arrays. It also allows to store up to seven snapshots of array contents of a given array and visualize differences between them. For complex applications in which the distribution of arrays changes many times during program execution, SPiDER provides an animated replay of the array redistribution

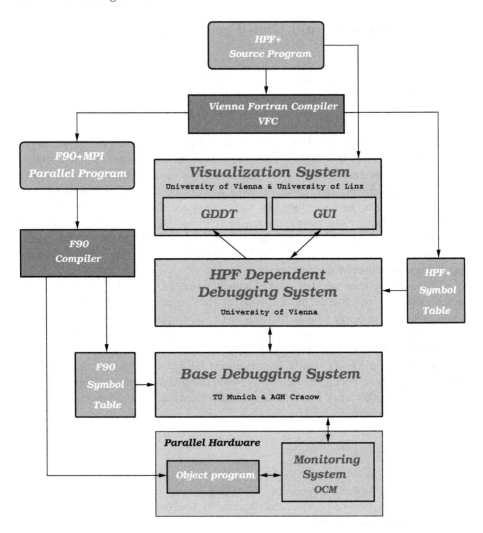

Fig. 1. Architecture of the HPF debugging system

sequence and allows to observe the migration of arbitrary array elements in a stepwise or continuous mode. Finally, SPiDER supports a load diagram that visualizes how many array elements have been mapped to every processor. This feature enables a programmer to examine how even data has been distributed across all processors.

Figure 1 shows the architecture of SPiDER with an emphasis on the support provided by VFC and low- and high-level debugging technology. The input programs of SPiDER are compiled with VFC to Fortran90 message programs. In order to generate an executable file, a vendor back-end Fortran90 compiler is used. The two-stage compilation process is reflected in the debugger architecture. The main parts of the system are the *Base Debugging System (BDS)* and the *HPF Dependent Debugging System (HDDS)*.

BDS operates as a low level debugger closely related to the target machine on which it is running on. It resolves all platform specific issues and hides them from the HDDS level. It also constitutes a clear, simple but unequivocal interface that provides functionality which allows to inspect the state of processes and values of data in the parallel program. BDS does not check for consistency of the running application with the HPF source code but provides information to HDDS about every process of the program. The design of BDS partially relies on the *DETOP* parallel debugger [17] and the *OCM* [18] monitoring system developed at LRR-TUM. HDDS works on top of BDS and provides a higher level functionality to allow viewing the associated HPF source code of the target parallel program and to interactively control and alter the application data. The interface of SPiDER to VFC is supported by a symbol table file which includes mapping information about mutually corresponding lines and symbols in HPF and the resulting Fortran90 message passing programs, and information about compiler transformations.

A programmer interacts with SPiDER by using the visualization system which consists of a *Graphical User Interface* (GUI) and a *Graphical Data Distribution Tool* (GDDT) for visualization of HPF data structures[14] (see Sect. 3.3).

The debugging commands offered by SPiDER can be subdivided into six classes:

1. **Execution control**: SPiDER enables to start, stop, and single step either the entire program or a specific process at any given time (see Figures 2 and 3).
2. **Inspection of program state**: These commands allow to retrieve information on the program's current state, e.g. the list of all existing processes, the current point of execution, back-trace of procedure calls, and the types and values of variables (distributed and replicated) or expressions (see Figures 2, 3, and 4).
3. **Visualization of distributed data**: These commands invoke GDDT to graphically visualize data distributions and array values (see Figures 2, and 3). Moreover, a history of data distributions and array value changes can be displayed.
4. **Modification of program state**: A set of commands is provided to modify the contents of variables and to change data distributions.
5. **Events and actions (breakpoints)**: Breakpoints (see Figures 2, and 3) may be set on source code lines or procedure entries for an arbitrary set of processes. A breakpoint consists of an execution event and an associated stop action. The event is raised whenever one of the selected processes reaches the given position in the source code. The stop action can either stop the process that raised the event, the processing node (on which a process is executing) or the entire program. These modes are essential in order to obtain consistent views of shared variables or the program's global state. Additionally, there are several events that are permanently monitored by SPiDER, e.g. exceptions or termination of a process.

6. **Miscellaneous**: There are also commands to display a source file, to set defaults, e.g. a default action for breakpoints, and to configure the graphical interface.

3.1   Data Distribution Steering

The capability to modify variable values in order to influence the behavior of a program is a very important feature of traditional debuggers. For long-running applications the programmer may inspect the program state at a given breakpoint and also control parameters that impact the program's performance. Specifying data distributions is of paramount importance to impact the performance of HPF programs. Therefore, the ability to steer the selection of data distributions provides the programmer with an excellent capability for program tuning. However, changing data distributions during program execution must be done with great care. Otherwise compiler assumptions about data distributions may become invalid, which can result in incorrect program behavior. Compilers perform various optimizations and transformations based on the assumption of a single data distribution (or possibly a set of them) that hold at a specific program point. If a programmer changes the data distribution during a debugging session such assumptions may become invalid. It mostly depends on the underlying compiler whether interactive redistribution of an array at a specific program point is valid or not. In the following we discuss important issues for interactive array redistribution under SPiDER.

In HPF the `DYNAMIC` directive is used to specify that the distribution of an array can be changed during program execution. All other arrays are assumed to be statically distributed (distribution cannot be changed during execution). For `DYNAMIC` arrays, compilers may assume that the associated distribution strategy is always unknown and, therefore, generate code that is distribution transparent, for instance its behavior does not depend on the distribution of arrays and refrain from performing any distribution-driven optimizations. However, advanced compiler technology may determine the set of possible distributions of an array at a given program point. This information can enable more optimized code generation which usually implies a reduced runtime overhead.

The execution of an SPMD parallel program commonly consists of interleaved phases of independent computation and communication phases. Note that independent computation phases are not restricted to code sections associated with the `INDEPENDENT` directive. The processes of a parallel program are not synchronized during a computation phase and every process may execute a different line of code at any given point in time. In many cases breakpoints serve as synchronization points where the debugger can provide a consistent view of the program execution and data (for instance, single execution point of processes and single value of replicated variables). However, there are exceptions based on the parallel nature of some HPF constructs that break the consistency of the program. The most typical example is a `DO INDEPENDENT` loop nest where every process executes a unique set of loop iterations. In order to enable a genuine parallel execution of `DO INDEPENDENT` loops, all data read or written by any process has to be local, otherwise non-local accesses would synchronize the execution. Invoking an array redistribution during execution of a DO INDEPENDENT loop would change the placement of array elements and as a consequence may invalidate the current work distribution.

VFC employs the inspector/executor strategy (see Sect. 2) to implement DO INDEPENDENT loops. A communication schedule specifies the non-local data needed to perform local computations. The loop nest is transformed in order to provide a uniform mechanism for accessing local and non-local data kept in buffers. By changing the distribution of a given array both communication schedule and associated buffers to access the array would be invalidated. The semantics of the program may be changed and incorrect results may be computed or the program may even crash. Another danger of changing a program's semantics stems from the REUSE clause which prevent redundant computation of inspector phases. Array redistribution could invalidate communication schedules and, therefore, also REUSE clauses. Although it is possible to recalculate the work distribution and resume execution of a loop nest, VFC and SPiDER currently disallow array redistribution during execution of a DO INDEPENDENT loop.

VFC provides SPiDER with important information (included in the HPF symbol table) to decide whether redistribution is allowed or not. Currently array redistribution is allowed based on the following constraints:

1. An array is associated with the DYNAMIC directive.
2. An array is not an alignee or an align target.
3. A breakpoint is set outside a DO INDEPENDENT loop nest,
4. Distribution driven compiler optimizations are turned off.

VFC determines these constraints and provides them to SPiDER through the HPF symbol table. The conditions are evaluated by the debugger at breakpoints and, depending on the result, a programmer is permitted to change the distribution of an array or not.

3.2 Graphical User Interface

SPiDER's graphical user interface comprises a debugger window (see "SPiDER window" in Figure 2) which consists of several frames: task frame, source code frame, state frame, output frame, and command frame. The source code frame shows the source of the currently debugged program. A green arrow (see Figure 2) points to the current statement where the debugger stopped all associated processes. Breakpoints are marked by red STOP icons. A programmer may click on a code line, variable name, or a breakpoint marker which pops up a menu offering all possible debugger commands for the given selection. For instance, if a line or a variable is selected, the menu will allow to set a breakpoint or to print the type or contents of the variable. If a breakpoint marker has been selected, the menu will enable deletion or modification of this breakpoint.

The task frame tabulates the list of processes (tasks) which currently execute the program shown in the source code frame. All commands invoked by a programmer under the debugger window will be applied to all selected processes in the task frame. In addition, there are also global commands that impact the entire application, e.g. a global stop.

The state frame displays the back-trace of procedure calls for all processes that are currently stopped. The command frame (see "SPiDER window" Figure 3) enables the programmer to enter debugger commands. The output frame shows various debugger output as a result of debugger commands entered by a programmer. In this frame SPiDER, for instance, outputs array values or data distributions.

A single debugger window is often sufficient and most convenient for debugging SPMD data parallel programs where all processes execute the same code. However, in the case where different processes are executing different parts of a program at a given time, it is very useful to simultaneously visualize all source code frames. Among others this feature may be useful if pure procedures are called in DO INDEPENDENT loops. Moreover, a coarse grain view of the entire program can be shown in one window, whereas a specific process could be debugged in a second window.

SPiDER has been designed to allow multiple debugger windows each of which may be associated with an arbitrary set of processes.

3.3   GDDT: Graphical Data Distribution Tool

GDDT [14] is used by SPiDER to visualize distributed arrays and their corresponding processor arrays. The development of GDDT has been largely driven by the needs of SPiDER, however, as of today it is a tool that can be used for other systems as well.

GDDT (*Graphical Data Distribution Tool*) has been designed for visualization and manipulation of distributed data structures which comprises the following features:

- visualization of data distributions,
- animation of redistributions histories,
- display of statistical information about data distributions,
- visualization of array values.

4   Applications

SPiDER has been fully implemented with all the functionality described in this paper. SPiDER is currently based on DETOP version 1.1, GDDT version 1.1, and VFC version 2.0. SPiDER currently runs under Sun Solaris 7. VFC generates message passing programs based on MPI library mpich 1.1.2. In this section we present two experiments in order to examine the usefulness of SPiDER which includes: a system for pricing of financial derivatives [6], developed by Prof. Dockner's group at the University of Vienna, and a system for quantum mechanical calculations of solids [3] developed by Prof. Schwarz and his group at the Vienna University of Technology.

4.1   Pricing of Financial Derivatives

The pricing of derivate products is an important field in finance theory. A *derivative* (or *derivative security*) is a financial instrument whose value depends on other, so called underlying securities [12]. Examples are stock options and variable coupon bonds, the latter paying interest rate dependent coupons. The pricing problem can be stated as follows: what is the price today of an instrument which will pay some cash flows in the future, depending on the development of an underlying security, e.g. stock prices or interest rates? For simple cases analytical formulas are available, but for a range of products, whose cash flows depend on a value of a financial variable in the past - so called *path dependent* products - Monte Carlo simulation techniques have to be applied [6]. By utilizing massively parallel architectures very efficient implementations can be achieved [13]. For a detailed description of the technique implemented see [6].

The group of Prof. Dockner at the Department of Business Administration, University of Vienna, developed the pricing system [6] as an HPF application. VFC was used to parallelize the pricing system and SPiDER to debug and to control the numerical behavior of this application.

In Figure 2 we show a snapshot of the SPiDER debugging session with the pricing system stopped in procedure TRAVERSE_DISCOUNT at a specific path in the Hull and White tree. The generated cash flow values are stored in array VALUE which consists of 5904 elements.

SPiDER provides a multiple process view of the pricing system. A programmer can either monitor and control a single process or inspect the entire program. SPiDER displays a list of all processes that are currently executing the program. A programmer can switch among them or select a group of processes based on which debugger commands can be invoked. In the source code frame the current execution point is displayed with several breakpoints set in procedure TRAVERSE_DISCOUNT. When execution reaches a breakpoint, either the processes for which the breakpoint has been set or all processes of the program are stopped. The state frame shows the current backtrace of procedure calls. It can be seen that the main program starts procedure au which in turn invoked procedure TRAVERSE_DISCOUNT. Window "Processor Array" shows processor array PR(1:4) with two processors PR(2:3) selected by a programmer. Window "Array Values" displays the element values for VALUE(2940:2970). The value range is between 14.19 and 89.63. Window "Data Array" shows the mapping relationship between processor and selected array elements.

4.2   Quantum Mechanical Calculations of Solids

A material science program package called WIEN97 [3] has been developed by the group of Prof. Schwarz, Institute of Physical and Theoretical Chemistry, Vienna University of Technology. Wien97 (calculates the electronic structure of solids) is based on density functional theory and the LAPW method which is one of the most accurate methods to investigate theoretically the properties of high technology materials.

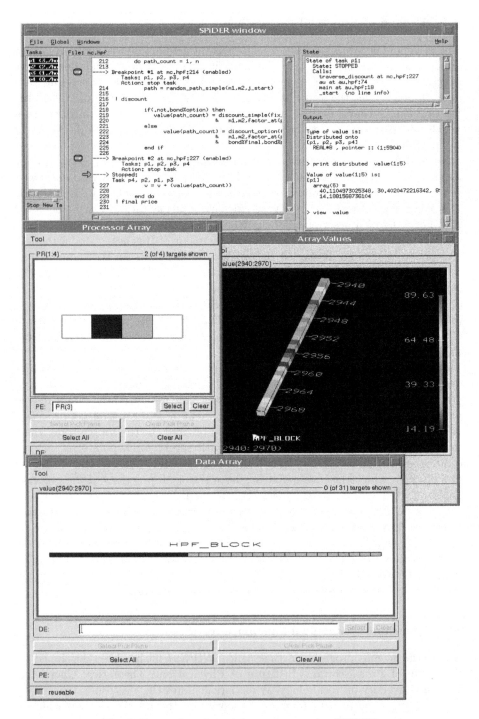

Fig. 2. Inspecting the pricing system under SPiDER

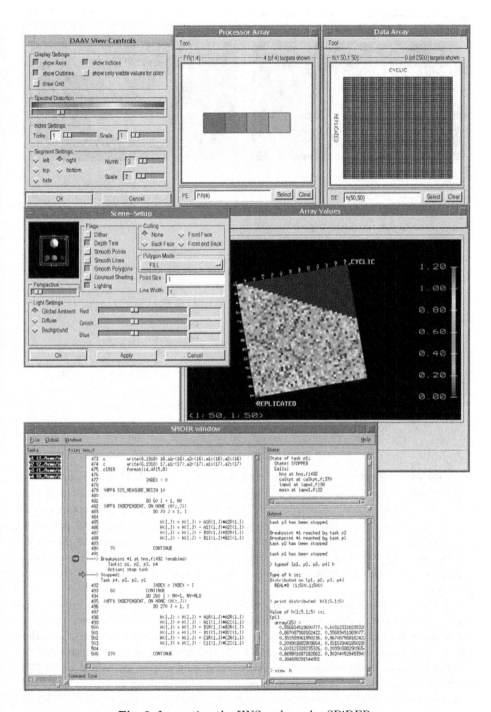

Fig. 3. Inspecting the HNS code under SPiDER

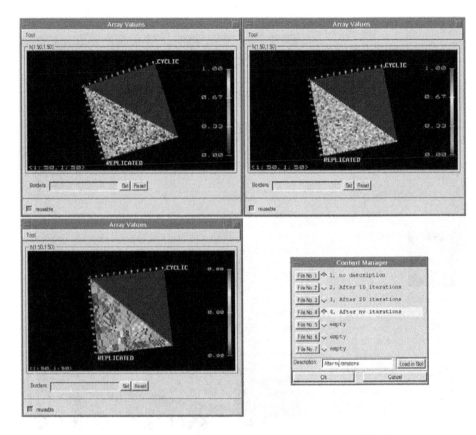

Fig. 4. Visualization of array values of the HNS code

One of the most computational intensive parts of WIEN97 comprises setting up the matrix elements of H and S, which are complicated sums of various terms (integrals between basis functions). A large fraction of this time is spent in the subroutine HNS, where the contributions to H due to the nonspherical potential are calculated. In HNS radial and angular dependent contributions to these elements are precomputed and condensed in a number of vectors which are then applied in a series of rank-2 updates to the symmetric (hermitian) Hamilton matrix.

H which is the main HNS array has been distributed CYCLIC [11] in the second dimension onto the maximum number of processors (HPF intrinsic function NUMBER_OF_PROCESSORS) – that are available on a given architecture. In order to achieve good work distribution, CYCLIC distribution has been chosen due to triangular loop iteration spaces. Figures 3 and 4 show two snapshots of an HNS debugging session under SPiDER. The parallel HNS version has been executed on a cluster of SUN workstations. Similar as for the pricing system, WIEN97 requires sophisticated support to visualize distributed arrays and the mapping relationship of data to processors.

Window "Data Array" in Figure 3 shows cyclic distribution of array H of the HNS code. The individual colors of array elements emphasize the owning processor in window "Processor Array". GDDT's rich set of display customization (slicing, scaling, and rotation) enables exploration of the view of array H. The graphical representation of distributed data is complemented by the visualization of array values. The global view of array values (see window "Array Values"), allows a programmer to quickly identify array elements with a possible inaccurate value. By incorporating GDDT's ability to store various array snapshots the position in the source code where an inaccurate value has been assigned can be found quite quickly.

Among others SPiDER has been used to locate an erroneous initialization of array H in the HNS code. All elements of H should have values in the range between 0 and 1. Moreover, only the lower left triangle of H should have values different from 0. Window "Array Values" of Figure 3 clearly displays array element values above 1 and also shows that array H is not triangular. Several array snapshots have been made which quickly enabled the programmer to detect that this bug was caused by an initialization procedure. Figure 4 shows the values of array H after eliminating this bug. The upper two windows show array elements at different iterations of a timing loop. The differences in values can be visualized by another feature of GDDT and is shown in the lower lower left window. Comparing array values at different execution points again allows to control the numerical behavior and in particular the convergence rate of the underlying algorithm.

5   Related Work

Despite of many activities in parallel software development, debugging parallel applications in particular debugging HPF applications has not been adequately supported so far.

There are some systems that visualize data distributions (e.g., *HPF-Builder* [16]) at compile time which are unable to show intricated details of dynamically changing data distributions. One of the most advanced systems in this field is *DAQV* [10], which has been designed for visualization of HPF programs. It is not a debugger by itself but rather a framework for accessing and modifying data at the run time in order to simplify visualization and computational steering. *CUMULVS (Collaborative User Migration User Library for Visualization and Steering)* [9] is a software framework that enables programmers to incorporate fault-tolerance, interactive visualization and computational steering into existing parallel programs. An experimental HPF debugger Aardvark [15] from DIGITAL is the most advanced system, that addresses many of the challenges involved. Aardvark introduces the concept of logical entities (an abstraction that exists within the debugger) that group together several related physical entities and syntesize a single view or behavior from them. Support for debugging HPF programs in most existing debuggers (e.g., *PDT* [5], *TotalView* [7]), is based on providing a display of the source code and global data visualization for viewing entire arrays and array segments allocated across processors. PDT supports global data visualization and replays for race conditions at the message passing level. TotalView provides process groups which are treated more like sets for set-wide operations than like a synthesis into a single logical entity. As a result no unified view of the call stacks exists.

6   Conclusions and Future Work

In this paper we have described SPiDER which is an interactive, source-level debugging system for both regular and irregular High Performance Fortran programs. SPiDER combines a base debugging system for message-passing programs with a high-level debugger that interfaces to an HPF compiler. A sophisticated visualization system has been developed and integrated into SPiDER for data distribution steering and animation as well as visualization and comparison of array values. The main novel features of SPiDER are the following:

- Besides regular applications SPiDER also supports irregular codes with highly dynamic behavior including indirect array accesses.
- Arrays can be dynamically redistributed at well-selected execution points which are controlled by the underlying compiler and SPiDER.
- Convenient facilities to navigate through distributed data arrays and logical processor arrays are provided with an emphasis on the mapping relationships between data and processors.
- An automatic replay feature enables the user to browse and replay array distribution sequences, which supports the examination of data redistributions during execution of a program.
- Array snapshots can be taken to store all values of an array at a specific execution point. Sophisticated visualization technology has been developed to examine and compare array snapshots which, for instance, enables the observation of the numerical behavior (e.g. convergence rate) of applications.
- The quality of data distributions can be examined using a load diagram, which visualizes how many data elements have been mapped to each process in a parallel program.

SPiDER combines the most useful capabilities of many existing debuggers and provides novel visualization and data distribution steering functionality for both regular and irregular data distributions.

In future work we will enhance SPiDER by presenting a single control flow of a program being debugged instead of a multiple process view. Moreover, we plan to extend existing SPiDER technology to support metacomputer applications written in JavaSymphony [8] based on OCM which is a distributed monitoring environment.

References

1. AURORA – Advanced Models, Applications and Software Systems for High Performance Computing, Part 1: Report on the first research period, April 10, 1997 - April 9, 2000. AURORA Report, October 1999.

2. S. Benkner. VFC: The Vienna Fortran Compiler. Scientific Programming, IOS Press, The Netherlands, 7(1):67–81, 1999.

3. P. Blaha, K. Schwarz, and J. Luitz. WIEN97, Full-potential, linearized augmented plane wave package for calculating crystal properties. Institute of Technical Electrochemistry, Vienna University of Technology, Vienna, Austria, ISBN 3-9501031-0-4, 1999.

4. P. Brezany, M. Bubak, P. Czerwiński, R. Koppler, K. Sowa, J. Volkert, and R. Wismüller. Advanced symbolic debugging of HPF programs with SPiDER. In Proc. of SC'99, ACM ISBN 1-58113-091-0, Portland, Oregon, USA, November 1999.

5. C. Clémençon, J. Fritscher, and R. Rühl. Visualization, Execution Control and Replay of Massively Parallel Programs within Annai's Debugging Tool. Technical Report TR-94-11, Swiss Center for Scientific Computing, 1994.

6. E. Dockner and H. Moritsch. Pricing Constant Maturity Floaters with Embeeded Options Using Monte Carlo Simulation. Technical Report AuR_99-04, AURORA Technical Reports, University of Vienna, January 1999.

7. Dolphin Interconnect Solution Inc. TotalView multiprocess debugger. User's Guide. Version 3.7.10, January 1998.

8. Thomas Fahringer. JavaSymphony: A System for Development of Locality-Oriented Distributed and Parallel Java Applications. In Proceedings of the IEEE International Conference on Cluster Computing CLUSTER 2000, Chemnitz, Germany, December 2000.

9. G. A. Geist, J. A. Kohl, and P. M. Papadopoulos. CUMULVS: Providing fault-tolerance, visualization and steering of parallel applications. International Journal of High Performance Computing Applications, 11(3):224–236, August 1997.

10. Steven T. Hackstadt and Allen D. Malony. DAQV: Distributed array query and visualization framework. Special issue on Parallel Computing, 196(1-2):289–317, 1998.

11. High Performance Fortran Forum. High Performance Fortran language specification, 1993.

12. J. C. Hull. Options, Futures, and Other Derivatives. Prentice Hall, April 1997.

13. J.M. Hutchinson and S.A. Zenios. Financial simulations on a massively parallel connection machine. The International Journal of Supercomputer Applications, 5(2):27–45, 1991.

14. R. Koppler, S. Grabner, and J. Volkert. Visualization of Distributed Data Structures for HPF-like Languages. Scientific Programming, spec. issue High Performance Fortran Comes of Age, 6(1):115–126, 1997.

15. D. C. P. LaFrance-Linden. Challenges in designing an HPF debugger. DIGITAL Technical Journal, 9(3):50–64, 1997.

16. Christian Lefebvre and Jean-Luc Dekeyser. Visualisation of HPF data mappings and of their communication cost. In Proc. VECPAR'98, Porto, Portugal, June 1998.

17. M. Oberhuber and R. Wismüller. DETOP - An Interactive Debugger for PowerPC Based Multicomputers. In P. Fritzson and L. Finmo, editors, Parallel Programming and Applications, pages 170–183. IOS Press, Amsterdam, May 1995.

18. R. Wismüller, J. Trinitis, and T. Ludwig. OCM — A Monitoring System for Interoperable Tools. In Proc. 2nd SIGMETRICS Symposium on Parallel and Distributed Tools SPDT'98, Welches, OR, USA, August 1998. To appear.

Experimental Version of Parallel Programs Translator from Petri Nets to C++

E.A. Golenkov, A.S. Sokolov, G.V. Tarasov, and D.I. Kharitonov

Institute for Automation and Control Processes, Radio 5, Vladivostok, Russia
demiurg@iacp.dvo.ru,
http://www.iacp.dvo.ru

Abstract. This article presents first steps in creating intellectual translator from Petri Net notation to C++. For this case Petri Nets have been adopted for programming needs and became capable to include functional programming commands and operators. Properties and operations on Coloured Petri Nets and Compositional Petri Nets were implemented in adopted version of Petri Nets, so that they could use advantages of hierarchical programming and data types. Translation to C++ procedure has been elaborated by a classical scheme: fragmentation, optimization and assembling, - and implemented in an experimental translator from Petri Nets to C++.

Keywords: Parallel systems, distributed systems, Petri Nets, parallel programming, computers clusters, supercomputing.

1 Introduction

On current state of computer evolution, computer clusters and supercomputers are widely used for solving not only scientific tasks but also business, economical and practical ones. That tendency is growing especially because of a progress in computer networks that makes it possible to manufacture clusters from ordinary components even at home. But programming of computer clusters differs from programming of stand alone computers. This is a quite difficult problem because a programmer has to decompose an algorithm on consecutive interactive processes and because parallel programs may have specific types of unusual errors. There are some models (shared memory, client-server), standards (MPI, PVM, OpenMP) and tools (HPF,HPC,Norma,T-System,DVM) for simplification parallel programming and improvement of parallelism degree in programs. Therefore we can say that programming of clusters is a job for highly skilled specialists.

Petri Nets is well known as a formalism for description and modeling of parallel and distributed systems. They are very attractive for application in parallel programming. Native visual representation, composition operations, interaction interfaces, explicit and implicit parallelism of different Petri Net dialects are useful for describing parallel programs, that are sometimes missing in other programming languages and tools. It is also useful to employ formal methods of

V. Malyshkin (Ed.): PaCT 2001, LNCS 2127, pp. 226–231, 2001.

analysis accumulated by the Petri Net theory. However the severe problem is that the Petri Net formalism is naturally parallel whereas computational units are programmed with the aid of sequential instructions. In this article we present an approach to translation of parallel constructs of Petri Nets into sequential instructions of functional language like C++. We also outline implementation of this approach in experimental version of translator.

2   Petri Nets Adaptation for Programming Needs

Petri Nets and their extensions [1] are usually based on set-theoretic notation, that is quite different from functional programming language semantics, so we were looking for another notation that could join together set-theoretic terms with programming constructions, we had found that XML suites this best. In order to produce appropriate notation we got definitions of consecutive and   parallel composition   operations from Compositional Petri Nets [4], places, arcs and transition attributes from Coloured Petri Nets [5] and type definitions, variable declarations, commands and operators from functional programming languages (C++).

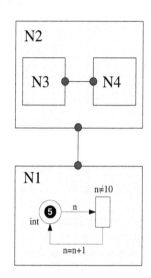

Fig. 1. Example of Petri Net

We defined Petri Net notation to consist of elements, that compose a structure of net, and a number of inscriptions corresponded to each element of the structure. Inscriptions are divided into two types: 1) visual inscriptions, that describes structure of elements size, positions, and naming, 2) qualitative, that describes elements behaviour in operations. The structure could consist of either sets of places, transitions and arcs (for plain Petri Net), or sets of nets and operations between them (for hierarchical Petri Net). Plain Petri Net elements could have qualitative inscriptions of the following types: *labels, token types, tokens, substitution and expression* (for arc), *predicate* (for transition), *SAP* (for places that form s-access points), *TAP* (for transitions that form t-access point). In hierarchical Petri Net only net elements could have qualitative inscriptions of types *TAP* and *SAP*, that represents inner net design in composition operations. We define *token types* to be C++ programming types and user defined programming types. *Substitution, expression* and *transition* are defined to be specified in C++ code too. It is not obligatory to use C++ semantics, that could be of any functional programming language, but having an aim to get further C++ code from a specification in terms of Petri Nets it is very convenient.

3   Translation from Petri Nets to C++

Typical program structure for solving problems with big amount of data is divided in next parts:

1. Gathering input data.
2. Decomposition of data between computational units.
3. Processing of data in computational units.
4. Assembling of data from computational units.
5. Presentation of answer to user.

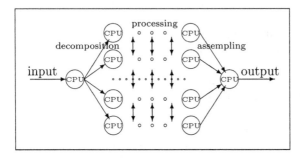

Fig. 2. Typical parallel task execution

These parts are quite different by type of data they are used in program algorithms. When using Petri Nets for description of program it is desirable to distinguish these parts in order not to overload description with redundant data and to reduce program definition by removing repeating parts. So we are thinking of real size programs in Petri Nets to consists of algorithms dealing with different aspects of data. Some of algorithms are processing data, and they could be called as pure algorithms, others that manipulates with data distribution and processes migration between computational units, could be called as templates. With such a scheme both templates and pure algorithms will not depend upon size of data, so that analysis and translation of them could be done by an appropriate translator. We had developed operations of decomposition and optimization that are preparing Petri Nets for such translation to C++.

Decomposition operation divides Petri Nets into a set of interacting sequential subnets of maximum length. The sequential subnet is a Petri Net, that saves number of tokens and interacts with other subnets only through the boundary elements, so that interaction is between more than two subnets.

Algorithm of decomposition is based on two concepts. First is the scope of token visibility: having token type and initial position we define it as set of places, arcs and transitions that could be reached by the token in all possible conditions. Second is the scope of token best visibility: having token type and initial position we define it as set of places, arcs and transitions that token always pass through in all possible conditions. To decompose net we need:

1. Find for each token in the net both scopes of visibility.
2. Intersect all tokens best visibility scopes and for each region form decomposition subnet.
3. Extract best visibility scopes from Petri Net.

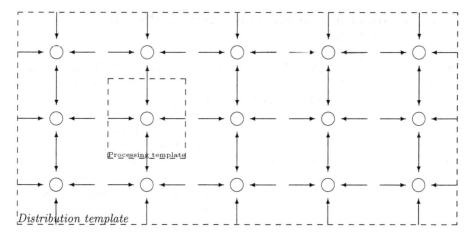

Fig. 3. Example of program template for computational grid

4. Define new tokens for places in previous tokens visibility scopes outgoing from best visibility scopes.
5. Repeat from first point until there are tokens in the net.

The main property of decomposition operation is an existence and uniqueness for any given Petri Net. So that after decomposition next operation - optimization, will deal with standard input data.

Optimization operation algorithm based on partial enumeration of all possible assemblings of decomposition subnets. Each assembling (or even assembling way) is evaluated by heuristic rules, and the best assembling is the final result of operation. In case of several equal estimated assemblings only one, that was found first will be the result. We had define three heuristic estimations:

1. for maximum length process, (the point is client-server application model);
2. for given number of approximately equal length processes, (the point is specific cluster architecture);
3. for minimum number of processes (the point is local area network application);

The aim of optimization operation is minimization of subnets number for execution in accordance with heuristic rules. This operation prepares for translation the specification of distributed algorithm with obvious processes and interactions between them.

A translation of optimized program representation from Petri Nets to C++ is a routine algorithm that could be interesting only from program development point of view.

4   Experimental Translator of Parallel Programs from Petri Nets to C++

The System consists of *Petri Net Editor* with a graphic user interface, three console applications (*Decomposition, Composition* and *Translation*), and two libraries (*Base Library* and *Petri Net program template*).

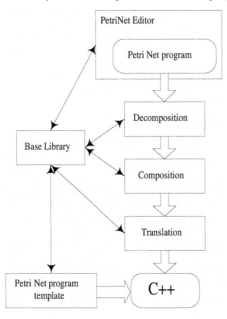

Fig. 4. System modules

Base Library is a set of C++ classes that is needed for using in the others components. It implements basic data structures such as list, array, tree, set, multiset and Petri net data structures. Together with these structures a number of basic operations to work with the structures have been defined there.

Petri Net Editor is used for Petri Net program specification and editing. It permits to work that could with many nets in the same time and programs you are designing that could be writing and reading to and from the file. To setup translation parameters the option dialog is used, in which you enter console tools location and properties (???). There are three translation buttons on a toolbar menu – Decomposition, Composition and Translation. To translate a program you need to push their consequently.

Decomposition, Composition and *Translation* tools implements decomposition, composition and translation phases accordingly. All these components work independently from each other and do not need a user interaction. They could be running both from the Petri Net Editor directly and command prompt manually as a stand-alone tool for producing certain translation phase. It is became possible because our system uses files for subsystems data communication. Decomposition and Composition write their results to file, stored by the Petri Net Editor and Translation tool creates C++ project in a directory specified by the user.

Petri Net file format is similar to XML [7] and can be easily converted to it, when standard XML specification of Petri Net will be completely defined.

Important part of the system is *Petri Net program template*. It is a stand-alone subsystem that represents a framework for Petri Net parallel programs. It implements all Petri Net abstractions in terms of C++. We develop special C++ classes to represent Petri Net processes, tokens, access points and etc. All Petri Net processes communications are handled by access points mechanisms. To provide processes interaction we have used MPI library.

In translation of Petri Net to C++ we have followed next principles:
- Subnet after composition phase is an independent process.
- Token is an independent data structure (class) describing a process state.
- Incoming arc in a transition is a separate class that prepares data for transition firing. It substitutes token class to transition predicate.
- Outgoing arc from transition is a special class that runs an expression and produces new tokens.

On the final phase of translation we inherit our generated program classes from the template and, hence, get a parallel C++ program that is designed in terms closed to Petri Net parallel mechanisms.

5 Conclusion

In this paper we investigated possibilities of Petri Net formalism in description parallel programs. An experimental version of translator from Petri Nets to C++ showed a possibility of creating efficient program environment based on Petri Nets. We can point out some directions for further work:

a) Program development with templates described by Petri Nets for clusters and supercomputers.

b) Application of existed analysis methods to program specifications.

References

1. Kotov V.E. Petri Nets. - Moscow: Science, 1984.
2. Hoar C. Interactive consecutive processes. - Moscow: World, 1989.
3. Anisimov N A: A Petri Net Entity as a Formal Model for LOTOS, a Specification Language for Distributed and Concurrent Systems. In: Mirenkov N.N. (ed) Parallel Computing Technologies, World Scientific, Singapore New Jersey London Hong Kong 1991, pp 440–450
4. Anisimov N.A., Koutny M. On Compositionality and Petri Nets in Protocol Engineering. In: In: Dembiński P, Średniawa M (eds.), Protocol Specification, Testing and Verification, XV. Chapman & Hall, pp.71-86, 1996.
5. Coloured Petri Nets. Basic Concepts, Analysis Methods and Practical Use. Volume 1, Basic Concepts K. Jensen, Monographs in Theoretical Computer Science, Springer-Verlag, 2nd corrected printing 1997.
6. Kotov V E: An Algebra for Parallelism Based on Petri nets. MFCS'78, Lect Notes Comput Sci, vol 64. Springer, Berlin Heidelberg New York 1978, pp 39–55
7. Meeting on XML/SGML based Interchange Formats for Petri Nets. Web page. Available on http://www.daimi.au.dk/pn2000/Interchange.
8. Melnikov V.E., Kharitonov D.I. On application of coloured access points for specification of autonomous vehichle. Th.: Third siberian congress on applied an industrial mathematics. INPRIM-98, Novosibirsk, 1998.
9. N.A.Anisimov, A.A.Kovalenko, G.V.Tarasov, A.V.Inzartsev, A.Ph.Scherbatyuk. A Graphical Environment for AUV Mission Programming and Verification. UUST'97, USA, 1997.
10. N.A.Anisimov, V.E.Melnikov, G.V.Tarasov, D.I.Kharitonov, P.V.Khrolenko, U.V.Vaulin, A.V.Inzartsev, A.Ph.Scherbatyuk. The using graphical language for AUV mission specification. Marine Technologies, Vladivostok, "Dalnauka", 1998

Typing the ISA to Cluster the Processor

Bernard Goossens

LIAFA, Université Paris 7, 2 place Jussieu, Paris Cedex 05, France
bg@liafa.jussieu.fr

Abstract. In this paper we propose a new separation of the processor units to avoid interunits communications for instruction dispatch, memory accesses and control flow computations. The motivation comes from the increasing importance of interchip signalling delays. The technique consists in separating the instruction set into types, e.g. integer, floating point and graphic, and the die into corresponding units, each including a private pc, an instruction cache, a prediction unit, a branch unit, a load/store unit and a data cache. Every type is able to fully handle data and pointer computations as well as typed address pointers. Hence the integer machine, the floating point one and the graphical one are very independent machines requiring no inter-machine communications. We justify our proposal by showing that the main communication paths can be highly reduced in length. We show that the fetch path length can be divided by 2, the data load path length can be decreased of 1/3 and computation units interconnection paths can be highly simplified, serving only for conversion purpose.

1 Introduction

Todays processors are built around 5 units: one instruction memory unit including an instruction cache, a fetch mechanism and a prediction subunit; three computing units (integer, floating point, graphic: the graphic unit can be further subdivided into an integer vector unit and a floating point vector unit); one data memory unit including load and store buffers and a data cache. Figure 1 left part shows how such a processor is organized on a die. The die is divided into three equal area parts, one devoted to the instruction memory unit, another devoted to the data memory unit and a third one containing the core, i.e. the three computing units. The size of the instruction cache has a direct impact on the processor cycle, with today a pipelined fetch unit delivering one fetch per cycle with a two cycles fetch latency [5,8].

Table 1 gives a *cacti* [2] estimation of the cache access times for different cache sizes and chips technologies (the times given are the data side ones in nano seconds, without output driver; computations parameters are: 128 output bits, 32 address bits, blocks of 32 bytes for caches up to 128KB and 64 bytes for larger caches, direct mapping for caches up to 8KB, associativity 2 for 16KB caches, 4 for 64KB caches and 8 for larger caches; for each line, the technology applied is the left one: for example on line one, the technology is 0.35μ).

V. Malyshkin (Ed.): PaCT 2001, LNCS 2127, pp. 232–242, 2001.

Table 1. Caches data path times

year	techno.	1KB	4KB	8KB	16KB	64KB	256KB	1MB	cpu cycle
1998	0.35/0.25μ	0.97	1.15	1.27	2.03	2.99	4.46	7.93	500/750Mhz 2/1.33ns
2000	0.25/0.18μ	0.70	0.82	0.91	1.45	2.14	3.18	5.67	1/1.5Ghz 1/0.66ns
2003	0.18/0.15μ	0.50	0.59	0.65	1.04	1.54	2.29	4.08	2/3Ghz 0.5/0.33ns
2005	0.15/0.13μ	0.42	0.49	0.54	0.87	1.28	1.91	3.40	4/6Ghz 0.25/0.16ns
2008	0.13/0.1μ	0.36	0.43	0.47	0.75	1.11	1.66	2.95	8/12Ghz 0.12/0.08ns
2010	0.1/...μ	0.28	0.33	0.36	0.58	0.86	1.27	2.27	16/...Ghz 0.06/...ns

If we assume a clock cycle doubling for each technology step, we can see that in 1998, a full fetch including cache block read and instruction selection and slotting, in a typical 16KB cache was possible in a cycle (as in the DEC 21164 [4]). In 2000, a fetch in a typical 64KB cache in a 600Mhz cpu (as in the DEC 21264) had a two cycles latency with a cache block read time of one cycle, hence the necessity of pipelining the fetch path (if the cache read time is larger than a cycle, wave pipelining [7] can be used to provide a cache throughput of one read per cycle as long as accurate addresses can be provided at the same rate). In a 1Ghz 0.18μ cpu, the first level cache must be reduced to 8KB to allow a single cycle read (as in the Pentium III [12]; the Pentium 4 [13] and the AMD Athlon [1] have larger L1 caches accessed in 2 cycles).

Moreover, driving the fetched instructions to the computing units is also a concern in todays cpus. For example the Pentium 4 dedicates a full cycle for this purpose. Tomorrow, in 2003/2005, in a 3Ghz cpu including an 8KB L1 instruction cache, if the path connecting the fetch machine to the computing units is not shortened, the drive time on its own will take two full cycles (to be added to the two cache read cycles).

This paper gives two hints to reduce fetch and load/store read path lengths in order to cope with the increased drive time. This paper is linked to the various works concerning processor clustering [6,11]. The main difference between the present approach and previous proposals is that we modify the ISA (Instruction Set Architecture). The consequence is that clustering is not only performed on the set of functional units but also on the fetch path and on the load/store path.

The paper is organized as follows: next section presents a two levels cache organization allowing simultaneous accesses to L1 and L2. Section 3 describes a new die layout clustered by data types. Section 4 explains which are the necessary ISA modifications. Section 5 discusses the paper proposal and compares it to the known works on cpu clustering, multithreading and on-chip multiprocessors.

2   A Two Levels Simultaneously Accessed Cache

On the die example presented on Fig. 1 left part, the fetch path is labeled 'f'. The fetch critical path goes from the center of the fetch unit (labeled *icache* on the figure) left edge where the pc is assumed to be located. It travels (say) to the fetch unit upper right corner where the fetched block is assumed to reside and

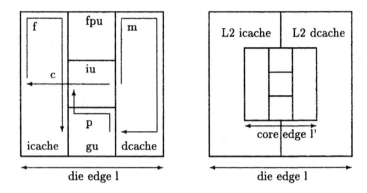

Fig. 1. Two processor dies

the fetched graphical instructions are propagated to the graphic unit (labeled *gu*) entrance which is assumed to be at the center of the unit left edge. This $5l/3$ path, where l is the die edge length ($l/2 + l/3 + 2l/3 + l/6$), corresponds to a worst case, a best one having an $l/3$ length (integer instruction placed at the center of the cache area). In a cpu today, this work is performed in two cycles, the first one being devoted to cache read (length $4l/3$) and the second one to instruction slotting (length $l/3$ and some decoding and selection logic). In such a cpu, the cycle is fixed to leave enough time for cache read, i.e. for a signal to cross a length $4l/3$ distance. Because the die edge l should be increased ([3]; 20mm in 2000, 28mm in 2005 and 40mm in 2010), as long as the cache read path is linked to l, the cycle time, if equal to the cache read time, should increase too (in other words, if we use the edge length increase to fill the die with cache, we increase the cycle time).

In the case of a memory access, an inter-computing-units communication takes place. The address computation is performed in the integer unit while the access itself may concern another unit register. The load path is labeled 'm' on the figure. It is longer than the fetch path because it involves a round trip. On the die example, the worst load distance is $2l$ starting at the center of the integer unit right edge (load address), going up to the data cache upper right corner where the block to be loaded is assumed to reside and going back to the center of the loading computing unit left edge, which is assumed to be the graphic one in the worst case ($l/2 + l/3 + 2l/3 + l/6 + l/3$). With today signalling delays, loading has at least a two cycles latency.

A first attempt to shorten the fetch and the load/store paths is to separate each cache in two levels. The die can be organized as shown on Fig. 1 right part. It includes a core corresponding to the left die, surrounded by two level 2 caches. The die edge is l (scaled to the technology process) and the core edge is l', with a wire delay of 1 cycle for a $4l'/3$ length (we link the cycle time to the l' length which should decrease as technology is refined). Such a design is close to the DEC 21164 or the Pentium III and 4 (except that the L2 cache in these processors is a unified cache). This two levels cache organization with a small

L1 cache was abandoned by DEC because the L1 cache had a too high miss rate and the first level miss detection incurred a too high penalty for the second level access time. It is still in use in the Pentium III but is also abandoned both in the AMD Athlon and in the Pentium 4 with a 64KB cache for the former and a 12Kops trace cache for the latter (the trace cache contains fixed length micro operations; it has a capacity roughly equivalent to a 64KB cache).

But as table 1 shows, such a cache capacity for 2003 clock speed will lead to a three to five cycles read latency (2 to 3 Ghz). On the other end, a cost effective two levels hierarchy starting with a small capacity L1 cache requires a reduced L2 access time. This can be done by performing both accesses (L1 and L2) simultaneously (the L2 access is stopped if the L1 hits) which implies keeping the L2 instruction cache distinct from the L2 data cache to avoid contention. In such a design, the L2 instruction cache can preferably be a victim cache as in the AMD Athlon (in case of a miss, the L1 cache loads the missing line and transfers to L2 the replaced line). In such a way, L1 miss detection does not add any penalty to L2 access time. In this design, a fetch that hits in the first level crosses a length $5l'/3$ with $4l'/3$ in a single cycle. For a L2 fetch, the distance is $2l - l'/3$ ($2l - l'$ for L2 access and $2l'/3$ to propagate L2 block to (say) the fpu). If we assume $l = 2l'$ as drawn on the figure, the L2 read ($3l'$) can be performed in 2 cycles (one more cycle is needed to slot instructions in their units, as in the case of a first level hit). As l' is decreased and l is increased, L2 reads may last much more than two cycles in finer technologies. When the gap becomes too important, it may be necessary to separate L2 in two levels, having three levels on-chip. However, by keeping the L1 caches constant in capacity, the l' length can scale with the technology allowing the cycle to scale too.

This is true only if the core does not increase (l' is not increased for architectural reasons). Unfortunately, actual trends with higher superscalar degrees is to add more and more functional units, along with new specialized ones such as the SIMD operators and bigger branch prediction hardware. Hence l' should not remain constant, implying that signal propagation inside the core itself may become a problem.

3   A New Die Layout

Figure 2 shows an alternative die organization that has three main differences with the layouts on Fig. 1: the caches first level have been duplicated, each copy being local to a computing unit; the fetch subunit and the prediction subunit have been duplicated with each copy placed on the left edge of each L1 instruction cache (there are three pc); eventually, the branch unit has been duplicated in every computing unit (the duplications are not apparent on the figure except for L1 caches).

The 'f' path starts from the center of an L1 unit left edge, goes up to the same L1 unit upper right corner and ends at the center of the corresponding computing unit left edge. The length is $2l'/3$, due to the locality of the fetch ($l'/6 + l'/3 + l'/6$). This is less than 1/2 of the Fig. 1 right die 'f' path length.

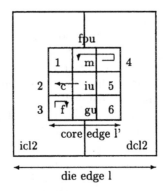

1,2,3: fpu,iu,gu instruction cache level 1
4,5,6: fpu,iu,gu data cache level 1

Fig. 2. A new die layout

In case of an L1 miss, the 'f' path length starts from the center of the L1 (say) graphic unit (gu) left edge, travels up to the L2 upper left corner (say), comes back to the starting point and ends at the center of the graphic computing unit left edge. Hence, it has length $2l$ $(2 * (l'/3 + l/2 + (l - l')/2) + l'/3)$ which is $l'/3$ longer than Fig. 1 right die 'f' path (the difference comes from the starting point of the fetch which is equidistant from each corner of the right die on Fig. 1 and but not on Fig. 2).

The 'm' path starts from the center of any computing unit right edge, goes to the corresponding L1 data unit upper right corner and travels back to the center of the same computing unit left edge $(l'/3 + l'/6 + 2l'/3 + l'/6)$. This is a length $4l'/3$ path (1/3 less than the right die 'm' path which has length $2l'$). In case of an L1 miss, the L2 access path has length $2l + 2l'/3$ $(2 * (l'/3 + (l - l')/2 + l'/3 + l/2) + l'/3)$. This is $2l'/3$ longer than right die 'm' path. The reason is that the address computation is local to the loading unit in the die on Fig. 2 instead of being performed in the integer unit in the right die on Fig. 1.

To fairly compare the two layouts, we must take in account that the L1 caches are partitioned in the new layout. This means that each unit has a private part that is 1/3 of the total L1 cache size. The cache miss rate is affected by this capacity reduction. Let r_1 be the L1 miss rate on Fig. 1 right die and r_2 the L1 miss rate on Fig. 2 die. The average fetch length on Fig. 1 right die is $5l'/3 * (1 - r_1) + (2l - l'/3) * r_1$ and the average fetch length on Fig. 2 die is $2l'/3 * (1 - r_2) + 2l * r_2$. The latter is better than the former as soon as $l < (3 - 6r_1 - 2r_2)/(6(r_2 - r_1))l'$. If for example $r_1 = 0.08$ and $r_2 = 0.16$, the new layout is better than the old one if $l < 4.6l'$ (when l gets very large compared to l', the L2 time becomes dominant; in such a case it is necessary to insert an intermediate level between L1 and L2; as L1 on Fig. 2, this intermediate level can be clustered).

The two layouts must also be compared for inter-unit communications. An inter-unit communication is involved when a conditional branch or indirect jump has not been correctly predicted. In this case, the corrected continuing fetch address is transfered from the branch unit to the prediction subunit (the branch unit can either be a separate unit or as assumed on Fig. 1, part of the integer unit). The prediction correction critical path, labeled 'c' on Fig. 1, can be assumed to be of length $2l/3$ ($2l'/3$ on the right die), going from the center of the integer unit right edge to the prediction subunit, located nearby the pc register, i.e. at the center of the fetch unit left edge. On Fig. 2, the 'c' path runs from the center of any computing unit right edge to the center of the corresponding L1 unit left edge. The path has a length of $l'/3$ which is half of the path on the Fig. 1 right die.

Also concerning the branch unit, the new set of predicated instructions [9] can lead to predicate interunit communications (e.g. a predicate obtained from the comparison of two floating point numbers and used in the branch unit). The predicate propagation critical path, labeled 'p' on Fig. 1, can be assumed to have length $2l/3$ ($2l'/3$ on the right die), starting from the center of the (say) graphic unit right edge and ending at the center of the integer unit left edge ($l/6 + l/3 + l/6$). Because the branch unit has been duplicated on the Fig. 2 die, no inter-unit predicate propagation is needed and the 'p' path may be removed.

4   ISA Typing

To allow a full separation of the computing machines, it is necessary to give each some instruction addresses computing facilities (branches and jumps targets computations) as well as some data addresses computing ones (data structures pointers). In such a way, a function can be fully handled by its hosting unit. For example, a floating point function such as SAXPY, that is made of floating point computation instructions, load and store ones and loop control ones, is entirely taken in charge by the fpu. This means that the fpu register file keeps the floating point arrays pointers and index as well as the floating point data. It also induces that the set of functional units includes an integer adder to handle address computations. The instruction set itself is enhanced to give to each computing machine proper branching, jumping, loading and storing instructions (with an address computation based on pointers locally available in the machine register file).

The following piece of code shows what SAXPY looks like when written with such an instruction set. As we can see, every instruction is prefixed with 'f'. This designates the fpu computing unit to be used to compute the function. The opcode suffix gives the operation to be performed that can be a true floating point one as in 'fmul' and 'fadd', a load or a store of a floating point data ('fld' and 'fst'), the computation of an integer value ('ficlr' and 'fiadd') or a comparison of integers in a conditional branch ('fibtrue'). The return instruction itself is typed, to distinguish a floating point function return from an integer one. The call instruction is also typed with the prefix giving both the caller and the callee types (for example, the fpu has three calls: 'ficall', 'ffcall' and 'fgcall' to call respectively a floating point, an integer or a graphic function). To handle calls and returns as well as predictions, two hardware stacks per unit are maintained. One, say RS, is the return address stack (as in actual speculative processors) and the other, say CS, is a continuing unit stack.

```
saxpy:          /*x:f1; y:f2; a:f3; n:f4*/
                /*for (i=0;i<n;i++)*/
                /*    y[i]+=a*x[i];*/
                ficlr f16              /*i=0*/
e0:             fld f17=M[f1+f16*4]    /*x[i]*/
                fmul f17=f17*f3        /*a*x[i]*/
                fld f18=M[f2+f16*4]    /*y[i]*/
                fadd f17=f17+f18       /*y[i]+=a*x[i]*/
                fst M[f2+f16*4]=f17    /*y[i]*/
                fiadd f16=f16+1        /*i++*/
                fibtrue (f16!=f4),e0   /*loop*/
                fret
```

A unit is made active when a call of its type is fetched (see Fig. 3 upper part; for example, if the fpu fetches a 'ficall', the integer unit is made active). The previous active unit code is pushed on top of CS (in the example, the fpu code is pushed on top of the integer unit CS stack; the return address is pushed on top of the fpu RS stack). The same unit remains active until the return instruction is fetched (in the example, a return from an integer function; in a return instruction, the target function type is not mentioned to allow returns to different function types). While a unit is active, the other ones are inactive (hence, units read one at a time in the instruction and data L2 caches). When a return is executed, the leaving unit pops the continuing unit from its CS stack. The leaving unit is disactivated (its fetch unit no more fetches) and the continuing unit is reactivated (its fetch unit pops the return address from its local prediction stack RS and restarts fetching). Disactivation and reactivation are performed within the same cycle, incurring no delay to switch the active unit.

Branches and jumps are predicted the same way than in a speculative processor (with one prediction subunit per type). A bad prediction correction is internal to a unit except for calls and returns. When a call is mispredicted, the calling unit resets the called one with the corrected address. When a return is mispredicted, first the falsely predicted continuing unit is disactivated and second, the true return address designates the true continuing unit (such a distinction requires that the OS separates the code region in typed segments; an alternative is to trap at fetch when a type t' instruction is fetched by a type t unit; this is further explained later). Such a typed coding highly relies on the compiler ability to recognize each function type. For example, in C, the SAXPY function would have the following prototype:

```
void saxpy(float x[], float y[], float a, int n)
```

This example shows that the function type itself (void) does not give the computing unit type. Moreover, the set of arguments is mixed. However, in this

```
              ...             ;fpu is the active unit
        ficall   max         ;push fpu on top of CS(iu)
                             ;push "a" on top of RS(fpu)
   a:         ...            ;fpu is the active unit
              ...            ;fpu is the active unit


   max:       ...            ;iu is the active unit
              ...            ;iu is the active unit
        iret                 ;pop CS(iu); pop RS(fpu)



        u...                 ;u is the active unit
        u...                 ;u is the active unit
        u...                 ;u is the active unit
        u'...                ;trap; u' becomes the active unit
        u'...                u' is the active unit
        u'...                u' is the active unit
        u'...                u' is the active unit
        u...                 ;trap; u becomes the active unit
        u...                 ;u is the active unit
```

Fig. 3. Typed function call and return

example the compiler should easily decide to match the function with the fpu. Some other cases might be more complicate for example when the function computes separate values of different types. Then, the compiler has to analyse the data dependencies to separate the function code into properly typed subfunctions. The connection between the subfunctions can be realized with a typed call instruction or by trapping. With the trapping technique, when a unit u (see Fig. 3 lower part) fetches an instruction belonging to unit u', a trap occurs that switches the active unit from u to u' (as if a typed call would have been fetched). This kind of trap occurs at fetch time. It incurs a one cycle delay (a block is fetched and a badly typed instruction is detected in it; it disactivates the active unit (u) and reactivates the continuing unit (u') with the trapping instruction address for pc; the instruction is refetched by the unit of its type (u')). The compiler should reorganize the code to minimize such types breaks (we must insist on the fact that mixing pointers and data does not lead to types breaks; as in the SAXPY example above, we can see that floating point pointers and indexes are handled by the fpu with its register file; for this reason, types breaks should be rare in the dynamic code run from our proposed ISA; as an example, the SAXPY code does not contain any type break).

The case of data is different. A function accesses data memory through its unit private cache. For example, a function handled by the fpu accesses floating point data and pointers on floating point structures in the fpu data cache. If a datum must be shared by two units, an explicit conversion must be performed that is coded with an import instruction that moves a register from an external unit to a register of the local unit. For example, this is the case in a conversion function. The function (see an example on Fig. 4 with the function *atof*) computes the conversion and leaves the converted value in one of its data registers.

```
atof:  ...              ;read an ascii word
       ...              ;and convert to a
       ...              ;floating point data
       ...              ;atof is computed by
       ...              ;the integer unit
       iret             ;fp data in R0, integer register


fpfun: ...
       ficall atof      ;call to the integer function atof
       fimport F0=R0;get the fp data
       ...              ;(inter-register files transfer)
```

Fig. 4. Inter-units importation

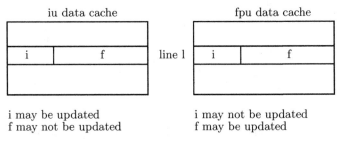

i may be updated   i may not be updated
f may not be updated   f may be updated

line l is duplicated in two caches, referenced for i by iu and for f by fpu

Fig. 5. A duplicated cache line

The caller (function *fpfun*) imports this register into its proper file (instruction *fimport*). The computing units are linked by a bus that only serves for this purpose. In such a way, a datum is typed and never has to be loaded for update in the cache of another type (it can be loaded as a side effect with other data sharing the same cache line in another cache but cannot be modified; for example, a structure composed of an integer and a floating point datum can be loaded in the integer unit data cache as well as in the fpu one; however, the integer, if handled by the integer unit cannot be modified by the fpu, nor can the floating point data be modified by the integer unit (see Fig. 5)). These restrictions ensure cache coherency without the need of snooping.

This typing of the computing units is compatible with any speculative and out-of-order execution mode as long as the techniques employed for implementation do not add any interunit communication except possibly some status signals.

5   Discussion

Different recent proposals have an impact on processor clustering. SMT-like multithreaded processors [15] have a very centralized organization, the different threads being merged into a unique shared core. This is an important drawback of SMT design that should lead to important inter-units communication delays. On-chip multiprocessors [10] cluster the die into independant processors that can communicate only through the shared part of their memory hierarchy (that can be on-chip or off-chip). The main disadvantage of this type of design comes from the resources redundancy imposed by the share-nothing choice and the inter-processors communications induced by the coherency protocol for the duplicated levels of the data memory hierarchy.

The Multicluster architecture [6], the Multiscalar architecture [14] and the Complexity-effective architecture [11] are examples of clustered single processor architectures. In each of them, the fetched instructions are dispatched to clusters. This is a first difference with this proposal. In these designs clustering does not concern the fetch unit, implying that the fetch latency does not get improved. A second difference is that we modify the ISA and they don't. For this reason, the cluster to which an instruction belongs is not opcode dependent (as it is in the present proposal) but is determined from two contradictory aims: avoid inter-cluster communications (this tends to centralize the instructions into a single cluster) and equilibrate cluster computation load (this tends to distribute instructions uniformly into clusters). Instructions forming a computation chain are oriented in the same cluster. Different chains are alternately placed in the available clusters. Instructions may have their sources in two different clusters implying an inter-cluster communication. This occurs often enough to impose one or more inter-cluster communication paths.

In fact their goal is not the same as our. They want to reduce the necessary core resources to allow a high superscalar degree (such as read and write ports on the register file). Each cluster takes in charge a subset of the superscalar degree (for example, a degree 16 machine could be composed of 4 degree 4 clusters). What we want is to decrease the number of inter-unit communications and to reduce the paths lengths. If a high superscalar degree is needed, then each computation unit has to be clustered itself (in the proposed design, each unit when it is active fetches as many instructions as the superscalar degree allows), which is out of the scope of this paper.

6   Conclusion

In this paper, we have first pointed out that inter-units communication paths and mainly fetch and load/store paths now impact processor performance. The fetch and the load/store paths can be shortened with a reduced size L1 cache. The L1 miss penalty can be reduced if the L1 and L2 caches are simultaneously accessed. We have also noted that even though the L1 cache is kept small to scale with the cpu cycle, the core area increases leading to an increase in the drive time along the paths connecting the caches to the computing units.

By typing the ISA, we have shown that it is possible to half the fetch path length. The instruction cache, the fetch unit, the branch prediction unit, the typed computing unit, the load/store unit and the data cache altogether form an independent machine that has quite no link with the other computing machines in the cpu, except inter-register import. During a cycle, a single machine is the active machine, i.e. the one that fetches. A machine is made active with a function call of its type, a function return or a fetch trap.

ISA typing should be useful to help to scale the processor cycle with the technology in future designs. With ISA typing, it is possible to reduce the pipelines depths by removing some or all of the drive stages. This means that the CPI can be better sustained despite the dramatic cycle reduction.

References

1. http://www.amd.com/products/cpg/athlon/pdf/architecture_wp.pdf
2. Steven J. E. Wilton and Norman P. Jouppi. An Enhanced Access and Cycle Time Model for On-Chip Caches. Compaq WRL Research Report 93/5, July 1994.
   http://www.research.digital.com/wrl/techreports/abstracts/93.5.html
   http://research.compaq.com/wrl/people/jouppi/cacti2.pdf
3. W.J. Dally and J.W. Poulton: Digital systems engineering. CUP 1998.
4. J. Edmondson et al.: Internal Organization of the Alpha 21164, a 300-MHz 64-bit Quad-issue CMOS RISC Microprocessor. Digital Technical Journal, vol. 7, no. 1: 119-135.
5. Richard E. Kessler: The Alpha 21264 microprocessor. IEEE Micro, 19 (2), March-April 1999, 24-36.
6. K. Farkas et al.: The multicluster architecture. Reducing cycle time through partitioning. Micro30, 1997
7. C.T. Gray, W. Liu and R.K. Cain III: Wave pipelining: theory and CMOS implementation. Kluwer academic publishers, Norwell, 1993.
8. ftp://www.hotchips.org/pub/hot7to11cd/hc98/pdf_1up/hc98_1a_johnson_1up.pdf
9. http://developer.intel.com/design/ia-64/manuals
10. K. Olukotun, B. Nayfeh, L. Hammond, K. Wilson, K. Chang: The case for a single-chip multiprocessor. ASPLOS7, 1996.
11. S. Palacharla and N. Jouppi: Complexity-effective superscalar processors. ISCA24, 1997
12. http://developer.intel.com/technology/itj/q21999/articles/art_2.htm
13. ftp://download.intel.com/pentium4/download/netburstdetail.pdf
14. K.K. Sundararaman, M. Franklin: Multiscalar execution along a single flow of control. ICPP 1997.
15. D.M. Tullsen, S.J. Eggers, H.M. Levy: Simultaneous multithreading: maximizing on-chip parallelism. ISCA22, 1995.

Send-Recv Considered Harmful?
Myths and Truths about Parallel Programming

Sergei Gorlatch

Technische Universität Berlin, Fachbereich Informatik,
Sekr. FR 5-6, Franklinstr. 28/29, D-10587 Berlin, Germany

Abstract. During the software crisis of the 1960s, Dijkstra's famous thesis *"goto considered harmful"* paved the way for structured programming, i.e. software development with well-defined and disciplined organization of control flow. In parallel programming, a new aspect – communication – has an important impact on the structure and properties of programs. This paper shows that many current difficulties of parallel programming are caused by complicated and poorly structured communication, which is a consequence of using low-level *send-recv* primitives. We argue that, like *goto* in sequential programs, *send-recv* should be avoided as far as possible and replaced by *collective operations* in the parallel setting. We argue against some widely held opinions about the apparent superiority of individual over collective communication and present substantial theoretical and empirical evidence to the contrary. The paper overviews some recent results on formal transformation rules for collective operations that facilitate systematic, performance-oriented design of parallel programs using MPI (Message Passing Interface).

1   Introduction

Nowadays, parallel and distributed systems have apparently ideal conditions for their development. The demand for such systems is great and growing steadily. Traditional supercomputing applications, *Grand Challenges*, require the solution of increasingly large problems, with new areas added recently, e.g. research on the human genome. The rapid growth of the Internet has given rise to geographically distributed, networked supercomputers (*Grids*) and to new classes of distributed commercial applications with parallelism on both the server and client side.

Every year, bigger and more powerful systems are built. Microprocessors are quickly becoming faster and cheaper, which enables more processors to be connected in one system. New networking hardware with smaller latency and greater bandwidth improves systems' scalability. Several levels of parallelism are available to the user: within a processor, between processors in an SMP or cluster, up to the parallelism among remote machines cooperating over the Internet.

Under such a favourable combination of conditions – strong demand and good hardware availability – it would be natural to expect substantial progress in the field of parallel and distributed software. However, program development for parallel and distributed systems remains a challenging and difficult task.

V. Malyshkin (Ed.): PaCT 2001, LNCS 2127, pp. 243–257, 2001.

One of the obvious reasons for this unsatisfactory situation is that today's programmers rely mostly on the programming culture of the 1980s and '90s, the Message Passing Interface (MPI) still being the programming tool of choice for demanding applications. The main merit of MPI is that it integrated and standardized major well-understood parallel constructs that were proven in practice. This put an end to the unacceptable situation where every hardware vendor provided its own set of communication primitives.

The major disadvantage of MPI – low-level communication management with the primitives *send* and *recv* resulting in a complicated programming process – has been known and criticized for years. Several attempts have been made to overcome this, DSM, HPF and OpenMP being the most prominent proposals. However, despite reported success stories, none of these approaches have ever achieved the popularity of MPI.

We believe that although MPI's main problem – low-level communication – was identified correctly, the chosen remedy – a complete banning of explicit communication statements from parallel programs – was probably not the right one. While simplifying the programming process, it makes the performance of parallel programs less understandable and hardly predictable.

The thrust of this paper is: *the problems of low-level communication should be solved not by excluding communication from parallel programs altogether, but rather by expressing communication in a structured way.*

2   Learning From History: "Goto Considered Harmful"

To decide what would be a better, more structured way of dealing with communication in parallel programs, let us turn to the history of "structured programming" in the sequential setting. During the 1960s, it became clear that the indiscriminate use of transfers of control was the root of much of the difficulty experienced by software developers. The breakthrough was made by Dijkstra in his famous letter *"goto* considered harmful" [9], where the finger of blame was pointed at the *goto* statement. The notion of so-called *structured programming* [7] became almost synonymous with "goto elimination".

Dijkstra's thesis did not appear in a vacuum. By that time, the research of Böhm and Jacopini [6] had formally demonstrated that programs could be written without any *goto* statements, in terms of only three control structures – sequence, selection and repetition. It was not until the 1970s that programmers started taking structured programming seriously, but even the first results were impressive, with software development groups reporting reduced development times as well as more frequent on-time and within-budget completion of software projects. The key to success was that structured programs are clearer, easier to debug and modify, and more likely to be bug-free. Newer languages like Java do not have a *goto* statement at all.

If we wish to learn from structured (sequential) programming, we have to answer the question: which concept or construct plays a negative role – similar to that of the *goto* – in the parallel setting?

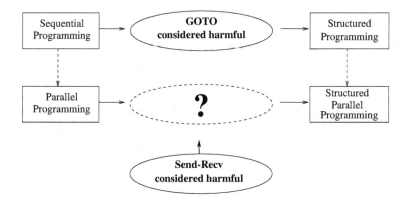

Fig. 1. Just as the indiscriminate use of the *goto* complicates sequential programs, *send-recv* statements cause major difficulties in parallel programming.

As implied in Figure 1 and demonstrated from Section 4 onwards, we believe that *send-recv* statements cause problems in parallel programming. We suggest, therefore, that *send-recv* be "considered harmful" and be avoided as far as possible in parallel programs.

3 Collective Operations: An Alternative to Send-Recv?

What would be the proper replacement for *send-recv*? In our opinion, it does not even need to be invented: we propose using *collective operations*, which are already an established part of MPI and other communication libraries. Each collective operation is a particular pattern specifying a mutual activity of a group of processes, like broadcasting data from one process to all others, gathering information from all processes in one process, and so on.

First prototypes of collective operations have been used since the 1970s. Languages and libraries like Minimax [19], CCL [2], PVM [10] definitely do not constitute an exhaustive list of such approaches. It was one of the main merits of the MPI standard that it combined in a uniform manner practically all collective operations that have been known and used for years.

For the sake of completeness, we show in Figure 2 the main collective operations of MPI for a group of four processes, P1 to P4.

Two upper rows of Figure 2 contain collective operations that specify pure communication (e.g. *broadcast, gather*, etc.); operations at the bottom of the figure, like *reduce*, perform both communication and computation. The binary operator specifying computations (+ in Figure 2) is a parameter of the collective operation: it may be either predefined, like addition, or user-defined. If the operator is associative, the collective operation can be implemented in parallel.

For collective operations to become a real alternative, they must demonstrate their clear advantages over the *send-recv* primitives for parallel programming. In the rest of the paper, we consider the following five challenges that should

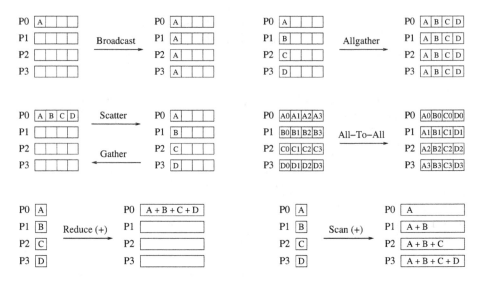

Fig. 2. Collective operations shown for a group of four processes. Each row of boxes represents data that reside in one process.

be addressed by every new approach in parallel programming; we use these challenges to prove the benefits of collective operations over *send-recv*.

Challenges for collective operations as an alternative to send-recv:

- *Simplicity:* Are "collective" programs simpler and more comprehensible?
- *Programmability:* Is a systematic program design process facilitated?
- *Expressiveness:* Can main application classes be conveniently expressed?
- *Performance:* Is the performance competitive with that using *send-recv*?
- *Predictability:* Are program behaviour and performance more predictable?

In the remainder of the paper, one section is devoted to each of the challenges. Each section opens by stating a commonly held, pro-*send-recv* opinion, which we somewhat polemically call a "Myth". We proceed by discussing theoretical and empirical results that refute the myth and conclude with the "Truth" based on the presented facts. This "myths and truths" structure enables us to draw a clear conclusion about the suitability of collective operations as an alternative to *send-recv*.

4   The Challenge of Simplicity

Myth : Send-recv primitives are a simple and convenient way of specifying communication in parallel programs.

To expose the invalidity of the simplicity myth, we use a simple example MPI program, Get_data1, shown in Figure 3 (top). This program is taken almost verbatim from a popular MPI textbook [21], where it directly follows the trivial `Hello World` example; thus, `Get_data1` can be viewed as one of the simplest truly parallel programs in the book. The C+MPI code in the figure accomplishes a simple task: one process (initiator) reads an input value, a, and broadcasts it to all other processes. To implement the broadcast more efficiently, the processes are organized in the program as a logical binary tree, with the initiator at the root of the tree. Communication in the program `Get_data1` proceeds along the levels of the tree, so that each non-initiator process first receives the value and then sends it on. The main part of the code (functions `Ceiling_log2`, `I_send`, `I_recv`) computes the height of the communication tree and finds the communication partners for each process, whereas the function `Get_data1` itself organizes communication along the levels of the tree.

Despite the fact that the program in Figure 3 is even shorter than in the book (we broadcast one piece of data instead of three and skip almost all comments), it is still long and complicated, considering the simplicity of the accomplished task. Furthermore, the program is error-prone: even a slight imprecision in determining the partner processes may cause a deadlock during program execution. Note that the described tree communication structure is not artificial, but rather expresses one of the efficient patterns that are widely used in parallel programming.

To demonstrate how collective operations simplify the program structure, we exploit the collective operation "broadcast": in the MPI syntax, it is `MPI_Bcast()`. The resulting "collective" version of the program is shown in Figure 3 (bottom). An immediate observation is that it is much shorter than the *send-recv* version, the size ratio being 6 vs. 34 lines of code. Skipping the part responsible for data input would result in an even more impressive saving: 3 vs. 31 lines.

The complexity of programming with *send-recv* has many more facets than just long program codes:

Firstly, the intricate communication structure induced by *send-recv* complicates the debugging process. Special tools are required, which provide the programmer with a detailed trace of program execution. This approach to debugging is cumbersome and has natural limitations: program behaviour is non-deterministic, and some errors can be detected only on particular machine configurations, which makes complete testing infeasible.

Secondly, if MPI is our language of choice then we have not just one *send-recv*, but rather 8 different kinds of *send* and 2 different kinds of *recv*. Thus, the programmer has to choose among 16 combinations of *send-recv*, some of them with very different semantics. Of course, this makes message-passing programming very flexible, but even less comprehensible!

Truth : The apparent simplicity of *send-recv* turns out to be the cause of large program size and complicated communication structure that make both the design and debugging of parallel programs difficult.

```
int Ceiling_log2(int x){ /* communication tree height */
   temp = x - 1; result=0;
   while (temp != 0) {
            temp = temp >> 1;
            result = result + 1 ;}
      return result;
} /* Ceiling_log2 */
int I_receive{ /* find partner to receive from */
   power_2_stage = 1 << stage;
   if ((power_2_stage <= my_rank) &&
            (my_rank < 2*power_2_stage)){
       *source_ptr = my_rank - power_2_stage;
       return 1;
   } else return 0;
} /* I_receive */
int I_send{ /* find partner to send to */
   power_2_stage = 1 << stage;
   if (my_rank < power_2_stage){
       *dest_ptr = my_rank + power_2_stage;
       if (*dest_ptr >= p) return 0;
       else return 1;
   } else return 0;
} /* I_send */
void Get_data1{
   if (my_rank == 0){ /* in the root process */
        printf("Enter a\n"); scanf("%f", a_ptr);
   }
   for (stage = 0; stage < Ceiling_log2(p); stage++)
        if (I_receive(stage, my_rank, &source))
            MPI_Recv(a_ptr, 1, MPI_FLOAT, source,
                               0, MPI_COMM_WORLD, &status);
        else if (I_send(stage, my_rank, p, &dest))
            MPI_Send(&a, 1, MPI_FLOAT, dest, 0, MPI_COMM_WORLD);
} /* Get_data1*/
```

```
void Get_data2{
   if (my_rank == 0) {
       printf("Enter a\n"); scanf("%f", a_ptr);
       }
   MPI_Bcast(a_ptr, 1, MPI_FLOAT, 0, MPI_COMM_WORLD);
   } /* Get_data2 */
```

Fig. 3. Example program with send-recv (top) and collective operation (bottom)

5   The Challenge of Programmability

Myth : The design of parallel programs is so complicated that it will probably always remain an *ad hoc* activity rather than a systematic process.

We address here what is probably the most challenging issue in parallel programming: To what extent are systematic design of parallel programs and formal reasoning about them possible? Programs with collective operations can be viewed as sequential compositions of comparatively simple parallel stages [12], similarly to the "batch" supersteps in BSP [24]. There are two kinds of stages: local computations in each process, and interprocess collective operations. Our goal is to reason about how can individual stages be composed into a complete program, with the ultimate goal of finding the best composition systematically.

We will briefly summarize some semantics-preserving transformations for specific compositions of collective operations (for more detail, see [11]). They have been formally proved using the functional Bird-Meertens formalism [5]. For our purposes, we present these transformations in the C+MPI notation.

The first transformation states that, if binary operators op1 and op2 are associative and op1 distributes over op2, then the following transformation of a composition of scan and reduction is possible:

$$\begin{bmatrix} \texttt{MPI\_Scan (op1);} \\ \texttt{MPI\_Reduce (op2);} \end{bmatrix} \implies \begin{bmatrix} \texttt{Make\_pair;} \\ \texttt{MPI\_Reduce (f(op1,op2));} \\ \texttt{if my\_pid==ROOT then Take\_first;} \end{bmatrix} \quad (1)$$

Here, the functions `Make_pair` and `Take_first` implement simple data arrangements that are executed locally, i.e. without interprocessor communication. The binary operator `f(op1,op2)` on the right-hand side is built using op1 and op2 from the left-hand side of the transformation. A similar transformation for two subsequent scan operations can be found in [11].

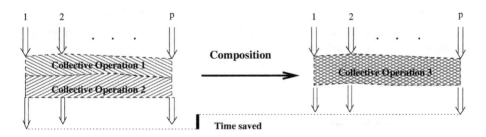

Fig. 4. Fusing two collective operations into one by a transformation like (1).

The effect of such transformations on an MPI program is that two subsequent collective operations are fused into one, with simple local computations beforehand and afterwards. This is illustrated in Figure 4 for a program with p processes.

Rule (1), and other similar transformation rules for collective operations presented in the sequel, have the following important properties:

- Their correctness is proved formally as mathematical theorems.
- They are parameterized by the occurring operators, like op1 and op2, and are therefore applicable to a wide variety of applications.
- They are valid for all possible implementations of the involved operations.
- They can be applied independently of the parallel target architecture.

Besides composition rules, there are also transformations that decompose one collective operation into a sequence of smaller operations. Here are two examples:

$$\texttt{MPI\_Bcast} \Rightarrow \begin{bmatrix} \texttt{MPI\_Scatter;} \\ \texttt{MPI\_Allgather;} \end{bmatrix}$$

$$\texttt{MPI\_Allreduce(op)} \Rightarrow \begin{bmatrix} \texttt{Red-scatter'(op);} \\ \texttt{MPI\_Allgather;} \end{bmatrix}$$

Composition and decomposition rules can sometimes be applied in sequence; here is an example of such a combined transformation:

$$\begin{bmatrix} \texttt{MPI\_Scan(op1);} \\ \texttt{MPI\_Allreduce(op2);} \end{bmatrix} \implies \begin{bmatrix} \texttt{Make\_pair;} \\ \texttt{Red-scatter(f(op1,op2));} \\ \texttt{Take\_first;} \\ \texttt{MPI\_Allgather;} \end{bmatrix}$$

We have demonstrated elsewhere [11] how transformation rules of the kind presented here can be exploited in the design of parallel algorithms. The idea is to start with an intuitive, obviously correct but probably inefficient version of an algorithm and proceed by applying semantically sound transformation rules, until an efficient algorithm is obtained. To choose the right rule to apply at a particular point in the design process, we need to study the impact of the design rules on program performance. We will address this problem in Section 8.

Truth : For collective operations, sound transformation rules can be developed. This enables a systematic program design process, in sharp contrast to the *ad hoc* programming using *send-recv* primitives. In the next sections, we demonstrate how the design process can be oriented towards predictable, higher performance.

6   The Challenge of Expressiveness

Myth : Collective operations are too inflexible and cannot express many important applications conveniently.

To refute this quite widely held opinion, we present in Table 1 several important applications, which according to the literature were implemented using exclusively collective operations without notable performance loss as compared with their counterparts using *send-recv*.

Table 1. Applications expressed using exclusively collective operations

Application	Communication/Computation Pattern
Polynomial Multiplication	Bcast (group); Map; Reduce; Shift
Polynomial Evaluation	Bcast; Scan; Map; Reduce
Fast Fourier Transform	Iter (Map; All-to-all (group))
Molecular Simulation	Iter (Scatter; Reduce; Gather)
N-Body Simulation	Iter (All-to-all; Map)
Matrix Multiplication (Fox)	Iter (Bcast (group); Map; Shift (group))
Matrix Multiplication (3D)	Allgather (group); Map; All-to-all; Map

Here, `Map` stands for local computations performed in the processes without communication; `Shift` is a cyclic one-directional exchange between all processes; `Iter` denotes repetitive action; `(group)` means that the collective operation is applied not to all processes of the program but rather to an identified subset of processes. In MPI, the groups are specified using the concept of communicators.

Additional strong confirmation of the expressive power of collective operations is provided by the PLAPACK package for linear algebra [25], which has been implemented entirely without individual communication primitives.

Truth : A broad class of communication patterns to be found in parallel applications is covered by collective operations, without any notable loss of performance.

7   The Challenge of Performance

Myth : Programs using *send-recv* are, naturally, faster than their counterparts using exclusively collective operations.

High performance is the first and foremost reason to exploit parallel machines. However, the performance of parallel programs is known to be an inexhaustible source of highly contradictory discussions. Examples are the continuous debates on superlinear speedup, as well as papers that analyze the many tricks used to deceive the community in terms of performance figures. They all show clearly how difficult it is to discuss performance matters in the parallel setting.

The usual performance argument in favour of individual communication is that collective operations are themselves implemented in terms of individual *send-recv* and thus cannot be more efficient than the latter. Although this is true to some extent, there are two important aspects here that are often overlooked:

1. The implementations of collective operations in terms of *send-recv* are written by the implementers, who are much more familiar with the parallel machine and its network than an application programmer can be. Recently, hybrid algorithms have been proposed, which switch from one implementation of a collective operation to another depending on the message size, number of processors involved, etc. A nice example is the MagPIe library

which is geared to wide-area networks of clusters [18]. Such optimizations are practically impossible at the user level in programs using *send-recv*. Some implementations of collectives exploit machine-specific communication commands, which are usually inaccessible to an application programmer.

2. Very often, collective operations are implemented not via *send-recv*, but rather directly in the hardware of a particular machine, which is simply impossible at the user level. This allows to fully exploit all machine resources and sometimes leads to rather unexpected results: e.g. a simple two-directional exchange of data between two processors using *send-recv* on a Cray T3E is two times slower than a version with two broadcasts [3]. The explanation for this phenomenon is that the broadcast is implemented directly on top of the shared-memory support of the Cray T3E.

Below, we argue against some commonly held opinions about the performance superiority of *send-recv* over collective operations, basing our arguments on empirical evidence from recent publications:

It is not true that *send-recv* is naturally faster than collective operations. Newer algorithms for collective communication [22] take into account specific characteristics of the interprocessor network, which can be then considered during the compilation phase of the communication library. In [23], the tuning for a given system is achieved by conducting a series of experiments on the system. In both cases, a nearly optimal implementation for a particular machine can be achieved automatically, without sacrificing portability. This is clearly almost impossible in an application program written using *send-recv*: the communication structure will probably have to be re-implemented for every new kind of network. It is further reported in [3] that the collective operation `MPI_Bcast` on a Cray T3E always beats *send-recv*.

It is not true that nonblocking versions of *send-recv*, `MPI_Isend` and `MPI_Irecv`, are invariably fast, owing to the overlap of communication with computation. As demonstrated by [3], these primitives in practice often lead to slower execution than the blocking version, because of the extra synchronization.

It is not true that the flexibility of *send-recv* allows smarter and faster algorithms than the collective paradigm. Research has shown that many designs with *send-recv* eventually lead to the same high-level algorithms as obtained by the "batch" approach [15]. In fact, batch versions often run faster [16].

It is not true that the routing of individual messages over a network offers fundamental performance gains as compared with the routing for collective operations. As shown formally by Valiant [24], the performance gap in this case becomes, with large probability, arbitrarily small for large problem sizes. A variety of theoretically interesting and practical techniques have been proposed – two-stage randomized routing, coalescing messages by destination, etc. – that attempt to exploit the full bandwidth of the network, at least to within a constant factor.

Truth : While absolute parallel performance achieved on a particular machine remains a complex and fuzzy issue, there is strong evidence that *send-recv* does not offer any basic advantages over collective operations in terms of performance. There are well-documented cases where collective operations are the clear winner. Furthermore, they offer machine-dependent, efficient implementations without changing the applications itself.

8   The Challenge of Predictability

Myth : The behaviour and performance of parallel programs are such complicated issues that information can only be obtained by actually running the program on a particular machine configuration.

The major advantage of collective operations is that we can not only design programs by means of the transformations presented in Section 5, but also estimate the impact of an applicable transformation on the program's performance.

Table 2. Impact of transformations on performance

Composition Rule	Improvement if
Scan_1; Reduce_2 → Reduce	always
Scan; Reduce → Reduce	$t_s > m$
Scan_1; Scan_2 → Scan	$t_s > 2m$
Scan; Scan → Scan	$t_s > m(t_w + 4)$
Bcast; Scan → Comcast	always
Bcast; Scan_1; Scan_2 → Comcast	$t_s > m/2$
Bcast; Scan; Scan → Comcast	$t_s > m(\frac{1}{2}t_w + 4)$
Bcast; Reduce → Local	always
Bcast; Scan_1; Reduce_2 → Local	always
Bcast; Scan; Reduce → Local	$t_w + \frac{1}{m} \cdot t_s \geq \frac{1}{3}$

Table 2 contains a list of transformations from [13], together with the conditions under which the application of a transformation improves performance.

Note that performance predictability is usually even more difficult to achieve than the absolute performance itself. To estimate performance, we must use some cost model and take into account a particular implementation of collective operations on the target machine. In the above table, a hypercube-like implementation of collective operations is presumed, and the cost model used has the following parameters: start-up/latency t_s, transfer time t_w and block size m. These parameters are used in the conditions in the right column of the table. The estimates were validated in experiments on a Cray T3E and a Parsytec GCel 64 (see [11] for details).

Since the performance impact of a particular transformation depends on the parameters of both the application and the machine, there are several alternatives to choose from in a particular design. Usually, the design process can be captured as a tree, one example of which is shown in Figure 5.

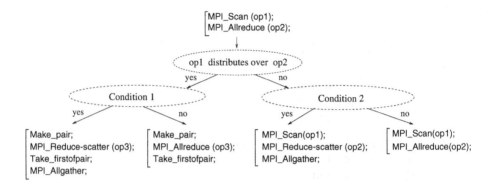

Fig. 5. The tree of design alternatives.

Conditions in the figure read as follows (see [11] for how they are calculated):

$$\text{Condition 1} = t_s < 2mt_w(\log p - 1)/\log p$$
$$\text{Condition 2} = t_s < m(t_w + 1 - (2t_w + 1)/\log p)$$

The best design decision is obtained by checking the design conditions, which depend either on the problem properties, e.g. the distributivity of operators, or on the characteristics of the target machine (number of processors, speed of the channels, etc.). For example, if the distributivity condition holds, it takes us from the root into the left subtree in Figure 5. If the block size in an application is small, `Condition 1` yields "no", and we thus end up with the second (from left to right) design alternative, where `op3 = f(op1,op2)` according to rule (1).

Note that the conditions in the tree of alternatives may change for a different implementation of the involved collective operations on the same machine.

Arguably, *send-recv* allows a more accurate performance model than collective operations do. Examples of quite detailed performance models, well suitable for finding new efficient implementations, are LogP and LogGP [17]. However, these models are often overly detailed and hardly usable for an application programmer, as demonstrated by comparison with batch-oriented models [4,14].

Truth: Collective operations contribute to the ambitious goal of predicting program characteristics during the design process, i.e. without actually running the program on a machine. This progress would be impossible with *send-recv*, which make the program's behaviour much less predictable. Furthermore, the predictablity of collective operations simplifies the modelling task at application level as compared with models like LogP.

9   Conclusion

This paper proposes – somewhat polemically – viewing *send-recv* primitives as harmful and, consequently, trying to avoid them in parallel programming. We have demonstrated the advantages of collective operations over *send-recv* in five major respects, which we call challenges: simplicity, expressiveness, programmability, performance and predictability. We have presented hard evidence that many widely held opinions about *send-recv* vs. collective operations are mere myths which can be refuted. We strongly believe that collective operations are a viable alternative that already works well for many parallel applications.

The following developments are necessary or are already under way in the drive to broaden the use of collective operations in parallel programming:

- More evidence should be collected about the applicability and usefulness of collective operations for parallel programming. In particular, we expect new parallel algorithms to be developed, with collective operations as the programming mechanism in mind.
- It may well be the case that the current set of collective operations provided by MPI needs adjustment to meet the requirements of programming practice.
- We plan to extend the results on transformation rules presented here, with the goal of building a complete algebra of collective operations.
- An experimental system for program development using transformation rules from Section 5 is described in [1].
- The research into new, efficient implementations for collective operations is very important to support their use in practice. Our current work also addresses new kinds of networks, including heterogeneous ones [17].
- Collective operations are successfully used not only in traditional communication libraries like MPI but also in new programming environments for distributed systems, including e.g. Java RMI [20].
- New applications of parallel computing, as well as new computational platforms such as *Grids* are promising candidates for collective operations.

In addition to the many arguments in this paper, our optimism with respect to the "collective communication thrust" is also based on the amazing similarities of its development to the history of the "structured programming thrust":

It is not easy to argue against a programming technology, like the *goto* or *send-recv*, that has been used for years by many programmers. However, in both cases an alternative is available which is also well known, so that no new constructs have to be learned by the users.

A new thrust is often opposed by practitioners, while theoreticians get euphoric. So-called "structured compilers" were developed to automatically translate any program with *goto*s into its structured equivalent. Similarly, there is at least one project now under way, whose goal it is to translate programs with *send-recv* into their equivalents with collective operations [8]. While such research definitely contributes to a better understanding of the relation between different programming styles, its practical utility is uncertain, for both the *goto* and *send-recv*. Our view is that the exclusive use of collective operations requires new parallel algorithms and a different programming methodology. A direct translation of old software can often result in poorly structured and inefficient programs. By analogy, Dijkstra advised against a mechanical translation into *goto*-less programs [9].

One of the major objections in both cases has been that both the *goto* and *send-recv* are "natural" mechanisms for expressing control flow and communication, respectively. We find this argument for *send-recv* elusive, for the following reason. The main parallel programming style, SPMD, presumes a "collective view" of the program. Since the number of processes is a parameter of an MPI program, it is difficult for the programmer to think in terms of particular processes: one does not even know how many of them are involved! Individual communication with *send-recv* disturbs this natural, collective view and should therefore be viewed as unnatural.

Other pro-*goto* and pro-*send-recv* arguments have been the feared losses in expressiveness and performance. In case of the *goto*, these arguments have been refuted by the progress in compilers and software engineering. In the case of *send-recv*, they will be hopefully refuted by theoretical and empirical evidence in favour of collective communication, as in this paper.

We conclude by paraphrasing Dijkstra's famous letter [9] which originally inspired our work. Applied to the parallel setting, it might read:

> The numerous versions of *send-recv*, as they stand for instance in MPI (non-blocking, ready, synchronous, etc.), are just too primitive; they are too much an invitation to make a mess of one's parallel program.

We strongly believe that collective operations have every potential to avoid this mess and to enable the design of well-structured, efficient parallel programs.

Acknowledgements

It is a pleasure to acknowledge the helpful comments of Christian Lengauer, Thilo Kielmann, Holger Bischof, Vladimir Korneev and Phil Bacon.

References

1. M. Aldinucci, S. Gorlatch, C. Lengauer, and S. Pelagatti. Towards parallel programming by transformation: The FAN skeleton framework. *Parallel Algorithms and Applications*, 16(2):87–113, 2001.
2. V. Bala et al. CCL: a portable and tunable collective communication library for scalable parallel computers. In *Proc. 8th Int. Conf. on Parallel Processing*.
3. M. Bernashi, G. Iannello, and M. Lauria. Experimental results about MPI collective communication operations. In *High-Performance Computing and Networking*, Lecture Notes in Computer Science 1593, pages 775–783, 1999.
4. G. Bilardi, K. Herley, A. Pietracaprina, G. Pucci, and P. Spirakis. BSP vs. LogP. In *Eighth ACM Symp. on Parallel Algorithms and Architectures*, pages 25–32, 1996.

5. R. Bird. Lectures on constructive functional programming. In M. Broy, editor, *Constructive Methods in Computing Science*, NATO ASI Series F: Computer and Systems Sciences. Vol. 55, pages 151–216. Springer Verlag, 1988.

6. C. Böhm and G. Jacopini. Flow diagrams, turing machines and languages with only two formation rules. *Comm. ACM*, 9:366–371, 1966.

7. O.-J. Dahl, E. W. Dijkstra, and C. A.R.Hoare. *Structured Programming*. Academic Press, 1975.

8. B. Di Martino, A. Mazzeo, N. Mazzocca, and U. Villano. Restructuring parallel programs by transformation of point-to-point interactions into collective communication. Available at http://www.grid.unina.it.

9. E. W. Dijkstra. Go To statement considered harmful. *Comm. ACM*, 11(3):147–148, 1968.

10. A. Geist et al. *PVM: Parallel Virtual Machine*. MIT Press, 1994.

11. S. Gorlatch. Towards formally-based design of message passing programs. *IEEE Trans. on Software Engineering*, 26(3):276–288, March 2000.

12. S. Gorlatch and C. Lengauer. Abstraction and performance in the design of parallel programs: overview of the SAT approach. *Acta Informatica*, 36(9):761–803, 2000.

13. S. Gorlatch, C. Wedler, and C. Lengauer. Optimization rules for programming with collective operations. In M. Atallah, editor, *Proc. IPPS/SPDP'99*, pages 492–499. IEEE Computer Society Press, 1999.

14. M. Goudreau, K. Lang, S. Rao, T. Suel, and T. Tsantilas. Towards efficiency and portablility. programming with the BSP model. In *Eighth ACM Symp. on Parallel Algorithms and Architectures*, pages 1–12, 1996.

15. M. Goudreau and S. Rao. Single-message vs. batch communication. In M. Heath, A. Ranade, and R. Schreiber, editors, *Algorithms for parallel processing*, pages 61–74. Springer-Verlag, 1999.

16. K. Hwang and Z. Xu. *Scalable Parallel Computing*. McGraw Hill, 1998.

17. T. Kielmann, H. E. Bal, and S. Gorlatch. Bandwidth-efficient collective communication for clustered wide area systems. In *Parallel and Distributed Processing Symposium (IPDPS 2000)*, pages 492–499, 2000.

18. T. Kielmann, R. F. Hofman, H. E. Bal, A. Plaat, and R. A. Bhoedjang. MagPIe: MPI's collective communication operations for clustered wide area systems. In *Proc. ACM SIGPLAN Symposium on Principles and Practice of Parallel Programming (PPoPP'99)*, pages 131–140, 1999.

19. Y. Kolosova, V. Korneev, V. Konstantinov, and N. Mirenkov. Yazik paralleljnykh algorithmov. In *Vychsliteljnye Sistemy*, volume 57. Nauka, 1973. In Russian.

20. A. Nelisse, T. Kielmann, H. E. Bal, and J. Maassen. Object-based collective communication in java. In *Joint ACM JavaGrande-ISCOPE 2001 Conference*, 2001.

21. P. Pacheco. *Parallel Programming with MPI*. Morgan Kaufmann Publ., 1997.

22. J.-Y. L. Park, H.-A. Choi, N. Nupairoj, and L. M. Ni. Construction of optimal multicast trees based on the parameterized communication model. In *Proc. Int. Conference on Parallel Processing (ICPP)*, volume I, pages 180–187, 1996.

23. S. S. Vadhiyar, G. E. Fagg, and J. Dongarra. Automatically tuned collective communications. In *Proc. Supercomputing 2000*. Dallas, TX, November 2000.

24. L. Valiant. General purpose parallel architectures. In *Handbook of Theoretical Computer Science*, volume A, chapter 18, pages 943–971. MIT Press, 1990.

25. R. van de Geijn. *Using PLAPACK: Parallel Linear Algebra package*. Scientific and Engineering Computation Series. MIT Press, 1997.

UNICORE: A Grid Computing Environment for Distributed and Parallel Computing

Valentina Huber

Central Institute for Applied Mathematics, Research Center Jülich,
Leo-Brandt-Str, D-52428 Jülich, Germany
v.huber@fz-juelich.de

Abstract. UNICORE (**UN**iform **I**nterface to **CO**mputer **RE**sources)
provides a seamless and secure access to distributed supercomputer resources. This paper will give an overview of the its architecture, security features, user functions, and mechanisms for the integration of existing applications into UNICORE. Car-Parrinello Molecular Dynamics
(CPMD) application is used as an example to demonstrate the capabilities of UNICORE.

1   Introduction

The increasing number of applications using parallel and distributed processing, e.g. planetary weather forecast or molecular dynamics research, require the
access to remote high performance computing resources through the Internet.
Figure 1 gives the overview upon the geographical distribution of user groups
working on the supercomputer complex of the John von Neumann Institute for
Computing (NIC) in Jülich.

On the other hand, one of the today's main difficulties is that the interfaces
to supercomputing resources tend to be both complicated and vendor specific.
To solve these problems, a project UNICORE [1] was funded in 1997 by the
German Ministry for Education and Research (BMBF). The goal of two-years
project and of the follow-on project UNICORE Plus [2] is to develop a seamless,
intuitive and secure infrastructure that make the supercomputer resources transparently available over the network. Project partners are the German Weather
Service (DWD), Research Center Jülich (FZJ), Computer Center of the University of Stuttgart (RUS), Pallas GmbH, Leibniz Computer Center, Munich (LRZ),
Computer Center of the University Karlsruhe (RUKA), Paderborn Center for
Parallel Computing (PC2), Konrad Zuse Center, Berlin (ZIB), and Center for
High Performance Computing at TU Dresden (ZHR). The project is structured
in eight sub-projects dealing with software development, quality management,
public key infrastructure (PKI), resources modeling, application specific support,
data management, job control flow, and meta-computing.

The main idea is to allow users to run jobs on the different platforms and
locations without the need to know details of the target operating system, data

V. Malyshkin (Ed.): PaCT 2001, LNCS 2127, pp. 258–265, 2001.

Fig. 1. User groups of NIC Jülich.

storage techniques, or administrative policies at the supercomputer sites. The graphical interface enables the user to create, submit and control jobs from the local Workstation or PC. UNICORE supports multi-system and multi-site applications for one job. This allows to use the optimal system and resources for the each part of a given problem. In the multi-step jobs the user can specify the dependencies between tasks, e.g. temporal relations or data transfer. Currently, execution of scripts, data transfer directives, and CPMD tasks in the batch mode are supported.

To create a seamless environment, jobs and resources are represented in abstract terms and units. The UNICORE servers translate the *Abstract Job Objects (AJOs)* into platform specific commands and options and schedules the tasks to honor dependencies. The autonomy of sites remains unchanged. The unique UNICORE user identifiers (certificates) will be mapped to local account names (Unix logins).

The developed software is installed at the German HPC centers for the target systems like CRAY T3E, T90, Fujitsu VPP, IBM SP2, Siemens hpcLine.

2   UNICORE System Architecture

UNICORE lets the user prepare or modify structured jobs through a graphical interface, the *UNICORE Client*, a Java-2 application, on a local UNIX Workstation or a Windows PC. The intuitive GUI for batch submission has the same look-and-feel independent of target system and provides the full information about resources to the user. Jobs can be submitted through the *Job Preparation*

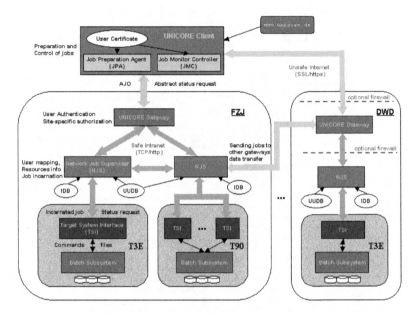

Fig. 2. UNICORE architecture.

*Agent (**JPA**)* to any platform of a UNICORE Grid, where the user has a local account, and the user can monitor and control the jobs through the *Job Monitor/Controller (**JMC**)*. Figure 2 presents the UNICORE system components and their interaction.

The *JPA* constructs a *AJO* with the definition of a job and contacts a *UNICORE Gateway* at a selected site. To support this selection, the *JPA* queries the availability of sites and the addresses of the corresponding gateways from the central UNICORE server (currently at `http://www.unicore.de`).

The Gateway, a small java-application running at the target site, authenticates the user through user's X.509 certificate and provides the user with the information about available resources at the site. It consigns a *AJO* to the appropriated *Network Job Superviser (**NJS**)* server.

Each target system or cluster of systems, is controlled by one NJS, also more then one NJS can be installed on a site. The NJS, a Java application, provides the resource information from the *Incarnation Database (**IDB**)* to the Gateway and checks the authorization of the user to use the requested resources from the *User Database (**UUDB**)*. It substitutes the site-independent *UNICORE login (Ulogin)*, which is based on a valid user certificate, with the corresponding local *Unix login (Xlogin)* on the destination system. For the target sites, which require additional security, e.g. DCE (Distributed Computing Environment), a *Site-specific Object (SSO)* of the *AJO* will be translated onto the corresponding procedures and commands to provide site-specific additional authentication. The NJS incarnates the abstract tasks destined for a local host into real batch jobs using the *IDB* and execute them through the *Target System Interface (**TSI**)* on the batch subsystem. The tasks to be run at a remote site will be passed to a peer Gateway.

The *TSI* is a daemon, a small perl-script, running on the target system, which submit the jobs to the local Batch Subsystem, e.g. NQS, and returns implicit output (stdout, stderr, log-files) from the jobs to the *NJS*, where they are retained for access by the user. Any temporary files, created during running of jobs, are automatically deleted. The Export files (see "Preparation of Jobs"), remain available at the location, specified by the user, on the target system or will be transferred to the local workstation or PC.

A low-level protocol layer between components, called the *UNICORE Protocol Layer (UPL)* provides authentication, SSL communication and transfer of data as byte-streams. The security is based on the Java implementations of SSL and the Java Cryptography Extensions [3] of the Institute for Applied Information Processing and Communications [4] at the Graz University of Technology. A high-level layer (AJO class library) contains classes to define UNICORE jobs, tasks, status and resource requests.

The authentication of users and components (Gateways and NJSes) is based on certificates issued by a UNICORE *Certification Authority (CA)*. It is located at LRZ in Munich and meets the regulations defined by the DFN-PCA (German Research Network - Policy Certification Authority) [5]. The partner centers run a *Registration Authority (RA)*.

3   Application Specific GUIs

The general basis for the integration of applications into UNICORE is the usage of the *ExecuteScript Task*. The *ExecuteScript* task contains the definition of a script, the sequence of commands to be executed on the target system, and the list of input and output files for the application. In addition the user can select several execution contexts, e.g. MPI-1, PVM, Debug, Profile, C, Fortran, etc. These contexts are predefined execution environments and are used for example to run parallel programs using MPI. The *UNICORE Client* provides the user with information about the available resources for each task and their limits, e.g. the minimum and the maximum number of processors on the selected machine. The *Transfer Task* is used for the transfer of files from one site to another one.

Furthermore, the users have the possibility to integrate new or already existing application specific GUIs as **plug-ins** into the *UNICORE Client*. The plug-ins are modules that are specifically written to extend the capabilities of the *UNICORE Client*. They use the standard function of the *UNICORE Client* for authentication, security, data transfer, submission and monitoring of jobs, and provide additional support for the applications, e.g. the specification of libraries, the preparation of the configuration files, etc.

Each application plug-in consist of some wrapper classes. The *plugin* class extends the *Job Preparation Menu* of the *UNICORE Client* with the options to add an application task to the job tree and provides the *UNICORE Client* with the information about other plug-in classes. The *TaskContainer* class constructs the AJO for the particular application task and the *JPAPanel* class presents

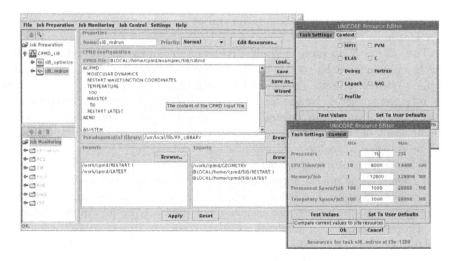

Fig. 3. GUI for the CPMD task.

the application specific GUI. The system plug-ins are located in the *unicore-client*/plugin directory. In addition the user can specify the plug-in directory for own plug-ins in the "*User Defaults*" dialog. The *UNICORE Client* scans these directories for plug-ins at start-up, loads them, and displays the application specific GUI in the *JPA* by the selecting of the corresponding icon representing an application task.

We selected the widely used Car-Parrinello Molecular Dynamics code [9] as a first application to be integrated in UNICORE. CPMD is an *ab initio* Electronic Structure and Molecular Dynamics program; since 1995 the development is continued at the Max-Planck Institute für Festkörperforschung in Stuttgart [11]. This application uses a large amount of CPU time and disk space and is the ideal candidate for a Grid application. Currently, multi processor versions for IBM Risc and Cray PVP systems and parallel versions for IBM SP2 and Cray T3E are available.

The developed CPMD interface provides the users with an intuitive way to specify the full set of configuration parameters (specification of the input and output data sets, pseudopotentials, etc.) for a CPMD simulation.

4   Preparation of Jobs

Figure 3 shows the input panel for one CPMD task, in this case a molecular dynamics run. It is divided into four areas: *Properties*, the configuration area for the CPMD calculation, data *Imports* and data *Exports*.

The *Properties* area contains global settings like the task name, the task's resource requirements and the task's priority. The resource description includes the number of processors, the maximum CPU time, the amount of memory, the required permanent and temporary disk space. The *JPA* knows about the minimum and the maximum values for all resources of the execution system, where the task is to be run, and incorrect values are shown in red.

The configuration area contains the application specific information. It includes the specification of the input file, required for the CPMD program [10]. The button *Generate* brings up the tool **CPMD Wizard**, developed at Research Center Jülich, which generates the CPMD input data automatically. Experienced users may use the data from existing jobs, stored on the local computer. The configuration data may be edited directly or through the Wizard. It is also possible to save data as a text file on the local disk.

For all atomic species, which will be used in the CPMD calculation, the path to the pseudopotential library has to be specified. The local pseudopotential files will be automatically transferred to the target system. Alternatively, the user can specify the remote directory for the pseudopotentials. If this field is empty, then the default library on the destination system will be used.

The *Imports* area describes the set of input files for the CPMD calculation, e.g. a restart file to reuse the simulation results from a previous step. The input files may reside on the local disk or on the target system. Local files marked *@LOCAL* are automatically transferred to the target system and remote files will be imported to the job directory.

The *Exports* area controls the disposition of the result files to be saved after the job completion. In the example some of the output files will be stored on the target system and others, marked *@LOCAL*, will be transferred to the local system and can be visualized there.

Before the CPMD job can be submitted to a particular target system, the interface automatically checks the correctness of the job. Prepared jobs can be stored to be reused in the future.

UNICORE has all the functions to group CPMD tasks and other tasks into jobs. Each task of a job may execute on a different target host of the UNICORE Grid. The job can be resubmitted to a different system by changing the target system. UNICORE controls the execution sequence, honoring dependencies and transfers data between hosts automatically.

Figure 4 represents an example of a CPMD job consisting of two steps: *si8_optimize* task for the wavefunction optimization of a cluster of 8 Silicon atoms and *si8_mdrun* task for molecular dynamics run. Both tasks will be executed on the same system, T3E in Jülich. The left hand side of the *JPA* represents the hierarchical job structure. The green color of the icons indicates the job as *Ready for submission*. The second task will be run only after the first one is completed. It uses the output files from the *si8_optimize* task to reuse the results of the wavefunction optimization. This dependency is shown on the right hand side and represents a temporal relation between the tasks.

5   Monitoring of Jobs

The user can monitor and control the submitted jobs using the job monitor part (*JMC*) of the *UNICORE Client*. The *JMC* displays the list of all jobs the user has submitted to a particular system. The job, initially represented by an icon,

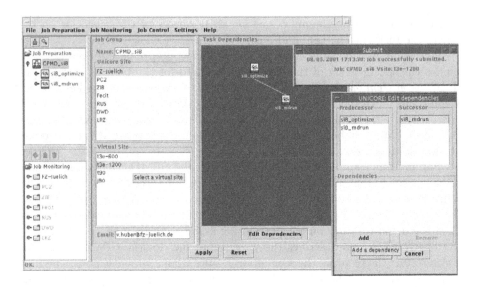

Fig. 4. CPMD job consisting of two tasks and dependency between them.

that can be expanded to show the hierarchical structure. The status of jobs or parts of jobs are given by colors: green - completed successfully, blue - queued, yellow - running, red - completed not successfully, etc. It is possible to delete a job, which has not begun execution, or to terminate running jobs.

After a job or a part of a job is finished, the user can retrieve its output. A completed job retains in the list of jobs until the user removes it.

Figure 5 presents the status of the jobs submitted to the T3E system in Jülich. The right hand side displays the summary standard output and standard error from two steps *si8_optimize* and *si8_mdrun* of *CPMD_si8* job.

6   Outlook

The technique of allowing independent task to execute simultaneously on different machines and independent child AJOs to execute simultaneously at different sites, supported by UNICORE, provides an alternative to the asynchronous parallelism. In addition, one of the sub-projects aims to extend the capability of UNICORE to allow the metacomputing in the usual sense, which typically requires support of synchronous message passing.

The technique used for the CPMD integration is extensible to numerous other applications. We plan to develop the interfaces for MSC-NASTRAN, FLUENT and STAR-CD applications. These interfaces are going to be integrated into the UNICORE Client for seamless submission and control of jobs. In the future it is planned to build a generic interface to allow easier integration of applications.

The first production-ready version of the UNICORE system has been deployed for operational use at the German HPC centers.

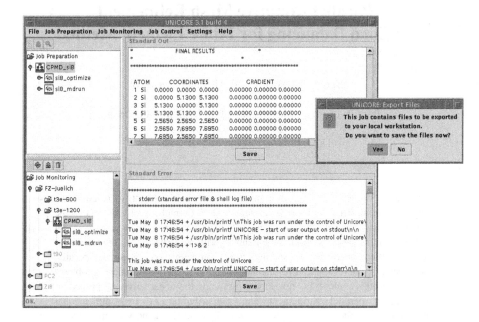

Fig. 5. The Job monitor displays the status of the jobs submitted to a particular system.

References

1. The Project UNICORE Web Page.
   http://www.kfa-juelich.de/zam/RD/coop/unicore
2. The Project UNICORE Plus Web Page.
   http://www.kfa-juelich.de/zam/RD/coop/unicoreplus
3. Java(TM) Cryptography Extension (JCE). http://java.sun.com/jce
4. Institute for applied Information Processing and Communications.
   http://jcewww.iaik.tu-graz.ac.at
5. Policy Certification Authority (PCA). http://www.cert.dfn.de/eng/dfnpca
6. J. Almond, D.Snelling: UNICORE: uniform access to supercomputing as an element of electronic commerce. FGCS **15** (1999) 539-548
7. J. Almond, D.Snelling: UNICORE: Secure and Uniform access to distributed Resources via World Wide Web. A White Paper.
   http://www.kfa-juelich.de/zam/RD/coop/unicore/whitepaper.ps
8. Romberg, M.: The UNICORE Grid Infrastructure.
   Proceedings of the 42nd Cray User Group Conference (2000)
9. Marx, D., Hutter, J.: Ab *Initio* Molecular Dynamics: Theory and Implementation Modern Methods and Algorithms of Quantum Chemistry. Proceedings of Winterschool, 21-25 February (2000) 329–478
10. Hutter, J.: Car-Parrinello Molecular Dynamics - An Electronic Structure and Molecular Dynamics Program. CPMD Manual (2000)
11. Research Group of Michele Parrinello.
    http://www.mpi-stuttgart.mpg.de/parrinello

Parallel Adaptive Mesh Refinement
with Load Balancing for Finite Element Method

Sergey Kopyssov and Alexander Novikov

Institute of Applied Mechanics UB of RAS, MSM Laboratory,
426001 Izhevsk, Russia
{kopyssov,an}@ipm.uni.udm.ru

Abstract. The efficient solution of many large-scale scientific calculations depends on unstructured mesh strategies. For example, problems where the solution changes rapidly in small regions of the domain require an adaptive mesh strategy. In this paper we discuss the main algorithmic issues to be addressed with an integrated approach to solving these problems on massively parallel architectures. We review new parallel algorithms to solve two significant problems that arise in this context: the refinement mesh and the linear solver. A procedure to support parallel refinement and redistribution of two dimensional unstructured finite element meshes on distributed memory computers is presented. The parallelization of the solver is based on a parallel conjugate gradient method using domain decomposition. The error indicator and the resulting refinement parameters are computed in parallel.

1   Introduction

The unstructured mesh strategies have proven to be very successful in reducing the computation and storage requirements for many scientific and engineering calculations. Massively parallel computers offer a cost-effective tool for solving such problems. However, many difficult algorithmic and implementation issues must be addressed to make effective use of this resource. In this paper, we review the major aspects of an unstructured mesh strategy and present an integrated approach to deal with these aspects on distributed memory machines. We also present computational results from a preliminary implementation of this approach. The irregular and evolving behavior of the computational load in adaptive strategies on complex domains becomes problematic when parallel distributed-memory machine implementations are considered. Complete parallelizations of these methods necessitate additional and difficult stages of partitioning, parallel refinement and the redistribution of the refined mesh. Many heuristics have been devised to partition the initial unstructured mesh and hence minimize the load imbalance and interprocessor communication among processors. The redistribution of the refined mesh can also be done by parallelizing similar partitioning heuristics.

V. Malyshkin (Ed.): PaCT 2001, LNCS 2127, pp. 266–276, 2001.

Adaptive finite element methods, driven by automatic estimation and control of errors have gained importance recently due to their ability to offer reliable solutions to partial differential equations. Starting with a coarse initial mesh

- the calculation of an approximate solution;
- the estimation of the distribution of the discretization error over the domain under consideration;
- the generation of an improved mesh by a complete remeshing of the domain (h-version of adaptivity);
- if the current partitioning indicates that it is adequately load balanced, control is passed back to the solver;
- otherwise, a repartitioning procedure is invoked to divide the mesh into subdomain;
- remapping the data ;

are executed repeatedly until the global error is within a desired tolerance. We propose an algorithm in which adaptivity and parallel computations, based on an automatic domain decomposition.

2 Parallel Adaptive Mesh Refinement

In this paper we consider adaptive refinement of triangular meshes by simple bisection. The longest side bisection of triangle is a partition of the triangle by the midpoint of its longest edge and the opposite vertex. An uncompatible edge is a common edge for triangle pair so that edge divided in one of triangles [1]. Other possible approaches, and more detail of the following algorithms, are given in [2,3]. In this paper, we present new parallel algorithm for the adaptive construction of nonuniform meshes.

The parallel mesh refinement is the refinement of distributed mesh. The initial mesh has been partitioned and distributed among processors. A mesh part will called a submesh. The partition was produced so that submeshs intersection was either a shared vertex or a shared edges. Refinement is made by longest side bisection. The refinement process consist of two steps:

Step 1. Divide all refinement triangles.

Step 2. Divide all triangles with uncompatible edges.

All triangles with uncompatible edges must be found for the second step. In the single processor case all search information are stored on the processor. In case of many processors an uncompatible edge may be a shared edge. If uncompatible edge is a shared edge than a processor in which a divided edge lie send message on the adjacent processor. Adjacent processor receive message but it is impossible find this edge using edge local number. A single numbering of mesh objects is required in this case. We used unique numbers produced from edge coordinates [4]. Unique numbers values are choose in the big range ($0...2^{31}$) and used in place of search keys. The search has been based on hashing with open addressing. Collisions in hash table has been resolved by linear probing. Edges unique numbers has been stored on every processor in edge hash table. Adjacent triangles numbers and processor membership of these triangles has been stored in two tables. These tables are adjusted with edge hash table. We differed an internal edges, a shared edges, a boundary edges and found adjacent triangles and submeshs by using this information:

Every processor realized next algorithm.

Step 1. Divide refinement triangles from this submesh.

Step 2. While uncompatible edges number of all mesh more than 0.

Step 2.1 While uncompatible edges number of this submesh more than 0.
        Divide triangles with uncompatible edges from this submesh.

Step 2.2 Define divided edges number.

Step 2.3 Exchange numbers values of shared edges which are divided
        in adjacent submeshs.

Step 2.4 Let uncompatible edges number is equal number of shared edges which
        are divided in adjacent submeshs.

        Let uncompatible edges are shared edges which are divided
        in adjacent submeshs.

Step 2.5 Define uncompatible edges number of all mesh.

Local mesh refinement decrease an effect of parallel FE equations system building and solving owing to the load unbalance. After parallel mesh refinement we had applied dynamic load balancing.

3 Dynamic Load Balancing

The dual graph representation of the initial computational mesh is one of the key features of this work. Parallel implementation of adaptive solvers requires a partitioning of the computational mesh such that each element belongs to an unique partition. Communication is required across faces that are shared by adjacent elements residing on different processors. Hence for the purposes of partitioning, we consider the dual of the original computational mesh. The elements of the computational mesh are the vertices of the dual graph. An edge exists between two dual graph vertices if the corresponding elements share a face. A graph partitioning of the dual thus yields an assignment of triangle to processors. The finite element mesh partitioning library ParMetis [5] has been used to obtain the element-balanced partitions. ParMetis is an MPI-based parallel library. We used algorithm for refining a k-way partitioning that is a generalization of the Kernighan-Lin/Fiduccia-Mattheyses (RefineKway). For partitioned mesh that are highly imbalanced in localized areas, diffusion-based load balancing scheme (LDiffusion) is used to minimize the difference between the original partitioning and final repartitioning by making incremental changes in the partitioning to restore balance. The next balances the load by computing an entirely different p-way partition, and then intelligently mapping the new partition to the old one such that the redistribution cost is minimized (Remap, MLRemap). Load balancing is required before the computation after every step refinement mesh. The performance results of various mesh partitioning algorithms are summarized (Fig.3-6).

4 Error Estimation

We have tested our algorithm using linear elasticity equations on a variety of geometry. For error estimation of problem smoothing the stress field, is used. The basic idea of error estimators is to substitute the field exact stress, which is generally unknown, by the field σ^h, obtained by means of recovery procedures. Usually, the conjugate approximation method [6] can be used, which consists in solving the following linear systems of equations

$$G\sigma_k^* = f, k = 1,2,3 \qquad (1)$$

where three systems of equations exist in (1), one for each stress component k. The coefficients of G are defined by :

$$G_{MN} = \int_\Omega \Psi_N \Psi_M d\Omega \qquad (2)$$

and are thus similar to those of a consistent mass matrix of the structure with unit mass density. f_{Nk} is the vector of the k component of nodal stresses, f_N is the k component of stress at node N. The coefficients of f_{Nk} are defined by :

$$f_{N_k} = \int_\Omega \Psi_N \sigma_k^h d\Omega \qquad (3)$$

Therefore, the expression for computing the approximate (estimated) relative error distribution can be expressed as

$$\left\| e_\sigma \right\|_{E(\Omega)}^2 = \int_\Omega \left(\sigma^* - \sigma^h \right)^T D^{-1} \left(\sigma^* - \sigma^h \right) d\Omega \qquad (4)$$

The contribution of all the elements in the mesh is given by

$$\left\| e_\sigma \right\|^2 = \sum_{e=1}^M \left\| e_\sigma \right\|_e^2 \qquad (5)$$

where M is total number of elements.

The relative percentage error in the energy norm for the whole domain can be obtained as

$$\eta = \frac{\left\| e_\sigma \right\|}{\left\| u \right\|} * 100\% \qquad (6)$$

where $\left\| u \right\|$ is given by

$$\left\| u \right\| = \sqrt{\left\| u^h \right\|^2 + \left\| e_\sigma \right\|^2} \qquad (7)$$

A criterion for an "optimal" mesh consists of requiring that the energy norm error be equidistributed among elements because it leads to meshes with high convergence. Thus, for each element

$$\|\bar{e}\| = \bar{\eta}\sqrt{\left(\|u^h\|^2 + \|e_\sigma\|^2\right)/M} \tag{8}$$

By defining the ratio

$$\xi_i = \frac{\|e\|}{\|\bar{e}\|}_i \tag{9}$$

it is obvious that refinement it need if

$$\xi_i > 1.0 \tag{10}$$

The selected element are refinement according to algorithm reduced in section 2.

5 Parallel Conjugate Gradient Method

Usually in finite element method it is considered, that a mesh and system of linear equation are assembled so that each node belongs to several elements. Let's assume return, the set of elements and element matrixes is teared. Let $A \in \mathbf{R}^{N \times N}$ be any global matrix and $\tilde{A}^e \in \mathbf{R}^{n \times n}$ an element contribution to A. We can write $A = \sum_{e=1}^{M} C_e^T \tilde{A}^e C_e$, where $C_e \in \mathbf{R}^{n \times N}$ is called a Boolean matrix and has the property

$$C^T = (C_1, C_2, ..., C_M)^T, \ C^T \in \mathbf{R}^{N \times m}, \ D = C\, C^T CC, \ D_e \in \mathbf{R}^{n \times n}$$

where D_e - diagonal matrix containing for each node of a number of elements, with which belongs to this node. Diagonal matrix $D \in \mathbf{R}^{m \times m}$ is composed from D_e^{-1} blocks. Block-diagonal matrix $\tilde{A} \in \mathbf{R}^{\times}$, $m = M \times n$, is composed from $\tilde{A}^e$ blocks. Matrix $\tilde{A}^e$ and vectors $\tilde{f}^e$ are incomplete, i.e. coefficients associated with nodes of element (subdomain) i and j do not contain the contributions form adjacent element (subdomain). We have termed the exchange of coefficients required to create complete vectors operation

$$q_k = C \sum_{i=1}^{P} C^T q_k \tag{11}$$

This operation represents the assembly and subsequent extraction of element vectors. Operation (11) is implemented through an exchange of data among the elements that share a global node. Element contributions may be assembled to subdomain. Each processor contains the portion m_i of the global vectors (e.g., p, u, r, etc.) required by the solution algorithm associated with the elements assigned to that processor.

Algorithm for solving the system for parallel computer can be implemented as indicated by following code:

- $\tilde{A} \in \mathbf{R}^{m_i \times m_i}, \mathbf{p}, \mathbf{r}, \mathbf{u}, \mathbf{q}, \tilde{\mathbf{q}} \in \mathbf{R}^{m_i}, \gamma_k, \rho_k, \beta_k, \alpha_k, \varpi, \theta, \gamma_{k_i}, \varpi_i, \theta_i, \rho_{k_i} \in \mathbf{R}^{1_i};$

$\mathbf{u}_0 = 0$, $\mathbf{r}_0 = C\bar{f}$, $\rho_0 = (\mathbf{r}_0, D\mathbf{r}_0)$, $\varepsilon = 10^{-8}$;

For $k = 0,1,2,\ldots$;

$$\mathbf{q}_k = \tilde{A}\mathbf{p}_k \tag{11}$$

$$\mathbf{q}_k = C\sum_{=} C^T \mathbf{q}_k \tag{12}$$

$$\omega_i = (\mathbf{q}_k, D\mathbf{q}_k) \tag{13}$$

$$\theta_i = (\bar{\mathbf{q}}_k, D\bar{\mathbf{r}}_k) \tag{14}$$

$$\gamma_{k_i} = (\bar{\mathbf{p}}_k, D\bar{\mathbf{q}}_k) \tag{15}$$

$$\gamma_k = \sum_{i=1}^{P} \gamma_{ki} \, , \omega = \sum_{i=1}^{P} \omega_i \, , \theta = \sum_{i=1}^{P} \theta_i \tag{16}$$

$$\alpha_k = -\frac{\rho_k}{\gamma_k} \tag{17}$$

$$\mathbf{u}_{k+} = \mathbf{u}_k - \alpha_k \mathbf{p}_k \tag{18}$$

$$\mathbf{r}_{k+1} = \mathbf{r}_k + \alpha_k \mathbf{q}_k \tag{19}$$

$$\rho_{k+1} = \rho_k + 2\alpha_k \theta + \alpha_k^2 \omega \tag{20}$$

$$\text{if } \frac{\rho_{k+1}}{\rho_0} < \varepsilon \text{ exit};$$

$$\beta_k = \frac{\rho_{k+1}}{\rho_k} \tag{21}$$

$$\mathbf{p}_{k+1} = \mathbf{r}_k - \beta_k \mathbf{p}_k \tag{22}$$

The element matrix and vector calculations can obviously be made in parallel. Note that the matrix-vectors products can be carried out at the element level within each subdomain. Let us further partition the matrix-vector product to distinguish nodes in interior from those on the interface. The matrix-vector product separates into two parts. Provided the interior submatrix-vector product is sufficiently large, this splitting may permit complete overlap of communication and computation. This strategy can be implemented efficiently using MPI procedures MPI_Isend and MPI_Irecv to perform non-blocked communications.

As against reference algorithm [7] a inner product of vectors of discrepancies on iteration was evaluated through three dot products (14) – (16) on previous step:

$$(r_{k+1}, r_{k+1}) = \sum_{i=1}^{m} r_{i_{k+1}} r_{i_{k+1}} = \sum_{i=1}^{m} (r_{i_k} + \alpha_k q_{i_k})(r_{i_k} + \alpha_k q_{i_k}) = \sum_{i=1}^{m} (r_{i_k} r_{i_k} + 2\alpha_k q_{i_k} r_{i_k} + \alpha_k q_{i_k} \alpha_k q_{i_k}) =$$

$$= \sum_{i=1}^{m} r_{i_k} r_{i_k} + 2\alpha_k \sum_{i=1}^{m} q_{i_k} r_{i_k} + \alpha_k^2 \sum_{i=1}^{m} q_{i_k} q_{i_k} = (r_k, r_k) + 2\alpha_k (q_k, r_k) + \alpha_k^2 (q_k, q_k),$$

The three inner products in (14) – (16) can now be calculated using only a single commutative operation to perform the three global summations.

Non-blocking communication and single communicative operation have reduced execution time on 15-25%.

We used this algorithm for solving system (1) with some k sides. In this case all vectors dimension is raised in k times. Iterations are completed when out condition for all processes are fulfilled. This computing organization decrease communications number.

6 Results

Consider now a crack problem in linear elasticity. The parameters of the structure are: $E = 1.0, v = 0.3$. Due to the symmetry, only a half of structure will be analyzed with an uniform initial mesh. The mesh is adaptivity refined according to the energy norm until the local error estimate for each triangle is less than a specified tolerance. Fourteen refinement steps are carried out using error estimators (1)-(10). The computational experiments are performed with linear elements and using an error tolerance $\eta = 4\%$. The coarse mesh and initial partitioning are shown in Fig. 1. In Fig. 2 refinement mesh is decomposed with the MLRemap algorithm   into eight subdomains. The linear systems for stiffness and error estimation problems are solved by using the parallel conjugate gradient method (12) - (23). Although the primary focus of this paper is the adaptive refinement algorithm, it is important to examine the performance of the algorithm both individually and from context of the complete problem solution. Thus, we have included the matrix assembly, linear solution, error estimation, mesh refinement, mesh partitioning and remapping in our experimental results (Fig. 3). The algorithm   without balancing was fulfilled more twice slowly. We can three major conclusions from plots. First, we find that the refinement time are compared to partitioning time. Second, the time to solve stiffness system and system (1) dominates the time to refine the mesh. Finally, we can see that the total adaption time is always less several percent of the total execution time. In Fig. 4 ,5 the quality of the obtained partitioning for each step is shown. Note, that the number of common edges (length of boundaries of subdomains) for all algorithms is approximately identical. In Fig. 6 the number of elements moved after everyone step is shown.

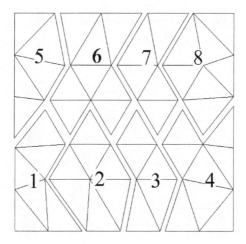

Fig. 1. Initial mesh partition (51 triangles, 37 nodes, $\eta = 33.48\%$).

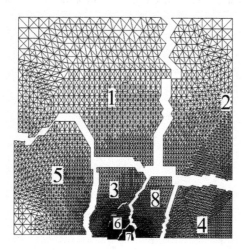

Fig. 2. Mesh after 14 refinement step (17224 triangles, 8744 nodes, $\eta = 3.89\%$).

Our experiments were run on up to 8 nodes of the Parsytec CC-8 machine at the Institute of Applied Mechanics. The machine is equipped with PowerPC 604 thin-nodes (133 MHz) with at least 64MB of memory. The top-level message-passing calls are implemented throught MPI [8].

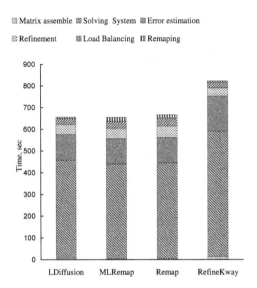

Fig. 3. Task execution time with some algorithm of load balancing

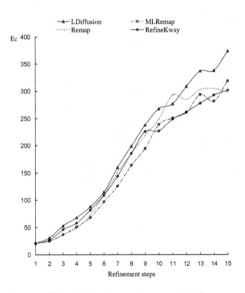

Fig. 4. Common edges quantity Ec.

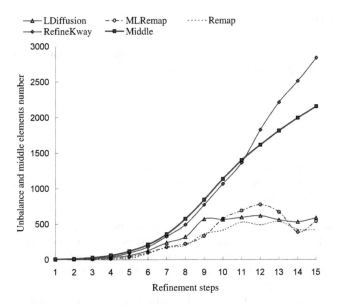

Fig. 5. Unbalance $\max_{i=1}^{P}(M_i) - \min_{i=1}^{P}(M_i)$ and middle elements quantity M/P.

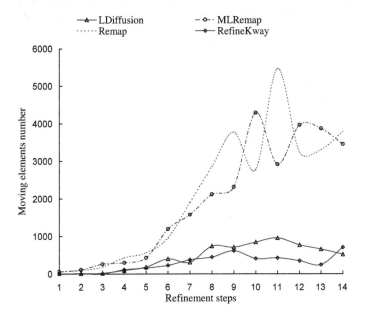

Fig. 6. Moving elements number.

Acknowledgements

This investigation was accomplished with support of Russia Foundation of Fundamental Investigation (project 99 –07-90455).

References

1. Rivara, M.-C.: Mesh refinement processes based on the generalized bisection of simplices. SIAM Journal of Numerical Analysis, 21 (1984) 604-613
2. Mitchell, W.F.: A comparison of adaptive refinement techniques for elliptic problems. ACM Transactions on Mathematical Software, 15 (1989) 326-347.
3. Jones, M. T., Plassmann, P. E.: Computational results for parallel unstructured mesh computations. Computing Systems in Engineering, 5 (1994) 297-309
4. Kopyssov, S. P., Alies, M. Yu., Novikov, A. K., Ustuzhanin, S. L.: Domain decomposition for Elastic Problem Solving with Dynamic Refinement Mesh Model. 2nd Russian Conference on High Performance Computing and Their Application. Moscow State University, Moscow (2000) 119-122
5. Karypis, G., Schloegel, K., Kumar V.: ParMetis Parallel Graph Partitioning and Sparse Matrix Ordering Library Version 2.0 University of Minnesota, Department of Computer Science / Army HPC Research Center Minneapolis, MN 55455
6. Oden, J.T: Finite elements of nonlinear continua. McGraw-Hill, New York (1972)
7. Ortega, J.: Introduction to Parallel and Vector Solution of Linear Systems, Plenum Publishing Co, 1988
8. MPI: A message-passing interface standard, University of Tennessee, Knoxville, Tennessee, 1.1 ed., (1995)

Concurrent Implementation
of Structurally Synthesized Programs

Sven Lämmermann, Enn Tyugu, and Vladimir Vlassov

Royal Institute of Technology, Department of Teleinformatics, Electrum 204
S-16440 Kista, Sweden
{laemmi,tyugu,vlad}@it.kth.se

Abstract. Specification for structural synthesis of programs (SSP) contains information needed for introducing concurrency into a synthesized program. We explain how this can be used in a multithreaded computing environment, in particular, in a Java environment. We discuss strategies of coarse-grained multithreaded execution of synthesized programs: composing threads and imposing parallelism on subtasks.

1 Introduction

A structurally synthesized functional program does not have constraints on execution order other than imposed by data dependencies and by logical constraints explicitly expressed in pre- and post-conditions of functions. From the other side, its specification contains explicit and easily usable information about all data dependencies that must be taken into account when synchronizing concurrent execution of its parts. This can be used for parallelization of structurally synthesized programs. Still, the existing implementations of the structural synthesis of programs (SSP) produce code for sequential execution in one single thread [5], although the first works on concurrent execution of programs obtained by structural synthesis appeared long ago [3]. Also the parallel computing models developed and investigated in [2] were quite close to the specifications for SSP, and could have been used for introducing concurrency into structurally synthesized programs. The ideas from [2] were to some extent used in the packages developed for parallel processing on the NUTS platform [6].

At present we have a new implementation of SSP on the basis of Java [1] that supports both multithreading, and an easy way to organize concurrent computations in the network of workstations. Consequently, technically good possibilities exist, both for using fine-grained and coarse-grained concurrency in the implementation of structurally synthesized algorithms. The question is how to parallelize computations automatically, because this is needed for programs, synthesized dynamically at run-time. First, we discuss our idea of synthesis of concurrent programs using dataflow synchronization in general, second, we consider a multithreaded implementation of structurally synthesized algorithms in Java. Finally, we discuss strategies of coarse-grained parallelization on the basis of information available in the specifications for SSP under the assumption that no help for parallelization can be taken at run-time from the user.

V. Malyshkin (Ed.): PaCT 2001, LNCS 2127, pp. 277–284, 2001.
© Springer-Verlag Berlin Heidelberg 2001

2   Multithreaded Execution of a Synthesized Program

The SSP uses a simple constructive logic that allows us to specify dataflow among functions. For instance, let us consider an example in a more restricted logic than SSP uses that still illustrates our approach. Input for synthesis is given as a collection of formulae that includes among others the following three formulae: $f : A \rightarrow B$, $g : U \rightarrow V$, and $h : B \wedge V \rightarrow X$, where $A \rightarrow B$, $U \rightarrow V$, and $B \wedge V \rightarrow X$ are specifications of functions f, g, and h. The dataflow between function f, g, and h is described by their respective specifications; i.e. the output of f (which is specified by B) and the output of g (specified by V) are used as inputs for h. The propositional variables A, B, U, V, and X are types that express the conceptual roles that their respective objects play in computations.

Current implementations of the SSP extract from a proof of existence of an object an algorithm, which is then translated into byte code [5] or source code of a particular target programming language [1]. In either case, the resulting program is sequentially executed in one single thread. The following figure depicts the synthesis process of a sequential program for computing an object specified by X.

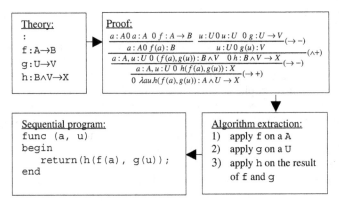

Fig. 1. Program synthesis

A concurrent implementation of a structurally synthesized algorithm is constructed of a set of dynamically created *guarded threads* and *shared input/output objects* that are used for communication between guarded threads. Shared input/output objects are available to guarded threads through an environment. A guarded thread represents a function selected from the proof of the existence of the result. The shared objects serve as "communication channels" for passing the result of one function (thread) to other functions (other threads). As in the dataflow computation model, a guarded thread can perform its computation if its required input objects in the computation exist and they are bound, so that the thread can get an input object and operate on it when needed. If a required input object is not available yet (it has not been bound yet), the thread is suspended while waiting for the input object to be bound. When the thread completes, it binds its computation result to its output object. It may happen that the output object still contains the result bound by a previous instance of the thread, i.e. the output object was not yet consumed by another thread. In dataflow, such situation is called data collision (or collision of tokens that represent the data). The simplest way to avoid data collisions is to suspend the thread that tries to bind its computation result to its respective output object until the output object can be reused for binding the computation result. This approach requires maintaining a queue of threads suspended on the shared object that cannot be reused. We use a more efficient mechanism to avoid data collisions, known as dynamic dataflow. Every instance of one and the same guarded thread is associated with a different instance of the environment. Every environment creates its own input/output objects. A guarded thread knows only those objects that are needed for input and output. A shared object can be considered as a "write-once" (or "bound-once") object.

A guarded thread does the following: 1) it waits until all objects needed as inputs become available, 2) if all objects are available then it executes, and 3) it binds its computation result to its respective output object. Let us assume that we have a programming platform with some means to realize dataflow synchronization – waiting for input values. A simple idea is to use dynamic dataflow synchronization on guarded threads that represent separately every function of the proof of the existence of the result. In this way one constructs a concurrent implementation of a structurally synthesized program, where each computational step (execution of one function) is encapsulated in a thread, which is illustrated in the following figure.

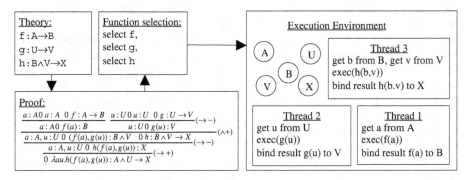

Fig. 2. Guarded threads

Due to dataflow synchronization (wait until an object is bound) thread 1 and 2 will run in parallel and thread 3 must wait until both threads 1 and 2 have finished their computation, i.e. have bound their outputs to the respective objects.

3   Guarded Threads

In this section we discuss the concurrent implementation of structurally synthesized programs in Java. Although Java is not designed for massively concurrent programming, we are still able to implement concurrent applications in Java. It supports threads and provides synchronization primitives that can be used to implement dataflow synchronization. We are well aware of that there are other programming languages that do better in terms of concurrent programming, the

Mozart [7] system, which implements Oz, for instance. The programming language Oz possesses a built in dataflow synchronization mechanism [8].

There are several ways of how to implement concurrent programs of structurally synthesized algorithms. For simplicity, and to keep our examples more comprehensible, we shall use easily understandable source code and avoid using sophisticated reflection tools. In our example, we assume that the functions f, g, and h are methods of the class MyClass. Their internal structure is uninteresting for us. First, we explain how we implement dataflow synchronization in Java. Data dependencies among functions are expressed by propositional variables of the respective specifications of the functions under consideration. For example, function h depends on function f and g specified by their common propositional variables B and V, where B and V occur in the premise of the specification of h and B (V resp.) occurs in the conclusion of the specification of function f (g resp.). In case of Java, propositional variables of specifications become parameters of methods of classes in extracted programs [1], where they are used as input (if they occur on the left hand side of the method specification) and output (if they occur on the right hand side of the method specification). To implement dataflow synchronization we simply encapsulate an input/output object in a wrapper object, which is an instance of an ObjectWrapper class. The ObjectWrapper class defines two methods, get and bind. Guarded threads use the method get to obtain an input object, and they use the method bind to bind their respective function result to its respective wrapper object. If a guarded thread invokes the method get on a wrapper object then this thread is blocked in the method call of get if the wrapper object has not yet bound an object, i.e. the method bind has not yet been invoked on this wrapper object. As soon as the method bind is invoked on this wrapper object, all guarded threads that are blocked in get will execute again. A guarded thread is simply a class that encapsulates the execution of a method. It invokes the method get on all wrapper objects that wrap the input objects of the encapsulated method (f), and invokes bind on that wrapper object that wraps the output object of the encapsulated method (f). The following code example is an implementation of the guarded thread class that encapsulates the method f (similar for the methods g and h).

```
class GuardedThread_f extends Thread {
    ConcurrentImpl env;
    GuardedThread_f (ConcurrentImpl env, int id) {
        super("Guarded Thread ID: [" + id + "]");
        this.env = env;
        this.start();
    }
    void run() {
        // get the value of A
        Object o = this.env.A.get();
        // execute the method f and bind the result to B
        this.env.B.bind(this.env.f(o));
    }
}
```

The method main of the class ConcurrentImpl (concurrent implementation) creates the execution environment (object of class ConcurrentImpl, wrapper objects) for the concurrent execution of needed guarded threads. After all guarded threads are created, the input objects of our synthesized concurrent program, which are proper objects for A and U, are bound to their respective wrapper objects. The program then waits until the result (which is a proper object for X) is computed.

```
class ConcurrentImpl extends MyClass {
    ObjectWrapper A = new ObjectWrapper();
        :
    ObjectWrapper X = new ObjectWrapper();
    // realization of A∧U->X
    public static void main(String[] args) {
        ConcurrentImpl env = new ConcurrentImpl();
        new GuardedThread_f (env, 1);
        new GuardedThread_g (env, 2);
        new GuardedThread_h (env, 3);
        // bind initial values
        env.A.bind(args[0]);
        env.U.bind(args[1]);
        // wait until goal X is computed
        System.out.println(env.X.get());
    }
}
```

Note that the implementations of our classes do not implement the control part of the synthesized algorithm explicitly. The computation of the result is guided by dataflow synchronization.

The SSP uses a logic that is much more expressive than we used here in our example. For instance, the formula $(U \rightarrow V) \wedge X \rightarrow Y$ specifies that we can compute a proper object for Y if we have a proper object for X and if we can find a realization of the subtask $(U \rightarrow V)$. This subtask receives a proper object for U from the function that receives this subtask as input, and computes a proper object for V. In Java one can implement subtasks as classes [1]. In case of concurrent implementations of structurally synthesized algorithms it is possible to implement subtasks as threads as well, which then themselves create guarded threads (similar to our main method of class ConcurrentImpl). The fact that subtasks are threads gives us the possibility to execute concurrently one and the same synthesized branch (subtask) by creating more than one object of the respecting subtask class. Imposing parallelism on subtasks will be discussed in section 4.2.

The general pattern of a class that realizes a subtask is very much similar to the class ConcurrentImpl. In addition a subtask class is also a thread class that implements a subtask method. This subtask method, which is invoked by the outer environment, starts the subtask thread.

The idea to use dataflow synchronization on guarded threads enables us to execute a synthesized algorithm in a maximally parallel way. From the other side, the fine granularity of threads may give heavy implementation overhead, and can be practical in the environments like Mozart, but not on Java platforms of today. The granularity of parallelization of structurally synthesized programs will be discussed in the following sections.

4   Coarse-Grained Parallelization

An obvious way to decrease the execution overhead for each function is to put several functions into one and the same thread – to decrease the granularity of threads. Some experience of coarse-grained parallel usage of synthesized programs exists already. In [5], programs for large simulation problems have been synthesized and run on a network of workstations. However, only pre-programmed parallelism of subtasks has been used in this case. We shall discuss the following two cases with the aim of using the coarse-grained parallelization completely automatically: 1) Composing threads, and 2) Imposing parallelism on subtasks.

Here we are going to use a representation of a structurally synthesized program in the form of a higher-order dataflow scheme (HODS) [4]. Nodes of a HODS are *functional nodes* and *control nodes*. The control nodes have subtasks. They not only exercise control over the execution order of synthesized branches, but perform computations as well. The figure shows such a scheme with four functional nodes b, c, d and e, and a control node a with one subtask Q. As usual for the SSP, we denote data dependencies as going in the direction of dataflow, showing explicitly also the data items as nodes of the scheme. We use small letters for representing data items.

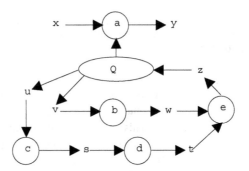

Fig. 3. Higher-order dataflow scheme

The scheme shows an algorithm for computing y from x by performing computations under the control of the node a. This node uses a subtask Q for computing z from u and v, possibly repetitively. When computing for the subtask, two branches: b and c;d can be performed concurrently. Parallelization is possible also for the subtasks: depending on the data dependencies in the node a, it may be possible to arrange the computations for each set of values of u and v (repeating computations for the subtask Q) concurrently. How much should be done concurrently, and what should be done at one site, depends on the properties of computations for each functional node. Any attempt to find an optimal solution leads to NP complete problems. Considering the large size of schemes we are handling in SSP (up to thousands of nodes), looking for optimal solutions is implausible. Therefore we consider the following heuristic techniques.

4.1   Composing Threads

We build threads in order to execute them concurrently and look for maximal sequences of steps that can be performed in one thread sequentially. A functional node in HODS may have several inputs, like the node a in figure 4. Therefore it may be included in different threads (see [3]). We have decided to compose threads in such a way that a thread can be run without synchronization with other threads after its execution had started (i.e. the synchronization is needed only for starting a thread). Therefore, a node with input from more than one thread (like the node a in figure 4) will be always the first in a thread. This is motivated by the fact that threads will be built only in the case when computations in nodes are so extensive that concurrency gives some performance advantage.

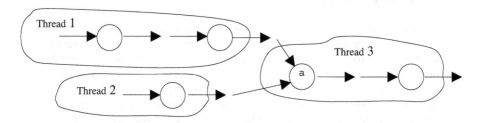

Fig. 4. Composing threads

4.2   Imposing Parallelism on Subtasks

Control nodes implemented in Java can be easily programmed in a multithreaded way. Knowing the usage of a control node, it may be possible to decide in advance whether its subtasks should be executed concurrently. It is possible as well to include several control nodes into a specification for synthesis that differ only by their implementation, and to use extra variables in a specification to show which implementation (sequential or concurrent) is needed in a particular case.

A rich set of control nodes for concurrent execution was developed for the distributed computing platform NUTS that has been described in [6]. Here we give an example of a control node for parallel processing of collections that implement the Java Enumeration interface, see figure below. A collection a is processed element by element, each time processing an element x of the collection and computing a new element y of the resulting array c. The subtask P specifies what has to be done with an element x from the collection a and to get an element of the array c. It is assumed that the subtask P is computationally heavy, and the computations for elements of the collection are performed in parallel.

5   Concluding Remarks

In this paper we have shown how to use the information already existing in a specification for structural synthesis of a program for concurrent implementation of the synthesized program. We see several possibilities of usage: multithreaded execution of functions, parallel execution of composed threads, and distributed implementation of a coarse grained concurrent program.

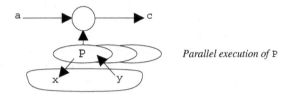

Fig. 5. Parallelism in control node

5   Concluding Remarks

In this paper we have shown how to use the information already existing in a specification for structural synthesis of a program for concurrent implementation of the synthesized program. We see several possibilities of usage: multithreaded execution of functions, parallel execution of composed threads, and distributed implementation of a coarse grained concurrent program.

The advantage of the proposed method relies in achieving concurrency without requesting additional information from a user, a comparatively small effort of implementation, and a composed program does not implement the control part of the synthesized algorithm explicitly, the computation of the program's result is guided by dataflow synchronization. Computational overhead implementing fine-grained parallelism may be high if pre-programmed functions are small. In this case, composing guarded threads should be taken into consideration.

References

[1] S. Lämmermann. Automated Composition of Java Software *TRITA-IT* AVH 00:03, ISSN 1403-5286. Dept. of Teleinformatics, KTH, 2000

[2] V. Malyshkin. Principles of synthesis of parallel programs on computational models witth arrays. Automated program synthesis. Aad. Sci. of Estonian SSR, Tallinn, 1983, p. 89 - 109.

[3] T. Plaks. Synthesis of parallel programs on computational models. Programming and Computer Software. v. 3, 1977, p. 282 - 290.

[4] E. Tyugu. Higher-Order Dataflow Schemas. Theoretical Computer Science, v.90, 1991, 185-198.

[5] E. Tyugu, M. Matskin, J. Penjam. Applications of structural synthesis of programs. In: J. Wing, J. Woodcock, J. Davies (Eds.) FM`99 - Formal Methods. World Congress on Formal Methods in the Development of Computing Systems, Toulouse, France, Sept. 1999. vol. I, LNCS No. 1708, Springer, 1999, p. 551 – 569

[6] V. Vlassov, et al. NUTS: a Distributed Object-Oriented Platform with High Level Communication Functions. Computers and Artificial Intelligence, v. 17, No. 4, 1998, p. 305 – 335.

[7] Seif Haridi, Peter Van Roy. Mozart: A Programming System for Agent Applications. Research Report, Dept. of Teleinformatics, KTH, October 1999

[8] Peter Van Roy, Seif Haridi, Per Brand, Gert Smolka, Michael Mehl, Ralf Scheidhauer. Mobile Objects in Distributed Oz. ACM Transactions on Programming Languages and Systems (TOPLAS), 19(5): 804-851 (1997)

An Associative Version of the Bellman-Ford Algorithm for Finding the Shortest Paths in Directed Graphs*

A.S. Nepomniaschaya

Institute of Computational Mathematics and Mathematical Geophysics,
Siberian Division of Russian Academy of Sciences,
pr. Lavrentieva, 6, Novosibirsk, 630090, Russia
anep@ssd.sscc.ru

Abstract. In this paper by means of a model of associative parallel systems with vertical data processing (the STAR–machine), we propose a natural straight forward implementation of the Bellman–Ford shortest path algorithm. We represent this algorithm as the corresponding STAR procedure, justify its correctness and evaluate time complexity.

1 Introduction

Problems of finding the shortest paths are among fundamental tasks of combinatorial optimization. An important version of the shortest path problem is the single–source problem. Given a directed n–vertex and m–arc weighted graph with a distinguished vertex s, the single–source shortest path problem is to find for each vertex v the length of the shortest path from s to v. When all arc weights are non–negative, the most efficient solution gives Dijkstra's sequential shortest path algorithm [3]. In [4], Ford generalizes Dijkstra's algorithm for graphs having negative arc weights but without cycles of the negative weight.

The most efficient solution of the single–source shortest path problem for general network topologies gives the Bellman–Ford algorithm [1,4]. On conventional sequential computers, it takes $O(n^3)$ time for complete connected graphs and $O(nm)$ time for sparse graphs [2].

In this paper, we study a matrix representation of the Bellman–Ford algorithm on a model of associative (content addressable) parallel systems of the SIMD type with vertical processing (the STAR–machine). To this end, we use a group of new basic procedures for updating graphs with the negative arc weights [8]. Here, we propose a natural straight forward implementation of the Bellman–Ford algorithm on the STAR–machine and justify its correctness. Assuming that each elementary operation of the model under consideration (its microstep) takes one unit of time, we obtain that the corresponding STAR procedure takes $O(hn^2)$ time, where h is the number of bits required for coding the maximal weight of the shortest paths from the source vertex.

---

* This work was supported in part by the Russian Foundation for Basic Research under Grant N 99-01-00548

V. Malyshkin (Ed.): PaCT 2001, LNCS 2127, pp. 285–292, 2001.

2   The STAR–machine

The model is based on a Staran–like associative parallel processor [5]. We define it as an abstract STAR–machine of the SIMD type with bit–serial (vertical) processing and simple single–bit processing elements (PEs) [6]. The model consists of the following components:

– a sequential control unit (CU), where programs and scalar constants are stored;

– an associative processing unit consisting of p single–bit PEs;

– a matrix memory for the associative processing unit.

The CU broadcasts an instruction to all PEs in unit time. All active PEs execute it simultaneously while inactive PEs do not perform it. Activation of a PE depends on the data.

Input binary data are loaded in the matrix memory in the form of two–dimensional tables in which each datum occupies an individual row and it is updated by a dedicated PE. The rows are numbered from top to bottom and the columns – from left to right. Both a row and a column can be easily accessed.

The associative processing unit is represented as h vertical registers, each consisting of p bits. The vertical registers can be regarded as a one–column array. The bit columns of the tabular data are stored in the registers which perform the necessary Boolean operations.

The STAR–machine run is described by means of the language STAR which is an extension of Pascal. Let us briefly consider the STAR constructions needed for the paper. To simulate data processing in the matrix memory, we use data types *word, slice,* and *table.* Constants for the types *slice* and *word* are represented as a sequence of symbols of $\{0,1\}$ enclosed within single quotation marks. The types *slice* and *word* are used for the bit column access and the bit row access, respectively, and the type *table* is used for defining the tabular data. Assume that any variable of the type *slice* consists of p components which belong to $\{0,1\}$. For simplicity, let us call "slice" any variable of the type *slice.*

Now, we present some elementary operations and predicates for slices.

Let X, Y be variables of the type *slice* and i be a variable of the type *integer.* We use the following operations:

SET(Y) sets all components of Y to $'1'$; CLR(Y) sets all components of Y to $'0'$; $Y(i)$ selects the i-th component of Y; FND(Y) returns the ordinal number i of the first (the uppermost) $'1'$ of Y, $i \geq 0$; STEP(Y) returns the same result as FND(Y) and then resets the first $'1'$ found to $'0'$.

In the usual way we introduce the predicates ZERO(Y) and SOME(Y) and the bitwise Boolean operations $X\ and\ Y$, $X\ or\ Y$, $not\ Y$, $X\ xor\ Y$.

Let T be a variable of the type *table.* We use the following two operations:

ROW(i, T) returns the i-th row of the matrix T; COL(i, T) returns the i-th column of T.

Remark 1. Note that the STAR statements are defined in the same manner as for Pascal. We will use them later for presenting our procedures.

3 Preliminaries

Let $G = (V, E, w)$ be a *directed weighted graph* with the set of vertices $V = \{1, 2, \ldots, n\}$, the set of directed edges (arcs) $E \subseteq V \times V$ and the function w that assigns a weight to every edge. We assume that $|V| = n$ and $|E| = m$.

A *weight matrix* for G is an $n \times n$ matrix which contains arc weights as elements. If $(v_i, v_j) \notin E$, then $w(v_i, v_j) = \infty$.

An *adjacency matrix* A for G is an $n \times n$ Boolean matrix in which $a_{ij} = 1$ if $(v_i, v_j) \in E$ and $a_{ij} = 0$, otherwise.

A *path* from u to v in G is a sequence of vertices $u = v_1, v_2, \ldots, v_k = v$, where $(v_i, v_{i+1}) \in E$ for $i = 1, 2, \ldots, k - 1$ and $k > 1$.

The *shortest path* between two vertices in G is a path with the minimal sum of weights of its arcs.

The *distance* from v_i to v_j is the weight of the shortest path between these vertices.

Now, recall three basic procedures from [6] implemented on the STAR–machine which will be used later on.

The procedure TMERGE(T, X, F) writes the rows of the given matrix T, selected by ones in the slice X, into the matrix F. Other rows of the matrix F are not changed.

The procedure TCOPY(T, h, F) writes the given matrix T, consisting of h columns, into the result matrix F.

The procedure TCOPY1(T, j, h, F) writes h columns from the given matrix T, beginning with its $(1 + (j - 1)h)$-th column, into the result matrix F, where $j \geq 1$.

The following three basic procedures from [8] use a given global slice X to select by ones positions of the rows which will be processed. These procedures are applied to an array which includes the negative integers. Such an array is represented as a matrix which saves only the magnitudes of the integers written in binary code and a slice which saves only the signs. We assume that every negative integer is indicated by one in this slice.

The procedure MIN$^*(T, X, Y, Z)$ uses the slice Y to save the signs of the matrix T. It defines positions of those rows of the matrix T, where minimal elements are located. This procedure returns the slice Z, where $Z(i) =' 1'$ if and only if either $X(i) =' 1'$, $Y(i) =' 0'$ and ROW(i, T) is the minimal element or $X(i) =' 1'$, $Y(i) =' 1'$ and ROW(i, T) is the maximal element.

The procedure HIT$^*(T, R, X, Y, Z, Z1)$ uses the slices Y and Z to save the signs of the given matrices T and R, respectively. It defines positions of the corresponding coincident rows of the matrices T and R considering the signs. This procedure returns the slice $Z1$, where $Z1(i) =' 1'$ if and only if $X(i) =' 1'$, ROW(i, T)=ROW(i, R) and $Y(i) = Z(i)$.

The procedure ADDV$^*(T, R, X, Y, Z, F, Z1)$ uses the slices Y and Z to save the signs of the matrices T and R, respectively. It performs the algebraic addition of the rows of the matrices T and R taking into account the signs. The procedure writes the magnitude of the result in the matrix F and the signs in the slice $Z1$.

4   Representing the Bellman–Ford Algorithm on the STAR–Machine

We first explain the main idea of the Bellman–Ford algorithm.

This algorithm sets temporary labels for the vertices so that on terminating the k-th iteration ($k \geq 1$) every label is equal to the length of the shortest path from the source vertex s to the corresponding vertex and this path includes no more than $k + 1$ arcs. To perform this, the algorithm saves a set of vertices U whose labels are changed at the current iteration.

To present the Bellman–Ford algorithm, we will use the following notations from [2].

For every vertex v_i, let us assume that $\Gamma(v_i) = \{v_j : v_i \to v_j \in E\}$ and $\Gamma^{-1}(v_i) = \{v_k : v_k \to v_i \in E\}$. If $U = \{v_1, v_2, \ldots, v_r\}$, then we have $\Gamma(U) = \bigcup_{i=1}^{r} \Gamma(v_i)$. Let $l^{k+1}(v_i)$ be the label for the vertex v_i after terminating the k-th iteration.

The Bellman–Ford algorithm runs as follows.

Initially $U = \Gamma(s)$, $l^1(s) = 0$, $\forall v_i \in \Gamma(s)$ $l^1(v_i) = w(s, v_i)$ and $l^1(v_j) = \infty$, otherwise.

For every vertex $v_i \in \Gamma(U)$, its label is updated at the k-th iteration ($k \geq 1$) as shown below:

$$l^{k+1}(v_i) = \min [\, l^k(v_i), \min_{v_j \in T_i} \{l^k(v_j) + w(v_j, v_i)\}\,], \tag{1}$$

where $T_i = \Gamma^{-1}(v_i) \cap U$. In other words, the set T_i includes those vertices for which the current shortest path from s consists of k arcs and there is an arc entering the vertex v_i. If $v_i \notin \Gamma(U)$, then $l^{k+1}(v_i) = l^k(v_i)$.

The termination of this algorithm is defined as follows:

(i) If $k \leq n-1$ and $l^{k+1}(v_i) = l^k(v_i)$ for all v_i, then the algorithm terminates. The labels for the vertices are equal to lengths of the shortest paths.

(ii) If $k = n - 1$ and $l^{k+1}(v_i) \neq l^k(v_i)$ for some v_i, then the algorithm terminates with the message: 'There is a cycle of the negative weight.'

If $k < n - 1$ and $l^{k+1}(v_i) \neq l^k(v_i)$ for some v_i, then $U = \{v_i : l^{k+1}(v_i) \neq l^k(v_i)\}$ and the $(k + 1)$-th iteration will be performed.

On the STAR–machine, the Bellman–Ford algorithm is represented as procedure BelFord. The graph G is given by means of a weight matrix T which stores only the weight magnitudes and a matrix Q which stores only the weight signs. Let us agree that each negative weight is indicated by one in the matrix Q. To represent $w_{i,j} = \infty$ in the matrix T, we choose an integer $r = \sum_{i=1}^{n} \gamma_i$, where γ_i is the magnitude of the maximal weight of arcs incident from the vertex v_i. Let inf be the binary representation of r and let h be the number of bits in this representation. Then the matrix T consists of hn bit columns and for every i the weights of arcs, entering the vertex v_i, are written in the i-th field having h bit columns. It should be noted that in view of formula (1) the length of the shortest path from s to every vertex of G is less than r.

The procedure BelFord uses the following input parameters:

the weight matrix T and the matrix of signs Q; the source vertex s; the number of bits h; the binary word inf for representing ∞.

The procedure returns the distance matrix D which stores only magnitudes of the distances and the slice Z which stores only the corresponding signs.

Note that the distance from s to v_i is written in the i-th row of D and $Z(i) =' 1'$ if and only if this distance is negative.

The procedure BelFord uses the following main variables:

an adjacency matrix A; a matrix $A1$ which is obtained after the transpose of the matrix A; a matrix M for computing the new labels for the vertices which are accessible from s at the current iteration; a matrix $M1$ for saving the new labels for the same vertices as the matrix M; a slice $Y1$ for storing positions of the vertices whose new labels are negative; a slice U for saving positions of the vertices whose labels are changed at the current iteration; a slice Y for saving positions of the vertices which are accessible from the vertex s at the current iteration.

The run of the procedure BelFord includes the following stages.

At *the first stage*, the matrices A and $A1$ are defined. Then the matrix D and the slice Z are initialised.

At *the second stage*, positions of the vertices v_i which are adjacent with s are stored in the slice U. The weights of the arcs (s, v_i) are the labels for the vertices v_i.

At *the third stage*, for every vertex v_i selected by one in the slice U, positions of all vertices $v_j \in \Gamma(v_i)$ are saved in the slice Y.

At *the fourth stage*, for every vertex v_p selected by one in the slice Y, the value $l^{k+1}(v_p)$ is defined as follows:

– first, positions of vertices $v_j \in T_p = \Gamma^{-1}(v_p) \cap U$ are defined in parallel;
– then, using the basic procedure ADDV*, the expression $l^k(v_j) + w(v_j, v_p)$ is computed for all vertices $v_j \in T_p$ in parallel, magnitudes of the results are saved in the corresponding rows of the matrix M and the signs in the slice $Z2$;
– finally, by means of the basic procedure MIN*, the position of $l^{k+1}(v_p)$ in the matrix M is selected. The magnitude of this value is stored in the p-th row of the matrix $M1$ and the sign in the p-th bit of the slice $Y1$.

At *the fifth stage* using the basic procedure HIT*, positions of the corresponding coincident rows of the matrices $M1$ and D are selected in parallel.

At *the sixth stage*, the termination of the procedure BelFord is verified in the same manner as described in the Bellman–Ford algorithm.

At *the seventh stage* by means of the basic procedure TMERGE, new values of the labels are written in the matrix D. Moreover, positions of vertices whose labels have been changed at the current iteration are stored in the slice U. After that, stage 3 is performed.

Remark 2. Note that positions of arcs, entering v_i, are selected by ones in the i-th column of the matrix A, while positions of arcs, outgoing from v_i, are selected by ones in the i-th column of the matrix $A1$.

Remark 3. Obviously, after terminating stage 4, new values $l^{k+1}(v_p)$ have been written in the matrix $M1$ for all v_p selected by ones in the slice Y.

5   Execution of the Procedure BelFord

To present the procedure BelFord, we need the following auxiliary procedures:

The procedure $ADJ(T, h, n, inf, A)$ returns the adjacency matrix A for the given matrix T. It runs as follows. For each i using TCOPY1, this procedure first selects the i-th field of T consisting of h bits. Then, using the basic procedure MATCH [7], it defines *positions* of the rows not coincident with the binary string inf and sets ones in the same positions of the i-th column of A.

The procedure $TRANS(A, n, A1)$ returns the matrix $A1$ being the transpose of the matrix A. It runs as follows. For each i it defines positions of ones in the i-th row of A and sets ones in the same positions of the i-th column of $A1$.

The procedure $INIT(T, Q, h, n, s, D, Z)$ returns the matrix D and the slice Z. It runs as follows. By means of the operation TRIM [6], it "cuts" the s-th row of the matrix T into n substrings, each consisting of h bits, and writes each i-th substring in the i-th row of D. Then, it defines positions of ones in the s-th row of the matrix Q and sets ones in the same positions of Z.

Now, we present the procedure BelFord.

```
proc BelFord(T,Q: table; h,n,s: integer; inf: word;
   var D: table; Z: slice);
var A,A1,M,M1,R: table;
   U,X,X1,Y,Y1,Z1,Z2: slice;
   i,k,p: integer; w: word;
1.   begin ADJ(T,h,n,inf,A);
2.      TRANS(A,n,A1);
3.      INIT(T,Q,h,n,s,D,Z);
4.      X:=COL(s,A1); U:=X;
```
/* Positions of vertices, being adjacent to the vertex s,
   are selected by ones in the slices X and U. */
```
5.      k:=1 to n-1 do
6.         begin TCOPY(D,h,M1);
7.            Y1:=Z; CLR(Y);
8.            while SOME(X) do
9.               begin p:=STEP(X);
10.                 X1:=COL(p,A1);
11.                 Y:=Y or X1
12.              end;
```
/* Positions of vertices which are accessible from s at the k-th
   iteration are selected by ones in the slice Y. */
```
13.              X:=Y;
```
/* The slice X is used to determine the new value for U. */
```
14.              while SOME(Y) do
```
/* At the k-th iteration, we will define the distance from s
   to every vertex selected by one in the slice Y. */
```
15.                 begin p:=STEP(Y);
16.                    X1:=COL(p,A);
```

```
17.                 X1:=X1 and U;
```
/* Positions of arcs, entering the vertex v_p, are selected
by ones in the slice $X1$. */
```
18.                 TCOPY1(T,p,h,R);
19.                 Z1:=COL(p,Q);
```
/* The weights of arcs entering the vertex v_p, are written
in the matrix R and their signs in the slice $Z1$. */
```
20.                 ADDV*(R,D,X1,Z1,Z,M,Z2);
```
/* The result of adding the corresponding rows of R and D,
selected by ones in $X1$, is written in M and the signs in $Z2$.*/
```
21.                 w:=ROW(p,D);
22.                 ROW(p,M):=w;
```
/* The p-th row of the matrix D is written in the p-th row
of the matrix M. */
```
23.                 Z2(p):=Z(p);  X1(p):='1';
```
/* Position of the p-th row is indicated by one in the slice $X1$,
and its sign is saved in the p-th position of the slice $Z2$. */
```
24.                 MIN*(M,X1,Z2,Z1);
25.                 i:=FND(Z1);  w:=ROW(i,M);
26.                 ROW(p,M1):=w;  Y1(p):=Z2(i)
```
/* The value $l^{k+1}(v_p)$ is saved in the p-th row of the matrix $M1$
and its sign in the p-th position of the slice $Y1$. */
```
27.               end;
28.           HIT*(D,M1,X,Z,Y1,Z1);
29.           Z2:=X and ( not Z1);
30.           if ZERO(Z2) then exit;
31.           if k=n-1 then
32.             begin message 'There is a cycle of negative weight';
33.                exit
34.             end;
35.           TMERGE(M1,Z2,D);  Z:=Y1;
```
/* New values for the labels are stored in the matrix D
and their signs in the slice Z. */
```
36.             X:=Z2;  U:=Z2
37.         end;
38.   end.
```

Theorem. *Let a directed weighted graph G be given as the matrix T which stores only the weight magnitudes and the matrix Q which stores only the weight signs. Let s be the source vertex, and there is no a directed cycle from s having the negative weight. Let every arc weight use h bits and let inf be the binary representation of infinity. Then the procedure BelFord(T,Q,h,n,s,inf,D,Z) returns the distance matrix D, in whose every i-th row there is the magnitude of the distance from s to v_i, and the slice Z which stores the signs of the corresponding distances. It takes $O(hn^2)$ time on the STAR–machine having no less than n PEs.*

The theorem is proved by induction on the number of iterations. We omit the proof because of lack of space.

Let us evaluate time complexity of the procedure BelFord. We first observe that the auxiliary procedures take $O(n)$ time each. Obviously, the procedure BelFord performs $n-1$ iterations. Since it updates no more than n vertices in each iteration and the basic procedures run in $O(h)$ time each [6–7], we obtain that the procedure BelFord runs in $O(hn^2)$ time on the STAR–machine with n PEs assuming that each elementary operation takes one unit of time.

6   Conclusions

We have proposed a matrix implementation of the classical Bellman–Ford short-est path algorithm on the STAR–machine being a model of associative parallel systems of the SIMD type with vertical processing. We have obtained that the procedure BelFord takes $O(hn^2)$ time on the STAR–machine having no less than n PEs assuming that each elementary operation takes one unit of time. It should be noted that the procedure BelFord performs $O(n^2)$ operations of ad-dition and $O(n)$ operations of comparison for complete connected graphs, while the Bellman–Ford algorithm executes $O(n^3)$ such operations on conventional sequential computers [2].

We are planning to select all cycles of the negative weights and to restore the shortest paths from s to every vertex v along with finding the distances by means of a simple modification of the procedure BelFord.

References

1. R. Bellman. On a Routing Problem. In: Quarterly of Applied Mathematics, **16**, No. 1 (1958) 87–90.
2. N. Christofides. Graph Theory, An Algorithmic Approach. Academic Press, New York (1975).
3. E.W. Dijkstra. A Note on Two Problems in Connection with Graphs. In: Numerische Mathematik, **1** (1959) 269–271.
4. L.R. Ford. Network Flow Theory. Rand Corporation Report P-923 (1956).
5. C.C. Foster. Content Addressable Parallel Processors. Van Nostrand Reinhold Com-pany, New York (1976).
6. A.S. Nepomniaschaya. Solution of Path Problems Using Associative Parallel Pro-cessors. In: Proc. of the Intern. Conf. on Parallel and Distributed Systems, IEEE Computer Society Press, ICPADS'97, Korea, Seoul (1997) 610–617.
7. A.S. Nepomniaschaya, M.A. Dvoskina. A Simple Implementation of Dijkstra's Short-est Path Algorithm on Associative Parallel Processors. In: Fundamenta Informati-cae, IOS Press, **43** (2000) 227-243.
8. A.S. Nepomniaschaya. An Associative Version of the Edmonds–Karp–Ford Shortest Path Algorithm. In: Bull. of the Novosibirsk Computing Center. Series: Computer Science. NCC Publisher, to appear.

Fusion of Concurrent Invocations
of Exclusive Methods*

Yoshihiro Oyama[1], Kenjiro Taura[2], and Akinori Yonezawa[2]

[1] Institute of Information Sciences and Electronics, University of Tsukuba
1-1-1 Tennoudai, Tsukuba, Ibaraki 305-8573, Japan
yosh@osss.is.tsukuba.ac.jp
[2] Department of Information Science, School of Science, University of Tokyo
7-3-1 Hongo, Bunkyo-ku, Tokyo 113-0033, Japan
{tau,yonezawa}@is.s.u-tokyo.ac.jp

Abstract. This paper describes a mechanism for "fusing" concurrent invocations of exclusive methods. The target of our work is object-oriented languages with concurrent extensions. In the languages, concurrent invocations of exclusive methods are serialized; only one invocation executes immediately and the others wait for their turn. The mechanism fuses multiple waiting invocations to a cheaper operation such as a single invocation. The programmers describe fusion rules, which specify method invocations that can be fused and an operation that substitutes for the invocations. The mechanism works effectively in the execution in synchronization bottlenecks, which are objects on which exclusive methods wait a long time for their turn. We have implemented a language that has the mechanism and tested the usefulness of the mechanism through experiments on a symmetric multiprocessor, the Sun Enterprise 10000. We have confirmed that the mechanism made programs with synchronization bottlenecks fast.

1 Introduction

Most of concurrent object-oriented languages and concurrent extensions to object-oriented languages have a mechanism for serializing concurrent method invocations invoked to the same object simultaneously. An example of the mechanism is synchronized methods in Java: only one synchronized method can execute on the object at one time. In this paper we use the term *exclusive method* to denote a method whose concurrent invocations to the same object are serialized.

This paper describes a scheme for efficient execution of dynamically serialized invocations of exclusive methods. This scheme "fuses" multiple invocations of exclusive methods to a cheaper operation such as a single invocation of an exclusive method. The scheme serves to reduce the number of executions of exclusive methods. For example, when a method invocation that adds one and a method invocation that adds two are waiting on a counter object, we replace

---

* An extended version of this paper is available via
http://www.osss.is.tsukuba.ac.jp/~yosh/publications/

V. Malyshkin (Ed.): PaCT 2001, LNCS 2127, pp. 293–307, 2001.
© Springer-Verlag Berlin Heidelberg 2001

these invocations with a method invocation that adds three to the counter. Another example occurs in GUI programs in which the repaint method is invoked to a window object. The scheme fuses multiple invocations of the repaint method that are invoked to one object almost at the same time into a single invocation of the method. Below we call this scheme *method fusion*. Method fusion works well particularly in the execution of *synchronization bottlenecks*, which are objects on which exclusive method invocations wait a long time for their turn.

The target of this work is concurrent object-oriented languages and concurrent extensions to object-oriented languages that are implemented on shared-memory multiprocessors.

Various techniques have been proposed so far for efficient execution of exclusive methods. They can be classified into two main groups. Those in one group concurrently execute a combination of exclusive methods that update a distinct set of variables [4,20,22]. Those in the other create replicas of synchronization bottlenecks [3,18]. Both techniques have a problem. The former cannot optimize a combination of exclusive methods that may update the same variable. For example, they cannot optimize multiple invocations of the add method described above. The latter do not allow the programmers to concisely describe dynamic changes in executed methods. Method fusion addresses the above problems.

The contributions of this work are shown below.

- We propose a novel optimization that makes the execution of serialized invocations of exclusive methods faster. We design a language that has an API to support the optimization. The language is called *Amdahl*.
- We develop an implementation scheme for Amdahl.
- We incorporate method fusion into the Amdahl compiler and confirm the usefulness of method fusion through experiments on 64-processor symmetric multiprocessors.

The rest of this paper is organized as follows. Section 2 gives the overview of method fusion and Sect. 3 describes our language Amdahl. Section 4 shows sample programs written in Amdahl. In Sect. 5 we discuss the design of Amdahl and in Sect. 6 we explain an implementation scheme for Amdahl. Section 7 gives our experimental results and Sect. 8 describes related work. Section 9 concludes this paper.

2   Overview of Method Fusion

The following Java program provides a good starting point for understanding method fusion.

```
class Counter {
  private int value;
  public Counter(int v) {  value = v;  }
  public synchronized void inc(int n) {  value += n;  }
  public synchronized void dec(int n) {  value -= n;  }
```

```
    public synchronized int get() {   return value;   }
}
```

A Counter object keeps an integer counter value. The method inc increments the counter value by its argument, and the method dec decrements the counter value by its argument. The method get returns the counter value.

The point to observe is that the execution of inc(x) and inc(y) has the same "effect" on the counter object as the execution of inc(x + y) with regard to the final value of the counter. Based on this observation, we attempt to "fuse" dynamically serialized invocations of inc(x) and inc(y) to an invocation of inc(x + y).

Amdahl programmers can describe *fusion rules*, which specify a pair of method invocations that can be fused and an operation that substitutes for the invocations[1]. For example, a fusion rule can be added to the definition of the Counter class as follows:

```
class Counter {
    ...
    fusion void inc(int x) & void inc(int y) {   inc(x + y);   }
}
```

The rule tells the compiler that

> execution of inc(x) and inc(y) can be replaced with execution of
> inc(x + y).

According to the rules, the compiler and runtime system may fuse two invocations of the method inc to one invocation of the method inc. The invocation inc(x + y), invoked as a result of the fusion, may further be fused with another invocation of the method inc.

3   The Amdahl Parallel Language

Our language Amdahl is C++ extended by adding threads and exclusive methods. It does not support inheritance.

3.1   Threads and Exclusive Methods

Amdahl has a primitive for thread creation. When the primitive is executed, a thread is created.

Multiple exclusive methods cannot execute concurrently on the same object. Non-exclusive methods, on the other hand, executes concurrently with any other methods. Exclusive methods have the keyword sync at the head of their declaration. The order in which threads call an exclusive method on the object is independent of the one in which threads actually execute it on the object (i.e., the FIFO scheduling order is not guaranteed). The recursive acquisition of the lock by its owner is not allowed.

---

[1] It may be possible to generate useful fusion rules automatically based on program analysis, but exploring this issue is not our concern here.

3.2   Fusion Rules

Amdahl programmers can define the behavior of method fusion by describing a set of fusion rules in class definitions. The syntax of fusion rules is shown below.

$$\texttt{fusion}\ t_p\ \ p(t_{x_1}\ x_1, ..., t_{x_m}\ x_m)\ \&\ t_q\ \ q(t_{y_1}\ y_1, ..., t_{y_n}\ y_n)\ \{$$
$$S$$
$$\}$$

p and q are method names. p may be the same as q. $x_1, ..., x_m, y_1, ...,$ and y_n are distinct variables. $t_{x_1}, ..., t_{x_m}, t_{y_1}, ...,$ and t_{y_n} are the types of the variables $x_1, ..., x_m, y_1, ...,$ and y_n, respectively. t_p and t_q are the types of the return value of the methods p and q, respectively. S is a statement. In the following part S is called a *body* of a fusion rule.

Let us explain the semantics of fusion rules. Assume that the above fusion rule is included in the definition of a class C. Furthermore, assume that two method invocations $p(t_{x_1}\ x_1, ..., t_{x_m}\ x_m)$ and $q(t_{y_1}\ y_1, ..., t_{y_n}\ y_n)$ have been invoked to the object O but both of them are waiting for the termination of another invocation executed on the object O. The fusion rule specifies that the execution of the two invocations can be replaced with the execution of the statement S.

The details of the semantics are given below.

- The statement S executes concurrently with any method invocations executing on the object O.
- The default receiver object of the method invocations in the statement S is the object O.
- An invocation of p and an invocation of q are fused irrespective of the order in which they are invoked. That is, the semantics of a fusion rule remain the same if the two invocation expressions in the rule are swapped. Consider a class definition with the following fusion rule.
    ```
    fusion void p(void) & void q(void) { ... }
    ```
    Adding the following rule to it is of no benefit.
    ```
    fusion void q(void) & void p(void) { ... }
    ```
- The statement S is executed by either the thread that invoked p or the one that invoked q.
- Values are returned to the caller of p and that of q as follows.

    Either t_p or t_q is the void type: The execution of S must be terminated with a return statement. The value of the return statement is returned to one of the callers of the fused method invocations whose return value is not of the void type.

    Neither t_p nor t_q is the void type: The execution of S must be terminated with an `mreturn` statement. `mreturn` is a primitive for returning two values. When S terminates with the statement
    ```
    mreturn a and b,
    ```
    a is returned to the caller of the method p and b is returned to the caller of the method q.

4   Sample Programs

GUI Event Handling. The following program fuses multiple invocations of the method `repaint` to one invocation of the method.

```
class Window {
  ...
  fusion void repaint(void) & void repaint(void) {
    repaint();
  }
}
```

Concurrent Buffers. The class `Buffer` makes an object that represents a buffer with an array. The class has the methods `put` and `get`. The code for checking buffer overflow and underflow is omitted. The following fusion rule allows us to "bypass" the manipulation of the array in the execution of a combination of `put` and `get` (we assume that buffers of the class `Buffer` do not give the users any guarantee of the order in which buffer elements are managed and further assume that the buffer overflow or underflow occurring when method fusion is absent does not need to be preserved when method fusion is used).

```
class Buffer {
  int length;
  obj* elements[MAXBUFFERLEN];
  ...
  sync void put(obj* o) {  elements[length++] = o;  }
  sync obj* get(void) {  return elements[--length];  }
  fusion void put(obj* o) & obj* get(void) {  return o;  }
}
```

5   Discussion

The primary purpose of method fusion is performance improvement. Though fusion rules can change the behavior of a program, we believe they should not. They should be performance hints. Otherwise a program will become error-prone and much less readable.

Fusion rules that keep the behavior of a program are called *transparent fusion rules*. To put it differently, programmers cannot know whether the fusion defined by a transparent fusion rule actually occurred. For example, the fusion rule in the class `Counter` shown in Sect. 2 is transparent. On the other hand, the fusion rules that make the program show the behavior that has never been observed in any execution of the original program are not transparent.

The definition of transparency depends on the definition of the *behavior* of a program and the definition of *equivalence* between behaviors. Consider the GUI code shown in Sect. 4. The fusion rule for the repaint method may reduce flickers in a GUI window. If the extent to which a window flickers is included in the behavior of the program, the fusion rule is not transparent because it varies the behavior. Otherwise it is transparent. Currently, we do not give a strict definition to the term "behavior." We would like to give one in the future.

It is one of our long-term goals to make the compiler accept as many transparent fusion rules as possible and reject as many non-transparent fusion rules as possible.

6 Implementation

This section first describes a method execution algorithm that does not support method fusion. We then extend the algorithm to support method fusion.

6.1 Basic Implementation Scheme

An *object lock* is associated with each object. Multiple invocations of exclusive methods to the same object are serialized using the object lock. Before a thread executes an exclusive method on an object, it acquires the object lock associated with the object. After a thread completes executing an exclusive method on an object, it releases its object lock. Every method invocation is executed by the thread that invoked it.

An object lock is represented by a *flag*, an auxiliary lock, and a doubly-linked queue of *waiting tasks*:

Flag A flag has either of two states, FREE or LOCKED. When an exclusive method is executing on the object, the flag of the object is set to LOCKED. Otherwise it is set to FREE.

Waiting tasks A waiting task is a data structure that represents a serialized method invocation (an invocation that has already been invoked but has not been executed due to the contention of the acquisition operations of the object lock). A waiting task contains a method ID and the arguments of the method. Below, it is also called *task*.

A queue of tasks is called a *waiting queue* below. Flags and waiting queues are manipulated exclusively with auxiliary low-level locks such as spin-locks.

A thread acquires an object lock as follows. First it reads the flag of the object lock. If the flag is FREE, the thread changes the flag to LOCKED, which means the object lock is successfully acquired. If the flag is LOCKED, the thread creates a task for the method invocation and enqueues it into the tail of the waiting queue. An enqueued task contains a synchronization data structure, through which threads can communicate notification. Then the thread waits until it receives notification from the synchronization data structure. After it receives one, it executes the inserted task.

A thread releases an object lock as follows. First the thread checks whether the waiting queue has a task. If it has no task, the thread changes the flag to FREE, which means the object lock is successfully released. Otherwise the

```
class Counter {
  int value;
public:
  sync int fa(int n) { /* fetch and add */
    int tmp = value;
    value += n;
    return tmp;
  }
  ...
  fusion int fa(int x) & int fa(int y) {
    z = fa(x + y);
    mreturn z and z - y;
  }
}
```

Fig. 1. A sample program. The code defines a counter that has the fetch-and-add operation.

thread dequeues a task out of the waiting queue and sends notification to the synchronization data structure associated with the task.

6.2 Implementation Scheme Extended to Support Method Fusion

Serialized invocations to an object are fused by the thread that tries to enqueue a task into the waiting queue of the object. Just before the enqueuing, the thread checks whether it can fuse the task to be enqueued (called the *enqueued task*) and the task at the tail of the waiting queue (called the *tail task*). Tasks in the queue other than the tail task are not checked. If it can fuse them, the thread dequeues the tail task out of the waiting queue, and then it reads the information stored in the two tasks and executes the body of the fusion rule applied. Otherwise, the tail task is not dequeued out of the waiting queue; the enqueued task is actually enqueued.

What can be fused is a combination of the tail task and the enqueued task. The tasks in the waiting queue except the tail task are not fused. There exists a performance trade-off among the strategies for choosing the tasks to be fused. One possible strategy is to check all of the tasks in the waiting queue. Although this extreme strategy likely increases the number of fusions, it also increases the cost of checking tasks as well. It seems almost impossible to devise a strategy that works effectively in all kinds of programs.

We explain the implementation of method fusion in more detail using the program in Fig. 1. Figure 2 shows how tasks are fused in the program[2]. Captions for the subfigures in Fig. 2 are given below.

---

[2] Although each thread has its own stack in Fig. 2, this is not essential. Our implementation scheme can also be applied to systems in which different threads reside in the same stack (e.g., Cilk [6], StackThreads/MP [19], and Schematic [14,15,17]).

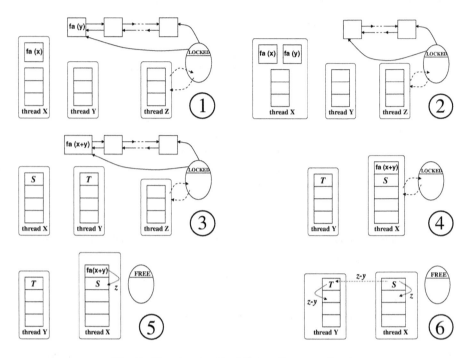

Fig. 2. How two method invocations are fused.

1. Thread Z is executing an exclusive method on the object. Thread Y enqueued a task that represents the invocation `fa(y)`. Thread Y is waiting for notification through the data structure associated with the task. Thread X is trying to invoke `fa(x)` to the object.
2. Thread X checks whether it can fuse the invocation `fa(x)` and the invocation `fa(y)`. Since they can be fused, the thread dequeues the tail task out of the waiting queue.
3. A frame S is pushed onto thread X's stack. In the frame S, thread X executes the body of the fusion rule. A frame T is pushed onto thread Y's stack. In the frame T, thread Y waits for a value to be sent by thread X and returns the value to the parent frame. A new synchronization data structure is created for communicating the value between thread X and thread Y. Thread X invokes `fa(x+y)`, fails to acquire the lock of the object, and consequently enqueues a task that represents `fa(x+y)` into the waiting queue.
4. Now thread X is executing the invocation `fa(x+y)`.
5. Thread X passes the return value of `fa(x+y)` to the frame S.
6. Thread X executes the mreturn statement. One of the values in the mreturn statement is returned to the parent frame of thread X. The other is sent to thread Y via the synchronization data structure. Thread Y receives the sent value and returns it to the parent frame (as if it itself executed `fa(y)`). When the thread fuses invocations of void-type methods, the threads communicate a dummy value in the same way.

In our implementation, each thread allocates tasks and synchronization data structures from the area pre-allocated at thread creation time. Areas for tasks and synchronization data structures do not have to be allocated dynamically with `malloc` or `new` because at most one task and one synchronization data structure is required for each thread at a time.

Our compiler does not support static fusions of multiple invocations that are statically determined to be called in succession.

7 Experimental Results

We have tested the usefulness of method fusion through experiments. We have incorporated the method fusion mechanism into the Amdahl-- compiler, which is a prototype version of the Amdahl compiler. The machine used in the experiments is a Sun Enterprise 10000 (UltraSPARC 250 MHz × 64, Solaris 2.7).

We use the following benchmarks.

Counter Each thread repeatedly invokes an exclusive method `inc`, which increments a counter value, to the counter object shared among threads. A fusion rule in the program specifies that multiple invocations of the method `inc` can be fused.

FileWriter This program creates a file object, which keeps a file descriptor and is shared among threads. The object has an exclusive method `strwrite`, which writes the string given in its argument to the data to the file represented by the file descriptor. The method flushes the buffered data in every invocation. Each thread repeatedly invokes the method `strwrite` to the object. A fusion rule in the program specifies that multiple invocations of the method `strwrite` can be fused. The runtime system will combine the two strings in the arguments of the invocations into a new string and invoke `strwrite` only once with the new string.

FileReader This program creates a disk object, which encapsulates a physical disk and is shared among threads. The object has an exclusive method `fileget`, which opens a file whose path is given in one argument, reads the file, and stores the content of the file into the character array given in the other argument. Each thread repeatedly invokes the method `fileget` to the object. A fusion rule in the program specifies that multiple invocations of the method `fileget` can be fused if they have the same path in their arguments. In the program, all invocations of the method `fileget` have the same path in their arguments.

ImageViewer This program reads an image file and displays it in a newly created window pixel by pixel. The program uses the GUI Toolkit GTK+ [8]. At the beginning of the program, pixels in the image are partitioned among threads. Each thread repeatedly draws a new pixel on the window and repaints the *row* that contains the pixel. A thread can repaint a row by invoking an exclusive method `repaint` to the object that represents the window[3]. A fusion rule in the program specifies that multiple invocations of the method `repaint` can be fused. It fuses multiple invocations of `repaint` into another invocation of `repaint` that repaints the area covering the rows that would otherwise have been repainted by the multiple invocations.

The benchmarks create a fixed number of threads at the beginning of the program. The number is the same as the number of processors. No thread is created during the succeeding execution. Since the amount of parallelism exposed in a program is the same as the number of processors, a thread that cannot immediately execute an exclusive method waits in a busy-wait loop without switching to other computing tasks. In the following description of the experiments, the term "thread" has the same meaning as the term "processor."

In all the benchmarks, the number of invocations of exclusive methods is always the same and independent of the number of threads.

We use at most 50 processors because the effect by other processes is often observed when using a larger number of processors. In the experiments running **ImageViewer**, we used a 14-processor Sun Enterprise because the GUI libraries required to run **ImageViewer** are absent in the 64-processor machine.

Figure 3 shows the execution times of the benchmarks. We compare four strategies for implementing exclusive methods: spin, mutex, custom, and fusion. Spin represents the programs using spin locks. Mutex indicates the programs using mutex locks provided by the operating system. Custom represents the programs that use the lock described in Sect. 6 and that do not support method fusion. Fusion represents the programs that use the lock described in Sect. 6 and that support method fusion.

Method fusion is effective in all the benchmarks except **Counter**: the programs supporting method fusion show the best performance in **FileWriter**, **FileReader**, and **ImageViewer**. In **Counter**, there is no strategy that shows the best performance on any number of processors. In **FileWriter**, as the number of processors increases, the execution time of fusion drops and then grow again. The method `fileget` in **FileReader** includes heavy operations such as opening a file, and hence the performance improvement ratio in **FileReader** is larger than that in any other benchmark. In the execution of **ImageViewer**, fusion shows the best performance when the number of processors is less than eight. In **ImageViewer**, not only fusion but also custom becomes faster as the number of processors increases. We are investigating why custom becomes faster.

Generally, in programs that have an object on which multiple invocations of exclusive methods are frequently serialized, the execution time increases according to the increase in the number of processors [13,16]. This phenomenon is observed in most of the programs.

Figure 4 shows the number of executions of exclusive methods. No fusion indicates the programs that do not support method fusion. Fusion indicates the

---

[3] Since GTK+ is not thread-safe, GTK+ library functions must be called from within an exclusive method. GTK+ provides a mechanism that makes GTK+ thread-safe. However, the mechanism simply serializes invocations to GTK+ library functions.

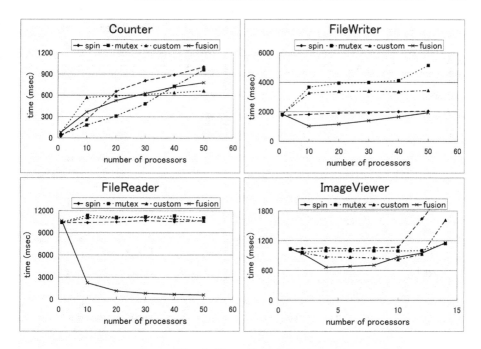

Fig. 3. Execution times.

programs that support method fusion. In **Counter**, there is a small reduction in the number of executions of exclusive methods. In **FileWriter**, as the number of processors increases, the number of executions of exclusive methods decreases steadily. This result means that the gradual increase in the execution time of fusion in **FileWriter** is not due to the decrease in the number of fusions, but is probably due to the increase in overhead. In **FileReader** and **ImageViewer**, the shape of the curve that represents the execution time is very similar to that representing the number of executions of exclusive methods.

We report the amount of time needed for executing the exclusive method once. A rough approximation of the amount is acquired by dividing the overall execution time measured on one processor by the number of executions of exclusive methods. The amount for each of the benchmarks above is 0.25, 17, 1035, and 137 microseconds, respectively.

8   Related Work

Parallel Execution of Associative Operations. There is an extensive literature on the techniques that extract parallelism among associative exclusive operations [3,5,9,12,18]. In systems using the techniques, each thread executes associative exclusive operations in parallel and accumulates the contributions of the operations in a thread-local area. The contributions of each thread are put together eventually. The techniques can only be applied to the regular program-

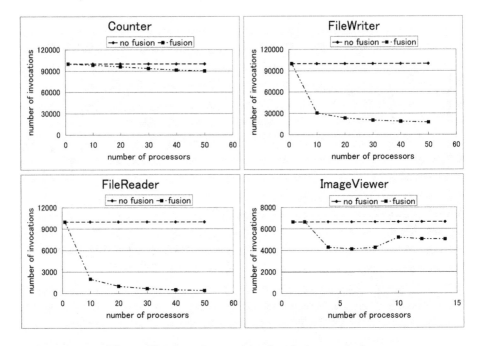

Fig. 4. Number of execution of exclusive methods.

ming models in which it is obvious at what point the contributions of operations should be put together. Method fusion can be applied to irregular execution models in which finding that kind of point is difficult. Another problem with these techniques is that they do not provide a way to change executed methods with a modest amount of code. The existing techniques above and method fusion are complementary; method fusion does not obviate their use, and vice versa. The techniques above are useful in some programs, while method fusion is useful in others.

Parallel Execution of "Non-interfering" Exclusive Methods. In several languages threads execute combinations of exclusive methods in parallel if the methods do not "interfere" with one another, and hence the semantics of the program are preserved even if concurrent invocation of them are not serialized [4,14,15,17,20,22]. Though their techniques are effective when the methods invoked in parallel do not interfere with one another, they are useless otherwise. On the other hand, method fusion works effectively when the methods invoked in parallel interfere with one another. Their techniques and method fusion are complementary.

Network Combining. The Network Combining technique has been proposed by Gottlieb et al. in their work for the NYU Ultracomputer [7]. In this technique, a network switch in a parallel computer combines multiple instructions flowing through the network into one instruction: only the combined instruction is sent from the switch. For example, two fetch-and-add instructions are combined into one fetch-and-add instruction. Their technique combines multiple *instructions*, keeping the semantics of sequential execution. Method fusion, on the other hand, combines multiple *method invocations*, currently making programmers responsible for keeping the semantics of their program.

Static Fusion of Multiple Operations through Program Transformations. There is much literature on program transformations that fuse multiple operations statically [1,2,5,10,11,21]. The techniques described in the literature detect *static occurrences* of the operations that are invoked consecutively, and transform them into a cheaper operation *statically*. Our technique, on the other hand, detects *dynamic occurrences* of the operations that can be executed consecutively, and it accordingly dispatch the control *dynamically* to a cheaper operation. Static fusion, unlike method fusion, does not accompany runtime overhead. Therefore static fusion is preferred wherever it can be used. Method fusion, on the other hand, can be applied to programs in which static fusion cannot be applied.

Our Previous Work. Our previous work [13,16] shows a scheme for efficiently executing parallel programs in which multiple invocations of exclusive methods are serialized frequently. The scheme improves the locality of memory references and the performance of lock operations. Unlike method fusion, the scheme does not change a multiset of executed method invocations. The scheme and method fusion are complementary.

9 Conclusion and Future Work

We have described language design for method fusion and showed an implementation scheme for method fusion. The method fusion mechanism fuses multiple critical sections that successively appear in a dynamic control flow across the thread boundaries. To our knowledge, a mechanism that can do this has to date not been proposed. We have confirmed the effectiveness of method fusion in experiments. Method fusion significantly improved the performance of the programs in which exclusive methods perform heavy operations such as I/O operations.

Method fusion is particularly effective in two kinds of programs. One is programs in which executing an operation twice can be replaced with executing the operation once. An example is a GUI program that executes repaint operations. The other is programs in which a pair of operations "neutralize" each other. An example of a pair is the put operation and the get operation for buffer objects.

We are actively exploring several future directions for method fusion. Firstly, we would like to develop a framework that helps programmers describe transparent fusion rules. Fusion rules described in real-world programs will be more complex than the ones given in this paper. Since static analysis techniques may not work well for complex fusion rules, it will be necessary to provide the environment that supports fusion rule debugging. Secondly, we would like to combine method fusion with inheritance. Thirdly, we would like to explore other implementation strategies than just choosing the task on the tail of the queue. Finally, we would like to improve the current implementation so that multiple manipulations of a waiting queue may run in parallel.

References

1. Richard S. Bird: Algebraic Identities for Program Calculation. The Computer Journal, 32(2) : 122–126, 1989.
2. David Callahan. Recognizing and Parallelizing Bounded Recurrences. In Proceedings of the Fourth International Workshop on Languages and Compilers for Parallel Computing (LCPC '91). Lecture Notes in Computer Science, Vol. 589. Springer-Verlag (1991) 169–185.
3. Andrew A. Chien. Concurrent Aggregates (CA). The MIT Press, 1991.
4. Andrew A. Chien, Udey Reddy, John Plevyak, and Julian Dolby. ICC++ – A C++ Dialect for High Performance Parallel Computing. In Proceedings of the Second JSSST International Symposium on Object Technologies for Advanced Software (ISOTAS '96). Lecture Notes in Computer Science, Vol. 1049. Springer-Verlag (1996) 76–95.
5. Allan L. Fisher and Anwar M. Ghuloum. Parallelizing Complex Scans and Reductions. In Proceedings of the ACM SIGPLAN '94 Conference on Programming Language Design and Implementation (PLDI '94), pages 135–146, 1994.
6. Matteo Frigo, Charles E. Leiserson, and Keith H. Randall. The Implementation of the Cilk-5 Multithreaded Language. In Proceedings of the ACM SIGPLAN 1998 Conference on Programming Language Design and Implementation (PLDI '98), pages 212–223, 1998.
7. Allan Gottlieb, Ralph Grishman, Clyde P. Kruskal, Kevin P. McAuliffe, Larry Rudolph, and Marc Snir. The NYU Ultracomputer – Designing an MIMD Shared Memory Parallel Computer. IEEE Transactions on Computers, 32(2):175–189, 1983.
8. GTK+ Home Page. http://www.gtk.org/.
9. Zhenjiang Hu, Masato Takeichi, and Wei-Ngan Chin. Parallelization in Calculational Forms. In Proceedings of the 25th ACM SIGPLAN-SIGACT Symposium on Principles of Programming Languages (POPL '98), pages 316–328, 1998.
10. Ken Kennedy. Telescoping Languages: A Compiler Strategy for Implementation of High-Level Domain-Specific Programming Systems. In Proceedings of International Parallel and Distributed Processing Symposium 2000 (IPDPS 2000), pages 297–304, 2000.
11. Yoshiyuki Onoue, Zhenjiang Hu, Hideya Iwasaki, and Masato Takeichi. A Calculational Fusion System HYLO. In IFIP TC2 Working Conference on Algorithmic Languages and Calculi, pages 76–106. Chapman&Hall, 1997.
12. OpenMP Architecture Review Board. OpenMP C and C++ Application Program Interface, 1998.
13. Yoshihiro Oyama. Achieving High Performance in Parallel Programs that Contain Unscalable Modules. PhD thesis, Department of Information Science, Graduate School of Science, University of Tokyo, 2000.

14. Yoshihiro Oyama, Kenjiro Taura, Toshio Endo, and Akinori Yonezawa. An Implementation and Performance Evaluation of Language with Fine-Grain Thread Creation on Shared Memory Parallel Computer. In Proceedings of 1998 International Conference on Parallel and Distributed Computing and Systems (PDCS '98), pages 672–675, 1998.

15. Yoshihiro Oyama, Kenjiro Taura, and Akinori Yonezawa. An Efficient Compilation Framework for Languages Based on a Concurrent Process Calculus. In Proceedings of Euro-Par '97 Parallel Processing, Object-Oriented Programming Workshop. Lecture Notes in Computer Science, Vol. 1300. Springer-Verlag (1997) 546–553..

16. Yoshihiro Oyama, Kenjiro Taura, and Akinori Yonezawa. Executing Parallel Programs with Synchronization Bottlenecks Efficiently. In Proceedings of International Workshop on Parallel and Distributed Computing for Symbolic and Irregular Applications (PDSIA '99), pages 182–204. World Scientific, 1999.

17. Yoshihiro Oyama, Kenjiro Taura, and Akinori Yonezawa. Online Computation of Critical Paths for Multithreaded Languages. In Proceedings of the 5th International Workshop on High-Level Parallel Programming Models and Supportive Environments (HIPS 2000). Lecture Notes in Computer Science. Vol. 1800. Springer-Verlag (2000) 301–313.

18. Martin C. Rinard and Pedro C. Diniz. Eliminating Synchronization Bottlenecks in Object-Based Programs Using Adaptive Replication. In Proceedings of 1999 ACM International Conference on Supercomputing (ICS '99), pages 83–92, 1999.

19. Kenjiro Taura, Kunio Tabata, and Akinori Yonezawa. StackThreads/MP: Integrating Futures into Calling Standards. In Proceedings of the 7th ACM SIGPLAN Symposium on Principles and Practice of Parallel Programming (PPoPP '99), pages 60–71, 1999.

20. Kenjiro Taura and Akinori Yonezawa. Schematic: A Concurrent Object-Oriented Extension to Scheme. In Proceedings of Workshop on Object-Based Parallel and Distributed Computation (OBPDC '95). Lecture Notes in Computer Science. Vol. 1107. Springer-Verlag (1996) 59–82..

21. Philip Wadler. Deforestation: Transforming programs to eliminate trees. Theoretical Computer Science, 73(2):231–248, 1990.

22. Masahiro Yasugi, Shigeyuki Eguchi, and Kazuo Taki. Eliminating Bottlenecks on Parallel Systems using Adaptive Objects. In Proceedings of International Conference on Parallel Architectures and Compilation Techniques (PACT '98), pages 80–87, 1998.

Computational Portal:
Remote Access to High-Performance Computing

Vladimir V. Prokhorov

Ph.D. in Math, Head of Laboratory, Institute of Mathematics and Mechanics,
Ural Branch of Russian Academy of Sciences, Ekaterinburg
S.Kovalevskoy, 16, Ekaterinburg GSP-384, 620219, RUSSIA
vpro@convex.ru

Abstract. The technology under consideration is called "Computational Proxy-Server" (CPS or "Computational Portal") and it is intended for remote computing. The technology makes it possible to simplify the process of access to high-performance computing resources via the Internet both for application-client and for human-client. The technology is based on distributed client-server architectures, agent technologies, component models, CORBA and COM architectures. The technology is oriented towards allotment of a primary service to client as a pair <software, hardware>. The approach allows to divide a pair <client – computing server> into two pairs: <client – CPS> and <CPS – computing server>. The technology is realized through a complex of software tools: CPS proper, HyperModeller and $^\pi J$.

1. Introduction

Application of heterogeneous complexes of hardware and software tools, including distributed high-performance computing resources, could increase efficiency of compound tasks development. In order to use such heterogeneous environment, it is necessary to solve a number of problems connected with convenient and effective computer-human interaction, with software interaction between remote hardware components, with reliability of distributed system while components could hang, etc. The Internet is natural environment for providing access to remote computing [1]. Last time, the web-technology, CORBA and COM architectures has been often used for remote access to high-performance computing resources. Component technologies are often used now. The technology of proxy computers is widely used for various Internet protocols. Technologies of visual programming and graphic user interface are widely spread in all areas of computer applications.

We propose a technology, which integrates three items: (1) *"Computational Proxy-Server"* (CPS or Computational Portal) – a technology of access to remote computational services via the Internet [4], (2) a technology of integrated visual programming, which is realized in authoring tool $^\pi J$ [5], and (3) a technology of open visual object-oriented assembling, which is implemented in a tool *HyperModeller* [6]. The technology is based on a component "π-technology" [2, 3] using functional, algorithmic, and object-oriented composition, web- and mail-access.

V. Malyshkin (Ed.): PaCT 2001, LNCS 2127, pp. 308–313, 2001.

2.   Basic Concept of the Technology

The software, realizing the technology, consists of 3 main items: software for client computer, software for proxy-computer (CPS), and software for computing server (CS). The common chart of CPS technology components is represented on the Fig.1.

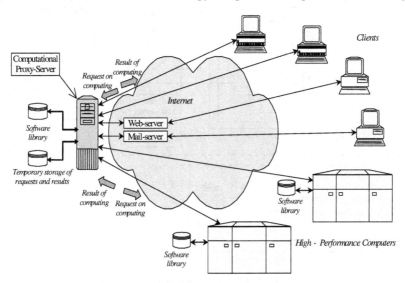

Fig. 1. The integrated chart of the computing proxy-server technology

CPS fulfills the following problems: – support of "a reference bureau" for functions provided to the client, – accept of the orders on computing with data transfer (under the protocols *COM* or *CORBA*, via *web-access* or via *email*), – making decision about the most expedient choice of the concrete computing server for concrete computing, – activation of computing on a computing server, – data transfer, – monitoring of computing process, making decision about change of the computing server (dynamic reconfiguration), – accumulation of experience in reliability of computing servers, – filing of resources provided by computing servers, – filing of programs for CS for storing in the library of CPS. The main components of CPS are represented on the Fig.2.

A client computer is connected with CPS via the Internet. It is equipped with appropriate software. The client can receive the list of provided resources, which are registered on CPS, can examine the state of tasks started before, and also can transmit an order for computing.

Authoring tool $^{\pi}J$ [5] can be used as a client for CPS. This one is a tool for programming in *Java, which* can be used as stay-alone tool, as add-on for *MS FrontPage*, and as a component of *HyperModeller* environment). The software supports various chart versions of Java: π-chart, flow-chart, etc. Operators of a graphic program could not only be Java operators, but also calls of **computing services**, provided by CPS. The tool allows using of external languages as sub-languages for a $^{\pi}J$ program (according to the π-technology).

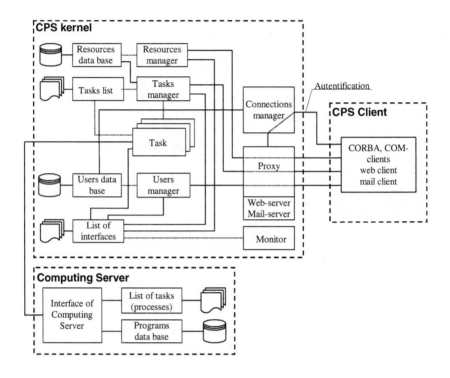

Fig. 2. The main components of CPS

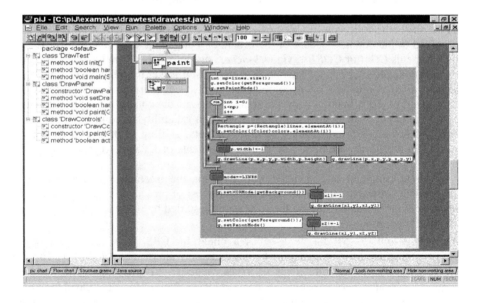

Fig. 3. A screenshot of authoring tool $^{\pi}J$

HyperModeller tool can also be used as a client for CPS. This one realizes an open object-oriented visual assembling technology. An application is assembled as a chart. The chart includes some elements connected by links. The elements could be, particularly, computing services provided by CPS, and modules created in $^{\pi}J$. Moreover, computational modules and input/output interface elements created in arbitrary languages (according to the π-technology) could be used as building bricks.

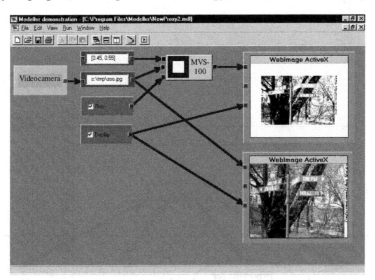

Fig. 4. A screenshot of HyperModeller chart, which uses picture processing on high-performance computer via CPS

Arbitrary *mail client* and *web-browser* can also be used as a client for CPS (see Fig.5).

Fig.6 illustrates possible relations between the tools' components in some hypothetic work. An element created in one component of the tools, could be used as a 'brick' for another component. For example, an object, created in HyperModeller (as a chart), could be used as an element of a program in $^{\pi}J$. This program could be principally used in its turn as an element of HyperModeller chart. Elements created in HyperModeller, in $^{\pi}J$ and hosted at CPS can be used to implement interface via *web-server*.

3.   Multimedia Computational Proxy-Server

It seems that one of fruitful applications of CPS is computer graphics and image processing (such as video compression, generation of animated scenes or rendering), because productivity of user computer is often less then it is necessary for efficient solution of such task. CPS can support in 2 main modes for these tasks: off-line and on-line (real time mode).

We call "Multimedia CPS" the application of Computational Proxy-Server technology for multimedia data stream processing in real time (Fig.7).

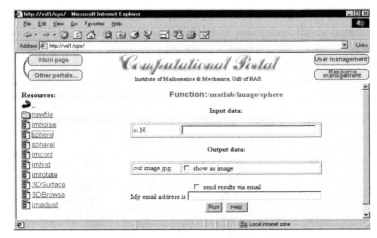

Fig. 5. Web-access to CPS computational service

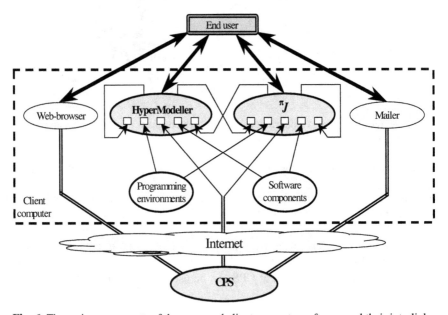

Fig. 6. The main components of the proposed client computer software and their interlinks.

Compression of video and audio flow by CPS in real time allows implementation of CPS for video-connection of remote clients using slow client computers and slow Internet channel.

As first step of the multimedia project, it has developed off-line audio-video codec for MPEG-4 ISO standard (the codec is realized in C++). The codec is registered as one of current CPS resources. Development of real-time MPEG-4 codec for CPS is in progress. The codec will use high-performance computing cluster (Institute of Mathematics and Mechanics Ural Branch RAS).

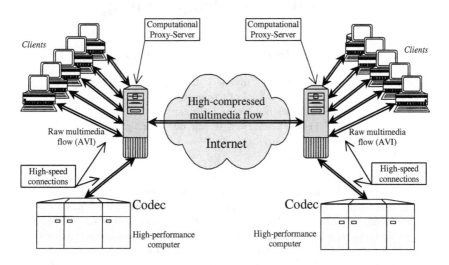

Fig. 7. Multimedia computational proxy-server

4. Conclusion

Experimental versions of CPS are published and operated on the Internet (http://cps.imm.uran.ru).

The author thanks Serge Izmailov, Dmitry Smirnov, Vadim Kosarev, Alexander Petukhov, Alexander Yakovlev, and Natalia Beresneva for participation in realization of the software.

The project is carried out with financial support of the Russian Foundation for Basic Research (code 99-01-00468).

References

1. Berners-Lee T. WWW: Past, Present, and Future. Computer. - 1998. - 29, N10. - P. 69-77.
2. Prokhorov V. PYTHAGORAS: Multienvironment Software. In: B.Blumenthal, J.Gornostaev, and C.Unger, Eds. Human-Computer Interaction. Lectures Notes in Computer Science (LNCS). Vol.1015. Springer Verlag, Berlin, Germany, 1995. - P.135-148.
3. Prokhorov, V. On the micro-context approach to construction of knowledge representation languages and human-computer interaction. Journal of Computer and Systems Sciences International. – 1997. - N5. - P.5-16.
4. Prokhorov, V. A technology of use of computing resources on the Internet on the basis of computing proxy-servers. In book.: Algorithms and software for parallel computing. Vol.2. - Ekaterinburg: Russian Acad. Sci./Ural Branch Publishing. – 1998. - P.256-267. (in Russian)
5. Prokhorov, V., Kosarev, V. Environment piJ for Visual Programming in Java. Information Visualisation IV99, IEEE Computer Society Press, Los Alamitos, CA, 1999.
6. Prokhorov, V., Smirnov, D., Kosarev, V. Visual multi-language tools for development of distributed environments. Journal of Control Systems and Machines International. - 1999, N6. - P.75-83.

Event Logic Programming

Rafael Ramirez and Andrew E. Santosa

National University of Singapore
School of Computing
S16, 3 Science Drive 2, Singapore 117543
{rafael,andrews}@comp.nus.edu.sg

Abstract. We present a new concurrent (constraint) logic programming language based on partially ordered event structures. A system is modeled as: (a) a set of concurrent processes, which are Prolog programs extended with *event goals* declaring program points of interest, and (b) a constraint store which imposes restrictions on the event goals execution order. The constraint store acts as a coordination entity which on the one hand encapsulates the system synchronization requirements, and on the other hand, provides a declarative specification of the system concurrency issues. This produces a powerful formalism which at the same time, overcome the deficiencies of traditional concurrent logic programming languages and preserve the benefits of declarative programming.

1 Introduction

The task of programming concurrent systems is substantially more difficult than programming for sequential machines. Unlike sequential (or transformational) programs, which merely terminate with a final result, concurrent (or reactive) programs produce results during their execution and may not even be expected to terminate. Thus, while in traditional sequential programming the problem is reduced to making sure that the program's final result (if any) is correct and that the program terminates, in concurrent programming it is not necessary to obtain a final result but to ensure that several properties hold during program execution. These properties are classified into safety properties, those that must always be true, and progress (or liveness) properties, those that must eventually be true. Partial correctness and termination are special cases of these two properties. We believe that the intrinsic difficulties in writing concurrent systems can be considerably reduced by

- using a declarative formalism to explicitly specify the system safety and progress properties, and
- treating these properties as orthogonal to the system base functionality.

This paper proposes a new concurrent (constraint) logic programming language which models a concurrent system as: (a) a set of concurrent processes, which are Prolog programs extended with event goals, and (b) a constraint store which imposes restrictions on the event goals execution order. The constraint

V. Malyshkin (Ed.): PaCT 2001, LNCS 2127, pp. 314–318, 2001.

store acts as a coordination entity which on the one hand encapsulates the system synchronization requirements, and on the other hand, provides a declarative specification of the system concurrency issues.

2   Related Work

Logic programming languages derive from the procedural interpretation of a subset of the first order predicate calculus. They offer a unifying style which allows them to be considered at the same time as specification languages, as formalisms for proving program properties, as well as programming languages. Concurrent constraint logic family of programming languages (e.g., CCP [7], Parlog [3], Concurrent Prolog [8], Guarded Horn Clauses [10]) preserve many of the benefits of the abstract logic programming model, such as the logical reading of programs and the use of logical terms to represent data structures. However, although concurrent logic programming languages preserve many benefits of the logic programming model, and their programs explicitly specify their final result, important program properties, namely safety and progress properties, remain implicit. These properties have to be preserved by using control features such as modes and sequencing, producing programs with little or no declarative reading.

It is also worth mentioning the language Linda [2]. Linda is related to the work reported here in the sense that it separates application functionality and concurrency control by providing a model for concurrency and communication via a shared tuple space. However, the tuple space has no logical reading on its own and it is up to the programmer to give meaning to the tuples on the tuple space. In general, this forces the specification of a system to be low level and makes impossible any formal treatment for synthesizing and verifying of specifications. There have been works on using tuple spaces as coordination mechanism in a logic programming framework [1,4,9] but these approaches inherit the lack of logical reading of the tuple spaces.

3   The Constraint Language

Many researchers, e.g. [5,6], have proposed methods for reasoning about temporal phenomena using partially ordered sets of events. Our approach to concurrent programming is based on the same general idea. The basic idea here is to use a constraint logic program to represent the (usually infinite) set of constraints of interest. The constraints themselves are of the form $X < Y$, read as "X precedes Y" or "the execution time of X is less than the execution time of Y", where X and Y are events, and $<$ is a partial order.

The constraint logic program is defined as follows. Constants range over events classes $E, F, \ldots$ and there is a distinguished (postfixed) functor $+$. Thus the terms of interest, apart from variables, are $e, e+, e++, \ldots, f, f+, f++, \ldots$. The idea is that e represents the first event in the class E, $e+$ the next event, etc. Thus, for any event X, $X+$ is implicitly preceded by X, i.e. $X < X+$. We denote by e_N the N-th event in the class E. Programs facts or *predicate constraints* are of the form $p(t_1, \ldots, t_n)$ where p is a user defined predicate and the t_i are ground terms. Program rules or *predicate definitions* are of the form $p(X_1, \ldots, X_n) \leftarrow B$ where the X_i are distinct variables and B a rule body whose variables are in $\{X_1, \ldots, X_n\}$. A program is a finite collection of rules and is used to define a family of partial orders over events. Intuitively, this family is obtained by unfolding the rules with facts indefinitely, and collecting the (ground) *precedence constraints* of the form $e < f$. Multiple rules for a given predicate symbol give rise to different partial orders. For example, since the following program has only one rule for p:

$$p(e, f).$$
$$p(E, F) \leftarrow E < F, \; p(E+, F+).$$

it defines just one partial order $e < f, e+ < f+, e++ < f++, \ldots$. In contrast,

$$p(e, f).$$
$$p(E, F) \leftarrow E < F, \; p(E+, F+).$$
$$p(E, F) \leftarrow F < E, \; p(E+, F+).$$

defines a family of partial orders over $\{e, f, e+, f+, e++, f++, e+++ \ldots\}$. We will abbreviate the set of clauses $H \leftarrow Cs_1 \ldots H \leftarrow Cs_n$ by the *disjunction constraint* $H \leftarrow Cs_1; \ldots; Cs_n$. in which disjunction is specified by the disjunction operator ';'.

The constraint logic programs have a procedural interpretation that allows a correct specification to be executed in the sense that events get executed only as permitted by the constraints represented by the program. This procedural interpretation is based on an incremental execution of the program and a *lazy* generation of the corresponding partial orders. Constraints are generated by the constraint logic program only when needed to reason about the execution times of current events.

4   Event Goals

In order to refer to the visit times at points of interest in the program we introduce event goals. An event goal has the syntax of an event name enclosed by angle brackets, e.g. <e>. Event goals appear in program clauses bodies.

Given a pair of events, constraints can be stated to specify the relative order of execution of event goals in all parts of the program. If the execution of a process P_1 reaches an event goal containing an event whose execution time is constrained to be greater than the execution time of a not-yet-executed event of an event goal in a different process P_2, then process P_1 is forced to suspend. In the presence of recursive definitions in a logic program event goals are typically executed several times. Thus, in general, an event e in an event goal G represents an event class, where each of its instances $e, e+, e++, \ldots$ corresponds to an execution of G (e represents the first execution, $e+$ the second, etc.).

When <e> is evaluated, the constraint store is checked to determine if event e is enabled, i.e., it is not preceded by another not-yet-executed event, then the constraint store is updated when necessary. The constraint store is updated when e is enabled by deleting all primitive constraints e < E. The evaluation of event goals are done atomically to preserve consistency of the constraint store.

We have adopted a design of using explicit concurrency in our language. Traditional concurrent (constraint) logic programming languages parallelism is implicit: every literal in a clause body represents a concurrent process. We believe that this can cause the creation of an unnecessary number of concurrent processes and thus, the creation of concurrent processes should preferably be done by an explicit primitive in the language. We provide the || operator which allows the programmer to explicitly spawn concurrent processes, which is similar to the &/2 operator of &-Prolog [4].

5   Conclusion

In this paper we have present a new concurrent (constraint) logic programming language based on temporal constraints among a set of events. In the language, concurrent processes are specified by Prolog programs extended with *event goals*. A constraint store contains a set of temporal constraints which impose restrictions on the event goals execution order. The constraint store acts as a coordination entity which on the one hand encapsulates the system synchronization requirements, and on the other hand, provides a declarative specification of the system concurrency issues. This produces a powerful formalism which at the same time, overcome the deficiencies of traditional concurrent logic programming languages and preserve the benefits of declarative programming, providing great advantages in writing concurrent programs and manipulating them while preserving correctness.

Current status: We have a prototype implementation of our language written in Parlog. Parlog was chosen as the implementation language since it provides mechanisms for creating concurrent processes and for process synchronization. The implementation is reported in an accompanied paper.

References

1. A. Brogi, P. Ciancarini: The concurrent language Shared Prolog. ACM Transactions on Programming Languages and Systems, **13(1)**, (1991), 99–123
2. N. Carriero, D. Gelernter: Linda in context. Communications of the ACM. **32(4)** (1989) 444–458
3. S. Gregory.: Parallel Logic Programming in Parlog: The Language and Its Implementation. Addison-Wesley. 1987.
4. M. Hermenegildo, D. Cabeza, and M. Carro: Using attributed variables in the implementation of concurrent and parallel logic programming systems. Logic Programming, Proc. Twelfth Int. Conf. on Logic Programming. (1995) 631–645
5. R. A. Kowalski and M. J. Sergot.: A logic-based calculus of events. New Generation Computing **4** (1986) 67–95
6. V. Pratt: Modeling concurrency with partial orders. Int. J. of Logic Programming, **15(1)** (1986) 33–71

7. V. A. Saraswat: Concurrent Constraint Programming. Logic Programming Series. MIT Press. 1992.
8. E.Y. Shapiro, editor: Concurrent Prolog: Collected Papers. MIT Press, 1987.
9. P. Tarau: Jinni: Intelligent mobile agent programming at the intersection of Java and Prolog. Proc. of PAAM '99. (1999)
10. K. Ueda: Guarded Horn clauses. E.Y. Shapiro, editor: Concurrent Prolog: Collected Papers. MIT Press. (1987) 140–156

Techniques for Increasing Performance of CORBA Parallel Distributed Applications

R. Shevchenko and A. Doroshenko

GradSoft, Ukraine
Hreschatik 32, ap 57, Kiev 01001, Ukraine
rssh@gradsoft.com.ua
Institute of Software Systems
National Academy of Sciences of Ukraine
Glushkov prosp., 40, Kiev 03187, Ukraine
dor@isofts.kiev.ua

Abstract. A time cost model for CORBA distributed applications performance is proposed and new insights on enhancing parallelism and performance optimisation techniques of distributed programs are given. Some results on measuring performance of experiment applications are presented. A new 4-tiered architecture based on our cost model against traditional 3-tiered one for Internet distributed applications is proposed.

1 Introduction

Rapid development of computer networks, introduction of technologies Intranet and universal distribution Internet services caused essential shifts in basic paradigms of designing of software systems that can be characterised by ever growing demands in performance and easy programming of distributed applications. These fundamental changes have caused development of whole classes of software architectures and middleware and CORBA (Common Object request Broker Architecture) is one of the distinguished one among them.

CORBA standard determines the architecture of distributed objects and interaction between them in heterogeneous networks [1]. CORBA gives a way of organisation of the distributed computation having a number of properties attractive for a designer such as precise object model, separation of object description from its implementation and call transparency. There are known a number of works to investigate performance issues in CORBA and propose methods to improve program efficiency [2-5]. However to our knowledge they deal insufficiently with development of quantitative performance models and programming methods in CORBA application design.

The purpose of this paper is to give a model and methodology for building high performance distributed CORBA applications suitable for practical use in industrial-strength software. The work relies on our experience of research and development of a CORBA based enterprise distributed software system [6]. We give a new insight on methods of enhancing parallelism and performance optimisation of distributed programs and illustrate presentation with experimental

V. Malyshkin (Ed.): PaCT 2001, LNCS 2127, pp. 319–328, 2001.

measuring performance of sample applications. The paper concludes with a proposal of a new 4-tiered architecture of Internet based distributed applications which enriches the traditional 3 tiered one with an extra logic component aimed to enhance system performance by means of various methods of minimisation of objects interaction time.

2   CORBA Objects Interaction and a Time Cost Model

General prerequisites of CORBA object requests broker interactions are specified by OMA architecture [7] as shown at figure below, where GIOP (General InterORB Protocol) is a protocol for data transfer between brokers. This architecture establishes following limitations on client-server interactions:

- interaction establishes permanent connection between the server and client while request processing; multiple request could be multiplexed over the same connection.
- method invocation is synchronous, that is once client's thread has executed remote method invocation it is blocked until the reply; asynchronous computation can be founded on existence of another (parallel) thread communicating a server thread by means of synchronous method invocation; Note, that in this article we do not talk about new CORBA AMI feature, which provide asynchronic methods invocation interface - this is subject for another analysis.
- implementation of the remote method may require sending some context needed for correct execution of the method, for example identifier of current transaction or information about codeset, used in current session;
- stages of request processing and their order are predefined.

Our analysis of time costs of request brokers shows that performance of a broker is mainly dependent on following functions underlying stages of request processing.

1. *Marshalling (demarshalling)* function $M(x)$ $(Dm(x))$ which implement coding (decoding) stages in request x processing. These functions are almost additive in space, $M(x|y) = M(x)|M(y)|pad(x,y)$, where $x|y$ is concatenation, $pad(x,y)$ is a quantity of bytes aligning y after x. Also they are almost linear in time $T_M(x|y) = T_M(x)+T_M(y)+\delta(x,y)$, where $T_M(x)$ is a time for coding x and $\delta(x,y)$ is negligible with respect to $T_M(x)$. Notice that the size of appropriate GIOP sequence $|M(x)| = K_{SM}|x|$ in bytes can be considered as proportional to size of request $|x|$ with a coefficient K_{SM}. Time for coding and decoding are considered as nearly equal. Coefficients K_{SM} not depend from ORB and fully defined by type of request and using coding (usially GIOP). $T_M(x)$ is depend from quality of ORB marshalling algorithm.

2. *Search objects* function. The main parameter that this function is dependent on is amount of objects supported in the system. So the time cost for invocation of this function can be designated $T_{FO}(o, N_o)$, where N_o is a size of objects table in the system.

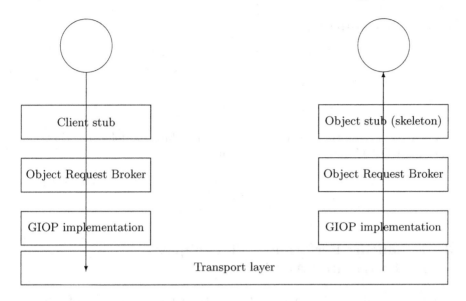

3. *Search methods* function. Searches in table of methods with time cost designated as $T_{Fm}(m, N_m(o))$, where m is method and $N_m(o)$ is a size of table of remote methods of the object.

4. *Activation object and invocation method* function estimated in time as $T_I(o, m)$ which includes time for servant invocation and, if needed, its thread initialisation.

5. *Network data transfer* function where K_s is mean value for a byte transfer time. Let there is a program code $y = o.m(x)$ with propagating a context c, where m is the method of remote object o with input parameter x and output y. To find estimation of time cost for this basic piece of code of distributed applications we need to define a number of time cost model constituents that are characterised in terms of functions introduced above:

- if designate $req(o, m, x, c)$ a function of sending appropriate request for $o.m(x)$ operation then coding request time can be estimated as;

$$T_M\left(req(o, m, x, c)\right) \approx T_M(o|m|x|c) \approx K_M \times (|o| + |m| + |x| + |c|)$$

- transferring request time:

$$T_S\left(req(o, m, x, c)\right) \approx K'_S \times (|o| + |m| + |x| + |c|)$$

- decoding request time:

$$T_{DM}\left(o, m, x, c\right) \approx K_M\left(|o| + |m| + |x| + |c|\right)$$

- time of search object in active object map, object activation, method invocation and evaluation of request:

$$T_{FO}\left(o, N_o\right) + T_{Fm}\left(m, N_m\left(o\right)\right) + F_I\left(o, m\right)$$

- time for reply transfer:

$$T_S\left(reply\left(y\right)\right) \approx T_S\left(y\right) \approx K_S' \times \left(|y| + |c|\right)$$

- time for reply decoding:

$$T_{DM}\left(y,c\right) \approx K_M \times \left(|y| + |c|\right)$$

Summarizing these time estimations, we can deduce the following timing cost model of CORBA remote method invocation:

$$T_{y=o,m(x)} = K_1 \times \left(|o| + |m| + |x| + |y|\right) + 2K_1 \times |c| + T_{FO}\left(o, N_o\right) +$$

$$+T_{FM}\left(m, N_M\left(o\right)\right) + \ T_I\left(o, m\right)$$

3   Enhancing Performance Techniques for Distributed Applications

There is difficult if not impossible to give the uniform definition of concept of efficiency suitable for all classes of applications. In each case of interest it can be a particular set of criteria. In this paper we consider timing characteristics a crucial for performance of most distributed applications. Among them are known: *computing performance* — speed of operation execution estimated as general time spent by the processor on any of a step of calculation performed; *application reactivity (responsiveness)* — a time interval between input by the user of the data and occurrence of the new information in his client's application; and *efficiency* — a degree of processor time utility as a share of actual calculation time of a task in general time of residence of the task in the system.

Below there are presented briefly a few examples of technique to improve performance characteristics followed by an application example illustrating their effect. Basically the methods concern optimisation of service interfaces design.

1. *Using composite operations.* Due to CORBA location transparency remote and local method invocations looks identical from application programmer point of view. But actually their time costs are different: in local case it is of T_I (time of invocation), in remote case this can be T_S (time of network data transfer). To reduce overhead an aggregation of multiple nonlocal method invocation into a composite one is exploited as shown in following code fragment. Let we have two subsequent invocations on remote object:

```
y1=o.req1(x1);
y2=o.req2(x2);
```

Define an object o operation $req12(x1, x2)$ as composition of $req1$ and $req2$. Then using our model the time cost of two sequential remote invocations is:

$$K_1\left(2|o| + |req1| + |req2| + |X_1| + |X_2| + |y_1| + |y_2|\right) + 2K_2|c|$$

$$+2T_{FO}\left(N_O\right) + 2T_{FM}\left(req, N_M\left(o\right)\right)$$

while in case of composite operation we have:

$$K_1\left(|o| + |x_1| + |x_2| + |y_1| + |y_2| + |req12|\right) + K_2|c|$$

$$+T_{FO}\left(N_O\right) + T_{FM}\left(N_M + 1\right) + T_I\left(o, req12\right).$$

So by using composite operations we can save time of

$$K_1|o| + K_2|c| + T_{FO}\left(N_O\right) + TFM\left(req12, N_{M+1}\right) + \Delta T_I\left(o, \left(req12, req1 + req2\right)\right);$$

that is equal to cost of empty remote invocation `void f(void)`. This transformation can improve all kinds of the timing characteristics of performance. Naturally the effect from composite operation is more significant in cases of coupling multiple invocations like in branch operation `if (o.m1(x)) o.m2(x); else o.m3(x)`. And the most effective this optimisation is for loop construct like:

```
for(ULong i=0; i<x.length();+i) r[i]=o.m(x[i]);+
```

In such case of homogeneous data arrays multiple operations like $m : O \times X \rightarrow Y$ can be defined as a single composite operation $m_{seq} : O \times X^N \rightarrow Y^N$ with obvious advantages of saving execution time. Examples of such technique can be found in CORBA Collection Services [8]. As our model shows this transformation is applicable (recommended) if T_s and T_M are the main constituents of application cost model. For implementation this optimisation is realised as server side composite operation equivalent to given sequence of methods invocations on the remote object.

2. *Nonblocking execution of coarse-grained computation in parallel threads.* This transformation is applied primarily if it is necessary to minimise time of reactivity of the application program. Let we have client source code is `y=o.m(x);F;ShowY(y)` where time consuming operation `m` is carried out on a server, following piece of code `F` is data independent on `y` and `ShowY(y)` is the closest operation which needs computed value of verb+y+. Then it is reasonable not to block the client program and to transform the code with: 1) replacing `y=o.m(x)` statement by starting equivalent ope ation in parallel thread on the client where the method `m` is actually performed, and 2) inserting wait-for statement just before the `ShowY(y)` to protect y variable form too early evaluation. A pattern for transformation of the code in Java can be like following:

```
RequestY()
{
Thread m_th = new Thread()
{    public void run()    {
          y=o.m(x);          }
 }; m_th.start();
}
 F
waitForY
{
if (!yReceived) {
```

```
    yWaiter.wait();
} ShowY(y)
}
```

This example exposes the simplest case of static source code transformation based on local analysis of program statements data independence. Advanced models with extended implications for parallelism extraction have been developed by authors in [9].

3. *Customisation of marshalling.* Cost of network transfer can be decreased by changing GIOP marshalling to customised one with more efficient characteristics by means of supply of adapter library for coding and decoding custom marshalled byte streams. Custom marshalling can be more efficient with respect to GIOP because we can use known structure of transferred data. Note that it is still possible to use CORBA network data transfer layer by encapsulation of the marshalled data stream into CORBA type `sequence<octet>`. This techniqe is also can be applied in case of object collocation [5], where we can simple skip marshalling/demarshalling stages.

We developed our own stream format called RC-stream for passing of relatively large data sets of known structure through low speed network. Adapters for writing and reading from RC stream are available to application programmer.

Let's denote difference in marshalling speed algorithm as ΔK_m, difference in multiplicator of marshalled data size as ΔK_t.

Now, we can compare difference in execution of 2 identical requests with 2 different marshallin constants: it would be

$$(\Delta K_m + \Delta K_t * K'_s)(|o| + |m| + |x| + |y| + 2|c|)$$

So, in ideal case parameters of marshalling algorithm must be depend from speed of data transfer: if we increase time of marshalling on, ΔK_M, than appropriative decreasing of request size must be bigger, than $\frac{\Delta K_M}{K_s}$ where K_s - speed of data tranfer in communication channel.

It's means, that custom marshalling is usefull in low-speed network environments, such as Internet.

4.*Elimination of metainformation.* CORBA provides reach facilities for building high-level general schemes of object interaction based on common design patterns. But their exploiting usually means expensive usage of metainformation such as passing `Any` type objects with type codes or using Interface Repository in runtime. Metainformation transfer leads to significant overhead. So it is desirable to use high-level generic components in performance critical subsystems and instead to use specialisation of general schemes where all information about object types is static, all calls to extra interfaces are known at compile-time and all parameters types are concrete.

To demonstrate the effect of our optimisation techniques some experiments were undertaken on 10 Mbs LAN processing a sample SQL Read-request to database consisting of 10000 records. The work of CORBA middle layer was to pass iteration over requested result set to CORBA front-end client. Identical front-ends clients and few different implementations of CORBA middle-layer server was tested. The request was coded in different languages with and without applying of RC-coding, with and without applying collocation on a machine. Also number of records retrieved during one remote method invocation was varied. Following combinations of these opportunities have been tested (shown in diagram legend below): 1. Server(++), Client (++), server and clients are collocated in one address space on single computer, sequence of records are marshalled with help of GIOP coding.

2. Server(++), Client (++), server and clients are collocated in one address space on single computer, sequence of records are marshalled with help of RC coding.

3. Server (++), Client (++), server and client are not collocated (i.e. situated in different address spaces), invocations are executed on single machine via LAN interface, sequence of records are marshalled with help of GIOP coding.

4. Server (++), Client (++), server and client are not collocated, invocations are executed on single machine via LAN interface, sequence of records are marshalled with help of RC coding.

5. Server (++), Client (++), calls are executed via LAN (10b), GIOP coding is used.

6. Server (++), Client (++), calls are executed via LAN (10b), RC coding is used.

7. Server (++), Client (Java), calls are executed via LAN (10b), GIOP coding is used.

8. Servers(++), Client (Java), calls are executed via LAN (10b),RC coding is used.

Results of time measurement with Sun Enterprise 450 under Solaris 2.6 and Oracle database acting as server, Pentium 300 under Windows NT acting as client are shown on the following Diagram 1.

On X-axis number of records passed in one remote invocation is shown, on Y-axis the time of processing requests and passing 1000 records in milliseconds is shown.

4   Internet Applications: Technique of Using Web Front-End

In this section we explain briefly the main idea of an application of our methodology in analysing Internet/Extranet applications: What is different between Intranet and Internet applications is the cost of network data transfer 10-100Mbs for LAN and 1-10 Kbs for Internet. Thus a good design of Internet application implies minimisation of network data transfer time T_S, while for Intranet application the time of invocation T_I can be more critical. One of consequence for making decisions in arch tecture design is to insert additional software layer for collecting data passed in large pieces of information in order to speed up integral performance of Internet application. Such Internet case architecture with four layers (Database, Logic, Server Front-End, Client) can be more efficient than traditional 3-tiered one consisting of Database, Server and Clients. Suppose that

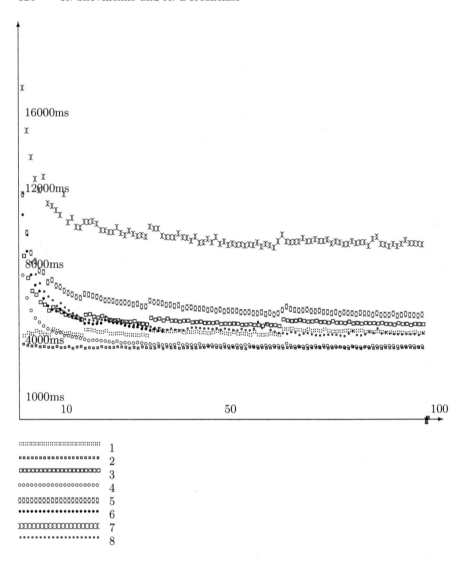

for organizing data in a single chunk it is needed to process N requests with method invocations of approximately equal time complexity. So for standard 3-tiered architecture we have following assessment of time evaluation:

$$T_{N(y=o,m(x))} = NK_1 \left(const + |x| + |y|\right) + NT_{y=o,m(x)}^L$$

Now consider the extra layer of logic where we have heterogeneous medium with transfer factor for external medium (Internet) and internal (LAN) as K_1 and K_1^* respectively. If WWW Servlet executes all invocations in LAN environment collecting all needed parameters with additional information and sending it to remote browser in a single chunk, then we obtain:

$$T^*_{N(o,m(x))} = K_1 \left(const + N|x| + N|y| + |z| \right) +$$

$$NK^*_1 \left(const + |x| + |y| \right) + NT^L_{y=o,m(x)} + T^L_Z$$

where is $|Z|$ a size of additional information added by servlet and T^L_Z is an overhead due to servlet and is an overhead due to servlet invocation. The difference will be:

$$T - T^* = K_1 \left((N-1) \, const - |z| \right) - NK^*_1 \left(const + |x| + |z| \right) - T^L_Z$$

Considering that $K^*_1 << K_1$ and the difference is of three orders of magnitude we can conclude LAN expenses is usually negligible in respect to the time of network transfer. So the benefit $T - T^*$ is surely positive and can be significant if the size of additional data is not enormous $|z| < (|x| + |y|)^* N$ and if time of operation is determined mostly by time of network data transfer.

5   Conclusion

We have presented a time cost model for CORBA distributed applications performance and proposed enhancing parallelism and performance optimisation techniques of distributed programs. This paper is inspired by practical experience of CORBA based industrial distributed software design project undertaken at GradSoft (Kiev, Ukraine). Some results on measuring performance of experiment applications reported in this paper shows that the model and techniques is a good basis for software architecture to ls development in support of high performance parallel and distributed computing [10]. Particularly a new 4-tiered architecture against traditional 3-tiered one is proposed for Internet distributed applications.

References

1. Object Management Group. formal/98-12-01 The Common Object request Broker: Architecture and Specifications. CORBA/IIOP 2.3.1, 712p. (ftp://ftp.omg.org/pub/formal/98-12-01.pdf)
2. D. C. Schmidt, T. Harrison. Evaluating the Performance of OO Network Programming Toolkits, C++ Report, SIGS Vol.8, No.7, July/August,1996, 8 p. (http://www.cs.wustl.edu/ schmidt/C++-report-doc-perf.ps.gz)
3. K. Maad. Efficient Bulk Transfers over CORBA. Uppsala University, Sveden, 1997 (http://www.docs.uu.se/ kmaad/streams.ps)
4. A. Vogel. Effecient Data Transfer with CORBA. Java Report, vol.8, 1998. (http://archive.javareport.com/9808/html/features/archive9806/corbatalk.html)
5. S. Vinoski. Collocation Optimizations for CORBA, C++ Report, SIGS, Vol. 11, No. 9, October, 1999.
6. R. Shevchenko, Analysis of Efficiency Enhancing Methods of CORBA Based Distributed Applications, Proc. 2-nd Int. Conf. on Programming, May 23-26, 2000, Kiev, Ukraine, pp. 226-240 (in Russian).

7. Object Management Group. OMA: A Discussion of the Object Management Architecture, January 1997, 44p (www.omg.org/library/oma/oma-all.pdf)
8. Object Management Group. formal/97-12-24. CORBA Services: Collection Service Specification (ftp://ftp.omg.org/pub/formal/97-12-09.pdf)
9. A. E. Doroshenko, Modeling synchronization and communication abstractions for dynamical parallelization, in "High-Performance Computing and Networking, Vienna, Austria, Apr.1997, Proc. Int. Conf., Lect. Notices. in Comput. Sci.,vol. 12 p.752-761.
10. A.E. Doroshenko, L.-E. Thorelli, V. Vlassov., Coordination Models and Facilities Could be Parallel Software Accelerators, in. "High Performance Computing and Networking" Proc.7-th Int. Conf HPCN'99, Lect. Notices. in Comput. Sci., 1999, pp. 1219-1222.

Manager-Worker Parallelism versus Dataflow in a Distributed Computer Algebra System*

Wolfgang Schreiner

Research Institute for Symbolic Computation (RISC-Linz)
Johannes Kepler University, Linz, Austria
Wolfgang.Schreiner@risc.uni-linz.ac.at
Tel. +43 732 2468 9966, Fax. +43 732 2468 9930

Abstract. We analyze two implementation variants of a parallel computer algebra algorithm in Distributed Maple. The original solution uses a manager-worker mechanism to control task scheduling, which requires an elaborate administration scheme. The new algorithm is based on a dataflow approach where all tasks are immediately started, automatically scheduled by the runtime system, and implicitly synchronized by task dependencies; non-determinism is effectively applied to provide more potential for parallelism. It turns out that the new version is not only more declarative (closer to the mathematical problem description) but also more efficient than the original solution.

1 Introduction

We have developed Distributed Maple [8,9] as a portable and easy to use environment for implementing parallel computer algebra algorithms. So far, it has been successfully applied to the parallelization of various basic methods and complex applications in computer algebra and algebraic geometry [12,11,6,13]. The system is based on previous experience of other authors with the parallelization of Maple applications [14,1,2].

A good deal of this effort has been to design the parallel algorithm, respectively to extract parallelism from a given sequential algorithm. However, even after the developer has devised the abstract algorithm, he is left with a number design decisions when constructing the concrete implementation: how to agglomerate independent activities to concurrent tasks, how to model the interactions between tasks, and how to schedule tasks for execution. This gives a wide spectrum of implementation strategies: from a program that explicitly controls task execution by a manager-worker scheme to a program that just creates all tasks and leaves the scheduling decisions to the runtime system.

As a matter of fact, in our previous work the decision which style to pursue was essentially left to the taste of the developer: some algorithms were parallelized in a high-level declarative style, while others were implemented by low-level imperative mechanisms. The later strategy was typically chosen because

---

* Supported by grant SFB F013/F1304 of the Austrian Science Foundation (FWF).

V. Malyshkin (Ed.): PaCT 2001, LNCS 2127, pp. 329–343, 2001.

of the opinion that keeping control over tasks yields a more efficient solution. However, due to the lack of comparative studies, there has up to now not been any well-founded basis for such a judgment.

In this paper, we make good this omission by developing for a problem that has been previously solved in the manager-worker style of parallel computing a new implementation that is based on the dataflow principle: the new program starts all tasks as early as possible and leaves all scheduling and synchronization issues to the runtime system. Our concern was to make the program as simple and declarative as possible, i.e., to keep it close to the mathematical problem description. For this case study, we have chosen the problem of computing the Dixon resultant; this is part of the `neighbGraph` function of the computer algebra package CASA [7] and was previously parallelized in a manager-worker style [11].

We have performed this work in preparation of a broader activity where we will compare parallel algorithms implemented in Distributed Maple with corresponding declarative versions written in para-functional language Glasgow Parallel Haskell GPH [3] which has been previously used for the parallelization of computer algebra algorithms [4]. We are going to use GPH as a coordination environment for scheduling computations among Maple kernels; for this purpose, we have already developed a GPH-Maple interface [10].

2   Distributed Maple

Distributed Maple is an environment for writing parallel programs on the basis of the computer algebra system Maple [9]. It allows to create tasks and to execute them by Maple kernels running on various machines of a network. Each node of a session comprises two components (see Figure 1):

Scheduler The Java program `dist.Scheduler` coordinates the node interaction. The scheduler process attached to the frontend kernel starts instances of the scheduler on other machines and communicates with them via sockets.

Maple Interface The program `dist.maple` running on every Maple kernel implements the interface between kernel and scheduler. Both components use pipes to exchange messages (which may embed any Maple objects).

The user interacts with Distributed Maple via the Maple frontend by a number of programming commands, in particular:

`dist[start]`$(f, a, ...)$ creates a task evaluating $f(a, ...)$ and returns a task reference t. Tasks may create other tasks and arbitrary Maple objects (including task references) may be passed as arguments and returned as results.

`dist[wait]`(t) blocks the execution of the current task until the task represented by t has terminated and returns its result. Multiple tasks may independently wait for and retrieve the result of the same task t.

This model is based on para-functional principles which is sufficient for many kinds of computer algebra algorithms. The environment also supports nondeterministic task synchronization for speculative parallelism and self-synchronized shared data objects which allow tasks to communicate by a global store.

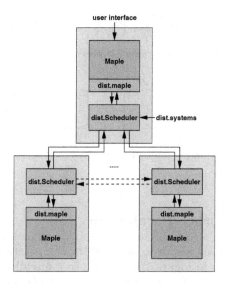

Fig. 1. Distributed Maple architecture

3 Problem and Sequential Algorithm

Our problem can be summarized as follows [5]: let p be a bivariate polynomial with rational coefficients x and z, i.e. $p \in \mathbb{Q}(x, z)$, and let $d_u^v \in \mathbb{Q}(x, z)$ denote the partial derivative $\frac{\partial p^{u+v}}{\partial x^u \partial z^v}$ of total order $u + v$. Our goal is to compute a sequence of univariate polynomials $[b_i]_{i=0}^n$ where $b_0(x)$ is the greatest square free divisor (gsfd) of $p(x, 0)$, $b_{i+1}(x)$ is the greatest common divisor (gcd) of $b_i(x)$ and of all $d_v^u(x, 0)$ with $u + v = i + 1$, and n is the smallest number such that $\deg b_n = 0$.

In the sequential algorithm, the partial derivatives of total order $i + 1$ are generated from (and overwrite) the derivatives of order i as shown in Figure 2:

$$(b, n) := \textbf{derivatives}(p)$$
$$i := 0$$
$$d_0 := p$$
$$b_0 := \text{gsfd}(d_0(x, 0))$$
$$\textbf{while } \deg(b_i) \neq 0 \textbf{ do}$$
$$\qquad d_{i+1} := \tfrac{\partial d_i}{\partial z}(x, z)$$
$$\qquad \textbf{for } j \textbf{ from } 0 \textbf{ to } i \textbf{ do}$$
$$\qquad\qquad d_j := \tfrac{\partial d_j}{\partial x}(x, z)$$
$$\qquad b_{i+1} := b_i$$
$$\qquad \textbf{for } j \textbf{ from } 0 \textbf{ to } i + 1 \textbf{ do}$$
$$\qquad\qquad b_{i+1} := \gcd(b_{i+1}, d_j(x, 0))$$
$$\qquad i := i + 1$$
$$\quad n := i$$
$$\textbf{end}$$

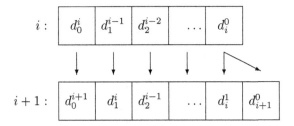

Fig. 2. Computation of derivatives of total order $i + 1$

4   Manager-Worker Parallelism

The main parallelization idea is to organize the computation of all d_u^v in a triangular matrix as shown in Figure 3: each line i contains all d_u^v with $u + v = i$, each column j contains all d_j^v, i.e., the matrix holds at position (i, j) the derivative d_j^{i-j}. We may thus compute all those positions (i, j) with $i \geq j$ in parallel whose data dependencies have been resolved, i.e., for which the result at $(i - 1, j)$ is available (if $i > j$) respectively the result at $(i - 1, j - 1)$ is available (if $i = j$).

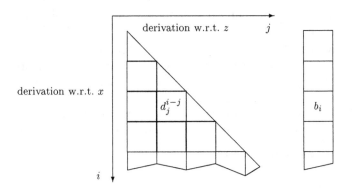

Fig. 3. The matrix of partial derivations

In order to allow an efficient implementation, the algorithm must increase the *granularity* of the parallel computation by letting each task compute multiple elements of the matrix: we partition the triangular matrix into square blocks of m^2 elements (for some blocking factor m) and let each task (i, j) compute the partial derivatives of the block with upper left corner (i, j). The blocks along the diagonal boundary of the triangular matrix are themselves triangular such that the corresponding tasks only need to compute $\frac{1}{2}(m^2 - m)$ elements.

All tasks are created by a manager program which itself computes iteratively the d_u^0, i.e., the derivatives along the diagonal boundary of the matrix. When the manager has computed all those derivatives that represent the diagonal boundary of a triangular block, it starts a corresponding task that computes this block. Whenever a task has terminated, the manager starts a new task for computing that square block that is adjacent to the lower boundary of the result block.

Actually, the result of a task need not be the values of all d_u^v in the corresponding block because we are only interested in

1. the last line of the block which is required by the task computing the adjacent block (this result need not be returned to the main program but can be put into a shared space from which the other task can retrieve it);
2. the greatest common divisor of each line of the block which is required to compute the greatest common divisor of the whole matrix line (this result is returned to the manager program).

Since the gcd is commutative and associative, the program may receive in any order the results computed by the tasks of line i and combine them with the current value of b_i. In a final step, b_{i+1} is then combined with b_i.

We utilize the p processors by the following *scheduling strategy*: Initially, the manager creates tasks for the first p triangular blocks. Whenever a task terminates, we "enable" the task that computes the adjacent square block; if a terminated task has computed a triangular block (and it was not one of the p initial tasks), we also enable the subsequent triangular block. Among all enabled blocks, we choose a block with minimum line index (its computation may make the computation of blocks with larger indices superfluous). When the termination criterion is detected in line i, only those tasks will be started that operate on lines with indices less than i; when no more task is active, the algorithm terminates.

The algorithm can be formalized as follows:

> $(b, n) :=$ **derivatives**(p)
> $T := \{\text{task } (im, im) : i = 0 \ldots p - 1\}$
> $n := \deg(p)$
>   **while** $T \neq \emptyset$ **do**
>   wait for some task $(i, j) \in T$ and remove it from T
>   update $b_i \ldots b_{i+m-1}$ and n
>   enable $(i + m, j)$
>   **if** $i = j$ **then** enable $(i + m, j + m)$ **end**
>   disable all (i, j) with $i \geq n$
>   **if** there is some enabled (i, j) with minimum i **then**
>   disable it and add task (i, j) to T
>   **end**
>   **end**
>   **for** i **from** 0 **to** $n - 1$ **do**
> $b_{i+1} := \gcd(b_i, b_{i+1})$
>   **end**
> **end**

We have implemented this algorithm in Distributed Maple [11]. Figure 4 illustrates by one example the dynamic behavior of the implementation (with

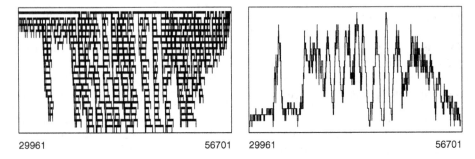

29961   56701   29961   56701

Fig. 4. Manager-worker parallelism

block size $m = 2$) on 20 Linux PCs with various processors connected by switched 100Mbit Ethernet lines: the left "machine diagram" displays on the vertical axis each machine participating in the session; each line in the diagram represents a task executed on a machine at a particular time. The right "utilization diagram" lists on the vertical axis the number of machines busy at a particular time. The sequential execution of this particular example took on a PIII@450MHz PC 552s; the corresponding parallel computation took 27s.

While the parallelization achieved significant speedup (mostly gained by the fact that the modified order of gcd computations turns out to be more efficient than the one in the sequential algorithm), the utilization diagrams show that there is much room for improvement: rarely all 20 machines are busy, in average only about 50% of the computing resources are utilized. Apparently, the manager is not able to issue parallel tasks at a rate that is sufficiently high to provide idle machines with work, i.e., the explicit task scheduling becomes a performance bottleneck. It also does not help to increase the block size: while the manager is then no more the bottleneck, simply too few tasks are generated to saturate all processors and the overall execution time increases.

5   Dataflow Parallelism

We now explore a new parallel solution where tasks are implicitly scheduled for execution whenever their data dependencies have been resolved. Having recognized the utilization problem, we also try to exhibit all parallelism inherent in the problem. In a nutshell, we are now heading for a *declarative* approach where the manager program only describes the collection of tasks that have to be executed and leaves the imperative details to the runtime system. Our goal is to have a program of bigger *elegance* that shall also yield good *performance*.

We start the new design by reorganizing the decomposition of the triangle matrix of partial derivatives as shown in Figure 5: we partition the matrix into uniform square blocks of size m^2 (for some blocking factor m) such that each block can be identified by the coordinate (i, j) of its upper point denoting d_i^j and contains all d_u^v with $0 \leq u < i + m$ and $0 \leq v < j + m$. Once d_i^j is known, all

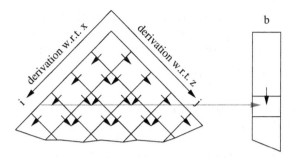

Fig. 5. Data dependencies

other elements of the block can be determined by derivation with respect to x or z, respectively. Like in the original algorithm, we compute within a block the gcd of all d_u^v with same sum $u + v$ which then contributes to the result vector b_{u+v}. Unlike in the original solution, the lines/columns of each block run diagonal to the computation of the derivatives as sketched by the grey arrow in Figure 5.

Since all elements in a block can be computed from the first element d_i^j, we can start the computation of a block when one of the following condition holds:

- $i = 0$ and d_i^{j-1} is known.
- $j = 0$ and d_{i-1}^j is known.
- $i > 0$ and $j > 0$ and
  - d_i^{j-1} is known *or*
  - d_{i-1}^j is known.

In other words, while a block $(0, j)$ at the right boundary of the triangle depends on its unique upper neighbor $(0, j - m)$ (because it needs d_0^{j-1}) and a block $(i, 0)$ at the left boundary depends on its unique upper neighbor $(i - m, j)$ (because it needs d_{i-1}^j), a block (i, j) in the inner of the triangle depends on *one* of its two upper neighbors $(i, j - m)$ and $(i - m, j)$ and can be computed whenever one of these neighbors has delivered d_i^{j-1} or d_{i-1}^j.

Let n_x be the degree of p in x, let n_z be the degree of p in z, and define $n := \min(n_x, n_z)$. Since $d_{n_x}^j$ and $d_i^{n_z}$ are constant, we know that b_n (the gcd of b_{n-1} and of all d_u^v with $u + v = n$) is constant and that therefore the computation terminates with some $k \leq n$. We therefore need to create only tasks (i, j) for which $i + j \leq n$; in the course of the computation it may turn out that $k < n$ and that therefore those tasks (i, j) with $i + j > k$ are not required any more and may be stopped. We denote by

$$\text{tasks}(k) := \{(i, j) : i + j = k \wedge i \bmod m = 0 \wedge j \bmod m = 0\}$$

the set of all task positions (i, j) such that $i + j = k$.

The manager program starts the tasks in some order compatible with the task dependencies and passes to each task (apart from the initial one which receives the input polynomial p) the references to those tasks that the new task potentially depends on. Then the program waits for all tasks (i, j) in the order of increasing $i + j$, combines the computed gcds with the vector b and signals by updating n whether the computation can be prematurely terminated. All tasks whose results are not required any more are then stopped:

$(b, n) :=$ **derivatives**(p)
$\quad n := \min(n_x, n_z)$
$\quad$ **for** k **from** 0 **to** n **by** m **do**
$\quad\quad$ **for** (i, j) **in** tasks(k) **do**
$\quad\quad\quad$ **if** $i = 0 \wedge j = 0$ **then** $t_{i,j} :=$ **start** task(i, j, m, p)
$\quad\quad\quad$ **else if** $i = 0$ **then** $t_{i,j} :=$ **start** task$_\mathrm{R}(i, j, m, t_{i,j-1})$
$\quad\quad\quad$ **else if** $j = 0$ **then** $t_{i,j} :=$ **start** task$_\mathrm{L}(i, j, m, t_{i-1,j})$
$\quad\quad\quad$ **else** $t_{i,j} :=$ **start** task$_\mathrm{I}(i, j, m, t_{i,j-1}, t_{i-1,j})$
$\quad\quad$ **end**
$\quad$ **end**
$\quad$ **for** k **from** 0 **to** n **by** m **do**
$\quad\quad$ $tset := \{t_{i,j} : (i, j) \in \text{tasks}(k)\}$
$\quad\quad$ **while** $tset \neq \emptyset \wedge n = \min(n_x, n_z)$ **do**
$\quad\quad\quad$ $t :=$ **select** $tset$
$\quad\quad\quad$ $(\_, \_, g) :=$ **wait** t
$\quad\quad\quad$ update $b_{i+j} \ldots b_{(i+m)+(j+m)}$ and n
$\quad\quad\quad$ $tset := tset\text{-}\{t\}$
$\quad\quad$ **end**
$\quad$ **end**
$\quad$ **for** k **from** $n + m$ **to** $\min(n_x, n_z)$ **by** m **do**
$\quad\quad$ **for** $(i, j) \in \text{tasks}(k)$ **do stop** $t_{i,j}$; **end**
$\quad$ **end**
$\quad$ **for** $t \in tset$ **do stop** t **end**
end

The initial task computes, starting with p, the first square of derivatives and returns the "boundary derivatives" d_{i+m}^j and d_i^{j+m} (for use by the neighbor tasks) and the gcd of the derivatives (for the manager program):

$(p_1, p_2, g) :=$ **task**(i, j, m, p)
$\quad$ compute all d_u^v with $i \leq u < i + m \wedge j \leq v < j + m$
$\quad$ $(p_1, p_2) := (d_{i+m}^j, d_i^{j+m})$
$\quad$ **for** k **from** 0 **to** $2m$ **do**
$\quad\quad$ $g_k := \gcd\{d_u^v : i \leq u < i + m \wedge j \leq v < j + m \wedge u + v = k\}$
$\quad$ **end**
end

The other tasks can then be formalized with the help of above description:

$(p_1, p_2, g) :=$ **task**$_\mathrm{L}(i, j, m, t)$ $\qquad$ $(p_1, p_2, g) :=$ **task**$_\mathrm{R}(i, j, m, t)$
$\quad$ $((p, \_), \_) :=$ **wait** t $\qquad\qquad\quad$ $((\_, p), \_) :=$ **wait** t
$\quad$ $(p_1, p_2, g) :=$ **task**$(i, j, m, \frac{\partial p}{\partial x})$ $\quad$ $(p_1, p_2, g) :=$ **task**$(i, j, m, \frac{\partial p}{\partial z})$
end $\qquad\qquad\qquad\qquad\qquad\qquad$ **end**

$(p_1, p_2, g) := \text{task}_I(i, j, m, tr, tl)$
  $t := \text{select}\{tr, tl\}$
  $\text{if } t = tr$
    $\text{then } (p_1, p_2, g) := \text{task}_R(i, j, m, t)$
    $\text{else } (p_1, p_2, g) := \text{task}_L(i, j, m, t)$
  end
end

An "inner" task selects non-deterministically the result of one of the two neighbor tasks (whichever is available first) and, depending on the selection, proceeds like a task on the right boundary respectively on the left boundary. Actually, a task (i, j) needs not return the boundary results d^j_{i+m} and d^{j+m}_i to the manager program (which is only interested in the gcd vector g); instead it may put the results into a shared space from which the other tasks may retrieve them (actually a task can do this ahead of the rest of its computation such that a subsequent task becomes enabled before its predecessor has terminated). Consequently, each task needs not receive references to other tasks but only the locations of shared data where it may find the boundary results. The main program creates these locations and passes to each task the location of its own result and the locations of the results it depends on. To avoid race conditions between producer and consumer, such a shared data item needs to be *self-synchronized*: as long as it is empty, the consumer gets blocked on an attempt to retrieve its content; the consumer is released only when the producer provides the content.

The main differences of the new algorithm to the original one are as follows:

1. **Matrix Decomposition:** the new algorithm uses a more regular decomposition. This has the advantage that each task computes the same number of derivatives m^2 the price that each task returns a gcd vector of double length. However, the new decomposition strategy is not a characterizing feature; both strategies can be applied in both algorithms.

2. **Task Synchronization:** the new algorithm uses implicit synchronization based on task dependencies. It thus becomes much simpler than the original one where dependencies were explicitly maintained to schedule exactly one task per processor at every time. Thus the new algorithm should yield more parallelism and overcome the utilization problem discussed in the previous section. On the other side, creating many tasks at once (many of which may become activated and blocked) means larger memory requirements. Thus greater simplicity and better processor utilization at the price of larger memory usage are the main distinguishing features of the new solution.

3. **Result Values:** in the new algorithm, each task returns two derivatives and a gcd vector as a result; the old algorithm returned a vector of derivatives together with the gcd vector. This is an inefficiency in the original algorithm that was not previously recognized because of a focus on the behavior of the sequential algorithm where all but one derivatives in a line are constructed from the previous line by derivation with respect to variable x. It would have also sufficed to communicate a single derivative (the left lower corner of the

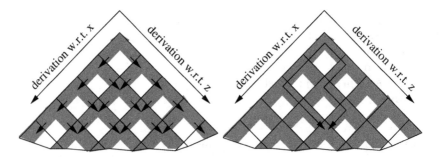

Fig. 6. Data dependencies and sample dependency paths

triangle/matrix) from one task to its successor, since the fist line of each square block can be computed by derivation with respect to z.

4. **Result Timing:** A task may put the computed boundary polynomials into a shared data space and thus enable the computation of two neighboring tasks tasks *before* it performs the remainder of its computation which is not required to enable other tasks. In this way, tasks may become active earlier and the utilization increase faster than in the original algorithm. As an illustration, the non-shaded areas in the left diagram in Figure 6 denote those elements of the derivation matrix which are *not* required to enable any task to compute its results. Again, a similar optimization might have been performed in the original algorithm.

5. **Non-determinism:** the new algorithm does not specify which of the two possible predecessor tasks returns the boundary polynomial that enables the further execution of an inner task. An inner task may thus be enabled by different paths of task dependencies as illustrated by the right diagram in Figure 6 that shows two possible paths that enable a particular task.

6. **Speculation:** the new algorithm exhibits more speculation than the original one, i.e., it starts more tasks whose result may turn out to be not required any more . In the original algorithm, on each of the p machines at most one task was active of a time, such that at most $p - 1$ tasks may become superfluous. In the new algorithm, about *all* tasks are initially created before starting to check for termination. Thus, depending on the actual input, many of the created tasks may become superfluous.

How far the speculated differences between original and new algorithm are actually relevant, is experimentally investigated in the following section.

6   Experimental Results

We have implemented in Distributed Maple the algorithm described in the previous section (including the optimization of using shared data spaces). The new implementation required about 140 lines of Maple code (70 lines for the main program) while the original one required 200 lines (140 for the main program); i.e. the size of the source code was reduced by 30% (50% for the main program).

Behavior. We have benchmarked the program in our local network with 20 Linux PCs with various Pentium class processors connected by switched 100MBit Ethernet lines; such a "Beowulf cluster" is currently the most suitable one for Distributed Maple applications. We have executed the sample benchmark problems as described in Section 4 and illustrate in Figures 7 two executions with block sizes $m = 4$ and $m = 5$ (which generally gave best results).

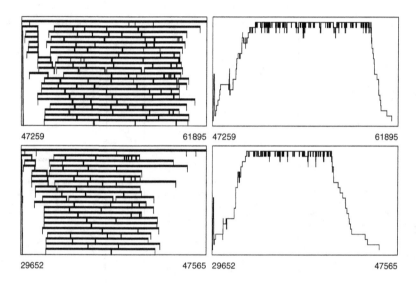

Fig. 7. Dataflow parallelism (block sizes 4 and 5)

All in all, the algorithm proceeds in the following phases:

1. all tasks are started and get immediately blocked (short activities on the left boundary of the machine diagram followed by empty space),
2. the first task is executed and lets other tasks resume execution which in turn let other tasks resume while the early tasks terminate again (task gap in the upper left part of the diagram);
3. more and more tasks get executed and utilization increases to maximum (task gap is filled),
4. many tasks are executed yielding maximum utilization (large block of tasks),
5. a few leftover tasks remain to be executed and the utilization drops to one (empty space on right boundary of diagram).

Figure 7 shows that the frontend node (top line) has several tasks executed at the very end of the computation while no more other nodes are active; this comes from multiple tasks that were early scheduled to the frontend and got blocked on data dependencies such that these tasks had to be later resumed and completed.

Comparing these diagrams with those for the old algorithm in Figure 4 illustrate dramatic differences: In the new algorithm with $m = 4$, after the startup phase which takes 20% of the execution time, all 20 machines get saturated and compute tasks for 65% of the whole computation time. After that, the utilization curve drops rather sharply such that the final phase takes only 15% of the computation. The overall utilization rate is about 75%. In the $m = 5$ case, the startup phase yields earlier higher utilization rate; however, load imbalances in the later phase (caused by slower machines) let the utilization curve drop earlier.

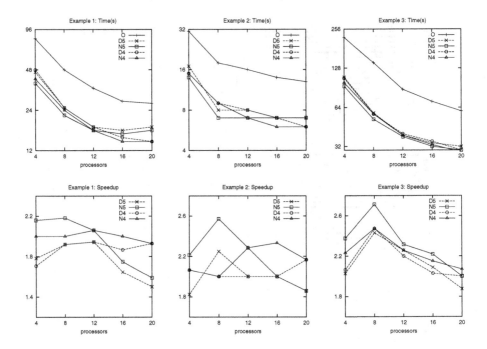

Fig. 8. Execution times and speedups

Execution Time. The actual execution times of the new algorithm in comparison with the execution of the old algorithm are listed in Figure 8: the top row of diagrams shows the execution time of the programs, the bottom row shows the speedup that the new algorithm gains *over the original one*. The comparison is based on the algorithm variants labelled as follows:

– O: the original algorithm.
– N4, N5: the new algorithm with non-deterministic task selection in the main program and in task$_I$ with block sizes $m = 4$ and $m = 5$.
– D4, D5: the new algorithm with deterministic selection in the main program $(t := \mathrm{first}(tset))$ and in task$_I$ $(t := tl)$ with block sizes $m = 4$ and $m = 5$.

All variants of the new algorithm are considerably faster than the original version with an average speedup (compared to the original version) of 1.8 (Example 1) respectively 2.2 (Examples 2 and 3). We could thus reduce the sequential execution time from 552s, 198s, respectively 1798s on a PIII@450MHz PC down to a parallel execution time of 14s, 6s, respectively 29s. The fact that the speedups are drastically superlinear is caused by the changed order in which the greatest common divisors are computed (also in the original parallel algorithm); this is a hint for a general algorithmic improvement of the sequential algorithm.

Block Size. Comparing the algorithm variants N4 and N5, we see that for smaller processor numbers ($p \leq 12$) N5 is better while N4 seems to have some advantage for larger processor numbers. This result is consistent with our previous observation that larger block sizes may cause some load imbalance in the final phases of the computation (which is more significant for larger processor numbers). A similar trend can be seen when comparing D4 and D5.

Non-determinism. For analyzing the effect of non-determinism on the changes of task dependencies, we have counted for a sample run with 20 machines the number of times that the non-deterministic task synchronization operation was called and how often it was not the first task that was selected because its result was not available (i.e., how often non-deterministic task selection actually made a difference compared to the deterministic variant): in the main program, it was in 44% of all non-deterministic calls not the first task that was selected; in $task_I$, this was in 19% of all calls the case. Thus there is a significant difference in synchronization dependencies, albeit two times more in the main program than in the individual inner tasks.

For analyzing the effect of non-determinism on the actual execution times, we compare the algorithm variants N5 with D5 and N4 with D4. We see that N5 is in many cases about 10% faster than D5, the application of non-deterministic brings a significant (but not dramatic) improvement in performance. In the comparison N4 versus D4, this effect is not that significant but still visible especially for smaller number of processors.

Figure 9 illustrate the differences in the dynamic behaviors of D5 and N5 by the trace of an execution with 20 processors. The difference between non-deterministic and deterministic execution is visually captured by additional "gaps" in the traces of individual machines for the deterministic variant; the non-deterministic variant keeps after an initial phase processors continuously busy. The large block sizes becomes especially significant in the later phases of the algorithm where few late tasks may hamper the completion of the algorithm. The smaller the block sizes are, the better the overall utilization becomes also in the final phases of the computation.

Speculation. In all three examples, the amount of speculation (tasks whose result was not required) was not significant. The only tasks (i, j) that ever became superfluous where those with maximum $i + j$, i.e., those at the bottom of the triangular matrix (because other tasks in that row already yielded a gcd with constant degree).

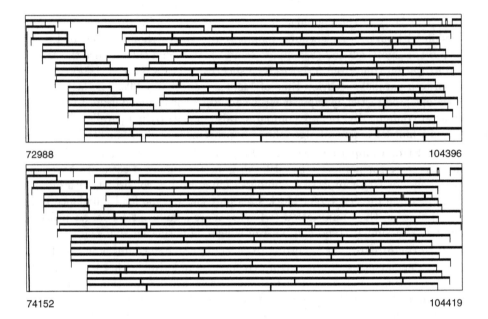

72988   104396

74152   104419

Fig. 9. Deterministic vs non-deterministic selection

7   Conclusions

We have rewritten a Distributed Maple application from a low-level imperative to a more high-level declarative style and compared the results. This has demonstrated that the *dataflow* style of computing with implicit task synchronizations can considerably improve the performance: we have achieved a *speedup of 2* compared to the original solution where the program explicitly schedules tasks for execution. While the original version is not able to saturate all processors, the dataflow solution yields good utilization even for a larger processor number. We have also shown that a declarative solution that uses *non-determinism* in order not to over-specify task dependencies may yield a *performance improvement of 10%* compared to a more imperative program that constrains data dependencies further than algorithmically required.

Both results demonstrate that also in Distributed Maple a more declarative solutions that does not care about scheduling decisions may be more efficient than one where the programmer tries to keep explicit control over all aspects of the computation. Thus parallel declarative programs need not be a priori less efficient than parallel imperative ones. The presented work has been performed in preparation of a study that will compare parallel algorithms implemented in Distributed Maple with corresponding declarative versions that will (on the basis of a recently developed Haskell-Maple interface) use the para-functional language Glasgow Parallel Haskell GPH.

References

1. L. Bernadin. Maple on a Massively Parallel, Distributed Memory Machine. In *PASCO'97 — Second Int. Symp. on Parallel Symbolic Computation*, pages 217–222, Maui, Hawaii, July 20–22, 1997. ACM Press.
2. A. Diaz and E. Kaltofen. FoxBox: A System for Manipulating Symbolic Objects in Black Box Representation. In O. Gloor, editor, *ISSAC'98 Int. Symp. on Symbolic and Algebraic Comp.* ACM Press, New York, 1998.
3. H.W. Loidl, P.W. Trinder, K. Hammond, S.B. Junaidu, R.G. Morgan, and S.L. Peyton Jones. Engineering Parallel Symbolic Programs in GPH. *Concurrency — Practice and Experience*, 11(12):701–751, 1999.
4. H.W. Loidl. LinSolv: A Case Study in Strategic Parallelism. *Proceedings of the Glasgow Workshop on Functional Programming*, Ullapool, Scotland, 1997.
5. C. Mittermaier. Parallel Algorithms in Constructive Algebraic Geometry. Master's thesis, Johannes Kepler University, Linz, Austria, 2000.
6. Christian Mittermaier, Wolfgang Schreiner, and Franz Winkler. A Parallel Symbolic-Numerical Approach to Algebraic Curve Plotting. In V. Gerdt and E. W. Mayr, editors, *CASC-2000, 3rd Int. Workshop on Computer Algebra in Scientific Computing*, Samarkand, Uzbekistan, October 5–9, 2000. Springer, Berlin.
7. M. Mnuk and F. Winkler. CASA - A System for Computer Aided Constructive Algebraic Geometry. In J. Calmet and C. Limongelli, editors, *DISCO'96 — Int. Symposium on the Design and Implementation of Symbolic Computation Systems*, volume 1128 of *LNCS*, pages 297–307, Karsruhe, Germany, 1996. Springer, Berlin.
8. Wolfgang Schreiner. Distributed Maple — User and Reference Manual. Technical Report 98-05, RISC-Linz, Johannes Kepler University, Linz, Austria, May 1998. http://www.risc.uni-linz.ac.at/software/distmaple.
9. Wolfgang Schreiner. Developing a Distributed System for Algebraic Geometry. In Barry H.V. Topping, editor, *EURO-CM-PAR'99 Third Euro-conference on Parallel and Distributed Computing for Computational Mechanics*, pages 137–146, Weimar, Germany, March 20-25, 1999. Civil-Comp Press, Edinburgh.
10. Wolfgang Schreiner and Hans-Wolfgang Loidl. GHC-Maple Interface, November 2000. http://www.risc.uni-linz.ac.at/software/ghc-maple.
11. Wolfgang Schreiner, Christian Mittermaier, and Franz Winkler. Analyzing Algebraic Curves by Cluster Computing. In Peter Kacsuk and Gabriele Kotsis, editors, *Distributed and Parallel Systems - From Instruction Parallelism to Cluster Computing, Proceedings of DAPSYS'2000, 3rd Austrian-Hungarian Workshop on Distributed and Parallel Systems*, pages 175–184, Balatonfüred, Lake Balaton, Hungary, September 10–13, 2000. Kluwer Academic Publishers, Boston.
12. Wolfgang Schreiner, Christian Mittermaier, and Franz Winkler. On Solving a Problem in Algebraic Geometry by Cluster Computing. In A. Bode et al (eds.), *Euro-Par 2000*, volume 1900 of *Lecture Notes in Computer Science*, pages 1196–1200, Munich, Germany, August 29 - September 1, 2000. Springer, Berlin.
13. Wolfgang Schreiner, Christian Mittermaier, and Franz Winkler. Plotting Algebraic Space Curves by Cluster Computing. In X.-S. Gao and D. Wang, editors, *ASCM'2000, 4th Asian Symposium on Computer Mathematics*, Chiang Mai, Thailand, December 17-21, 2000. World Scientific Publishers, Singapore/River Edge.
14. K. Siegl. Parallelizing Algorithms for Symbolic Computation Using ‖MAPLE‖. In *Fourth ACM SIGPLAN Symposium on Principles and Practice of Parallel Programming*, pages 179–186, San Diego, California, May 19-22, 1993. ACM Press.

Communication Interface CoIn

Evgueni Sidorov, Sergey Bobkov, and Sergey Aryashev

Research Institute for System Studies,
Russian Academy of Sciences,
Moscow, Russia
{esidorov,bobkov,aserg}@cs.niisi.ras.ru

Abstract. The paper presents a communication interface CoIn. The interface is developed in the Research Institute for Systems Studies of Russian Academy of Sciences. The interface is intended for building high perfomance distributed computer systems, massive parallel processor computers and clusters.

1 Introduction

High perfomance parallel computer systems require more powerful communication subsystems than the conventional IPC tools of ordinary operating systems can provide. Specialized communication interfaces are being developed, that accords best to the classes of tasks and quality of inter-process communications inherited in high performance parallel computer systems.

Communication interface CoIn represents a kind of such communication subsystem. The interface is developed with taking into account the expirience of a number of firms dealing with such systems. CoIn is based on such open standards and specifications as Virtual Interface (VI), InfiniBand, and Myrinet.

Virtual Interface is an open specification developed by Intel, Compaq and Microsoft [1]. The VI represents an architecture for the interface between high perfomance network hardware and computer systems. The goal of this architecture is to improve the performance of the distribed applications by reducing the latency associated critical message passing operations. This goal is attained by substantially reducing the system software processing required to exchange messages compared to traditional network interface architectures.

The InfiniBand Archeticture Specification is developed by a group of vendors, with Intel, IBM, Compaq, Dell, Hewlett-Packard, Microsoft and Sun Microsystems among them [2]. InfiniBand describes a first order interconnect technology for interconnecting processor nodes and I/O nodes to form a system area network [3].

Myrinet represents the architecture of a high-performance inter-computer packet switching network [4]. Specification of Myrinet was developed by Myricom Inc. The standard includes, either directly or by reference, the specification of the Data Link level, timing information, character set, signals, and the details of the connectors.

V. Malyshkin (Ed.): PaCT 2001, LNCS 2127, pp. 344–349, 2001.

2   Architectural Scope of CoIn

Traditional network architectures does not provide the performance requred by
modern distributed applications, largely due to the host-processing overhead of
kernel-based transport stacks. These problems are addressed in the CoIn architecture by moving the network much closer to the application, increasing its
functionality, and better matching its features to application requirements. The
CoIn architecture looks like a four-layer communication stack (see Fig. 1).

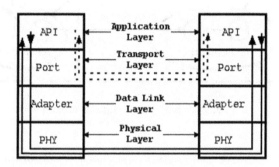

Fig. 1. Four-layer communication stack.

The API layer includes applications running in parallel on the nodes of the
system. The Transport layer is represented by ports. The ports are global objects through which applications interface with each other. The Data link and
Physical layers can be of two types. In case the interfacing ports are located
within the same operating system, these ports communicate through the conventional IPC, called shared memory. In case the interfacing ports are located on
different nodes of the computer, the ports communicate through the Myrinet-like
communication media.

In the traditional network architecture, the operating system virtualizes the
network hardware into a set of logical communication endpoints available to
network consumers. The OS multiplexes access to the hardware among these
endpoints. In most cases, the operating system also implements protocols that
make communication between endpoints reliable. This model permits the interface between the network hardware and the operating system to be very simple.
The drawback of this organization is that all communication operations require
a call or trap into the operating system kernel, which can be quite expensive
to execute. The demultiplexing process and reliability protocols also tend to be
computationally expensive.

The CoIn architecture eliminates the system-processing overhead of the traditional model by providing each consumer process with a protected, directly
accessible interface to the network hardware - a Port. Each port represents
a communication endpoint (see Fig. 2). A process may own one or multiple

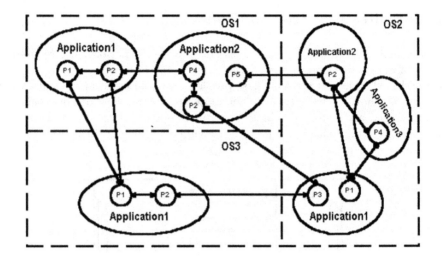

Fig. 2. Port-based comminucation model.

ports exported by one or more network adapters. A network adapter performs the endpoint virtualization directly and subsumes the tasks of multiplexing, de-multiplexing, and data transfer scheduling normally performed by an OS kernel and device driver. An adapter may completely ensure the reliability of communication between interfacing ports. Alternatively, this task may be shared with transport protocol software loaded into application process. The adapter has a direct access to the virtual memory space of processes involving CoIn. Adapter can perform transfers directly from virtual memory of one process into virtual memory of other process eliminating the need for calls or traps into the operating system kernel.

The CoIn is a message-passing interface. All data transfers are done through message passing between ports. Interface supports two kinds of communication operations:

1. Send/Receive
2. Remote Direct Memory Access

In the first case, the communicating processes should be aware of each other, and each control structure for Send operation on the sending side should be accompanied with the corresponding Receive descriptor on its peer at the receiving side. The RDMA operations can be performed just remotely without need for notifying the peer process. These operations are faster than operations of the Send/Receive model. Alternatively, the RDMA operations can be performed with notifications of the peer process.

The CoIn has three levels of reliability. Different ports within one process can have different levels of reliability. Communications can be done only between the ports with the same reliability levels.

Ports can communicate either in datagram mode or in mode with logical connection. Besides, any port can be assigned a logical partition number. Only ports from the same logical partition can communicate.

3   Adapter – Intellectual Communication Controller

An adapter performs a substantial part of communication functions. A generelized model of adapter is shown in Figure 3.The model corresponds to the model of adapter in the Virtual Interface architecture [1].

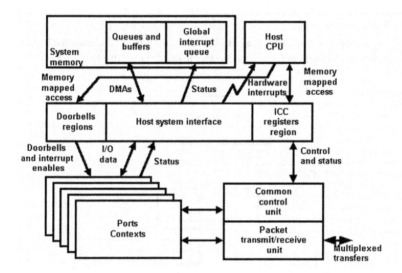

Fig. 3. Generelized model of adapter.

A host processor has access to adapter through the memory region of the I/O memory space. Processor can access only a register set of the ICC, adapter memory and doorbell regions.

The adapter has direct access to the virtual memory space of the processes. Adapter can handle the following objects in the memory:

– operation descriptor queues
– completion queues
– buffers of shared memories
– global interrupt queue

These objects can be directly accessed by the adapter, and thus they must be registered in the operating system. Being registered in the operating system means that the page of memory is protected from swapping and reordering, and information on the virtual to physical address translation for this page must be placed into the adapter.

Adapter can generate hardware interrupts to the host processor. These interrupts are traped and handled by the corresponding kernel agent of the operating system.

Functionally adapter includes the units as follows:

- Host System Interface
- Common Control Unit
- Ports Contexts Storing and Processing Unit
- Packet Transmit/Receieve Unit

All these units cooperating with each other can effectively perform communication operations of different kinds in partially autonomous mode. In this mode the host CPU is underloaded from performing a substantial part of communication interface functions. However, there is a mode when the host CPU controls all the functions of the adapter. In this mode the CPU deals with registers of the adapter and manages all data flows through the adapter.

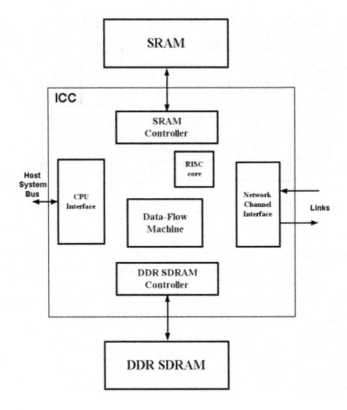

Fig. 4. Architecture of Intellectual Communication Controller

Architecturally adapter includes Intellectual Communication Controller (ICC) and local memory arrays. All communication functions are implemented by the ICC. Memory arrays are used for temporary packet storing and for storing control and service information, In addition, the memory is used by the RISC-core of ICC for program and data storing.

ICC includes the following units:

- System Bus Interface
- Communication Media Channel Interface
- Local Memory Controllers
- RISC-core
- Data-Flow Machine

Communication functions can be implemented exclusively with the RISC-core of ICC at micro-code level. In addition, the most time critical functions can be implemented in hardware. The Data-Flow Machine represents a set of hardware implemented communication functions.

4   Conclusion

A communication interface CoIn was presented. The interface can be used for developing parallel computer systems, massive parallel processor systems and clusters. The interface represents an architecture different from the traditional network architectures. The architecture to the better extent satisfies the demands of high perfomance parallel computer systems executing strongly tighted distributed tasks.

References

1. Virtual Interface Architecture Specification. Version 1.0. Compaq Computer Corp., Intel Corporation, Microsoft Corporation.December 16, 1997
2. InfiniBand Cavalry to the Rescue. By Infiniband Trade Assiciation. Buses and Boards, September/October 2000
3. InfiniBand Architecture Specification Volume 1. Release 1.0. October 24, 2000. Final
4. Myrinet-on-Vme Protocol Specification Draft Standard. VITA 26-199x, Draft 1.1. August 31, 1998
5. The GM Message Passing System. Myricom Inc. 1999

Design of a Tool for Providing Dynamic Network Information to an Application*

Masha Sosonkina[1] and Gan Chen[1]

Department of Computer Science, University of Minnesota, Duluth,
320 Heller Hall, 10 University Drive, Duluth, Minnesota 55812-2496
{masha,gchen}@d.umn.edu

Abstract. We propose a design of a simple tool that can be used by
a distributed application to discover the relevant network information
dynamically. The simplicity is a key design feature: the tool can be used
without multiple modifications of the application code. The timely notification of the application is performed using a callback mechanism which
minimizes the application idle time. The network information is gathered
and analyzed simultaneously with application execution. We show that
empowering an application with a knowledge of network characteristics
provides insights into possible application adaptation mechanisms and
into the causes of communication delays.

Keywords: network information collection, callback application notification, application adaptations.

1 Introduction

The need for distributed resources has been widely accepted in scientific community for performing computationally-intensive tasks. Applications are made
portable across various interconnecting technologies. However, for a distributed
application it is difficult to attain a good performance on different interconnections since they are often shared among several communicating programs. The
performance of the interconnections varies with static (configuration) characteristics and dynamic network conditions that change depending on the network
load and communication distance. At present, the majority of the network protocols permit no reservation of network resources for the application use. A growing
number of distributed applications is computationally-intensive scientific applications which have no means to learn the network information and to request a
particular amount of network resources. For such and many other applications,
it is desirable to have a mechanism that provides the network information transparently to the application programmer or user, so that the burden of handling
the low level network information is shifted to a network developer. Many research projects have focused on this pressing and complex task (see, e.g., [2], [7],

---

* This work was supported in part by the Minnesota Supercomputing Institute

V. Malyshkin (Ed.): PaCT 2001, LNCS 2127, pp. 350–357, 2001.
© Springer-Verlag Berlin Heidelberg 2001

[3], and [11]) targeting different network architectures and configurations. With a knowledge of network performance, the application may adapt itself to perform the communication more efficiently. The adaptation features are, of course, application-specific. For a scientific application, it may be beneficial to perform more local computations (iterations) waiting for the data to arrive [10]. For a file transfer, an adaptation may consist of choosing a server with a better connection [4].

Our first goal is to supply an application with the network information only *if this information becomes critical*, i.e., when the values for the network characteristics to be observed fall outside of some feasible bounds. The feasibility is determined by an application and may be conveyed to the network information collector as parameter. Note that these bounds might not be attained under the particular network conditions since the end-to-end reservations are difficult to enforce in the "best effort" network protocols with different administrative systems owning parts of the network. This *selective notification* approach is rather advantageous both when there is little change in the dynamic network characteristics and when the performance is very changeable. In the former case, there is no overhead associated with processing unnecessary information. In the latter, the knowledge of the network may be more accurate since it is obtained more frequently.

The second goal is to augment the application execution with this knowledge of the network while requiring minimum modifications of the application and without involving the user/programmer into the network development effort. We accomplish this goal by using callback mechanisms, implemented similarly to the description in [6].

This paper is organized as follows. Section 2 describes the design of our network information collection and justifies the design choices made. Section 3 presents a few experiments with a user application. The concluding remarks appear in Section 4.

2   Design of Network Information Collection and Application Notification (NICAN)

We consider a host-based design in which the information about the network is collected in the endpoints. The primary justification for this approach is that it does not require any access to the routers from the user and assumes no particular software configuration on a router. Thus application programmers can easily utilize our tool without network manager's help. The first aspect of the design is that each host, which participates in the distributed computation, may have its own NICAN that alerts the host when certain events happen in the network connection. When initializing NICAN on a computing node, an application may request NICAN to monitor one or several network characteristics, such as an effective throughput on an external (network) interface of the node or the latency between this node and a neighbor node participating in distributed computation. Such characteristics may be passed as parameters to NICAN, and thus form a "multirequest", i.e., a single request that contains a number of network events which NICAN is capable of monitoring.

The signaling mechanism of NICAN delivers network information in a timely fashion such that there is no instrumenting of an application with, say, call-queries directed to the network interface. In fact, the initialization of the NICAN tool may be the *only* non-application specific modification required in the application code to interface with NICAN. The application is alerted only if the network characteristics monitored fall outside the certain bounds, which could be either inserted in the multirequest by the application at NICAN initialization or taken as defaults by NICAN. Such types of bounds as maximum and minimum values of the effective network bandwidth (throughput) and latency seem the most common among distributed applications and are often sufficient for an application to make decisions on proper adaptations to the network conditions. Thus our design enables application notification with the information based on the boundary values of these types. Similar to the case described in [6], our design needs a new signaling mechanism that passes to the application the information processed by NICAN. (This is not always possible with the standard signaling techniques of an operating system such as Unix.) If NICAN sends a signal to an application, then an application may need to engage its adaptive mechanisms. To minimize changes inside the application code, we propose to encapsulate application adaptation in a notification handler (signal handler) invoked upon the signal receipt. This signal handler can contain an adaptation code with a possible access to some application variables. One way to implement this access is to use shared memory paradigm as provided by Unix.

Once initialized by an application, local NICAN runs independently from the application. Therefore it may probe the network as often as deemed necessary without causing an application to wait for the result as it happens in the query-based mechanisms. The callback approach decouples the network analysis from the application execution which may lead to more precise results of the analysis. Multiple probes of the network are recorded to estimate the network performance over a longer period of time. They may also be useful for the prediction of network performance in such common cases as when an iterative process lies at the core of application.

In NICAN, a process of collecting the network information is separated from its other functions, such as notification, and is encapsulated into a module that can be chosen depending on the types of the network, network software configuration, and the information to be collected. For example, assume that the current throughput is requested by an application during its execution. Then, if the network has the Simple Network Management Protocol (SNMP) [5] installed, NICAN will choose to utilize the SNMP information for throughput calculation. Otherwise, some benchmarking procedure – more general than probing SNMP but also more costly – could be applied to determine the throughput. To determine the latency between two hosts, the system utilities such as `ping` and `traceroute` can be used. NICAN collects latency independently of throughput. Thus, the collection of these two network characteristics is performed simultaneously if the information on both latency and throughput is requested. The modular design enables an easy augmentation of the collection process with new options, which ensures its applicability to a variety of network interconnections.

Figure 1 summarizes our design by depicting a general host-based view of NICAN architecture, which consists of the interface between NICAN and application, the notification mechanism, and the data collection and analysis components. Solid arrows represent the initialization of NICAN from an applications and the launch of the collection module from NICAN. The flows of the application multirequest, NICAN signals, and shared memory accesses are shown as dashed arrows. A detailed information on the design and implementation can be found in [1].

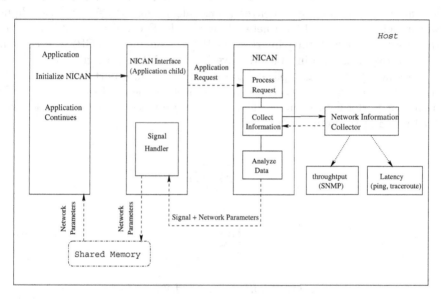

Fig. 1. NICAN architecture

3   Experiments

We have built a prototype of NICAN that uses several different procedures-modules for network information collection. This makes the tool useful for a variety of network types and available network management software. Here we present a set of experiments in which NICAN calculates the bandwidth available to a host by using the information provided by the Simple Network Management Protocol. The SNMP agent can be installed on a host, thus requiring no router access by the user. SNMP collects a set of data in the internal database (MIB). Our prototype of NICAN polls the database periodically. (The time period of polling is determined automatically by NICAN.) Then NICAN sends a signal to an application according to the specified criteria, which is passed as parameters to NICAN. In this experiment, we have used the following criterion: *Report "peak" throughput if it is above 8.5 Mbps AND if the change in throughput is less than 10% AND Report throughput only once.* We call this criterion the *first peak* throughput criterion. The number 8.5 Mbps has been taken based on the characteristics of the network which we used for the experiments. It is a Local Area Network accessed using Ethernet protocol with nominal bandwidth of 10 Mbps. In Figure 2, the interconnection of the hosts we used for testing is presented. NetPIPE [8] is considered as an example of user application. NetPIPE is a network benchmarking program that utilizes the network heavily. Specifically, this application sends over a TCP connection a message of increasing size and measures the time of its delivery, thus calculating the effective throughput, which includes also TCP and network overheads. For a distributed application that uses Message Passing Interface (MPI) [9] (on top of TCP), the communication overhead also includes the overhead for MPI. Since most of the high performance computing applications use MPI to ensure portability across distributed environments, measuring and monitoring the MPI overheard may be useful for performance tuning. Thus NICAN provides a way to interact with MPI-based distributed applications.

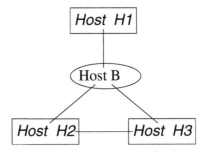

Fig. 2. Interconnection of the hosts used in the experiments

The bandwidth measurements taken by NetPIPE and NICAN are shown in Figure 3. Note that the throughput calculated by NICAN is almost always an upper bound on the bandwidth calculated by NetPIPE. This can be explained by the presence of the transport layer protocol TCP overhead in the measurements by NetPIPE. At the same time, the bandwidth calculated by NICAN is the actual number of all incoming and outgoing packets on the external network interfaces divided by the polling interval. The difference between the measurements is especially pronounced in the beginning of execution, for small messages, and when the bandwidth limitations are reached for large messages which need segmentation. Note that the bandwidth measured by NetPIPE is roughly the same regardless of the LAN topology, whereas the effect of an extra hop (via host B in Figure 2) is noticeable compared with the higher bandwidth values recorded by NICAN along the direct H2–H3 link.

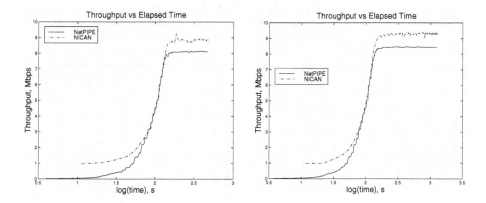

Fig. 3. Simultaneous NetPIPE and NICAN bandwidth measurements: between host H1 and H2 (left), between host H2 and H3 (right)

In our experiments, having the bandwidth delivered by NICAN as a (close) upper bound on the bandwidth of the application ensures that the application does not exhaust the network capacity and can make timely adaptations. We have supplied NetPIPE with a notification handler to react to the *first peak* bandwidth signal delivered by NICAN. In particular, the handler stops the growth of the transmitted messages so that the maximum bandwidth perceived by Net-PIPE is sustained without excessive consumption of computational and network resources. Figure 4 zooms on the occurrence of the *first peak* bandwidth notification. The bandwidth values measured by NetPIPE remain very close with and without invoking adaptation mechanism (solid and dashed lines, respectively, in Figure 4, left), which indicates that the peak bandwidth is reached for a particular message size. NICAN (dashed-dotted and dotted lines) detects the peak bandwidth and notifies NetPIPE at about $t_p = 10^{2.22}$ seconds. On the other hand, for NetPIPE, the times to transmit a message (Figure 4, right) differ greatly beyond t_p.

For the MPI version of NetPIPE (called NetPIPE-MPI), the adaptation is even more important. As seen in Figure 5 (left), adaptive NetPIPE-MPI (solid line) predicts more accurately the maximum throughput of the link. The poor prediction of the non-adaptive application (dashed line) can be attributed to the effects of the MPI buffer configuration, which is system- and implementation-specific. In particular, during the long periods of buffer handling, the link load decreases while the time recording continues. If the MPI buffering delays are overlapped with the communication of some other data, then the throughput (dash-dotted line in Figure 5, right) recorded by NICAN increases reaching nearly the link capacity. Note that the presence of another communicating program (in this case, the TCP version of NetPIPE, the starting point of which is indicated by the circle 0 in Figure 5, right) affects the calculations done by NetPIPE-MPI since NetPIPE-MPI is unaware of competing communication program. On the other hand, the NICAN output suggests that the *first-peak* throughput criterion is achieved and that the adaptations based on this criterion can be invoked.

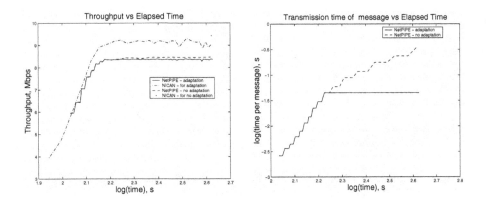

Fig. 4. Performance of NetPIPE with and without invoking adaptation mechanism: bandwidth measurements between H1 and H3 (left) and time to transmit a message (right)

4   Concluding remarks

We have outlined a design of Network Information Collection and Application Notification (NICAN) that emphasizes simplicity of use, modularity, and a call-back application notification mechanism. The tool can estimate the required network parameters either by polling an existing network management software or benchmarking the network connection. A selective notification of an application is implemented using a callback mechanism which provides the ability to pass as parameters the required criteria when the tool is initialized within a given application. Our experiments performed with a tool prototype already show the potential of NICAN. In the future, we plan to conduct extensive experiments on the tool-application interaction, provide a more sophisticated network parameter analysis, and focus on the support for heterogeneous computing platforms.

References

1. G. CHEN, *Providing dynamic network information to distributed applications*, May 2001. Master's Thesis.

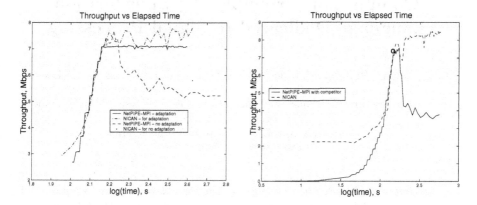

Fig. 5. Simultaneous NetPIPE-MPI and NICAN bandwidth measurements: NetPIPE-MPI version with adaptations (left), NetPIPE-MPI competing with another communicating application (right)

2. D. GUNTER, B. TIERNEY, B. CROWLEY, M. HOLDING, AND J. LEE, *NetLogger: A toolkit for distributed system performance analysis*, in Proceedings of the IEEE Mascots 2000 Conference, 2000.
3. B. LOWEKAMP, N. MILLER, D. SUTHERLAND, T. GROSS, P. STEENKISTE, AND J. SUBHLOK, *A resource query interface for network-aware applications*, Cluster Computing, 2 (1999), pp. 139–151.
4. N. MILLER AND P. STEENKISTE, *Collecting network status information for network-aware application*, in Infocom'00, Tel Aviv, 2000.
5. *NET SNMP project.* Web Site, http://net-snmp.sourceforge.net/.
6. B. D. NOBLE, *Mobile data access*, Tech. Rep. CMU-CS-98-118, School of Computer Science, Carnegie Mellon University, Pittsburgh, PA 15213, 1998. Ph.D. Thesis.
7. W. NORTON AND A. ADAMS, *Project NetSCARF*, ConneXions, 10 (1996).
8. Q. SNELL, A. MIKLER, AND J. GUSTAFSON, *NetPIPE: A network protocol independent performance evaluator*, in IASTED International Conference on Intelligent Information Management and Systems, 6 1996.
9. M. SNIR, S. OTTO, S. HUSS-LEDERMAN, D. WALKER, AND J. DONGARRA, *MPI - The complete Reference*, vol. 1, The MIT Press, second ed., 1998.
10. M. SOSONKINA, *Runtime adaptation of an iterative linear system solution to distributed environments*, in Applied Parallel Computing, PARA'2000, vol. 1947 of Lecture Notes in Computer Science, Berlin, 2001, Springer-Verlag, pp. 132–140.
11. R. WOLSKI, *Forecasting network performance to support dynamic scheduling using the Network Weather Service*, in 6th IEEE Symp. on High Performance Distributed Computing, 1997, pp. 316–325.

Compilation Principle of a Specification Language Dedicated to Signal Processing

Julien Soula[1], Philippe Marquet[1], Alain Demeure[2], and Jean-Luc Dekeyser[1]

[1] Laboratoire d'Informatique Fondamentale de Lille, Université de Lille, France
http://www.lifl.fr
[2] Thomson Marconi Sonar, Sophia-Antipolis, France
http://www.tms-sonar.com

Abstract. ARRAY-OL, developed by Thomson Marconi Sonar, is a programming language dedicated to signal processing. An ARRAY-OL program specifies the dependencies between array elements produced and consumed by tasks. In particular, temporal dependencies may be specified by referencing elements that belong to an infinite dimension of an array.
A basic compilation strategy of ARRAY-OL on a workstation has been defined. This basic compilation does not allow the generation of efficient code for any ARRAY-OL application; specifically those defining infinite arrays. We propose to transform such applications to hierarchical ARRAY-OL applications that may be compiled with ARRAY-OL basic strategy. We introduce a formal representation of ARRAY-OL applications, which is a relation between points of $\mathbb{Z}^n$ spaces; code transformations are applied at this level. In this paper we show how the transformation process is used during the compilation phase of a representative application.

1 Introduction

ARRAY-OL[1], developed by Thomson Marconi Sonar [5], is a programming language dedicated to signal processing (SP). The SP application doamin is characterized by systematic, regular, and massively data-parallel computations.

ARRAY-OL applications are edited in a graphic environment of specification. ARRAY-OL application specification is built on two stages: a global stage describes the application through a directed graph where the nodes (tasks) exchange arrays; a local stage details the calculations performed on the array elements by each node. An ARRAY-OL application directly expresses dependencies between elements of arrays. In particular, temporal dependencies may be specified by references to elements along an infinite dimension of an array. Section 2 presents ARRAY-OL language.

ARRAY-OL compilation targets both dedicated embedded multi-processor computers and workstations or clusters of workstations in a purpose of simulation and debugging of applications.

---

[1] ARRAY-OL™ is a trademark of Thomson Marconi Sonar. It stands for Array Oriented Language.

V. Malyshkin (Ed.): PaCT 2001, LNCS 2127, pp. 358–370, 2001.

A basic strategy of compilation of ARRAY-OL on a workstation was defined. This compilation mechanism can not handle all ARRAY-OL applications. In particular, the manipulation of arrays of infinite dimension is impossible and the use of large arrays is expensive. This compiler is presented in Section 3.

We propose tools to transform ARRAY-OL applications. A given ARRAY-OL application program will be rewritten such that the initial version of the compiler is able to handle (or, at least, to handle more effectively).

These transformations work at the level of a formalism of relations between points of $\mathbb{Z}^n$ spaces: the ODT[2]. The representation of an ARRAY-OL task by the ODT defines the links/dependencies between the elements of the output arrays of the task and those of the input arrays. The transformation principle is detailed in Section 4. Section 5 illustrates the approach with an example. The ODT and their manipulations are studied in Sections 6 and 7. Section 8 compares our approach with others.

2   The ARRAY-OL Language

We briefly introduce the main characteristics of the ARRAY-OL language [5]. An ARRAY-OL application is made up of a task hierarchy [7]. The tasks are themselves data-parallel: they handle arrays.

An ARRAY-OL application is successively expressed in two models. A first global model defines the task scheduling in the form of dependencies between tasks and arrays. A second local model details the elementary actions the tasks realize on array elements.

2.1   Global Model

The global model defines and names arrays and tasks. The arrays are used to organize the dependence graph of tasks on a level: each task takes its inputs from the defined arrays and produces one or more arrays.

The task specification and the detail of the array element usage are hidden at this specification stage.

Array: A Structure for Signal Processing. SP applications are organized around a regular and potentially infinite stream of data. ARRAY-OL captures this stream in arrays with a possible infinite dimension.

Some spatial dimensions of arrays used in SP correspond to sensors. Such sensors may be organized in a circle. Consequently, ARRAY-OL array dimensions wrap around.

2.2   Local Model

For a given task, the local model specification details the operations and accesses to input and output arrays.

---

[2] Opérateurs de Distribution de Tableau (Array Distribution Operators).

An ARRAY-OL task links its output array elements to its input array elements. The role of the task is to produce all the values of its output arrays.

These values are produced through *patterns*. A pattern is a subset of the elements of one array. An output pattern is produced by applying the code associated to the task on patterns of the input arrays. So, a task implantation consists of an iterator constructor; these iterations are independent.

Since ARRAY-OL is restricted to the specification of SP applications, the shape of the patterns, the array tiling by the patterns, and the task code are dedicated to this domain: ad hoc specifications are proposed.

Fitting: Pattern Definition. Patterns are arrays. Equidistant elements in a pattern are equidistant in the array.

A pattern may be defined by an origin in the array and a set of vectors (fitting vectors; one vector is associated to each dimension of the pattern). The other points of the pattern are defined in the array by shifting the origin along the fitting vectors as much as required by the pattern size.

Paving: Tiling of an Array with Its Patterns. Two equidistant output patterns are produced by two equidistant input patterns.

The array paving with patterns is given by a first pattern in each array and a set of paving vectors. The other patterns are defined by a shift of the initial pattern along the paving vectors as much as needed in order to cover the master array. By definition, two patterns of an output array may not overlap.

Component Library. For each paving iteration, a task extracts the input pattern from the input arrays and applies a function on these patterns to produce output patterns. These patterns are then stored in the output arrays.

The task is either a new hierarchy of tasks or an elementary transformation (ET). A library of predefined ET is available for usual signal operations (FFT, integration...). An ET takes patterns as input and returns patterns; it may be parametrized, for example by the size of the patterns.

2.3   ARRAY-OL Specification Language

ARRAY-OL is a specification language. The programmer specifies dependencies in both models. In the global model, the dependencies between tasks are given by the input and output arrays. In the local model, the dependencies are given in term of patterns.

In this context, the compiler starts directly from these dependencies to generate code.

3   The aol2c++ Compiler

The aol2c++ compiler is used to produce C++ code in order to execute an ARRAY-OL application on a workstation by straightforward translation. This strategy limits the set of ARRAY-OL applications the compiler may handle. The ARRAY-OL code transformation presented in Section 4 will allow us to widen the set of ARRAY-OL applications covered by the compiler.

3.1 Execution Scheme of an ARRAY-OL Application

The simulation of an ARRAY-OL application on a workstation reads the input arrays and produces the output arrays in the file system. The intermediate arrays are allocated in memory.

Infinite arrays are handled by slides of n values. The value of n is supplied on the command line at execution time.

The simulation triggers the ARRAY-OL tasks in an order computed by a dependence analysis. An ARRAY-OL task is an indivisible execution unit: it is fully executed before the next task starts.

3.2 Main Structure of the Generated C++ Code

A C++ function is generated for each ARRAY-OL task. This function is parametrized by the input and output patterns of the task and the possible parameters of the task.

An ET code is fetched from the component libraries.

For a hierarchical task, the function locally defines and allocates the intermediate arrays. A dependence analysis produces a scheduling of the sub-tasks. The code of each sub-task consists of allocating the input and output patterns and iterating over the paving. The body of the loop:

- copies the array points in the operand patterns;
- calls the function corresponding to the task;
- copies the output pattern points in the arrays.

In particular, the generated code that manages the read and write of a pattern takes a paving iteration vector and iterates on the fitting, using the following formula to compute the index of an array point:

$$(\mathcal{M}_p.q + \mathcal{M}_f.d + \mathcal{O}) \bmod m, \tag{1}$$

q and d design the paving and fitting iterators; $\mathcal{M}_p$ and $\mathcal{M}_f$ design the paving and fitting matrix; m and $\mathcal{O}$ design the array dimensions and origin.

3.3 Code Generation Key Points

We detail some interesting points of the general compilation process.

Array Scanning. An ARRAY-OL application specification does not impose an order on array element iterations (especially for multi-dimensional arrays). The compiler must ensure a coherent order with the allocation of the array in a virtual paged memory.

Static Shortcut of Pattern Copy. Input/output patterns of a hierarchical task are only useful to read/write patterns of the sub-tasks (sub-patterns). Therefore, no copy of the patterns is needed at this level. The sub-patterns are built directly from the arrays: the sub-task receives references to the whole arrays associated with the origins of the current patterns. At compile time, we combine the two specifications of the paving/fitting of the task and sub-task to produce a new paving/fitting specification.

In this context, a sub-task code is no more independent of the calling task. A sub-task used in different contexts will be cloned for each of its uses.

Point Coordinate Computation. The computation of the coordinates of an array point is based on the equation (1). Nevertheless, the computation of the coordinates for the set of points corresponding to a pattern, is not performed by a systematic application of the matrix product: an incremental computation is implemented.

The coordinates of a point on a given iteration dimension is produced from the coordinates of the previous point with the paving vectors increments $\mathcal{F}'$. These vectors are computed, at compile time, from the fitting vectors $\mathcal{F}$ and the pattern sizes D: $\mathcal{F}'_i = \mathcal{F}_i - \sum_{j<i} D_j \times \mathcal{F}_j$.

Modulo Usage. ARRAY-OL arrays are wrapped around. A modulo operation is necessary on the coordinates of all points of an array. The cost of this modulo is prohibitive.

A simple calculation [2] allows us to identify whether a set of points obtained by Cartesian iterations of vectors cause array overflows or not. This restricts the set of arrays for which a modulo operation is needed. The property is checked at compile time for the whole array, and also at runtime for each pattern.

3.4 Limitations and Extension of the Compiler

The `aol2c++` compiler has a number of limitations. We illustrate these limitations and introduce the strategy chosen to get rid of them.

Task Unity and Infinity Handling. An ARRAY-OL task is executed from beginning to end before another task begins. As a consequence, the operands of a task must be completed before the triggering of the task.

The fact a task waits for its argument completeness limits the use of infinite arrays taht in ARRAY-OL. Only ARRAY-OL applications made up of a single task may handle arrays with an infinite dimension.

The execution scheme is expensive; other execution strategies may be considered: a "pipeline" execution will trigger a task on a part of its operands to produce a part of its results; these results may be used by another task to complete a part of its work... Such an execution does not necessitate a full allocation of the intermediate arrays.

Compiler Extension. In order to be able to deal with a wider set of ARRAY-OL applications (applications handling huge or infinite arrays), we propose to keep the basic compiler strategy implemented in aol2c++ but to operate a preliminary transformation on the ARRAY-OL source.

This transformation step will produce, from a given ARRAY-OL program, an ARRAY-OL program that the aol2c++ compiler may effectively handle.

Our Intermediate Language, ARRAY-OL/aol2c++. The set of ARRAY-OL sources that aol2c++ may compile defines a subset of ARRAY-OL. We use this subset as an intermediate language in our code transformation/compilation process. This approach offers numerous advantages.

First, we propose basic transformation operators of ARRAY-OL code. The operators may be applied interactively in the frame of the GASPARD environment [3]. The programmer may then evaluate the quality of the transformation (visualization of the memory size needed for the execution of a task, etc.). This interactive semi-automatic usage is an experimental platform that allows the definition of transformation strategies.

Application compiled by aol2c++, i.e. applications produced by the code after the transformation process, consists of a main loop over the time. The body of this loop is itself made up of a linear loop that accesses array elements. This is a good formalism for applications which aim for a parallel execution. Furthermore, the form of the code naturally identifies sequences of tasks which produce a result (i.e. patterns) from an input pattern. This property may be exploited to map the arrays on a distributed memory.

In particular, this formalism is used to implement ARRAY-OL applications on a dedicated architecture developed by Thomson.

Finally, this method allows a code transformation to change the scheduling of an application without having to rewrite a new implementation of the ARRAY-OL compiler.

4 ARRAY-OL Code Transformation Principle

We propose a transformation operator of an ARRAY-OL application that introduce supplementary hierarchy levels in the application. We consider a set of operand patterns that are able to trigger a sequence of tasks, each one producing the whole number of patterns. Operand arrays are then cut into *macro-patterns*: macro-patterns are subsets of operand array elements allowing a task to produce at least one output pattern.

New loops on macro-patterns ensure the processing of the whole operand arrays (Figure 1). The definition of these loops on the macro-patterns relies on an extension of the paving and fitting notions, namely the macro-paving and macro-fitting.

Such a strategy has already been implemented at Thomson Marconi Sonar on some applications in order to implant them on a dedicated architecture. We automate the transformations.

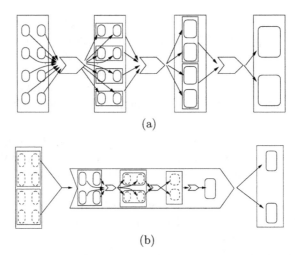

(a)

(b)

Fig. 1. Rewriting of (a) an ARRAY-OL application of three successive tasks in (b) a hierarchical ARRAY-OL task composed of three sub-tasks. Observe the possible reduction of the intermediate array size. Rectangles denote arrays. They are cut into patterns which are used and produced by tasks (denoted by arrow-like polygons)

The validity of the hierarchization relies on the dependencies: input macro-patterns of an iteration must contain enough points to allow the computation of the task sequence of the hierarchy and to produce the output macro-patterns.

The ODT formalism is a representation of the dependencies between input and output of an ARRAY-OL task. The principle is to code a set of ARRAY-OL tasks with ODT, to transform these ODTs, and to find an ODT form of an ARRAY-OL hierarchy.

5   ARRAY-OL Code Transformation Example

As explained above, our main goal is to automatically compute a hierarchy from a set of tasks. We are going to illustrate our transformations on a representative example of signal processing. We will produce just one hierarchy from an initial sequence of two tasks.

5.1   Beam Forming

The application consists of providing frequencies and location correlations (so called *beam*) from a continuous flow of data. It is based on elementary signal transformations: FFT (Fast Fourrier Transformation) and discrete integration.

- The *Hydrophones*, an ($h = 1024 \times T = \infty$) array, is the input of the application. It delivers a continuous flow of data from a set of 1024 captors.
- The first task computes FFT for each captor and period of 512 units of time. It fills *Frequencies*, an ($h = 1024 \times T = \infty \times f = 256$) array.

– The second task computes a beam for each period, frequency and set of captors (one captor out of 4 in a cyclic linear range of 64). It outputs *Beams*, an $(t = 1024 \times T = \infty \times f = 256)$ array.

The direct `aol2c++` compilation produces code that cannot be run. The application specification must be transformed.

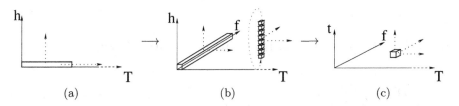

Fig. 2. Sequence of the three arrays ((a) *Hydrophones*, (b) *Frequencies*, (c) *Beams*). One input/output pattern and the paving directions have been represented for each array. On *Frequencies*, the compact pattern is written and the sparse cyclic one is read

5.2   Code Transformations

Break of the Flow. As mentioned above, the temporal dimension should be broken into recurrences in order to link partial execution of the two tasks. In the example, the recurrence length on the *Hydrophones* temporal axis would be 512: it would compute all FFTs of a period. Each recurrence will then provide the full hydrophone and frequency dimensions of *Frequencies* for the given period. Eventually the second task will compute the whole beam dimension for the period value under consideration.

Reduction of Temporary Data. The two sub-tasks generated from the initial tasks work now on finite arrays. Nevertheless, other cuttings could alleviate the memory requirements.

The computation of a *Beams* pattern requires an input pattern on *Frequencies*. This pattern computation needs the 64 FFT of the corresponding period (one FFT by hydrophone). Thus, each iteration will produce a single beam and needs only an $(h = 64 \times f = 256)$ intermediate array.

Reduction of Redundancies. The major problem of the previous solution comes from the redundant computations. First of all, the first sub-task produces the full frequency dimension on *Frequencies*; it implies that the second sub-task may compute the beams for all frequencies. On the other hand, some input patterns of *Frequencies* overlap on hydrophone dimension. For the whole application, the same FFT is recomputed 63 times. To avoid this, all overlapping patterns are gathered in a single pattern. Each period is divided in 4 input/output meta-patterns: the input patterns are the sets of 256 hydrophones (one in 4); the output patterns are the sets of 256 beams (one in 4) with the whole frequency dimension. The *Frequencies* sub-array stores the results of the 256 FFT.

In this scheme, there are no redundancies and the intermediate array size is ($h = 256 \times f = 256$). If this size is less than the memory resources, this transformed application represents the best balance between memory usage and computation overhead.

6   ODT Representation of an ARRAY-OL Task

The ODT formalism allows the specification of dependencies between input and output operands of ARRAY-OL tasks [4,6].

The set of the ODT is built by composition of basic operators. Each operator defines a mathematical relation between two $\mathbb{Z}^n$ spaces. These relation operators look like filters which cut, let through, or duplicate input links. An input point may be mapped with zero, one, or several (and even an infinity of) output points. Relation operators are presented in Table 1.

Table 1. Basic relation operators of the ODT

Gauge	$\begin{pmatrix} \overrightarrow{\min}, \ \overrightarrow{\max} \\ \mathbf{G} \end{pmatrix}$	$\mathbb{Z}^n \longrightarrow \mathbb{Z}^n$ $\overrightarrow{\min} \leq \overrightarrow{x} < \overrightarrow{\max} \mapsto \overrightarrow{x}$
Shift	$\begin{pmatrix} \overrightarrow{\text{shift}} \\ \mathbf{S} \end{pmatrix}$	$\mathbb{Z}^n \longrightarrow \mathbb{Z}^n$ $\overrightarrow{x} \mapsto \overrightarrow{x} + \overrightarrow{\text{shift}}$
Projection with $\mathcal{M}$, a $m \times n$ matrix enclosing possibly non integer values. $\quad |\mathcal{M}|$		$\mathbb{Z}^n \longrightarrow \mathbb{Z}^m$ $\overrightarrow{x} \mapsto \lfloor \mathcal{M}.\overrightarrow{x} \rfloor$
Modulo with $\overrightarrow{m} > \overrightarrow{0}$.	$\begin{pmatrix} \overrightarrow{m} \\ \mathbf{M} \end{pmatrix}$	$\mathbb{Z}^n \longrightarrow \mathbb{Z}^n$ $\overrightarrow{x} \mapsto (x_i \bmod m_i)$
Replication with $\overrightarrow{m} > \overrightarrow{0}$.	$\begin{pmatrix} \overrightarrow{m} \\ \star \end{pmatrix}$	$\mathbb{Z}^n \longrightarrow \mathbb{Z}^n$ $\overrightarrow{0} \leq \overrightarrow{x} < \overrightarrow{m} \mapsto (x_i + k_i.m_i) \quad \forall k_i \in \mathbb{Z}$
Segmentation with $\mathcal{M}$, a $m \times n$ matrix enclosing possibly non integer values.	$\overline{\mathcal{M}}$	$\mathbb{Z}^m \longrightarrow \mathbb{Z}^n$ $\overrightarrow{x} \mapsto \overrightarrow{y} \ ; \ \overrightarrow{x} = \lfloor \mathcal{M}\overrightarrow{y} \rfloor$

The relation operators are close to ARRAY-OL characteristics: the gauge defines the arrays boundaries; the projection combines paving and fitting vector sets; the shift comes from the shifting of the origin; the modulo is used for toroidal array dimensions.

The relation operators of replication and segmentation are respectively the symmetrics of modulo and projection. (The gauge and the shift are their own symmetric.)

The ODT representation of an ARRAY-OL task consists of two expressions that represent: the links between the iteration space and, at one side, the operand arrays and, at the other side, the resultant arrays. Each of these expressions is the composition of a gauge that limits the paving and fitting iterations, a projection made of the paving/fitting vectors, a modulo on the array sizes, and possible shift depending on array origins. For example, the ODT of the first task of the beam forming (Section 5) is:

$$
\begin{pmatrix} 512 \\ \infty \\ M \end{pmatrix} \cdot \begin{vmatrix} 1 & 0 & 0 \\ 0 & 512 & 1 \end{vmatrix} \cdot \begin{pmatrix} 512 \\ \infty \\ 512 \end{pmatrix} \begin{matrix} \} \text{iteration} \\ \} \text{boundaries} \\ \} \begin{matrix} \text{operand} \\ \text{pattern size} \end{matrix} \end{matrix} \qquad
\begin{pmatrix} 512 \\ 256 \\ \infty \\ M \end{pmatrix} \cdot \begin{vmatrix} 1 & 0 & 0 \\ 0 & 0 & 1 \\ 0 & 1 & 0 \end{vmatrix} \cdot \begin{pmatrix} 512 \\ \infty \\ 256 \end{pmatrix} \begin{matrix} \} \text{iteration} \\ \} \text{boundaries} \\ \} \begin{matrix} \text{result} \\ \text{pattern size} \end{matrix} \end{matrix}
$$

$$\underbrace{\qquad\qquad\qquad}_{\text{operand ODT expression}} \qquad\qquad \underbrace{\qquad\qquad\qquad}_{\text{result ODT expression}}$$

The two iteration spaces are homogenized (by gauge normalization and introduction of zeros in projection matrix):

$$
\begin{pmatrix} 512 \\ \infty \\ M \end{pmatrix} \cdot \begin{vmatrix} 1 & 0 & 0 & 0 \\ 0 & 512 & 0 & 1 \end{vmatrix} \cdot \begin{pmatrix} 512 \\ \infty \\ 256 \\ 512 \end{pmatrix}_{G} \qquad
\begin{pmatrix} 512 \\ 256 \\ \infty \\ M \end{pmatrix} \cdot \begin{vmatrix} 1 & 0 & 0 & 0 \\ 0 & 0 & 1 & 0 \\ 0 & 1 & 0 & 0 \end{vmatrix} \cdot \begin{pmatrix} 512 \\ \infty \\ 256 \\ 512 \end{pmatrix}_{G}
$$

$$\underbrace{\qquad\qquad\qquad}_{\text{operand ODT expression}} \qquad\qquad \underbrace{\qquad\qquad\qquad}_{\text{result ODT expression}}$$

It is then possible to compose the operand ODT with the symmetric of the result ODT. The resulting expression is just a link from the output points to the input points:

$$
\begin{pmatrix} 512 \\ \infty \\ M \end{pmatrix} \cdot \begin{vmatrix} 1 & 0 & 0 & 0 \\ 0 & 512 & 0 & 1 \end{vmatrix} \cdot \begin{pmatrix} 512 \\ \infty \\ 256 \\ 512 \end{pmatrix}_{G} \cdot \underbrace{\overline{\begin{vmatrix} 1 & 0 & 0 & 0 \\ 0 & 0 & 1 & 0 \\ 0 & 1 & 0 & 0 \end{vmatrix}} \cdot \overline{\begin{pmatrix} 512 \\ 256 \\ \infty \\ \star \end{pmatrix}}}_{\text{result ODT symmetric}}
$$

The general ODT form of an ARRAY-OL task is:

$$
\begin{pmatrix} M_1 \\ M \end{pmatrix} \cdot \begin{pmatrix} S \\ S \end{pmatrix} \cdot |\mathcal{P}_{op}| \cdot \begin{pmatrix} G \\ G \end{pmatrix} \cdot \overline{\mathcal{P}_{res}} \cdot \begin{pmatrix} M_2 \\ \star \end{pmatrix} \tag{2}
$$

7   Composition of Two ARRAY-OL Tasks

Consider two consecutive tasks T_1 and T_2: T_1 produces an array A_2 from an array A_1, T_2 produces A_3 from A_2. The ODT of the tasks are:

$$T_1 \rightarrow \begin{pmatrix} M_1 \\ \mathbf{M} \end{pmatrix} \cdot \begin{pmatrix} S_1 \\ \mathbf{S} \end{pmatrix} \cdot \left| \mathcal{P}_{op,1} \right| \cdot \begin{pmatrix} G_1^q \\ G_1^d \\ \mathbf{G} \end{pmatrix} \cdot \overline{\mathcal{P}_{res,1}} \cdot \begin{pmatrix} M_2 \\ \star \end{pmatrix}$$

$$T_2 \rightarrow \begin{pmatrix} M_2 \\ \mathbf{M} \end{pmatrix} \cdot \begin{pmatrix} S_2 \\ \mathbf{S} \end{pmatrix} \cdot \left| \mathcal{P}_{op,2} \right| \cdot \begin{pmatrix} G_2^q \\ G_2^d \\ \mathbf{G} \end{pmatrix} \cdot \overline{\mathcal{P}_{res,2}} \cdot \begin{pmatrix} M_3 \\ \star \end{pmatrix}$$

A hierarchization consists in merging the two tasks, in order to find a task T_{12} that directly produces A_3 from A_1. This task will be composed of two sub-tasks T_1' and T_2', transformations of the original tasks. The ODT of T_{12} is the composition of T_1 and T_2 ODT:

$$\begin{pmatrix} M_1 \\ \mathbf{M} \end{pmatrix} \cdot \begin{pmatrix} S_1 \\ \mathbf{S} \end{pmatrix} \cdot \left| \mathcal{P}_{op,1} \right| \underbrace{ \begin{pmatrix} G_1^q \\ G_1^d \\ \mathbf{G} \end{pmatrix} \cdot \overline{\mathcal{P}_{res,1}} \cdot \begin{pmatrix} M_2 \\ \star \end{pmatrix} \cdot \begin{pmatrix} M_2 \\ \mathbf{M} \end{pmatrix} \cdot \begin{pmatrix} S_2 \\ \mathbf{S} \end{pmatrix} \cdot \left| \mathcal{P}_{op,2} \right| \cdot \begin{pmatrix} G_2^q \\ G_2^d \\ \mathbf{G} \end{pmatrix} }$$

$$\cdot \, \overline{\mathcal{P}_{res,2}} \cdot \begin{pmatrix} M_3 \\ \star \end{pmatrix}$$

The hierarchization process will transform this expression into an ODT form of an ARRAY-OL task (2). The transformation is detailed in [2].

The outline of the transformation is to produce a symmetric segmentation $\overline{\mathcal{P}_{res,1}}$ and to join the result with the following projection $\left| \mathcal{P}_{op,2} \right|$. This is a legal transformation because of the constraints and limitations of ARRAY-OL. Nevertheless, the operation may produce non integer values. Therefore, we gather several patterns and consider a bounding box to retrieve an integer form.

We compose the resulting form with the original paving/fitting matrix $\mathcal{P}_{op,1}$ and $\mathcal{P}_{res,2}$. The paving and fitting parts of this iterator becomes the paving and fitting of the task T_{12}. The fitting part is also split in two parts to form the paving of the two sub-tasks T_1' and T_2'.

8   Related Work

The ARRAY-OL language and the ODT formalism belong to linear algebra, integer programming and constraint systems. Tools other than the ODT may be used in that context:

– An ALPHA [12] application is defined by a system of affines recurrence equations (SARE). To implement such applications on systolic architectures, interactive transformations are considered such as changes of basis and toggling between broadcast and pipeline. The system may also generate a scheduling and an allocation of arrays.

– PIPS [11] is a FORTRAN77 automatic parallelizer. It includes dependence analysis, code transformations and SPMD code generation.

Both of the above use a formalism based on polyhedra. Indeed, since a polyhedron defines a space area by bounding it with a set of affine hyper-plans[3], it provides a reasonable represention of an iteration set of a loop nest.

Several software packagess handle polyhedra. The ones that are usefull for compilation have to handle parametrized polyhedra defined by integer constraints. The POLYLIB [13] handles parametrized rational polyhedra (image by affine function, convex hull, integer points count...). PIPS, ALPHA and others rely on this library. On the other hand, PIP [8] solves parametrized integer programming problems; it is used by several automatic parallelizers such as PAF [9], BOUCLETTE [1] and SUIF [10].

Although the ODT are less expressive than the polyhedra (with the exception of the notion of modulo), they are sufficient to formalize the ARRAY-OL language. Moreover, our transformation process produces ARRAY-OL source. Restricting us to a formalism closer to ARRAY-OL simplifies the finalization of the transformations.

9   Conclusion

ARRAY-OL is a parallel language dedicated to signal processing. A code transformation strategy is implemented to overcome the limitations of a first basic compiler (inability to handle infinite arrays, poor performance on huge arrays).

We have proposed a formalism to represent ARRAY-OL applications. In this formalism, we defined a basic transformation operator of an ARRAY-OL code into a hierarchical ARRAY-OL code. This transformation has been implemented in GASPARD, a graphical environment for ARRAY-OL application specification. It allows us to interactively transform ARRAY-OL tasks.

Several representative applications have already been transformed. Significant gains have been reported.

From these experiments, we are developing strategies to automatically apply this operator in the rewriting of a whole ARRAY-OL application.

The proposed code transformations produce an ARRAY-OL hierarchy of tasks. The iterations of this hierarchy are independent: we have found a number of independent flows equal to the number of patterns in the array. We are developing such code transformations to control the mapping of arrays on a given number of threads/processes.

References

1. Pierre Boulet. Bouclettes: A Fortran loop parallelizer. In *HPCN'96*, pages 784-791. Lecture Notes in Computer Science vol. 1067, 1996.

---

[3] An affine hyper-plan is a affine sub-space with one dimension less and therefore cuts space into two parts.

2. Jean-Luc Dekeyser, Alain Demeure, Philippe Marquet, and Julien Soula. Array-OL compilation by code transformation. Research Report 99-15, LIFL, Université de Lille, France, December 1999.

3. Jean-Luc Dekeyser, Philippe Marquet, and Julien Soula. Video kills the radio stars. In *Supercomputing'99 (poster session)*, Portland, OR, November 1999. (http://www.lifl.fr/west/gaspard/).

4. Alain Demeure. Les ODT: Propositions de notation pour décrire des opérateurs de distribution de tableaux. Research report, Thomson Marconi Sonar, Sophia-Antipolis, France, 1998.

5. Alain Demeure. Anne Lafage, Emmanuel Boutillon, Didier Rozzonelli, Jean-Claude Dufourd, and Jean-Louis Marro. Array-OL: Proposition d'un formalisme tableau pour le traitement de signal multi-dimensionnel. In *Gretsi*, Juan-Les-Pins, France, September 1995.

6. Alain Demeure (Thomson Marconi Sonar). Procédé de placement automatique des tâches d'une application dans une machine de traitement de signal. Brevet 9912574, 1999.

7. Alain Demeure (Thomson Marconi Sonar). Procédé de saisie graphique dans une forme hiérarchisée. Brevet 9902906, 1999.

8. Paul Feautrier. Parametric Integer Programming. *RAIRO Recherche Opérationnelle*, 22:243-268, September 1988.

9. Paul Feautrier. Toward automatic distribution. In *ACM International Conference on Supercomputing (ICS)*, Tokyo, Japan, July 1993.

10. Stanford Compiler Group. Suif Compiler System. World Wide Web document, http://www-suif.stanford.edu/.

11. François Irigoin, Pierre Jouvelot, and Rémi Triolet. Semantical interprocedural parallelization: An overview of the PIPS project. In *1991 International Conference on Supercomputing*, Cologne, Germany, June 1991.

12. Hervé Le Verge, Christophe Mauras, and Patrice Quinton. The ALPHA language and its use for the design of systolic arrays. The *Journal of VLSI Signal Processing*, 3(3):173-182, September 1991.

13. Doran K. Wilde. A library for doing polyhedral operations. Research Report 785, IRISA, Rennes, France, December 1993.

An Approach to Composing Parallel Programs

Lars-Erik Thorelli and Vladimir Vlassov

Department of Microelectronics and Information Technology, Royal Institute of Technology
Isafjordsgatan 39, S-164 40, Kista, Sweden
{le,vlad}@it.kth.se

Abstract. Principles for coordination and composition of parallel/distributed programs are discussed. We advocate a synchronizing shared memory model (EDA) for coordination and an algebraic approach to building programs using a linking language (LL) based on module composition, restriction and renaming. A prototype system ErlEda illustrating these principles is described. The system uses the concurrent programming language Erlang and its distributed environment as a basis. We illustrate the approach using the Dirichlet problem.

Introduction

An increasing number of computation intensive applications require the power of parallel computers, and a variety of distributed applications already make a large impact on modern society. However the complexity of programming parallel/distributed systems is a significant obstacle, making development of new applications for parallel/distributed computer systems costly and error-prone. This motivates the search of new concepts and platforms that would enable parallel/distributed programs to be conveniently designed from sequential components without sacrificing either efficiency or robustness. In this work we propose and demonstrate the use of new principles for the composition and coordination of parallel/distributed programs. In this paper we concentrate on software engineering and execution efficiency aspects.

We consider a programming model for parallel and distributed computing that combines aspects of the shared memory programming model and the object-oriented paradigm. The shared memory model defines a shared address space that can be accessed by processes via ordinary loads and stores, thus providing convenient but unstructured communication between processes. To maintain desired ordering in parallel execution and preserve essential data and control dependencies in a parallel program, synchronization such as locks, flags and barriers must be provided.

The object-oriented paradigm states that an object can carry a thread of execution and that the object's state is encapsulated in variables that are local to the object even though some may point to other objects. The state of the object can be observed and changed by some external thread only via message passing. Object orientation supports structured design and efficient software development. Achieving high execution efficiency for such programming models in a parallel/distributed environment is however real challenge.

A basic idea of the model introduced in this article is to unify some local variables of interacting objects to be shared among them. Such variables constitute a state

V. Malyshkin (Ed.): PaCT 2001, LNCS 2127, pp. 371–378, 2001.

common to these objects. The variables are accessed via accessor functions that synchronize implicitly according to the type of the variable. The linking of objects via shared variables allows efficient combination of fine-grain communication and synchronization among object threads similar to dataflow execution.

Coordination: The EDA Model

Assuming that a parallel program contains a number of cooperating entities or processes, the question arises how these entities coordinate their work. A number of models have been proposed, including various message- passing schemes and shared memory approaches. The Linda tuple space model [4] offers another approach. The term "coordination language/model" was coined in connection with Linda [5].

We propose using the EDA model [14, 10, 13] that provides a unified approach to shared memory, synchronization and communication, in other words, to coordination. Shared data is provided but can be accessed only in a constrained way. There is no global shared address space available to the processes; each process can access certain shared variables, or acquaintances [1], on a "need to know" basis.

Following [10, 13], shared variables are of three different *synchronization types*, I-data, X-data, and S-data, which all impose different constraints in the way accesses may be performed. *I-data* are used for enforcing data dependency: a read operation on an empty variable will lead to suspension, and assignment is allowed only once. The concept of I-data is inspired from, but not identical to, I-structures [3]. A write operation on a full variable is discarded, thus supporting a kind of OR-parallelism.

X-data are used for mutual exclusion and synchronous communication: reads and writes must be performed in a strictly alternating sequence. A process attempting an access violating this order will be delayed until another process has changed the state of the accessed variable. *S-data* allow stream communication. A writing process can assign successive values to an S-type variable; these will be queued and available for read operations. Each read removes one value from the stream. Processes accessing a stream need not be suspended, except in the case of reading from an empty stream.

A slightly more general model is achieved if the type restriction is removed, i.e. if all access operations are allowed on a shared variable. For instance, a producer of a stream can conveniently achieve flow control by interspersing Sstores with Xstores at suitable intervals. This approach was taken in the mEDA model [12] where in addition Sfetches from an empty stream are non-blocking (returning the value 'empty'), and operations Ufetch/Ustore have been added for unsynchronized accesses.

Like Linda, EDA provides a medium for coordination between processes that do not know of each other. This gives a clean separation between the executing components of a program and promotes reuse. Efficiency is an issue of concern when using Linda, since reading or extracting data requires a matching process. As noted e.g. in [5], the open nature of the communication medium compromises security. Both these drawbacks are absent with EDA. Compared to conventional shared memory, the introduction of different synchronization types and/or operations enables more efficient implementations, avoiding or reducing memory coherence overhead which is a heavy burden in large-scale shared memory systems with conventional semantics.

Composition

In this section we discuss the issue of how to compose a program. We advocate an algebraic approach where program modules may be combined to form new modules.

A module is a set of processes and shared variables. Some of the variables are exported i.e. their names and associated type information are visible to the outside, whereas the remaining variables are hidden. The module may also have imports, i.e. shared variables that are referenced by processes in the module but are not contained in it. Two modules A and B may be combined to a new module if their exports are disjoint, i.e. have distinctly named variables. Some imports required by A may be satisfied by B and vice versa. An executable program is a module without imports.

To formalize, let us call the sets of exports and imports of a module M *exps*(M) and *imps*(M), respectively. The combination of modules A and B is denoted A | B. Then

- A | B is defined if $exps(A) \cap exps(B) = \{\}$ (the empty set)
- $exps(A \mid B) = exps(A) \cup exps(B)$
- $imps(A \mid B) = imps(A) \setminus exps(B) \cup imps(B) \setminus exps(A)$

The combination A | B can be seen as the juxtaposition of an instance of A and an instance of B, and the connection of identically named imports and exports.

Combination is the main operation of our language LL (linking language) for composing programs [11]. Other operations are restriction and renaming. The language can be seen as a form of process algebra restricted to static operations [7, 8].

Let A denotes a module and s a set of names. The restriction of A by s is denoted A\s and is the same module as A except that variables whose names are included in s are no longer exported. This operation is essential for information hiding.

Let A denotes a module and I a one-one mapping of names to names. We write A[I] to denote a module equal to A but whose imported or exported variables have been renamed using I.

The linking language LL allows hierarchic composition of modules and facilitates reuse of software. Primitive modules are modules not composed of other modules. Given a set of primitive modules for an application area, different application programs can be built using LL by combining instances of these modules.

A Prototype System

This section describes a prototype system ErlEda for parallel program development, based on the principles described above. Our description concentrates on the coordination and composition facilities and their implementation. The prototype is based on the Erlang programming language and system developed at Ericsson [2]. Erlang is a programming language designed for building real-time and distributed applications. It was developed by the company Ericsson and has inherited many properties from functional programming languages. It uses dynamic typing and is garbage-collected. It features lists and tuples as built-in data types. A freeware version of the system is available on Internet (http://www.erlang.org/). Erlang offers a process concept and means of communication and synchronization. Scheduling is provided for free. Processes can be spawned at run-time. Processes communicate using asynchronous message passing. There are no global data; only process identifiers (pids) are global. There is support for error handling and the creation of robust programs. Erlang supports programs distributed over several hosts (nodes). This feature is used in the implementation of ErlEda.

Distribution

The processes and shared variables of an ErlEda program are distributed over a set of nodes in a logically transparent way. Logical transparency means that the semantics of a program will not be affected by how its objects and shared variables are distributed. This property facilitates programming, though the distribution will affect performance. Our approach is to leave it to the user to specify, for each node, which EDA processes and shared variables should be allocated to it. With present technology it is not very important to consider network topology, thus we assume the target system to consist of a set of equal and fully connected nodes. The user specifies *N* LL expressions if the program is to be executed on *N* nodes. An option would be to use automatic allocation of the program, based on its total LL description possibly together with some information of frequency of shared variable accesses.

Dynamic load balancing by means of re-allocation of processes and shared variables during execution is less useful since it would mean discarding our knowledge of the program´s static structure provided by the LL description. Also, in most cases the communication overhead would be too high.

Processes and Shared Variables

Erlang processes represent EDA processes, henceforth called *objects*, and the behavior of the object is specified by an Erlang function. Some of the arguments of the function represent the acquaintances of the object, while others constitute its local, mutable state. An ErlEda program has an essentially fixed configuration of EDA objects interrelated by means of acquaintances to shared variables. Dynamic evolution of the configuration is possible under certain conditions, but this feature is not relevant for our discussion.

The Erlang module called de   (short for *distributed eda*) implements the access operations on shared data. For example, I-fetching the value of shared variable V to local variable X is expressed by X = de:ifetch(V). In the following we omit the "de:" prefix for the shared data operations.

In all there are six main access operations, ifetch, istore, xfetch, xstore, sfetch, and sstore. As Erlang is a typeless language as far as data types are concerned, so is ErlEda. A shared variable may be bound to a number, an atom, a tuple or a list. It may also be empty (unbound). If V in the example above is empty then the executing object will be suspended until another object assigns a value to it.

The EDA shared memory is managed by the set of EDA daemon processes, one per node. Remote I-data variables fetched by an object are cached locally for future references by objects in the same node.

The Linking Language

A program distributed over N nodes is represented in the linking language by a list of N components, each of which specifies a module allocated to one node. An ErlEda module contains objects and shared variables. The module is represented by an Erlang tuple {*ShVars*, *Objects*, *Exports*, *Imports*}, where *ShVars* enumerates the shared variables, *Objects* the arguments and function names of the objects, *Exports* specifies which of the shared variables should be visible outside the module, and *Imports* lists the remote references needed by this module. The loader program will check that the modules in the list are consistent and that all imports demanded by one node is satisfied by another node. If this is the case, the remote references will be resolved and the N node program will be constructed and started. Note that this internode linking amounts to a final combination operation with N operands.

The linker and loader are themselves programmed in Erlang and constitute an Erlang module `ll`. Table 1 summarizes its main functions. The linking language LL in our system consists of these functions embedded within Erlang.

Table 1. LL functions of the ErlEda system

LL function	Effect
build(V, O, E)	Builds a module with shared variables V, objects O, and exported sh. var:s E
combine(M1, M2)	Builds the module M1 | M2
comblist(L)	Builds the combination of the modules of list L
restrict(M, S)	Builds the module M \ S
rename(M, Old, New)	Builds a version of M where name Old is replaced by New
rename(M, OldNewList)	As above but performs simultaneous replacements according to OldNewList, a list of pairs
bind(M, Arg, Val), bind(M, ArgValList	Builds a version of M where imported name(s) Arg is bound to value(s) Val
cat(A, N)	Forms a new name by concatenating A and N. N is typically a natural number.

An Example: The Dirichlet Problem

In this section we show how a typical computational problem can be described, partitioned and executed on a set of m nodes (workstations).

Given is a 2D grid of numerical values, where the boundary points have constant values and the interior points at time $(t+1)$ are determined as the average of the four neighboring points at time t. We assume n^2 interior points, and $4\times (n+1)$ boundary points, making a total of $(n+2)^2$ points. All interior points are zeros initially, and the constant boundary value is chosen as 100.

The problem will here be partitioned column-wise, so that the program will be composed of a left boundary column, a right boundary column, and m partitions each containing w interior columns, where $m\times w$ equals n. Assume $m \geq 2$ and $n/m \geq 2$. Each partition will iterate over its part of the grid. For each iteration the partition will have to exchange its boundary columns with those of its neighbors. For simplicity, the number of iterations is fixed to 100. A partition will hold a local array where the leftmost and rightmost columns are local copies of neighboring columns in other partitions. In addition, a partition will contain and export shared variables Lout, Rout, and import shared columns Lin, Rin. (Hint: "L" and "R" indicate direction of information flow - leftward or rightward).

The result of the computation is collected and printed by a collector object.

We show the code for a partition in outline:

```
part(I1, W, N, Lin, Lout, Rin, Rout, Res) ->
    State = vec(W, addon(100, vec(N, 0), 100)),
%Initial state
%   Iterate NIter times:
    Final = iterate(100, State, Lin, Lout, Rin, Rout),
%   Send final result to collector object:
    send(Final, I1, Res), receive bye -> bye end.
send([H|T], I, S) -> sstore({I, H},S), send(T, I+1, S);
send([], I, S) -> ok.
iterate(0, State, Lin, Lout, Rin, Rout) -> State;
iterate(NIter, State, Lin, Lout, Rin, Rout) ->
%   Exchange boundary colums with neighbours:
    xstore(hd(State), Lout), xstore(last(State), Rout),
    State1 = addon(xfetch(Rin), State, xfetch(Lin)),
    iterate(NIter-1,laplace(State1),Lin,Lout,Rin, Rout).
```

The function laplace computes a new state by averaging over neighboring points and is omitted here. Figure 1 outlines the partitioning of the program over the m nodes. Here the b boxes represent the left and right boundaries of the grid, the box P(j) the j'th partition, and the C box the collector.

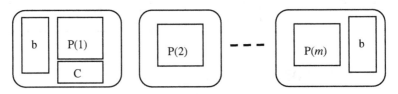

Fig. 1. Partitioning the Dirichlet program over *m* nodes.

The module P(j) exports shared variables Lout, Rout and imports shared variables Lin, Rin. To connect these, global names are introduced. We use r0, r1, ..., rm for the right bound connections, and l0, l1, ...lm for the left bound ones. By renaming the Lin variable of P(j) and the Lout variable of P(j+1) to lj, and the Rout variable of P(j) and the Rin variable of P(j+1) to rj, the desired connections are established.

Table 2 summarizes the modules from which complete programs are built.

To create and allocate the program for n=16, m=2 we create a list with two components. Assume that variables Lboundary, Rboundary, ... have been bound to the corresponding module descriptions (Table 2).

Table 2. Primitive modules for Dirichlet programs

Name	Sh. Vars	Objects	Exports	Imports
lboundary	Rout	boundcol(lin,rout,n)	rout	lin, n
rboundary	Lout	boundcol(rin,lout,n)	lout	rin, n
partition	lout,rout	part(i1,w,n, lin,lout,rin,rout,res)	lout,rout	i1,w,n,lin,rin,res
collector	Res	coll(res, n)	res	n

```
Part1 = bind(Partition, [{i1,1}, {w,8}, {n,16}]),
Part2 = bind(Partition, [{i1,9}, {w,8}, {n,16}]),
[comblist(
  [rename(bind(Lboundary,n,16), [{lin,10}, {rout,r0}]),
   rename(Part1,[{lin,11},{lout,10},{rin,r0},
{rout,r1}]),
   bind(Collector,n,16)]),
 combine(
  rename(Part2,[{lin,12},{lout,11},{rin,r1},
{rout,r2}]),
  rename(bind(Rboundary,n,16), [{rin,r2}, {lout,12}]))]
```

The following Erlang function "sys" composes such a system with arbitrary n and m ($n = wm$, $m \geq 2$, $w \geq 2$). Note the use of the LL function cat() to form new names and the use of the Erlang function constructor "fun(x) ->expression(x) end" to express the partitions P(i).

```
sys(M, N) ->
    W = N div M,
    P = fun(I) ->
            P2 = rename(bind(Partition, [{w, W}, {n, N}]),
                  [{lin, cat(l, I)}, {lout, cat(l, I-1)},
                    {rin, cat(r, I-1)}, {rout, cat(r, I)}]),
            bind(P2, i1, W*(I-1)+1)
    end,
    Parray = listof(P,2,M-1), %creates [P(2),...,P(M-1)]
      append([
        [comblist([
        rename(bind(Lboundary,n,N),[{lin,10},{rout,r0}]),
          P(1), bind(Collector,n,N)])],
        Parray,
        [combine(P(M),
  rename(bind(Rboundary,n,N),[{rin,r2},{lout,12}]))]]).
```

Given the resulting list of modules as argument, the system loader will create and allocate each module on a separate node. Then all inter-module references will be resolved, and the execution of the modules will be started.

Conclusions

We have shown how an environment for parallel/distributed programming can be based on the coordination medium of the EDA shared memory together with the linking language LL for composing programs. The resulting system is powerful and easy to use. The different access types offered by EDA makes the system more general than the message-passing based systems common today, yet avoiding the overhead of general cache coherence. The algebraic approach of LL supports hierarchic system design and reuse of software components and subsystems.

Our prototype system is based on the Erlang language and system. Erlang offers a convenient platform for building distributed systems, but our principles can be accommodated in most environments. In [12] an implementation based on PVM [6] is described which however does not support the linking facilities. The performance of any system based on our principles will mainly be determined by the efficiency of the communication mechanisms offered by the hardware and operating system.

The concept of a linking language can also support resource binding before execution. When the static structure of the program is known before run-time the system can allocate resources more efficiently. For instance, the optimal allocation of a given program on a given distributed system has been investigated in [9], based on a cost model accounting for computation, communication, and synchronization.

References

1. Agha, G.: Concurrent Object-Oriented Programming. CACM, **33** (1990) 125-141.
2. Armstrong, J., Virding, R., Williams, M.: Concurrent Programming in Erlang. Prentice-Hall (1993).
3. Arvind and Thomas, R. E.: I-structures: An Efficient Data Structure for Functional Languages. Technical Report LSC/TM-178, MIT Laboratory for Computer Science (1980).
4. Carriero, N., Gelernter, D.: Linda in Context. CACM, **32** (1989) 444-458.
5. Carriero, N., Gelernter, D.: Coordination languages and their significance. CACM, **35** (1992) 97-107.
6. Geist, A., et.al.: PVM: Parallel Virtual Machine, The MIT Press (1994).
7. Milner, R.: Flowgraphs and flow algebras. Journal of the ACM, **26** (1979) 794-818.
8. Milner, R.: Communication and Concurrency, Prentice Hall (1989).
9. Moritz C. A., Thorelli, L.-E.: A Static Mapping System for Logically Shared Memory Parallel Programs. 5-th Euromicro Workshop for Par. and Dist. Proc., London, UK, (1997).
10. Thorelli, L.-E.: The EDA Multiprocessing Model. Tech. Rep. TRITA-IT-R 94:28. Dept. of Teleinformatics, Royal Inst. of Technology, Stockholm, Sweden (1994).
11. Thorelli, L.-E., Liib, D.: A Language for Composing Program Modules. Tech. Rep. TRITA-IT-R 95:21, Dept. of Teleinformatics, Royal Inst. of Technology, Stockholm, Sweden (1995).
12. Vlassov, V., Thorelli, L.-E.: A Synchronizing Shared Memory: Model and Programming Implementation. Proc. 4th European PVM/MPI Users' Group Meeting. Springer-Verlag, LNCS **1332** (1997) 159-166.
13. Vlassov, V., Thorelli, L.-E.: Synchronizing Communication Primitives for a Shared Memory Programming Model. Euro-Par'98. Springer-Verlag, LNCS **1470** (1998) 682-687.
14. Wu, H.: Extension of Data-Flow Principles for Multiprocessing. Tech. Rep. TRITA-TCS-9004 (Ph D thesis). Royal Inst. of Technology, Stockholm, Sweden (1990).

Web-Based Parallel Simulation
of AGVs Using Java and JINI

Rong Ye, Wen-Jing Hsu, and Ze-Hua Liu

Centre for Advanced Information Systems,
School of Computer Engineering, Nanyang Technological University,
639798, Singapore
yerong@bigfoot.com, Hsu@ntu.edu.sg

Abstract. The vision of Computational Grids promises an exciting future for the distributed simulation community. In this project we make a small but practical step toward the grand vision of distributed simulation by using certain prevailing Internet technologies to enable access of simulation services anytime and anywhere. Specifically, this project focuses on accessing distributed simulation of AGVs (Automated Guided Vehicle) in container port operations through the World Wide Web. The objectives are to explore and address relevant issues, evaluate various approaches, demonstrate a workable version. We initially construct the AGV simulation system in an indirect communication model and identify its merits and demerits. Then, we explore the use of JINI technology for an efficient and robust direct communication architecture.

1 Introduction

The vision of computational grid has been well expanded in the book by Ian Foster and Carl Kesselman *The Grid: Blueprint for a new Computing Infrastructure*[6], which simply put, is an infrastructure that provides dependable, consistent, pervasive and inexpensive access to high-end computational capabilities. This will result in increased delivered computation by five orders of magnitude within a decade brought about by increased demand-driven access to computational power, increased utilization of idle capacity, greater sharing of computational results, and new problem solving techniques and tools.

Meanwhile, in the past decade, the "Internet revolution" has been the most significant technological development. The technological development has crossed all the frontiers of time and space and truly reduced the world into a global village. Presently the development of the Internet appears to be driven by the momentum created by the "network-centric model"[3], the ultimate goal of which is to turn the network into the computer and turn the client into a "thin" client, i.e. shifting computing burden from the client to server. It brings about the concept of balancing the computational burdens throughout the network amongst clients and servers with minimum resources expended on each specific client. Although arising from a different context, mainly driven by the rise of PC and Internet, this network-centric computing concept actually coincides with that of the Computational Grids which has been championed by people from super-computing

V. Malyshkin (Ed.): PaCT 2001, LNCS 2127, pp. 379–384, 2001.

arena. In this project we make a small step toward the vision by using some of the prevailing Internet technologies. Specifically, the project focuses on Web-based distributed simulation of AGVs by using JINI and Java. The objectives are to explore and address relevant issues, evaluate various approaches, demonstrate a workable JINI-enabled version for a distributed AGV simulation system.

The rest of paper is organized as follows: Section 2 briefly introduces a traditional AGV simulation system and its Web-enabled counterpart; Section 3 presents an *ad-hoc* 3-tier approach; Section 4 elaborates on an efficient and robust JINI-enabled framework; Section 5 concludes the paper and discusses future work.

2   Container Port Simulation

To manage the complexities of the processes at the port, container operations include scheduling of the port operations, allocation of resources and various traffic control schemes. An AGV simulation system concentrates on all or part of the above aspects. The statistics collected in the simulation would give useful information to both the route layout designers and the routing algorithm designers for the AGVs.

We have developed a prototype AGV simulation system[8]. It could run on SGI, SUN SPARC Workstation or other UNIX systems.

The user could specify the number of AGVs involved and various other control parameters at the beginning of a simulation run. Afterwards, the user can observe the visualization output of simulation execution. In the end, results are analyzed and reports are presented to the user. Usually, the user will invoke the simulation system with different parameters and repeat them many a time before coming to a conclusion.

We now port the original system to the Web and Internet by utilizing latest Internet technologies such as JAVA and JINI in the following sections.

We employ the "server fat approach" which means the critical computing is done on the server, usually a high performance machine, so as to tackle the complicated computing involved in a simulation in time. A Java "wrapper" program is developed for our legacy non-Java AGV simulation service. The GUI part inclusive of both input and output handling is ported onto the Web-Browser by means of Java applets. In our framework, the client is the Web-Browser, or more specifically the applet embedded in an HTML page; the server is a Java-coded or a JINI-enabled simulation service. Figure 1 is a snapshot of visualization outputs of a running AGV simulation on a Web-Browser.

3   An *Ad-Hoc* Approach

To support Web-based applications, it has become a rather standard practice to adopt a 3-tier architecture(see Fig. 2)[5].

We developed an initial *ad-hoc* version based on a generic approach, where the Middle-tier servers mediate between sophisticated back-end services and the Web front-ends. This approach applies an indirect communication model. By name, the clients will talk with the back-end services through a so-called "bridge". This model has both merits and demerits. Clearly, the biggest problem is that the "bridge" may become a bottleneck in the system with the number of links increased.

The user downloads Java applets from the Web server. The applets will then connect the client machine to a Lookup Service and send requests to the server. In response to a service request, the Lookup Service locates and forwards requests to the relevant AGV simulation service provider.

On the high performance computer side, an Application Server Daemon is responsible for registering itself in a Lookup Service and waiting for incoming requests. Upon receiving a request, the Daemon will invoke the high performance computing application with the given parameters. Finally, the results will be transferred back to the the clients via the Lookup Service server.

This version was developed by using JDK(Java Development Kit) with TCP/ IP as its communication protocol. Besides the shortcomings tagged with the indirect communication model, there are other drawbacks. The system has to deal with joining and leaving process of any particular AGV service provider. The most difficult part is to handle all kinds of faults or exceptions, such as a sudden crash of a service provider, failures of a subnetwork.

4   A Structured Approach: JINI-Enabled Framework

JINI is a framework for building scalable, robust and truly distributed systems using Java [2,4]. Using JINI is a new approach to demonstrate the concept of Web-enabled AGV simulation system. The JINI approach provides a number of benefits including instant availability of services, impromptu community software and high flexibility and fault tolerance.

By employing Java and JINI technology, we have designed, analyzed, and implemented a JINI-enabled framework for Web-based distributed AGV simulation system.

JINI-enabled version adopts a direct communication model, where the clients will communicate with back-end services directly through a proxy provided by the service. A proxy is an arbitrary serializable Java object in the service item. It contains the information of how to interact with the service.

The advantage of the direct scheme is obvious: firstly, there is no more "bridge"-like bottleneck; secondly, the communication delay will be reduced greatly [1]. A possible disadvantage of the direct communication model is related to the security issue. Malicious attacks to the back-end server are possible because the server's network address is published in its proxy. We here assume that the back-end machine itself has been well protected from intrusion.

4.1   System Architecture: Services Federation

Figure 3 shows a schematics of a so-called AGV simulation service federation which consists of one or more JINI Lookup Services.

For AGV Service Providers (see Fig. 3):

– *register*: The AGV service providers will join the federation by registering themselves in one or more JINI Lookup Services in the federation. This step could occur at any time when a high performance machine starts up and is willing to provide a service. The service programs may be one that has been installed on the machine or one downloaded from an AGV services repository. If the services programs are downloaded from a services repository, firstly, they should be configured to be able run on the local machine. That may involve compiling, linking and other necessary processing.

For Service Agents (see Fig. 3):

1. *Step (1)*: Firstly, the Service Agent should register itself in one or more Lookup Services so as to expose itself to clients and to be ready for serving. Meanwhile, it registered its interest in AGV Service in the federation.
2. *Step (2)*: Then, the agent will collect matched AGV Service Providers' proxies in the federation. When a new Service Provider comes to join the federation or a Service Provider leaves the federation, the JINI Lookup Services will notify the agent of the change. In this way, the agent could always keep a collection of all live Service Providers' proxies without polling individuals in the federation.

4.2 Distributed AGV Simulation Serving Scenario

Figure 4 shows the scenario of how the Web-enabled distributed AGV simulation system serves a user.

1. A user accesses the portal Web page of the AGV service, downloads Java applets and logs on the federation.
2. The applet will then connect the user machine to a JINI Lookup Service and search the Service Agent. When a Service Agent is located, the applet will forward the user's requirements to the Agent.
3. After that, the Agent will utilize all available AGV simulation computing resources to execute AGV simulation tasks according to the user's requirements. Multiple independent modules or multiple batch jobs will be performed concurrently.
4. The clients could monitor the execution of an individual task and observe its visualization output through the back-end server's proxy.

On the high performance computer side, upon receiving a request, a Service Provider Daemon will invoke the high performance computing application with the given parameters from the agents and finally the results will be transferred back to the requester.

Obviously, the "batch work" feature of simulation executions makes distributed multiprocessing possible. With the enforced system, we now are able to apply the agent approach to the following two categories of AGV simulation scenarios.

– *Iterative simulation and batch jobs* As we mentioned earlier, usually, a simulation run will be repeated for many a time with same parameters or different options before reaching a more objective result. In both cases, the agents system could dynamically distribute "batch tasks" among the service providers in the federation thus provide clients with a timely service.

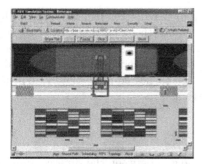

Fig. 1. A Sample Session in Automated Guided Vehicle Simulation

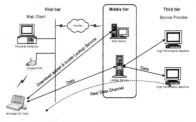

Fig. 2. 3-tier View of Web-Based Simulation System

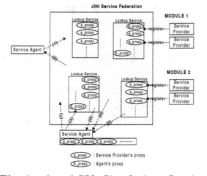

Fig. 3. An AGV Simulation Services Federation

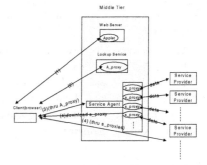

Fig. 4. Service Access Protocol in the Agent-Based Framework

- *Time-parallel simulation* This is an alternative way to Space-Parallel decomposition of simulation. The key idea is to decompose the simulation along the time dimension for multiprocessing [7]. Usually, the computing involved in intervals is independent. From another point of view, we have a batch of jobs again.

4.3   Scheduling and Self-Healing System

Clearly, scheduling is an important issue in our system. First of all, the agent will estimate a weight value for each service provider based on an estimation function:

$$V_{provider} = f(NumOfProc, PeakPerf, Workload, Latency, Credit, \ldots)$$

NumofProc represents the number of the service provider's physical processors; *PeakPerf* denotes its peak performance; *Workload* indicates its current computing workload; and *Latency* means the communication delay. These parameters are dynamic information.

Credit is an additional information. Each Service Provider is tagged with a *Credit* value which is evaluated by the Agent depending on the number of failures of the Service Provider in earlier scenarios. Important and nontrivial tasks are always dispatched to a Service Provider with a high *Credit* value.

With JINI technology, a provider joining or leaving the federation could be observed by the agent. The agent will recalculate the weight values of service providers and refresh the ordered list regularly. If any task is currently assigned to a failed service provider, it will be reassigned to another provider. Meanwhile, any newly joined resource will be noticed and be harnessed immediately. In other words, it is an adaptive and self-healing system.

5   Conclusions and Future Work

This project arises from the need to bridge the gap between the supercomputers and the general users by utilizing some of the prevailing Internet technologies. Through a JINI-enabled distributed AGV simulation services community, the remote client could access the AGV simulation resources on a network even on the Internet with a common Web-Browser. The following are recaps of our main contributions:

- We have evaluated two approaches in terms of their suitability to the Web-based AGV simulation application.
- A Web-based and JINI-enabled distributed AGV simulation system has been implemented with Java and JINI technologies resulting in intelligence, self-heal, improved efficiency, high scalability, high reliability, fault tolerance, and with security measure.

References

1. Hyok Kim, Hongki Sung, and Hoonbock Lee: Performance Analysis of the TCP/IP Protocol Under UNIX Operating Systems for High Performance Computing and Communications. HPC ASIA'97 IEEE. (1997) 499 -504
2. Ken Arnold, Bryan Osullivan, Robert W Scheifler and Jim Waldo: The Jini Specification. Addison-Wesley (1999)
3. Bernard Conrad Cole: The Emergence of Net-centric Computing: Network computers, Internet Appliances, and Connected PCs. Prentice Hall (1999)
4. W. Keith Edwards: Core Jini. Prentice Hall (1999)
5. Jeri Edwards: 3-Tier Client/Server At Work (revised edition). Robert Ipsen (1999)
6. Ian Foster: The Grid: Blueprint for a New Computing Infrastructure. Morgan Kaufmann (1999)
7. David M. Nicol and Richard M. Fujimoto: Parallel simulatio today. Annals of Operations Research, 53:249-285, 1994
8. Voon-Yee Vee, Rong Ye, Shah Sneha Niranjan and Wen-Jing Hsu: Meeting Challenges of Container Port Operations for the Next Millennium. Report for Supercomputer Programming Contest(CrayQuest'99), Singapore. (1999), Gold Award Winner
9. Voon-Yee Vee, Rong Ye, Liu Zehua, Shah Sneha Niranjan, Wen-Jing Hsu and Frank Reichert: Web-Based Parallel Computations: Challenges and Opportunities of HPC in the Network-Centric Era. Report for Supercomputer Programming Contest (CrayQuest'2000), Singapore. (2000) Grand Champion (Industry Category)

On the Parallelezation of Domain Decomposition Methods for 3-D Boundary Value Problems*

V.N. Babin, V.P. Il'in, and A.S. Pylkin

Institute of Computational Mathematics and Mathematical Geophysics,
Siberian Division of Russian Academy of Sciences,
pr. Lavrentieva, 6, Novosibirsk, 630090, Russia
pylkin@ssd.sscc.ru

Abstract. An investigation of parallel domain decomposition methods for interactive solution of 3D boundary value problem is presented. The various variants of algorithms are considered: the different values of subdomain overlapping, the different numbers of subdomains and processors, accelerated and non-accelerated two-level iterations. The dependence of speedup on the computational parameters is discussed on the base of numerical experiment at the multiprocessor computer Fujitsu-Siemense RM600.

Keywords: parallel implementation, multiprocessor, speedup, domain decomposition method, boundary value problem

1 Introduction

We consider numerical solution of grid three-dimensional boundary value problems obtained by finite element, finite difference or finite volume approximations, see [1]. The conventional approach for solution of obtained linear algebraic systems of equations with sparse matrices of very large order consists of using the incomplete factorization with conjugate gradient methods [2], which provide the number of iterations $O(h^{-1/2})$ but do not garantee a scaling speedup in parallel direct implementation at the multiprocessor computer system. The cardinal improvement of situation is made by the application of domain decomposition [3] based on the simultaneous solution of subsystems into computational subdomains and organizing the external iteration with the sequential data transfers between neighbour processors. Here the topological equivalence of subdomains and computer net is supposed (subdomain $\Longleftrightarrow$ processor).

The goal of presented paper is experimental investigation of efficiency of domain decomposition methods for the solution of model three-dimensional boundary value problems at the multiprocessor computer Fujitsu-Siemense' RM 600. The various variants of algorithms are considered: the different values of subdomain over lapping, the different numbers of subdomains and processors, accelerated and non-accelerated iterations.

In section 2 we described the parallelized algorithms. The section 3 presents the discussion of the numerical results.

---

* The work is supported by the RFBR grants N 99-01-00579, N 99-07-90422

2   The Description of the Algorithms

We consider numerical solution of three-dimensional boundary value problem for
the diffusion equation

$$-\frac{\partial}{\partial x} a \frac{\partial u}{\partial x} - \frac{\partial}{\partial y} b \frac{\partial u}{\partial y} - \frac{\partial}{\partial z} c \frac{\partial u}{\partial z} = f(x, y, z),$$
$$(x, y, z) \in \Omega; \quad a, b, c > 0,$$
(1)

in parallelepipedoidal computational domain $\Omega = (x_0, x_{L+1}) \times (y_0, y_{M+1}) \times (z_0 \times z_{N+1})$ under Dirichlet condition at the boundary Γ

$$u|_\Gamma = g(x, y, z).$$
(2)

By means of simple finite difference or finite volume (see [1]) or finite element
approximations at the regular grid

$$x_i = x_{i-1} + h_i^x, \quad y_j = y_{j-1} + h_j^y, \quad z_k = z_{k-1} + h_k^z,$$
$$i = 1, 2, ..., L + 1, \quad j = 1, 2, ..., M + 1, \quad k = 1, 2, ..., N + 1$$
(3)

we obtain the algebraic grid system of linear 7-point equations, see [1]:

$$(Av)_{i,j,k} = \left(p_0 v_0 - \sum_{l=1}^{6} p_l v_l \right)_{i,j,k} = f_{i,j,k}^h,$$
$$i = 1, ..., L, \quad j = 1, ..., M, \quad k = 1, ..., N,$$
(4)

where the local indeces $0, 1, ..., 6$ are corresponded to the central (i, j, k)-th of grid
stencil and its neighbours with multi-indeces $(i - 1, j, k)$, $(i, j - 1, k)$, $(i + 1, j, k)$,
$(i, j + 1, k)$, $(i, j, k - 1)$, $(i, j, k + 1)$ respectively. The right hand sides $f_{i,j,k}^h$ take
into account boundary condition (2) and the matrix A is seven diagonal sym-
metric positive definite matrix. The coefficients $(p_l)_{i,j,k}$ before the terms $(v_l)_{i,j,k}$,
which correspond to boundary nodes, are supposed to be zero and corresponding
boundary values are included in $f_{i,j,k}^h$.

The main part of computational complexity of solution of multidimensional
boundary value problem consists of numerical solving the very large linear algebraic systems of equations with sparse structured matrices. One of the most
efficient approach for the scaled parallel implementation is domain decomposition method which in the simplest form can be discribed as follows.

Let we have rectangular computer net with the $p \cdot q$ processors. The map-
ping of algorithms at the computer architecture consists into definition of $p \cdot q$ corresponding subdomains. The grid computational domain is presented as
$\Omega = \bigcup \Omega_{l,m}, \ l = 1, ..., p, \ m = 1, ..., q$ where parallelepipedoidal subdomain
is $\Omega_{l,m} = [i_l^b, i_l^e] \times [y_m^b, j_m^e]$ for all indeces $k = 0, 1, ..., N + 1$. The differences
$\Delta i = i_{l-1}^e - i_l^b \geq -1$ and $\Delta j = j_{m-1}^e - j_m^b \geq 1$ are integer measure of overlapping.

For simplicity we consider the uniform domain decomposition, i.e. each (l, m)-
th subdomain has the same number of nodes $K_{l,m} = (i_l^e - i_l^b)(j_m^e - j_m^b)(N + 2)$
and overlapping sizes $\Delta i, \Delta j$. We define the measure of overlapping

$$\delta = lm K_{l,m} / (LMN),$$
(5)

which characterizes the reduntant computations in DDM.

The simplest version of iterative domain decomposition method, i.e. block Jacoby algorithm, can be written as

$$
\begin{aligned}
A_{l,m}\hat{v}_{l,m}^{n} = A_{l,m}^{(1)}v_{l-1,m}^{n-1} + A_{l,m}^{(2)}v_{l,m-1}^{n-1} + \\
A_{l,m}^{(3)}v_{l+1,m}^{n-1} + A_{l,m}^{(4)}v_{l,m+1}^{n-1} + f_{l,m} \equiv g_{l,m}^{n-1},
\end{aligned}
\tag{6}
$$

where n is the number of (external) iterations, $A_{l,m}$ and $\hat{u}_{l,m}$ are the square matrix and subvector which orders equal to the number $K_{l,m}$ of nodes in subdomain $\Omega_{l,m}$. The rest four matrices are responsible for the connections with the neigbour subdomains. Let $S_{l,m}$ is the total number of nonzero entries in the sum of the matrices $A_{l,m}^{(1)} + ... + A_{l,m}^{(4)}$, which characterizes the measure of communication time at each external iteration.

The vector $\hat{u}_{l,m}^{n}$ means the preliminary new iterative value, modified by the formula

$$
v_{l,m}^{n} = \tau_n \hat{v}_{l,m}^{n} + (1 - \tau_n)v_{l,m}^{n-1}
\tag{7}
$$

of Chebyshev acceleration with parameters τ_n or by cojugate gradient approach, see [2]. The stopping criteratia for iterations (6), (7) is tolerance condition for the residual

$$
\|r^n\|/\|r^0\| \le \varepsilon_e, \quad r^n = f^h - Av^n.
\tag{8}
$$

Each system in (l,m)-th subdomain is solved by means of some internal iterative process

$$
B_{l,m}(v_{l,m}^{n,t} - v_{l,m}^{n,t-1}) = g_{l,m}^{n-1} - A_{l,m}v_{l,m}^{n,t-1}, \quad v_{l,m}^{n,0} = v_{l,m}^{n-1},
\tag{9}
$$

where $B_{l,m}$ is corresponding preconditioning matrix and some acceleration procedure is applied to (9) similar to (7).

The internal iterative process continue until to the given number of iterations n_i or it is interrupted by own tolerance criteria

$$
\|r_{l,m}^{n,t}\|/\|r_{l,m}^{n,0}\| \le \varepsilon_{i,n}, \quad r_{l,m}^{n,t} = g_{l,m} - A_{l,m}v_{l,m}^{n,t-1}.
\tag{10}
$$

In general, under condition (10) the numbers of internal iterations t_n can be different for different subdomains, but we mean its maximum value in this case.

The total number of arithmetic operations in such two-level method is defined as

$$
Q_{l,m} = (n_{l,m}q_l + \sum_{k=1}^{n} t_k q_i)l\,m,
\tag{11}
$$

where $n_{l,m}$ is the number of external iterations, q_i is the number of operations at each internal iteration and q_l notes an additional volume of operations at one external iteration (in one subdomain), which are propertional to $K_{l,m}$.

3   The Analysis of Efficiency

If τ_a and τ_c are average times of one arithmetic operation and tranfer of one value between processors then the total time of implementation of numerical solution of system (4) equals

$$T_{l,m} = Q_{l,m}\tau_a + n_{l,m}S_{l,m}\tau_c. \tag{12}$$

There is an evident consequence of this formula in the sence of influence of grid subdomain shape on the relative contribution of communication losses. Namely, because the numbers of arithmetic operations in (12) is proportional to $(lm)^\gamma$, $\gamma \geq 1$, and communication time is proportional to $l + m$, the optimal situation is $l = m$ when all subdomains have the same square cross-sections.

For the fixed total number LMN of meshpoints and given overlapping measures Δi, Δj, increasing the number lm of subdomains and processors increases the number of external iterations and decreases the numbers of internal ones.

For the fixed LMN and lm the increasing of overlapping values decreases the number of external iterations $n_{l,m}$ but increases the number of internal iterations t_n, the communication time and reduntant coefficient δ in (5). So, the problem of optimization of DD algorithm is complicated enough and is hardly investigated theoretically, because various tactics of choosing the tolerance criteria for internal iterations can be used, and estimation of condition numbers for variably preconditioned iterative processes is open question in the matrix theory.

The analize of speedup factor $R_{l,m} = T_{l,m}/T_1$ and coefficient of efficiency $E_{l,m} = R_{l,m}/(lm)$ can be different in terms of definition of denominator T_1. More direct definition of T_1 is the execution time of the same DD method at one processor. But in fact DDM is not the best algorithm for sequential implementation, and estimation of $R_{l,m}$ can be done more pessimistic, if we use, for example, algebraic multigrid method for solution of (4) which is badly parallelezable but has almost optimal order of computational efficiency.

The another motivation of multiprocessor implementation of DDM consists of collecting together the computational resources of several processors for solution of the big problems which can not be solving efficiently at one processor (for example, it demands the huge flopping because of deficite of CPU).

The dramatically high speedup can be obtained due to existance of the fast cash memory if its size is not sufficient for the runming of the problem at one processor but it can be used efficiently in multiprocessor regime. in a such case the super-linear speedup, i.e. $R_{l,m} > lm$ and $E_{l,m} > 1$, can be achieved typically.

We consider the results of numerical experiments for the model Dirichlet boundary value problems (1), (2) with constant coefficients $a = b = c = 1$.

The solutions were sought at the square grids for different L, M, N and "line" processor nets with $m = 1$ and $l = 1, 2, 4, 8$. The simplest Jacoby iterative method was used for the external iterations with $\varepsilon_e = 0.5$ and for internal iterations with the fixed values $n_i = 5, 10, 20$. In the Tables 1–4 the numbers of external iterations n_e and CPU times T_l are presented. The computations were made at the Fujitsu-Siemense RM 600 E30 SMP-system containing 4.2GByte

Table 1. Numerical results for DDM without overlapping, grids $L \cdot 64 \cdot 64$, $n_i = 5, 10, 20$

p	L	n_L	$T_p(sec)$
1	64	223, 111, 55	124, 120, 123
2	128	288, 149, 81	161, 163, 179
4	256	289, 150, 81	165, 173, 183

Table 2. The results for DDM without overlapping, grids $L \cdot 150 \cdot 150$, $n_i = 5, 10, 20$

p	L	n_L	$T_p(sec)$
1	50	272, 136, 68	637, 635, 635
2	100	858, 440, 232	2085, 2104, 2274
4	200	1153, 592, 312	3084, 3053, 3266

Table 3. Numerical results for DDM with overlapping $\Delta i = 10$, grids $L \cdot 64 \cdot 64$, $n_l = 5, 10, 20$

p	L	n_L	$T_p(sec)$
1	64	167, 83, 41	94, 91, 93
2	128	216, 111, 60	122, 123, 135
4	256	216, 112, 60	125, 131, 138

Table 4. Numerical results for DDM with overlapping $\Delta i = 10$, grids $L \cdot 150 \cdot 150$, $n_i = 5, 10, 20$

p	L	n_L	$T_p(sec)$
1	50	204, 102, 51	481, 479, 480
2	100	643, 330, 174	1574, 1589, 1717
4	200	864, 444, 234	2328, 2305, 2466

of shared memory and 8 processors R10000 running at frequency of 250 mhz. System software includes Reliant UNIX operating system, C/C++ and Fortran compilers and MPICH 1.2.0 software.

The presented results provide the following conclusions.

a. The simultaneous increasing the grid numbers L by factor p and the numbers of processors increase the number of external iterations n_e and CPU time proportionally to p^α, $\alpha \approx 1/2$. It provides a good enough speedup and efficiency of parallelized domain decomposition method.

b. The improvement of general convergence rate of iteration process demands using the acceleration of external iterations, an implementation of more fast internal solver instead the simplest Jacoby algorithm and dynamical control of two level iterations. It can be done on the base of advanced incomplete factorization methods and application of preconditioned conjugate gradient methods

[2]. The problem of optimization of parallel DDM needs on additional theoretical as experimental investigations.

c. The further increasing of speedup can be achieved by means more careful mapping of algorithm structure into the computer architecture on the base of simubtaneous implementation of data multicommunications and arithmetic operations in fast cash distributed or shared memory. The considered approaches can be used efficiently for more general boundary value problems, including nonlinear or nonstationary differential equations instead of (1). It should increase the total computational complexity of algorithm but not decrease the speedup of the parallel implementation.

References

1. V.P.Il'in. Finite difference and finite volume method for elliptic equations. Novosibirsk, IM SDRAS Publ., 2000, 344 pp. (in Russian).
2. V.P.Il'in. Incomplete factorization methods. Singapore, World Sci Publ., 1992, 190pp.
3. V.P.I'in. On the strategies of parallelezation in mathematical modeling. Programming, N 1, 1999, 41-46.

Parallel Generation of Percolation Beds Based on Stochastic Cellular Automata

Stefania Bandini, Giancarlo Mauri, and Giulio Pavesi

Dept. of Computer Science, Systems and Communication
University of Milan–Bicocca
Milan, Italy
{bandini,mauri,pavesi}@disco.unimib.it

Abstract. Percolation is the process that causes a a solvent (e.g. water) to pass through a permeable substance and to extract a soluble constituent. Cellular Automata provide a very powerful tool for the simulation and the analysis of percolation processes. In some cases, however, the most challenging problem is perhaps to reproduce correctly within the automaton the features of the percolation bed, that is, the porous medium the solvent flows through. In this paper we present a computational model for the controlled generation of two–dimensional percolation beds based on stochastic Cellular Automata, and we show how it has been applied to the generation of percolation beds suitable for the simulation of pesticide percolation in the soil. In particular, the approach we present permits to keep under control the shape and the size of the single components of the bed (e.g. grains), and their position. In order to reproduce percolation beds of feasible size, and to manage large automata, the model has been implemented on a cluster of workstations.

1 Introduction

Percolation is the process that causes a a solvent (for example, water) to pass through a permeable substance, and to extract a soluble constituent. Percolation processes have been thoroughly studied both from theoretical [1] and applicative [2] viewpoints. Percolation theory defines and offers formal frameworks for the creation of abstract, analytical, and computational models dealing with a wide range of phenomena.

The computer simulation of percolation phenomena occurring in porous media is a very challenging problem, for which several computational models and techniques have been introduced, from finite elements algorithms to Cellular Automata (CA) [3]. The latter provide a very powerful tool for the simulation of percolation processes, for instance, in case of coffee [4], pesticides [5] and carbon black rubber compounds [6]. In these models, some cells of the automaton reproduce the percolation bed, that is, the porous medium the solvent flows through, while others are empty or contain the solvent. Reproducing in the automaton the features of real percolation beds, however, can be a very challenging task. When available, microscope images of real case studies can be used directly or as

V. Malyshkin (Ed.): PaCT 2001, LNCS 2127, pp. 391–400, 2001.

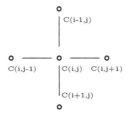

Fig. 1. The von Neumann neighborhood of cell $C(i, j)$.

a model to be reproduced, both for the shape and the size of the single components (for example, grains of coffee), and their position within the bed. In some cases, however, experimental data are hard or expensive to obtain. Therefore, a computer–based method for the generation of percolation beds reproducing as much as possible the features of real cases could be a very useful tool. In particular, in this paper we focus on the generation of percolation beds reproducing *soil*, that have been used for the simulation of pesticide percolation.

2   The Model

Informally, CA can be viewed as parallel computing machines made of a large number of processors, called cells, that perform simple operations, opposed to traditional sequential computers based on a single processing unit that executes complex operations. Cells are usually arranged on a regular grid. CA evolve through a sequence of discrete time steps. At a given time, every cell is characterized by a *state*, belonging to a finite set. The state of the cells is updated simultaneously at each step according to a given *update rule*. The rule determines the new state of each cell according to the current state of the cell itself and the state of the neighboring cells, located on adjacent nodes of the grid. In our model cells are arranged on a two–dimensional $N \times M$ square grid, and we adopted the von Neumann neighborhood, where every cell has four neighbors. More in detail, the neighbors of the cell located in position (i, j) in the grid are the cells in positions $(i - 1, j)$, $(i + 1, j)$, $(i, j - 1)$, and $(i, j + 1)$ (see Fig. 1).

In this paper, we present a computational model based on Stochastic Cellular Automata (that is, CA whose update rule is probabilistic) for the controlled generation of two–dimensional patterns, that permits to keep under control the morphological properties (shape and size) of the patterns produced. The cells of the automaton can assume two states: *empty* or *occupied*. Patterns are formed by adjacent occupied cells (*components*), and are dynamically generated starting from a single occupied cell that assumes the role of an initial *seed*, while the remaining cells of the automaton are empty. When the automaton is started, the seed starts growing, with a process similar to cell mitosis, and generates new components into adjacent empty cells. The reproductive potential of the seed is expressed with an integer number of *reproductive abilities*, that determines the final size of the pattern. In fact, each reproduction uses one reproductive ability;

therefore, the maximum number of components that can be generated equals the number of reproductive abilities assigned to the initial seed. A newly generated component takes some reproductive abilities from its parent component, becoming in this way able to produce offspring components by itself. Once a cell has become occupied by a component, it cannot revert its state back to empty.

The choice of the neighboring cells that will contain a new component, that is, the direction of growth of the pattern, is controlled by a probabilistic mechanism that can be fine tuned in order to obtain patterns with different shape. That is, a probability value is associated with each of the four possible growth directions. Thus, each evolution of the CA starting with the same probability distribution produces (with high probability) a different pattern. Anyway, all patterns generated with the same probability distribution have the same macroscopic properties, that is, look similar to the human eye.

The automaton can be initialized with more than one seed. In this case, each pattern is characterized by a different *id number*. A cell can belong to at most one pattern, and all the cells belonging to the same pattern have the same id number. A different number of reproductive abilities, and different growth probabilities can be assigned to each seed, in order to obtain patterns of different size and shape within the same automaton. Whenever an empty cell has neighbors with different id numbers trying to generate a new component in its position, its occupation is determined by competition among candidate parents.

In the following section we present the formal description of the model for the generation of a single pattern. Then, we show how the model can be extended to more than one pattern. Finally, we show how the model has been applied to the generation of artificial percolation beds for the simulation of pesticide leaching in the soil.

3   Generating a Single Pattern

We now give the formal definition of the automaton. The CA is defined by a 5–tuple $\mathbf{CA} = \langle R, H, Q, f, I \rangle$, where:

1. $R = \{(i, j) \mid 0 \leq i \leq N - 1; 0 \leq j \leq M - 1; N, M \in \mathbb{N}\}$, is a two–dimensional $N \times M$ lattice;
2. H is the von Neumann neighborhood;
3. $Q = \langle ID, \mathbf{CAP}, \mathbf{P} \rangle$ is the finite set of the values of variables of state, where:
   (a) ID is the cell identifier, 0 in case of an empty cell, 1 otherwise;
   (b) $\mathbf{CAP} = \langle N, S, W, E \rangle$ are integers representing the number of reproductive abilities respectively towards north, south, west, and east;
   (c) $\mathbf{P} = \langle P_N, P_S, P_W, P_E \rangle$ are the probabilities of directing the reproductive abilities towards north, south, west and east, that is, the probabilities associated with the four possible directions of growth, such that $\sum_{i \in \{N, S, W, E\}} P_i = 1$.
4. $f : Q \times Q^{|H|} \rightarrow Q$ is the state transition function (update rule);
5. $I : R \rightarrow Q$ is the initialization function.

Fig. 2. The structure of a cell of the automaton.

The structure of a cell of the automaton is shown in Fig. 2. From now on, we will refer with $\mathbf{C}(i,j)$ to the cell located at coordinates (i,j), with $ID(i,j)$ to its identifier, with $N(i,j)$, $S(i,j)$, $W(i,j)$, and $E(i,j)$ to the number of reproductive abilities contained in each of its four portions, with $\mathbf{P}(i,j) = \langle P_N(i,j), P_S(i,j), P_W(i,j), P_E(i,j) \rangle$ to the probability values associated with the four directions.

The initialization function I picks a cell (k,l), usually located near the center of the automaton, sets its ID to one (it becomes occupied), and sets the other parameters corresponding to the reproductive abilities and the probabilities defined by the user. Every other cell (i,j) of the automaton has ID set to zero, no reproductive abilities, and probability values $\mathbf{P}(i,j) = \mathbf{P}(k,l)$.

The transition function f is the composition of two functions. Therefore, $f = h \circ g$, where $g : Q \times Q^{|H|} \to Q$ is defined as follows:

$$g(\mathbf{C}(i,j), S(i-1,j), N(i+1,j), W(i,j+1), E(i,j-1)) = \mathbf{C}'(i,j)$$

with $\mathbf{C}'(i,j) = \langle ID'(i,j), \mathbf{CAP}'(i,j), \hat{\mathbf{P}}(i,j) \rangle$, where:

$$ID'(i,j) = ID(k,l)$$

If $ID(i,j) = 0$, then (k,l) are the coordinates of the cell corresponding to the maximum of $\{N(i+1,j), S(i-1,j), W(i,j+1), E(i,j-1)\}$ (the highest bidder among the neighbors). Otherwise, $(k,l) = (i,j)$. That is, if an empty cell has at least one neighbor with ID set to one, and able to reproduce in its direction, it becomes occupied. Otherwise, the ID does not change, and remains one or zero. An occupied cell (newly or not) collects reproductive abilities from occupied neighbors. That is:

$$N'(i,j) = \begin{cases} S(i-1,j) & \text{if } ID'(i,j) = ID(i-1,j) = 1 \\ N(i,j) & \text{otherwise} \end{cases}$$

If the ID of the cell at the previous step was zero and the cell becomes occupied for effect of function g, then the number of the reproductive abilities inherited from the parent neighbor (at least one) is decreased by one, used by cell (i,j) itself to become occupied. Also, $\hat{\mathbf{P}}(i,j) = \mathbf{P}(i,j)$, that is, probabilities are left unchanged by g. The function $h : Q \to Q$ is defined as follows:

$$h(\langle ID(i,j), \mathbf{CAP}(i,j), \mathbf{P}(i,j) \rangle) = \langle ID'(i,j), \mathbf{CAP}'(i,j), \hat{\mathbf{P}}(i,j) \rangle$$

Fig. 3. Growth of a seed with 5000 reproductive abilities, $P = 1/4$ in each direction, at step 5, 10, 50, 100, 200, and 500.

where $ID'(i,j) = ID(i,j)$ (the identifier does not change). The actual change takes place in the distribution in the four portions of the reproductive abilities collected at the previous step (if any). That is, given $T_N = N(i,j) + S(i,j) + W(i,j) + E(i,j)$, we have:

$$N'(i,j) = \sum_{k=1}^{T_N} r_k^N$$

where r_k^N are T_N random variables such that $\forall r_k^N$, $\Pr[r_k^N = 1] = P_N(i,j)$. Then, set $T_S = T_N - N'(i,j)$, we have:

$$S'(i,j) = \sum_{k=1}^{T_S} r_k^S$$

where $\forall r_k^S$, $\Pr[r_k^S = 1] = P_S(i,j)$. In the same way, given $T_W = T_N - S'(i,j)$,

$$W'(i,j) = \sum_{k=1}^{T_W} r_k^W$$

with $\forall r_k^W$, $\Pr[r_k^W = 1] = P_W(i,j)$. Finally, given $T_E = T_W - W'(i,j)$:

$$E'(i,j) = T_E$$

Also, h might change the four probabilities $\mathbf{P}(i,j)$. One possible way could be to rotate the probabilities, for example, by setting $\hat{P}_N(i,j) = P_E(i,j)$, $\hat{P}_W(i,j) = P_N(i,j)$, and so on. The final shape of the patterns generated by the automaton is determined by the initial probabilities assigned to the starting seed and how they are changed during the evolution. For example, if the probabilities are initially set to $1/4$ in each direction and left unchanged by function h, the result is the uniform growth of the pattern in the four directions, with a final shape that looks circular, as shown in Fig. 3. Different simulations would lead (with high probability) to a slightly different result, that anyway would still look circular to the human eye.

4   The Multi Pattern Model

In order to let more than a single pattern grow within the same automaton, we
have to make some changes in the model introduced in the previous section. The
user may now define different classes of patterns (each one possibly corresponding
to a different growth probability distribution) he wants to generate, the size of the
patterns belonging to each class (usually picked at random between minimum
and maximum values), and how many patterns he wants for each class (the
exact number, or assigning a probability value to each class). The initialization
function has now to plant more than one seed; this can be simply implemented
by choosing a cell at random, checking whether it is occupied or not, and, in
the latter case, defining the initial parameters of the seed according to the user's
input.

An occupied cell belongs to only one pattern. In order to be able to recognize
which pattern a cell belongs to, the *ID* is now defined as an integer (greater than
zero, not greater than the number of the patterns). Each pattern is therefore
formed by cells with the same *ID*. The *ID* is assigned to the patterns by the
initialization step, that simply associates a different *ID* number with each seed.

Moreover, an empty cell might now have neighbors belonging to different
patters trying simultaneously to expand toward its direction, generating a new
component in its position. The transition function has therefore to be modified
in order to solve this possible conflict. The idea is the following: the cell takes
the *ID* of the highest bidder, that is, the neighbor which has more reproductive
abilities in the portion adjacent to the empty cell. Ties are broken arbitrarily.
Also, occupied cells can trade abilities with neighbors with the same *ID*. The
transition sub–function g therefore becomes:

$$g(\mathbf{C}(i,j), S(i-1,j), N(i+1,j), W(i,j+1), E(i,j-1)) = \mathbf{C}'(i,j)$$

with $\mathbf{C}'(i,j) = \langle ID'(i,j), \mathbf{CAP}'(i,j), \hat{\mathbf{P}}(i,j) \rangle$, where:

$$ID'(i,j) = ID(k,l)$$

$$\hat{\mathbf{P}}(i,j) = \mathbf{P}(k,l)$$

If cell (i,j) is empty, and at least one neighbor has reproductive abilities in the
portion adjacent to (i,j), then (k,l) are the coordinates of the cell corresponding
to the maximum of $\{N(i+1,j), S(i-1,j), W(i,j+1), E(i,j-1)\}$ (the highest
bidding neighbor). Otherwise, $(k,l) = (i,j)$. Also,

$$N'(i,j) = \begin{cases} S(i-1,j) & \text{if } ID'(i,j) = ID(i-1,j) \\ N(i,j) & \text{otherwise} \end{cases}$$

The terms $S'(i,j)$, $W'(i,j)$ and $E'(i,j)$ are defined in a similar way. As in the
single–pattern case, if $ID(i,j) = 0$ and $ID'(i,j) > 0$ the abilities inherited from
the parent cell are decreased by one. The transition sub–function h remains
unchanged.

Table 1. Different types of soil texture and corresponding grain size.

Soil	Grain Diameter
Clays	$< .002$ mm
Silts	$.002 - .02$ mm
Sands	$.02 - 2$ mm
Coarse Fragments	> 2 mm

5   Generation of Soil Percolation Beds

Pesticides have become essential elements for modern agriculture, in order to obtain production yields sufficient to satisfy the growing needs of the increasing world population. More than two million tons of pesticide products derived from 900 active ingredients are used each year worldwide. The extensive use of pesticides can entail risks for the environment and non–target organisms, including humans. When applied to crops, pesticides are absorbed by soil. Then, when water flows through the soil because of rain or floods, pesticides can be released into it. Water containing pesticide may reach the groundwater layer because of gravity. Since groundwater is usually the source of common tap water, it is straightforward to understand the polluting danger deriving from the excessive use of pesticides. For percolation beds used in simulations of this case study, experimental data concern shape and size of the grains composing the bed. Soil separates (individual grains of soil mineral materials) can be divided into three main particle size classes, shown in Table 1. Size fractions are generally determined either by sieving or by Stokes settling rates. Soil is usually classified according to the percentage of clay, silt, and sand grains it contains. Thus, percolation beds can also be composed of different classes of grains. It has been experimentally observed (by microscope images) that the larger are the grains, the more regular is their shape. Clay grains are very irregular, while sand grains (the largest) are more or less spherical. The percentage of the percolation bed occupied by grains usually ranges from 40% to 60%. The position of the grains in the bed is based on the following rule–of–thumb (based on geologists' advice): voids between grains cannot be larger than the maximum size of the grains in the bed.

The size of grains is reproduced in our model as follows. We let the size of the smallest grain composing the bed correspond to the size of a cell of the automaton. Therefore, the number of abilities assigned to a seed ranges from 0 (the smallest grain possible) to $R = M/m$, where M and m are the maximum and minimum grain size allowed, respectively. For example, in case of silt percolation beds, the largest grain can be 100 times larger than the smallest one. Therefore, the number of abilities assigned to each seed is selected at random between 0 and 100 according to the probability distribution given by the user. For example, we can have uniform probability over the size range. In case of percolation beds composed by different grain types, we first select the seed type at random (with probabilities proportional to the percentage of grains of each type we want in

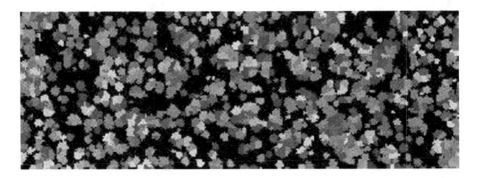

Fig. 4. Example of a silt percolation bed, generated by the multi–pattern model.

the bed), then assign to it the reproductive abilities. The shape of the grains can be reproduced in our model by setting the growth probabilities to 1/4 in each direction, that, as we have shown, tends to generate circular patterns. Also, the smallest is the pattern generated, the more irregular is its shape, as in the real case.

The final position of the grains in the percolation bed is influenced by the choice of the cells containing the initial seeds. Seeds cannot be too close, since in this case they would not have enough room to grow. The effect would be a percolation bed with some parts packed with grains and some under–populated regions, violating the rule determining the maximum size of empty spaces. We solved this problem with a simple trick: whenever we plant a seed in the automaton and we mark its cell as occupied, we also mark the surrounding cells as "unavailable" for seeds, in order to prevent another seed to be too close the current one. The size of the forbidden area roughly corresponds to the average size of a grain. Even if this rule does not guarantee that too many grains are packed together, the experimental results have been satisfactory. An example is shown in Fig. 4.

The initial particle size of the mineral fraction influences many processes of soil development and the properties of the resulting soil. Coarser (larger) materials generally have high hydraulic conductivities, while finer materials have low hydraulic conductivities, that is, let less water (and thus less pollutants) reach the groundwater layer. Thus, the sandier is the soil (that is, the larger are the grains composing it), the higher is the risk for water containing pesticides to reach the groundwater layer. These results have been reproduced in our model [7], leading us to conjecture that the morphological properties of the percolation beds have been captured successfully.

6   The Parallel Implementation

In order to generate percolation beds of feasible size and to model real conditions, a very large automaton has often to be employed, and the update rule has to be applied a large number of times. For example, in percolation bed of silt, each cell represents a square portion of soil with a side of 2 μm. This makes the algorithm time and memory consuming even for the most powerful sequential machines. Therefore, we implemented our model on a cluster of workstations, using the MPI (Message Passing Interface) library.

The two-dimensional grid forming the automaton is divided vertically into n layers, where n is the number of processors available. Basically, each processor updates a slice of the automaton. That is, processor p will take care of cells belonging to rows from $\frac{N}{n}(p-1)$ to $\frac{N}{n}p-1$, where N is the overall number of rows. Thus, at each update step the processors update simultaneously the cells belonging to their part, divided in rows numbered from 1 to N/n.

Rows 1 and N/n of each layer have to be updated according (also) to the state of cells belonging to other processors. For this reason, we added rows 0 and $(N/n)+1$ to each part. These two rows are composed of so–called *ghost cells*. Before each update step, processor number p communicates the state of its cells of row 1 to processor number $p-1$, and the state of the cells of row N/n to processor number $p+1$. It also receives the state of the cells of row N/n from processor $p-1$, that form its own row 0, and the state of the cells of row 1 from processor $p+1$, that form its own row $(N/n)+1$. In this way, each processor can update its border rows copying in its ghost cells the state of the neighboring cells belonging to different processors. In order to parallelize also the communication among processors, we make processor p communicate first with $p+1$, then with $p-1$ if p is even; vice versa if p is odd.

The parallel implementation of the update routine of the automaton can be summed up as follows, where p is the processor number:

1. if (p is odd):
   (a) send row 1 to processor $p-1$;
   (b) receive row 0 from processor $p-1$;
   (c) send row N/n to processor $p+1$;
   (d) receive row $(N/n)+1$ from processor $p+1$;
2. else (p is even)
   (a) receive row $(N/n)+1$ from processor $p+1$;
   (b) send row N/n to processor $p+1$;
   (c) receive row 0 from processor $p-1$;
   (d) send row 1 to processor $p-1$;
3. Update cells;

7   Conclusions

Among the problems arising in the design and development of computer environments for the simulation of percolation in porous media, the correct representation of percolation beds is a crucial issue. The model we presented, that controls both the properties of single components and their overall position, can provide an efficient tool for this task, as shown in this work for the case of soil percolation beds.

References

1. D. Stauffer, A. Aharony. Introduction to Percolation Theory. Taylor & Francis, London, 1992.
2. M. Sahimi. Applications of Percolation Theory. Taylor & Francis, London, 1994.
3. M. Sahimi (ed.). Flow Phenomena in Rocks: from Continuum Models to Fractals, Percolation, Cellular Automata and Simulated Annealing. *Rev. of Modern Physics*, **65**(4), 1993.
4. C. Borsani, G. Cattaneo, V. de Mattei, U. Jocher, B. Zampini. 2D and 3D Lattice Gas Techniques of Fluid–Dynamic Simulations. In S. Bandini, R. Serra, F. Suggi Liverani (eds.), *Cellular Automata: Research Towards Industry*, Springer Verlag, Berlin, 1998.
5. S. Bandini, G. Mauri, G. Pavesi, C. Simone. A Parallel Model Based on Cellular Automata for the Simulation of Pesticide Percolation in the Soil. In V.Malyshkin (ed.), *Parallel Computing and Technologies*, Lecture Notes in Computer Science 1662, Springer Verlag, Berlin, 1999.
6. S. Bandini, M. Magagnini. Parallel Simulation of Dynamic Properties of Filled Rubber Compounds Based on Cellular Automata. *Parallel Computing*, **27**(5), 643–661, 2001.
7. S. Bandini, G. Mauri, G. Pavesi, C. Simone. Parallel Simulation of Reaction Diffusion Phenomena in Percolation Processes: a Model Based on Cellular Automata. *Future Generation Computer Systems*, **17**(6), 679–688, 2001.

Parallel Simulation of 3D Incompressible Flows and Performance Comparison for Several MPP and Cluster Platforms

Oleg Bessonov[1], Dominique Fougère[2], and Bernard Roux[2]

[1] Institute for Problems in Mechanics of Russian Academy of Sciences,
101, Vernadsky ave., 117526 Moscow, Russia
[2] Laboratoire de Modélisation en Mécanique à Marseille, L3M–IMT, La Jetée,
Technopôle de Château-Gombert, 13451 Marseille Cedex 20, France
bess@ipmnet.ru, {fougere,broux@l3m.univ-mrs.fr}

Abstract. This paper describes a parallelization method for the numerical simulation of 3D incompressible viscous flow in a cylindrical domain. Implementation details are discussed for efficient parallelization on distributed memory computers with relatively slow communication links. The developed parallel code is used for the performance evaluation of several computers of different architectures, with the number of processors used from 1 to 16. The obtained results are compared to the measured computational and communication characteristics of these computers.

1 Introduction

Modern distributed memory parallel computers are characterized by very high computational potential. Therefore they are very attractive for the solution of time-consuming non-steady 3D CFD problems. In contrast, the communication speed of interconnection networks is usually much lower than necessary to exploit fully the intrinsic parallelism of numerical algorithms. With the rapid development of superscalar RISC microprocessors, the gap between computational speed and interconnection capacity becomes even wider. Therefore, much attention should be paid on the development of numerical methods and parallelization algorithms that are economical from the point of view of data exchanges.

For simulations of flows in 3D regular domains (rectangular or cylindrical), the Finite Difference (FDM) and Finite Volume (FVM) methods have proved to be very efficient [1]. Straightforward implementations of these methods normally use a substantial fraction of "explicit" time integration codes, that don't need data exchanges during the computational steps. Only a small part of data, the separator (boundary) planes between subdomains, belonging to different computational nodes, need to be transferred after completion of every timestep.

Unfortunately, a realistic simulation of incompressible viscous flows can't be performed by pure explicit code due to timestep constraints, especially for flows with highly diffusive processes (e.g. low Prandtl melt flow in crystal growth applications). The implicit methods should be incorporated, that involve solving

V. Malyshkin (Ed.): PaCT 2001, LNCS 2127, pp. 401–409, 2001.

3-diagonal linear systems in every spatial direction (for the economical ADI approach). Another numerical difficulty of incompressible flow simulation arises from the physical nature of pressure. The pressure Poisson equation must be solved globally in the entire domain on every timestep. In order to avoid expensive iterative methods, the direct Fourier method is often used that involves Fast Fourier transfer (FFT) steps and 3-diagonal sweeps. Parallelization of FFT requires full data exchange between nodes and is therefore very uneconomical. In order to reduce amount of data exchanges, several approaches have been suggested by different authors [2,3]. However, these algorithms are either much less accurate than necessary, or less economical than the Fourier method (they would need, for example, $O(N^2)$ operations vs. $O(N \log(N))$ for 1D transform).

The present work is based on the previous effort on parallelization of 3D CFD problem [4] where one-dimensional decomposition of a computational domain was considered. Now, the analysis has been extended to multidimensional decomposition, with the consideration of all arising questions. To avoid excessive data exchanges, a new method for solving Poisson equation has been developed, based on a cyclic reduction of arising linear systems in frame of the FACR approach [5]. As a result, the algorithmically and numerically economical implementation has been obtained for the number of processors up to 16.

Another part of this paper is devoted to the comparative analysis of performance and parallelization efficiency for different distributed memory machines – massive parallel computers (MPP) and SMP clusters, using this new code as a benchmark. Some previous work has been performed in this area [6]. The current analysis is based on the evaluation of parallelization efficiency of the presented code for different number of processors (2, 4, 8, 16) and problem sizes in comparison with the measured computational and communication characteristics.

2   Description of the Numerical Method

The numerical problem considered here is the solution of 3D non-stationary Navier-Stokes equations in Boussinesq approximation for incompressible viscous flow in a cylindrical domain. This sort of simulation is used in crystal growth applications, like semiconductor melt flows in Czochralski apparatus [7].

The velocity-pressure formulation and FVM discretization are employed, with the decoupled solution of momentum, pressure and temperature equations using the Fractional step (pressure correction) method. The time integration scheme is partially implicit, with the implicit treatment of the most critical terms using ADI (Alternating directions implicit) approach. The pressure Poisson equation is normally solved by efficient Fourier method, that involves FFTs in two spatial directions and 3-diagonal systems solutions in the last direction. This numerical method is fully direct and doesn't involve costly iterative steps.

From the point of view of data processing, the computations are organized by the following way:

- The cylindrical computational domain is considered as a 3-dimensional array (φ, z, r). All computations are performed in the most efficient manner, using

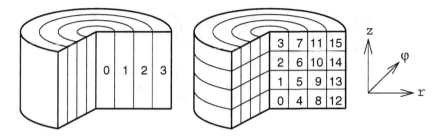

Fig. 1. 1D and 2D decompositions of a computational domain

the 1-st index of array as the innermost one in Fortran loops. An iteration of the outer loop can be considered as computations in a plane (φ, z), that is moving in the direction r as a "frontal plane of computations" [4].

- All explicit parts of the algorithm are trivial and simply form 2D loops within this plane of computations.
- The implicit part is split into solving 3-diagonal linear systems in all 3 directions (φ, z, r), each consisting of 2 sweeps (forward and backward) in corresponding direction. All sweeps in the directions φ and z involve processing of data located within 2D plane of computations. Sweeps in the direction r look like a slow motion of this plane in forward or backward direction.
- The Fourier method comprises FFTs in the directions φ and z, that again involve processing within a plane of computations, and solving 3-diagonal systems in the direction r, implemented as for the implicit step.

3   Parallelization of the Algorithm

The parallelization method is based on the splitting a computational domain in the last 2 directions, r and z. The current implementation includes the following variants: 1×1, 2×1, 4×1, 4×2 and 4×4 (Fig. 1), from 1 to 16 CPUs (with a possible extension to 8×4 for 32 CPUs).

Consider first the parallelization method for 1-dimensional splitting.

- Computational domains are overlapped, with one neighbour's plane (2D array of data) stored in a node for each boundary. This is necessary for calculation of some terms in discretized equations.
- All parts of the numerical algorithm involving calculations only within a plane of computations (φ, z) are processed independently in each node and don't need data exchanges. These parts include all explicit steps, implicit sweeps in the directions φ and z, and FFTs in these directions. Data exchanges between adjacent processor nodes are performed only between these steps (when necessary), transmitting full 2D arrays of data.
- Sweeps in the direction r can't be parallelized in frame of the conventional 3-diagonal solver. Instead, the twisted factorization is used for 2 processors, or two-way parallel partition method [8,4] for 4 or more processors. These

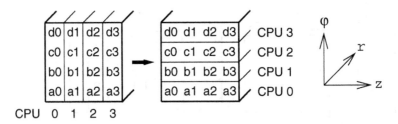

Fig. 2. Blocked transposition for parallelization of FFT in the direction z

methods employ more complicated way of Gauss elimination procedure, that can be done simultaneously in all subdomains. These modified sweeps are performed as frontal planes of computations, with exchange of full 2D data arrays between adjacent nodes when necessary. Parallel solution of 3-diagonal system on 4 processors requires 3 to 6 such exchanges (depending on the sort of 3-diagonal matrix).

As a result, the parallelized numerical method is algebraically identical to the sequential one. This is different from the iterative domain decomposition approach, when the efficiency depends on convergence properties of the algorithm and can be violated by the splitting.

The above method has demonstrated the good parallelization efficiency [4,6]. However, the increased complexity of solving 3-diagonal systems limits the number of processors by 4, at most 8. The natural way to overcome this limitation is to extend decomposition into the 2-nd spatial direction (z). This would increase the limitation to $4 \times 4 = 16$ processors.

The parallelization procedure and data distribution for the direction z are similar to those of the direction r for almost all steps of the algorithm. However, FFTs in the direction z can't be efficiently parallelized because multiple transmissions of all processed data are required. The way to reduce the number of data transfer is to split a computational domain in the last spatial direction (φ) and rearrange data for this operation. Figure 2 illustrates this rearrangement (blocked transposition) for 4 processors, when 3/4 of all data are involved into an exchange.

The following steps of the algorithm – FFT in the direction z, 3-diagonal sweeps in the direction r, and inverse FFT in z – are performed on rearranged data independently in each processor. Finally, another transposition is required in order to return resulting data into the initial distribution. As a result, the parallelized procedure for the Fourier method would look as follows:

$$\text{FFT}(\varphi), \text{ transposition}, \text{ FFT}(z), \text{ 3-diag}(r), \text{ FFT}(z), \text{ transposition}, \text{ FFT}(\varphi)$$

4   New Method for Solving Poisson Equation

The described procedure requires an exchange of 3D data arrays between processors, while for the other steps of the algorithm only 2D boundary planes must be transferred. Since the speed of interprocessor communications of modern parallel computers is much lower than their computational performance, this step would involve long delays and dramatically reduce the efficiency of parallelization.

In order to lower the required amount of data transfer, the new method for solving pressure Poisson equation has been developed. The method is employed to 2D linear systems obtained after performing FFTs in the direction φ. It is based on the FACR (Fourier analysis with cyclic reduction) approach [5] and consists of 3 stages: cyclic reduction of the original matrix, solution of the reduced linear system by the Fourier method, and substitution of results into the remaining equations.

The method of cyclic reduction is used for simplifying 3-diagonal and blocked 3-diagonal linear systems. One iteration of this method halves the number of equations in a system by the following way:

$$
\begin{aligned}
x_{i-2} + A\,x_{i-1} + \quad x_i \qquad\qquad\qquad &= y_{i-1} \\
x_{i-1} + A\,x_i + \quad x_{i+1} \qquad\quad &= y_i \\
x_i + A\,x_{i+1} + x_{i+2} &= y_{i+1}
\end{aligned}
$$

If we multiply every second equation (i-th in this case) by $-A$ and add two adjacent equations to it, we obtain the reduced linear system:

$$
x_{i-2} + (2 - A^2)\,x_i + x_{i+2} = y_{i-1} - A\,y_i + y_{i+1}
$$

Substituting $A^{(1)} = 2 - A^2$ and $y_i^{(1)} = y_{i-1} - A\,y_i + y_{i+1}$, we obtain the system of equations of the same type and can therefore employ the cyclic reduction procedure again. After several iterations, the resulting system can be solved by any convenient method, with the following backsubstitution steps in order to find the remaining unknowns.

In our case, the blocked 3-diagonal system is solved, where A is a 3-diagonal matrix itself. As a result, the new matrices $A^{(1)}$, $A^{(2)}$ etc are no more 3-diagonal. However, they can be factored into simple 3-diagonal matrices, and the resulting systems can be resolved by several repetition of 3-diagonal algorithm.

Every iteration of the cyclic reduction increases the complexity of the numerical algorithm and sophisticates the data exchange pattern. As a compromise, the 2-step cyclic reduction scheme has been chosen, with the 4-fold reduction of matrix size and amount of data exchanges in Fourier method. Despite the slight increase of data transfers in another parts of the algorithm, the resulting amount of transmissions is now on the reasonable level and doesn't influence so much the efficiency of parallelization.

5   Some Technological Aspects of Parallelization

Parallel computational code expressed in high level language (Fortran in our case) has much more complicated structure than the sequential one. This complexity arises in particular from the increased number of sorts of subdomains with a variety of boundary conditions: external (physical), and internal (between subdomains). In order to simplify the code flow, the alternating numbering scheme

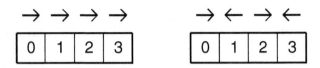

Fig. 3. Standard (left) and alternating (right) numbering schemes

is proposed. If, for example, the domain is split into 4 subdomains in some direction, data elements (data points) in this direction are numbered in alternating order (Fig. 3). Due to this, codes in every two adjacent nodes (0 and 1, 2 and 3) become more unified, and the total number of different boundary conditions is reduced. More important, all data exchanges are performed uniformly in all nodes. Additionally, the alternating numbering scheme naturally corresponds to the two-way parallel partition method for solving 3-diagonal linear systems.

Another improvement of the algorithm concerns the solution of 3-diagonal linear systems with constant coefficients, that happens in the discretized pressure Poison equation and some other cases. For this sort of systems, the LU matrix decomposition can be performed in advance, thus reducing the computational work and eliminating data exchanges of matrix elements in parallel solution.

The next point is a choice of communication library. The most standard one is the MPI. Unfortunately, some parallel systems may lack a MPI implementation at all, or may offer more efficient option like SHMEM, GM or MPL. For this reason, the library-independent approach has been chosen, with a set of intermediate data exchange routines used instead of MPI. All library-specific calls are encapsulated within these routines. As a result, a parallel application program becomes system-independent. In order to adapt to any new communication protocol, only a small set of routines must be rewritten. Sometimes, there exist incompatibilities in different implementations of the same library, or some compiler problems, and the library-independent approach is useful in this case.

This approach also allows to accomplish some specific optimizations of data exchanges without modification of application code, such as splitting blocks to be transferred into smaller parts, or regulating duplex mode of transmission by some way. Another thing necessary for parallel optimization is the renumbering (remap) of allocated processor nodes, that can be important for better adaptation of a parallel computer topology (SMP-nodes, 2D-grids etc) to the structure of an algorithm.

Up to now, the intermediate communication routines have been adapted to the following protocols: NX (Intel i860), Parix (Parsytec), PVM, MPL (IBM SP2), SHMEM (Cray T3E, SGI) and MPI, the latter in different incompatible implementations.

6   Comparison of Different Parallel Computers

During the last years, many new parallel machines have appeared, including the novel class – multiprocessor node (SMP) parallel computers and clusters.

Table 1. Characteristics of the analyzed parallel computers

parallel platform and interconnect	CPUs per node	CPU cache size	theor. peak MFLOPS	real code MFLOPS	comm. library	comm. duplex MB/s	ratio MB/s to MFLOPS
IBM SP2-375 Colony switch	16	8M	1500	297	MPL	80–175 –	0.27–0.59 –
IBM SP2-120 SP switch	1	128K	480	120	MPL	– 28	– 0.23
Alpha 21264-667 Myrinet	2	4M	1333	347	MPI	90 41–73	0.26 0.12–0.20
PC PIII-550 2×Ethernet100	2	512K	550	84.5	MPI	39 5.8–10	0.46 0.07–0.12
SGI O2000-300 shared memory	256	8M	600	125	MPI	30–45 –	0.24–0.36 –

Combining several processors in a single node with common shared memories allows to isolate traffic between neighbour processors within this node, thus reducing internode communications. Also, the speed of intra-node exchanges is usually several times higher due to "directcopy" transfer in memory.

The presented parallel code has been used for evaluating parallel performance of several computers, mainly of this new class, in order to reveal their communication behaviour and applicability to this class of numerical problems. Additionally, an investigation of single processor performance and communication network characteristics has been performed. Main characteristics of all analyzed computers and some results of this investigation are presented in Table 1.

The MFLOPS rates were measured by the single-processor version of the presented code, for the problem size 70 MB ($128 \times 64 \times 92$). In order to represent the real life situation for SMP nodes, and to account shared memory conflicts, the appropriate number of copies of this program were running simultaneously.

The communication speed was measured by transferring large arrays of data ($32 - 64$ KB) in duplex mode. Both intra-node and internode exchanges are shown (top and bottom, respectively). When appropriate, measurements were performed in two regimes: heavy, when all CPU pairs exchange simultaneously, and light, when only one pair communicates without conflicts (shown as ranges).

Table 2 and Fig. 4 present the parallelization efficiency results for 2 problems: of the fixed size (70 MB), and the scalable one (70 MB per processor).

For the fixed size problem, a superlinear speed-up can be seen for SP2-375 due to big L2-cache. When the subproblem's size becomes comparable with the size of a cache, most data arrays fit into it entirely, and the computational speed increases sharply, compensating (fully or partially) the parallelization overhead.

In general, these results illustrate a good correlation between communication-to-computation speed ratio and parallelization efficiency. However, for a big number of processors (16, and sometimes 8) there is some unexpected drop in efficiency for the scalable problem (IBM SP2-375, Alpha cluster, SGI O2000).

Table 2. Parallelization efficiency (%) for the fixed and scalable problems

parallel platform	fixed size problem				scalable problem			
	2	4	8	16	2	4	8	16
IBM SP2-375	98.9	98.0	105.5	102.3	96.2	86.4	79.6	71.5
IBM SP2-120	94.1	87.0	82.2	74.7	95.2	91.4	87.9	84.9
Alpha cluster	91.8	82.4	83.5	75.2	90.5	82.3	82.2	71.8
PC cluster	89.0	82.0	78.6	66.4	90.8	86.2	78.8	74.5
SGI O2000	–	–	–	–	94.0	85.3	77.8	57.0

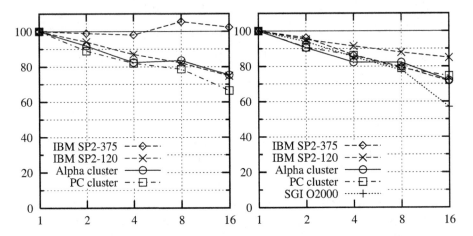

Fig. 4. Efficiency (%) for the fixed (left) and scalable (right) problems

For the Alpha cluster, this can be explained by differences in processor node's speed exceeding 5 % in some cases, and also by non-uniform (in time) behaviour of communication network. The IBM SP2-375 is supposed to suffer from multi-user environment when user processes migrate between SMP-nodes during their runs. The most unstable computer happens to be the 256-processor O2000. Due to its NUMA memory organization, even the performance of a single-processor job would vary by 50 % or more in different runs. For this reason, it was impossible to obtain any reliable results for this machine for the fixed size problem.

The classical and well-balanced IBM SP2-120 with single-processor nodes demonstrates very uniform and monotonic behaviour in all regimes.

The most interesting observations have been obtained for the dual Ethernet PC cluster. Despite its communication network is less balanced than that of the Alpha cluster (Table 1), the PC cluster demonstrates comparable level of parallelization efficiency due to better intra-node exchanges.

With a proper organization of parallel algorithms, this sort of systems may compete to Myrinet-based PC clusters [9] with much more expensive communication hardware. More advances implementations of PC clusters, build upon dual PIII and Athlon platforms (1 GHz or more) and interconnected by gigabit Ethernet, look as promising and economical solutions for coming years.

7   Conclusion

The method presented in the paper allows to parallelize 3D CFD codes for simulation of incompressible flows in regular domains. Despite the partially implicit nature of such codes and relatively low communication speed of modern computers' interconnects, this method ensures a reasonable level of parallelization efficiency. The method follows SPMD model and can be easily adapted to different architectures. The comparative performance analysis of several computers performed with the new code reveals their important characteristics and illustrates the correlation between communication speed and parallelization efficiency.

This work was partially supported by the program "Réseau de coopération universitaire et scientifique Franco-Germano-Russe" of the French Ministry of National Education, and by the Russian Foundation for Basic Research (grant RFBR-01-01-00745). The access to parallel computers was given by CINES, France, and JSCC (Joint SuperComputer Center), Russia.

References

1. Numerical simulation of 3-D incompressible unsteady viscous laminar flows: a GAMM workshop / ed. by M. Deville et al. Notes on Numerical Fluid Mechanics, **36**, Vieweg (1992)
2. F. Marino, E. Swartzlander. Parallel implementation of multidimensional transforms without interprocessor communication. IEEE Transactions on Computers, **48** (9) (1999) 951–961
3. L. Borges, P. Daripa. A fast parallel algorithm for the Poisson equation on a disk. J. Comput. Phys. **169** (2001) 151–192
4. O. Bessonov, V. Brailovskaya, V. Polezhaev, B. Roux. Parallelization of the solution of 3D Navier-Stokes equations for fluid flow in a cavity with moving covers. Proceedings / PaCT-95, Lecture Notes in Computer Science, **964** (1995) 385–399
5. C. Temperton. On the FACR(l) algorithm for the discrete Poisson equation. J. Comput. Phys. **34** (1980) 314–329
6. O. Bessonov, B. Roux. Optimization techniques and performance analysis for different serial and parallel RISC-based computers. Proceedings / PaCT-97, Lecture Notes in Computer Science, **1277** (1997) 168–174
7. V. Polezhaev, O. Bessonov, N. Nikitin, S. Nikitin. Convective interaction and instabilities in GaAs Czochralski model. J. Crystal Growth (2001), to appear
8. C. Walshaw, S.J. Farr. A two-way parallel partition method for solving tridiagonal systems. University of Leeds, U.K., School of Computer Studies Research Report Series, Report 93.25 (1993)
9. F. Cappello, O. Richard, D. Etiemble. Performance of the NAS benchmarks on a cluster of SMP PCs using a parallelization of the MPI programs with OpenMP. Proceedings / PaCT-99, Lecture Notes in Computer Science, **1662** (1999) 339–350

Distributed Simulation of Hybrid Systems with HLA Support

Andrei Borshchev, Yuri Karpov, and Pavel Lebedev

Experimental Object Technologies www.xjtek.com, and
St. Petersburg Technical University, Russia
{andrei,karpov,pavel}@xjtek.com

Abstract. As engineers are confronted with designing increasingly complex systems composed of interconnected components of diverse nature, traditional methods of modeling and analysis become cumbersome and inefficient. In the paper we discuss one of the approaches to modeling and distributed simulation of hybrid (discrete/continuous) systems. We use hybrid state machines, where sets of algebraic-differential equations are assigned to states, to model complex interdependencies between discrete and continuous time behaviors. This framework is fully supported by UML-RT/Java tool AnyLogic developed at Experimental Object Technologies. We use High Level Architecture (HLA), a de-facto standard for distributed simulation, as a communication and synchronization media for distributed hybrid simulation components. Integration of simulations developed with AnyLogic into HLA is considered.

1   Introduction

A large class of systems being developed has both continuous time and discrete time behavior. In fact, any system that interacts with physical world falls in that class. Chemical, Automotive, Military, Aerospace are areas most frequently mentioned in this respect. To model such systems successfully and to get accurate and reliable results from simulation experiments one needs an executable language naturally describing hybrid behavior, and a simulation engine capable of simulating discrete events interleaved with continuous time processes. Additional problems arise with simulating hybrid systems in a distributed environment.

There is a number of tools, commercial and academic, capable of modeling and simulating systems with mixed discrete and continuous behavior (so called hybrid systems), for a good survey we refer to [2] and [9]. We believe that the most convenient way of hybrid system modeling is to specify continuous behavior as a set of algebraic-differential equations associated with a state of a state machine. When a state changes as a result of some discrete event, the continuous behavior may also change. In turn, a condition specified on continuously changing variables could trigger a state machine transition – so called change event. State machines run within objects that communicate in discrete way, e.g. by message passing, as well as by sharing continu-

V. Malyshkin (Ed.): PaCT 2001, LNCS 2127, pp. 410–420, 2001.

ous-time variables over unidirectional connections. Complex hybrid system modeling may require distributed simulation due to system complexity, performance and interoperability requirements, etc. Developed simulation should interoperate with other components, possibly created with different tools. This could be achieved by using some M&S standard. This would also allow creation of distributed simulations, where components run on different machines and different platforms [12]. We believe that High Level Architecture (HLA) for Modeling and Simulation developed by US DoD ([4], [5] and [6]) is the most suitable for this purpose.

In the paper we present AnyLogic, a tool for modeling and simulation of hybrid systems and a way of HLA support integration in the tool simulation engine [3]. To demonstrate AnyLogic ability to model and simulate hybrid systems, we present a simple example – two tanks system [9]. We examine problems aroused with distributed simulation of this system in AnyLogic using HLA.

The paper is organized as follows. Section 2 presents AnyLogic tool and its modeling language. A hybrid system example and its modeling in AnyLogic environment is described in section 3. Section 4 gives an overview of AnyLogic simulation engine integration into HLA. Distributed model of two-tanks system designed in HLA is also described here together with problems of hybrid system simulation in distributed environment. Section 5 concludes the discussion.

2   AnyLogic and Its Modeling Language

AnyLogic [1] architecture is shown in Fig. 1.

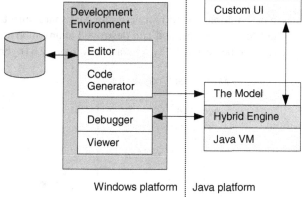

Fig. 1. Architecture of AnyLogic Modeling and Simulation Environment

Windows-based Development Environment includes graphical model Editor and Code Generator that maps the model into Java code. The model runs on any Java platform on the top of AnyLogic Hybrid Engine. A running model exposes an interface to control its execution and to retrieve information via a text-based protocol over TCP/IP. That interface is used by Viewer and Debugger that runs on Java platform as well. The model supports connection of multiple clients from arbitrary (e.g. remote) locations.

We have chosen a subset of UML for Real Time as a modeling language, and extended it to incorporate continuous behavior. The language supports two types of UML diagrams: collaboration diagrams and statechart (state machine) diagrams with some changes. In collaboration diagrams we have added unidirectional continuous connections between objects (capsules in UML-RT) and the corresponding interface elements – input and output variables.

The main building block of a hybrid model is called active object. The object interface elements can be of two types: ports and variables. Objects interact by passing messages through ports, or by exposing continuous time variables one to another.

Object may encapsulate other objects, and so on to any depth. Encapsulated objects can export ports and variables to the container interface, see Fig. 2.

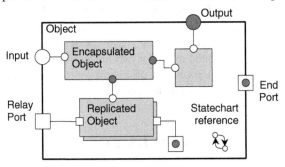

Fig. 2. AnyLogic Structure Diagram extending UML-RT with continuous connections

An object may have multiple concurrent activities that share object local data and object interface. Activities can be created and destroyed at any moment of the model execution. An activity can be described by a Java function or by a (hybrid) statechart.

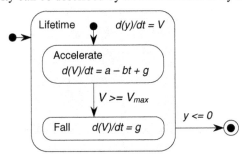

Fig. 3. AnyLogic Hybrid Statechart

In addition to standard UML attributes of states and transitions, in hybrid statecharts one can associate a set of differential and algebraic equations with a simple and/or composite state of a statechart, and you can also specify a condition over continuously changing variables as a trigger of a transition. The currently active set of equations and triggers is defined by the current simple state and all its containers.

The example hybrid statechart in Fig. 3 is a simple model of an object that accelerates vertically up until it reaches the speed of Vmax, and then falls under the impact of gravity until it touches the ground (y <= 0), where it ceases to exist.

3   Hybrid System Example

Consider a system consisting of two tanks and a controller (Fig 4). Three valves controls water injection in tank 1 (*v1*), water flow from tank 1 to tank 2 (*v2*), and water flow from tank 2 outside the system (*v3*). Controller tracks water level in both tanks (h_1 and h_2) and generates commands to open or close valves. The main task is to avoid droughts or overflows of tank 2. (AnyLogic demo with this and other examples is available from http://www.xjtek.com.)

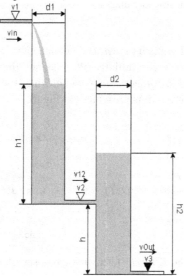

Fig. 4. Two tanks system example

As we can see from the system description, there are two components: two tanks and the controller. Structure diagram of two tanks component of AnyLogic system model is presented in Fig. 5. Output variables *h1* and *h2* are used to expose water levels in tanks 1 and 2 respectively.

$$d(h1)/dt = (vIn - v12)/S1, \quad d(h2)/dt = (v12 - vOut)/S2, \tag{1}$$
$$S1 = \pi(d1/2)^2, \quad S2 = \pi(d2/2)^2,$$

$$h = 0.39, \ d1 = 0.12, \ d2 = 0.05, \ vIn = 400/1000/3600, \text{ heights of both} \tag{2}$$
$$\text{tanks are } 1.0, \ l^+ = 0.9, \ l^- = 0.3$$

Ports *vXOn* and *vXOff* are used to receive commands for appropriate valves. Variables *k1*, *k2*, *p1* and *p2* are used in hybrid statecharts *trackV1*, and *trackV2* to model water flow through valves *v2* and *v3* while they are in transit from opened to closed states and vice versa.

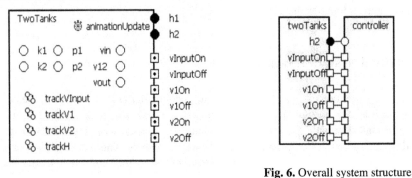

Fig. 5. Two tanks component structure diagram.

Fig. 6. Overall system structure

Fig. 7 presents hybrid statechart *trackV1*. Controller component consists of one statechart implementing its logic (initially fill tanks and then track water level in tank 2), opening valve *v3* when *h2* goes below *l* and closing it when *h2* rises above *l⁺*. The overall system structure diagram is presented on Fig. 6.

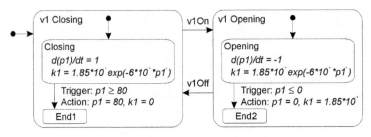

Fig. 7. *TrackV1* activity (hybrid statechart)

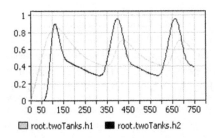

Fig.8. Simulation results of AnyLogic model of two tanks problem.

Note the continuous variable connection on *h2* between components. Simulation results of the system with equations (1) and parameters (2) are presented in Fig. 8.

4   Distributed Simulation with HLA Support

The High Level Architecture (HLA) is a standard framework that supports simulations composed of different distributed simulation components. The HLA was developed by the Defense Modeling and Simulation Office (DMSO) of the Department of Defense (DoD) to meet the needs of defense-related projects, but it is now increasingly being used in other application areas [11]. The primary goal of such architecture is to facilitate simulation interoperability and reuse across a broad range of applications [7,8]. Recent adoption of the HLA as an IEEE standard will strengthen positions of this architecture among other modeling and simulation standards. There are examples of the successful creation of distributed simulations composed of components developed using different tools [10].

The HLA follows a framework approach and is defined by three major elements:
- Rules [4] govern the behavior of the overall distributed simulation (Federation) and their members (Federates);
- An Interface Specification [5] prescribes the interface between each federate and the Runtime Infrastructure (RTI), which provides communication and coordination services to the federates;
- An Object Model Template [6], which defines the way federations and federates have to be documented (using the Federation Object Model and the Simulation Object Model, respectively). Federations can be viewed as a contract between federates on how a common federation execution is intended to be run.

In simulation, HLA plays a role similar to one CORBA, COM+, etc. play in object oriented distributed software development.

4.1   Integrating Simulation Engine of Any Logic and HLA

Integrating HLA support in AnyLogic will give the user the possibility of rapid creation of prototypes of component simulations (federates) and development of distributed simulations (federations) using convenient and powerful graphic environment of AnyLogic. When a prototype developed in AnyLogic proves its ability to deal with the problem it is intended to solve, one or more of the federates could be re-implemented using, for example, raw HLA interface on one of the high-performance languages such as C++. We believe that such approach for federation development could reduce the time and cost of simulation development and avoid many errors on early phases of the development process.

HLA integration in AnyLogic requires careful consideration. The most difficult problems arise in distributed simulation because of hybrid nature of simulated system components.

AnyLogic simulation algorithm could be represented as follows:

1. If there are current events (events that are
   scheduled to occur at the current model time),
   then randomly select one and execute it. This
   step is called event step. The properties of
   the event step are:
   - No model time elapses
   - Some actions defined within the model may be
     executed
   - As a result, the state of the model may change
2. Otherwise (no current events scheduled), the model
   time could be advanced to the time of the next
   discrete event scheduled (if any).The properties
   of this time step are:
   - The model time progresses
   - The discrete state of the model remains unchanged
   - Active algebraic-differential equations are
     solved numerically and the variables are
     changed correspondingly
   - Awaited change events (predicates on continuously
     changing variables which could change discrete
     state of the system) are tested for
     occurrence. This event is scheduled as current
     event and the algorithm proceeds to Step 1.

If we wish to build time regulating and/or time constrained federate with Any-
Logic, we should modify simulation engine to allow coordinated time advancements
of all distributed simulation participants. The most general technique to achieve such
coordination is using zero lookahead value (for time regulating federates) and Next
Event Request Available (NERA) HLA Time Management service call. NERA(t)
service allows delivery of all queued RO messages. It grants time advancement to the
time t (if no more TSO messages will be delivered with time stamp less then t) or to
the time t1<t, where t1 is the lowest time stamp of all scheduled TSO messages. Then
it delivers this TSO message to the federate. Usage of NERA service call allows sending and/or receiving additional TSO messages scheduled at the current time and allows seamless integration of local AnyLogic and HLA simulation engines.

AnyLogic simulation algorithm with HLA support could be represented as follows:

1. t = t0. Detect discrete change events;
2. if there are current events, then
       Choose one and execute it
       NextEventRequestAvailable (t0)
       Awaiting TimeAdvanceGrant(t0) callback
       Goto 1
3. t1 = findNextContinuousEvent(t0,min{Tnext,Tmaxstep})
4. NextEventRequestAvailable(t1)
5. Awaiting TimeAdvanceGrant(t2) callback (t2 <= t1)
6. t0 = t2
7. Goto 1

Here Tnext is the time of the next event scheduled, and Tmaxstep is a constant.

AnyLogic provides user-accessible service for determination of time stamp of the next continuous or discrete event. Extension of AnyLogic simulation engine with such services allows integration of HLA support as an add-on package.

4.2   Distributed Simulation of Two Tanks Problem with AnyLogic

HLA support module for AnyLogic that is currently under development allowed us to build distributed simulation of described two tanks system model. System has been represented as one object class `TwoTanksSystem` with attributes `Tank1Level` and `Tank2Level`. Interaction class `ValveState` with parameters `Valve` and `IsOpen` allows federation participants to change valve states of the instance of the system. The HLA federation consists of three federates: two tanks simulator federate, controller federate, and viewer federate providing visualization of the process. Two tanks simulator federate publishes object class `TwoTanksSystem` with both attributes, creates and registers one instance of that class and updates its attributes. It also subscribes to `ValveState` interaction and translates it to the messages to appropriate ports (*vXOn* and *vXOff*). Controller federate subscribes to object class `TwoTanksSystem` with both attributes and later will discover object instance created by two tanks simulator. It also publishes interaction class `ValveState` to be able to send interactions of this class. AnyLogic models of system components have been wrapped by another ActiveObjects responsible for registration or discovery of instance of appropriate HLA object class, updating instance attribute values (periodically), and translating commands previously sent via ports to and from HLA interactions. Additional ActiveObject called HLATimeAdvancer has been added to every federate to synchronize local simulation engine time with federation time by requesting HLA RTI for time advancements as described in previous section.

Distributed simulation of the model shows overflows of tank 2. Because model logic has been left unchanged, the problem source is in breaking connections between two tanks and the controller (Fig 6). Connections between ports of the components have been represented as interactions between distributed components. Sending or receiving message to/from port is a discrete event, thus no information has been lost by such representation. But transmission of continuous time variable *h2* only in discrete moments of time (periodic updates) with update period greater then some Δt will not allow controller properly react to the change in water level. Previous update may indicate normal level (below *l*), but the next one may show very high level or even overflow. This is an instance of more general sensitivity problem.

So, we are facing problem with exposition of continuous time variable in distributed simulation of hybrid system and detecting condition defined on it in another distributed component.

There are no significant conceptual problems with building distributed simulations of discrete event systems according to system state updates. Situation changes when one or more components have continuous time or mixed (hybrid) behavior, which they want to expose to other components.

The problem is to represent hybrid system as a discrete event system at the level of distributed components interactions.

Three general approaches could be proposed: value polling, sampling along time or value axis, and an approach which provides ability for one component to define a predicate on a variable, which is to be evaluated locally at another component along with notification when such event occurs.

First two mentioned approaches are quite obvious. Their disadvantage is that they can't solve the problem of guaranteed correct detection of conditions defined over continuously changing interface variables. Below we propose an approach, called Remote Predicate Evaluation, which can cope with those difficulties.

4.3   Detecting Conditions Defined
over Continuously Changing Interface Variables

Polling and sampling update methods are good enough when we need to monitor behavior of components, e.g. for building external viewers, statistic collecting, tracking objects, and other situation awareness needs. However, these update methods are not very good for detecting conditions defined over continuously changing interface variables (like $h2$ in the distributed two tanks system).

There are situations when we are interested in the value of a predicate (condition) defined on a continuous time variable. This, for example, may affect discrete state of the system or trigger some actions associated with this event in other components. Remote Predicate Evaluation (RPE) is the method when such predicate could be checked locally within the component, which exposes the variable(s) while solving algebraic-differential equations. It could provide required accuracy in determining the moment of time when this event occurs. Besides it allows distributed model designer to lower the probability of sensitivity problem appearance and minimizes overhead caused by frequent variable value updates (only the fact of event detection is announced to other interested components). Finite amount of information is required to transfer both a predicate and a notification over the network.

It could be recommended to design distributed simulation in the way that components "encapsulate" their continuous behavior, exposing continuous time variables (attributes) only for the needs of situation awareness, visualization and remote statistic collection at relatively low rate. Detection of all required events identified during simulation (federation) design and development is then performed inside the component and the corresponding notification is sent to all interested components.

Sometimes, however, simulation components model devices with analog output, which is continuous by its nature (e.g., electrical current or voltage interface). A model designer may not know a priori which conditions will be interesting for components connected to this device during distributed simulation execution. In this case a mechanism for dynamic creation and modification of predicates on output variables can be implemented.

If the designer has a priori knowledge of the form of the predicate, she could parameterize it and allow other components to change parameters during simulation execution, tuning this component for their needs. In HLA this effect could be achieved, for example, by declaring attributes with transferable ownership representing predicate parameters. Or it could be implemented using specialized interaction exchange protocol.

The latter method was implemented with prototype HLA support add-on to Any-Logic for distributed simulation of above-mentioned two tanks problem. Controller tracks value of h_2 and when it reaches some dangerously high level L^+, it commands appropriate valve to open. In other words, controller component defines predicate on continuous variable h_2 in the form $h_2 > L^+$. Since h_2 is modeled in another component, the h_2 update method can directly affect the time delay before open valve command is issued and thus can lead to tank 2 overflow (this is just what we've got during distributed simulation using sampling). The same system simulated as a single AnyLogic model does not show such overflow. Here we can see that distributed simulation of hybrid system can show wrong results just because of continuous variable update delay.

The solution of this problem is to allow controller federate define L^+ value for the two tanks federate. We have done this by defining HLA interaction with parameter specifying L^+ value. After interaction reception two tanks federate changes parameter of the predicate on h_2 ($h_2 > L^+$) and evaluates it during solving system of differential equations. After predicate becomes true (an event detected), the federate updates values for h_1 and h_2 and the controller detect this event with minimal possible error. As the predicate is evaluated "remotely" by the federate simulating continuous time variable, we call this method Remote Predicate Evaluation. It showed its ability to deal with the described problem for this particular example of distributed simulation.

RPE has several obvious limitations. For example, it cannot help if we have predicate on more than one continuous time variable simulated by different distributed components. For this case revision of model partitioning into distributed components could be advised. Obviously, subcomponents tightly coupled by continuous variables should be placed in the same distributed component.

5   Conclusion

Hybrid statemachines approach implemented in AnyLogic modeling and simulation environment is a powerful and convenient formalism to describe behavior of the real world systems. AnyLogic itself is a very flexible tool, it is essentially an environment for programming on Java with modeled system visual specification support in terms of simulation class library. This property of AnyLogic makes it relatively easy to develop HLA support extensions and enable components created with this tool participate in distributed simulations.

There is a single common standard of distributed simulation in military domain. But there's no such standard in civil domain. HLA adoption as IEEE standard will improve situation. It can help with interoperability and reuse of simulations created with different tools. HLA is suitable for discrete event systems, but problems arise with distributed hybrid systems modeling with HLA. Distributed execution of components connected on continuous time variables and detection of events related to them may lead models to demonstrate results which differs drastically from the simulation of the same system locally. One example of such problem has been demonstrated and solution named Remote Predicates Evaluation has been proposed.

References

1. AnyLogic 4.0 User Manual. Available from http://www.xjtek.com/products/anylogic/40/
2. Astrom, J., Emqvist, H., Mattson, S.E.: Evolution of Continuous-time Modeling and Simulation. In: Proceedings of the 12th European Simulation Multiconference, ESM'98, Manchester, UK (1998)
3. Borshchev, A.V., Kolesov, Yu.B., Senichenkov, Yu.B.: Java Engine for UML Based Hybrid State Machines. In: Proceedings of the Winter Simulation Conference 2000, WSC'00, December 10-13, Orlando, FL, USA (2000)
4. IEEE P1516, Draft Standard [for] Modeling and Simulation (M&S) High-Level Architecture (HLA) – High Level Architecture Rules.
5. IEEE P1516.1, Draft Standard [for] Modeling and Simulation (M&S) High-Level Architecture (HLA) - Federate Interface Specification
6. IEEE P1516.2, Draft Standard [for] Modeling and Simulation (M&S) High-Level Architecture (HLA) - Object Model Template (OMT)
7. Li, B., Li, X., Chai, X., Qing, D.: A HLA Integrated Development Environment. Society for Computer Simulation Conference, (July 1999)
8. Allen, R., Garlan, D., Ivers, J.: Formal Modeling and Analysis of the HLA Component Integration Standard. In: Poceedings of the 6th International Symposium on the Foundations of Software Engineering (FSE-6) (1998)
9. Kovalewski et al.: A Case Study in Tool-aided Analysis of Discretely Controlled Continuous Systems: the Two Tanks Problem. In 5th International Workshop on Hybrid Systems, Notre Dam, USA (1997)
10. Steffen Straßburger: On The HLA-based Coupling of Simulation Tools. Available online from http://isgsim1.cs.uni-magdeburg.de/hla/paper/HLASimTools.pdf
11. Thomas Schulze, Steffen Straßburger, Ulrich Klein: Migration of HLA into Civil Domains: Solutions and Prototypes for Transportation Applications. Available online from http://isgsim1.cs.uni-magdeburg.de/hla/paper/S7305-05.pdf
12. Günther Seliger, Dirk Krützfeldt, Peter Lorenz, and Steffen Straßburger: On the HLA- and Internet-based Coupling of Commercial Simulation Tools for Production Networks. Available online from http://isgsim1.cs.uni-magdeburg.de/hla/paper/ICWMS99.pdf

Application of the Parallel Computing Technology to a Wave Front Model Using the Finite Element Method

André Chambarel and Hervé Bolvin

Laboratory of Complex Hydrodynamics, 33 rue Louis Pasteur
F-84000 Avignon, France
andre.chambarel@univ-avignon.fr

Abstract. The Time Domain Reflectometry probe is a new technique applied to moisture measurement. It is a wave guide stuck in the ground. The wave crosses a variable electric properties medium . We develop a model based on the resolution of Maxwell's equations which allows to determine the electromagnetic field and the energy density. The problem of a wave front propagation presents a very large CPU cost. So we develop a parallel computing approach based on C++ Objects Oriented Programming , Finite Element Method and selected data technique. We associate the SIMD technology with the MPI C++ library for software implementation. High performances computing are obtained.

1 Introduction

Water resource management for plants is becoming an increasingly acute problem. This is associated with pollution phenomena usually caused by fertilizers. It is therefore essential to have a precise idea as to the soil's moisture content, both at surface and underground levels. Various techniques have been used to this effect, e.g. the uneasy technique of sampling. The latest generation of instruments [1] under development is based on Time Domain Reflectometry − TDR −. These instruments come as two or three parallel metal rods driven into the ground down to little over three feet − or 1 m −. An electrical impulse is applied to the end bit above ground surface. The impulse propagates along the rods. Measurement and processing of the signal obtained by reflection should theorically allow the determination of local moisture levels. In this paper we shall present a parallel computing method for the numerical study of an electromagnetic echography of the ground. So we use the Maxwell's equation model by a Finite Element approach.

2 General Presentation of the Model

The wave guide (Fig. 1) is represented by two parallel electrodes and the electric conductivity of these is infinite. The free space around the electrodes can be an ohmic conductor. The electrical impulse is applied to the end bit above ground surface and we study the Transverse Magnetic mode -TM- in the wave guide.

We formulate the Maxwell's equations with the usual notations (1). For a numerical model we prefer to use adimensional equations. The Maxwell's equations

V. Malyshkin (Ed.): PaCT 2001, LNCS 2127, pp. 421–427, 2001.

show a non dimensional parameter Rm . The non dimensional Maxwell's equations (**E, H**) become [2]:

$$[\mu_r]\frac{\partial \overline{H}}{\partial t} = -\overline{curl\, E} \qquad div([\mu_r]\overline{H}) = 0$$

$$[\varepsilon_r]\frac{\partial \vec{E}}{\partial t} = \overrightarrow{curl\,H} - Rm\,.[\gamma_r]\vec{E} \qquad div\,([\varepsilon_r]\vec{E}) = 0 \qquad (1)$$

3 Finite Element Formulation

The 2D model is presented in Figure 1. We discretize with triangular linear elements. We have 13,985 triangular elements and 7,300 nodes. 29,200 differential equations are generated by a Finite Element process [3].

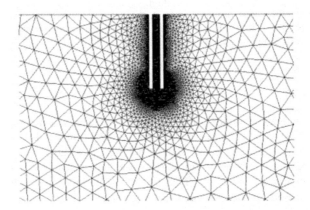

Fig. 1. Geometrical model and mesh of the medium.

3.1 The Code FAFEMO and the Automatic Multigrid System (AMS)

We use an efficient C++ Object Oriented Programming for the Finite Element code called FAFEMO (Fast Adaptive Finite Element Modular Object) [4]. This technology allowes the implementation of very low sized solvers (29 Kb – 700 lines). In this context, our numerical calculus uses a technique called the AMS . For each time step, the determination of the computational area and the selection of the elements dedicated to each processor are determined on the full grid [5].

3.2 Grid Optimization

The AMS expert system should be built for each problem. Mathematical, numerical and physical considerations can be used. Before the parallelization of the algorithm the finite element grid should be optimized. In our example the celerity c of the wave is known. Only the active elements are selected according to the front position. We denote a time dependent active grid. In our case the active degrees of freedom number and the element number increase in time.

The working of the AMS reduces previously the size of the differential system before the application of the parallel technology.

4 Numerical Resolution

After a classical assembling operation where index (G) denotes the global values, the differential system of reduced size is as follow :

$$[M].\frac{d}{dt}\begin{Bmatrix}H^{(G)}\\E^{(G)}\end{Bmatrix}=\begin{Bmatrix}F_H^{(G)}\\F_E^{(G)}\end{Bmatrix}-[K].\begin{Bmatrix}H^{(G)}\\E^{(G)}\end{Bmatrix} \qquad (2)$$

Under these conditions we can test the semi-implicit method. We use a *matrix-free technique* [5] , the mass matrix and the stiffness matrix never being built. We notice a high performance level for the CPU and the storage costs for vectors only.

4.1 Principle of Parallelization

The principal CPU cost corresponds to computing of the elementary matrices (me,ke,fe) and secondarily the time step updating. In the example of an unsteady problem, the analytical discretization of the problem with the Finite Element Method gives the following scalar product [3]:

$$\sum_{NE} \langle \delta ue \rangle.([me]\left\{\frac{due}{dt}\right\}+[ke]\{ue\}-\{fe\})=0 \quad \text{with} \quad NE=1..ne \qquad (3)$$

If p is the number of processors, we select a list of elements Nk by the AMS expert system:

$$\bigcup_{k=1}^{p} Nk = NE \quad \text{and} \quad Ni \cap Nj = 0 \quad \text{for } i \ne j \qquad (4)$$

Each elementary matrix can be assembled into a global matrix by a classical Finite Element process [3]. With p processors the dispatching of elements in the following list is :

processor j: list Nj

$$\sum_{Nj}\left|M_e^j\right|=\left|M_j\right| \quad \sum_{Nj}\{\Psi_e^j\}=\{\Psi_j\} \quad j=1...N_p \qquad (5)$$

4.2 Parallel Algorithm

In this case the Bernstein's conditions are verified. So we have a correct load balancing if the list of elements is similar for each processor. The arrays definition depends on the technology. We use the SIMD – Single Instruction Multiple Data-associated with the MPI - Message Passing Interface - C++ library. The communications between the processors exist only at the end of the time step. Only the global diagonal mass matrix would be constructed before the updating of the solution. After each processor builds its part of the differential system and the below algorithm allows the updating of the solution {U}. A parallel semi-implicit algorithm is used:

$$t_n = 0$$

$$while \ (t_n \leq t_{max})$$

$$\begin{Bmatrix} for \ j=1 \ to \ p & \{\Delta U_n^i\}_j = \Delta t_n . [M_n^i]^{-1} . \{\Psi_j (U_n + \alpha.\Delta U_n^{i-1}, t_n + \alpha.\Delta t_n)\} \\ i=1, 2, ... \quad until \quad \|\Delta U_n^i - \Delta U_n^{i-1}\| \leq tolerence \end{Bmatrix}$$

$$\{U_{n+1}\} = \{U_n\} + \{\Delta U_n\}$$

$$t_{n+1} = t_n + \Delta t_n$$

$$end \quad while$$

where α is the upward time-parameter. Eventually if $\alpha < 0.5$ a stability condition is required [6].

5 Numerical Results

In this case, we choose an example of variable electric properties in space. Around point (y_0, z_0) there is a spot of electric singularity and the ε (y , z) value is modified by a mathematical model of a moisture spot.

Figure 2   presents the active zone at time t = 1.3 and figure 3 presents the adimensionnal electromagnetic energy at the same time. The electric singularity profile is a white circle. If the time is greater than L/c, then the electromagnetic field extends beyond the end of the wave guide. Figure 3   shows the coming out of the electromagnetic wave in the free space. We notice a large dissymmetry because of the electric particularity of the medium. The celerity of the electromagnetic wave decreases strongly in this zone and a more important part of the wave is reflected toward the entrance of the wave guide (Fig. 3). It therefore provokes a variation in the impedance of the wave guide, in particular, as seen at the entrance.

Figure 4 and 5 show respectively the part of elements dedicated to processor #1 and processor #2. We have here a graphical resemblance with the domain decomposition method because the numeration of the elements by the mesh generator is sequential. Table 1 presents the numerical caracteristics of our parallel computing. This results concern the full grid but the AMS expert system can reduce the equation's number by active grid optimization (Fig. 2).

The code FAFEMO associated with the AMS capabilities allows to use a very low sized memory. Table 2 presents some results of the used memory.

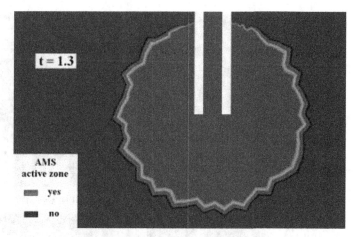

Fig. 2. Computational area at time t = 1.3 .

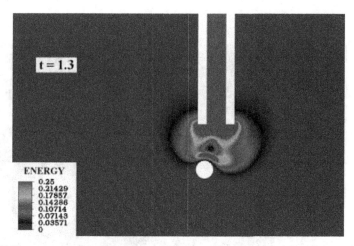

Fig. 3. Electromagnetic energy in presence of an electric singularity at time t = 1.3.

Table 1. Summary of the calculs properties.

Equations	CPU time	Nb. of processors	Speed up (%)
29200	29 mn 31 s	1	—
29200	16 mn 42 s	2	88 %

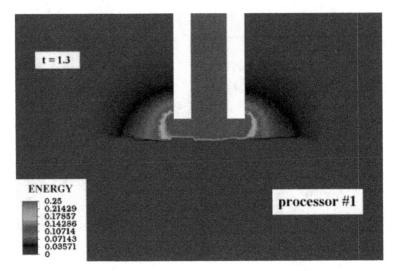

Fig. 4. Part of elements dedicated to processor #1.

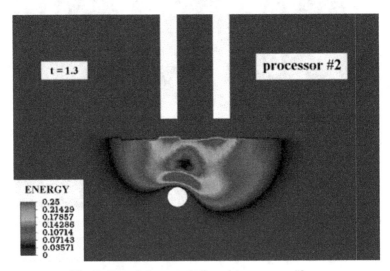

Fig. 5. Part of elements dedicated to processor #2.

Table 2. Summary of used memory.

Processor	Source Code	Memory Full Grid	Memory partial Grid
#1	29 Kb	3.8 Mb	1.8 Mb
#2	—	3.5 Mb	1.6 Mb

6 Conclusion

Generally the wave propagation with a front is always a difficult numerical problem with a large CPU cost. We present a general Finite Element formulation for Maxwell's equations in the case of propagation phenomenon . An electromagnetic wave propagates along the wave guide with the object determining the variable electric properties of the space crossed. This process is performed by the AMS with a time dependent number of unknowns. At these techniques we associate a parallel computing technology based on the selected data with SIMD and MPI technologies. The first tests of calculus are performed with an usual PC 2-Processors Pentium 1 GHz. In this way the CPU and memory cost are reasonable. This paper shows that the Finite Element Method, the Object Oriented Programming and the selected data by AMS expert system constitute a coherent set of techniques for an easy use in engineering problems.

References

1. Spaans, E.J.A., Backer, J. : Examining the use of Time Domain Reflectometry for measuring liquid water-content in frozen soil. Water Ressources Research, Vol. 31, n°12 (1995) 2917-2925.
2. Fleckinger, E. : Electromagnétisme. Editions Masson, Paris (1991).
3. Dhatt, G., Touzot G. : Une présentation de la méthode des éléments finis. Editions Maloine S.A., Paris (1981).
4. Chambarel, A., Onuphre, E. : Parallel computation of an unsteady compressible flow . Parallel Computing Technologies : Proceedings of the 4th International Conference. Lecture Notes in Computer Sciences, Vol. 1277. V. Malyshkin edition, Springer-Verlag. (1997) 377-382.
5. Chambarel, A., Ferry E.: Finite Element formulation for Maxwell's equations with space dependent electric properties. Revue Européenne des Eléments Finis, Vol. 9, n° 8 (2000) 941-967.
6. Anderson, D.A., Tannehill, J.C., Pletcher, R.H. : Computational Fluid Mechanics and Heat Transfer . Hemisphere Publishing Corporation Editor (1984).

A General Parallel Computing Approach Using the Finite Element Method and the Objects Oriented Programming by Selected Data Technique

André Chambarel[1] and Dominique Fougère[2]

[1] Complex Hydrodynamics Laboratory, Faculté des Sciences, 33 rue Louis Pasteur
F-84000 Avignon, France
andre.chambarel@univ-avignon.fr

[2] Laboratory of Modeling in Mechanics L3M , La jetée, Technopole de Château-Gombert,
8 rue F. Joliot Curie
F-13451 Marseille Cedex 20, France
fougere@l3m.univ-mrs.fr

Abstract. We develop a coherent set of techniques for parallel computing. We use the Finite Element Method associated with the C++ Objects Oriented Programming with only one database. A technique of data selection called AMS – Automatic Multigrid System – is used for the determination of the data dedicated to each processor. This method is performed by a SIMD technology associated with the MPI capabilities. This parallel computing is applied to very large CPU cost problems particularly the unsteady problems or steady problems using iterative methods. Different results in Computational Fluid Dynamics are presented.

1 Introduction

In this paper we will present a parallel computing method for engineering problems by a Finite Element approach. Several methods are used for the parallel computing, such as the domain decomposition [1]. We propose a coherent set of techniques for an easy implementation including:
– Finite Element Method,
– C++ Objects Oriented Programming,
– Selection data technique,
– Matrix free technique and iterative method.

We develop an easy method for parallel computing which seems to be a natural way to perform intensive computation. Our purpose is to carry out parallel algorithms without modifying the object structure of the solvers and the data structure. To answer this requirement, we use a selected data method resulting in suitable load balancing with the choice of lists of elements. This technique is independent of the geometry, and can be applied in general cases. This new concept is a natural way for the standardization of parallel codes. In fact, parallelization is here applied to the resolution of the nonlinear system by matrix free algorithm. The domain of potential applications is very wide and several examples are presented [2].

V. Malyshkin (Ed.): PaCT 2001, LNCS 2127, pp. 428–435, 2001.

Among different hardware concepts the SIMD – Single Instruction Multiple Data – architecture has proved to be the most promising for parallel computer. This technology is used for the high performance computing especially when problems such as solving large set of differential equations are dealt with [3]. A SIMD parallel computer consists of a set of processors connected with a fast communication network. Each processor performs the same program with different data. In our work the different data are obtained with a single file and each processor selects its concerned data. For the parallel programming we use the MPI – Message Passing Interface – library.

2 Structure of Code

Figure 1 shows the general structure of the compact code. It is organized into three classes corresponding to the functional blocks of the Finite Element Method's different stages. With these classes we built three objects that are connected by a single heritage. So the transmission of the parameters between the objects is defined by a list technique.

We use efficient C++ Objects Oriented Programming for the Finite Element code called FAFEMO (Fast Adaptive Finite Element Modular Object) [4]. This technology allows an implementation of very low sized solvers. In our examples their sizes are about 31 Kb – 900 C++ lines –. Each solver is dedicated to a problem and can be considered as an element of an algebraic structure [5].

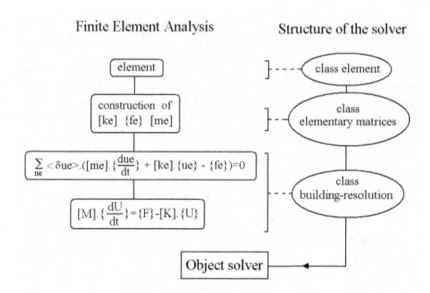

Fig. 1. Object structure of a standard solver.

3 Method of Parallel Computing

3.1 Principle of Parallelization

The principal CPU cost corresponds to the elementary matrices computing and secondarily to the time step updating. In the example of an unsteady problem, the analytical discretization of the problem with the Finite Element Method is given by the following scalar product [6]:

$$\sum_{NE} \langle \delta ue \rangle.([me]\{\frac{due}{dt}\} + [ke]\{ue\} - \{fe\}) = 0 \quad \text{with} \quad NE = 1..ne \tag{1}$$

Generally the matrix free technique is used and we consider only the elementary residuum $\{\psi e\}$:

$$\sum_{NE} \langle \delta ue \rangle.([me]\{\frac{due}{dt}\} - \{\psi e\}) = 0 \tag{2}$$

If p is the number of processors, we select a list of elements Nk:

$$\bigcup_{k=1}^{p} Nk = NE \quad \text{and} \quad Ni \cap Nj = 0 \quad \text{for } i \neq j \tag{3}$$

Each elementary matrix can be assembled into a global matrix by a classical Finite Element process [5]. We obtain:

$$\sum_{k=1}^{p} [Mk] = [M] \quad \text{global mass matrix} \quad \text{and} \quad \sum_{k=1}^{p} \{\Psi k\} = \{\Psi\} \quad \text{global residuum} \tag{4}$$

In this case the Bernstein's conditions are verified [4]. So we have a correct load balancing if the list's size of elements are similar for each processor. The communications between the processors exist only at the end of the time step. Each processor builds his part of the differential system and the below algorithm allows the updating of the solution $\{U\}$. A semi-implicit algorithm is used [6]:

$t_n = 0$

$while \quad (t_n \leq t_{max})$

$$\begin{cases} for \ j = 1 \ to \ p \quad \{\Delta U_n^i\}_j = \Delta t_n.[M_n^i]^{-1}.\{\Psi_j(U_n + \alpha.\Delta U_n^{i-1}, t_n + \alpha.\Delta t_n)\} \\ \quad i = 1, 2, ... \quad until \quad \|\Delta U_n^i - \Delta U_n^{i-1}\| \leq tolerence \end{cases}$$

$\{U_{n+1}\} = \{U_n\} + \{\Delta U_n\}$

$t_{n+1} = t_n + \Delta t_n$

$end \quad while$

where α is the upward time-parameter. If $\alpha < 0.5$ a stability correction is required [6]. For the above algorithm we dispose of a technique [7] for an easy diagonalization of the matrix [M].

3.2 Technique of Parallelization

Each solver is endowed with a capability called AMS (Automatic Multigrid System). It is an expert system with several possibilities. The applications of this capability are very large:
-       Multiprocessor computing (in this paper),
-       Wave front,
-       Multidomain calculus,
-       Moving boundary,
-       Multigrid simulation, ...
    According to the problem, the AMS expert system can choose different analytical or geometrical components (Fig. 2):
if the element *i* is (dis)activated (active_element[i]=false/true):
-    all nodes of this element are (dis)activated:
-    (active_node[j]=false/true, j=1 .. nn)
-    all degrees of freedom of each node j are (dis)activated:
-    (active_dof[k]=false/true, k=1 .. nd)
    The converse is true.
    In the case of parallel computing the AMS expert system chooses here the elements dedicated to each processor for the sharing of the scalar product (1).

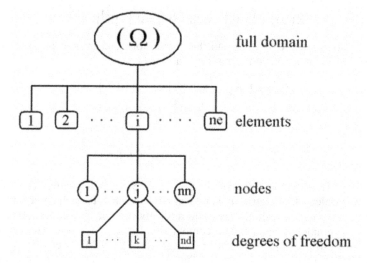

Fig. 2. Taxinomy of the Finite Element parameters.

    In fact we can summarize the principal stages of parallelization:
-    A first stage consists to create an expert system for the selection of the data for each processor.
-    In the second stage each processor calculates the concerned elementary matrix without communication per step.
-    In the third stage each secondary processor sends its assembled elementary matrices to the principal processor. So it can update the step.

4 Application

The classical test problem is the flow of a dilatable fluid in a square cavity [1]. We use the AMS capabilities for multiprocessor computing with a two- or four-processors computer with the precedent algorithm. It also presents a driven cavity flow and thermo-convection flow [8]. With the usual notations [1], the adimensional Navier-Stokes equations can be written:

$$\frac{\partial u_j}{\partial x_j} = 0$$

$$\frac{\partial u_i}{\partial t} + \frac{1}{Pr}.u_j.\frac{\partial u_i}{\partial x_j} = -\frac{\partial p}{\partial x_i} + \frac{\partial^2 u_i}{\partial x_j^2} + Ra.T.\delta_{i3} \tag{5}$$

$$\frac{\partial T}{\partial t} + \frac{1}{Pr}.u_j.\frac{\partial T}{\partial x_j} = \frac{1}{Pr}.\frac{\partial^2 T}{\partial x_j^2}$$

We use a classical Galerkin formulation associated with the Taylor-Hood element [9], for a steady problem the Navier-Stokes equations (5) become a nonlinear system:

$$[K(U)]\{U\} = \{F\} \quad \text{with} \quad \{\Psi\} = \{F\} - [K]\{U\} \tag{6}$$

An iterative method is used and the above nonlinear system is resolved into the iterative following algorithm using the relations (4):

$$\text{for } j = 1 \text{ to } p \quad \{\Delta U_j^i\} = [A]^{-1}.\{\Psi_j(U^i)\}$$
$$\{U^{i+1}\} = \{U^i\} + \{\Delta U_j^i\}$$

$$i = 1, 2, \ldots \quad \text{until} \quad \text{Max}_j \left\| \Delta U_j^i \right\| \le \text{tolerence}$$

where $[A]^{-1}$ is a diagonal preconditioner [10]. So this algorithm is similar to an unsteady problem. It is matrix free and can be dispatched to each dedicated processor. Thereby, no communications are required between the processors. Each of them performs a completely independent computation for each iteration. This is particularly well adapted to the object structure of the solver. The SIMD architecture is used for the parallel computing management. The AMS capabilities select the data for each processor. The corresponding software is developed with the MPI C++ library. We should notice that the parallel solver is almost the same as the one used in a sequential process. These examples are performed on a Silicon Power Challenge computer.

The different stages of the parallel computing are applied to CFD problems. Different cases of driven square cavities with thermoconvection are presented in figures 3, 4 and 5. The structured mesh is here 20 x 20 i.e. 800 triangles and the velocity vectors are plotted. In this case, we use 2 or 4 processors and the list of elements is shared in 2 or 4 equal parts. Initially we have separated vortices and each picture is an algebraic representation of different stages of the previous iterative process. When the iterations number increases, the separate vortices merge and give the exact solution [1]. We have here a graphical resemblance with the domain decomposition method because the numeration of the elements is sequential according to the coordinates axis. These results are similar to that of the reference [1].

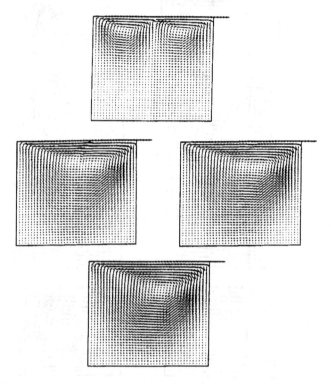

Fig. 3. Velocity vectors in a driven cavity calculated with 2 processors.

Table 1. Summary of calculus properties.

Nb of processors	Equations	CPU time-10 iterations	Speed up
1	2554	2 mn 43 s	—
2	2554	1 mn 33 s	90 %
4	2554	0 mn 47 s	87 %

The efficiency of the parallel computing is summarized in the Table 1.

5 Conclusion

An easy method of parallel computing for engineering problems is proposed. It consists to use a coherent set of techniques including :

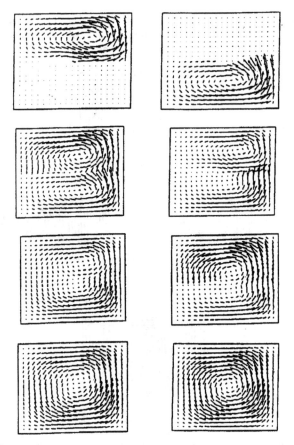

Fig. 4. Velocity vectors of a thermoconvection problem calculated with 2 processors.

- Finite Element Method,
- C++ Objects Oriented Programming by FAFEMO software,
- Selection data technique by AMS expert system,
- Matrix free algorithms.

 In this context the implementation of the concerned low sized solvers is very easy. The SIMD architecture associated with the MPI-C++ library is used. So we dispose of an efficient method for the parallelization of differential systems coming from the Finite Element Method. The performances are interesting. We notice particularly the low sized memory and the good load balancing. Different examples in Computational Fluid Dynamics are presented.

References

1. Yeckel, A., Smith, J.W., Derby, J.J.: Parallel finite element calculation of flow in a three dimensional lid-driven cavity using the CM-5 and T3D. Int. J. Num. Methods in Fluids, Vol. 24 (1997) 1449-1461.

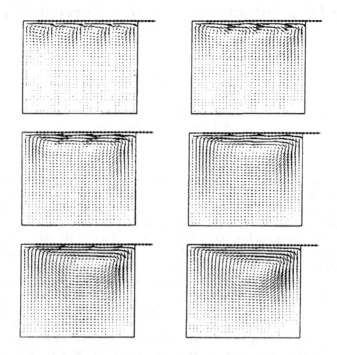

Fig. 5. Velocity vectors in a driven cavity calculated with 4 processors.

2. Gresho, P.M.: On the theory of semi-implicit projection methods for viscous incompressible flow and its implementation via a finite element method that also introduces a nearly consistent mass matrix. Int. J. Numer. Meth.Fluids, Vol. 11 (1990) 621-659.
3. Hempel, R., Calkin R., Hess, R., Joppich, W., Keller, U., Koike, N., Oosterlee, C.W., Ritzdorf, H., Washio, T., Wypior, P., Ziegler, W.: Real applications on the new parallel system NEC Cenju-3. Parallel Computing, Vol. 22 (1996) 131-148.
4. Chambarel, A., Onuphre, E.: Parallel computation of an unsteady compressible flow by the Finite Element method. Lecture Notes in Computer Sciences, Springer-Verlag, Berlin Heidelberg New York (1997).
5. Chambarel, A., Onuphre, E.: Finite Element software based on Object Programming. International Conference of the twelfth I.A.S.T.E.D., Annecy France, May 18-20, 1994.
6. Dhatt, G., Touzot, G.: Une présentation de la méthode des éléments finis. Editions Maloine S.A., Paris (1981).
7. Chambarel, A., Ferry, E.: Finite Element formulation for Maxwell's equations with space dependent electric properties. Revue européenne des Eléments Finis, Vol. 9, n° 8 (2000) 941-967.
8. Turek, S.: Tools for simulating non stationary incompressible flow via discretely divergence-free finite element model. Int. J. Numer. Meth. Fluids, Vol. 18 (1994) 71-105.
9. Taylor, C., Hood, P.: A numerical solution of the Navier-Stokes equations using the Finite Element technique. Computer & Fluids, Vol. 1 . Pergamon Press (1973) 73-100.
10. Van der Vorst, H.A.: Bi-CGSTAB, A fast and smoothly converging variant of Bi-CG for the solution of non-symmetric linear systems. S.I.A.M. J. Sci. Statist. Comput., Vol.13 (1992) 631-644.

Parallel Implementation of a Corrected DSMC Method

Svetlana Ignatieva[1] and Vladimir Memnonov[1]

St.Petersburg State University, Dep. math. mech., Bibliotecnaya sq.2, St.Petersburg, St.Peterhov, 198504, Russia

Abstract. In the paper it is suggested a correction of the Bird's algorithm in the DSMC method. It takes account of real distribution of collision events inside the time steps Δt and actual trajectories for the collided particles there thus diminishing asymptotical order of the error in time evolution from $O(\Delta t)$ to $O((\Delta t)^2)$. However the structure of the algorithm turned out to be more complicated and parallel implementation of it becomes a new problem. As some solution of this problem the corrected DSMC method in its domain decomposited version was applied for simulation of unsteady flow in a two-dimensional cavity with a moving bottom. The numerical results of this simulation presented in the paper show a noticeable artificial acceleration of changes for system parameters by the uncorrected version in comparison with the corrected one as the former locates all collision events from the previous collisional time step at one time point at the beginning of the space motional step. The difference between their results in calculation of the mean velocity circulation along the identical loops in its time development increases proportionally to value of the time step $O(\Delta t)$ used and to mean molecular collision number on the distance from the source of perturbation to a measuring point.

1 Introduction

Monte Carlo simulation is widely used in rarefied gas dynamics for solution of very different problems. The most successful provs to be version of it introduced by G.A.Bird [1],[2] and known as direct simulation Monte Carlo (DSMC) method. In this version molecular collisions and their space motion are splitted within a small time step Δt into two separate, one after another, computable processes. So that after a collision time step the collided molecules with its newly acquired velocities just from the very beginning of the subsequent space motional time step are moved to its new space positions. Thus all collision events are located at one time point in the step beginning instead of being distributed somehow within it as in real evolution. Thus the error of the DSMC method is of order $O(\Delta t)$. In order to diminish this error it was introduced a trajectory correction [3], [4] which is shortly described in the next section along with its further development and some consequences for parallel implementation of the corrected DSMC method.

V. Malyshkin (Ed.): PaCT 2001, LNCS 2127, pp. 436–441, 2001.

2   Background and Trajectory Correction

As it was underlined in papers [3],[4] an important point of the DSMC method
is the assumption that molecules are located equally probable inside their cells.
This is related to the nature of the gasdynamical measurements where particle density inside of small space volumes with linear size say R_1 could not be
determined during the measurements. So that for any state of the gas system
such kind of an assumption is also understood not contradicting yet long-term
scientific experience.

It should be also mentioned that the time of the gasdynamical measurements
is limited from below. And characteristic times of all the processes must be
much larger than some time interval Δt_1, commonly $\Delta t_1 \approx R_1/c$, where c is
a characteristic speed. It is true, for instance, for local optical Doppler's shift
measurements of the molecular velocity in a cell. Usually all parameter's changes
during this time step Δt_1 are so small that the system could be considered as
quasi–stationary within it. By choosing DSMC decoupling time step Δt being of
order of this value Δt_1 we can take advantage of using some results of Khinchine
[5] for stationary random processes.

Indeed in [3],[4] it was introduced random collisional fluxes – the probabilities
of some encounter for a pair of molecules in a cell for the time between t and
$t + dt$ during collisional time interval Δt. Superposition of all such fluxes in a
cell forms a stochastic process. Through asymptotical estimates it was shown
[6] that constituent random fluxes mutually independent, stationary, ordinary
and with limited after-effect. So that applicability conditions for the Khinchine's
limit theorem [5] were verified. The superposition of these random fluxes proves
to be then a Poisson process, the number of collisions in a cell K_c being the
Poisson variate.

In fact due to decoupling of the molecular space motion and mutual molecular
collisions, a collided particle in the Bird's algorithm moves straight from the
very beginning of the subsequent space motional time interval Δt with its newly
obtained velocity $\mathbf{c'_j}$, instead of running at least over two asymptotes of a real
trajectory first with an old velocity $\mathbf{c_j}$ and then with the new one $\mathbf{c'_j}$ after an
apex at the collision time point t_c somewhere inside Δt. The probability of
the apex location because of the mentioned above stationarity does not depend
upon time hence the probability of an encounter between t and $t + dt$ within Δt
is equal to $dt/\Delta t$. So time point of an encounter t_c can be simulated simply by
$t_c = rnd()*\Delta t$, rnd() being the next random number. The complete displacement
$\mathbf{s_j}$ which includes such a collision is given by

$$\mathbf{s_j} = \mathbf{c_j}t_c + \mathbf{c'_j}(\Delta t - t_c)$$

As one needs here the values of both velocities before $\mathbf{c_j}$ and after an encounter $\mathbf{c'_j}$ it is natural to calculate the space motion of collided particles within
the collisional time step. The probability of two collisions during Δt for the same
molecule being proportional to $O((\sigma n v \Delta t)^2)$ where σ is molecular collision cross
section, n - concentration, v - relative speed, is considered to be vanishing small

and neglected. So the error in time is correspondingly proportional to $O(\Delta t^2)$. Though expressions for nonstationary corrections and collisions for molecules from different cells have already been obtained in [3] for simplicity they will not be applied here.

This is the main difference of the present correction from the traditional Bird's algorithm [1],[2]. In papers [3], [4] for the sake of diminishing computational cost it was used simplified version of the trajectory correction with the average displacement $E(\mathbf{s_j})$ instead of complete simulation which through perhaps excessive simplification has allowed in that time to maintain the structure of the Bird's algorithm. Yet true complete simulation demands to change its structure and parallel implementation of this corrected DSMC method then presents a new problem. The next section describes parallel, domain decomposited implementation of the corrected DSMC method for the flow in a two-dimensional cavity. The last section contains conclusions.

3   An Unsteady Flow Simulation

In order to estimate the practical significance of this correction a two-dimensional unsteady flow in the square cavity with a moving bottom and diffusively reflecting walls was simulated by the DSMC method both with and without it. Simulation domain is shown in Fig.1a) , where the linear size of the square was equal to 32 mean free paths (mfp) of an initial state. During simulations the domain was divided into 9216 square cells with the cell size being equal to one third of mean free path and constant moving bottom velocity Uw was equal to 0.6 of the most probable velocity of the initial state v_T, $v_T = \sqrt{2kT/m}$, where k—Boltzmann's constant, T—initial temperature and m—molecular mass. Time step Δt was equal to 0.04, 0.08 or 0.16 of mean free time (mft) of a molecule. Molecules supposed to interact as hard spheres.

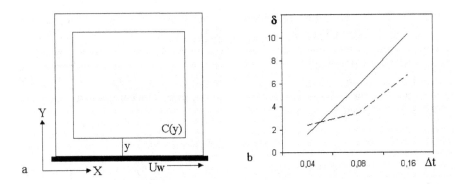

Fig. 1. a) Simulation domain. b) Relative error δ for the uncorrected version in comparison with the corrected one. The solid is for y=1.9mfp and the dashed one for y=0.4mfp

The whole flow field was equally decomposited between four processors. After completing the simulation of an initial state first for a cell it was determined number of the potential collisions, which is the expectation of variate K_c and is given by the formula of the Bird's NTC method [2]. Then for those of them which were experianced real collision according to that method it was checked whether the beginning asymptote of its trajectory with an old velocity had intersected the boundary walls. If it was the case then collision is considered still as falsh, otherwise it was a real encounter. Then it was checked whether second trajectory asymptote has intersected the border lines of the processor or the boundary walls. In the last case the apropriate reflections from the walls were simulated. While for the former the data of the molecule were written and afterwords transfered to the pertinent processor through 'recv' and 'send' operations of the MPI. The results of the reflections were again checked for intersections and so on. Thus the complete trajectories for collided particles were constructed. The probability of two collisions for the same molecule, as it has been already above mentioned, was neglected. So that the probability of a second collision for the molecules, which have had a falsh encounter because of wall perturbation, after that time point, was neglected too. Now after all the collided molecules have been moved over their real trajectories the remaining in the cell particles are moved according to their velocities freely. Completing this procedure for every cell in the flow field, one has to do only indexing by determining new molecular numbers in cells. Thus traditional splitting procedure is entirely avoided.

The results of the simulations have shown that approximately 6-8% of collisions are affected by walls or borders. For instance for a cell near a wall and far from the processor borders in a test simulation 6.6% of the whole collision number were not realized because their trajectories were perturbed by an encounter with the wall before collision time point t_c. For a cell near a processor border 7.8% of collisions hapened to occur in that neighboring processor's space. Yet their trajectories were followed up to the very end and then its data were transfered to the pertinent processor. And finally for a cell located exactly at the corner between a wall and a border 7.7% of collisions were not realized and 7% occured in the different processor's domain. Now going over to gas dynamical quantities it is usefull to consider circulation over rectangular loops $C(y)$ for the averaged in a cell molecular velocity $\mathbf{V}$ related to the value of Uw and divided by their lengths L, $Q(y)$,

$$Q(y) = \frac{1}{UwL} \oint_{C(y)} \mathbf{V} \, d\mathbf{r} \tag{1}$$

with different distances y from the moving wall to the nearest part of the contour, see Fig.1a).

Circulation $Q(y)$ is depicted at the parts a) and b) of the Fig.2, corresponding to $\Delta t = 0.04mft$ and $\Delta t = 0.16mft$ respectively. The dashed and solid curves represent the uncorrected and corrected versions with the different distances from the moving surface y: the curve 1 for $y = 0.4mfp$, the curve 2 for $y = 1.9mfp$ and the curve 3 for $y = 4.9mfp$. As one can see from the Fig.2 the uncorrected version showes higher $Q(y)$ values. It could be easily understood by taking into consideration that the perturbations from the moving wall are being transfered through the collisions of the particles. Starting in this version from the very beginning of the space motional time step Δt already with its new velocities obtained after a collision, which in real evolution is distributed somehow during the whole that interval, the molecules are thus transporting perturbations ahead of the real evolution.

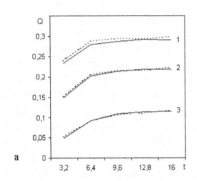 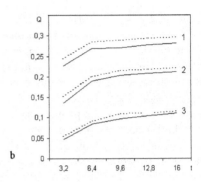

Fig. 2. Circulation Q(y): a) for $\Delta t = 0.04$mft and b) for $\Delta t = 0.16$mft, curves 1 for y = 0.4mfp, curves 2 for y = 1.9mfp and curves 3 for y = 4.9mfp. Dashed and solid curves are uncorrected and corrected versions respectively.

Some exceptions in the Fig.2a) for the curves 3 could be explained by en-hanced scattering in that case due to insufficients both the sample size and the time interval of simulation in the case where the most part of the contour is unreachable during that interval. The difference between these versions has ap-preciably increased with enlargement of time step Δt. This is seen by comparing parts a) and b) of the Fig.2 which presents the same quantities but Δt in the last case being four times as higher as in the previous one.

On the part b) of the Fig.1 it is depicted relative error $\delta = (Qun./Qc. - 1) * 100\%$. The lower lying curve corresponds here to $y = 0.4 mfp$ and much higher values are belong to $y = 1.9 mfp$ thus confirming the importance of the distance for the accumulation of an overall error.

4   Conclusions

The results presented in previous sections show that the trajectory correction recovers the joint development inside Δt of the decoupled in DSMC processes by properly mapping the collision events onto subsequent space motional time step. The uncorrected version, on the contrary, accelerates the whole evolution locating all collisions at one time point at the beginning of the space motional step instead of distributing them somehow within it. As natural consequence of it the error in time of the Bird's algorithm increases asymptotically proportionally to the order $O(\Delta t)$. The intoduced in the paper trajectory corrected version has this order equal to $O(\Delta t^2)$. The values of the time step Δt used and the mean molecular collision number on the distance from the source of perturbation to a measuring point are important parameters of the DSMC method related to its accuracy.

Acnowledgement

The authors would like to thank Yu.P.Galyuck for important hints on debugging the parallel code. This work was partially supported by the RFBR grant N01-01-00315 and by the grant "Integration" B 0008.

References

1. Bird G.A., Molecular Gas Dynamics. Clarendon Press, Oxford, 1976.
2. Bird G.A., Molecular Gas Dynamics and the Direct Simulation of the Gas Flows. Clarendon Press, Oxford, 1994.
3. Memnonov V.P., Direct Simulation Monte Carlo Method: Another Version of Reunion for Decoupled Processes. Proc. of the 3rd St.Petersburg Workshop on Simulation.Ed.'s S.M.Ermakov and V.B.Melas, SPbSU Publ.House 1998, 101–106.
4. Memnonov V.P., Direct Simulation Monte Carlo Method: Different Procedure for Joining of Decoupled Processes(in Russian)// Mathematical modeling, 1999, **11**, n3, 77–82.
5. Khinchine A.Ya., Mathematical Models in the Theory of Queueing. Griffing, London, 1960.
6. Memnonov V.P., Some Asymptotical Estimates in the DSMC Method. In Proc. of 2nd St.-Petersburg Workshop on Simulation. Ed.'s S.M.Ermakov and V.B.Melas, SPbSU Publ. House 1996, 118–119.

Parallel Algorithms
for Non-stationary Problems:
Survey of New Generation of Explicit Schemes*

Yuri M. Laevsky[1], Polina V. Banushkina[2], Svetlana A. Litvinenko[1], and
Alexander A. Zotkevich[1]

[1] Institute of Computational Mathematics and Mathematical Geophysics SB RAS,
6, Lavrentiev ave, 630090, Novosibirsk, Russia
`laev@labchem.sscc.ru`
[2] Novosibirsk State University
2, Pirogov st., 630090, Novosibirsk, Russia

Abstract. In the paper the new approach to design parallel algorithms
for the modelling of the multi-scale non-stationary processes is proposed.
Our technique is based on the explicit multi-level difference schemes with
the local stability conditions. We study a number of the methods which
are realized efficiently with multi-computer systems and are applied to
some problems from combustion theory.

The advantages of the explicit methods from the parallelisation point of view are
well known. But very stiff stability conditions were the reason to exclude such
algorithms from computational practice, essentially for the diffusion problems.
From the other hand, there are many examples where the use of implicit schemes
are failed. For instance, implicit methods for the flame propagation problems
require the discretization time step, which coincides with the step of the stable
explicit scheme. The reason of this effect is in local unstability in the small
subdomain with combustion process. It means that the large time step in implicit
scheme does not provide an acceptable accuracy.

Thus, we consider a new class of explicit schemes with different time steps in
space subdomains with local stability conditions. Below we present some methods in vector–matrix form. All these algorithms may be considered as domain
decomposition methods. Our consideration is partially based on the ideas described in [1–4]. From a variety of the existing methods of parallelization of
algorithms, the algorithms considered here are parallelized by the domain decomposition method and by the explicit form of schemes. Briefly, the essence of
this method consists in the following. The basic data of a problem are distributed
among nodes (branches of a parallel algorithm), and the algorithm is the same
in all the nodes, but operations of this algorithm are distributed according to
the data, available in these nodes. The distribution of operations of an algorithm

* The work was supported by the RFBR (grant 01-01-00819), the Programm "Russian
  Universities" (grant 991116), the Russian-Holland Programm NWO-RFBR (grant
  047.008.007)

V. Malyshkin (Ed.): PaCT 2001, LNCS 2127, pp. 442–446, 2001.

consists, for example, in assignment of different values by a variable of the same cycle in different branches, or in performance in different branches of the different number of loops of the same cycles, etc. Homogeneous distribution of data among nodes (branches) serves a basis for the balance between the time needed for calculation, and the time needed for interactions of branches.

Let all unkown variables be devided into two groups. Then the matrix, corresponding to the diffusion grid operator, is presented in a block form

$$A = \begin{pmatrix} A_{11} & A_{12} \\ A_{12}^T & A_{22} \end{pmatrix}.$$

The two-level scheme of Dirichlet type is following:

$$\frac{u_1^{n+1} - u_1^n}{\Delta t} + A_{11}u_1^n + A_{12}u_2^n = f_1^n, \tag{1}$$

$$u_1^{n+\frac{k}{m}} = u_1^n + \frac{k}{m}(u_1^{n+1} - u_1^n), \tag{2}$$

$$\frac{u_2^{n+\frac{k+1}{m}} - u_2^{n+\frac{k}{m}}}{\tau} + A_{12}^T u_1^{n+\frac{k}{m}} + A_{22}u_2^{n+\frac{k}{m}} = f_2^{n+\frac{k}{m}}, \tag{3}$$

where $\Delta t = m\tau$, $n = 0, 1, \ldots$, $k = 0, \ldots, m-1$. Here the vector u_1^n corresponds to the variables in the "external subdomain", $u_2^{n+\frac{k-1}{m}}$ corresponds to the variables in the "internal subdomain" and equalities (2) are the linear interpolation in the interface. It means that in the "internal subdomain" we solve the Dirichlet problem. The scale difference is provided by strong inequality

$$\|A_{11}\| \ll \|A_{22}\|.$$

The main theoretical result is localization of stability conditions:

$$\Delta t \|A_{11}\| = O(1), \qquad \tau \|A_{22}\| = O(1).$$

Accuracy of scheme (1)–(3) is $O(\Delta t)$ in "external subdomain" and $O(\tau)$ in "internal subdomain". Now we will present the scheme with an accuracy $O((\Delta t)^2)$ in "external subdomain" and practically without additional arithmetical costs. Here we used the result from article [5]. Let v_1^n be auxiliary vectors and $v_1^0 = u_1^0$. Then we consider the following scheme:

$$\frac{v_1^{n+1} - u_1^n}{\Delta t} + A_{11}v_1^n + A_{12}u_2^n = f_1^n, \tag{4}$$

$$v_1^{n+\frac{k-1}{m}} = v_1^n + \frac{k-1}{m}(v_1^{n+1} - v_1^n), \tag{5}$$

$$\frac{u_2^{n+\frac{k}{m}} - u_2^{n+\frac{k-1}{m}}}{\tau} + A_{12}^T v_1^{n+\frac{k-1}{m}} + A_{22}u_2^{n+\frac{k-1}{m}} = f_2^{n+\frac{k-1}{m}}, \tag{6}$$

$$\frac{u_1^{n+1} - u_1^n}{\Delta t} + A_{11}\frac{v_1^n + v_1^{n+1}}{2} + A_{12}\frac{u_2^n + u_2^{n+1}}{2} = \frac{1}{2}(f_1^n + f_1^{n+1}), \tag{7}$$

where $k = 1, \ldots, m$. More accurate variant of such type schemes is to use the corrector in "internal subdomain" too:

$$\frac{v_1^{n+1} - u_1^n}{\Delta t} + A_{11} v_1^n + A_{12} u_2^n = f_1^n, \tag{8}$$

$$v_1^{n+\frac{k-1}{m}} = v_1^n + \frac{k-1}{m}(v_1^{n+1} - v_1^n), \tag{9}$$

$$\frac{v_2^{n+\frac{k}{m}} - u_2^{n+\frac{k-1}{m}}}{\tau} + A_{12}^T v_1^{n+\frac{k-1}{m}} + A_{22} v_2^{n+\frac{k-1}{m}} = f_2^{n+\frac{k-1}{m}}, \tag{10}$$

$$\frac{u_2^{n+\frac{k}{m}} - u_2^{n+\frac{k-1}{m}}}{\tau} + A_{12}^T \frac{v_1^{n+\frac{k-1}{m}} + v_1^{n+\frac{k}{m}}}{2} + A_{22}\frac{v_2^{n+\frac{k-1}{m}} + v_2^{n+\frac{k-1}{m}}}{2} =$$
$$= \frac{1}{2}(f_2^{n+\frac{k-1}{m}} + f_2^{n+\frac{k}{m}}), \tag{11}$$

$$\frac{u_1^{n+1} - u_1^n}{\Delta t} + A_{11}\frac{v_1^n + v_1^{n+1}}{2} + A_{12}\frac{u_2^n + u_2^{n+1}}{2} = \frac{1}{2}(f_1^n + f_1^{n+1}), \tag{12}$$

In many combustion problems there are more than two scales. For instance, in the gas filtration problem at least three essentially different time–space scales. For such problems we propose the Neumann type multi–level scheme. All unkown variables are devided into p groups and now the matrix, coorresponding to the diffusion grid operator, is presented in a block–tridiagonal form. Then let

$$A_{l,l} = A_{l,l}^{(l-1)} + A_{l,l}^{(l)}, \quad l = 2, \ldots, p,$$

where $A_{l,l}$ are the diagonal blocks and $A_{1,1}^{(1)} = A_{1,1}$. Let us introduce the 2×2-block matrices

$$A_l = \begin{pmatrix} A_{l,l}^{(l)} & A_{l,l+1} \\ A_{l,l+1}^T & A_{l+1,l+1}^{(l)} \end{pmatrix}, \quad l = 1, \ldots, p-1,$$

and $A_p = A_{p,p}^{(p)}$. Now we have p different scales and corresponding condition is

$$\|A_1\| \ll \cdots \ll \|A_p\|.$$

And finally, let us introduce some index notations. Let $m_2, \ldots, m_p$ be some natural numbers. Then $r_1 = 1$, $r_l = m_l r_{l-1}$ and $\alpha_1 = n$, $\alpha_l = \alpha_{l-1} + n_l/r_l$, $l = 2, \ldots, p$. The values α_l are the functions of the parameters $n_k = 0, \ldots, m_k$, $k = 2, \ldots, l$. Let us consider the following multi–level difference scheme:

$$\frac{u_1^{n+1} - u_1^n}{\tau_1} + A_{1,1} u_1^n + A_{1,2} u_2^n = f_1^n, \tag{13}$$

$$\frac{u_l^{\alpha_l + \frac{1}{r_l}} - u_l^{\alpha_l}}{\tau_l} + A_{l-1,l}^T u_{l-1}^{\alpha_{l-1}} + A_{l,l}^{(l-1)} u_l^{\alpha_{l-1}} + A_{l,l}^{(l)} u_l^{\alpha_l} + A_{l,l+1} u_{l+1}^{\alpha_l} = f_l^{\alpha_l},$$

$$n_k = 0, \ldots, m_k - 1, \quad k = 2, \ldots, l, \quad l = 2, \ldots, p - 1, \tag{14}$$

$$\frac{u_p^{\alpha_p + \frac{1}{\tau_p}} - u_p^{\alpha_p}}{\tau_p} + A_{p-1,p}^T u_{p-1}^{\alpha_{p-1}} + A_{p,p}^{(p-1)} u_p^{\alpha_{p-1}} + A_{p,p}^{(p)} u_p^{\alpha_p} = f_p^{\alpha_p},$$

$$n_p = 0, \ldots, m_p - 1, \tag{15}$$

where the sequence of the time–steps are given by the equalities

$$\tau_1 = \Delta t, \quad \tau_l = \tau_{l-1}/m_l, \quad l = 2, \ldots, p.$$

It is easy to see that in distinguish to schemes (1)–(3), (4)–(7) and (8)–(12) here we do not use interpolation on the interface and in the "internal subdomain" we solve the Neumann problem. Particularly two–level scheme has the form

$$\frac{u_1^{n+1} - u_1^n}{\tau_1} + A_{1,1} u_1^n + A_{1,2} u_2^n = f_1^n,$$

$$\frac{u_2^{n + \frac{k+1}{m}} - u_2^{n + \frac{k}{m}}}{\tau_2} + A_{1,2}^T u_1^n + A_{2,2}^{(1)} u_2^n + A_{2,2}^{(2)} u_2^{n + \frac{k}{m}} = f_2^{n + \frac{k}{m}},$$

where $k = 0, \ldots, m - 1$, $m = m_2$. For scheme (13)–(15) we have proved a localization of stability conditions:

$$\tau_l \|A_l\| = O(1), \quad l = 1, \ldots, p.$$

Now we will present Dirichlet–Neumann type algorithm with the other adjoint condition on the interface. Namely we use adjoint condition based on the penalty method. This algorithm approximates some auxiliary problem with discontinues solution, and a convergence to the solution of the original problem is provided by small positive parameter ε. For simplicity we present two–level variant of the method. Firstly let us devide all variables into three groups: the variables in the opened "external subdomain", the variables in the interface and the variables in the opened "internal subdomain". Then diffusion grid operator has the form

$$A = \begin{pmatrix} A_{1,1} & A_{1,\Gamma} & 0 \\ A_{1,\Gamma}^T & A_{\Gamma,\Gamma}^{(1)} + A_{\Gamma,\Gamma}^{(2)} & A_{\Gamma,2} \\ 0 & A_{\Gamma,2}^T & A_{2,2} \end{pmatrix},$$

where Γ is the interface. Let

$$A_1 = \begin{pmatrix} A_{1,1} & A_{1,\Gamma} \\ A_{1,\Gamma}^T & A_{\Gamma,\Gamma}^{(1)} \end{pmatrix}, \qquad A_2 = \begin{pmatrix} A_{\Gamma,\Gamma}^{(2)} & A_{\Gamma,2} \\ A_{\Gamma,2}^T & A_{2,2} \end{pmatrix},$$

In accordance with these notations we consider two groups of the variables. Let us note that we include the variables on the interface into the both groups. Then the explicit scheme of the penalty method has the form

$$\frac{u_1^{n+1} - u_1^n}{\tau} + A_1 u_1^n + \frac{1}{\varepsilon} (B_{1,1} u_1^n - B_{1,2} u_2^n) = f_1^n, \tag{16}$$

$$u_1^{n+\frac{k}{m}} = u_1^n + \frac{k}{m}(u_1^{n+1} - u_1^n), \tag{17}$$

$$\frac{u_2^{n+\frac{k+1}{m}} - u_2^{n+\frac{k}{m}}}{\tau} + A_2 u_2^{n+\frac{k}{m}} +$$

$$+ \frac{1}{\varepsilon}\left(B_{2,2} u_2^{n+\frac{k}{m}} - B_{1,2}^T u_1^{n+\frac{k}{m}}\right) = f_2^{n+\frac{k}{m}}, \tag{18}$$

where the operator

$$B = \begin{pmatrix} B_{11} & -B_{12} \\ -B_{12}^T & B_{22} \end{pmatrix}$$

corresponds to the internal Newton type boundary conditions in differential problem:

$$\varepsilon \frac{\partial u_1}{\partial \nu_1} + u_1 - u_2 = 0, \quad \frac{\partial u_1}{\partial \nu_1} + \frac{\partial u_2}{\partial \nu_2} = 0 \quad \text{on} \quad \Gamma.$$

The theory of a convergence with respect to the small parameter ε is based on the estimate

$$\|u - u_\varepsilon\|_{L_2(\Omega)} = O(\varepsilon),$$

where u and u_ε are the solutions of the original and the perturbed problems, respectively.

References

1. V.I.Drobyshevich and Yu.M.Laevsky. An algorithm of solution of parabolic equations with different time–steps in subdomains. Rus. J. of Numer. Anal. and Math. Modell. – 1992. – V.7, No.3. – P.205–220.
2. Yu.M.Laevsky. The decomposition of domains for parabolic problems with discontinuous solutions and the penalty method. Comp. Maths Math. Phys. – 1994. – V.34, No.5. – P.605–619.
3. V.D.Korneev and S.A.Litvinenko. The domain decomposition parallel algorithm for multi-dimensional parabolic equations. Bull. of the Novosibirsk Computing Center. – Ser. Computing Science. – 1999. – Is.10. – P.25–35.
4. Yu.M.Laevsky and P.V.Banushkina. The compound explicit schemes. Siberian J. Numer. Math. – 2000. – V.3, No. 2.– P.165–180 (in Russian).
5. G.V.Demidov and E.A.Novikov. Effective algorithm for the integration of non–stiff systems of ordinary differential equations. Numerical Methods in Mathematical Physics. – 1979, Novosibirsk. – Computing Center of SB RAS. – P.69–83 (in Russian).

Tool Environments in CORBA-Based Medical High Performance Computing*

Thomas Ludwig, Markus Lindermeier, Alexandros Stamatakis, and
Günther Rackl

Technische Universität München (TUM), Informatik
Lehrstuhl für Rechnertechnik und Rechnerorganisation (LRR-TUM)
Arcisstr. 21, D-80333 München
{ludwig,linderme,stamatak,rackl}@in.tum.de

Abstract. High performance computing in medical science has led to important progress in the field of computer tomography. A fast calculation of various types of images is a precondition for statistical comparison of big sets of input data. With our current research we adapted parallel programs from PVM to CORBA. CORBA makes the integration into clinical environments much easier. In order to improve the efficiency and maintainability we added load balancing and graphical on-line tools to our CORBA-based application program.

1 Introduction

Imaging in medical science is an important issue that shows an increasing connection with high performance computing. Relevant picture series from imaging hardware like magnetic resonance tomographs or positron emission tomographs are usually computed on powerful servers and stored in specialized picture archiving systems.

Recently, workstation clusters became more and more popular as they provide a good price-performance ratio. Furthermore, many operations that are performed on these picture series exhibit a maximum parallelism. In many cases no interprocess communication is required and the parallelization is handled at the granularity level of the individual pictures.

As soon as the parallel imaging servers are used in production mode we are faced with two more problems. One is the load of the individual nodes of the cluster. It should be balanced in order to guarantee an optimal use of the computational power of the cluster. Second, the imaging software has to interact with other software components in a medical environment and thus has to meet certain standards of reliability and interoperability.

The paper will present an approach where we base our parallelization of the imaging software on a distributed object-oriented middleware system (in our case

* This work is partly funded by the *Deutsche Stifterverband*, Kurt-Eberhard-Bode Stiftung

V. Malyshkin (Ed.): PaCT 2001, LNCS 2127, pp. 447–455, 2001.
© Springer-Verlag Berlin Heidelberg 2001

Load Management System

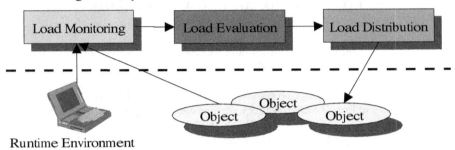

Fig. 1. The components of a load management system

CORBA) to take advantage of component integration. A load balancing mechanism is integrated into a specific CORBA ORB to provide optimal performance to the application programs.

2 The Load Management System

Load management systems can be classified according to their implementation. They may be integrated into the application, the runtime system, or a separate service. The first case is called application level, the second one system level, and the third one service level load management. We decided to make a system level implementation because it provides maximum flexibility and transparency to the user.

In general, load management systems can be split into three components: The load monitoring, the load distribution, and the load evaluation component. They fulfill different tasks and work at different abstraction levels. This eases the design and the implementation of the overall system. Figure 1 shows the components of a load management system and a runtime environment containing some application objects.

The load monitoring component provides both, information on available computing resources and their utilization, and information on application objects and their resource usage. This information has to be provided dynamically, i.e. at runtime, in order to obtain knowledge about the runtime environment and its objects. The computing resources in distributed environments may be shared by middleware based applications and legacy applications.

Load distribution provides the functionality for distributing workload. Load distribution mechanisms for system level load management are initial placement, migration, and replication.

Initial placement stands for the creation of an object on a host that has enough computing resources in order to efficiently execute an object. Initial placement may be applied to all kinds of objects because it is done at creation time.

Migration means the movement of an existing object to another host that promises a more efficient execution. It may be applied to all kinds of objects, too. However, migration is applied to existing objects, so the object state has to be considered. The object's communication has to be stopped and its state has to be transferred to the new object. Finally, all communication has to be redirected to the new object.

Replication is similar to migration but the original object is not removed, so some identical objects called replicas are created. Further requests to the object are divided up among its replicas in order to distribute workload (requests) among the replicas. Replication is restricted to replication safe objects. This means that an object can be replicated without applying a consistency protocol to the replicas. A precise definition of the term replication safe can be found in [7].

Finally, the load evaluation component makes decisions about load distribution based on the information provided by load monitoring. The decisions can be reached by a variety of strategies. The aim of the diverse strategies is to improve the overall performance of the distributed application by compensating load imbalance. There are two main reasons for load imbalance in distributed systems. First, background load can substantially decrease the performance of a distributed application. Second, request overload that is caused by too many simultaneously requesting clients increases the request processing time and thus, decreases the performance of the overall application. Both sources of load imbalance have to be considered by a load management system.

Distributed object oriented environments like CORBA [10] or DCOM [2] are based on some kind of object model. In general, the object models imply some transparency requirements [8]. Location transparency demands that the location of an object is unknown to its user. The middleware transparently connects client and server. Access transparency postulates that all objects in a distributed system are accessed in the same way. The middleware is responsible for providing uniform access to all objects, independent of their implementation or runtime environment. These transparency requirements have to be fulfilled by load management systems, too. Therefore, load distribution has to be transparent to the user. Our load management system provides full migration and replication transparency which means that migration and replication are completely transparent to the user.

The load management concepts described so far are universal and may be applied to diverse distributed object-oriented environments. The implementation of these concepts strongly depends on the underlying middleware architecture. We decided to make an implementation for CORBA because it is the most popular middleware architecture.

In CORBA, objects are connected to the middleware by the POA (Portable Object Adapter). The object adapter provides the functionality for creating and destroying objects, and for assigning requests to them. The POA is configured by the developer via so called policies. The ORB (Object Request Broker) provides the functionality for creating object adapters and for request handling. A request to an object arrives at the ORB which transmits it to the appropriate POA. Subsequently, the object adapter starts the processing of the request by an implementation of the object (Servant).

The load management functionality, especially load monitoring and load distribution, have to be integrated into the ORB and the POA because we decided to make a system level implementation. Therefore, we added some policies and interfaces to the POA in order to enable state transfer and the creation of replicas. The monitoring of the runtime environment is performed via the Simple Network Management Protocol (SNMP) [11] which is a well established standard in network management.

A new policy called `ControlFlowPolicy` that controls the creation and destruction of CORBA objects is added to the POA. The policy value `USER` indicates that objects are created by the programmer. The value `SYSTEM` indicates that objects are created on demand by the CORBA runtime environment. This enables the transparent creation of new objects in case of migration and replication. Therefore, the programmer has to provide a `ServantFactory` interface that enables the creation and destruction of Servants analogous to the Factory design pattern [4]. The POA's `RequestProcessingPolicy` is extended with the value `USE_SERVANT_FACTORY` that causes the POA to use the `ServantFactory` for object creation and destruction.

Migration and replication of objects that hold state require state transmission as described before. Therefore, some persistence mechanism has to be provided. A new policy, the `PersistencePolicy` is added to the POA. The policy value `USE_PERSISTENT_SERVANT_FACTORY` indicates that an extension of the `ServantFactory` interface, the `PersistentServantFactory`, is used in order to create and destroy objects. Additionally, the `PersistentServantFactory` provides the functionality to extract an object's state and to recreate objects from that state. This approach enables the application of various persistence mechanisms like the Persistent State Service [9] or proprietary mechanisms like Java serialization.

Finally, request redirection is performed by the CORBA Location Forward mechanism [5]. It enables to hand over object references to clients by raising an `ForwardRequest` exception. The client runtime transparently reconnects to the forwarded reference. This guarantees migration and replication transparency.

3   The Medical Image-Processing Application

A medical image-processing application is chosen for exploration of concept purposes. The realignment process forms part of the Statistical Parametric Mapping (SPM) application developed by the Wellcome Department of Cognitive Neurology in London [6]. SPM is used for processing and analyzing tomograph image sequences, as obtained for example by functional Magnetic Resonance Imaging (fMRI) or Positron Emission Tomography (PET). Such image sequences are used in the field of neuroscience, for the analysis of activities in different regions of the human brain during cognitive and motoric exercises.

Realignment is a cost intensive computation performed during the preparation of raw image data for the forthcoming statistical evaluation. It computes a 4×4 transformation matrix for each image of the sequence, for compensating the effect of small movements of the patient, caused e.g. by his breath. The images are realigned relatively to the first image of the sequence.

The realignment algorithm for image sequences as obtained by fMRI will briefly be presented. One has to distinguish two cases.

First Case: Realignment of one sequence of images: The reference data set and the first matrix is obtained by performing a number of preparatory computations using the image data of the first image. The matrices for all remaining images are calculated using the reference data set.

Second Case: Realignment of multiple sequences of images: The reference data set and the first matrix of the first sequence are calculated. Thereafter, the first images of all remaining sequences are realigned relatively to the first image of the first sequence and its reference data set. Finally, the realignment algorithm as described in the first case is applied to all sequences independently.

At this point the only precondition for the calculation of the transformation matrix is the availability of the reference data set, which is calculated only once for each sequence. Once the reference data set(s) is(are) available, the matrices of the sequence(s) can be computed independently.

The manually parallelized realignment application is already available as sequential C++, C++/CORBA and C++/PVM program. Previous work shows, that the overhead induced by CORBA is not prohibitive for its deployment in clinical environments.

For the following steps it is necessary to transform the sequential C++ program into a Java program because some components of our tool environment only provide Java interfaces. This program transformation is performed using the Java Native Interface (JNI). An interesting intermediate result is that the deployment of JNI does not lead to any performance decrease for the specific program [12].

4   Integrating the Application into the Tool Environment

In order to improve performance and scalability of the image-processing application we decided to integrate it into our load management system.

As already mentioned in section 3 the availability of a Java program is a necessary prerequisite for the integration into the load management system, since it only provides services for Java/CORBA programs. The sequential Java realignment application is transformed into a distributed Java/CORBA application.

Figure 2 depicts the structure of the CORBA application. The service offered by the server object is the `compute()` service, which calculates the transformation matrix for an image. The state of a server object consists of a reference data queue (cache). Therefore it is replication safe since it can be replicated without

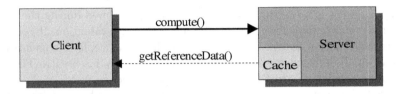

Fig. 2. The structure of the medical image-processing application

applying a consistency protocol to its replicas, i.e. the required cache data can easily be reestablished. A `getReferenceData()` service is offered by each client and provides the specific reference data to the server if it is not already cached.

The basic adaptation of the Java/CORBA application to the load balancer is straightforward. Minor chnages to the code are necessary in order to add the `ServantFactory` and `PersistantServantFactory` methods to the server object. In addition to those modifications the system is extended by various additional components for testing particular aspects of the load management system. The mechanism itself was integrated into the Java-based JacORB [1].

The second part of our tool environment consists of the Middleware Monitoring Tool (MIMO) [3] and the graphical on-line visualization tool MiVis (Middleware Visualization). The integration of these tools is straight forward, too. MIMO provides some standard events like object creation, object deletion, object interactions, and additionally defines generic events. Furthermore, MIMO provides the infrastructure for designing active tools, i.e. tools that manipulate the monitored application. Initially we specify the data to be monitored, for example client and server hosts, client and server objects, server object load, server host load, application object interactions, and load balancing actions like migration and replication. This information is provided by a MIMO adapter that is used to instrument the application and the load management system.

MiVis is a graphical on-line visualization tool that is based on the MIMO monitoring system. It provides a framework that enables the development of new display types which can be plugged into the tool core. We developed a new display that is used for the visualization of the new monitoring events described before. Figure 3 presents the basic layout of the graphical on-line tool. Client and server objects are located within the respective rectangles representing the client and server hosts. In addition, server object load (numerical representation) and server host load values are depicted (numerical and graphical representation). The CORBA method `compute()` is represented as blue arrow (black in Fig. 3) with a counter and `getReferenceData()` as offset turquoise arrow. Replications and Migrations are represented as yellow (white in Fig. 3) and red arrows respectively. Replication and Migration actions can be initiated manually too, by a drag and drop function.

The combination of MIMO and MiVis provides a flexible and extensible infrastructure for the development and the maintenance of large scale distributed applications. Together with our monitoring system performance and scalability of applications can be substantially improved.

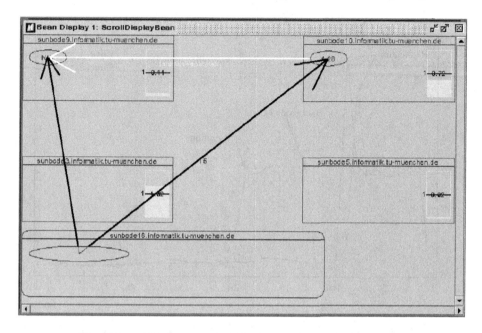

Fig. 3. Visualization of a replication and of object interactions

5   Evaluation

In order to evaluate the efficiency of the presented load management concept and its implementation, a test case is shown.

The hardware consists of three machines with equal configuration. There is no background load on the machines. The examined CORBA application is the medical image-processing application described in section 3 with two simultaneously requesting clients. The application is replication safe as already mentioned in section 4. Thus, migration and replication can be applied to this application.

Figure 4 shows the processing time per image against the number of the processed image for both clients. At the beginning, one server object is created and placed on a machine (initial placement) and the clients start requesting the server. The image processing time is equivalent for both clients now because the server alternately processes their requests. After a while the load management system recognizes that the server is overloaded because both clients permanently request the server. Accordingly, replication is performed, i.e. a second server object (replica) is created and each client gets a replica on its own. In consequence of the replication, the image processing time of each client decreases about 50%. Some time later background processor load is generated on the machine that is used by the second client's replica. Hence, the image processing time of the second client substantially increases. Again, the load management system recognizes the processor overload and migrates the affected replica to the third machine which was not used so far. The consequence is that the image processing time returns to its normal level.

Processing Time / Image [Sec.]

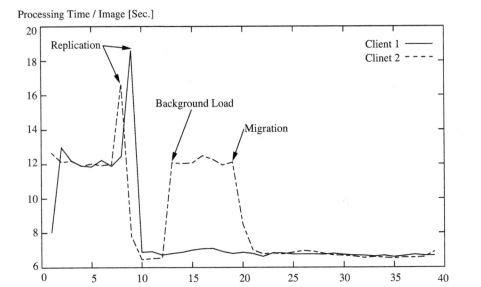

Fig. 4. The load managed medical image-processing application

The test case shows how the load management system is able to deal with different kinds of overload. Request overload is compensated by replication, whereas background load is compensated by migrating an object to a less loaded host. Consequently, the load management systems improves the performance and the scalability of the medical image-processing application.

6   Conclusion and Future Work

The combination of load balancing and graphical user interface provides a powerful environment for the production oriented image processing in medical environments. Workstation clusters can be used as high performance servers for reconstruction and statistical analysis of tomography pictures. Our CORBA-based approach allows the integration of image processing into the workflow of clinical routine. Future steps in this field will cover aspects of fault tolerance, where the computing environment will have integrated mechanisms for fail-soft and recovery.

References

1. G. Brose. JacORB: Implementation and Design of a Java ORB. In *International Conference on Distributed Applications and Interoperable Systems (DAIS'97)*. Chapman & Hal, 1997.
2. G. Eddon and H. Eddon. *Inside Distributed COM*. Microsoft Press, 1998.

3. G. Rackl. *Monitoring and Managing Heterogeneous Middleware.* PhD thesis, Technische Universität München, 2001.
4. E. Gamma, R. Helm, R. Johnson, and J. Vlissides. *Design Patterns.* Addison Wesley, 1994.
5. M. Henning. Binding, Migration, and Scalability in CORBA. *Communications of the ACM*, 1998.
6. K. Friston. SPM. Technical report, The Wellcome Department of Cognitive Neurology, University College London, 1999.
7. M. Lindermeier. Load Management for Distributed Object-Oriented Environments. In *International Symposium on Distributed Objects and Applications (DOA'2000)*, Antwerp, Belgium, 2000. IEEE Press.
8. OMG (Object Management Group). A Discussion of the Object Management Architecture. Technical report, http://www.omg.org, 1997.
9. OMG (Object Management Group). CORBAServices: Common Object Services Specification. Technical report, http://www.omg.org, 1998.
10. OMG (Object Management Group). The Common Object Request Broker: Architecture and Specification — Revision 2.3.1. Technical report, http://www.omg.org, 1999.
11. W. Stallings. *SNMP, SNMPv2, SNMPv3, and RMON 1 and 2.* Addison Wesley, 1998.
12. A. Stamatakis. Interoperable Tool Deployment for the Late Development Phases of Distributed Object-Oriented Programs. Master's thesis, Technische Universität München, 2001.

Parallel Algorithms for the Analysis of Biological Sequences

Giancarlo Mauri and Giulio Pavesi

Dept. of Computer Science, Systems and Communication
University of Milan–Bicocca
Milan, Italy
{mauri,pavesi}@disco.unimib.it

Abstract. In the last few years, molecular biology has produced a large amount of data, mainly in the form of sequences, that is, strings over an alphabet of four (DNA/RNA) or twenty symbols (proteins). For computational biologists the main challenge now is to provide efficient tools for the analysis and the comparison of the sequences. In this paper, we introduce and briefly discuss some open problems, and present a parallel algorithm that finds repeated substrings in a DNA sequence or common substrings in a set of sequences. The occurrences of the substrings can be approximate, that is, can differ up to a maximum number of mismatches that depends on the length of the substring itself. The output of the algorithm is sorted according to different statistical measures of significance. The algorithm has been successfully implemented on a cluster of workstations.

1 Introduction

On April 6th 2000, Celera Genomics announced to the world that the sequencing phase of the genome of a human being was completed. These news made the headlines all over the world, and even if it was to be taken with a grain of salt[1], Celera's announcement had and is still having a great impact on science, religion, and politics. Although important, the news were for many people already involved in molecular biology and computational biology just the tip of an iceberg. In the last few years, molecular biologists have produced a large amount of data, and more are going to come in the near future. For instance, since last April, the genomes of *Drosophila Melanogaster* (fruit fly) [1] and *Arabidopsis Thaliana* (thale cress) [2] have already been completed. Coming up next: the mouse genome.

Biological data come in the form of DNA or protein sequences. The standard assumption is that the sequences contain all the information needed to obtain biologically meaningful results, abstracting away the reality of DNA and proteins as flexible three–dimensional molecules interacting with one another in a

---

[1] If we figure the genome as a book, the sequencing stage has produced millions of pages, alas, with no page numbers on them. The assembly phase, that is, putting the pages in the right order, has yet to be completed.

V. Malyshkin (Ed.): PaCT 2001, LNCS 2127, pp. 456–468, 2001.

Table 1. Average genome sizes.

Epstein–Barr virus	0.172×10^6 bytes
Bacterium (*E.coli*)	4.8×10^6 bytes
Beer Yeast	14.4×10^6 bytes
Nematode Worm	100×10^6 bytes
Thale Cress	100×10^6 bytes
Fruit Fly	165×10^6 bytes
Homo Sapiens	3300×10^6 bytes

dynamic environment. For computer scientists, this is a real godsend (at least at the beginning, until they find out what problems they have to face), that allows them to enter such a fascinating world and at the same time to work on a data structure they are very familiar with: the *string*. When dealing with DNA or RNA, strings are built over an alphabet of four symbols, corresponding to the four DNA nucleotides. For proteins, we have an alphabet of twenty symbols, corresponding to the twenty different amino acids that build them. Leaving aside problems related to the generation of the data itself (such as sequence assembly problems), there are scores of different challenging problems deriving from the analysis of biological sequences, whose solution can provide efficient and powerful tools for the biological community (for a complete survey, see [3]).

Most of the problems admit polynomial time solutions. However, when dealing with whole chromosomes or even genomes, the size of the data is such that even linear algorithms become time consuming. Some figures are shown in Table 1. On the other hand, in some cases a parallel version of the algorithm is trivial to implement; therefore, running an algorithm even on a small cluster of workstations can yield significant improvements on the time required by the sequential version.

2   Open Problems

One of the most widely studied problems is finding various types of *repetitive* structures in biological strings. One of the most striking features of DNA (or to a lesser degree, proteins) is the number of repeated substrings that occur in genomes. It has been estimated that families of reiterated sequences account for about one third of the human genome. A short discussion on types and roles of repeated structures in DNA can be found in [3]. The main difficulty lies in the fact that repeats of the same pattern can be *approximate*, that is, may present mutations, insertions, or deletions of symbols. If we restrict our attention to mutations, the problem can be formalized as follows.

Problem 1 *Given an alphabet Σ, a string S on Σ, and two integers e and q, find all the patterns that occur at least q times in S with at most e mismatches.*

A closely related problem, at least when it comes to its solution, is to find *common* substrings in a set of strings. For example, if some sequences share the same biological function, the common substrings could hint at which parts are responsible for the function itself. Again, if we allow only mismatches, the problem can be formalized as follows.

Problem 2 *Given an alphabet Σ, a set of strings $S_1, \ldots, S_k$ on Σ, and two integers e and q, find all the patterns that occur in at least q strings with at most e mismatches.*

Alas, when dealing with biological sequences, things are not that simple. For example, in proteins, some amino acids have similar chemical and physical properties, while others are significantly different. Therefore, mismatches in the strings should be also weighted according to the similarities between pairs of amino acids. Moreover, as we already mentioned, each occurrence of a pattern could present the insertion and/or deletion of some symbols. Thus, problem 1 becomes:

Problem 3 *Given an alphabet Σ, a string S on Σ, an error threshold $e \in \mathbb{R}$, an integer q, and a distance measure $\mathcal{D}$, find all the patterns that occur at least q times in S such that, for every occurrence, the distance between the pattern and the occurrence measured according to $\mathcal{D}$ is less than or equal to e.*

For example, in proteins distance between amino acids can be measured according to PAM or BLOSUM matrices, that define a distance value for each pair of amino acids. Thus, given two strings $S_1 = s_1^1 \ldots s_k^1$ and $S_2 = s_1^2 \ldots s_k^2$ of equal length, the distance $\mathcal{D}$ between the two strings is the sum of the distances between the corresponding symbols s_i^1 and s_i^2. When insertions and deletions are taken into account, the measure of distance usually used is the *edit distance*. Given two strings (of arbitrary length), the edit distance is defined as the minimum number of edit operations (mutation, insertion or deletion of a symbol) needed to transform one string into the other. If we apply Hamming distance to Problem 3 we have again Problem 1. Problem 2 can be extended in a similar way.

Clearly, the complexity of the problems we introduced depends on the distance measure adopted. If we use Hamming distance, a naïve algorithm that generates all patterns of length k on Σ and checks whether they satisfy the constraints takes $O(|\Sigma|^k en)$ time, where $O(en)$ time is usually required to find the occurrences of each pattern. Some improvements have been introduced for the latter, but the main drawback is the $|\Sigma|^k$ factor, due to the exhaustive enumeration of the patterns. The $O(|\Sigma|^k en)$ time bound has been improved in [4], where it is reduced to $O(|\Sigma|^e k^e n)$ by means of *suffix trees*, a data structure that exposes the internal structure of a string in a very deep and meaningful way. Further improvements can be obtained by introducing some heuristics that somehow prune the search space, or that impose some restrictions on the location of the mismatches, for example, forcing them to occur at the same positions in each occurrence. The main drawback of heuristic methods is the fact that some "interesting" patterns can be missed altogether. We believe that heuristic approaches are suitable to perform a quick analysis of the data, while exhaustive enumeration, implemented as efficiently as possible, is perhaps the best choice if a thorough once–for–all analysis is needed.

The algorithm we present in this paper solves Problems 1 and 2, and can be seen as an extension of the one presented in [4]. In the next section we introduce the data structure the algorithm is based on, while in sections 4, 5 and 6 we present the algorithm and two different parallel versions.

3 Suffix Trees

A suffix tree $\mathcal{T}$ for an n–character string $S = s_1 \ldots s_n$ is a rooted directed tree with exactly n leaves numbered 1 to n. Each internal node, other than the root, has at least two children. Each edge is labeled with a nonempty substring of S. Two edges leaving the same node cannot have labels beginning with the same character. For any leaf i, the concatenation of the edge labels on the path from the root to leaf i exactly spells the suffix of S starting at position i, that is, it spells out $s_i \ldots s_n$.

The definition of suffix tree just given, however, does not guarantee that a suffix tree exists for every string S. The problem is that if one suffix of S matches a prefix of another suffix, then the tree cannot be built, since the path for the first suffix would not end up in a leaf. This problem can be avoided by assuming that the last symbol of the string does not appear elsewhere in the string, i.e., by appending to the string a termination symbol that does not belong to the string alphabet, as shown in Fig. 1.

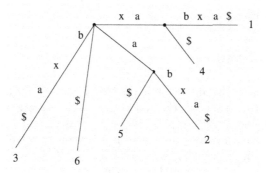

Fig. 1. Suffix tree for string xabxa. Symbol $ is used as termination. Without the termination, suffix xa would not end up in a leaf, since it is also a prefix of xabxa.

A suffix tree for a string can be built with different methods [5,6] in time linear on the length of the string. As a matter of fact, the only linear time solution for many string problems can be obtained only by using suffix trees or analogous text–indexing structures. It is also straightforward to prove that the space required by the tree (depending on the number of its nodes) is $O(n)$.

Given a string S of length n on a finite alphabet Σ, once the suffix tree for S has been built searching for a pattern p in the string is straightforward. Starting from the root, we match the symbols of p along the unique path in the tree until either p is exhausted, or no more matches are possible. In the former case, the leaves in the subtree below the last match are numbered with a starting location of p in the string. If we are interested only in counting the number of occurrences of patterns, we can also annotate each node of the tree with the number of leaves in the subtree below it. This can be done, once the tree has been built, with a linear time (since we have $O(n)$ nodes) depth–first traversal of the tree. If the pattern is m symbols long, the search takes $O(m)$ time, with an overall time complexity of $O(n + m)$, equaling "classic" pattern matching algorithms like Boyer–Moore [7] or Knuth–Morris–Pratt [8]. Suffix trees, however, are appealing when we want to search for many different patterns in the same string. Traditional pattern matching algorithms pre–process the pattern instead of the string and require, for each pattern, $O(m)$ time for the preprocessing and $O(n)$ time for the actual search. This approach might become time consuming in practice when $n \gg m$, as in the case of biological sequences. With suffix trees, instead, the $O(n)$ time is required only once, for the construction of the structure. Once the tree has been built, searching for each pattern takes only $O(m)$ time. Moreover, the theoretical linear time bound for the construction of the tree has proven itself to be very efficient in practice.

We can also search for a pattern p with at most e mismatches in a similar way. In this case, we match p along different paths on the tree at the same time, keeping track of the number of mismatches encountered on each path. Whenever the number of errors on a path is greater than e, we discard that path. If we complete p, the surviving paths represent all the occurrences of p in S with at most e mismatches.

4   The Algorithm

The starting point of the algorithm is the search method for approximate occurrences of a pattern outlined at the end of the previous section. Given a string S, its suffix tree $\mathcal{T}$ and a pattern p, we will call *locus* of p in $\mathcal{T}$ the end (along an edge) in $\mathcal{T}$ of the path corresponding to p. We want to solve a slightly different version of Problem 1: given an *error ratio* ϵ, with $0 \leq \epsilon < 1$, we want to find all the patterns p that occur at least q times in S with at most $\lceil \epsilon |p| \rceil$ errors, where $|p|$ denotes the length of p. We also assume that a maximum length M of patterns to be sought has been given as input.

First of all, we build the suffix tree $\mathcal{T}$ for S, and annotate each node with the number of occurrences of the corresponding substring. The core of the algorithm is the recursive procedure **expand**, outlined in Fig. 2. Suppose we have found on $\mathcal{T}$ the paths corresponding to approximate occurrences of a pattern $p = p_1 \ldots p_n$, that is, a set of pointers to the loci on $\mathcal{T}$ of patterns whose Hamming distance from p is less than or equal to $\lceil \epsilon |p| \rceil$. We will denote with $Actual_p$ this set of pointers. Also, we have associated with each pointer the Hamming distance from

expand$(p, s, Actual_p, Future_p)$

```
 1.  p' = ps
 2.  Occ(p') = 0
 3.  Fut(p') = 0
 4.  Actual_p' = ∅
 5.  Future_p' = ∅
 6.      For all q ∈ Actual_p ∪ Future_p do
 7.          For all q' ∈ Next(q) do
 8.              if the last symbol pointed by q' matches s
 9.                  error(q') = error(q)
10.              else
11.                  error(q') = error(q) + 1
12.              end if
13.              if error(q') ≤ ⌈ε|p'|⌉
14.                  add q' to Actual_p'
15.                  Occ(p') = Occ(p') + count(q')
16.                  Fut(p') = Fut(p') + count(q')
17.              else if error(q') ≤ ⌈εM⌉
18.                  add q' to Future_p'
19.                  Fut(p') = Fut(p') + count(q')
20.              end if
21.          end if
22.      end for
23.      end for
24.
25.  if Occ(p') ≥ minocc
26.      report(p')
27.  end if
28.
29.  if Fut(p') ≥ minocc
30.      For all σ ∈ Σ
31.          expand(p', σ, Actual_p', Future_p')
32.      end for
33.  end if
34.
35.  return
```

Fig. 2. The pseudo–code of the procedure **expand**. $Next(q)$ returns a set of pointers to the endpoints of paths obtained by extending by one symbol the path pointed by q; $count(q)$ returns the number of occurrences of the substring whose path is pointed by q; report(p') saves the pattern p', that satisfies the input constraints and has to be output to the user; $minocc$ is the minimum number of occurrences required.

p of the corresponding substring. The overall number of approximate occurrences of p is given by the sum of the occurrences of the substrings spelled by the paths in $Actual_p$, that can be read in the nodes entered by the last edges on the paths. Furthermore, we keep another list of pointers (called $Future_p$), corresponding to the paths spelling patterns whose Hamming distance from p is greater than $\lceil \epsilon |p| \rceil$ but less than or equal to $\lceil \epsilon M \rceil$. This is the list of *future occurrences* of p. That is, p might be the prefix of a longer pattern, that can admit at most $\lceil \epsilon M \rceil$ mismatches. These paths, however, do not contribute to the number of occurrences of p.

Now we try and expand p by one symbol. That is, for each symbol $\sigma \in \Sigma$, we match σ against the next symbol on the paths pointed by $Actual_p$ and $Future_p$. If a path ends just before a node T of the tree, we match σ against the first symbol on each edge leaving T. Whenever we encounter a mismatch, we increase the previous error along the path by one. Otherwise, the error remains unchanged. If the new error is less than or equal to $\lceil \epsilon(|p| + 1) \rceil$, we add the corresponding pointer to $Actual_{p'}$, the set of actual occurrences of $p' = p_1 \ldots p_n \sigma$; if it is greater than $\lceil \epsilon(|p|+1) \rceil$ but less than or equal to $\lceil \epsilon M \rceil$, we add it to $Future_{p'}$; otherwise we discard the path. If the new symbol added to the path is the termination, we discard the path as well. At the end, once all the actual and future occurrences of p have been checked, we have built the sets of actual and future occurrences of p', and computed its actual number of occurrences ($Occ(p')$) and the number of potential future occurrences ($Fut(p')$). If $Fut(p')$ is at least q, and the length of p' is less than M, we expand p' in the same way, otherwise we continue with p moving on to the next symbol in Σ. Notice that neither p or p' are required to occur exactly in S. The algorithm starts by expanding the empty pattern from the root of the suffix tree.

4.1   Sorting the Output

So far, we have been concerned with the size of the input, and how to develop an efficient algorithm. But, if we examine its output, that is, the list of patterns that satisfy the constraints given as input by the user, we have to face another issue. The output is usually *huge*, especially when the input sequence is long, and the minimum number of occurrences required is low. For example, *Saccharomices Cerevisiae* Chromosome I contains more than $200,000$ base pairs. If we ask the algorithm to report all the patterns, of maximum length 10, that occur at least twice in it with no errors, we obtain $153,397$ patterns. Trying to make some sense from the output could turn into a nightmare for the hapless biologist. One possible solution is to associate with each pattern a measure of *significance*, trying to reflect as much as possible its biological importance, and to sort the output accordingly. For example, we may consider biological sequences as random strings emitted by a source according to an unknown probability distribution over the symbols of the alphabet. When errors are not allowed a complete survey on this topic can be found in [9], and an algorithm, based on suffix trees, that finds "significant" patterns according to different measures is presented in [10]. In the latter, measures of significance compare in different ways the number of occurrences of a pattern with an expected value. Perhaps, the simplest one is the following:

$$z_1 = Occ(p) - \mathrm{E}[Occ(p)]$$

where $Occ(p)$ is the number of occurrences of a pattern p in a string, and $E[Occ(p)]$ is the corresponding expected value computed according to a given distribution of probability. The higher is the value of z_1, the more "surprising" is the number of occurrences of p. On the other hand, if z_1 has negative value, p appears less than expected. More sophisticated measures can be defined, like the following:

$$z_2 = \frac{Occ(p)}{E[Occ(p)]}$$

$$z_3 = \frac{(Occ(p) - E[Occ(p)])^2}{(E[Occ(p)])}$$

$$z_4 = \frac{(Occ(p) - E[Occ(p)])}{\sqrt{Var(Occ(p))}}$$

When approximate occurrences are taken into account, we think that a measure of significance should consider not only the number of occurrences of a pattern, but also how well conserved the pattern is. A pattern of length k that occurs q times with no errors should be considered more significant than another pattern, of the same length, that occurs q times as well but with e errors in each occurrence. Another factor that should be considered is *where* mutations have occurred. A pattern where mismatches occur, for example, in the central e positions should be more significant than another one where mutations are randomly distributed, since it can be seen as composed by two perfectly conserved parts. We now show how these considerations have been implemented in the algorithm.

Given a pattern $p = p_1 \ldots p_m$, we denote with $\mathcal{H}(p, e)$ the set of patterns within Hamming distance e from p. Let S be a string over an alphabet Σ. We assume that S has been generated by a random memoryless source with a given probability distribution on Σ. For each symbol $\sigma_i \in \Sigma$, we estimate the probability of σ_i to be generated by the source with the maximum likelihood estimator:

$$\pi_S(\sigma_i) = \Pr[\sigma_i \text{ appears in } S] = \frac{count(\sigma_i)}{|S|} \tag{1}$$

where $count(\sigma_i)$ denotes the number of occurrences of σ_i in S. The probability $\Pi_S(p)$ that p occurs in S with no errors is therefore given by:

$$\Pi_S(p) = \Pr[p \text{ occurs in } S] = \prod_{i=1}^{m} \pi_S(p_i) \tag{2}$$

Allowing overlaps, the number of occurrences of p in S (denoted by $Occ_S(p)$) is a random variable with binomial distribution, whose expected value is given by:

$$E[Occ_S(p)] = \Pi_S(p) \cdot (|S| - |p| + 1)$$

When approximate occurrences are allowed, that is, we allow at most e errors for p, the *a priori* probability of finding a valid occurrence of p is:

$$\Pi_S(p, e) = \sum_{p' \in \mathcal{H}(p,e)} \Pi_S(p')$$

The corresponding expected value for $Occ_S(p, e)$ (the number of occurrences of p in S with at most e mismatches) is given by:

$$E[Occ_S(p, e)] = \Pi_S(p, e) \cdot (|S| - |p| + 1)$$

If we use the value $\Pi_S(p, e)$, however, we lose information on how p actually appears in S. Therefore, we compute the expected value of $Occ_S(p, e)$ according to the a *posteriori* probability:

$$\hat{\Pi}_S(p, e) = \sum_{p' \in \mathcal{O}_S(p,e)} \Pi_S(p')$$

where $\mathcal{O}_S(p, e)$ is the set of patterns in $\mathcal{H}(p, e)$ that appear at least once in S. That is, we sum only the probabilities of patterns corresponding to actual occurrences of p in S. In this way, the more a pattern is conserved, the less is its probability to occur in S, and the higher is its significance value according to the measures defined above. Moreover, computing the a posteriori probabilities is straightforward. We just have to add to each pointer we use in the expand procedure the probability value of the corresponding path. Thus, the a posteriori probability of a pattern p is given by the sum of the probability values associated with the pointers in $Actual_p$. When a pointer q is expanded to q', the probability of the path pointed by q' can be computed by multiplying the probability of the path pointed by q by the probability of the symbol added by q'. In this way, whenever a pattern satisfies the input constraints we can compute its significance value according one of the measures defined before. The variance of $Occ(p)$ used in z_4 can be approximated by neglecting terms due to overlaps, that is, with the variance of the binomial distribution $(|S| - |p| + 1)\hat{\Pi}_S(p, e)(1 - \hat{\Pi}_S(p, e))$.

4.2   Time Complexity

The first step, the construction of the tree, takes $O(n)$ time. Let M be the maximum pattern length allowed and $e = \lceil \epsilon M \rceil$. For each call to the expand procedure, there are at most $O(n)$ different paths to be checked, each one in constant time. Moreover, we stop expanding a pattern whenever the number of future occurrences is less than q. Thus, the complexity of the algorithm depends on the number of patterns that have to be expanded, that can be estimated, as in [4], by $\sum_{i=1}^{e} \binom{M}{i} (|\Sigma| - 1)^i \leq |\Sigma|^e M^e$. The overall time complexity is therefore $O(|\Sigma|^e M^e n)$. The sorting stage takes $O(\nu \log \nu)$ time, where ν is the number of valid patterns reported by the algorithm.

4.3   Speedups

In practice, there are different ways to prune the search space, in order to get faster, even if less precise, results. For example, we may ask the algorithm to consider only patterns that occur at least once *exactly* in the sequence. It is sufficient to check, in the expand procedure, whether there is one path with error zero, corresponding to the exact occurrences of the pattern. This reduces significantly the search space. The risk is to miss completely a significant pattern, that has mutated in every occurrence. We can also run the algorithm in *prefix mode*: given a pattern $p = p_1 \dots p_m$ and an error ratio ϵ, for every valid occurrence $p' = p'_1 \dots p'_m$ of the pattern we must have:

$$\forall i \in \{1, \dots, m\} \ \ \mathcal{D}(p_1 \dots p_i, p'_1 \dots p'_i) \leq \lceil \epsilon i \rceil$$

That is, an occurrence of the pattern is valid iff it is a valid occurrence for each of its prefixes. In this way, we require mismatches to be uniformly distributed along the pattern. To implement this, we just have to discard the $Future_p$ list of pointers, maintaining only $Actual_p$. The risk is to lose some potentially valid occurrences. Anyway, the parameters of the algorithm can be fine tuned in order to reduce the probability of missing significant patterns to negligible values [11]. Moreover, in this case we need not provide the algorithm with an explicit value for the maximum length of the patterns.

5 Extensions

We now briefly sketch how the algorithm has been extended in order to solve Problems 2 and 3. For the common substrings problem on a set of k strings, we build a *generalized suffix tree*, as in [3], where each node is annotated with a k–bit string. The substring spelled out by the path from the root to a given node occurs in the i–th string of the set iff the i–th bit of the node is set. This can be done with a $O(kn)$ time pre–processing of the tree. During the pattern searching phase, instead of summing the counters of the nodes, we OR the bit strings, obtaining two bit strings for the actual and future occurrences of the patterns. Then, instead of checking the actual and future counters, we check how many bits are set in the two bit strings. If there are more than q bits set (actual or future), we expand the pattern. Significance measures based on the number of sequences a pattern appears in and the corresponding expected value can also be defined, as in the single sequence case.

The algorithm can also be run with different error measures. The basic version simply gives an error value of $+1$ to mismatches, and 0 to matches. These values can be redefined by providing the algorithm with appropriate scores for every pair of symbols, as introduced in the discussion of Problem 3. Then, instead of defining a maximum number of mismatches, we have to define an error threshold T, possibly as a function of the pattern length.

6 Parallel Implementation

For the parallel version of the algorithm, we considered two possible alternatives: dividing the set of patterns among the processors, assigning a different subset to each one, or breaking the sequence(s), making each processor work on a different region. Both versions have been implemented on a cluster of five workstations, using the Message Passing Interface (MPI) library.

6.1 Dividing the Patterns

As we have seen, the algorithm is composed of three parts: construction of the suffix tree, pattern discovery, and sorting of the output. Leaving aside for the moment the theoretical time complexity of the three stages, we have noticed that, in practice, the most time consuming part is the second one, that is, finding the patterns. As a matter of fact, building the tree (pruned to the maximum length of the patterns sought), also with a non–optimal implementation of the construction algorithm requires at most a few seconds even for sequences of millions of base pairs. Moreover, sorting thousands of patterns requires a few seconds. Finally, the annotated suffix tree, pruned at the maximum length needed, usually fits with no problems into the main memory of a medium size workstation, leaving enough room for the data structures required by the matching and sorting stage. All these considerations have led us to implement one parallel version of the algorithm as follows.

First of all, each processor builds its own copy of the suffix tree, pruned at a maximum pattern length given by the user. Then, each processor starts to search for his set of patterns. That is, patterns are distributed among the processors in order to obtain a workload as balanced as possible. For example, suppose we have as input a DNA sequence where the four symbols have (approximately) the same frequency, and we want to run the algorithm on four processors. The first processor scans its own copy of the tree for all the patterns starting with A, the second one for those starting with C, and so on. If we have eight processors at our disposal, the first one will search for patterns starting with AA and AC, the second one for those starting with AG and AT, and so on.

This simple heuristic can be extended also to the case of non–uniform probability distributions over the symbols of the alphabet. Again, we suppose we are working on the DNA alphabet $\Sigma = \{A, C, G, T\}$, and we want to run the algorithm on P processors. First, we generate all the strings on Σ of length k in lexicographic order. Let $p^1, p^2, \ldots, p^{4^k}$ be the strings. For each of them, we also compute the probability $\Pi_S(p^i)$ to occur in S according to Equations 1 and 2. Then, processor number one searches for patterns starting with p^1, p^2, and so on, until the sum of the probabilities of the prefixes used equals or is greater than $1/P$. At the same time, processor number two scans the list of k–letter patterns until it finds the first pattern p^i such that $\sum_{j=1}^{i-1} \Pi_S(p^j) \geq 1/P$. Then, it starts searching for patterns starting with p^i, p^{i+1}, and so on, until it meets a pattern p^f such that $\sum_{j=i}^{f} \Pi_S(p^j) \geq 1/P$. In the same way, processor number l will search for the first p^i such that $\sum_{j=1}^{i-1} \Pi_S(p^j) \geq (l-1)/P$, and will proceed in the same way.

After completing the searching step, each processor sorts the patterns found according to the measure adopted. If the workload has been balanced correctly, we expect all processors to complete this step more or less at the same time. Note that no communication among processors has been needed so far. At this point, all processors communicate to the same processor their sorted list of patterns, together with the significance values. The lists are finally merged together into a single sorted list, that is output to the user.

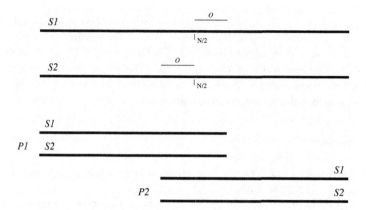

Fig. 3. Sequence splitting between two processors. Two sequences $S_1 = s_1^1 \ldots s_N^1$ and $S_2 = s_1^2 \ldots s_N^2$ of equal length N have been given as input, as well as the overlap parameter o. Processor 1 finds common patterns in the two sub–sequences $s_1^1 \ldots s_{N/2+o}^1$ and $s_1^2 \ldots s_{N/2+o}^2$, while processor 2 works on $s_{N/2-o}^1 \ldots s_N^1$ and $s_{N/2-o}^2 \ldots s_N^2$

6.2   Breaking the Sequences

This approach has been considered for the common substrings problem. In DNA sequences that share the same biological function, common substrings usually appear in the same order in each sequence. Therefore, if a common pattern occurs at the beginning of a sequence, we expect it to occur at the beginning of every other sequence. The idea is thus the following: each processor finds common substrings among corresponding regions of the sequences. For example, suppose that two strings $S_1 = s_1^1 \ldots s_{n_1}^1$ and $S_2 = s_1^2 \ldots s_{n_2}^2$ have been given as input. If the algorithm runs on two processors, we make processor 1 work on the first halves of the two strings, that is $S_1 = s_1^1 \ldots s_{\frac{n_1}{2}}^1$ and $S_2 = s_1^2 \ldots s_{\frac{n_2}{2}}^2$, while processor 2 will search for common patterns in $s_{\frac{n_1}{2}+1}^1 \ldots s_{n_1}^1$ and $s_{\frac{n_2}{2}+1}^2 \ldots s_{n_2}^2$.

To avoid missing "interesting" patterns that occur near the middle of the sequences, each half is extended by a region that overlaps with the other, whose size can be given as input to the algorithm. An example is shown in Fig. 3. This idea can be easily extended to more than two processors. This approach is appealing when the strings to be processed are very long, for example whole chromosomes from different organisms. Notice that no communication among processors is needed: each one works by itself, and outputs its list of patterns.

7   Conclusions

We presented an algorithm that finds repeated patterns in a string or common substrings in a set of strings, suitable for the analysis of DNA and RNA sequences. Pattern occurrences can be approximate, that is, can present a number of mismatches that depends on the pattern size. The set of patterns that satisfy the input constraints is output by the algorithm sorted according to different significance measures. A parallel version of the algorithm has been easily implemented on a cluster of workstations. Furthermore, we hinted at some ways to speed up the execution of the algorithm. We think that the algorithm, implemented even on a small number of computers, can provide to the biological community a useful tool for sequence analysis.

References

1. M. D. Adams *et al.* The genome sequence of Drosophila Melanogaster. *Science* **287**(2000), pp. 2185–2195.
2. The Arabidopsis Genome Initiative. Analysis of the genome sequence of the flowering plant Arabidopsis Thaliana. *Nature*, **408**(2000), pp. 796–815.
3. D. Gusfield. Algorithms on Strings, Trees and Sequences: Computer Science and Computational Biology. Cambridge University Press, New York, NY, 1997.
4. M. F. Sagot. Spelling approximate repeated or common motifs using a suffix tree. *Proc. of Latin '98*, Springer Verlag LNCS 1380, pages 111-127, 1998.
5. E. Ukkonen. On–line construction of suffix trees. *Algorithmica*, **14**(1995), pp. 249–260.
6. P. Weiner. Linear pattern matching algorithms. In *Proceedings of the 14th IEEE Symp. on Switching and Automata Theory*, pp. 1–11, 1973.
7. R. S. Boyer, J. S. Moore. A fast string searching algorithm. *Communications of the ACM*, **20**(1977), pp. 762–772.
8. D. E. Knuth, J. H. Morris, V. B. Pratt. Fast pattern matching in strings. *SIAM Journal of Computing*, **6**(1977), pp. 323–350.
9. G. Reinert, S. Scabath, M.S. Waterman. Probabilistic and statistical properties of words. *Journal of Computational Biology*, **7**(2000), pp. 1–48.
10. A. Apostolico, M. E. Bock, S. Lonardi, X. Xu. Efficient detection of unusual words. *Journal of Computational Biology*, **7**(2000), pp. 71–94.
11. G. Pavesi, G. Mauri, G. Pesole. An algorithm for finding signals of unknown length in DNA sequences. In *Proceedings of the 9th International Conference on Intelligent Systems for Molecular Biology (ISMB 2001)*, to appear.

Some Parallel Monte Carlo Algorithms*

G.A. Mikhailov

ICMMG of SB RAS,
Pr. Lavrentieva, 6, Novosibirsk, 630090, Russia
gam@sscc.ru

Abstract. The use of M independent computational processors by distributing random samples among them decreases the cost of the Monte
Carlo method by M times, as the final summation and averaging of the
results are practically inessential. This approach is especially effective
when using the 'double-randomization' method for solving the problems
with random parameters. When M is large, the necessary amount of
random numbers is also very large, and it is especially expedient to use
the combined random-pseudorandom secuence. For global estimating a
solution in the metric C by simulation of series of trajectories from different points, it is reasonable to use the same random numbers for each
point. The fact decreases the necessary amount of random numbers.

1 Introduction

It is obvious that the use of M independent computational processors by distributing random samples among them decreases the cost of the Monte Carlo
method by M times, as the final summation and averaging of the results are
practically inessential. Realization of different sample sizes by different processors is *admitted*, but here it is expedient to use the optimal averaging formula:

$$\bar{x} = \frac{\sum_{i=1}^{M} n_i \bar{x}_i}{\sum_{i=1}^{M} n_i}$$

where n_i is the sample size for the i-th processor and $\bar{x}_i$ is the corresponding
mean.

The massive distribution of random samples is extremely effective for the
Monte Carlo solution of problems with random parameters because 'double randomization' (see Sect. 4) results in the essential increasing of the probabilistic
space dimension.

When M is large, the necessary amount of random numbers is also very
large,and it is especially expedient to use the combined random-pseudorandom
sequence considered in Section 2.

This work is mainly related to solving of linear and weakly nonlinear integral
and differential equations by simulation of the proper random trajectories [1-3].

---

* The work was supported by RFBR (00-01-00797, 99-07-90422) and IG SD RAS 2000
- N 43

V. Malyshkin (Ed.): PaCT 2001, LNCS 2127, pp. 469–479, 2001.

Note that for global estimating a solution in the metric C by simulation of series of trajectories from different points, it is reasonable to use the same random numbers for each point (see Section 3). The fact decreases the necessary amount of random numbers.

In conclusion of this section note that there is not the ideal parallel algorithm for simulation of a stochastic ensemble of N interactig particles. But usually here the asymptotical deterministic error is equal to $C_1 N^{-1}$ and the corresponding probabilistic error is equal to $C_2 N^{-\frac{1}{2}}$. Therefore it is expedient to realize this simulation independently $(C_2/C_1)^2 N$ times by different processors with final averaging.

2   Specific Simulation of Ramdom Numbers

As a rule, simulation of a random variable with a given distribution is carried out by transformations of one or a number of independent values of a random number α uniformly distributed in the interval (0,1), i.e. by the formula: $\xi = \varphi(\alpha_1, ..., \alpha_n)$.

The sequence of 'sample' values of α is usually obtained on a computer by number-theoretic algorithms, of which the most widely used is the so-called 'method of residues', in the form

$$u_0 = 1, \quad u_n \equiv u_{n-1} M (\mathrm{mod}\, 2^r), \quad \alpha_n = u_n \cdot 2^{-r}.$$

Here r is the order of the mantissa of the computer. Often $M = 5^{2p+1}$ is used [1-3], where

$$p = \max\{q : 5^{2q+1} < 2^r\}.$$

Numbers of this type are called 'pseudo-random numbers'; they are verified by statistical testing and by solving typical problems (see [1-3]). The length of the period of the above version of the method of residues is 2^{r-2}. Physical generators, tables of random numbers and quasi-random numbers are also used in the Monte Carlo method.

The following special order of using pseudo-random numbers is expedient to correlate different computations. It is related to conventional methods of verifying the multidimensional uniformness. The sequence $\{u_n\}$ is supposed to be divided into the subsequences of the length m, beginning with the numbers u_{km}, $k = 0, 1, 2, ...$, and each subsequence is used to construct the corresponding random trajectory. Clearly,

$$u_{(k+1)m} \equiv u_{km} M^m (\mathrm{mod}\, 2^r).$$

So, to simulate the k-th trajectory we use the multiplicative pseudo-random sequence beginning with

$$\alpha_{km} = u_{km} \cdot 2^{-r}.$$

Here, it is sensible to use 'real' random numbers instead of α_{km}. This combined method has the theoretical basis provided $M \to \infty$ [4] (see so [3]).

Real random numbers can be produced by physical generators. It is possible to improve their distribution by summarization modulo one (congruent summation), i.e., using the expression

$$\alpha = \text{fract}\left(\sum_{i=1}^{n} \alpha_i\right),$$

where $\{\alpha_i\}$ are numbers from a physical generator. It is known that the distribution of α very quickly converges to uniform distribution, if n increases.

More, the termwise congruent summation of the random numbers produced by independent (or weakly dependent) random generators is very efficient, as the next statement shows.

Let $\{p_i^{(n)}(\cdot)\}$ be the probability density functions in $[0, 1]^n$ corresponding to the independent random number generators, 'convolution' corresponds to 'summation'.

Theorem 1. *If for $i = 1, 2, ..., m$, $m \geq 2$, the distribution densities $p_i^{(n)}(\cdot)$ of independent random vectors in $[0, 1]^n$ are square integrable and $p_{(m)}^{(n)}(\cdot)$ is their congruent m-fold convolution, then*

$$\|p_{(m)}^{(n)}(\cdot) - 1\|_{L^\infty} \leq \prod_{i=1}^{m} \|p_i^{(n)}(\cdot) - 1\|_{L^2} \quad \forall n.$$

$\square$

Proof. The Theorem is the direct collorary of the Theorem A.1 from [3]. $\square$

When simulating trajectories, these 'expensive' real α are used as initial numbers for the method of residues with M as large as possible. It *seems that this combined method is the most promising when using many processors.*

Additionally remark, that during approximately 35 years the version of the method of residues with $M = 5^{17}$ and $r = 40$ was successfully used for solving different mathematical physics problems. The numerical results of the statistical testing of this version are presented in [1].

Similar positive results were obtained for the above-mentioned special order of using these numbers with $m = 1024$.

3   Global Estimates of Solutions

In order to construct a global estimate of the function

$$\varphi(x) = \int_Y g(x, y) P(dy)$$

in the bounded domain D, one can estimate it's values in nodes of a rectangular grid with step H by the Monte Carlo method and then perform linear filling. We denote the estimate thus obtained by $\tilde{\varphi}(x)$. Generally speaking, the function $\tilde{\varphi}(x)$ is a random field, whose distribution is due to the sample size (i.e. the number of realizations of the Monte Carlo estimates), to the way of constructing the estimate ξ, and to step h.

The problem on the convergence of $\tilde{\varphi}$ to φ in some metric can be solved by considering the quantity

$$B(\varphi, \tilde{\varphi}) = \mathrm{E}\|\varphi(x) - \tilde{\varphi}(x)\|_{L(D)},$$

where $L(D)$ is a corresponding Banach space (see, for example, [3]). This problem is connected with the complexity of the estimation algorithm, i.e. with the average number of operations that provides the validity of the inequality $B(\varphi, \tilde{\varphi}) < \delta$. Estimating $B(\varphi, \tilde{\varphi})$ is the simplest for the space $L_2(D)$:

$$
\begin{aligned}
B^2(\varphi, \tilde{\varphi}) &= \left(\mathrm{E}\left\{ \int_D [\varphi(x) - \tilde{\varphi}(x)]^2 dx \right\}^{1/2} \right)^2 \\
&\leq \int_D \mathrm{E}[\varphi(x) - \tilde{\varphi}(x)]^2 dx = \int_D \mathrm{D}\tilde{\varphi}(x)dx + \int_D \mathrm{E}[\varphi(x) - \tilde{\varphi}(x)]^2 dx.
\end{aligned}
\tag{1}
$$

In particular, expression (1) confirms the importance of the uniform minimization of the value $\mathrm{D}\xi$. We assume that the second-order derivatives of the function $\varphi(x)$ are uniformly bounded in D. Then

$$B^2(\varphi, \tilde{\varphi}) \leq d/n + C_0 h^4.$$

Therefore the problem of minimizing the complexity can be here formulated in the form:

$$S_0 = nt_0 h^{-k} \to \min_{n,h}, \quad d/n + c_0 h^4 = \delta^2,$$

where k is the phase space dimension, n is the sample size, h is the grid step, the meaning of d is seen from (1), and $t_0 = t\,\mathrm{mes}(D)$, where t is the input for one realization of ξ. The optimal order of values h, n and S_0 is as follows:

$$h_0^* \asymp \delta^{1/2}, \quad n_0^* \asymp \delta^{-2}, \quad S_0^* \asymp \delta^{-(2+k/2)}.$$

In this case the estimate $B(\varphi, \tilde{\varphi}) < \delta$ is valid and therefore $\tilde{\varphi}$ converges to φ in the metric L_2.

One can obtain similar results for the metric $C(D)$ by using the theorems of embedding the space $W_2^l(D)$ in the space $C(D)$, provided $2l > k$. This condition implies that using the first-order derivatives suggests $k = 1$, i.e. allows one to consider the convergence of the estimate of the solution of a one-dimensional equation (or a multi-dimensional equation in a given straight line). In this case the inequality holds

$$\|\varphi - \tilde{\varphi}\|_C^2 < K\left[\int_D [\varphi(x) - \tilde{\varphi}(x)]^2 dx + \int_D [\varphi'(x) - \tilde{\varphi}'(x)]^2 dx \right].$$

Since the variance of the difference of independent random quantities is equal to the sum of their variances, one must use the following inequality when making an independent estimate of values at nodes of the given grid:

$$\mathrm{D}\tilde{\varphi}'(x) < \frac{d(x)}{nh^2} \ .$$

In addition, since $\tilde{\varphi}'$ is a step function, one needs to consider the relation

$$\int_D [\varphi'(x) - \tilde{\varphi}'(x)]^2 dx < C_1' h^2.$$

Thus, it is appropriate to consider the following estimate asymptotically for $h \to 0$:

$$\|\varphi - \tilde{\varphi}\|_C^2 < \frac{d_1}{nh^2} + C_1 h^2.$$

This estimate leads to the following problem of complexity minimization:

$$S_1 = nt_0 h^{-k} \to \min_{n,h}, \quad \frac{d_1}{nh^2} + C_1 h^2 = \delta^2. \tag{2}$$

The optimal values are of the following order of magnitude:

$$h_1^* \asymp \delta, \quad n_1^* \asymp \delta^{-4}, \quad S_1^* \asymp \delta^{-5}.$$

Thus, in a one-dimensional case the complexity of global estimation of the solution in $C(D)$ is quadratic with respect to the estimate in $L_2(D)$.

The complexity of the estimation in $C(D)$ can be considerably reduced by using a dependent estimate of values of φ that provides the relation

$$|\tilde{\varphi}(x) - \tilde{\varphi}(x+h)| < Ch, \quad h \to 0$$

with the probability 1. In this case, instead of (2), we obtain the problem

$$S_1 = nt_0 h^{-1} \to \min_{n,h}, \quad d_2/n + C_2 h^2 = \delta^2,$$

where

$$h_2^* \asymp \delta, \quad n_2^* \asymp \delta^{-2}, \quad S_2^* \asymp \delta^{-3}.$$

There are various ways of correlating the estimates in the Monte Carlo method (see section 1 and [1-3]).

4 Double Randomization

1. Various examples introducing additional randomness for constructing effective simulation algorithms can be found in the literature devoted to the Monte Carlo methods (see, for example, [3]). This section is concerned with randomized algorithms for estimating probabilistic characteristics of equations with random parameters.

Randomized estimation for the statistical moments of the solution is presented below. Assume functional equation $L\phi = f$ to be solved by the Monte Carlo method on the basis of simulation of a stochastic process. (Denote the trajectories of this process by ω). This means that random variables $\xi_k(\omega)$ are constructed so that

$$M\xi_k(\omega) = J_k, \quad k = 1, 2, ..., m,$$

where J_k are the functionals of ϕ to be evaluated (M denotes the mathematical expectation).

Let the operator L and the function f depend on a random field σ (for example, a random medium in transfer theory, random force in elasticity theory, etc.). Also,

$$\xi_k = \xi_k(\omega, \sigma), \quad J_k = J_k(\sigma)$$

and

$$M[\xi_k(\omega, \sigma)|\sigma] = J_k(\sigma),$$

where the variables ω and σ are generally not independent.

Consider the problem of evaluating the quantities

$$J_k = EJ_k(\sigma), \quad R_{kj} = E[J_k(\sigma)J_j(\sigma)], \quad k, j = 1, ..., m,$$

where E denotes the mathematical expectation with respect to the distribution of σ.

The following obvious method is known for evaluating these mathematical expectations. First, realizations of σ are constructed: then the equation $L_\sigma \phi_\sigma = f_\sigma$ is solved precisely enough for each realization by a numerical or an analytical technique. Finally, statistical estimates of the desired quantities are calculated. However, this approach fails for complicated multi-dimensional problems because the computational cost of an explicit solution of the equation considered is too high. Therefore, it is useful to apply sometimes a method of 'double randomization'. In our case, this technique follows from the following relations:

$$EJ_k(\sigma) = EM\xi_k(\omega, \sigma) = M_{(\omega, \sigma)}\xi_k(\omega, \sigma), \tag{3}$$
$$E[J_k(\sigma)J_j(\sigma)] = M_{(\omega_1, \omega_2, \sigma)}[\xi_k(\omega_1, \sigma)\xi_j(\omega_2, \sigma)],$$

where ω_1 and ω_2 are conditionally independent trajectories, constructed for one fixed realization of σ and the subscript of the expectation symbol indicates the distribution to which it corresponds. Clearly, we have to assume the existence of the total expectations exposed in (3), i.e.,:

$$M_{(\omega, \sigma)}|\xi_k(\omega, \sigma)| < +\infty, \quad M_{(\omega_1, \omega_2, \sigma)}[|\xi_k(\omega_1, \sigma)\xi_j(\omega_2, \sigma)|] < +\infty.$$

Relations of Eq. (4.1) show that to estimate the quantities J_k it is sufficient to construct only one trajectory for a fixed σ, while the estimation of the quantities R_{kj} requires two conditionally independent trajectories. To optimize the randomization technique, it is natural to use the 'splitting method' (see, for example, [5]). In this method, the quantities J_k are estimated as follows. First, one constructs n conditionally independent trajectories (i.e. a vector $\omega = (\omega_1, ..., \omega_n)$, with σ fixed), and then a random variable

$$\zeta_k^{(n)}(\omega, \sigma) = \frac{1}{n} \sum_{i=1}^{n} \xi_k(\omega_i, \sigma)$$

is used instead of $\xi_k(\omega, \sigma)$. The optimal value of n is calculated by the formula (see, for example, [5])

$$n = \sqrt{\frac{a_2}{a_1} \cdot \frac{t_1}{t_2}},$$

where

$$a_1 = \mathrm{E}(\mathrm{M}\xi_k)^2 - \mathrm{J}_k^2, \quad a_2 = \mathrm{ED}\xi_k \,,$$

t_1 is the average computing time for a fixed realization of σ, and t_2 is the average computing time for a fixed realization of ω.

2. As a particular case of using the formulae (3) it is possible to consider ran-domization of the collision estimate [1-3]

$$\xi = \sum_{n=0}^{N} Q_n h(x_n),$$

where

$$Q_0 = \frac{f(x_0)}{\pi(x_0)}, \quad Q_n = Q_{n-1} \frac{k(x_{n-1}, x_n)}{p(x_{n-1}, x_n)}$$

Here $\{x_n\}$ is the Markov chain with functional characteristics $\pi(x_0)$ and $p(x', x)$ and $k(x', x)$ is the kernel related to the integral equation $\varphi = K\varphi + f$. Let $\widetilde{k}(x_{n-1}, x_n), \widetilde{f}_0, \widetilde{h}_n$ be independent unbiased estimates of the corresponding val-ues $k(x_{n-1}, x_n), f(x_0), h(x_n)$ (for instance, random estimates of integrals, which express those values), $\widetilde{Q}_n$ is the corresponding unbiased estimate of the weight Q_n and K_1 is the integral operator with the kernel function $\mathrm{E}|k(x', x)|$. If $\rho(K_1) < 1, \mathrm{E}|\widetilde{h}| \in L_\infty, \mathrm{E}|\widetilde{f}| \in L_1$, then [1]

$$I_h = (\varphi, h) = \mathrm{M}\widetilde{\xi},$$

where $\widetilde{\xi} = \sum_{n=0}^{N} \widetilde{Q}_n \widetilde{h}_n$. Besides in [1] it is shown, that

$$\mathrm{E}\widetilde{\xi}^2 = (\chi, h[2\varphi^* - h]) + (\chi, \mathrm{D}\widetilde{h}),$$

where χ is the Neumann series for the equation

$$\chi'(x) = \int_X \frac{\mathrm{E}\widetilde{k}^2(x', x)}{p(x', x)} \chi'(x') dx' + \frac{\mathrm{E}\widetilde{f}^2(x)}{\pi(x)}, \quad \text{or} \quad \chi' = K_p' \chi' + \mathrm{E}(\widetilde{f}^2/\pi),$$

if $\rho(K_p') < 1, \mathrm{E}\widetilde{f}^2/\pi \in L_1$.

If evaluating $h(x)$ is only randomized, then

$$\mathrm{D}\widetilde{\xi} = \mathrm{D}\xi + (\chi, \mathrm{D}\widetilde{h}),$$

where χ is determined as usual [1]. It is possible to show that the relation $\rho(K_p') < 1$ implies the relation $\rho(K_1') < 1$.

3. Further a class of Monte Carlo algorithms for solving large scale linear al-gebraic systems with dense matrixes based on randomization of matrix-vector multiplication is considered [6] (see so [3]). Varying the number of non-zero rows in random sparse matrixes involved from N to 1 (N being the number of equa-tions) one can proceed from deterministic successive approximations method to

Neumann-Ulam scheme [1] (with transition probabilities p_{ij} all equal to $1/N$), thus, the statistical error being easily controlled. The general scheme with sufficient conditions for variance boundness is considered. The method is intended for solving stochastic problems.

Consider a system of linear algebraic equations

$$A u = g, \tag{4}$$

here $u, g \in \mathbb{R}^N$, A is nonsingular $N \times N$ matrix. Suppose that stationary iterative method for solving this system can be constructed. It means that (4) can be transformed to

$$u = K u + f,$$

with the spectral radius of K less than unity, and thus the successive approximations

$$u^{(n+1)} = K u^{(n)} + f,$$

$$u^{(0)} \quad \text{given},$$

converging to the unique solution of (4). The results below are independent of whether the elements of matrix K available in explicit form or not.

Let $S^{(1)}, S^{(2)}, \dots, S^{(n)}, \dots$ be an infinite sequence of independent realizations of the random matrix S such that $ES = K$. Define the sequence of random vectors $\xi^{(n)}$ setting

$$\xi^{(n+1)} = S^{(n)} \xi^{(n)} + f, \tag{5}$$

$$\xi^{(0)} = u^{(0)},$$

Since $S^{(n)}$ and $\xi^{(n)}$ are independent within this construction we get $E\xi^{(n)} = u^{(n)}$ for all n.

Let $J = \{j_1, j_2, \dots, j_L\}$ be a random set of L different natural numbers less or equal to N, where j_1 is chosen with equal probabilities among all this numbers, j_2 is chosen with equal probabilities among the numbers remained, etc. For all first indexes i put

$$s_{ij} = \begin{cases} \frac{N}{L} k_{ij}, & \text{if } j \in J, \\ 0 & \text{otherwise}. \end{cases}$$

Thus, the random matrix S constructed has L non-zero columns which are equal to corresponding columns of matrix K, multiplied by N/L. For all i, j

$$E s_{ij} = \frac{N}{L} k_{ij} \cdot P\{j \in J\} = k_{ij}.$$

Due to the special form of random matrix S to calculate random vector $\xi^{(n+1)}$ (see (5) one needs only L components of $\xi^{(n)}$ to be calculated on the previous step with, in turn, only L components of $\xi^{(n-1)}$ involved. Hence, the amount of computational work needed to calculate k components of $\xi^{(n+1)}$ is proportional to $kL + nL^2$. If $L = 1$ then the algorithm described coincides with the standard Neumann-Ulam scheme (or 'collision estimate') with transition probabilities all equal to $1/N$. If $L = N$ it becomes the successive approximation method with no randomization at all (vectors $\xi^{(n)}$ are equal to $u^{(n)}$ for all n). Note, that the conditions of the boundness of the values $E(\xi^{(n)})^2$ are considered in [6] (see so [3]).

5   Internal Parallelezation

1. It is clear that the use of a simple parallel summator can essentially raise the efficiency of the 'global walk-on-grid' method in solving difference equations. At the same time such a device supplemented with a purely arithmetic parallel processor computing the values of the kernel also can essentially reduce the cost of the general method of local estimates [1-3] in solving multi-dimensional integral equations; here the local estimate method becomes essentially more effective than the usual 'frequency polygon' method. The computer costs can be similarly decreased when solving a number of problems by using weights [1-3] and when numerically simulating the random fields by summarizing the independent realizations of the initial random functions [5].

2. Now consider the simulation of a particle free-path in the medium with a piece-wise-constant total cross-section [1-3]. Let a set of surfaces is determined so that the i-th surface is the boundary only of two subdomains with numbers k_i and l_i, i.e., there is the correspondence: $i \to (k_i, l_i)$, $i = 1, ..., N$. In each given subdomain a cross-section is constant. Let a particle start from a point r in the i-th subdomain in the direction ω, i.e., along the ray

$$r(t) = r + \omega t, \quad t > 0.$$

Using standard geometric algorithms (see, for instance, [1-3]), it is possible to calculate the corresponding distances from the point r till all the surfaces of the system under consideration. Obviously, a simple arithmetic parallel multiprocessor system is here essentially useful. As a result we obtain the sequences:

$$t_1, t_2, ..., t_n,$$
$$f(k^{(1)}, l^{(1)}), (k^{(2)}, l^{(2)}), ..., (k^{(n)}, l^{(n)}),$$

where $\{t_s\}$ are above-mentioned distances in increasing order, and $\{(k^{(s)}, l^{(s)})\}$ are the numbers of subdomains which are separated by the corresponding surfaces. Further, the sequence

$$m_1 = j, m_2, ..., m_n \tag{6}$$

of numbers of intersected domains can be determined by the following recursive procedure:

$$\text{if} \quad m_s = k^{(s)} \quad \text{then} \quad m_{s+1} = l^{(s)} \quad \text{else} \quad m_{s+1} = k^{(s)}, s = 1, ..., n - 1.$$

Note that in the case $m_{s+1} = k^{(s)}$ the equality $l^{(s)} = m^{(s)}$ has to be valid if the initial geometrical information is true. Using the sequence (6) we can sample a free-path length [1-3]; here it is useful to previously compute in the parallel manner all the values

$$\delta\tau_s = (t_s - t_{s-1})\sigma_{m_s}, \quad t_0 = 0, \quad s = 1, ..., n.$$

If the system contains a part with a regular net of cells, then it is expedient to use for this part the maximal cross-section method [5]. Such a combined simulation of a free-path length is in detail considered for the case of a hexagonal net in [5], where the net is reduced to the parallelepipedal form, and the operation 'entier' is used for the determination of the elementary subdomain numbers.

Finally note, that if

$$\sigma(r) = \sum_{i=1}^{m} \sigma_i(r),$$

then the free-path length l can be sampled by the formula:

$$l = \min(l_1, ..., l_m),$$

where $\{l_k\}$ are independent random free-path lengths corresponding to the cross-sections $\{\sigma_k(r)\}$.

3. When simulating the 'walk on spheres' process it is necessary to determine the distance from a given point r to the boundary of the region under consideration (see [1,3]). This distance is expressed by the formula

$$d(r) = \min(d_1(r), ..., d_N(r)),$$

where $\{d_i(r)\}$ are the distances form r to the elementary surfaces, which are the parts of the boundary. It is expedient to use here a simple multiprocessor system. Usually the region is artificially divided into the parts so that if a point is included in one of them, then it is necessary to compute only some corresponding distances $\{d_i(r)\}$.

To simulate 'walk on spheres' it is necessary to sample the isotropic unit vector. In n-dimensional case it is expedient to use for this purpose the following well-known relation between the Gaussian distribution and the isotropic direction: if $\eta_1, ..., \eta_n$ are standard independent Gaussian random variables, then the vector $\bar{\eta} = (\eta_1, ..., \eta_n)$ is isotropic [1].

References

1. S.M.Ermakov and G.A.Mikhailov: Statistical Modelling. Nauka, Moskow (1982) (in Russian).
2. M.H.Kalos and P.A.Whitlock: Monte Carlo Methods. Vol. 1: Basics. John Wiley, New Jork, 1986.
3. G.A.Mikhailov: Parametric Estimates by the Monte Carlo Method. VSP, Utrecht, 1999.
4. I.M.Sobol: On one approach to the calculation of multidimensional integrals. Problems of Computational and Applied Mathematics **38** (1970), 100-111, Tashkent (in Russian).

5. G.A.Mikhailov: Optimization of Weighted Monte Carlo Methods. Springer, Berlin - Heidelberg (1992).
6. Yu.V.Bulavsky and S.A.Temnikov: Randomized method of successive approximations. Jn: Mathematical Methods in Stochastic Simulation and Experimental Design, St. Petersburg University Publishing House (1996) pp. 64-68.

Implementation of the Parallel Four Points Modified Explicit Group Iterative Algorithm on Shared Memory Parallel Computer

M. Othman[1] and A.R. Abdullah[2]

[1] Department of Communication Technology and Network,
University Putra Malaysia, 43400 UPM Serdang, Selangor D.E., Malaysia
`mothman@fsktm.upm.edu.my`
`http://www.fsktm.upm.edu.my/~mothman`
[2] Department of Industrial Computing,
University Kebangsaan Malaysia, 43600 UKM Bangi, Selangor D.E., Malaysia

Abstract. The four points modified explicit group ($\mathcal{MEG}$) method for solving 2D Poisson equation was introduced by Othman and Abdullah [6] which was shown to be the most superior as compared to the four points-$\mathcal{EDG}$ and $\mathcal{EG}$ methods due to Abdullah [1] and Evans *et al.*, [4], respectively. These methods were found to be suitable for parallel implementation, see Evans and Yousif, [5], Yousif and Evans, [8]. In this paper, the implementation of the four points $\mathcal{MEG}$ algorithm with the red black (RB) and four colors (4C) strategies for solving the same equation on shared memory parallel computer are presented. The experiment results of the test problem are included and compared with the parallel four points-$\mathcal{EG}$ and $\mathcal{EDG}$ algorithms.

1 Introduction

The parallel point iterative algorithm which incorporates the full-sweep approach for solving a large and sparse linear system has been implemented successfully by Barlow and Evans, [2], Evans, [3]. While the half-sweep approach was introduced by Abdullah [1] for the derivation of the four points $\mathcal{EDG}$ method. Since the $\mathcal{EDG}$ method is explicit, it is suitable to be implemented in parallel on any parallel computer. While, the parallel $\mathcal{EG}$ and $\mathcal{EDG}$ methods have been developed extensively by Evans *et al.* [5] and Yousif, *et al.*, [8], respectively. For instance, Yousif and Evans, [8] implemented the parallel four, six and nine points $\mathcal{EDG}$ methods for solving 2D Poisson equation. All the parallel either point or block iterative algorithms were implemented on MIMD Sequent B8000 computer system at Parallel Algorithm Research Center (PARC), Loughborouh University of Technology, United Kingdom.

In recent year, the four points $\mathcal{MEG}$ iterative method was derived from the standard five points formula with the grid spacing h and $2h$, and the rotated five points formula. Furthermore, the method is shown to be the most superior as compared to the four points-$\mathcal{EDG}$ and $\mathcal{EG}$ methods, see Othman and Abdullah, [6].

V. Malyshkin (Ed.): PaCT 2001, LNCS 2127, pp. 480–489, 2001.
© Springer-Verlag Berlin Heidelberg 2001

2 Derivation of the Four Points Modified Explicit Group ($\mathcal{MEG}$) Method

Many important physical phenomena such as the electromagnetic and the incompressible potential flow fields are presented in elliptic equation. A typical representative is the Poisson's equation as,

$$u_{xx} + u_{yy} = f(x, y), \quad (x, y) \in \Omega, \tag{1}$$

subject to the Dirichlet boundary conditions and satisfying the exact solution, $u(x, y) = g(x, y)$, for $(x, y) \in \partial\Omega$, which normally resulted in a large and sparse linear system. Hence, the iterative method is considered as suitable approach for solving such a linear system.

Let's consider Eq. (1) on the solution domain Ω with the grid spacing h in both directions, $x_i = x_0 + ih$ and $y_j = y_0 + jh$, for all $i, j = 0, 1, \ldots, n$. Eq. (1) can be approximated at any point (x_i, y_j) in many ways. The discretized form of Eq. (1) with the finite difference approximation will results to the standard five points formula as,

$$v_{i+1,j} + v_{i-1,j} + v_{i,j+1} + v_{i,j-1} - 4v_{i,j} = h^2 f_{i,j}, \tag{2}$$

where $v_{i,j}$ is an approximation to the exact solution $u(x_i, y_j)$ at the grid points $(x_i, y_j) = (ih, jh)$ and $f_{i,j} = f(x_i, y_j)$. Eq. (1) also can be discretized using the same approximation formulae with the grid spacing $2h$ and leads to the following equation,

$$v_{i+2,j} + v_{i-2,j} + v_{i,j+2} + v_{i,j-2} - 4v_{i,j} = 4h^2 f_{i,j}. \tag{3}$$

Another type of approximation derived from the rotated five point approximation can be obtained by rotating the $x-y$ axis clockwise by $45°$. Thus, rotated approximation for Eq. (1) become,

$$v_{i+1,j+1} + v_{i-1,j-1} + v_{i+1,j-1} + v_{i-1,j+1} - 4v_{i,j} = 2h^2 f_{i,j}. \tag{4}$$

All the Eqs. (2), (3) and (4) have a local truncation errors of order $\mathcal{O}(h^2)$.

From Figure 1, the solution at any group of four points type $\bullet$ in the solution domain can be solved using Eq. (3) and this will result in a (4×4) system of equations,

$$
\begin{bmatrix}
4 & -1 & 0 & -1 \\
-1 & 4 & -1 & 0 \\
0 & -1 & 4 & -1 \\
-1 & 0 & -1 & 4
\end{bmatrix}
\begin{bmatrix}
v_{i,j} \\
v_{i+2,j} \\
v_{i+2,j+2} \\
v_{i,j+2}
\end{bmatrix}
=
\begin{bmatrix}
v_{i-2,j} + v_{i,j-2} - 4h^2 f_{i,j} \\
v_{i+4,j} + v_{i+2,j-2} - 4h^2 f_{i+2,j} \\
v_{i+4,j+2} + v_{i+2,j+4} - 4h^2 f_{i+2,j+2} \\
v_{i-2,j+2} + v_{i,j+4} - 4h^2 f_{i,j+2}
\end{bmatrix}. \tag{5}
$$

The Eq. (5) can be inverted and leads to a four points $\mathcal{MEG}$ equation,

$$
\begin{bmatrix}
v_{i,j} \\
v_{i+2,j} \\
v_{i+2,j+2} \\
v_{i,j+2}
\end{bmatrix}
= \frac{1}{24}
\begin{bmatrix}
7 & 2 & 1 & 2 \\
2 & 7 & 2 & 1 \\
1 & 2 & 7 & 2 \\
2 & 1 & 2 & 7
\end{bmatrix}
\begin{bmatrix}
v_{i-2,j} + v_{i,j-2} - 4h^2 f_{i,j} \\
v_{i+4,j} + v_{i+2,j-2} - 4h^2 f_{i+2,j} \\
v_{i+4,j+2} + v_{i+2,j+4} - 4h^2 f_{i+2,j+2} \\
v_{i-2,j+2} + v_{i,j+4} - 4h^2 f_{i,j+2}
\end{bmatrix}, \tag{6}
$$

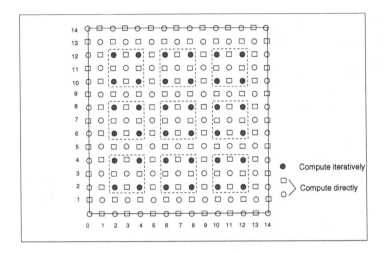

Fig. 1. The solution domain Ω of the four points $\mathcal{MEG}$ iterative method.

whose individual explicit equations are given by,

$$
\begin{aligned}
v_{i,j} &= \tfrac{1}{24}(7L_1 + W_2 + L_3) \\
v_{i+2,j} &= \tfrac{1}{24}(W_1 + 7L_2 + L_4) \\
v_{i+2,j+2} &= \tfrac{1}{24}(L_1 + W_2 + 7L_3) \\
v_{i,j+2} &= \tfrac{1}{24}(W_1 + L_2 + 7L_4)
\end{aligned}
\tag{7}
$$

where,

$$
\begin{aligned}
L_1 &= v_{i-2,j} + v_{i,j-2} - 4h^2 f_{i,j}, & L_2 &= v_{i+4,j} + v_{i+2,j-2} - 4h^2 f_{i+2,j}, \\
L_3 &= v_{i+4,j+2} + v_{i+2,j+4} - 4h^2 f_{i+2,j+2}, & L_4 &= v_{i-2,j+2} + v_{i,j+4} - 4h^2 f_{i,j+2}, \\
W_1 &= 2(L_1 + L_3), & W_2 &= 2(L_2 + L_4).
\end{aligned}
$$

Due to the independency and large size of mesh points as notified by Othman and Abdullah, [6], it can theoretically save the execution time approximately a quarter if the iteration over the solution domain is carried out only on the points which undergo the process of iterations. After the convergence criteria is achieved, the solutions at the remaining mesh points are executed directly at once starting from points type $\square$ followed by $\circ$ using Eqs. (4) and (2), respectively. Hence, we can define the four points $\mathcal{MEG}$ iterative method as the following algorithm,

1. Group all the $\bullet$ points into a four points group such that the iterative evaluations will only involve points within the group as shown in Figure 1.
2. Iterate the intermediate solutions of the points within the group on the solution domain using the following equation,

$$
\begin{bmatrix} \bar{v}_{i,j} \\ \bar{v}_{i+2,j} \\ \bar{v}_{i+2,j+2} \\ \bar{v}_{i,j+2} \end{bmatrix}^{(k+1)}
= \frac{1}{24}
\begin{bmatrix} 7L_1 + 2W_2 + L_3 \\ 2W_1 + 7L_2 + L_4 \\ L_1 + 2W_2 + 7L_3 \\ 2W_1 + L_2 + 7L_4 \end{bmatrix}^{(k)} ,
$$

where L_1, L_2, L_3, L_4, W_1 and W_2 are described in Eq. (7).

3. Implement the relaxation procedure,

$$
\begin{bmatrix} v_{i,j} \\ v_{i+2,j} \\ v_{i+2,j+2} \\ v_{i,j+2} \end{bmatrix}^{(k+1)} = \omega \begin{bmatrix} \bar{v}_{i,j} \\ \bar{v}_{i+2,j} \\ \bar{v}_{i+2,j+2} \\ \bar{v}_{i,j+2} \end{bmatrix}^{(k+1)} + (1 - \omega) \begin{bmatrix} v_{i,j} \\ v_{i+2,j} \\ v_{i+2,j+2} \\ v_{i,j+2} \end{bmatrix}^{(k)}.
$$

where ω is the relaxation factor.

4. Check the convergence. If converge evaluate solution at the remaining points (i.e. □ followed by ∘) using,

4.1. $v_{i,j} = \frac{1}{4}(v_{i+1,j+1} + v_{i-1,j-1} + v_{i+1,j-1} + v_{i-1,j+1} - 2h^2 f_{i,j})$,   and,

4.2. $v_{i,j} = \frac{1}{4}(v_{i+1,j} + v_{i-1,j} + v_{i,j+1} + v_{i,j-1} - h^2 f_{i,j})$,

respectively. Otherwise, repeat the iteration cycle (i.e. goto step (2));

5. Stop.

3   Parallel Strategies and Implementation

Since all groups of four points in the solution domain are identical, the data partitioning approach is suitable in the implementation of the method and all the identical tasks (i.e. groups) can be executed in parallel. Again, the static scheduling is employed in this implementation.

There are several strategies of parallelizing the four points $\mathcal{MEG}$ method have been investigated and only two of them produce very good results. They are described as follows,

3.1   Red Black (RB) Strategy

From Figure 2a, all the groups T_i, for all $i = 1, 2, \ldots, (\lfloor \frac{n}{4} \rfloor)^2$ are allocated to the available processors in RB ordering strategy. Then iterate all the groups in the following order,

$$T_1, T_2, T_3, T_4, T_5, T_6, T_7, T_8 // T_9, T_{10}, T_{11}, T_{12}, T_{13}, T_{14}, T_{15}, T_{16} //,$$

where the $//$ indicates the synchronization point take place. In this strategy, there are only two stages of iterative evaluations which start from a block (T_1, T_2, T_3, T_4, T_5, T_6, T_7, T_8) then followed by a block (T_9, T_{10}, T_{11}, T_{12}, T_{13}, T_{14}, T_{15}, T_{16}) with synchronization points at the end of each stage to ensure that the updated values are used in the subsequent iterations. Each group T_i is assigned to one processor at a time. Every processors independently iterate on its own group of points and then check for its own local convergence. If this is not achieved, its local flags are initialized to zero and repeat the cycle. If the local convergence is achieved for all the processors (i.e. all local flags are set to one), then a global convergence test is performed.

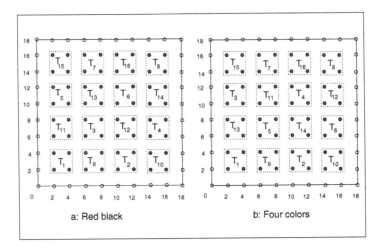

Fig. 2. a-b show the RB and 4C ordering strategies, respectively for $n = 18$.

If converge globally then the solution of the remaining points in the solution domain are evaluated directly at once starting from points type □ followed by ○ using Eqs. (4) and (2), respectively. The direct evaluations are also executed in parallel. Otherwise, increased the number of iteration and repeat the iteration cycle.

3.2   Four Colors (4C) Strategy

Groups of four points T_i, for all $i = 1, 2, \ldots, (\lfloor \frac{n}{4} \rfloor)^2$ are allocated to processors in 4C ordering strategy as shown in Figure 2b. Iterate each group T_i in the following order,

$$T_1, T_2, T_3, T_4//T_5, T_6, T_7, T_8//T_9, T_{10}, T_{11}, T_{12}//T_{13}, T_{14}, T_{15}, T_{16}//.$$

A block (T_1, T_2, T_3, T_4) is allocated first to the available processors, then after all the calculations in a block are completed, the synchronization point will take place to ensure that the updated values of each points in the group are used in the subsequent iteration. Then the second block (T_5, T_6, T_7, T_8) is allocated to the available processors followed by the third block and finally the fourth block. Each processor will checks for its local and global convergence, the same way as described in the RB strategy.

4   Experimental Results

All the methods described above were applied to the following equation as a model of problem which was used by Abdullah, [1], Evans and Biggins, [4], Evans and Yousif, [5], Othman and Abdullah, [6], Yousif and Evans, [8]. The model is defined in a unit solution domain Ω and described as $u_{xx} + u_{yy} = (x^2 + y^2)e^{xy}$

Table 1. The iteration numbers and maximum errors of the parallel four points-$\mathcal{EG}$, $\mathcal{EDG}$ and $\mathcal{MEG}$ algorithms.

n	Methods	Strategies	ω	Ite no.	Max. error
	$\mathcal{EG}$	RB	1.72	72	4.63×10^{-6}
26	$\mathcal{EDG}$	HZL	1.69	69	2.46×10^{-4}
	$\mathcal{MEG}$	RB	1.51	38	2.21×10^{-5}
		4C	1.51	38	2.21×10^{-5}
	$\mathcal{EG}$	RB	1.84	135	1.25×10^{-6}
50	$\mathcal{EDG}$	HZL	1.83	129	6.64×10^{-5}
	$\mathcal{MEG}$	RB	1.71	72	5.28×10^{-6}
		4C	1.71	72	5.28×10^{-6}
	$\mathcal{EG}$	RB	1.89	201	5.75×10^{-7}
74	$\mathcal{EDG}$	HZL	1.88	198	3.03×10^{-5}
	$\mathcal{MEG}$	RB	1.79	103	2.35×10^{-6}
		4C	1.79	103	2.35×10^{-6}
	$\mathcal{EG}$	RB	1.92	280	3.27×10^{-7}
98	$\mathcal{EDG}$	HZL	1.91	265	1.72×10^{-5}
	$\mathcal{MEG}$	RB	1.84	139	1.32×10^{-6}
		4C	1.84	139	1.32×10^{-6}

subject to the Dirichlet boundary conditions and satisfying the exact solution $u(x, y) = e^{xy}$, $(x, y) \in \partial\Omega$.

Throughout the experiments, a tolerance of the $\varepsilon = 10^{-10}$ in the local convergence test was used. The experimental values of ω were obtained within ± 0.01 by running the program for different values of ω and choosing the one(s) that gave the minimum number of iterations. The experiments were carried out on the several mesh sizes, $26, 50, 74$ and 98.

As comparisons, the parallel four points-$\mathcal{EG}$ and $\mathcal{EDG}$ algorithms are implemented by using the RB and horizontal zebra line (HZL) strategies, respectively, see Evans and Yousif, [5], Yousif and Evans, [8]. The implementation of the parallel four points $\mathcal{MEG}$ algorithm with the RB and 4C strategies as described in the previous section. Table 1 lists the strategy, optimum value of ω, iteration numbers and maximum errors for all the methods. Table 2 shows the total execution time, speedup and efficiency of two different strategies for the parallel four points-$\mathcal{MEG}$ algorithm whilst in Table 3 shows the total execution time, speedup and efficiency of all the algorithms. The temporal performance of the parallel four points $\mathcal{MEG}$ algorithm with two different strategies was plotted and shown in Figure 3.

5   Summary

The results obtained in Table 1 have shown that the parallel four points $\mathcal{MEG}$ algorithm with both strategies produce good performance as indicated by the

Table 2. The total execution time, speedup and efficiency of the RB and 4C strategies for the parallel four points-$\mathcal{MEG}$ algorithm.

n	No. proc.	RB strategy			4C strategy		
		Time	Speedup	Eff.	Time	Speedup	Eff.
	1	0.4892	1.0000	1.0000	0.5712	1.0000	1.0000
	2	0.3232	1.5132	0.7566	0.3783	1.5096	0.7548
26	3	0.2410	2.0297	0.6766	0.3007	1.8992	0.6331
	4	0.2290	2.1355	0.5339	0.2883	1.9810	0.4953
	5	0.2040	2.3972	0.4794	0.2786	2.0498	0.4099
	1	3.3535	1.0000	1.0000	3.4750	1.0000	1.0000
	2	1.9481	1.7214	0.8607	2.0335	1.7088	0.8544
50	3	1.5046	2.2288	0.7429	1.5909	2.1842	0.7280
	4	1.2462	2.6909	0.6727	1.3818	2.5148	0.6287
	5	1.0259	3.2687	0.6537	1.1151	3.1162	0.6232
	1	10.2211	1.0000	1.0000	11.2431	1.0000	1.0000
	2	5.6746	1.8012	0.9006	6.3113	1.7814	0.8907
74	3	4.5797	2.2318	0.7439	5.0533	2.2249	0.7616
	4	3.3514	3.0498	0.7625	3.7929	2.9642	0.7410
	5	2.8063	3.6421	0.7242	3.1346	3.5867	0.7173
	1	25.4072	1.0000	1.0000	26.0720	1.0000	1.0000
	2	13.6590	1.8601	0.9300	14.0254	1.8589	0.9295
98	3	9.8203	2.5872	0.8624	10.1011	2.5811	0.8604
	4	7.6705	3.3123	0.8281	7.9514	3.2789	0.8197
	5	6.5450	3.8819	0.7764	6.7519	3.8614	0.7723

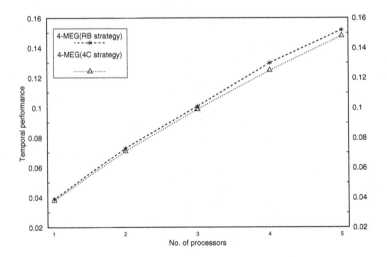

Fig. 3. Temporal performances of the four points-$\mathcal{MEG}$ algorithms with the RB and 4C strategies for $n = 98$.

Table 3. The total execution time, speedup and efficiency of the RB and 4C strategies for the parallel four points-$\mathcal{MEG}$ algorithm.

n	No. proc.	$\mathcal{EG}$			$\mathcal{EDG}$			$\mathcal{MEG}$		
		Time	Speedup	Eff.	Time	Speedup	Eff.	Time	Speedup	Eff.
	1	3.3578	1.0000	1.0000	1.6083	1.0000	1.0000	0.4892	1.0000	1.0000
	2	1.8864	1.7800	0.8900	0.9137	1.7601	0.8800	0.3232	1.5132	0.7566
26	3	1.6913	2.4360	0.8120	0.7208	2.2310	0.7437	0.2410	2.0297	0.6766
	4	1.0677	3.1448	0.7862	0.5509	2.9192	0.7298	0.2290	2.1355	0.5339
	5	0.9560	3.5120	0.7024	0.4855	3.3121	0.6624	0.2040	2.3972	0.4794
	1	24.7121	1.0000	1.0000	11.9701	1.0000	1.0000	3.3535	1.0000	1.0000
	2	13.1447	1.8800	0.9400	6.4959	1.8427	0.9214	1.9481	1.7214	0.8607
50	3	9.9030	2.4954	0.8318	5.0679	2.3619	0.7873	1.5046	2.2288	0.7429
	4	8.5260	3.1984	0.7996	3.7137	3.2232	0.8085	1.2462	2.6909	0.6727
	5	6.2920	3.9275	0.7855	3.0976	3.8642	0.7724	1.0259	3.2687	0.6537
	1	80.9406	1.0000	1.0000	38.0573	1.0000	1.0000	10.2211	1.0000	1.0000
	2	43.0283	1.8811	0.9401	20.4488	1.8611	0.9306	5.6746	1.8012	0.9006
74	3	30.9051	2.6190	0.8730	15.1991	2.5039	0.8346	4.5797	2.2318	0.7439
	4	23.6157	3.4274	0.8568	11.8230	3.2189	0.8047	3.3514	3.0498	0.7625
	5	19.8476	4.0781	0.8156	9.7313	3.9108	0.7822	2.8063	3.6421	0.7242
	1	205.0506	1.0000	1.0000	97.1684	1.0000	1.0000	25.4072	1.0000	1.0000
	2	104.4336	1.9597	0.7989	49.9837	1.8944	0.9472	13.6590	1.8601	0.9300
98	3	73.7539	2.7802	0.9267	37.0179	2.6249	0.8749	9.8203	2.5872	0.8624
	4	60.5976	3.3838	0.8459	28.6531	3.3912	0.8478	7.6705	3.3123	0.8281
	5	49.8785	4.1110	0.8222	24.1652	4.0210	0.8042	6.5450	3.8819	0.7764

number of iteration and maximum errors. However, the total execution time of the algorithm with the RB strategy is slightly faster than the 4C strategy as shown in Table 2. It is also indicated in the temporal performance graph plotted in Figure 3. This is due to the fact that the RB strategy required less number of synchronization for every completed iterative cycle as compared to the 4C strategy.

In Table 3 and Figure 4, we found that the total execution time of the parallel four points $\mathcal{MEG}$ algorithm regardless of the number of processors is faster than the parallel four points-$\mathcal{EG}$ and $\mathcal{EDG}$ algorithms. This is because the number of mesh points which undergoes the iterative evaluations are approximately a quarter over the total mesh points in the solution domain. In view of this, we found that the speedup and efficiency of the parallel $\mathcal{MEG}$ algorithm is not as good as the other two algorithms and it can be improved by increasing the size of mesh points in the solution domain. Additionally in Figure 5, the temporal performance of the parallel $\mathcal{MEG}$ algorithm has shown the highest values as compared to the other algorithms. In other words, the parallel four points $\mathcal{MEG}$ algorithm is the most superior and effective method among the three algorithms particularly for solving 2D Poisson equation.

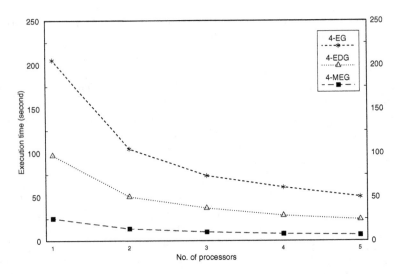

Fig. 4. Total execution time versus no. of processors of the four points-$\mathcal{EG}$, $\mathcal{EDG}$ and $\mathcal{MEG}$ algorithms when $n = 98$.

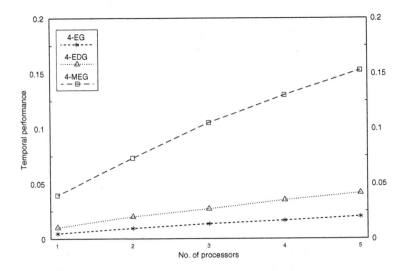

Fig. 5. Temporal performances of the four points-$\mathcal{EG}$, $\mathcal{EDG}$ and $\mathcal{MEG}$ methods when $n = 98$.

It can be summarized that the parallel four points $\mathcal{MEG}$ algorithm with the RB strategy is the most superior among the three algorithms as the size of mesh points getting larger. In the future, the algorithm will be implemented on the networked of workstations (Anderson, *et al.*, [7]) and the paper will be reported soon.

References

1. Abdullah, A.R.: The Four Explicit Decoupled Group ($\mathcal{EDG}$) Method: A Fast Poisson Solver. Intern. Journal of Computers Mathematics, **38** (1991) 61–70.
2. Barlow, R.H., Evans, D.J.: Parallel Algorithms for the Iterative Solution to Linear System. Computer Journal, **25**(1) (1982) 56-60.
3. Evans, D.J.: Parallel S.O.R. Iterative Methods. Parallel Computing, **1** (1984) 3-18.
4. Evans, D.J., Biggins, M.J.: The Solution of Elliptic Partial Differential Equations by A New Block Over-Relaxation Technique. Intern. Journal of Computers Mathematics, **10** (1982) 269-282.
5. Evans, D.J., Yousif, W.S.: The Implementation of the Explicit Block Iterative Methods on the Balance 8000 Parallel Computer. Parallel Computing, **16** (1990) 81-97.
6. Othman, M., Abdullah, A.R.: An Efficient Four Points Modified Explicit Group Poisson Solver. Intern. Journal of Computers Mathematics, **76** (2000) 203-217.
7. Anderson, T.E., et al.: A Case for NOW (Networks of Workstations). IEEE Micro, **15**(2) (1995) 54-64.
8. Yousif, W.S., Evans, D.J.: Explicit De-coupled Group Iterative Methods and Their Parallel Implementations. Parallel Algorithms and Applications, **7** (1995) 53-71.

A Parallel Expressed Sequence Tag (EST) Clustering Program

Kevin Pedretti, Todd Scheetz, Terry Braun, Chad Roberts, Natalie Robinson, and Thomas Casavant

Parallel Processing Laboratory,
and The Coordinated Laboratory for Computational Genomics,
Dept. of Electrical and Computer Engineering University of Iowa,
Iowa City IA 52242, USA

Abstract. This paper describes the UIcluster software tool, which partitions Expressed Sequence Tag (EST) sequences and other genetic sequences into "clusters" based on sequence similarity. Ideally, each cluster will contain sequences that all represent the same gene. If a naïve approach such as an NxN comparison (N is the number of sequences input) is taken, the problem is only feasible for very small data sets. UIcluster has been developed over the course of four years to solve this problem efficiently and accurately for large data sets consisting of tens or hundreds of thousands of EST sequences. The latest version of the application has been parallelized using the MPI (message passing interface) standard. Both the computation and memory requirements of the program can be distributed among multiple (possibly distributed) UNIX processes.

1 Introduction

Clustering is the process of taking a set of elements and partitioning them into meaningful groups. In the high throughput gene sequencing activities of our laboratories, we generate large numbers of short sequences – Expressed Sequence Tags (ESTs) – and partition them into sets based on similarity. The importance of this problem bears on several aspects, but the principal of these are creating non-redundant indices of genes and assessing the novelty of sequencing. If done in a naïve fashion, such as a NxN comparison, this problem would be intractable for the data set sizes we produce (50K–300K ESTs). Although there are several existing software system [7,5,1,6] available that perform sequence clustering accurately, our program is unique in its ability to efficiently and accurately cluster EST sequences. Over the past four years, we have developed techniques to speed up the computation by using increasingly sophisticated heuristics along with parallel processing techniques. The usefulness of our program, UIcluster, has been demonstrated in the identification of more than 100,000 unique/novel clusters across three species (human, mouse, and rat).

V. Malyshkin (Ed.): PaCT 2001, LNCS 2127, pp. 490–497, 2001.

2   Expressed Sequence Tags (ESTs)

From a biological perspective, ESTs are partial transcripts of genes. Specifically, they are sequenced from cDNA (complementary DNA) clones, synthesized from polyA-selected whole-cell RNA. To prepare for EST sequencing, mRNA molecules are extracted from cells and converted into cDNA through reverse transcription. The cDNAs are then cloned into a vector and electroporated into bacteria for growth, amplification, and storage. A collection of such cDNAs is referred to as a library. Each cDNA library potentially contains many unique and previously undiscovered genes. However, significant redundancy within a library (multiple copies of the same mRNA) and between libraries is normal.

High throughput EST sequencing for gene identification involves sequencing the 3' end of randomly chosen cDNA clones from a cDNA library. The use of a poly-T primer during reverse transcription allows for the preferential creation of cDNAs with a poly-A tail at their 3' ends. Thus, sequencing can start from a known position (within poly-A tail).

For the purposes of this paper, and from the computational perspective, an EST is a character string made up of letters from the alphabet A, C, T, G, X, N where A, C, T, and G represent the four nucleotide bases of DNA and X and N represent bases within repetitive (low-complexity) segments or that are of indeterminate identity. ESTs are typically between 400 to 1000 letters, or bases, long. Comparing pairs of ESTs and looking for similarity is the basic element of clustering. This comparison is complex because the underlying sequencing technology is error prone – bases can be inserted, deleted, or misread. Studies of our EST sequences have indicated that the error rate for EST sequencing is approximately 5% for misread errors, and 1-2% for insertion/deletion errors.

3   Uses of Clustering

Clustering is used to assess the gene discovery rate of sequencing done from cDNA libraries. For single library assessment, the entire set of ESTs obtained from that library is used as a input for clustering. Clustering partitions the set into subsets, or clusters, based on similarity. Each EST is a member of at most one cluster. Novelty is computed as the number of clusters identified divided by the number of sequences clustered.

This computation is used to calculate both incremental and overall novelty rates (roughly corresponding to gene discovery rates) for individual cDNA libraries and for EST projects as a whole. Incremental novelty calculations are performed daily to monitor the sequencing efforts and to determine when cDNA library subtractions should occur [2]. This procedure can dramatically increase novelty rates. However, the subtraction process is time consuming and cannot be performed on a continual basis.

Figure 1 shows an example of the effectiveness of these procedures for a progression of four cDNA libraries, named C0, C1, C2p, and C3. Each sharp increase in novelty rates corresponds to a subtraction on the preceding library being performed.

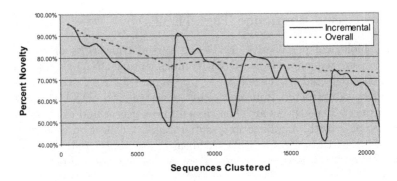

Fig. 1. Incremental library novelty

Another significant use of clustering is the generation of non-redundant gene indices, or UniGene sets [7]. As mentioned previously, ideally each cluster will uniquely represent a gene. Thus, the goal in constructing a UniGene set is to bring together all of the ESTs sequenced for a given gene into a single cluster. This information is useful for reducing redundant processing and for the annotation of EST sequences.

4 Program Evolution

UIcluster has evolved as our laboratory's processing requirements have increased. Three generations of the clustering program have been developed to date. The first revision was developed to work well for moderately sized data sets of ESTs. As our data sets grew, this version required more than a days computation time to cluster the entire set of ESTs. The main goal of the second version of the program was improved performance for large data sets. A third, parallelized version provided higher performance and several additional features has recently been released. All revisions of UIcluster may be freely obtained from our project web site (http://genome.uiowa.edu).

The basic clustering program flow proceeds as follows: 1) read one sequence from the input file, 2) compare the sequence against every existing cluster, 3) based on sequence similarity, either add it to an existing cluster or make it the first member of a new cluster. This process is repeated until every sequence in the input file is examined. In step 3, the EST is only added to an existing cluster if the specified similarity criteria is met. The similarity criteria is runtime configurable and is of the form N out of M bases. For example, 38 out of 40 bases would mean two sequences are judged to be similar if there is at least one window of 38 out of 40 bases in common, allowing insertion, deletion, and mismatch errors. The speed of the program is directly effected by these parameters. Higher error tolerance $(M - N)$ increases program execution time significantly as does larger window sizes (M).

```
Sequence: GCCACTTGGCGTTTTG
Hashes:
          Hash 1: GCCACTTG = 48406
          Hash 2: CCACTTGG = 44869
          Hash 3: CACTTGGC = 27601
          Hash 4: ACTTGGCG = 39668
          Hash 5: CTTGGCGT = 59069
          ...etc.
```

Fig. 2. Example of hashing a sequence

4.1 Revision 1.0

Revision 1.0 was useful for relatively small data sets ($< 30,000$ ESTs). The program was structured so that clusters were stored in a 2-D linked list. Each EST read from the input file was compared against a single representative element from each cluster. The longest EST from each cluster was used as a representative element for that cluster.

Evaluating the N of M similarity criteria for two sequences is computationally intensive. As a performance optimization, we used a hashing technique to eliminate comparisons that will obviously be unsuccessful (i.e., the N of M criteria will not be met). A *hash* is simply an integer that uniquely represents a short string of characters. The general equation used to generate a hash is given by (1).

$$H = \sum_{i=0}^{\zeta-1}(K^i * \phi_i) \tag{1}$$

In this equation, H is the generated hash value, ζ is the string length, K is the alphabet size, and ϕ_i is the integer value assigned to the letter at position i in the string being hashed. The string length ζ that can be used to generate hashes is limited by the word size of the computer. For the DNA alphabet, each base requires 2-bits to represent it ($\lceil \log_2 K \rceil$ where $K = 4$ for DNA). Thus, the maximum value of ζ using a single word on a 32-bit machine is 16.

When a sequence is hashed, equation 1 is used on every ζ length sub-string. Figure 2 shows the first six hashes generated for a sample sequence with $\zeta = 8$.

When an EST is clustered, the N of M similarity criteria is only evaluated for cluster representatives that contain one or more hashes in common with the EST being clustered. The length of the hash probe used is an important parameter that can significantly affect performance. Longer hash lengths will result in better performance for a given similarity criteria. It must also be chosen carefully so that potential similarities are not missed. The formula for calculating the maximum hash size is shown in (2). The rational for this equation is that for any chosen similarity criteria N of M, there is at least one contiguous, error-free region of ζ bases. Thus, the comparison of two sequences can be accelerated by first searching for short exact matches of length ζ bases between the pair (i.e. searching for identical hashes). If such a match is found, a more exhaustive

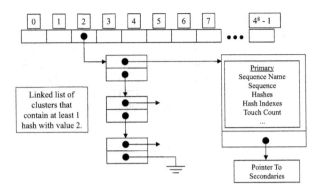

Fig. 3. Global hash table

search that permits errors can be performed. If no length ζ hashes are identified, then the two sequences cannot possibly contain a window of M bases with N bases in common.

$$\zeta = \left\lfloor \frac{M}{M - N + 1} \right\rfloor \qquad (2)$$

The calculation to generate the hashes for a sequence is only performed once since the hash lists are stored in memory. However, the hashes are accessed many times during the programs execution. This amortizes the computational overhead of generating the hashes.

4.2   Revision 2.0

The main improvement in revision 2.0 was the implementation of the global hash table (GHT). As our EST data sets grew larger, the sequential nature of the traversal of the cluster representative linked list for every input sequence became a bottleneck. The GHT optimizes the program at a higher level than individual sequence comparisons by filtering the entire search space of cluster representatives into a subset of high-potential candidate targets.

When a new sequence is clustered, a list of hashes is generated for each ζ base window of its sequence. Each hash in the list is then used as an index into the GHT. Figure 3 shows a GHT with 4^8 elements, corresponding to $\zeta = 8$. Each element in the table points to a linked list of clusters that contain at least one occurrence of the hash equal to its index. In figure 3, there are three clusters that contain the hash 2. If the sequence being clustered also has a hash of two, the touch count field of each cluster linked from the second element in the GHT is incremented. If the touch count field of a cluster exceeds a run-time configurable threshold, a detailed sequence comparison is performed between the input sequence and the candidate cluster. This procedure is based on the premise that two similar sequences will likely have many hashes in common.

Care must be taken to adjust the touch count threshold appropriately. For a given similarity criteria (e.g. 38 out of 40 bases) and hash length ζ, if the

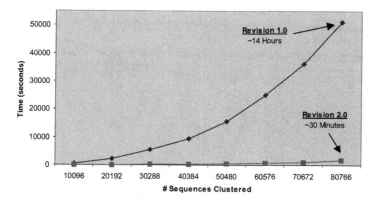

Fig. 4. Execution time of Revision 1.0 vs. Revision 2.0

threshold is too low the speedup due to the GHT will be small. Conversely if the threshold is too high, some sequence similarities will be missed.

Figure 4 shows the execution time for both revisions of the clustering program with an input data set of 80,766 rat EST sequences. Revision 2.0 demonstrates 28x speedup while calculating virtually identical results. The major trade-off of the GHT optimization is memory utilization. However, on a 2GB machine we have been able to cluster data sets as large as 1 million ESTs. While theoretically the first revision could handle data sets this long, the computation time required would make it impractical.

4.3   Revision 3.0

The latest version of the clustering program has been parallelized to split up the computational and memory requirements across several computers (compute nodes). The main reasons for doing this are for added performance and so that the program can scale to larger problem sizes without being constrained by the memory limitations of a single computer. The MPI (message passing interface) [4] communication standard has been used for inter-process communication.

In this mode of execution, each cluster is stored on exactly one compute node. A given sequence is read in from the input file and processed in parallel on each compute node. This results in a parallel search of the cluster space. Once each node has finished its search, each node's best match is collectively communicated to all compute nodes. The node with the best match stores the sequence in its memory space. If no match is found on any of the compute nodes, the input sequence becomes a new cluster and is assigned to one of the compute nodes. Clusters are balanced evenly across the compute nodes.

Figure 5 illustrates the parallel speedup obtained for clustering a data set of approximately 81,000 rat EST sequences. The three curves represent three different runs of the program using different parameter sets. The first curve (labeled 1) corresponds to the default parameters used in our processing pipeline.

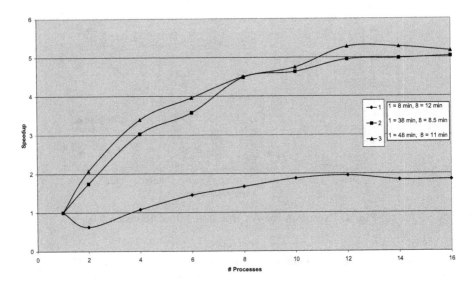

Fig. 5. Parallel speedup

The second curve (labeled 2) adds the extended search option. By default, an EST is added to the first cluster it found to be similar to and the search is halted. This option enables the identification of all similar cluster representatives for each EST clustered. The third curve (labeled 3) enables the reverse complement checking option of the program.

Since the implementation uses a collective communication at the end of every sequence clustered, the amount of computation required for each sequence is important. As the grain size increases, better performance should be observed since relatively less communication is being performed.

The times in minutes for the single and 8 node run for each case are shown in the figure. Performance scales poorly for the first case, actually decreasing when using two compute nodes. This is most likely due to the computation being unevenly distributed and the communication overhead. With more compute nodes, performance increases somewhat but is never greater than double that of the serial case. The larger grain size of the second case results in significantly improved speedup. The third curve scales similarly since the grain size is only slightly increased for this case.

5   Conclusion

The evolution of an EST clustering program has been discussed in this extended abstract. Background information on the problem has been presented along with details of two sequential implementations and a parallel implementation. Planned extensions to `UIcluster` include utilizing the recently released human genome sequence [3,8] to improve the accuracy of clustering, and to aid in identification of alternative splice forms and intron/exon boundaries. Other extensions planned include improved performance for long sequences (e.g., full length cDNA sequences), automatic cluster merging, and tools for manual curation of clustering results by expert human operators.

References

1. Adams M.D., Kerlavage A.R., Fleishmann R.D., Fuldner R.A., Bult C.J., Lee N.H., Kirkness E.F., Weinstock K.G., Gocayne J.D., White O., et al. (1995) Initial assessment of human gene diversity and expression patterns based upon 83 million nucleotides of cDNA sequence. Nature 377:3-17
2. Bonaldo M.F., Lennon G., Soares M.B. (1996) Normalization and subtraction: two approaches to facilitate gene discovery. Genome Research 6:791-806
3. International Human Genome Sequencing Consortium (2001) Initial sequencing and analysis of the human genome. Nature 409:860-921
4. Message Passing Interface Form (1994) MPI: A message-passing interface standard. University of Tennessee Technical Report CS-94-230
5. Miller R.T., Christoffels A.G., Gopalakrishnan C., Burke J.A., Ptitsyn A.A., Broveak T.R., Hide W.A. (1999) A comprehensive approach to clustering of expressed human gene sequence: The Sequence Tag Alighment and Consensus Knowledgebase. Genome Research 9:1143-1155
6. Parsons J.D., Brenner S., Bishop M.J. (1992) Clustering cDNA Sequences. Computational Applications in Bioscience 8:461-466
7. Schuler G.D. (1997) Pieces of the puzzle: expressed sequence tags and the catalog of human genes. Journal of Molecular Medicine 75:694-698
8. Venter J.C., Adams M.D., Myers E.W., Li P.W., Mural R.J., Sutton G.G., et al. (2001) The sequence of the human genome. Science 291:1304-1351

Protein Sequence Comparison on the Instruction Systolic Array

Bertil Schmidt[1], Heiko Schröder[1], and Manfred Schimmler[2]

[1] School of Computer Engineering, Nanyang Technological University, Singapore 639798
{asbschmidt,asheiko}@ntu.edu.sg
[2] Institut für Datenverarbeitungsanlagen, TU Braunschweig,
Hans-Sommer-Str. 66, 38106 Braunschweig, Germany
masch@ida.ing.tu-bs.de

Abstract. Molecular biologists frequently compare an unknown protein sequence with a set of other known sequences (a database scan) to detect functional similarities. Even though efficient dynamic programming algorithms exist for the problem, the required scanning time is still very high, and because of the exponential database growth finding fast solutions is of highest importance to research in this area. In this paper we present a new approach to biosequence database scanning on the instruction systolic array to gain high performance at low cost. To derive an efficient mapping onto this architecture, we designed a fine-grained parallel sequence comparison algorithm. This results in an implementation with significant runtime savings on Systola 1024, a parallel computer of this particular architecture.

1   Introduction

Scanning protein sequence databases is a common and often repeated task in molecular biology. The need for speeding up this treatment comes from the exponential growth of the biosequence banks: every year their size scaled by a factor 1.5 to 2. The scan operation consists in finding similarities between a particular query sequence and all the sequences of a bank. This operation allows biologists to point out sequences sharing common subsequences. From a biological point of view, it leads to identify similar functionality.

Comparison algorithms whose complexities are quadratic with respect to the length of the sequences detect similarities between the query sequence and a subject sequence. One frequently used approach to speed up this time consuming operation is to introduce heuristics in the search algorithms [1]. The main drawback of this solution is that the more time efficient the heuristics, the worse is the quality of the results [15].

Another approach to get high quality results in a short time is to use parallel processing. There are two basic methods of mapping the scanning of protein sequence databases to a parallel processor: one is based on the systolisation of the sequence comparison algorithm, the other is based on the distribution of the computation of pairwise comparisons. Systolic arrays have been proven as a good candidate structure for the first approach [3,8,16], while more expensive supercomputers and networks of workstations are suitable architectures for the second [6,13].

Special-purpose systolic arrays provide the best price/performance ratio by means of running a particular algorithm [10]. Their disadvantage is the lack of flexibility

V. Malyshkin (Ed.): PaCT 2001, LNCS 2127, pp. 498–509, 2001.
© Springer-Verlag Berlin Heidelberg 2001

with respect to the implementation of different algorithms. Instruction systolic arrays (ISAs) have been developed in order to combine the speed and simplicity of systolic arrays with flexible programmability [11]. Originally, the main application field of ISAs was supposed to be scientific computing. However, in the mid 90s the suitability of the ISA architecture for other applications was recognised, e.g. [5, 17-21]. In this paper we illustrate how an ISA can be used for efficient biosequence database scanning. We designed a parallel algorithm for sequence comparisons that is tailored towards the capabilities of the ISA. This leads to a high-speed implementation on Systola 1024, a parallel computer of this particular architecture.

This paper is organised as follows. In Section 2, we introduce the basic sequence comparison algorithm for database scanning and highlight previous work in parallel sequence comparison. Section 3 provides a description of the ISA concept as well as the Systola 1024 architecture. The new parallel algorithm and its mapping onto the parallel architecture are explained in Section 4. The performance is evaluated and compared to previous implementations in Section 5. Section 6 concludes the paper with an outlook to further research topics.

2   Parallel Sequence Comparison

Surprising relationships have been discovered between protein sequences that have little overall similarity but in which similar subsequences can be found. In that sense, the identification of similar subsequences is probably the most useful and practical method for comparing two sequences. The Smith-Waterman algorithm [22] finds the most similar subsequences of two sequences (the local alignment) by dynamic programming.

The algorithm compares two sequences by computing a distance that represents the minimal cost of transforming one segment into another. Two elementary operations are used: substitution and insertion/deletion (also called a gap operation). Through series of such elementary operations, any segments can be transformed into any other segment. The smallest number of operations required to change one segment into another can be taken into as the measure of the distance between the segments.

Consider two strings $S1$ and $S2$ of length $l1$ and $l2$. To identify common subsequences, the Smith-Waterman algorithm computes the similarity $H(i,j)$ of two sequences ending at position i and j of the two sequences $S1$ and $S2$. The computation of $H(i,j)$ is given by the following recurrences:

$$H(i, j) = \max \begin{cases} 0 \\ E(i, j) \\ F(i, j) \\ H(i-1, j-1) + Sbt(S1_i, S2_j) \end{cases} \quad ,1 \leq i \leq l1, 1 \leq j \leq l2$$

$$E(i, j) = \max \begin{cases} H(i, j-1) - \alpha \\ E(i, j-1) - \beta \end{cases} \quad ,0 \leq i \leq l1, 1 \leq j \leq l2$$

$$F(i, j) = \max \begin{cases} H(i-1, j) - \alpha \\ F(i-1, j) - \beta \end{cases} \quad ,1 \leq i \leq l1, 1 \leq j \leq l2$$

where *Sbt* is a character substitution cost table. Initialisation of these values are given by:

$$H(i,0) = E(i,0) = 0, \quad 0 \leq i \leq l1$$
$$H(0,j) = F(0,j) = 0 \quad 0 \leq j \leq l2$$

Multiple gap costs are taken into account as follows: α is the cost of the first gap; β is the cost of the following gaps. Fig. 1 illustrates an example with gap costs $\alpha = 1$ and $\beta = 1$ and *Sbt* defined as:

$$Sbt(x,y) = \begin{cases} 2 & \text{if } (x = y) \\ -1 & \text{otherwise} \end{cases}$$

Each position of the matrix H is a similarity value. The two segments of $S1$ and $S2$ producing this value can be determined by a backtracking procedure (see Fig. 1).

	Ø	A	T	C	T	C	G	T	A	T	G	A	T	G
Ø	0	0	0	0	0	0	0	0	0	0	0	0	0	0
G	0	0	0	0	0	0	2	1	0	0	2	1	0	2
T	0	0	2	1	2	1	1	4	3	2	1	1	3	2
C	0	0	1	4	3	4	3	3	3	2	1	0	2	2
T	0	0	2	3	6	5	4	5	4	5	4	3	2	1
A	0	2	2	2	5	5	4	4	7	6	5	6	5	4
T	0	1	4	3	4	4	4	6	5	9	8	7	8	7
C	0	0	3	6	5	6	5	5	5	8	8	7	7	7
A	0	2	2	5	5	5	5	4	7	7	7	10	9	8
C	0	1	1	4	4	7	6	5	6	6	6	9	9	8

Fig. 1. Example of the Smith-Waterman algorithm to compute the local alignment between two DNA sequences ATCTCGTATGATG and GTCTATCAC. The matrix $H(i,j)$ is shown for the computation with gap costs $\alpha = 1$ and $\beta = 1$, and a substitution cost of +2 if the characters are identical and −1 otherwise. From the highest score (+10 in the example), a traceback procedure delivers the corresponding alignment (shaded cells), the two subsequences TCGTATGA and TCTATCA.

The dynamic programming calculation can be efficiently mapped to a linear array of processing elements. A common mapping is to assign one processing element (PE) to each character of the query string, and then to shift a subject sequence systolically through the linear chain of PEs (see Fig. 2). If $l1$ is the length of the first sequence and $l2$ is the length of the second, the comparison is performed in $l1+l2-1$ steps on $l1$ PEs, instead of $l1 \times l2$ steps required on a sequential processor. In each step the computation for each dynamic programming cell along a single diagonal in Fig. 1 is performed in parallel.

A number of parallel architectures have been developed for sequence analysis. In addition to architectures specifically designed for sequence analysis, existing programmable sequential and parallel architectures have been used for solving sequence problems.

Special-purpose systolic arrays can provide the fastest means of running a particular algorithm with very high PE density. However, they are limited to one single algorithm, and thus cannot supply the flexibility necessary to run a variety of algorithms required analyzing DNA, RNA, and proteins. P-NAC was the first such machine and computed edit distance over a four-character alphabet [14]. More recent examples, better tuned to the needs of computational biology, include BioScan, BISP, and SAMBA [3,8,16].

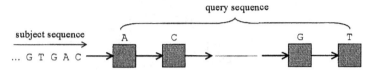

Fig. 2. Sequence comparison on a linear processor array: the query sequence is loaded into the processor array (one character per PE) and a subject sequence flows from left to right through the array. During each step, one elementary matrix computation is performed in each PE.

Reconfigurable systems are based on programmable logic such as field-programmable gate arrays (FPGAs) or custom-designed arrays. They are generally slower and have far lower PE densities than special-purpose architectures. They are flexible, but the configuration must be changed for each algorithm, which is generally more complicated than writing new code for a programmable architecture. Splash-2 and Biocellerator are based on FPGAs, while MGAP and PIM have their own reconfigurable designs [2,7,9,10].

Our approach is based on instruction systolic arrays (ISAs). ISAs combine the speed and simplicity of systolic arrays with flexible programmability [11], i.e. they achieve a high performance cost ratio and can at the same time be used for a wide range of applications, e.g. scientific computing, image processing, multimedia video compression, computer tomography, volume visualisation and cryptography [5,17-21]. The Kestrel design presented in [4] is close to our approach since it is also a programmable fine-grained parallel architecture. Unfortunately, its topology is purely a linear array (compared to a mesh in our approach). This has limited so far its widespread usage to biosequence searches and a computational chemistry application.

3   ISA Concept and Systola 1024

The ISA [11] is a mesh-connected processor grid, where the processors are controlled by three streams of control information: instructions, row selectors, and column selectors (see Fig. 3). The instructions are input in the upper left corner of the processor array, and from there they move step by step in horizontal and vertical direction through the array. This guarantees that within each diagonal of the array the same instruction is active during each clock cycle. In clock cycle $k+1$ processor $(i+1,j)$ and $(i,j+1)$ execute the instruction that has been executed by processor (i,j) in clock cycle k.

The selectors also move systolically through the array: the row selectors horizontally from left to right, column selectors vertically from top to bottom. Selectors mask the execution of the instructions within the processors, i.e. an instruction is executed if and only if both selector bits, currently in that processor, are equal to one. Otherwise, a no-operation is executed.

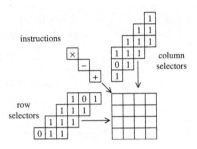

Fig. 3. Control flow in an ISA

Every processor has read and write access to its own memory. Besides that, it has a designated *communication register* (*C-register*) that can also be read by the four neighbour processors. Within each clock phase reading access is always performed before writing access. Thus, two adjacent processors can exchange data within a single clock cycle in which both processors overwrite the contents of their own C-register with the contents of the C-register of its neighbour. This convention avoids read/write conflicts and also creates the possibility to perform *aggregate functions* within one instruction (or a constant number of instructions).

Aggregate functions on a processor array are associative and commutative functions to which every processor provides an argument value. As they are commutative and associative, aggregate functions can be evaluated in many different ways (orders). The ISA supports top-down column operations and left-right row operations, due to the systolic flow of the instructions. Thus, an aggregate function can be implemented on the ISA by executing it firstly in all columns, placing the corresponding results within the last processor within each column, and secondly applying the aggregate function to these results in the last row, executing it within the last row (left-to-right). Simple examples of aggregate functions are the sum of all and the maximum of all. Other important operations that can be executed particularly well on the ISA are *row broadcast* (left-to-right), *column broadcast* (top-down) and *ringshift operations*. These are the key operations within the algorithm presented in this paper and hence they are explained below.

Row broadcast: Each processor reads the value from its left neighbour. Since the execution of this operation is pipelined along the row, the same value is propagated from one communication register to the next, until it finally arrives at the rightmost processor. Note that the row broadcast requires only a single instruction.

Row ringshift: The contents of the C-registers can be ringshifted along the processor rows by two instructions. Every two horizontally adjacent processors exchange data (using one read left and one read right operation). Because of the instruction flow from west to east this implements a ringshift. Of course, a column ringshift can be executed in the same way.

Systola 1024 is a low cost add-on board for standard PCs [12]. The ISA on the board is integrated on a 4×4 array of processor chips. Each chip contains 64 processors, arranged as an 8×8 square. This provides 1024 processors on the board.

In order to exploit the computation capabilities of this unit, a cascaded memory concept is implemented on Systola 1024 that forms a fast input and output environment for the parallel processing unit. For the fast data exchange with the ISA there are rows of intelligent memory units at the northern and western borders of the array called *interface processors* (IPs). Each IP is connected to its adjacent array processor for data transfer in each direction. The IPs have access to an on-board memory by means of special fast data channels, those at the northern interface chips with the northern board RAM, and those of the western chips with the western board RAM. The northern and the western board RAM can communicate bidirectionally with the PC memory over the PCI bus. The data transfer between every two memory units within this hierarchy is controlled by an on-board controller chip (see Fig. 4).

At a clock frequency of $f = 50$ MHz and using a word format of $m=16$ bits each (bitserial) processor can execute $f/m = 50/16 \cdot 10^6 = 3.125 \cdot 10^6$ word operations per second. Thus, one board with its 1024 processors performs up to 3.2 GIPS.

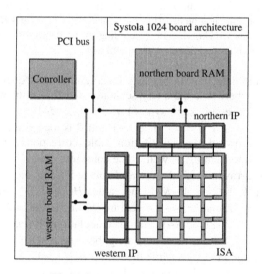

Fig. 4. Data paths in Systola 1024

4   Mapping of Sequence Comparison onto the ISA

Systolic parallelisation of the Smith-Waterman algorithm on a linear processor array is well-known (see Section 2). In order to extend this algorithm to a mesh-architecture, we take advantage of ISAs capabilities to perform row broadcast and row ringshift in a very efficient way (see Section 3). Since the length of the sequences may vary (several thousands in some cases, however commonly the length is only in hundreds), the computation must also be partitioned on the $N \times N$ ISA. For sake of clarity we firstly assume the processor array size N^2 to be equal to the query sequence length M, i.e. $M=N^2$.

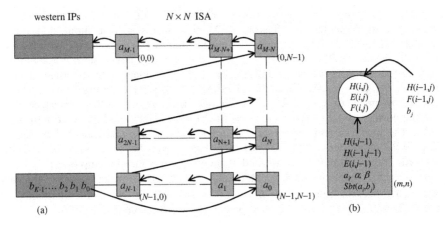

Fig. 5. (a) Data flow for aligning two sequences A and B on an $M=N{\times}N$ ISA: A is loaded into the ISA one character per PE and B is completely shifted through the array in $M+K-1$ steps. Each character b_j is input from the lower western IP and results are written into the upper western IP. **(b)** For the computation of $H(i,j)$, $E(i,j)$, and $F(i,j)$, the values $H(i-1,j)$, $F(i-1,j)$, and b_j are received from the neighbouring PE (according to the data flow in (a)), while $H(i,j-1)$, $H(i-1,j-1)$, $E(i,j-1)$, a_i, α, β, and $Sbt(a_i,b_j)$ are stored locally.

Fig. 5a shows the data flow in the ISA for aligning the sequences $A = a_0 a_1 ... a_{M-1}$ and $B = b_0 b_1 ... b_{K-1}$, where A is the query sequence and B is a subject sequence of the database. As a preprocessing step, symbol a_i, $i = 0,...,M-1$, is loaded into PE (m,n) with $m = N-i$ div $N-1$ and $n = N-i$ mod $N-1$ and B is loaded into the lower western IP. After that the row of the substitution table corresponding to the respective character is loaded into each PE as well as the constants α and β. B is then completely shifted through the array in $M+K-1$ steps as displayed in Fig. 5a.

In iteration step k, $1 \le k \le M+K-1$, the values $H(i,j)$, $E(i,j)$, and $F(i,j)$ for all i, j with $1 \le i \le M$, $1 \le j \le K$ and $k=i+j-1$ are computed in parallel in the PEs (m,n) with $m = N-i$ div $N-1$ and $n = N-i$ mod $N-1$. For this calculation PE (m,n) receives the values $H(i-1,j)$, $F(i-1,j)$, and b_j from its eastern neighbour $(m,n+1)$ if $n < N-1$, or from PE $(m+1,0)$ if $n = N-1$ and $m < N-1$, while the values $H(i-1,j-1)$, $H(i,j-1)$, $E(i,j-1)$, a_i, α, β, and $Sbt(a_i,b_j)$ are stored locally (see Fig 5b). The lower right PE $(N-1,N-1)$ receives b_j in steps j with $0 \le j \le K-1$ from the lower western IP and zeros otherwise.

Because of the efficient row ringshift and row broadcast, these routing operations can be accomplished in constant time on the ISA. Thus, it takes $M+K-1$ steps to compute the alignment cost of the two sequences with the Smith-Waterman algorithm. However, notice that after the last character of B enters the array, the first character of a new subject sequence can be input for the next iteration step. Thus, all subject sequences of the database can be pipelined with only one step delay between two different sequences. Assuming k sequences of length K and $K = O(M)$, we compute K sequence alignments in time $O(K{\cdot}M)$ using $O(M)$ processors. As the best sequential algorithm takes $O(K{\cdot}M^2)$ steps, our parallel implementation achieves maximal efficiency.

Because of the very limited memory of each PE, only the highest score of matrix H is computed on Systola 1024 for each pairwise comparison (see Fig. 1). Ranking the compared sequences and reconstructing the alignments are carried out by the front end PC. Because this last operation is only performed for very few subject sequences, its computation time is negligible. In our ISA algorithm the maximum computation of the matrix H can be easily incorporated with only a constant time penalty: After each iteration step all PEs compute a new value max by taking the maximum of the newly computed H-value and the old value of max from its neighbouring PE. After the last character of a subject sequence has been processed in PE $(0,0)$, the maximum of matrix H is stored in PE $(0,0)$, which is written into the adjacent western IP.

So far we have assumed a processor array equal in size of the query sequence length ($M=N^2$). In practice, this rarely happens. Assuming a query sequence length of $M = k \cdot N$ with k a multiple of N or N a multiple of k, the algorithm is modified as follows:

1.   **k ≤ N:** In this case we can just replicate the algorithm for a $k{\times}N$ ISA on an $N{\times}N$ ISA, i.e. each $k{\times}N$ subarray computes the alignment of the same query sequence with different subject sequences.

2.   **k > N:** A possible solution is to assign k/N characters of the sequences to each PE instead of one. However, in this case the memory size has to be sufficient to store k/N rows of the substitution table (20 values per row, since there are 20 different amino acids), i.e. on Systola 1024 it is only possible to assign maximally two characters per PE. Thus, for $k/N > 2$ it is required to split the sequence comparison into $k/(2N)$ passes:

The first $2N^2$ characters of the query sequence are loaded into the ISA. The entire database then crosses the array; the H-value and F-value computed in PE $(0,0)$ in each iteration step are written into the adjacent western IP and then stored in the western board RAM. In the next pass the following $2N^2$ characters of the query sequence are loaded. The data stored previously is loaded into the lower western IP together with the corresponding subject sequences and from there sent again into the ISA. The process is iterated until the end of the query sequence is reached. Note that, no additional instructions are necessary for the I/O of the intermediate results with the processor array, because it is integrated in the dataflow (see Fig. 5a). The additionally required data transfer between IPs and board RAM can be performed concurrently with the computation (see Section 5 for more details).

To achieve even higher performance we mapped the database scanning application on a cluster of 16 Systola 1024 boards (see Fig. 6). The cluster consists of 16 PCs (Pentium II 450) connected via a Gigabit-per-second LAN (using Myrinet M2F-PCI32 as network interface cards and Myrinet M2L-SW16 as a switch). For parallel application development we use the MPI library MPICH v. 1.1.2.

For distributing of the computation among the PCs we have chosen a static split load balancing strategy: A similar sized subset of the database is assigned to each PC in a preprocessing step. The subsets remain stationary regardless of the query sequence. Thus, the distribution has only to be performed once for each database and does not influence the overall computing time. The input query sequence is broadcast to each PC and multiple independent subset scans are performed on each Systola 1024 board. Finally, the highest scores are accumulated in one PC.

This strategy provides the best performance for our homogenous architecture, where each processing unit has the same processing power. However, a dynamic split load balancing strategy as used in [13] is more suitable for heterogeneous environments.

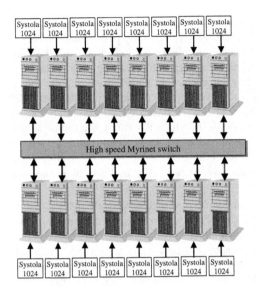

Fig. 6. Architecture of a hybrid parallel system: A coarse-grained cluster of 16 PCs with Systola 1024 PCI boards

5   Performance Evaluation

A performance measure commonly used in computational biology is *millions of dynamic cell updates per second* (MCUPS). A CUPS represents the time for a complete computation of one entry of the matrix *H*, including all comparisons, additions and maxima computations. To measure the MCUPS performance on Systola 1024, we have given the instruction count to update two *H*-cells per PE in Table 1.

Table 1. Instruction count to update two *H*-cells in one PE of Systola 1024 with the corresponding operations.

Operation in each PE per iteration step	Instruction Count
Get $H(i-1,j)$, $F(i-1,j)$, b_j, max_{i-1} from neighbour	20
Lookup $Sbt(a_i,b_j)$ in internal memory	16
Compute $t = \max\{0, H(i-1,j-1) + Sbt(a_i,b_j)\}$	4
Compute $F(i,j) = \max\{H(i-1,j)-\alpha, F(i-1,j)-\beta\}$	8
Compute $E(i,j) = \max\{H(i,j-1)-\alpha, E(i,j-1)-\beta\}$	8
Compute $H(i,j) = \max\{t, F(i,j), E(i,j)\}$	8
Compute $max_i = \max\{H(i,j), max_{i-1}\}$	4
Sum	**68**

Because new *H*-values are computed for two characters within 68 instruction in each PE, the whole 32×32 processor array can perform 2048 cell updates in the same time. This leads to a performance of

$$\frac{2048}{68} \times f \text{ CUPS} = \frac{2048}{68} \times \frac{50}{16} \times 10^6 \text{ CUPS} = 94 \text{ MCUPS}$$

Because MCUPS does not consider data transfer time and query length, it is often a weak measure that does not reflect the behaviour of the complete system. Therefore, we will use execution times of database scans for different query lengths in our evaluation.

The involved data transfer in each iteration step is: input of a new character b_j into the lower western IP of each $k \times N$ subarray for query lengths ≤ 2048 (case 1. in Section 4) and input of a new b_j and a previously computed cell of H and F and output of an H-cell and F-cell from the upper western IP for query lengths > 2048 (case 2. in Section 4). Thus, the data transfer time is totally dominated by above computing time of 68 instructions per iteration step.

Table 2. Scan times (in seconds) of TrEMBL 14 for various length of the query sequence on Systola 1024, a PC cluster with 16 Systola 1024, and a Pentium III 600. The speed up compared to the Pentium III is also reported.

Query sequence length	256	512	1024	2048	4096
Systola 1024	294	577	1137	2241	4611
speed up	*5*	*6*	*6*	*6*	*6*
PC Cluster of 16 Systolas	20	38	73	142	290
speed up	*81*	*86*	*91*	*94*	*92*
Pentium III 600 MHz	1615	3286	6611	13343	26690

Table 2 reports times for scanning the TrEMBL protein databank (release 14, which contains 351'834 sequences and 100'069'442 amino acids) for query sequences of various lengths with the Smith-Waterman algorithm. The first two rows of the table give the execution times for Systola 1024 and the cluster with 16 boards compared to a sequential C-program on a Pentium III 600. As the times show, the parallel implementations scale almost linearly with the sequence length. Because of the used static split strategy the cluster times scale also almost linearly with the number of PCs. A single Systola 1024 board is 5-6 times faster than a Pentium III 600. However, a board redesign based on technology used for processors such as the Pentium III (Systola 1024 has been built in 1994 [12]) would make this factor significantly higher.

Fig. 7 shows time measurements of sequence comparison with the Smith-Waterman algorithms on different parallel machines. The data for the other machines is taken from [4]. Systola 1024 is around two times faster than the much larger 1K-PE MasPar and the cluster of 16 Systolas is around two times faster than a 16K-PE MasPar. The 1-board Kestrel is 4-5 times faster than a Systola board. Kestrel's design [4] is also a programmable fine-grained parallel architecture implemented as a PC add-on board. It reaches the higher performance, because it has been built with 0.5-μm CMOS technology, in comparison to 1.0-μm for Systola 1024. Extrapolating to this technology both approaches should perform equally. However, the difference between both architectures is that Kestrel is purely a linear array, while Systola is a mesh. This makes the Systola 1024 a more flexible design, suitable for a wider range of applications, see e.g. [5, 17-21].

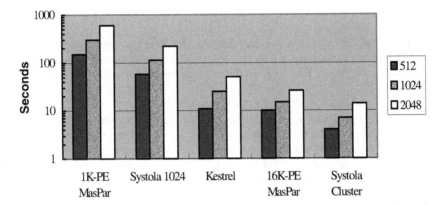

Fig. 7. Time comparison for a 10Mbase search with the Smith-Waterman algorithm on different parallel machines for different query lengths. The values for 1K-PE MasPar, Kestrel, and 16K-PE MasPar are taken from [4], while the values for Systola are based on the TrEMBL 14 scanning times (see Table 2) divided by a normalisation factor of 10.

6   Conclusions and Future Work

In this paper we have demonstrated that the ISA concept is very suitable for scanning biosequence databases. We have presented the design of an ISA algorithm that leads to a high-speed implementation on Systola 1024 exploiting the fine-grained parallelism inherent to the sequence comparison problem. By additionally using a coarse-grained distribution of the database within a cluster of Systola 1024, we can achieve supercomputer performance at low cost.

The exponentially growth of genomic databases demands even more powerful parallel solutions in the future. Because comparison and alignment algorithms that are favoured by biologists are not fixed, programmable parallel solutions are required to speed up these tasks. As an alternative to special-purpose systems, hard-to-program reconfigurable systems, and expensive supercomputers, we advocate the use of specialised yet programmable hardware whose development is tuned to system speed.

Our future work in parallel computing will include identifying more applications that profit from this type of processing power consisting of a combination of fine-grained and coarse-grained parallelism, like scientific computing and multimedia video processing. The results of this study will influence our design decision to build a next-generation Systola board consisting of one large 128×128 ISA or of a cluster of 16 32×32 ISAs.

References

1. Altschul, S.F., Gish, W., Miller, W., Myers, E.W, Lipman, D.J.: Basic local alignment search tool, J. Mol. Biol., 215 (1990) 403-410.
2. Borah, M., Bajwa, R.S., Hannenhalli, S., Irwin, M.J.: A SIMD solution to the sequence comparison problem on the MGAP, in Proc. ASAP'94, IEEE CS (1994) 144-160.
3. Chow, E., Hunkapiller, T., Peterson, J., Waterman, M.S.: Biological Information Signal Processor, Proc. ASAP'91, IEEE CS (1991) 144-160.

4. Dahle, D., Grate L., Rice, E., Hughey, R.: The UCSC Kestrel general purpose parallel processor, http://www.cse.ucsc.edu/research/kestrel/papers/pdpta99.pdf in Proc. PDPTA'99 (1999).

5. Dittrich, A., Schmeck, H.: Givens's Rotation on an Instruction Systolic Array, Proc. Parcella'88, LNCS 342, Springer (1988) 340-346.

6. Glemet, E., Codani, J.J.: LASSAP, a Large Scale Sequence compArison Package, CABIOS 13 (2) (1997) 145-150.

7. Gokhale, M. et al.: Processing in memory: The Terasys massively parallel PIM array, Computer 28 (4) (1995) 23-31.

8. Guerdoux-Jamet, P., Lavenier, D.: SAMBA: hardware accelerator for biological sequence comparison, CABIOS 12 (6) (1997) 609-615.

9. Hoang, D.T.: Searching genetic databases on Splash 2, in Proc. IEEE Workshop on FPGAs for Custom Computing Machines, IEEE CS, (1993) 185-191.

10. Hughey, R.: Parallel Hardware for Sequence Comparison and Alignment, CABIOS 12 (6) (1996) 473-479.

11. Lang, H.-W.: The Instruction Systolic Array, a parallel architecture for VLSI, Integration, the VLSI Journal 4 (1986) 65-74.

12. Lang, H.-W., Maaß, R., Schimmler, M.: The Instruction Systolic Array - Implementation of a Low-Cost Parallel Architecture as Add-On Board for Personal Computers, Proc. HPCN'94, LNCS 797, Springer (1994) 487-488.

13. Lavenier, D., Pacherie, J.-L.: Parallel Processing for Scanning Genomic Data-Bases, Proc. PARCO'97, Elseiver (1998) 81-88.

14. Lopresti, D.P.: P-NAC: A systolic array for comparing nucleic acid sequences, Computer 20 (7) (1987) 98-99.

15. Pearson, W.R.: Comparison of methods for searching protein sequence databases, Protein Science 4 (6) (1995) 1145-1160.

16. Singh, R.K. et al.: BIOSCAN: a network sharable computational resource for searching biosequence databases, CABIOS, 12 (3) (1996) 191-196.

17. Schimmler, M., Lang, H.-W.: The Instruction Systolic Array in Image Processing Applications, Proc. Europto 96, SPIE 2784 (1996) 136-144.

18. Schmidt, B., Schimmler, M.: A Parallel Accelerator Architecture for Multimedia Video Compression, Proc. EuroPar'99, LNCS 1685, Springer (1999) 950-959.

19. Schmidt, B., Schimmler, M., Schröder, H.: Long Operand Arithmetic on Instruction Systolic Computer Architectures and Its Application to RSA cryptography, Proc. Euro-Par'98, LNCS 1470, Springer (1998) 916-922.

20. Schmidt, B., Schimmler, M., Schröder, H.: The Instruction Systolic Array in Tomographic Image Reconstruction Applications, Proc. PART'98, Springer (1998) 343-354.

21. Schmidt, B.: Design of a Parallel Accelerator for Volume Rendering. In Proc. Euro-Par'2000, LNCS 1900, Springer (2000) 1095-1104.

22. Smith, T.F., Waterman, M.S.: Identification of common molecular subsequences, J. Mol. Biol. 147 (1981) 195-197.

SCI-Based LINUX PC-Clusters as a Platform for Electromagnetic Field Calculations

Carsten Trinitis, Martin Schulz, Michael Eberl, and Wolfgang Karl

Lehrstuhl für Rechnertechnik und Rechnerorganisation (LRR)
D-80290 München, Germany
{Carsten.Trinitis,Martin.Schulz,Michael.Eberl,Wolfgang.Karl}@in.tum.de
http://smile.in.tum.de/

1 Introduction

When designing high voltage equipment like power transformers, it is of essential importance to precisely and efficiently calculate eddy-current problems in a transformer to determine possible losses. A method suitable for such simulations is the Boundary-Element method (BEM) [2]. As far as the simulation is concerned, for electrical devices operating continuously under alternating current, time-harmonic states are of interest. These lead to an elliptic transmission problem for the eddy-current Maxwell equations. With some modifications, the linear equation system resulting from the boundary element discretization is well-conditioned. For realistic problems, however, the discretization leads to very large, non-symmetric systems of linear equations. To deal with such large equation systems, iterative solution techniques such as GMRES [9] must be employed. However, for certain combinations of materials occurring in electrical engineering (such as e.g. iron and copper parts) the parallel boundary integral equation system and its discretizations are ill-conditioned, primarily caused by the physical parameters in the problem formulation. In order to cope with such problems, the Seminar for Applied Mathematics at the ETH Zürich, Switzerland has developed a preconditioner for the eddy-current system of second kind Boundary Integral Equations [4] which has been integrated into the framework of the boundary element field simulation code POLOPT [1]. For this code, it is important to deploy a network with both high bandwidth and low latency like the Scalable Coherent Interface (SCI) [6] achieving significantly improved performance over standard Ethernet. With such a cluster installed at ABB Corporate Research, Heidelberg, it is now possible to perform realistic eddy current calculations in a shorter amount of time.

2 Physical Background and Simulation Process

Eddy currents are often generated in transformers and cause power losses and heat problems. Faraday's Law implies that a changing flux produces an induced electric field even in empty space. Inserting a metal plate into this empty space produces electric currents (eddy currents) in the metal. If the induced currents

V. Malyshkin (Ed.): PaCT 2001, LNCS 2127, pp. 510–513, 2001.

are created by a changing magnetic field, the eddy currents will be perpendicular to the magnetic field. By constructing a transformer core of alternating layers of conducting and nonconducting materials, the size of the induced loops is reduced which in turn reduces the energy loss.

Mathematically, the conventional approach to the calculation of eddy currents is based on the formulation of the boundary value problem with respect to a vector magnetic potential. This is justified for two-dimensional problems when the vector magnetic potential has only one component. In three dimensional problem space, however, the potential is a three dimensional vector like the field itself. Thus, Maxwell's equations should be used directly, with respect to field vectors. As can be seen in [4], this eventually yields a system of second kind boundary integral equations on a conductor surface by using the so called $H - \phi$ formulation [7]. When applying the Boundary Element Method (BEM) for these equations, a linear equation system is obtained. However, this system is still ill-conditioned and can hence not be solved with the General Minimal Residual Method (GMRES) [9], which is the solver being used in POLOPT. Therefore, a preconditioner is applied in [4] so that after preconditioning the equation system can be solved with GMRES: First, a coefficient matrix is generated by POLOPT which can be done in parallel since the generation of a line is independent from any other line. Then the parallel preconditioner and solver described in [4] are applied. Typical sizes for the equation systems are in the range of 3-4-5 orders of magnitude with densely populated coefficient matrices.

3   High Performance Cluster Computing

In the last few years, clusters built from commodity-of-the-shelf (COTS) components have become increasingly popular and have found their way from pure research use to industrial production environments. Existing specialized cluster interconnects, such as Myrinet[3], and SCI [6] provide a considerably higher bandwidth and much lower latencies. All of them are based on the principle of user–level communication, enabling applications to directly benefit from the improved communication performance leading to a significantly improved overall performance comparable to expensive tightly coupled multi–processors, but at a fraction of their cost.

In this work, PC clusters interconnected using the Scalable Coherent Interface (SCI) are used. SCI is an IEEE standardized [6] state-of-the-art SAN technology allowing for link speeds of up to 667 MB/s and a process-to-process communication bandwidth of up to 85 MB/s and latencies less than 2 μs.

In order to allow applications to exploit SCI's capabilities, several projects aim at providing both standard communication libraries like MPI [8] and low-level communication mechanisms like Sockets in a way fully exploiting the underlying hardware capabilities and avoiding excessive protocol stacks, like TCP/IP. Typically over 90% of the raw performance can be achieved using these approaches.

In 1999, ABB Corporate Research Center in Heidelberg, Germany installed a cluster of 8 LINUX based 500MHz Pentium-III class PCs connected via both Fast Ethernet and SCI. Each node is equipped with 1 GB of physical memory. For the parallel version of POLOPT, the SCI-based MPI implementation ScaMPI [5] from SCALI AS has been used. It is fully MPI 1.1 specification compliant and highly optimized for SCI-based architectures. Its raw performance on the target architecture used for this work is around $5\,\mu s$ in MPI end–to–end latency and 80 MB/s in bandwidth, which is about 94 % of the raw performance of SCI on the ABB setup. This shows that ScaMPI enables applications to directly leverage on the high performance of the underlying interconnection fabric without the high protocol overhead visible in traditional systems.

4   Practical Examples and Results

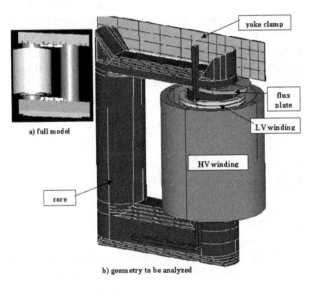

Fig. 1. Transformer model

The transformer that has served as a benchmarking example is depicted in Figure 1. The task is to calculate the distribution of power losses caused by eddy currents in the yoke clamping plates in order to detect possible temperature hot spots. To guide the magnetic flux and to manipulate the loss distribution, the yoke is extended by a so called flux plate. The yoke clamps are modeled as solid parts. The full model consisting of the magnetic core, the yoke clamps, the flux plate and the HV windings has been analyzed with all materials assumed as linear. The obtained peak values were 10.071 kA for the Low Voltage winding (30 turns) and 482.175kA for the High Voltage winding (1 turn), respectively. From these values, the eddy currents in two different parts of the yoke clamp have been calculated. The required number of unknowns and the resulting working set sizes can be seen in Table 1.

The calculations have been performed on the ABB LINUX cluster. Due to the high permeability values of the materials, it is necessary to actually solve the equation system twice [4]. The computation times have been measured for both Fast Ethernet and SCI. As can be seen from from Table 1, a speedup of 1.3-1.4 is obtained by using the SCI network technology significantly reducing runtime.

Table 1. Computation times and speedup for transformer example

Part	Unknowns	Size	Network	Solver 1	Speedup	Solver 2	Speedup
1	11547	2 GB	Fast Ethernet	1289 sec	1.0	1533 sec	1.0
1	11547	2 GB	SCI	932 sec	1.4	1080 sec	1.4
2	15291	3.6 GB	Fast Ethernet	2636 sec	1.0	2843 sec	1.0
2	15291	3.6 GB	SCI	2025 sec	1.3	2179 sec	1.3

5 Conclusions and Outlook

In this paper we have described the process of eddy-current simulations based on new algorithms developed by ETH Zürich. Using a high bandwidth and low latency network like SCI, a significant speedup in the solver computation times has been achieved. Recently the LINUX PC cluster has been upgraded to 16 nodes yielding a total main memory of 16GB. Therefore, it will be possible to compute even larger eddy current problems as the coefficient matrices will fit into the cluster's main memory.

References

1. Z. Andjelic. *POLOPT 4.5 User's Guide*. ABB Corporate Research Center Heidelberg, 1996.
2. R. Bausinger and G. Kuhn. *Die Boundary-Element Methode (in German)*. Expert Verlag, Ehingen, 1987.
3. N. Boden, D. Cohen, R. Felderman, J. Seizovic A. Kulawik, C. Seitz, and Wen-King Su. Myrinet: A Gigabit–per–Second Local Area Network. *IEEE Micro*, 15(1):29–36, February 1995.
4. G. Schmidlin, Ch. Schwab et al. Preconditioning second kind boundary integral equations for 3-d eddy current problems (unpublished). Technical report, ETH Zurich, Zurich, Switzerland, 2000.
5. L. Huse, K. Omang, H. Bugge, H. Ry, A. Haugsdal, and E. Rustad. *SCI: Scalable Coherent Interface. Architecture and Software for High-Performance Compute Clusters*, volume 1734 of *LNCS State-of-the-Art Survey*, chapter 14, ScaMPI — Design and Implementation. Springer Verlag, October 1999. ISBN 3-540-66696-6.
6. IEEE Computer Society. IEEE Standard for the Scalable Coherent Interface (SCI). IEEE Std 1596-1992, 1993. IEEE 345 East 47th Street, New York, NY 10017-2394, USA.
7. I.D. Mayergoyz. Eddy current problems and the boundary integral equation method. *Computational Electromagnetics*, pages 163–171, 1996.
8. Message Passing Interface Forum (MPIF). MPI: A Message-Passing Interface Standard. Technical Report, University of Tennessee, Knoxville, June 1995. http://www.mpi-forum.org.
9. Y. Saad and M.H. Schultz. GMRES: A generalized minimal residual algorithm for solving nonsymmetric linear systems. In *SIAM J.Sci. Stat. Comput.*, pages 856–869. 1989.

Author Index

Lecture Notes in Computer Science

For information about Vols. 1–2065
please contact your bookseller or Springer-Verlag